HISTORIC HOUSES
CASTLES & GARDENS

THE ORIGINAL GUIDE TO THE TREASURES OF GREAT BRITAIN & IRELAND

Pashley Manor Gardens, *Ticehurst, East Sussex*
Winner of Christie's / HHA Garden of the Year Award presented in 2000

a
JOHANSENS
publication

INSURANCE FOR YOUR LIFESTYLE

In the important areas of insurance and risk management, you want a company who can deliver tailored, personal insurance solutions, not merely off-the-shelf policies. When that company is a Johansens Preferred Partner, you expect an additional level of expertise and quality.

Marsh Private Client Services have built a loyal client base over many decades of serving discerning individuals who like the way we do business.

Backed by the globally respected broking strength of the world's leading insurance broking and risk management group, our clients know they can rely on us to provide the right products at the right price, tailored to their own special requirements.

Global reach with a personal touch

- **Motor**
- **Home**
- **Travel**
- **Fine Art**
- **Estates**
- **Farms**

- **Personal Accident**
- **Healthcare**
- **Dental**
- **Legal Protection**
- **Pets and equestrian**

Specialist areas:

- **Buildings and Contents**
  Including larger, distinctive homes through to weekend retreats and overseas properties. Personal valuables, antiques, collections, fine art and jewellery.

- **Motor**
  For all vehicles including private, commercial and agricultural, including prestige and performance cars.

- **Countryside**
  Farms, estates and country properties, plus risks associated with all country pursuits including fishing, shooting and equestrian.

- **Horses and Pets**
  Vets fees and liabilities for dogs, cats and horses.

Telephone today:
01462 428000

Marsh Private Client Services, Garden House, 42 Bancroft, Hitchin, Herts SG5 1DD Tel: 01462 428000 Fax: 01462 428008

Contents

The Bridge at Blenheim Palace,
Oxfordshire

Jardin du Château de Villiers, Chassy,
France

National Collection of Fashion, V&A,
London

UNITED KINGDOM   AMERICA

0800-89-00-11
AT&T Direct® Service

The easy way to call home from the U.K.

FOR EASY CALLING WORLDWIDE:
1. Just dial the AT&T Access Number for the country you are calling from.
2. Dial the phone number you're calling.
3. Dial your AT&T Calling Card, AT&T Corporate, AT&T Universal, MasterCard,® Diners Club,® American Express,® or Discover® card number.

Global
connection
with the AT&T
Network

AT&T
direct
service

Foreword by Ian Harris
Stately Homes and the Antiques Roadshow

'Love and marriage…go together like a horse and carriage'… Well, maybe not so often these days; but the love match between the BBC's Antiques Roadshow and Stately Homes seems one made in heaven. It's quite long-lasting as marriages go: 23 years, and the happy couple see no end in sight!

Stately homes do lend an aura which is sadly lacking from the anonymous and more-or-less identical sports halls that form the backcloth to so many programmes. Increasingly (and bravely, considering our climate) the programmes are recorded in the gardens, and it's usually difficult to predict whether to pack the Panama or the thermal underwear.

One such programme was recorded at *Athelhampton*, in Dorset, which, as I see when thumbing through last year's Guide, won the *Christie's/HHA Garden of the Year Award* in 1998. The gardens at Athelhampton include a topiary garden with tall clipped obelisks surrounding a central fountain, the river Piddle flowing through, and marvellous old roses. I like houses that have a few plants for sale, because they are often a little out-of-the ordinary, and a good souvenir of an enjoyable day. There were even a few decent pieces of jewellery for me to record.

The other nice thing about recording at stately homes is that being a member of the BBC team seems to give you carte blanche to wander about the house at will, when the crowds have thinned out in the late afternoon, as the houses are often closed to the public on recording days.

Eastnor Castle, in the Malvern Hills, where we did a Roadshow last year, is an externally austere stone built mediaeval style four-corner-turreted battlemented pile built above a lake in 1812. Inside are huge, high-ceilinged rooms decorated in slightly faded High Victorian Gothic grandeur. Suits of armour sightlessly glare at you; indeed, there's a helmet lying on a table in the Hall (it deserves a capital H) that you are invited to try on, if you are not too claustrophobic. It was scattered with hinges, pivots, fastening hooks etc; I thought I'd end up like the Man in the Iron Mask, and never get it off again.

Inside, because it had been one of the coldest and most miserable of July days, with only a miracle keeping off the rain, we crept from bedroom to bedroom in the gloom of low cloud and anti-UV blinds. Time had marched on, as all the rooms had their own bathrooms: the comfortably old-fashioned sort, not the Victorian repro lots of us try for these days, but the real thing, with huge cast iron baths and mahogany loo seats. The bathrooms were as large as most people's bedrooms, and quite comprehensively furnished with dressing tables, chairs, even the occasional settee.

When we did a Roadshow at *Chatsworth* in Derbyshire, their

Graces wandered around taking a keen interest in what was happening and chatting to the experts and technical people. This doesn't always happen; sometimes the owners seem to prefer to be away. At supper, I was sat next to the curator of the Chatsworth jewellery and silver collection, so we had a lot to talk about. Normally we tend to catch a train straight home after a day's recording, but as we were invited to a private view of the strong-rooms on the Friday morning, we stayed.

Well, wow! The silver was impressive, in floor-to-ceiling deep glazed cupboards lining the walls of the strong-room. We were shown something like a coin cabinet with numerous narrow drawers, each drawer containing about 100 rings set with cameos, intaglios, carved gems, diamonds and precious stones. At the time, the curator was working on an inventory of the cabinet's contents; in the past it had never been considered necessary. What they had, they had, and in the past, when in Polite Society you didn't discuss politics, money or sex (which is about all we do talk about these days), it probably would have been considered in bad taste to know what you possessed by actually listing it all.

By the way, it's not the Royal 'we'. Usually, my wife Natalie and I do the Roadshows together. Working at reception, usually one of a team of three, she looks at everything that comes in, and directs people to the appropriate expert. On many occasions she could tell them not to bother to queue up for another hour or more, but they don't want that. They want their chat with Henry Sandon, John Bly, Hilary Kay, or whomever the Roadshow has made into a familiar personality. Therefore, on the strong-room visit we were together as usual; just as well, as I would have looked a bit silly in one of the spectacular Devonshire tiaras!

The *Arundel Castle* Roadshow was recorded inside the Castle, in the massive hall. This is unusual, because even the grandest of houses seldom has a room big enough to house us, the cameras, reception, hundreds of queuers, the BBC sales booth, St John's Ambulance (in case someone faints at the value of their object, or more realistically, the heat and the wait) a Police desk (there may be a few dodgy characters lurking) miles of cables, and all the ancillary bits and pieces needed for the Show.

We all spend 80% of our Roadshow days being nice to people about objects of little interest or value. What is seen on the screen is the distillation of maybe thousands of items looked at on any particular day. What makes it all worthwhile is the excitement of finding something special, and the pleasure you give its owner when you do; so long may the Roadshow flourish!

Your guide to holiday relaxation.

Put your mind at rest that any fine wine that you choose from Barrels & Bottles' Johansens selection will be of the very highest quality from some of the world's finest estates.

Rest

Cabernet Sauvignon

As the preferred wine merchant for Johansens group Barrels & Bottles wish you a very relaxed holiday in the Johansens recommended cottage of your choice.

Relax

Chardonnay

Whether enjoying our wines whilst you are on holiday or ordering for home delivery Barrels & Bottles can deliver next day anywhere in the U.K.

Simply call our dedicated Johansens Freephone line.

Riesling

Enjoy

How to use this guide

If you want to identify a historic property, garden, museum or gallery whose name you already know, look for it in the Index of all properties from page 377.

If you want to find a historic property, garden, museum or gallery in England, Ireland, Scotland or Wales, you can:
• Turn to the maps at the back of the book from page 385.
• Look through the guide for the county you require; they are sorted in alphabetical order. The properties are then listed alphabetically wherever possible.

Properties in Belgium, France, Germany and The Netherlands have their approximate positions labelled on the illustrated maps in each country introduction.

Starting from page 322, there are a number of properties listed in certain categories: properties open by appointment only, Cambridge and Oxford Universities, film locations, garden specialists, plants for sale, art collections, weddings, "top teas", open all year, conference facilities and accommodation.

Please turn to pages 350–367 for illustrated mini listings of all Johansens Recommended Traditional Inns, Hotels & Restaurants in Great Britain, Hotels in Europe & the Mediterranean, as well as a full listing of all Recommended Hotels and Country Houses in Great Britain & Ireland.

Publisher:	David Northover
Regional Contributors:	Martin Greaves
	Warren Knock
	Audrey & Alan H. Smith
Publishing Manager:	Phoebe Hobby
Production Director:	Daniel Barnett
Production Controller:	Kevin Bradbrook
Sub-editor:	Stephanie Cook
Senior Designer:	Michael Tompsett
Designer:	Kerri Bennett
Map Illustrations:	Linda Clark
Special Promotions Editor:	Fiona Patrick
Sales & Marketing Director:	Tim Sinclair
Marketing Executive:	Adam Crabtree
Sales Administrator:	Susan Butterworth
Managing Director:	Andrew Warren

Published by Johansens Ltd
Therese House, Glasshouse Yard, London EC1A 4JN
Tel: +44 (0)20 7566 9700 Fax: +44 (0)20 7490 2538 E-mail: info@johansens.com

Find Johansens on the Internet at: www.historichouses.co.uk

Copyright © 2001 Johansens Ltd.
Johansens is a subsidiary of the Daily Mail and General Trust plc
ISBN 1-903665-00-0

Printed in England by St Ives plc
Colour origination by Catalyst Creative Imaging

Distributed in the UK and Europe by Johnsons International Media Services Ltd, London (direct sales) & Windsor Books, Oxford (bookstores). In North America by Hobsons DMI, Cincinnati (direct sales) and Hunter Publishing, New Jersey (bookstores). In Australia and New Zealand by Bookwise International, Wingfield, South Australia.

Key to Symbols

	The National Trust
	The National Trust for Scotland
	Historic Scotland
	English Heritage
	CADW
	Historic Houses Association
	HITHA
	Park
	Garden
	Refreshments
	Children's Playground
	Accommodation Available
	Meals Available
	Picnic Area
	Wedding Licence
	Disabled Access
	Guided Tours
	Gift Shop
	Nurseries – Plants for Sale
	Live Entertainment
	House by Appointment Only
	Haunted
	Conference Facilities
	Used for Filming
	Special Group Rates

What does your paper say about you?

Jeremy Hoskins, hotelier, chooses Conqueror* Contour in Oyster, printed in colour.

Starring role. Jeremy Hoskins combed the Conqueror* range to discover the perfect texture for his hotel's letterhead. Ideal for brochures, menus, wine-lists and letterheads, as well as for all corporate and conference stationery, the colours, textures and weights of the Conqueror* range are the best in the business. For a free sample pack or advice on the Conqueror* range and where to find it, call +44 (0) 1256 728 665 or visit www.conqueror.com now. You'll get five stars for presentation.

conqueror®

A Family Passion - the Rothschilds at Waddesdon Manor

A conversation with Beth Rothschild on her special relationship with this beautiful estate

Beth Rothschild on the Parterre at Waddesdon Manor (©Eleanor Bentall)

Waddesdon Manor was built at the end of the 19th century by Baron Ferdinand de Rothschild in the style of a French early 16th-century château. Baron Ferdinand was an inspired collector, and the house was designed to accommodate his fine collection of French 18th-century furniture, Sèvres porcelain, English portraits and other exceptional examples of the decorative arts. When Ferdinand died in 1898, he left Waddesdon Manor to his sister, Miss Alice. Upon her death, the house passed to James de Rothschild, a cousin from the French arm of the family. James inherited a substantial part of his father Baron Edmond's great collection. In 1957, in order to ensure its future in perpetuity, Waddesdon was bequeathed to the National Trust by James de Rothschild, although his widow, Dolly, continued to manage the house until her death in 1988.

The garden today is essentially the one laid out by Baron Ferdinand and his French landscape designer, Elie Lainé. When Baron Ferdinand bought the estate in 1874, the central hill was mostly farmland with few trees. Over the next ten years a dramatic transformation took place. The crown of the hill was levelled and planted with mature trees, drives and banks were created, and formal gardens were planted and decorated with sculpture. Baron Ferdinand's sister, Alice (1847-1922), maintained the 19th century form of the garden and added rare specimen trees and shrubs. However, by the time the property was bequeathed to the National Trust in 1957, the area of the garden had been reduced and the famous formal Parterre on the south side had been partly grassed over.

In 1990, Lord Rothschild initiated an extensive programme of building and restoration work with the aim of returning the garden and park to their original design. Most significantly, this has included the restoration of the Parterre on the South Terrace, which has returned to its traditional Victorian form using raised ribbon bedding schemes. Lord Rothschild's daughter, Kew graduate Beth Rothschild, has overseen the restoration of the Parterre, and continues to play an active role in the development of the garden.

"I have always been passionate about gardening... there was no question where my career would be"

Born in London, Beth Rothschild never had any doubts concerning her career. "I have always been passionate about gardening", she remembers. "There was no question where my career would be. I simply loved plants and gardens, and from the age of eight I used to scrape all my pocket money together and spend it on plants." When she was fourteen, her parents even built her a greenhouse on the roof of their London house. At the age of sixteen, Beth started her horticultural career by landing her first 'gardening' job: at the garden centre of

Aerial view of Waddesdon Manor (©Flying Pictures)

Clifton Nurseries. "It was a whole year of moving soil and staking roses…", she laughs. "And I was allowed to sweep the greenhouse!" She then joined the landscape design team, and later went on to gain a National Certificate in Horticulture from Oaklands College. Encouraged by her great-aunt Miriam, whom she always regarded as her mentor, Beth spent one year in Israel, working with Dr Michael Avishai at the Jerusalem Botanic Gardens. "I chose Israel for my first work experience abroad because of my family's roots there. Besides, I wanted to get into the course at Kew, and work experience at a Botanic Garden was one of the entry requirements." The project, in which they specifically concentrated on the introduction of wild flora as garden plants, lasted one year, and afterwards, Beth spent a few months at a Kibbutz. "They knew about my gardening experience, so that's what I was doing. And since I had farming experience as well, they also put me onto lambing. I spent the days in the garden and the nights delivering lambs!"

On her return to England, Beth Rothschild worked as a freelance landscape gardener before embarking on her studies at the Royal Botanical Gardens, Kew. Before and during her studies, she spent time travelling to America, China, Maccau, Hong Kong, the Philippines, Australia and New Zealand, collecting plants and seed and looking at gardens. When she left Kew in 1989, Beth was awarded the Thornton Smith Travel Scholarship and spent two years in Mexico, collecting plants in the dry forests of Jalisco and the cloud forests of Colima as part of a project to evaluate the local flora. She became especially interested in reforestation, and travelled extensively during the dry season in Guatemala and Costa Rica, looking at related projects.

Asked which part of the world appealed most to her, Beth doesn't hesitate for one second: "Mexico, without the hint of a doubt! And Guatemala as well. I was simply amazed by the diversity of the vegetation, the whole flora and fauna. They have absolutely untouched temperate forest there, which I had never seen before, and haven't seen anywhere since. I also loved the customs, the way people lived, and their relationship with nature. Part of me definitely belongs there!"

Her extensive travelling has obviously influenced Beth Rothschild in her understanding of landscape gardening. "The effect travelling had on me was simply that it gave me a better understanding of plants in general and the importance of plants in their natural habitat." This understanding is especially reflected in her involvement with restoration and conservation projects. "My greatest concern is the conservation of nature. This is what drives me."

One of the conservation projects Beth Rothschild has carried out over the last five years was the restoration of an olive grove overlooking the sea on the coast of Corfu. Her aim has been to put back the native flora which was previously lost during building work. Plants were collected locally to try to restore the natural ecological balance of the area.

"My greatest concern is the conservation of nature. This is what drives me"

Her favourite project, however, will always be the restoration of the Parterre at Waddesdon Manor, which she started while she was still at Kew. "Once upon a time, there was this beautiful Victorian parterre, which had

The Parterre (Andrew Peppard, ©National Trust, Waddesdon Manor)

then been forgotten and neglected over the years. I was really fortunate to have had the opportunity to restore it back to its former beauty, and create a historic example of a particularly fine Victorian garden. I have been involved in so many different projects at Waddesdon, planting trees, doing structural restoration work and so on, but I have to say the Parterre is definitely the project I feel most protective about."

"To be involved in the restoration of the Parterre was such a pleasure and honour for me"

One of Beth Rothschild's most recent projects at Waddesdon Manor was the opening of the Children's Garden in 1999. "After 12 years of working at Waddesdon Manor, I came to realise that the garden didn't offer anything attractive for children. I thought we should start to improve Waddesdon Manor for family visitors by widening the garden experience for children and by introducing a designated playing area. There was a playground, but it was a rather sad patch full of mud, which didn't offer much inspiration for playing. I knew

Children's Garden (©Beth Rothschild)

we could do better than that!" Inspiration for the design of the garden also came by talking directly to children."I thought it was very important to involve children in this project. I worked mainly with my own children, asking them how they imagined things to be and what they would like. I also worked with the children from the local school, which inspired me a lot. We're still at stage one, however, and a lot more needs to be done to reach stage two!"

The design of the garden allows for both play and education, with the focus on 'learning through playing'. There is a range of low hedges surrounding the gardens, which are cut in contrasting shapes and colours: red, silver and gold. "They're cut in children's heights, of course", Beth explains. "There will be features like a children's door in a hedge, which is only accessible for children, so that they can climb through and meet their parents at the other side."

Aside from the ongoing restoration and building works at Waddesdon, there are other current projects that provide entertainment for the visitor. The Parterre is

South Front and Parterre (©2000 by John Bigelow Taylor, N.Y.C.)

replanted twice a year, and a trial bed to the east of it is used to develop new planting schemes for each season. "This is a very special project in connection with the current celebrations to mark the new Millennium", explains Beth enthusiastically. "Each year, for the next four years, we will collaborate with a major artist to create something special in the garden." Last year, the American painter John Hubbard contributed a special painting, which the design team translated into plants,

Carpet Bedding (by Vivian Russell ©National Trust, Waddesdon Manor)

creating a 'living painting' in the Parterre.

This year, the designer Oscar de la Renta will create a 'Rainbow of Colours', for which carpet bedding plants will be used. This colourful spectacle can be admired at Waddesdon Manor between June and October 2001.

Text: Waddesdon Manor / Stephanie Cook

*For more information on Waddesdon Manor, please see page 34, or visit the website at **www.waddesdon.org.uk***

electricity is the same all over the UK it's the people you deal with which make the difference

Maverick Energy specialise in the business of electricity supply.

Having been energy consultants and brokers for 7 years we know what you need, and want, in terms of customer care.

To safeguard our beliefs in how the industry could be, we've become a licensed electricity supplier using simple principles. A competitive price offer with straightforward, timely and accurate billing - backed up with solid, tangible customer care.

Doing what needs to be done, by whom, when agreed, as agreed, and keeping you informed is what gives us a 97% annual retention rate of customers.

You will struggle to find a better Energy Team to work with.

Contact us to receive an excellent electricity price for your premises.

maverick
ENERGY

27 Shamrock Way, Hythe Marina Village, Hythe, Hampshire, SO45 6DY.
T **02380 841555**   F **02380 841777**
Email: sales@maverickenergy.co.uk Website: www.maverickenergy.co.uk

 preferred energy supplier

THE CHURCHES CONSERVATION TRUST

Caring for historic churches throughout England

St Mary's, Lead,
North Yorkshire

St Mary's is just one of the 50 exceptional churches chosen by The Churches Conservation Trust to illustrate the gems it has in its care. *Your Starter for 50* churches all have something specially interesting or beautiful about them – and can be visited *free* throughout the year. Our map shows where they all are.

The job of The Churches Conservation Trust is to repair and preserve churches throughout England of outstanding architectural and historic interest when they are no longer needed for regular parish use. In many, you can see the results of conservation work we have undertaken to protect crumbling stone, or ancient stained glass or even mediaeval wall paintings.

We welcome visitors to all our churches; some are opened daily, others have more limited opening times and still others have nearby keyholders. Opening arrangements for the featured churches are included overleaf.

We have over 300 churches but why not begin your exploration by sampling the glories of our selected *Starter for 50*?

BRISTOL

Bristol, St John ▼

St John's is the sole survivor of four Bristol churches built on the city wall in the 12th century and its picturesque tower and spire surmount the old North Gate. Above an earlier 14th century vaulted crypt, the present Perpendicular church was founded by Walter Frampton (d 1388) whose tomb and fine effigy are in the north wall of the chancel. The small, but impressively tall interior has interesting and lovely fittings, mostly 17th century, and an air of mercantile splendour.

Bottom of Broad Street at intersection with Nelson Street, ST587732.
Open Tues-Fri 11-4.
or 07931 578 068.

CORNWALL

St Anthony-in-Roseland, St Anthony ▶

St Anthony's stands behind Place, looking across the creek to St Mawes, and is unusual in surviving in its 13th century form without later additions. Pevsner thought it 'the best example in the county of what a parish church was like in the 12th and 13th centuries.' The ingenious 1850 restoration was carried out by Revd C W Carlyon, an amateur architect, and a cousin of the Sprys of Place whose monuments are in the church. There is a fine Norman doorway which may have come from Plympton Priory nearby.

20m SW of St Austell off A3078 and opp. St Mawes, SW855320.
Open daily.

Boris Baggs

CUMBRIA

◀ Brougham, St Ninian

Known locally as Ninekirks, this lovely church is reached down a long track off the A66, and stands in fields above a bend in the River Eamont. In 1660 Lady Anne Clifford completely rebuilt the Norman church and it remains a fascinating example of what is known as Gothic Survival style, with furniture and fittings almost untouched. The simple whitewashed interior has clear glass in most windows and a stone-flagged floor. The family pews, complete with canopies, the box pews and benches, communion rails and screen, and the three-decker pulpit are all of late 17th century oak and of excellent quality.

3m E of Penrith off A66, NY559299. Open daily.

Boris Baggs   *Boris Baggs*

DORSET

▼ Winterborne Tomson, St Andrew

In a gentle farmyard setting, built of grey stone and flint with a bell-turret of board and tile, this small 11th century village church is a delight. It enchants on sight and is all one could hope for inside. Archbishop Wake of Canterbury presented the box pews, pulpit and other furnishings early in the 18th century and most are still there, under a barrel-roof whose arches continue over the apse. They are all of oak, bleached through the years to a magical silvery grey. The church was gently repaired in 1931 using money raised from the sale of Thomas Hardy manuscripts.

8m W of Wimborne Minster off A31, SY885974.
Open daily.

KENT

Sandwich, St Peter ▶

The tower and Flemish cupola of this great town centre church, as well as the gable of its south-eastern vestry, all show the influence of 16th and 17th century refugees from the Low Countries. But other parts of this church have stood for 900 years, so much of what we see was fashioned in the 1200s and 1300s. Mediaeval roofs, exquisite 14th century tombs under arches and a host of treasures, ancient and modern, may be enjoyed in this lofty, light and airy church, where we learn much about the history and life of the town and Cinque Port. St Peter's has a busy programme of events throughout the year.

In town centre, TR331580. Usually open daily, or key available next door.

Christopher Dalton

LINCOLNSHIRE

◀ Kingerby, St Peter

Set by fields in leafy countryside, this is a beautiful and unspoilt church. Its solid rustic tower may date from the 12th century or even earlier and the rest is mainly from the 13th and 14th. The nave roof timbers date from the 17th century. Three splendid 14th century monuments to the Disney family survive, two in the south aisle and one in the chancel. The church also had a north aisle, now long demolished. The church escaped Victorian restorers and the appealing simplicity of the interior remains.

5m NW of Market Rasen, TF057929.
Open daily.

NORFOLK

Hales, St Margaret ▽

Known far and wide for its thatched roofs and round tower, Hales is Norfolk's best example of a 12th century Norman church essentially in its original form, with fascinating arcading around the apse, a magnificent north doorway of somewhat later date and a very good one to the south too. There are wall paintings including a St Christopher, the remains of a 15th century screen and a beautiful 15th century font. Despite its solitary position, remote from its village, it remains a place of pilgrimage for architectural students and church crawlers alike.

12m SE of Norwich and W of A146, TM384962.
Usually open daily April-Sept,
or keyholder nearby.

Christopher Dalton   *Christopher Dalton*

NORFOLK

King's Lynn, St Nicholas Chapel ▲

This striking building, splendidly light and spacious within, was built as a chapel of ease to St Margaret's. The fine tower is Early English, with a spire added by Sir George Gilbert Scott in 1869, but most of the church you see was finished in 1419. Its glories include a superb two-storied south porch, vaulted and richly ornamented, huge east and west windows and a very beautiful angel roof. There are fine fittings and interesting monuments, many commemorating Lynn merchants through the centuries.

St Anne's St, TF618205.
Key at True's Yard, call Andrew Lane
01553 770 479.

SUSSEX

▲ Warminghurst, The Holy Sepulchre

Up a narrow lane and on a walled bank with fine views to the south, Warminghurst church is one of the delights of Sussex. A simple mainly 13th century sandstone building, its 18th century interior is magical and unforgettable. A triple-arched screen, under a tympanum carrying a splendid Royal Arms robed in crimson drapery, separates nave from chancel; a complete set of box pews and a clerk's pew and pulpit fill the nave; there are hatchments and monuments from the 18th century and earlier; and the natural wood furnishings and uneven floor are all lit through clear glass.

10m N of Worthing off A24, TQ117169.
Keyholder nearby 01903 892 353.

WEST YORKSHIRE

Harewood, All Saints ▽

All Saints stands in the park of Harewood House and was built around 1410. Sir George Gilbert Scott's restoration in 1862–63 reordered the interior considerably to accord with the Victorians' idea of a mediaeval church. Inside, the building is severe and the lack of decorative carving contrasts strongly with its greatest treasures: the six superb alabaster tombs and pairs of effigies of the owners of Harewood and nearby Gawthorpe, dating from 1419 to 1510. These provide a unique display of costume, armour and funerary design during those years. There is good Victorian glass by Kempe and others.

6m N of Leeds off A61, SE314451
Open 10-6 April-October, 7 days a week. At other times call 0113 288 6331

Boris Baggs

Boris Baggs   *Christopher Dalton*

NORTH YORKSHIRE

Lead, St Mary ▲

Known as the Ramblers' Church this peaceful and well-visited place lies close to the battlefield of Towton where the wearisome Wars of the Roses ended. The field around is full of low earthworks, indicating the site of a manor house for which this was surely the chapel. It is tiny and rustic and the 14th century single cell building with a bell-cote is fitted with 18th century woodwork and earlier open benches. The floor includes mediaeval coffin lids and the font may be from an earlier church.

10m SE of Wetherby off B1217, SE464369.
Open daily.

WORCESTERSHIRE

Lower Sapey, St Bartholomew Old Church ▲

This humble two cell building is a rare survival: a rustic Norman or late Saxon church, memorably set in beautiful and remote country next to a 17th century farmhouse and close to the site of a Saxon settlement. Some alterations were made in the 14th century, others in the 18th, but the importance and charm of this church is that little has changed from its early times. Years of neglect followed the building of a new church in the 1870s, but the efforts of local people and its vesting in the Trust in 1994 secured its future.

13m NW of Worcester off B4204, SO699602.
Open daily.

Your Starter for 50 churches in the care of The Churches Conservation Trust

All churches on the map are opened regularly or have keyholders nearby*. Further details may be obtained by ordering the leaflets below.

- ● Churches featured in the article
- ● Other *Starter for 50* Churches

Newcastle Upon Tyne ■
● Bywell
● Brougham   Middlesbrough ■

Skelton-cum-Newby ●
Harewood ● ● York Holy Trinity
● Lead
Leeds

● Waterloo   ■ Manchester   Kingerby ●
Liverpool ■ ● Warburton   Snarford ●
● Macclesfield   Lincoln
Chester ■

● Kedleston

● Battlefield   King's Lynn Booton ●
Shrewsbury ●   ● Stapleford   ● Wiggenhall   Norwich St John ●
● Wroxeter   Norwich ■
● Bridgnorth   ● Hales
■ Birmingham   Bungay ■
● Lower Sapey   ● Icklingham
Worcester ■   Cambridge ■
Billesley   ● Cambridge St Peter
Holme Lacy ●   Duxford ●

Gloucester ■   Eastleach Martin ●
Ozleworth ●   Inglesham ●
London ■
● Bristol St John   Cooling ●
● Cameley
Parracombe ●   ● Albury   Sandwich St Peter ●
Dover ■
Fisherton ● Delamere   ● Itchen Stoke
North Stoke ● ● Warminghurst
● Tarrant Crawford   ● Chichester ■ Brighton
● Winterborne Tomson   ● Church Norton
● Exeter
Torbryan ●
■ Plymouth
Truro
● Roseland-St-Anthony

*Please remember that emergency building work may mean that we need to close a church temporarily for safety reasons.

Complete and send to The Churches Conservation Trust, 89 Fleet Street, London, EC4Y 1DH

Name .... Title ....

Address .... Postcode ....

Please send me: *Your Starter for 50* leaflet(s). Please tick beside the area(s) you are interested in

North ☐   South West ☐   South East ☐   Central ☐   East ☐

Full List of Churches in the care of The Churches Conservation Trust ☐

County leaflets, please specify county(ies)..

JHS1

Scotland in Trust

The National Trust for Scotland celebrates its 70th anniversary

Nobody can doubt the extraordinary variety and richness of Scotland's heritage and nowhere is it better shown than in the properties owned and cared for by The National Trust for Scotland. This year the Trust celebrates its 70th anniversary and is taking the opportunity to look back over its own history with the publication of a new book as well as looking forward to the next decades of conserving the best of Scotland's heritage.

Founded in 1931, the Trust was established to act as a guardian of Scotland's magnificent heritage of architectural, historic and scenic treasures and to encourage public access to them. At first, the Trust had no properties and 32 members; now it cares for some 120 properties and benefits from the support of over 228,000 members, making it Scotland's leading conservation charity. The portfolio of properties ranges from castles and mansions, beautiful gardens and romantic islands to historic battlefields, spectacular mountains and fascinating examples of Scotland's industrial past. They are all held "for the benefit of the nation" to be enjoyed by both natives and visitors and each year over 2 million people enjoy the treasures on offer. Members have the double benefit of knowing that they are helping to keep these treasures safe for future generations to enjoy whilst also enjoying free access to all properties for a year.

Bannockburn - Statue of Robert the Bruce (©The National Trust for Scotland)

Many of the Trust's "Great Houses" encapsulate the organisation's aim to preserve places of historic interest or natural beauty – the former being the buildings and the latter, the gardens and estates which often surround them. One such example is **Culzean Castle**, in South Ayrshire, where Robert Adam's castle, built between 1772 and 1790 is set in Scotland's first Country Park, comprising 563 acres, and stretching from shoreline to mature parklands and gardens.

Within each house is an exceptional range of contents displaying the best of the fine and decorative arts. **Fyvie Castle**, in the North East, for instance, contains an important collection of portraits including works by Raeburn and Gainsborough, while **Brodick Castle**, located on the Isle of Arran, is known for its porcelain and silver collections. Many give an insight into the lives of the families who have lived in these historic properties through the generations reminding visitors that they always have been family homes. It is not unusual to have the feeling of "stepping back in time' to bygone ages, for example, by experiencing 17th century life in Edinburgh at **Gladstone's Land**, 18th

Aerial view of Culzean Castle, South Ayrshire (©The National Trust for Scotland)

century life in the city's New Town at The **Georgian House**, or early 20th century domestic life in Glasgow at the **Tenement House**!

Scotland's tumultuous history is reflected in the Trust's properties through the conservation of land which itself has borne witness to historic acts – namely Bannockburn, Glencoe and Culloden. Strenuous efforts have been made to present each site with care and dignity and, where possible, an interpretation centre puts into context the events which have happened there and shaped Scotland's history.

Some of the Trust's more unusual properties – including two mills and a printing works - remind visitors of Scotland's rich industrial heritage. Records show that a mill has occupied the site of **Barry Mill**, near Carnoustie, since 1539 and **Preston Mill**, in East Lothian, continued in commercial use until 1957. Both mills give an impression of what it would have been like to work there, while **Robert Smail's Printing Works**, in the Borders, shows how printing was done at the beginning of this century and even offers the opportunity to try typesetting by hand!

The National Trust for Scotland is the country's largest garden owner, with over 700 acres under intensive cultivation supporting 13,500 different types of plant. Almost every style of Scottish garden

history is represented. As well as maintaining such historic gardens, the Trust plays an important role in training with its School of Practical Gardening, based at **Threave Garden** in Dumfries and Galloway, giving invaluable experience to students each year.

Of its gardens, **Inverewe** in Ross-shire, is probably the Trust's best known. Here, even the location is exceptional, with a setting on a peninsula on the shores of Loch Ewe. Inverewe is an oasis of colour and fertility where exotic plants from many countries flourish. Himalayan rhododendrons and Tasmanian eucalyptus can be found together with plants from Chile, South

Culzean Castle (©The National Trust for Scotland)

www.historichouses.co.uk

Africa and New Zealand, all enjoying the effects of the North Atlantic Drift which brings unusually warm currents to the shores of this sea loch.

Scotland's countryside is renowned for its spectacular and varied scenery and for the wildlife which lives there. The Trust cares for some of the finest and most important examples of this heritage, and this combination of landscape and wildlife attracts visitors throughout the year. It is possible to see and enjoy spectacular species – Golden Eagles, massive seabird colonies and red deer – at some properties, whilst the varied plant life and more familiar animals of the countryside can be discovered at others. There is an active programme of management for the wildlife and special work is undertaken for wildlife under threat.

Crathes Castle, Banchory, Aberdeenshire (©The National Trust for Scotland)

The Hill House, Helensburgh (©The National Trust for Scotland)

The Trust's Rangers are skilled and practical naturalists with a strong commitment to the conservation of the Scottish countryside. "Conservation Volunteers", who give up time to carry out diverse tasks, such as repairing footpaths and dry stone walls, undertake further practical conservation work.

The largest acquisition in the Trust's history was the 77,500-acre **Mar Lodge Estate**, part of the core area of the Cairngorm Mountains, which it took into its ownership in April 1995. The main priority on the estate is the conservation of its outstanding natural heritage qualities in harmony with allowing public access and maintaining its traditional sporting use. A reduction in deer numbers will encourage the natural regeneration of the native Caledonian pine forest, which is of national importance.

As well as owning properties on Scotland's mainland, the Trust also cares for a number of islands. Among these are **St Kilda**, 110 miles out in the Atlantic and designated Scotland's first World Heritage site in 1987; **Fair Isle**, situated between Orkney and Shetland and famed for its birdlife and knitwear; and **Staffa**, with its Fingal's Cave, immortalised by Mendelssohn in his celebrated "Hebrides" Overture.

The Trust advocates life-long learning and aims to inform people, of all ages and backgrounds, about the natural and cultural development of Scotland. Hopefully, with the variety on offer, the National Trust for Scotland has something that can be enjoyed by every visitor or native, and through the Trust's work, Scotland's past can enjoy a secure future.

Ian Gardner
Head of Public Affairs

Brodie Castle, Forres, Moran (©The National Trust for Scotland)

THE NATIONAL
GARDENS SCHEME

GARDENS OPEN FOR CHARITY

INNOVATIVE OR CLASSIC, THE NATIONAL GARDENS SCHEME EMBRACES THEM ALL,

FROM INTIMATE CITY COURTYARDS TO COTTAGE PLOTS AND LANDSCAPES.

FIND NOVEL SOLUTIONS TO ALL KINDS OF GARDEN PROBLEMS AND ENJOY PRIVILEGED

INSIGHT INTO INVENTIVE PLANTING SCHEMES. INTERESTING AND UNUSUAL PLANTS ARE

OFTEN AVAILABLE, ALONG WITH EXPERT TIPS FROM THE PEOPLE IN THE KNOW.

GARDENS
OF ENGLAND AND WALES
OPEN FOR CHARITY

This book is sponsored by
CARR SHEPPARDS
CROSTHWAITE

2001

THE NATIONAL GARDENS SCHEME

Plan your visits with **'Gardens of England and Wales Open For Charity'**, the best-selling annual guide published by the NGS, which lists days when fine private gardens open their gates to the public for charity. The 'Yellow Book', as it is familiarly known, includes short descriptions of the gardens and county maps and is available at all major booksellers and on the NGS website.

Garden Finder, a search and mapping facility on the NGS website, provides even more detail about the gardens, often including photographs. Find exclusive openings on the **NGS website http://www.ngs.org.uk**

For more information, or to find out about opening your own garden please contact:

Catherine Stepney, Public Relations Administrator, The National Gardens Scheme

Hatchlands Park, East Clandon, Surrey GU4 7RT

T 01483 211535 **F** 01483 211537 **Email** ngs@ngs.org

✸ Heritage Education Trust ✸
Sandford Awards - sponsored by Johansens

"Palaces and Castles, Cathedrals and Parsonages, Breweries and Hop Farms, Historic Houses and Cottages all show the richness and variety of Britain's built heritage."

Since 1982, The Heritage Education Trust has recognised and promoted the excellence of educational services offered in Historic Houses, Castles and Gardens, Museums and Galleries, through the granting of Sandford Awards for Heritage Education.

The Awards are made annually by the Heritage Education Trust. They recognise the provision of quality education in and about historic buildings, artefacts and landscape. They are non-competitive, recognising quality and excellence. There is no stipulation for entry on the size of the property, or the extent of the educational services provided.

Any historic property, artefact and historic landscape is eligible; as an illustration, previous Sandford Award winners include Blenheim Palace, Glamis Castle, Manchester Jewish Museum, Royal Armouries - Tower of London, Canterbury Cathedral, Clipper Ship Cutty Sark and Wigan Pier.

Entry is, in the first place, by the completion of a pro forma application, then, after consideration for qualification, Judges will be allocated to visit, assess and report back to the main Judges' Panel, whose recommendations are passed to the Directors for their final decision. The Judges all have educational backgrounds and include Ofsted inspectors, educational consultants, property education officers and administrators.

The Sandford Awards are an independently judged, quality assured assessment of heritage education in historic properties. They are recognised and recommended by The Historic Houses Association and The National Trust.

Schools and other educational groups are encouraged to look for historic properties displaying the Heritage Education Trust logo to signify that they are Sandford Award holders and thus deliver a quality heritage education service.

Heritage Education

Recent surveys of the public's perspective of the historic landscape of Britain have identified the great affinity in which heritage is held in these isles. Not only do we respect and treasure our heritage, but we are also aware of the need to conserve it for future generations. It is through education at all levels that this current esteem is passed on to the decision-makers of tomorrow.

Heritage is not just about bricks and mortar, it provides revenue and employment; it encourages the continuance of craftsmanship; it helps us to make informed choices, and share values within the community. It is the base line for the delivery of a meaningful education.

The Heritage Education Trust seeks to further the provision of this quality education and to link the users - both schools and the public in general and the providers at all suitable historic properties. The need to show good practice in both spheres has been identified so that teachers will know where to take their students for a worthwhile learning experience, whilst the properties develop programmes from examples of work undertaken at similar sites and by visiting schools. The well-motivated property owner or administrator often works in isolation in establishing their service. The Trust is seeking to address this need and provide a network of symbiotic partnerships, which will benefit not only students but visitors of all ages to make their visits enjoyable, entertaining and educational.

For further details on The Heritage Education Trust or The Sandford Awards for Heritage Education contact:

Gareth Fitzpatrick
Chief Executive, Heritage Education Trust
Boughton House, Kettering
Northamptonshire NN14 1BJ
www.heritageontheweb.co.uk/het

The Sandford Awards are sponsored by Johansens. The Heritage Education Trust is a Company limited by guarantee and registered as a charity.

Sandford Awards 2000

The Heritage Education Trust was pleased to recognise the achievements of properties from across the nation, from Perth in Scotland to East Sussex and Devon, a wide range of sites are represented. The grandeur of Alnwick Castle, Northumberland and the Palace of Scone in Perth contrast with the more humble, but equally important homes of country writers Wordsworth and Brontë all are set in the historic landscapes that gave such inspiration.

The spiritual life of The Cathedral Church of St Peter in Exeter is far removed from the more temporal life shown in the Bass Museum in Burton upon Trent. The historic houses and galleries that also featured give a more traditional view of Britain's built heritage, but all recipients show to future generations the important wealth of history to be found in these Isles.

The Sandford Awards for Heritage Education

Award Winners 2000

ALNWICK CASTLE, Northumberland

THE BASS MUSEUM, Staffordshire

BEAULIEU, Hampshire

BODIAM CASTLE, East Sussex

THE BRONTE PARSONAGE MUSEUM, West Yorkshire

THE CATHEDRAL CHURCH OF ST. PETER, Exeter

DOVE COTTAGE, Cumbria

DULWICH PICTURE GALLERY, London

HOLDENBY HOUSE, Northamptonshire

KINGSTON LACY HOUSE, Dorset

KILLERTON HOUSE, Devon

MUSEUM OF KENT LIFE, Kent

SCONE PALACE, Scotland

Sandford Award Holders

The following properties received Sandford Awards in the years in brackets after their names in recognition of the excellence of their educational services and facilities and their outstanding contribution to Heritage Education. Two or more dates indicate that the property has been reviewed and received further recognition under the system of quinquennial review introduced by the Heritage Education Trust in 1986.

Alnwick Castle, Alnwick, Northumberland (2000)

The Argory, Co. Tyrone, Northern Ireland (1995)

Aston Hall, Birmingham, (1993,1998)

Avoncroft Museum of Buildings, Bromsgrove, Worcestershire, (1988,1993, 1998)

Bass Museum Visitor Centre & Shire Horse Stables, Burton-upon-Trent, Staffs (1990, 1995, 2000)

Beaulieu, Hampshire (1978, 1986, 1991, 2000)

Bedford Museum and the Cecil Higgins Art Gallery, Bedford (1988, 1993,1998)

Bewdley Museum, Worcestershire (1992,1997)

Blakesley Hall Museum, Birmingham (1993,1998)

Blenheim Palace, Woodstock, Oxon, (1982,1987,1992,1997)

Bodiam Castle, East Sussex, (1995, 2000)

Boughton House, Kettering, Northamptonshire (1988,1993,1998)

Bowhill House & Country Park, Selkirk, Borders, Scotland (1993,1998)

Bronte Parsonage Museum, Haworth, West Yorkshire (2000),

Buckfast Abbey, Buckfastleigh, Devon (1985,1990,1995)

Buckland Abbey, Yelverton, Devon (1995,1996)

Cannock Chase Heritage Centre (formerly Museum of Cannock Chase), Cannock (1998)

Cannon Hall Museum and Country Park, Barnsley (1999)

Canterbury Cathedral, Canterbury, Kent (1988,1993,1998)

Castell Henllys Iron Age Fort, Pembrokeshire National Park (1999)

Castle Museum, York, North Yorkshire (1987,1993,1998)

Castle Ward, County Down, Northern Ireland (1980,1987,1994)

The Cathedral Church of St Peter in Exeter, Devon, (2000)

Cathedral & Abbey Church of St Alban, St Albans, Hertfordshire (1986, 1991, 1996)

Chester Cathedral, Chester (1998)

Chiltern Open Air Museum, Chalfont St Giles, Buckinghamshire (1994, 1999)

Chirk Castle, Chirk, Clwyd, Wales (1994, 1999)

Clipper Ship Cutty Sark, Greenwich (1998)

Clive House Museum, Shrewsbury, Shropshire (1992,1997)

Coldharbour Mill, Working Wood Museum Cullompton, Devon (1989,1994)

Combe Sydenham, Nr Taunton, Somerset (1984,1989,1994,1999)

Corfe Castle, Dorset (1998)

Crathes Castle and Gardens, Kincardineshire, Scotland (1992,1997)

Croxteth Hall & Country Park, Liverpool, Merseyside (1980, 1989, 1994, 1999)

Culzean Castle & Country Park, Ayrshire, Scotland (1984,1989,1994,1999)

Dove Cottage & the Wordsworth Museum, Grasmere, Cumbria (1990, 1995, 2000)

Dulwich Picture Gallery, London (1990,1995, 2000)

Duncomber Park, Helmsley, Yorkshire (1999)

Dunham Massey Hall, Altrincham, Cheshire (1994)

Elscar Heritage Centre, Barnsley, South Yorkshire (1999)

Erddig Hall, Nr Wrexham, Clwyd, Wales (1991,1996)

Exeter Cathedral, Devon (1995)

Fishbourne Roman Palace, Chichester, West Sussex (1999)

Flagship Portsmouth, Portsmouth (1996)

Ford Green Hall, Stoke-on Trent (1996)

Florence Court, Co Fermanagh, Northern Ireland (1995)

Georgian House, Edinburgh, Scotland (1978)

Gladstone's Land, Edinburgh, Scotland (1995)

Glamis Castle, Glamis, Forfar, Scotland (1997)

The Goodwood Estate, Goodwood (1998)

Harewood House, Leeds, West Yorkshire (1979,1989,1994)

Sir Harold Hillier Gardens and Arboretum, Ampfield, Hampshire (1993, 1998)

The Heritage Centre, Macclesfield (1998)

Holdenby House, Northamptonshire (1985, 1990, 1995, 2000)

Jewellery Quarter Discovery Centre, Birmingham (1996)

Killerton House, Devon, (2000)

Kingston Lacy House, Wimborne, Dorset (1990, 1995, 2000)

Laundry Cottage, Normanby Hall Country Park, South Humberside (1994)

Lichfield Cathedral & Visitors' Study Centre, Staffs (1991,1996)

Llancaiach Fawr Living History Museum, Nelson, Mid Glamorgan (1994,1999)

Macclesfield Museums, Macclesfield (1988,1993,1998)

Manchester Jewish Museum, Manchester (1998)

Margam Country Park, Port Talbot, Wales (1999)

Moseley Old Hall, Wolverhampton, (1983, 1989, 1994, 1999)

Museum of Kent Life - Cobtree, Kent (1995, 2000)

National Waterways Museum, Gloucester (1991, 1996)

New Lanark, Lanark, Scotland (1999)

Norton Priory, Cheshire (1992,1997)

Oakwell Hall Country Park, Birstall, West Yorkshire (1988,1993,1998)

The Old School, Bognor Regis (1996)

The Priest's House Museum, Wimborne Minster, Dorset (1993,1998)

Quarry Bank Mill, Styal, Cheshire (1987,1992,1997)

The Queen's House, Greenwich (1995)

Rockingham Castle, nr Corby, Northamptonshire (1980,1987,1992,1998)

Roman Baths and Pump Room, Bath, Avon (1994,1999)

Rowley's House Museum, Shrewsbury, Shropshire (1993, 1998)

Ryedale Folk Museum, Hutton le Hole, North Yorkshire (1993, 1998)

Scone Palace, Perth, Scotland, (2000)

The Shugborough Estate, Staffordshire (1987, 1992, 1997)

South Shields Museum and Art Gallery (Arbeia Roman Fort), (1996)

Springhill, Co Londonderry (1995)

St Peter's Village Tour, Broadstairs (1998)

Sutton House, Hackney (1996)

Tatton Park, Knutsford, Cheshire (1979,1986, 1991, 1996)

Tenement House, Glasgow (1996)

Thackray Medical Museum, Leeds, Yorkshire (1999)

Tower of London, Tower Bridge, London (1978,1986,1991,1996)

Victorian School of the 3 Rs, Llangollen (1996)

Weald and Downland Open Air Museum, Chichester (1996)

Wigan Pier, Wigan, Lancashire, (1987,1992,1997)

Wightwick Manor, Wolverhampton, (1986,1991,1996)

Wimpole Hall & Home, Near Cambridge, Cambridgeshire (1988,1993, 1999)

York Castle Museum, York (1998)

FINE ESTATE JEWELLERY

Bedfordshire

The chalk grassland and sandhills of Bedfordshire's gently undulating countryside are a pleasant setting for its busy towns, thatched hamlets and mediaeval villages.

Historic Bedford lies on the River Ouse, in the centre of the county. This location, much contested in the reign of King Alfred, is now an attractive riverside town where the only battles that occur are between oarsmen along its watercourse. A statue of John Bunyan pays tribute to the rebellious author of The Pilgrim's Progress, written here whilst Bunyan was imprisoned in the 1600s.

Many stately homes and gardens enjoy views over the rich rural landscape and are rewarding places to visit. The county is home to a varied population of wildlife, flora and fauna, as well as the inhabitants of its several nature reserves and world-famous animal parks.

In contrast, bustling towns such as Luton and Dunstable are home to much of its 560,000 strong population, preserving the peace of the picturesque 12th and 13th century villages that surround them.

JOHN BUNYAN MUSEUM AND BUNYAN MEETING FREE CHURCH

Mill Street, Bedford, Bedfordshire MK40 3EU
Tel & Fax: 01234 213722

Experience the life and times of the famous 17th century preacher, pastor and author of 'The Pilgrim's Progress'. The collection includes copies of Bunyan's most celebrated work in over 170 languages and many of his personal possessions. The church, with its magnificent bronze entrance doors and 20th century stained glass windows, should be included in your visit. Sunday Services are held at 11am & 6:30pm. **Open:** Museum: March-end Oct: Tues-Sat 11am-4pm (last entry 3.45pm). Closed Good Fri. Group bookings & school parties by prior arrangement throughout the year. Teachers' research packs available. **Admission:** Free.

map 4 E2

SWISS GARDEN

Old Warden, Biggleswade, Bedfordshire
Tel: 01767 626255/627666 (Bedfordshire County Council)

The Swiss Garden was designed in the 1820s with serpentine paths winding around ponds and over wrought iron bridges, through glades and over lawn. As you stroll through this woodland garden you'll find a fernery-grotto, a thatch seat, the Swiss Cottage and other tiny buildings dotted around this miniature alpine landscape. Peacocks wander amid the slendid trees and shrubs. In spring, daffodils add colour to the many shades of green, followed by rhododendrons and azaleas. A little later roses twine around the arches and finally brilliant acres announce the late summer. Designed to delight, a garden to bring visitors back. **Open:** Mar-Sept. Sun & B.H. 10-6pm. Other Days 1-6pm. Jan, Feb & Oct. Sun 11-3pm. **Admission:** Adults £3, Conc £2, Family £8 (2 adults 2 conc). Group discounts and private hire available. **E-mail:** swissgarden@deed.bedfordshire.gov.uk

map 4 E2

WOBURN ABBEY

Woburn, Bedfordshire,
Tel: 01525 290666 Fax: 01525 290271
(The Marquess of Tavistock and the Trustees of the Bedford Estates)

Woburn Abbey is the home to the Marquess and Marchioness of Tavistock and their family. The art collection, one of the most important in the country, includes paintings by Van Dyck, Gainsborough and Reynolds. In the Venetian Room there are 21 views of Venice by Canaletto. There is also French and English 18th century furniture, silver and gold and exquisite porcelain. There are 9 species of deer in 3,000 acre deer park including the Pere David deer, saved from extinction here at Woburn. The Flying Duchess Pavilion serves lunches, snacks and teas and there are gift shops and an Antiques Centre. **E-mail:** woburnabbey@aol.com

map 4 E2

WREST PARK GARDENS

Silsoe, Bedfordshire MK45 4HS
Tel: 01525 860152 (English Heritage)

Take a fascinating journey through a century and a half of gardening styles. Enjoy a leisurely stroll by the Long Water, canals and Leg O'Mutton Lake and explore a charming range of garden buildings, including the baroque Archer Pavilion, Orangery and classical Bath House. Discover bridges and ponds, temples and altars, fountains and statues in over 90 acres of carefully landscaped gardens, laid out before a fabulous French-style Victorian Mansion. There is an informative audio-tour available. **Location:** 10 miles south of Bedford. **Open:** 31 Mar-30 Sept Oct: 10–6pm (5pm in Oct), weekends and Bank Holidays only. Last admission one hour before closing time. **Admission:** Adult £3.50, Conc £2.65, Child £1.75 (15% discount for groups of 11 or more). Family ticket £8.80.

map 4 E2

CECIL HIGGINS ART GALLERY

Castle Close, Castle Lane, Bedford
Tel: 01234 211222 Fax: 01234 327149

Housed in an elegantly converted and extended Victorian Mansion, original home of the Higgins family of wealthy Bedford brewers, the Cecil Higgins Art Gallery is home to one of the most outstanding fine and decorative art collections outside London. The Gallery offers: • A remarkable collection of British and European watercolours from the 18th to the 20th centuries and international prints from Impressionism to the present. Includes works by Rembrandt, Turner, Blake, Cotman, Rossetti, Burne-Jones, Whistler, Renoir, Picasso, Dalí, Moore, Warhol, Hockney. The exhibition changes regularly. • A distinguished group of ceramics and glass from the Renaissance to the 20th century, with particular focus on 18th century porcelain, Whitefriars glass and ceramics of the Arts and Crafts movement. • Authentically reconstructed Victorian room settings in the Victorian mansion, suggesting the life of a prosperous 1880's household. • The William Burges room, a complete Gothic experience, with Burges' own furniture in a full decorative setting, inspired by his designs. • Hands-on activities for children and workshops for all ages. • Changing exhibitions from the collection and elsewhere. • Programme of events, lectures, performances and more. • Fully guided tours available for groups on request (charges vary). • A shop selling high quality souvenirs and work by local designers. **Open:** Tues–Sat 11am–5pm; Sun & Bank Holiday Mon 2–5pm (last admission 4.45pm). Closed Mondays, Good Friday, 25 & 26 December & 1 Jan. **Admission:** Adults £2 (includes visit to Bedford Museum), Children & Concessions free. **E-mail:** chag@bedford.gov.uk

map 4
E2

Berkshire

Those who visit this beautiful and serene county will find some of England's most famous heritage and its most subtle charm.

Windsor, one of the homes of the royal family, is situated in the east of the county's 60-mile stretch to the west of London. Its narrow cobbled streets, whose ancient buildings house boutique shops, traditional cafés and fine restaurants, are watched over by impressive Windsor Castle, an awe-inspiring stone fortress standing on high ground in the centre of the city.

Across the River Thames, which flows through the length of the county on its journey east to London, is Eton, home to the famous public school, founded by Henry VI in 1440.

Berkshire's history dates back to the Bronze Age, when an area of high ground known as the Ridgeway formed a major trade route between the east and west. Now a popular walking trail, it continues to afford magnificent views across the Berkshire Downs. Numerous idyllic Thames Valley towns lie in the pretty countryside along the river to the north of the county, where cosy pubs and picturesque churches abound.

The Savill Garden

 ## ETON COLLEGE
Windsor, Berkshire SL4 6DW, UK
Tel: 01753 671177 Fax: 01753 671265

Founded in 1440 by Henry VI, Eton College is one of the oldest schools in the country. Visitors are invited to experience and share the beauty and traditions of the College. **Open:** Times are governed by both the dates for term and holidays on the school calendar, but the College will be open to visitors from the end of March until the beginning of October. Guided Tours during the season are available for individuals at 2.15 and 3.15pm daily. Guided Tours for groups by prior arrangement with the Visits Manager, Mrs Hunkin (Tel: 01753 671177 Fax: 01753 671265). **E-mail:** visits@etoncollege.org.uk **Internet:** www.etoncollege.com

map 4
C4

 ## DORNEY COURT
Dorney, Nr Windsor, Berkshire SL4 6QP
Tel: 01628 604638 Fax: 01628 665772 (Mrs Peregrine Palmer)

'One of the finest Tudor Manor Houses in England' – Country Life. Built about 1440 and lived in by the present family for over 450 years. The rooms are full of the atmosphere of a very much lived in home with early English Oak furniture, portraits spanning 600 years, stained glass and needlework. **Location:** 2 miles W of Eton & Windsor in village of Dorney on B3026. From M4 use exit 7. **Open:** May: Bank Hol Mons & preceding Sun. 1.30-4.30, Aug every afternoon except Sat 1.30-4.30. **Admission:** Adults £5, Children over 9 £3. Parties by arrangement throughout the year. **Refreshments:** Teas at the Plant Centre in Walled Garden. PYO fruit from June–end Aug. **E-mail:** palmer@dorneycourt.co.uk **Internet:** www.dorneycourt.co.uk

map4
D4

MAPLEDURHAM HOUSE & WATERMILL
Nr. Reading, Berkshire, RG4 7TR Tel: 01189 723 350
Fax: 01189 724 016 (The Mapledurham Trust)

Late 16th century Elizabethan home of the Blount family. Original plaster ceiling, great oak staircase, fine collection of paintings and private chapel in Strawberry Hill Gothick added in 1797. The 15th century Watermill is fully restored and producing flour and bran which are sold in the gift shop. **Location:** 4 miles NW of Reading on North bank of River Thames. Signposted from A4074. **Open:** Easter–end Sept. Midweek parties by arrangement. **Admission:** Please phone for details. **Refreshments:** Tearooms serving cream teas. **Events/ Exhibitions:** By arrangement. **Conferences:** By arrangement. **Accommodation:** 11 self-catering holiday cottages. Wedding receptions by arrangement. Car parking and picnic area. **E-mail:** mtrust1997@aol.com **Internet:** www.mapledurham.co.uk

map 4
D4

HIGHCLERE CASTLE

Nr Newbury, Berkshire RG20 9RN
Tel: 01635 253210 Fax: 01635 255315

Designed by Charles Barry in the 1830s at the same time as he was building the Houses of Parliament. This soaring pinnacled mansion provided a perfect setting for the 3rd Earl of Carnarvon, one of the great hosts of Queen Victoria's reign. Old master paintings mix with portraits by Van Dyck and 18th century painters. Napoleon's desk and chair rescued from St Helena sits with other 18th century furniture. The 5th Earl of Carnarvon, discovered the Tomb of Tutankhamun with Howard Carter. The castle houses a unique exhibition of some of his discoveries which were only rediscovered in the castle in 1988. The current Earl is the Queen's Horseracing Manager. In 1993 to celebrate his 50th year as a leading owner and breeder 'The Lord Carnarvon Racing Exhibition' was opened and offers a fascinating insight into a racing history that dates back three generations. The magnificent parkland, with its massive cedars, was designed by Capability Brown. The Secret Garden has a romance of its own with a beautiful curving lawn surrounded by densely planted herbaceous gardens. A place for poets and romantics. Guided tours are often provided, free of charge, to visitors. **Location:** 4.4 miles S of Newbury on A34, Jct 13 off M4 about 2 m from Newbury. **Open:** 1 July–31 Aug, 7 days a week 11–5pm, last adm. 4pm, Sat last adm. 2.30pm. Closed 21/22 July. **Refreshments:** Lunches, teas, ices, soft drinks. **Conferences:** Business conferences, management training courses, film and photographic location. Licensed for civil weddings. Ample car park and picnic area adjacent to Castle. Suitable for disabled persons on ground floor only. Visitors can buy original items in Castle Gift Shop. No dogs are permitted in the house or gardens except guide dogs. No photography in the house. Occasionally subject to closure. **E-mail:** theoffice@highclerecastle.co.uk **Internet:** www.highclerecastle.co.uk

map 4
C5

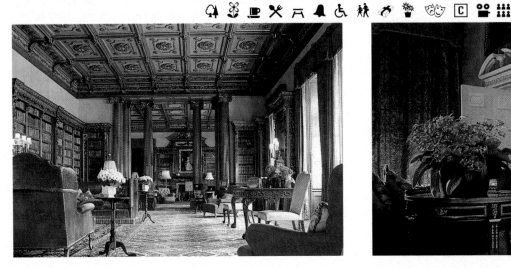

MUSEUM OF READING
The Town Hall, Blagrave Street, Reading, Berkshire RG1 1QH
Tel: 0118 939 9800

Visit the refurbished Museum of Reading which now features twelve exciting galleries. The new spaces include the world's first biscuit gallery dedicated to Huntley & Palmers, a Victorian Art Gallery, a sculpture gallery and the Green Space environment gallery. Additionally, the museum features rich Roman displays, including stunning mosaics, pottery and the Silchester gallery of Roman life. Mosaic, the museum shop sells high quality gifts at affordable prices. Please call us for further details and a free leaflet, or visit our website. **Open**: Tuesday–Saturday 10-4pm; Thursday late opening 10-7pm; Sunday & Bank Holiday Mondays 11–4pm. (Closed Mondays).

Internet: www.readingmuseum.org.uk

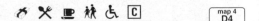

map 4
D4

SAVILL GARDEN
Windsor Great Park
Tel: 01753 847518

World renowned woodland garden of 35 acres, situated in the tranquil surroundings of Windsor Great Park. The garden contains a fine range of rhododendrons, azaleas, camellias and magnolias; with adjoining rose gardens and herbaceous borders. Autumn provides a great feast of colour and the whole garden offers much of great interest and beauty at all seasons. Queen Elizabeth Temperate House. **Location:** To be approached from A30 via Wick Road and Wick Lane, Englefield Green. **Station(s):** Egham (3 m). **Open:** Daily 10–6pm Mar–Oct, 10–4pm Nov–Feb (closed Dec 25/26). **Admission:** Adults: Apr–May £5, June–Oct £4, Nov–Mar £3. Concessions for Senior Citizens and Groups. **Refreshments:** Licensed self-service restaurant. Well stocked plant centre/gift shop. Ample parking.

map 4
E4

TAPLOW COURT
Berry Hill, Taplow, Nr Maidenhead, Berks SL6 0ER
Tel: 01628 591215 Fax: 01628 773055 (SGI–UK)

Set high above the Thames affording spectacular views. A pre-Domesday manor. Remodelled mid-19th century by William Burn, retaining earlier neo-Norman Hall. 18th century home of Earls and Countesses of Orkney and more recently of Lord and Lady Desborough who entertained "The Souls" here. Tranquil gardens and grounds with Cedar Walk. Anglo-Saxon burial mound. Permanent and temporary exhibitions. Arts Festivals. **Location:** OS Ref. SU907 822. M4/J7 off Bath Road towards Maidenhead. 6m off M40/J2. **Open:** House and grounds: Easter Sunday and every Sunday and Bank Holiday Monday until the end of July, 2–6pm. Please ring to confirm opening. **Admission:** No charge. Free parking.

map 4
D4

BASILDON PARK
Lower Basildon, Reading RG8 9NR
Tel: 0118 984 3040 Fax: 0118 984 1267 (The National Trust)

Elegant classical 18th century house designed by Carr of York. Overlooking the River Thames is the Octagon drawing room containing fine furniture and pictures. The grounds include formal and terrace gardens, pleasure grounds and woodland walks. **Open:** Mar 31-4 Nov, Wed–Sun & BH Mon 1–5.30pm. (Closed Good Friday). Park, garden & woodland walks as house. Note: House & grounds close at 5pm on 17–18 August. **Admission:** House, park & garden: Adult £4.30, child £2.15, family ticket £10.50. Park & garden only: Adult £1.80, child 90p, family ticket £4.50. **E-mail:** tbdgen@smtp.ntrust.org.uk

WELFORD PARK
Welford, Newbury RG20 8HU
Tel: 01488 608203 (J.H.L. Puxley)

Queen Anne house with later additions. Attractive gardens and grounds. **Location:** 6 miles NW of Newbury and 1 mile N of Wickham village off B4000. **Station:** Newbury. **Open:** Late spring and August Bank Holidays and 1–26 June inclusive from 11am–5pm. **Admission:** Adults £3.50, OAPs and under 16s £2. Interior by prior appointment only.

map 4
C4

WINDSOR CASTLE

Windsor, Berkshire SL4 1NJ

Tel: Visitor Office 01753 869898 Information Line (24 hours): 01753 831118 Fax: 01753 832290

Windsor Castle, Buckingham Palace, and the Palace of Holyroodhouse are the Official residences of the Sovereign and are used by The Queen as both home and office. The Queen's personal standard flies when Her Majesty is in residence. Furnished with works of art from the Royal Collection, these buildings are used extensively by The Queen for State ceremonies and official entertaining. They are opened to the public as much as these commitments allow. A significant proportion of Windsor Castle is opened to visitors on a regular basis including the Upper and Lower Wards, the North Terrace with its famous view towards Eton,

Queen Mary's Dolls' House, the State Apartments including St. George's Hall, the Crimson Drawing Room and other newly restored rooms. **Open:** Everyday except Good Friday, Christmas Day, Boxing Day, and during any State or Royal visits. Nov–Feb 9.45–4.15pm (last admission 3pm) Mar–Oct 9.45–5.15pm (last admission 4pm). St. George's Chapel is closed to visitors on Sundays as services are held throughout the day. Worshippers are welcome. **Admission:** Adults £11, Children (under 17) £5.50, Senior Citizens (over 60) £9. Family ticket (2 adults and 2 under 17) £27.50. **Internet:** www.the-royal-collection.org.uk

The King's Bedchamber The Royal Collection © 2000, H. M. Queen Elizabeth II/John Freeman

St. George's Hall The Royal Collection © 2000, H. M. Queen Elizabeth II/Mark Fienne

map 4 E4

Buckinghamshire

Hughenden Manor

Just a stone's throw from London, Buckinghamshire has, fortunately, managed to remain largely undeveloped.

The magnificent Chiltern Hills, perhaps the county's best known geographical feature, are set in acres of stunning countryside, along with numerous picturesque villages and market towns.

Henley-on-Thames, which lies on the intersection of Oxfordshire, Berkshire and Buckinghamshire, has hosted the Royal Regatta annually since 1839. The regatta (Wednesday 4th to Sunday 8th July 2001) is the most prestigious event in the British rowing calendar, and attracts a number of overseas crews, although many spectators come simply to soak up the atmosphere and the Pimm's.

The nearby River and Rowing Museum (see entry under Oxfordshire) is just along the bank from Leander Club, which numbers Sir Steven Redgrave amongst its members, and will provide a fascinating introduction to the sport.
A number of other sports can be enjoyed in the county, including golf, fishing, horse riding and walking, as well as hot air ballooning.

BUCKINGHAMSHIRE COUNTY MUSEUM
Church Street, Aylesbury, Bucks HP20 2QP
Tel: 01296 331441 Fax: 01296 334884

You're sure to have a fun-packed day at Buckinghamshire County Museum. The museum complex contains permanent exhibitions about the County, stunning art galleries and, of course, the award-winning Roald Dahl Children's Gallery, full of hands-on activities. **Open:** Main Museum: Mon–Sat 10–5pm. Sun 2–5pm. Roald Dahl Children's Gallery: As above except Mon–Fri during off–peak term time which is 3–5pm only. **Admission:** Main Museum: Adults £1.50, Children free. Museum & Roald Dahl Children's Gallery: Adults £3.50 (£2.50 off–peak), Children 3–16 yrs £2.50 (£1.50 off–peak). Location: An hour by train from London Marylebone or 25 mins off the M25 via the A41. Near St Mary's Church (5mins walk from station). **E-mail:** museum@buckscc.gov.uk

map 4 D3

CLIVEDEN
Taplow, Maidenhead, SL6 0JA, Bucks
Tel: 01628 605069 Fax: 01628 669461 (The National Trust)

On cliffs above the Thames, this estate has magnificent views over the river. The great 19th century mansion (now let as a hotel) was once the home of Nancy, Lady Astor. There are a series of gardens, each with its own character and featuring roses, topiary, water gardens, statuary, and formal parterre. **Open:** Entire Estate: 15 Mar–31 Oct: daily 11–6pm. 1 Nov–31 Dec: daily 11–4pm. House (three rooms open): Apr–Oct: Thurs & Sun 3–5.30pm. Entry by timed ticket from information kiosk. **Admission:** Woodland Car Park only £3, Family Ticket £7.50. Grounds: £5, Family ticket £12.50. House £1 extra. Licensed conservatory restaurant and shop. **E-mail:** www.tclest@smtp.ntrust.org.uk

map 4 D4

HUGHENDEN MANOR
High Wycombe, Bucks HP14 4LA
Tel: 01494 755573 Infoline: 01494 755565 (The National Trust)

The home of Queen Victoria's favourite Prime Minister, Benjamin Disraeli. Much of his furniture, pictures and books remain and there are beautiful walks through the surrounding park and woodland. The garden is a recreation of the colourful designs of his wife, Mary Anne. **Open:** House: 1–30 Mar, Sat & Sun only, 1 Apr–31 Oct, daily except Mon & Tues (closed Good Fri, but open Bank Hol Mon) 1–5pm. Garden: same days as house 12–5pm. Park & Woodland: open all year. **Admission:** House & garden: £4.20, Family ticket £10.50. Garden only £1.50, Children 75p. Park & Woodland free. Tearoom and shop available.

map 4 D3/4

NETHER WINCHENDON HOUSE
Aylesbury HP18 0DY
Tel: 01844 290199
(Robert Spencer Bernard Esq.)

Medieval and Tudor manor house with 18th century Strawberry Hill Gothic additions. Home of Sir Francis Bernard, Governor of New Jersey and Massachusetts, 1760. **Location:** 1 mile N of A418 Aylesbury/Thame Road, in village of Lower Winchendon, 6 miles SW Aylesbury. **Stations:** Aylesbury (7 miles). Haddenham and Thame Parkway (2 miles). **Open:** 1–28 May and 26 & 27 Aug, 2.30–5.30pm. Last party each day at 4.45pm. Parties at any time of year by written appointment. **Admission:** Adults £4, Children (under 12) and OAPs £2 (not weekends or bank holidays). HHA members free. **Refreshments:** By arrangement. Correspondence to Robert Spencer Bernard Esq.

map 4
D3

THE OLD GAOL MUSEUM
Market Hill, Buckingham, Buckinghamshire MK18 1JX
Tel/Fax: 01280 823020

Displays include local geology, archaeology and social history and the story of the county yeomanry. New, state-of-the-art glass roof and education resource centre (Tourist Information Centre). **Exhibitions:** Temporary exhibitions and events held throughout the year. **Open:** Mon–Sat 10am–4pm.

map 4
D2

STOWE HOUSE
Stowe, MK18 5EH
Tel: 01280 818282

Formerly the home of the Dukes of Buckingham, this is a house adorned with the traditions of aristocracy and learning. For over one and a half centuries up to the great sale of 1848, the Temples and Grenvilles almost continuously rebuilt and refurbished it in an attempt to match their ever growing ambitions with the latest fashions. Restoration to the North front and colonnades until 9 Oct 2002. Around the mansion is one of Britain's most magnificent landscape gardens now in the ownership of the National Trust. **Location:** 4 miles north of Buckingham town. **Stations:** Milton Keynes. **Open:** In 2001, the House will be open to the public on the following dates; 24 Mar-16 Apr;Wed-Fri 2-5pm and Sat-Sun 10-1pm, 8 Jul-31 Aug; Wed/Thurs 2-5 pm. Fri-Sun 10-1pm, 14 Dec-23 Dec; Fri-Sat 10-1pm. For other dates and groups (by appointment, 17 Apr-6 Jul and 3 Sep-21 Oct.) please telephone Christine Shaw on: 01280-818282 first to check. **Admission:** Adults £3 and Children (under 16) £1.50. Guide books and souvenirs available from Stowe Bookshop situated in the Menagerie on the South Front – open Mon–Fri, 10–12noon and 1–4.30pm.

C

map 4
D2

STOWE LANDSCAPE GARDENS
Buckingham, Bucks MK18 5EH
Tel: 01280 822850. Fax: 01280 822437 (The National Trust)

One of the first and finest landscape gardens in Europe. Adorned with buildings by Vanbrugh, Gibbs and Kent, including arches, temples, a Palladian bridge and other monuments, the sheer scale of the garden must make it Britain's largest work of art. "New for 2001: Four newly restored monuments, including Wolfe's Obelisk".**Open:** 3 Mar–28 Oct (closed 26 May) & 1-23 Dec (Wed-Sun, and BH Mons), 10am-5.30pm. Gardens may close in bad weather. **Admission:** Gardens £4.60. Family £11.50. Licensed tearoom. **E-mail:** tstmca@smtp.ntrust.org.uk

WINSLOW HALL
Winslow, Buckinghamshire, MK18 3HL
Tel: 01296 712 323 (Sir Edward & Lady Tomkins)

Built 1698–1702. Almost certainly designed by Sir Christopher Wren. Has survived without any major structural alteration and retains most of its original features. Modernised and redecorated by the present owners. Good 18th century furniture, mostly English. Some fine pictures, clocks and carpets. Several examples of Chinese art, notably of the Tang period. Beautiful gardens with many unusual trees and shrubs. **Location:** At entrance to Winslow on A413, the Aylesbury road. **Station(s):** Milton Keynes or Aylesbury (both 10 miles). **Open:** By appointment only throughout the year. **Admission:** Adults £5, Children free. **Refreshments:** Catering by arrangement.

map 4
D2

WADDESDON MANOR

Nr. Aylesbury, Buckinghamshire, HP18 0JH
Tel: 01296 653211 Fax: 01296 653208

Waddesdon Manor was built (1874-1889) for Baron Ferdinand de Rothschild to entertain his guests and display his vast collection of art treasures. It has won many awards including the Silver Award for Best Overall Property, the Europa Nostra Garden Award and the Best Gift Shop 1999. The French Renaissance-style château houses one of the finest collection of French 18th century decorative arts in the world and an important collection of English portraits. The garden has one of the finest Victorian gardens in Britain, renowned for its seasonal displays, colourful shrubs, mature trees and Parterre. The Rococo-style aviary houses a splendid collection of exotic birds and thousands of bottles of vintage Rothschild wines are found in the wine cellars. Many events are organised throughout the year including special interest days, wine tasting and garden workshops. **Location:** A41 between Aylesbury & Bicester. **Open: Grounds, aviary, restaurant and shops:** 28 Feb-23 Dec, Wed-Sun & Bank Hol. Mons, 10-5pm. **House (including wine cellars):** 28 Mar–4 Nov, Wed-Sun & Bank Hol Mons 11–4pm. (Recommended last admission 2.30pm). Bachelors' Wing open Wed, Thurs & Fri. **Admission: House & Grounds:** Adult £10, Child £7.50. **Grounds only:** Adult £3, Child £1.50. Bachelors' Wing £1. National Trust Members free. Timed tickets to the House can be purchased on site or reserved up to 24 hours in advance by phoning 01296 653226, Mon–Fri 10–4pm. Advance booking fee: £3 per transaction.

map 4
D3

www.historichouses.co.uk

Cambridgeshire

The Cambridgeshire countryside is mostly fenland – flat expanses with drained marshes so fertile that the earth is known as "black gold". Picturesque rivers wind their way through the lush greenery, making the region ideal both for walking and for watersports. The magnificent cathedral at Ely overlooks the fens; indeed, the town is reputed to take its name from the Saxon "elig", meaning "Eel Island". The Fen Rivers Way runs all the way from Ely to Cambridge, but more recreational walkers may prefer the gentler Town and Riverside Trail.

Cambridge itself is a medieval city that has prospered throughout its history. Its 13th century university has always been one of the world's great centres of learning, and has kept pace with the changing times. As a result, Cambridge now has a flourishing high-tech industry, attracted to the region by groundbreaking work at the university. Nevertheless, the centre of the city remains pleasantly untouched by modern developments, and visitors can still wander through quiet streets marvelling at the wonderful architecture of the colleges.

Wansford

ELTON HALL

Elton, Peterborough PE8 6SH
Tel: 01832 280468 Fax: 01832 280584 (Mr & Mrs William Proby)

This romantic house has been the home of the Proby family for over 350 years. Excellent furniture and outstanding paintings by Gainsborough, Reynolds, Constable and other fine artists. There are over 12,000 books, including Henry VIII's prayer book. Wonderful gardens, including restored Rose Garden, knot and sunken gardens and recently planted Arboretum. Stunning new Gothic Orangery. Bressingham Plant Centre is in the walled Kitchen Garden. Location: On A605, 8 miles W of Peterborough. **Open:** 27-28 May, and Weds in June, July and Aug: Weds, Thurs, Sun Aug Bank Hol Mon 2-5pm. **Admission**: Adults £5, accompanied children free. Garden only: Adults £2.50, accompanied children free.

map 9 F7

ELY CATHEDRAL

The Chapter House, The College, Ely CB7 4DL
Tel: 01353 667735 Fax: 01353 665658

A wonderful example of Romanesque architecture. The Octagon and the Lady Chapel are of particular interest. There are superb medieval domestic buildings around the Cathedral. Stained glass museum, brass rubbing centre, shops and restaurants. **Location:** 15 miles N of Cambridge city centre via the A10. **Open:** Summer: 7–7pm. Winter: Mon–Sat, 7.30–6pm, Sun and week after Christmas, 7.30–5pm. Sun services: 8.15am, 10.30am and 3.45 pm. Weekday services: 7.40am, 8am & 5.30pm (Thurs only also 11.30am & 12.30pm). **Admission:** Charges apply.

map 5 F1

THE FITZWILLIAM MUSEUM

Trumpington Street, Cambridge CB2 1RB
Tel: 01223 332900 Fax: 01223 332923

The Fitzwilliam Museum has magnificent permanent collections of international importance, including antiquities from Ancient Egypt, Greece and Rome; English and European pottery and glass; furniture, clocks, fans and armour; coins, medals, manuscripts and rare printed books; paintings, including masterpieces by Simone Martini, Domenico Veneziano, Titian, Rubens, Van Dyck, Canaletto, Gainsborough, Constable, Monet and Picasso, portrait miniatures and 20th century art, and changing displays of drawings, watercolours and prints. Temporary exhibitions, guided tours, gallery talks, concerts and other events; shop and café. **Open:** Tues-Sat 10-5pm; Sun 2.15-5pm. Closed: Mons and 24 Dec-1 Jan inclusive. **Admission:** Free. **E-mail:** fitzmuseum-enquiries@lists.cam.ac.uk **Internet:** www.fitzmuseum.cam.ac.uk

map 5 F1/2

ISLAND HALL

Post Street, Godmanchester PE29 2BA
Tel: 020 7491 3724 (Mr Christopher & Lady Linda Vane Percy)

An important mid 18th century mansion of great charm, owned and restored by an award-winning Interior Designer. This family home has lovely Georgian rooms with fine period detail and interesting possessions relating to the owners' ancestors since their first occupation of the house in 1800. A tranquil riverside setting with formal gardens and ornamental island forming part of the grounds in an area of Best Landscape. Octavia Hill wrote "This is the loveliest, dearest old house, I never was in such a one before". Home-made teas. **Open:** Island Hall will be open from May–Sept (except Aug) 2001 to groups by appointment only. **Admission:** £3.50 per head (when over 30 persons), £4.00 per head (when 15–30 persons), under 15 persons minimum charge £60.00.

map 4
E1

KETTLE'S YARD

Castle Street, Cambridge CB3 0AQ
Tel: 01223 352124 Fax: 01223 324377

20th Century Art in a domestic setting with furniture, decorative arts, pebbles and shells. Artists include Alfred Wallis, Ben Nicholson, Barbara Hepworth, Christopher Wood and Henri Gaudier-Brzeska. Contemporary exhibitions in the gallery. **Opening Times**: Gallery Tues–Sun 11.30–5pm. House Tues–Sun 2–4pm. **Admission:** Free. Location: The corner of Castle Street and Northampton Street. **Exhibitions/Events**: 7–8 exhibitions p.a. Leaflet produced. Parties please phone. **Internet**: www.kettlesyard.co.uk **E-mail:** mail@kettlesyard.cam.ac.uk

map 5
F1

KIMBOLTON CASTLE

Kimbolton, Cambridgeshire
Tel: 01480 860505 Fax: 01480 861763 (Governors of Kimbolton School)

Tudor manor house associated with Katherine of Aragon, completely remodelled by Vanbrugh (1708–20); courtyard c.1694. Fine murals by Pellegrini in chapel, boudoir and on staircase. Gatehouse by Robert Adam. Parkland. **Location:** 8 miles NW of St Neots on B645; 14 miles N of Bedford. **Station(s):** St Neots (9 miles) **Open:** Easter Sun & Mon, Spring Bank Hol Sun & Mon, Summer Bank Hol Sun & Mon, also Sun 29 July, 5, 12, 19, & 26 Aug 2–6pm **Admission:** Adults £2.50, Children & OAPs £1.50. **Conferences:** By negotiation. Guided tours for groups of 20 or more by arrangement on days other than advertised.

map 4
E1

KING'S COLLEGE

King's Parade, Cambridge CB2 1ST
Tel: 01223 331212

Visitors are very welcome, but remember that this is a working College. Please respect the privacy of those who work, live and study here at all times. Recorded messages for services, concerts and visiting times: 01223 331155. **Open:** Out of term time – Mon–Sat, 9.30–4.30pm. Sun, 10–5pm. In term: Mon–Fri, 9.30–3.30pm. Sat, 9.30–3.15pm. Sun, 1.15–2.15pm, 5–5.30pm. **Admission:** Adults £3.50, Children (12–17) £2.50, Children under 12 free if part of a family unit, Students £2.50. Guided tours are only available through Cambridge Tourist Office Tel: 01223 457574.

map 4
E1

THE MANOR

Hemingford Grey, Huntingdon, Cambs PE18 9BN
Tel: 01480 463134 Fax: 01480 465026 (Mr & Mrs Peter Boston)

Built about 1130 and made famous as Green Knowe by the author Lucy Boston this house is reputedly the oldest continuously inhabited house in the country and much of the Norman house remains. It contains the Lucy Boston patchworks. The garden has topiary, one of the best collections of old roses in private hands, large herbaceous borders with many scented plants and a variety of Dykes Medal winner irises. **Open:** House: all the year by appointment. Garden: open daily all year 10–6pm (dusk in winter). **Admission:** House and Garden: Adults £4, Children £1.50. Garden only: Adults £1, Children 50p.

map 4
F1

NORRIS MUSEUM

The Broadway, St.Ives, PE27 5BX
Tel: 01480 497 314

The Norris Museum tells the story of Huntingdonshire from earliest times. There are fossils and models of the Ichthyosaurs and Plesiosaurs that lived here 160 million years ago, together with remains of Mammoths from the Ice Ages; archaeology from the Stone Age to Roman and Saxon times and local history from the Middle Ages onwards, including lace making and ice skating. Our art gallery displays paintings of local scenes by local artists and is also used for a programme of special temporary exhibitions. The attractive museum building is set in a picturesque riverside garden. **Open:** Mon-Fri 10am-1pm & 2–5pm; Oct-Apr closes at 4pm. Sat 10-12 noon. May-Sep, Sat-Sun 2-5pm. **E-mail:** norris.st-ives-tc@co-net.com

map 5
F1

OLIVER CROMWELL'S HOUSE

29 St. Mary's Street, Ely, Cambridgeshire
Tel: 01353 662062 Fax: 01353 668518 (East Cambridgeshire District Council)

Oliver Cromwell's House is set in the heart of Ely, deep in the Cambridgeshire Fens. Displays show how Cromwell's family would have lived in the 17th century, and brings to life some of the episodes of his career. Suitable for a family visit, with a dressing up box and Haunted Bedroom for children to enjoy, the house has lots to offer and also gives an insight into the continuing struggle to drain and maintain the fens. Home to the Ely Tourist Information Centre, the house is the first point to call for a visit to the area. **Open:** Summer: 1 Apr–31 Oct, Daily, 10–5.30pm. Winter: 1 Nov–31 Mar, Mon to Sat, 10–5pm. Suns 12–4pm in winter.

map 4
F1

PETERBOROUGH CATHEDRAL

The Chapter Office, Minster Precincts, Peterborough, Cambridgeshire PE1 1XS
Tel: 01733 343342 Fax: 01733 552465 (The Dean & Chapter)

Visit Peterborough Cathedral one of the finest Norman buildings in Europe, with a magnificent early English West Front. Marvel at the unique 13th century painted ceiling , admire the exquisite fan vaulting., visit the burial places of two Queens and find out much more from the visitors Exhibition now open in the North Aisle. Group guided tours bookable in advance. The Cathedral Shop and Beckets Restaurant are open all year round in the Precincts and the Tourist Information Centre is also here. Education Centre opens Spring 2001. **Open:** All year, Mon–Sat 8.30–5.15pm; Sun 12–5.15pm. Donations are requested.

map 9
F7

UNIVERSITY BOTANIC GARDEN

Cory Lodge, Bateman Street, CB2 1JF
Tel: 01223 336265 Fax: 01223 336278 (University of Cambridge)

Forty acres of outstanding gardens with lake, glasshouses, winter garden, chronological bed and nine National Collections, including Geranium and Fritillaria. **Location:** 1 mile S of Cambridge centre. Entrance on Bateman Street. **Stations:** Cambridge Railway Station 1/4 mile. **Open:** Open all year except Christmas Day and Boxing Day 10–6pm (summer), 10–5pm (autumn & spring), 10–4pm (winter). **Admission:** Charged weekends and Bank Holidays throughout the year and weekdays Mar 1–Oct 31. All parties must be pre-booked. Pre-booked school parties and disabled people free. No reductions for parties. **Refreshments:** Tearoom in the Gilmour Building. No dogs except guide dogs. Guided tours by the Friends of the Garden available by arrangement. **E-mail:** gardens@hermes.cam.ac.uk **Internet:** www.plantsci.cam.ac.uk/botgdn/index.htm

map 4
F1

Cheshire

Chester

Cheshire runs from the windswept moors of the Peak National Park to the internationally important Dee and Mersey estuaries. In between there is rich agricultural land, woodland and lowland heath, laced with rivers and canals.

The county town of Chester lies on a bend of the River Dee, and was founded by the Romans 2000 years ago. Today, visitors can admire a mediaeval wall surrounding its winding streets and historic buildings.

Garden lovers will not be disappointed either: Cheshire plays host to one of the world's biggest garden events - the Royal Horticultural Society Flower Show at Tatton Park.

ARLEY HALL AND GARDENS

Arley, Northwich, Cheshire CW9 6NA
Tel: 01565 777353 Fax: 01565 777465 (Lord & Lady Ashbrook)

Arley Hall, a Jacobean Victorian house, is set amongst a 2,000 acre estate with attractive stable block, 15th century barn and chapel. The award-winning gardens, bordering the park, offer many unique features including clipped Quercus Ilex, Rootery, double herbaceous border, two walled gardens and contain collections of shrub roses, exotic trees and shrubs, rhododendrons and azaleas. **Location:** 5 m N of Northwich; 6 m W of Knutsford; 7 m S of Warrington; 5 m off M6 at junctions 19 & 20; 5 m off M56 at junctions 9 & 10. Nearest main roads A49 and A50. **Open:** Easter–30 Sept, Gardens & Grounds: Tues–Sun & BH Mons, 11am–5pm. Hall only open Sun & Tues 12–5pm. **Refreshments:** Restaurant, gift shop & plant nursery. **Events/Exhibitions:** Antiques, crafts, food & wine fairs, Garden Festival & plant fairs, outdoor concerts. **Conferences:** Corporate events, filming, weddings, themed events. Dogs welcome.

map 6 C1

CAPESTHORNE HALL

Nr. Macclesfield, Cheshire
Tel: 01625 861 221 Fax: 01625 861 619 (Mr & Mrs W. A. Bromley-Davenport)

Capesthorne Hall has been the home of the Bromley Davenport family and their ancestors since Domesday times. The present hall dates from 1719 and contains a great variety of paintings, sculptures and furniture. The gardens, lakes and park contain many interesting features including a Georgian Chapel and an old ice house. **Location:** 3½ miles south of Alderley Edge on A34. **Open:** Hall and Gardens: April–October, Wednesday, Sunday and Bank Holidays (afternoons). **Refreshments:** Butler's Pantry plus catering by arrangement. **Admission:** Adults £6.50, Children £3.00. Special events throughout the year. Also available for corporate hospitality, civil weddings and receptions.

map 8 B5

ADLINGTON HALL

Nr Macclesfield, Cheshire SK10 4LF
Tel: 01625 820875 Fax: 01625 828756 (Mrs C Legh)

Adlington Hall is a Cheshire Manor and has been the home of the Leghs since 1315. The Great Hall was built between 1450 and 1505, the Elizabethan 'Black and White' in 1581 and the Georgian South Front in 1757. The Bernard Smith Organ was installed c1670. A 'Shell Cottage', Yew Walk, Lime Avenue, recently planted maze and rose garden. Recently restored follies include a Chinese bridge, Temple to Diana and T'ing House. Occasional organ recitals. **Location:** 5 miles N of Macclesfield on the Stockport/Macclesfield Road (A523). **Station(s)** Adlington (½m). **Open:** Throughout the year to groups by prior arrangement. Also open to public in June/July 2001 Mon & Wed 2–5pm. **Admission:** Hall and Gardens Adults £4.50, Children £1.75 (over 20 people £4.00). **Refreshments:** At the Hall. Car park free.
E-mail: enquiries@adlingtonhall.com **Internet:** www.adlingtonhall.com

map 8 B4

BEESTON CASTLE
Tel: 01829 260464
(English Heritage)

Experience one of the most spectacular castle views in England. On a clear day you can gaze across eight counties. From Beeston Crag, 500 feet above the Cheshire plain, you can see from the Pennines in the East to Wales in the West! Inspired by tales of impregnable hilltop strongholds in the Holy Land, it was a royal fortress until it fell to a 12-month siege in the Civil War. Climb the dominating keep of Beeston Castle. Is Richard II's treasure really buried here - or is the real wealth of Beeston its 4,000-year history? **Location:** 11 m SE of Chester on minor road off A49 or A41. Train: Chester 10m. Bus: Tel 01244 602666. **Open:** All year, 1 Apr–30 Sept daily, 10am–6pm. 1–31 Oct daily, 10am–5pm. 1 Nov–28 Mar daily, 10am–4pm. Closed 24–26 Dec & 1 Jan. **Admission:** Adult £2.90, Conc £2.20, Child £1.50, under 5 yrs free. Groups of 11+: 15% discount. **Internet:** www.english-heritage.org.uk

map 6 C1

BRAMALL HALL
Bramhall Park, Bramhall, Stockport, Cheshire, SK7 3NX
Tel: 0161 485 3708 Fax: 0161 486 6959 (Stockport Metropolitan Borough Council)

This magical Tudor manor house is set in 70 acres of parkland, with lakes, woods and gardens. The house contains 16th century wall paintings, Elizabethan fine plaster ceilings, Victorian kitchens and servant's quarters. Excellent stables, tearoom and gift shop. **Location:** 4 miles S of Stockport, off A5102. **Stations:** Cheadle Hulme. **Open:** Good Fri–30 Sept, Mon–Sat, 1–5pm. Sun & BHols, 11–5pm. 1 Oct–1 Jan, Tue–Sat, 1–4pm. Sun & BHols, 11–4pm. Closed 25–26 Dec. 2 Jan–Easter, Sat & Sun, 12–4pm. Parties by arrangement, including out of hours bookings. **Admission:** Adults £3.50, Children/OAPs £2. **Refreshments:** Stables, tearooms. **Events/Exhibitions:** Full events programme. **Conferences:** Available for corporate entertaining and civil marriages. Disabled access on ground floor, shop and tearooms.

map 8 B4

CHOLMONDELEY CASTLE GARDEN
Malpas, Cheshire, SY14 8AH
Tel: 01829 720383/202 (The Marchioness of Cholmondeley)

Extensive ornamental gardens dominated by romantic Gothic Castle, built in 1801 of local sandstone. Imaginatively laid out with fine trees and water gardens, it has been extensively replanted from the 1960s with azaleas, rhododendrons, magnolias, cornus, acer and many other acid loving plants. As well as the beautiful water garden, there is a rose garden and many mixed borders. Lakeside picnic area, children's play areas, rare breeds of farm animals, including llamas. Ancient private chapel in the park. **Location:** Off A49 Whitchurch/Tarporley Road. **Open:** Sun 1 Apr–Sun 30 Sept 2001: Wed, Thur, Sun & Bank Hol Mon 11.30–5.30pm (last entry 5pm). Closed Good Friday 13 April. **Admission:** Adults £3, Children £1.50. Coach parties of 25+ at reduced rates. **Enquiries to:** The Secretary, Cholmondeley Castle (House not open to public), Malpas, Cheshire SY14 8AH.

map 6 C/D1

DORFOLD HALL
Nantwich CW5 8LD
Tel: 01270 625245 Fax: 01270 628723 (Mr Richard Roundell)

Jacobean country house built 1616. Beautiful plaster ceilings and panelling. Interesting furniture and pictures. Attractive gardens including spectacular spring garden and summer herbaceous borders. Guided tours. **Location:** 1 mile W of Nantwich on A534 Nantwich/ Wrexham Road. **Stations:** Nantwich (1½ miles). **Open:** Apr–Oct Tues and Bank Holidays Mons 2–5pm. At other times by appointment only. **Admission:** Adults £4.50, Children £3.

map 6 D1

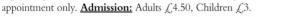

NT Photographic Library, Nick Meers

DUNHAM MASSEY HALL
Altrincham, Cheshire
Tel: 0161 941 1025 Fax: 0161 929 7508 (The National Trust)

18th century house extensively re-worked in the early 20th century resulting in one of Britain's most sumptuous Edwardian interiors with collections of walnut furniture, paintings and magnificent Huguenot silver. One of the North West's great gardens with an Orangery, Victorian bark house and well house. The surrounding deer park was laid out in the early 18th century and contains a series of beautiful avenues and pools. **Admission:** NT members free. House and Garden: Adult £5, Child £2.50, Family £12.50. Booked parties £4. House or garden only: Adult £3.20, Child £1.60. Car entry: £3 per car. **Open:** House and garden open 31 Mar–4 Nov daily except house closed Thur & Fri. House open 12–5pm Apr–Sept, 4pm in Oct. Open 11am BH Mon & preceding Sun. Garden open 11–5.30pm Apr–Sept, 4.30pm in Oct. Deer park, restaurant & shop open daily all year.

map 6 B1

LITTLE MORETON HALL
Congleton, Cheshire CW12 4SD
Tel: 01260 272018 (The National Trust)

Begun in 1450, Little Moreton is regarded as the finest timber-framed moated manor house in England. The Chapel, Great Hall and Long Gallery, together with the Knot Garden, make Little Moreton a great day out. Try the local historic recipes in the restaurant and visit the shop with its extensive range of gifts. Parties welcome. Live music and tours with supper for booked parties. Great Hall decorated for an Elizabethan Yuletide with Christmas Festivities, seasonal refreshments and shopping. Open Air theatre in July. **Open:** 31 Mar–4 Nov, Wed–Sun, Bank Holiday Monday 11.30–5pm. 10–25 Nov, Sat, Sun 11.30–4pm. 1–22 Dec, Sat, Sun 11.30–4pm Free entry. Tel: 01260 272018. **Admission:** Adult £4.40, Child £2.20, Family £11.

map 8 B5

MACCLESFIELD SILK MUSEUM
ROE STREET, MACCLESFIELD, SK11 6UT
TEL: 01625 613210 FAX: 01625 617880

The Silk Museum is situated within a Grade II former non-denominational Sunday school. It tells the story of the development of the Silk industry by audio-visual programme, graphics, models, costume and textiles. Nearby Paradise Mill Museum is the location of 26 hand jacquard silk looms in their original setting. Knowledgeable guides, many of whom worked in the silk industry, demonstrate the intricate process involved in weaving. Room sets and graphic panels depict life in the mill in the 1930s. Shop selling silk goods, novelties. Refreshments. Pre-booked parties are welcome. Lively education service. **Open:** Mon-Sat, 11am-5pm & Sun 1-5pm. Closed Sun Jan–Mar, Dec 25-26, Jan 1, Good Fri. Paradise Mill: Tue–Sun 1-5pm, Apr–Oct. Tue–Sat 1–4pm Nov–Mar. **E-mail:** postmaster@silk-macc.u-net.com **Internet:** www.silk-macclesfield.org

map 8 B5

NESS BOTANIC GARDENS
Ness, Neston, South Wirral, Cheshire CH64 4AY
Tel: 0151 353 0123 Fax: 0151 353 1004

Pioneers in the world of plants since 1898. Beautiful Botanic Garden for all seasons with extensive displays of trees and shrubs, including Rhododendrons and Azaleas. Renowned heather, rock, terrace, water, rose and herb gardens. Visit our coffee shops which provide home-made cakes and light meals. Gift shop, plant sales area, visitor centre and picnic area. **Admission:** Charge. **Location:** 6 miles from exit 4, M53, 5 miles from western end M56, off A540 Hoylake–Chester Road. Please phone for admission rates and opening times.

map 6 C2

LYME PARK
Disley, Stockport, Cheshire SK12 2NX
Tel: 01663 726023 Fax: 01663 765035

A fine Elizabethan house with eighteenth and nineteenth century additions, set in historic gardens at the edge of a lake. The décor spans four centuries, and includes a collection of English clocks. Surrounding the house is a 1,400 acre deer park. Open: Please call for details of opening times. **Admission:** House and Garden: £5, House only: £4. Garden only: £2.50. Combined family ticket: £15.

NETHER ALDERLEY MILL
Congleton Road, Nether Alderley,
Macclesfield, Cheshire SK10 4TW
Tel: 01625 523012 Fax: 01625 527139 (The National Trust)

Have you visited this unique medieval flour mill? Original Elizabethan timbers support a stone flagged roof. The fully restored Victorian machinery is driven by tandem overshot wooden waterwheels and runs daily subject to availability of water. Flour grinding demonstrations on Sunday afternoons. Groups welcome (booking essential). Guided tours on request. Enjoy the sights and sounds of a working mill on a fascinating visit! **Location:** 1½ miles south of Alderley Edge on A34. **Open:** April, May and Oct: Wed, Sun and Bank Holiday Mon, 1–4.30pm. June–Sept: Tues–Sun & Bank Holiday Mon, 1–5pm.

map 8 B5

NORTON PRIORY MUSEUM & GARDEN
Tudor Road, Manor Park, Runcorn, Cheshire WA7 1SX
Tel: 01928 569895 (The Norton Priory Museum Trust)

The beautiful 38 acre woodland gardens with an award winning walled garden are the setting for the now demolished mansion of the Brookes, built on the site of a former Augustinian priory. Excavated remains of the priory & the atmospheric 12th century undercroft can be found with displays on the medieval priory, the later houses and gardens in the museum. Contemporary sculpture is situated in the grounds. **Location:** From M56 (junction 11) turn towards Warrington and follow Norton Priory road signs. **Open:** Daily all year. Apr–Oct, Sat, Sun & Bank Hols 12–6pm; Mon to Fri 12–5pm; Nov–Mar, daily 12–4pm. Walled Garden open Mar–Oct. Closed 24/25/26 Dec, 1 Jan. Special arrangements for groups. **Admission:** Adults £3.75, Conc £2.50, Family £9.80 (2 adults & up to 3 children under 16). Pre-booked groups(20+) £2.20.

map 6 C1

PEOVER HALL AND GARDENS
Over Peover, Knutsford, WA16 9HN

Elizabethan House dating from 1585. Mainwaring Chapel. There are approximately 15 acres of gardens including 5 walled gardens. Lily pond, rose, herb, white and pink gardens, moat, C19 Dell, rhododendron walks, church walk, pleached lime avenues, fine topiary work. Grade I listed Carolean Stables and C18 landscaped park. **Location:** 4 m S of Knutsford. Turn off A50 at Whipping Stocks Inn, down Stocks Lane. Follow signs for Peover Hall and Church. The Estate entrance can be found off Goostrey Lane, clearly signed. **Open:** Hall, Gardens & Stables every Monday (except Bank Holiday) 2–5pm. Guided tours of Hall at 2.30 & 3.30pm. Gardens & Stables only every Thursday 2–5pm. Other days by appointment: contact I Shepherd on 01565 632358. **Admission:** Hall & Gardens £3, Gardens only £2. **Refreshments:** Cream teas available on Monday afternoons only. No dogs allowed.

map 8
A4

TABLEY HOUSE
Knutsford, Cheshire, WA16 0HB.
Tel: 01565 750 151 Fax: 01565 653 230
Owners: The Victoria University of Manchester

Finest Palladian mansion in the NW designed by John Carr of York for the Leicester family. The staterooms show family memorabilia, furniture by Gillow, Bullock and Chippendale and the first collection of English paintings ever made. **Location:** 2 miles W of Knutsford, entrance on A5033 (M6 Junction 19, A556). **Open:** Apr–end Oct: Thurs, Fri, Sat, Sun and Bank Hols, 2–5pm. (Last entry 4.30pm). Free car park. Main rooms and the Chapel suitable for the disabled. **Admission:** Adults £4. Children/Students with card £1.50. **Refreshments:** Tearoom and shop facilities. ALL ENQUIRIES TO THE ADMINISTRATOR. **Conferences:** Small meetings, civil wedding licence.

map 6
C1

TATTON PARK
Knutsford, Cheshire WA16 6QN
Tel: 01625 534400 Fax: 01625 534403 (Cheshire County Council)

One of the most splendid historic estates in the United Kingdom. The 1000 acres of parkland are home to herds of red and fallow deer and provide the setting for a Georgian Mansion, Gardens, Tudor Old Hall and a working Farm. These attractions, plus private functions and a superb events programme attract over 700,000 visits a year. Archaeologists have found evidence of occupation at Tatton since 8000 BC with the discovery of flints in the park. There is also proof of people living here in the Iron Age, Roman times, Anglo-saxon and Medieval periods. The Neo-Classical Mansion, by Wyatt, is the jewel in Tatton's crown and was built in stages from 1780-1813. The family collection of Gillow furniture, Baccarat glass, porcelain and paintings by Italian and Dutch masters is found in the splendid setting of the magnificent staterooms. The Victorian kitchens and cellars provide a fascinating insight into life as it would have been"downstairs". The Gardens extend over 50 acres and feature rare species of plants, shrubs, & trees. They are considered to be one of the most important gardens within the National Trust. Features include:Conservatory by Wyatt, Fernery by Paxton plus the Japanese and Italian terraced gardens. The rare collection of plants including rhododendrons, tree ferns, bamboo and pines are the result of 200 years of collecting. Home farm has traditional breeds of animals including rare sheep, cattle, pigs and horses. At the Old Hall, tours show visitors how life would have been in centuries past. **Open: Park & Gardens:** Open all year except Mondays but including Bank Holidays (Closed Christmas Day). **Farm:** Apr-Sep, Tues-Sun; Oct-Mar, Sundays only. **Mansion & Old Hall:** Apr–Oct, Tues-Sun. Phone for further details.

map 6
C1

Cornwall

Padstow

Cornwall is a county rich in myth, where the visitor can walk in the footsteps of Merlin and King Arthur, or trace the story of Tristan and Isolde. The coastline is breathtakingly beautiful, from the dramatic cliffs at Tintagel and Land's End to the quiet harbours at Padstow and St Ives. Inland, the county is no less attractive and equally varied: the austere beauty of Bodmin Moor is in stark contrast to the lush sub-tropical gardens at St Mawes. The countryside around the historic town of Launceston is dotted with charming, sleepy villages such as North Petherwin, which featured in the Domesday book, and where visitors to the church of St Padernus can view the recently restored Holy Well.

ANTONY HOUSE AND GARDEN

Torpoint, Cornwall PL11 2QA
Tel: 01752 812191

A superb early 18th century mansion set in beautiful parkland and gardens overlooking the river Lynher. The ancestral home of the Carew family for over five hundred years, Antony contains a number of fine paintings, tapestries and embroideries. The nearby woodland garden features camellias, magnolias, rhododendrons and azaleas. **Open:** 3 Apr–31 May and 4 Sept–1 Nov: Tues–Thurs and Bank Holiday Mon. June, July, Aug: Tues–Thurs and Sun, 1.30–5.30pm. **Admission:** Adult £4.20, Family £10.50.

BOSVIGO

Bosvigo Lane, Truro, Cornwall
Tel: 01872 275774 Fax: 01872 275774 (Michael and Wendy Perry)

Unlike most Cornish Gardens, Bosvigo is a 'summer' garden. Shrubs take second place to herbaceous perennials, carefully planted to give a succession of colour from Jun through 'til Sept. The gardens comprise a series of walled or hedged 'rooms' all around the Georgian house (not open). Each room has its own colour theme. A Victorian conservatory houses a collection of semi-tender climbers and plants–a delightful place to sit and relax. This is a plantsman's garden–the harder you look, the more plants you will see. Featured in many books, magazines and on television. Selected as a 'Millennium Garden' by the Daily Telegraph. "One of the best examples of British Gardening in the UK in the year 2000." - Stephen Lacey, garden writer and broadcaster. **Open:** Mar–end Sept, Thur–Sat, 11–6pm. **Admission:** Adults £3, Children 5–15yrs £1, under 5s free. Sorry, no dogs.

map 2
C6

BURNCOOSE NURSERIES & GARDEN

Gwennap, Redruth TR16 6BJ
Tel: 01209 860316 Fax: 01209 860011 (C H Williams)

The Nurseries are set in the 30 acre woodland gardens of Burncoose. 12 acres are laid out for nursery stock production of over 3000 varieties of ornamental trees, shrubs and herbaceous plants. Specialities include camellias, azaleas, magnolias, rhododendrons and conservatory plants. The Nurseries are widely known for rarities and unusual plants and have won numerous gold medals at Chelsea and many other flower shows. Mail order catalogue £1.50 (posted). **Location:** 2 miles southwest of Redruth on the main A393 Redruth to Falmouth road between the villages of Lanner and Ponsanooth. **Open:** Mon–Sat 9–5pm, Sun 11–5pm. Gardens and tearooms open all year (except Christmas Day). **Admission:** Nurseries free, Gardens £2. **E-mail:** burncoose@eclipse.co.uk **Internet:** www.burncoose.co.uk

map 2
C6

CAERHAYS CASTLE AND GARDENS

Caerhays Gorran, St Austell PL26 6LY
Tel: 01872 501310 Fax: 01872 501870

One of the very few Nash built castles still left standing - situated within approximately 60 acres of informal woodland gardens created by J C Williams, who sponsored plant hunting expeditions to China at the turn of the century. Noted for its camellias, magnolias, rhododendrons and oaks.

English Heritage Listing: Grade One, Outstanding. **Open:** House: 19 Mar–27 Apr. mon–fri(excluding B.H.) 2–4pm,booking recommended. Gardens: 12 Mar–18 May. 10–4pm. Charity openings (gardens only) 25 Mar, 15 Apr, 7 May. 10–4pm. **Admission:** House £3.50, Gardens £3.50. Both £6. Group guided tours of gardens with head gardener £4.50 (Can be arranged outside normal openingtimes). **E-mail:** estateoffice@caerhays.co.uk **Internet:** www.caerhays.co.uk

map 2
C6

COTEHELE

St Dominick, Saltash, Cornwall PL12 6TA
Tel: 01579 351346 Fax: 01579 351222

A fine mediaeval house, Cotehele stands on the steep wooded slopes of the river Tamar. Visitors can admire tapestries, suits of armour, and oak furniture inside the house, whilst outside there is a series of gardens containing exotic and delicate plants. A nearby museum tells the story of Tamar's maritime past. **Open:** House: 31 Mar–4 Nov, daily (except Fri) 11am–5pm. Garden: All year, 10.30am – dusk. **Admission:** House: Adult £6.20. Garden only: Adult £3.40. **E-mail:** cctlce@smtp.ntrust.org.uk

LANHYDROCK HOUSE

Bodmin, Cornwall
Tel: 01208 73320 Fax: 01208 74084 (The National Trust)

Lanhydrock, one of Cornwall's grandest houses, dates back to the 17th century but much was rebuilt after a fire in 1881 destroyed all but the north wing, which includes the magnificent Long Gallery with its extraordinary plaster ceiling. A total of 49 rooms are on show today, including servants' bedrooms, kitchens, the nursery suite and the grandeur of the dining-room. Surrounding the house are formal Victorian gardens, wooded higher gardens where magnolias, rhododendrons and camellias climb the hillside. **Open:** Gardens and Park only: 17Feb–31 Oct . House: 31 Mar–31 Oct daily 11–5.30pm. Closes 5pm in October. House closed Mons (except Bank Hol Mons). **Admission:** House and gardens: Adult £6.80, Child £3.40. Garden and grounds only: Adult £3.70, Child, £1.85. Family ticket (2 adults + 3 children) £17. Pre-arranged parties £5.80, Child£2.90.

map 2
D5

JAMAICA INN AND MUSEUMS

Bolventor, Launceston, Cornwall PL15 7TS
Tel: 01566 86250 Fax: 01566 86177 (Five Star Taverns Ltd)

Made immortal by Dame Daphne du Maurier's novel, come and visit Jamaica Inn and Museums.

Daphne du Maurier's Smugglers at Jamaica Inn

Here, we introduce you to the life and works of Daphne du Maurier, and our arch villain, Demon Davey, the Vicar of Altamun, invites you to enter an exciting presentation of the story of Jamaica Inn told in tableaux, sound and light. Finally, on to see probably the finest collection of smuggling relics, dating from today back into the mists of time. **Tel/Fax:** 01566 86025

Mr Potter's Museum of Curiosity

One of the last truly Victorian Museums in England, consisting of assembled items of curiosity global. Come and browse around our fascinating museum founded in 1861, by the famous taxidermist, Walter Potter, containing his humorous tableaux, 'The Death of Cock Robin', 'House that Jack Built', 'Kittens Wedding', 'Guinea Pigs Cricket Match' and many others. Packed also with over 10,000 unusual and rare curios worldwide - General Gordon's autograph, two-headed pig sought by witches, ancient Egyptian mummified crocodile, native whistle made with human arm bone, three-legged chicken, postilion boots, a church made of feathers etc. **Tel/Fax:** 01566 86838

Open: Museums open February half term to December. Refreshments available from the Inn.

map 2
D5

MUSEUM OF SUBMARINE TELEGRAPHY

Eastern House Porthcurno, Penzance, Cornwall TR19 6JX
Tel: 01736 810966 Fax: 01736 810966

In 1870, the British end of the first undersea telegraph cable to Bombay landed at Porthcurno. By the early 20th century, this tiny Cornish cove was home to the world's largest telegraph station. Displays describe Porthcurno's important role in the development of the world telegraph network. Housed in a unique underground building constructed during the Second World War. Superb collection of telegraph apparatus, working World War II telegraph office. Local social history. Interactive displays, audio-visuals, temporary exhibitions, talks, archive, shop, guided tours. **Open:** 10am–5pm. Jan–Mar: Sun, Mon, Tues; Apr–Oct: Sun–Fri; Jul–Aug: all week. Nov–Dec: Mon. **Admission:** Adult £4, Concession £3.50, Child/Student £2.50, Family £10.50. **Internet:** www.porthcurno.org.uk

map 2
B7

NORTH CORNWALL MUSEUM & GALLERY

The Clease, Camelford, Cornwall PL32 9PL
Tel & Fax: 01840 212954

The museum shows many aspects of life in North Cornwall from 50-100 years ago. There are sections on the tools in various trades and on the domestic side a wide range of exhibits from clothes to early vacuum cleaners. **Open:** 2 April-29th September: Monday-Saturday 10-5pm.

map 2
D5

ROYAL CORNWALL MUSEUM

River Street, Truro
Tel: 01872 272205 Fax:: 01872 240514

The Royal Cornwall Museum is the flagship museum for Cornwall. Situated 100 meters from the City Centre, it offers eight galleries of permanent & temporary exhibitions, an extensive gift & book shop and a superb cafe with indoor and courtyard seating. Collections include a world renowned mineral collection, archaeology, local history, fine and applied art, an extensive ceramics collection and a new gallery of Cornwall's natural history. Activities include an education program, holiday activities for adults & children, lectures & special events. **Open:** All year round, Mon-Sat, 10-5pm. except B.H. mons. **Admission:** Adult £3, Children Free, Conc £2.

E-mail: enquiry@royal-cornwall-museum.freeserve.co.uk

map 2
E6

PENCARROW
Washaway, Bodmin PL30 3AG

Tel: 01208 841369 Fax: 01208 841722 (The Molesworth-St Aubyn Family)

Georgian house and listed gardens, still owned and lived in by the family. A superb collection of 18th century pictures, furniture and porcelain. Mile long drive and Ancient British Encampment. Marked walks through beautiful woodland gardens, past the great granite Victorian Rockery, Italian and American gardens, Lake and Ice House. Approximately 50 acres in all. Over 700 different rhododendrons, also an internationally known specimen conifer collection. **Open: House:** 1 Apr–14 Oct, 1.30–4.30pm (last entry), 11am from 28 May through to 27 Aug, Sun –Thurs. **Gardens:** 1 Mar–31 Oct daily, dawn to dusk. **Admission:** Adults – House & Gardens £5, Gardens only £2.50. Children – House £2.50, Gardens: children and dogs very welcome and free. Group rate 20% off. NPI National Heritage Award Winner 1997, 1998 & 1999. **E-mail:** pencarrow@aol.com **Internet:** www.pencarrow.co.uk

map 2 D5

PENDENNIS CASTLE
Falmouth, Cornwall TR11 4LP
Tel: 01326 316594 (English Heritage)

Facing the castle of St Mawes, with glorious views over the mile wide mouth of the River Fal, Pendennis Castle has stood in defence of our shores for almost 450 years. Take a guided tour through the tunnels to the Second World War Gun Battery. Explore the First World War Guardroom with its cells and see a Tudor gun deck in action complete with the sights and sounds of battle. A trip on the delightful ferry to St Mawes will make your day even more enjoyable. **Location:** On Pendennis Head 1m SE of Falmouth. **Open:** 1 Apr–31 Oct: daily 10am–6pm or dusk if earlier. 1 Nov–28 Mar: daily 10am–4pm. Closed 24–26 Dec & 1 Jan. **Admission:** Adult £3.80, Conc £2.90, Child £1.90. 15% discount for groups of 11 or more.

map 2 C6

ST MAWES CASTLE
St Mawes, Falmouth, Cornwall TR2 3AA
Tel: 01326 270526 (English Heritage)

Designed with three huge circular bastions resembling a clover leaf, Henry VIII's picturesque fort stands in delightful sub-tropical gardens.

Here you can see a remarkable collection of plants from all corners of the world. Climb to the battlements and experience the breathtaking views across the bay to Falmouth and take a trip on the ferry across the estuary to Pendennis Castle. **Location:** In St Mawes on A3078. **Open:** 1 Apr–31 Oct: daily 10am–6pm (5pm in October). 1 Nov–31 Mar: Fri–Tues, 10am–4pm. Closed 1–2pm and 24–26 Dec & 1 Jan. **Admission:** Adult £2.70, Conc £2, Child £1.40. 15% discount for groups of 11 or more.

map 2 C6

ST MICHAEL'S MOUNT
Marazion, Nr Penzance, Cornwall
Tel: 01736 710507/01736 710 265 (The National Trust)

Home of Lord St Levan. Medieval and early 17th century with considerable alterations and additions in 18th and 19th century. **Location:** ½ mile from the shore at Marazion (A394), connected by causeway. 3 miles E Penzance. **Open:** 1 April–31 Oct, Mon–Fri, 10.30–5.30pm (last adm 4.45pm). **Weekends:** The castle and grounds are open most weekends during the season. These are special charity open days when National Trust members are asked to pay. Nov to end of Mar: Guided tours as tide, weather and circumstances permit. (NB: ferry boats do not operate a regular service during this period. **Admission:** Adults £4.50, Children £2.25, Groups £4.10, for 20 or more paying people.

map 2 B6

TRELOWARREN HOUSE & CHAPEL

Mawgan-in-Meneage, Helston, Cornwall, TR12 6AD
Tel: 01326 221366 Fax: 01326 221834 (Sir Ferrers Vyvyan, Bt.)

Home of the Vyvyan family since 1427. Part of the house dates from early Tudor times. The Chapel, part of which is pre-Reformation and the 17th century part of the house are leased to the Trelowarren Fellowship, an ecumenical charity, for use by them as a Christian residential healing and retreat centre. (Phone for details). The Chapel and main rooms containing family portraits are open to the public at certain times. Sunday services are held in the Chapel during the holiday season. Please phone The Warden for details of opening times and prices.

TRERICE

Newquay, Cornwall, TR8 4PG
Tel: 01637 875404 Fax: 01637 879300

Trerice is a small Elizabethan manor which houses a collection of old clocks, along with fine furniture and ceramics. **Open:** 1 Apr–16 Jul and 12 Sept–4 Nov: daily (except Tues and Sat). 17 Jul–11 Sept: Sun–Fri, 11am–5.30pm. **Admission:** £4.30

TATE ST IVES

Tate St Ives, Porthmeor Beach, St Ives, Cornwall TR26 1TG
Tel: 01736 796226 Fax: 01736 794480

Experience a unique introduction to modern art, where paintings & sculpture can be seen in the surroundings which inspired them. The gallery presents changing displays from the Tate collection, focusing on the post-war modern movement St Ives is famous for and includes the works of Alfred Wallis, Ben Nicholson, Peter Lanyon, John Wells, Terry Frost and Wilhelmina Barns-Graham. Tate St Ives also runs the Barbara Hepworth Museum & Sculpture garden. Special exhibitions feature Patrick Heron, Antony Gormley and Ian Hamilton Finlay. **Admission:** Adults £3.95, Conc £2.50 Seniors & Children free. **Open:** Tues–Sun 10.30–5.30pm and Mons in Jul and Aug. Bank holidays 10.30–5.30pm. Closed 24–26 December. **Facilities:** Rooftop café, gallery shop, education services, guided tours, events and activities, full disabled access. **Internet:** www.tate.org.uk

`map 2 B6`

TINTAGEL CASTLE

Tintagel, Cornwall PL34 0HE
Tel: 01840 770328 (English Heritage)

A visit to Tintagel is a marvellous family experience combining legend, myth and magic. Located on Cornwall's dramatic Northern coast, this legendary castle of King Arthur is a place of mystery and romance, with breathtaking views of the Cornish coastline that inspire the imagination. Excavations prove the link between this area and the 6th century Mediterranean. **Location:** ½ mile from Tintagel Village along rough track. **Open:** 1 Apr–31 Oct daily 11am–6pm (5pm in Oct); 1 Nov–28 Mar daily 10am–4pm. Closed 24–26 Dec & 1 Jan. **Admission:** Adult £3, Concession £2.30, Child £1.50. Group discount 15% for groups of 11 or more.

`map 2 D5`

TREVARNO ESTATE GARDENS & NATIONAL MUSEUM OF GARDENING

Trevarno Manor, Helston, Cornwall TR13 0RU
Tel: 01326 574274 Fax: 01326 574282

An unforgettable gardening experience combining beautiful Victorian and Georgian gardens with the splendid fountain garden conservatory, unique range of craft workshops and the amazing National Museum of Gardening. Relax in the tranquil gardens, follow the progress of major restoration projects, visit the craft areas including handmade soap workshop and organic herbal workshop, explore Britain's largest and most comprehensive collection of antique tools, implements, memorabilia and ephemera. **Location:** Leave Helston on Penzance Rd, signed from B3302 and N of Crowntown. **Open:** 10.30–5pm exc. Christmas Day. **Admission:** Gardens: Adult £3.50, OAP/Disabled £3.20, Child (5–14) £1.25.

`map 2 B6`

Cumbria

Loweswater

The most famous of Cumbria's many charms is undoubtedly the Lake District National Park. The northern half of the Park is bordered by England's four highest mountains, Scafell, Scafell Pike, Helvellyn and Skiddaw, whilst to the south are over 600 square miles of glorious and contrasting scenery, stretching from Grasmere to Arnside. A huge number of activities can be enjoyed in the Park, from cycling to canoeing, and from rock-climbing to water-skiing.

Carlisle, set in the north of the county, is a fine cathedral city steeped in history, where visitors can retrace the steps of Bonnie Prince Charlie and Robert the Bruce.

THE BEATRIX POTTER GALLERY

The Square, Hawkshead, Ambleside, Cumbria
Tel: 015394 36355 Fax: 015394 36187 (The National Trust)

The Beatrix Potter Gallery in the beautiful, picturesque village of Hawkshead houses original Beatrix Potter art. There is an annually changing exhibition of subjects and illustrations from Beatrix Potter's story books plus original manuscripts from the National Trust collection. The building was once the office of her husband, the solicitor William Heelis, and the interior remains largely unaltered since his days. There is a wonderful cosy feel to the interior with its lime-washed walls and its beautiful polished wooden floors. The ground floor houses original items from the solicitor's office and the art work is displayed upstairs. **Open:** 1 Apr–1 Nov daily except Fri & Sat (open Good Fri), 10.30am–4.30. Last admission 4pm. **Admission:** Adults £3, Children £1.50, Family £7.50. Car & coach parking in village car park. There is a National Trust Shop close by, selling traditional NT merchandise as well as Beatrix Potter specific merchandise. The property also sells property-specific merchandise including limited-edition prints taken from the exhibitions. These are unique to the property and cannot be purchased elsewhere.

map 10 E6

BROUGHAM CASTLE

Tel: 01768 862888
(English Heritage)

Come to the gentle banks of the River Eamont and stroll through the wonderful ruins of this 13th-century fortress. Climb the Keep and enjoy wonderful panoramic views. Find out about the charismatic Lady Anne Clifford, who restored the castle in the 17th century. Enjoy the lively exhibition where you'll see relics from the nearby Roman fort. Free parking; exhibition; toilets; gift shop. Picnics welcome. **Location:** By car: 1 ½ miles SE of Penrith on minor road off A66. By train: Penrith Station 2 miles away. **Open:** 1 Apr–30 Sept daily 10am–6pm. 1–31 Oct daily 10am–5pm. **Admission:** Adults £2.10, Concessions £1.60, Children £1.10. Under 5 yrs free. 15% discount for groups of 11 or more. **Internet:** www.english-heritage.org.uk

map 11 F5

 ## CARLISLE CASTLE
Carlisle, Cumbria CA3 8UR
Tel: 01228 591922 (English Heritage)

This impressive medieval castle, where Mary Queen of Scots was once imprisoned, has a long and tortuous history of warfare and family feuds. A portcullis hangs menacingly over the gatehouse passage, there is a maze of passages and chambers, endless staircases to lofty towers and you can walk the high ramparts for stunning views. There is also a medieval manor house in miniature: a suite of medieval rooms furnished as they might have been when used by the castle's former constable. The castle is also the home of the Museum of the King's Own Border Regiment (included in admission price). **Location:** In Carlisle town, at N end of city centre. **Open:** 1 Apr–30 Sept: daily 9.30am–6pm. 1–31 Oct: daily 10am–5pm. 1 Nov–28 Mar: daily 10am–4pm. Closed 24–26 Dec. **Admission:** Adult £3.10, Child £1.60, Concession £2.30. 15% discount for groups (11+).

Maryport Maritime Museum

Keswick Museum & Art Gallery

MARYPORT MARITIME MUSEUM
1 Senhouse Street, Maryport, Cumbria CA15 6AB
Tel: 01900 813738 Fax: 01900 819496

Open: Easter–31 Oct: Mon–Thurs 10-5pm. Fri & Sat 10-1pm & 2-5pm. Sun 2-5pm. Nov-Easter: Mon-Sat 10-1pm & 2-4.30pm. **Admission:** Free.

KESWICK MUSEUM & ART GALLERY
Station Road, Fitz Park, Keswick Cumbria CA12 4NF
Tel: 017687 73263 Fax: 017687 80390

Open: Easter–31 Oct: Daily 10-4pm including Bank Holidays. **Admission:** Adults £1, Conc 60p. Group Discounts.

HELENA THOMPSON MUSEUM
Park End Road, Workington Cumbria CA12 4DE
Tel: 01900 326255 Fax: 01900 326256

Displays include costumes, pottery and local history. **Open:** Easter–31 Oct: Mon-Sat 10.30-4pm. 1 Nov-Easter: Mon-Sat 11-3pm. **Admission:** Free.

WORKINGTON HALL
c/o Tourism Section, Allerdale Borough Council, Allerdale House, Workington Cumbria CA14 3YJ. Tel: 01900 326408

Discover this striking ruin's fascinating heritage. **Open:** Easter–31 Oct: Daily 12-4pm including Bank Holidays. **Admission:** Adults £1, Conc 80p, Family £2.50. Group Discounts.

CUMBERLAND PENCIL MUSEUM
Southey Works, Keswick, Cumbria CA12 5NG
Tel: 017687 73626 Fax: 017687 74679

The pencil story, from the discovery of graphite to present day methods of pencil manufacture, told with exhibitions and a video presentation of modern day pencil production in our Keswick factory. Video demonstrating techniques and uses of Derwent pencils. World's largest pencil. Children's drawing area. Well-stocked gift shop. Parking. **E-mail:** museum@acco-uk.co.uk **Internet:** www.pencils.co.uk

DALEMAIN HISTORIC HOUSE & GARDENS
Nr Penrith, Cumbria CA11 0HB

Tel: 017684 86450 Fax: 017684 86223 (Robert Hasell-McCosh)

Impressive Mediaeval, Tudor and Georgian house, home to the Hasell family since 1679. Fascinating interiors with fine furniture, family portraits, ceramics, dolls houses, old toys, Mrs Mouse's house and the Westmorland & Cumberland Yeomanry Museum. Delightful Gardens with many rare plants and old fashioned roses. Featured as Lowood Institution, Jane Eyre's school, in LWT's recent television production. Free parking and admission to the Licensed Restaurant and Tea Room in the Mediaeval Hall (log fire), the Gift Shop and the Plant Sales. Country Walk towards Dacre Church and Castle. **Open:** 25 Mar–7 Oct 2001. Sun to Thur 10.30–5pm. House: 11–4pm. **E-mail:** admin@dalemain.com **Internet:** www.dalemain.com

Abbot Hall Art Gallery

ABBOT HALL ART GALLERY
Kendal, Cumbria LA9 5AL
Tel: 01539 722464 Fax: 01539 722494

Abbot Hall is a jewel of a building in a beautiful setting on the banks of the River Kent, surrounded by a park and overlooked by the ruins of Kendal Castle. This is one of Britain's finest small art galleries and a wonderful place in which to see and enjoy changing exhibitions in the elegantly proportioned rooms of a Grade I Listed Georgian building. The collection includes a fine collection of Lake District watercolours, including works by Ruskin and Turner. The diverse collection includes works by George Romney, Ben Nicholson, Lucian Freud and Bridget Riley. Free parking for cars an coaches. **Open:** 7 days a week 8 Feb–21 Dec 2001 10.30am–5pm (reduced hours in winter). **Admission:** Adult £3, OAP £2.80, Child £1.50, Family £7.50. **E-mail:** info@abbothall.org.uk **Internet:** www.abbothall.org.uk

BLACKWELL–THE ARTISTIC HOUSE
Bowness on Windermere, Cumbria LA23 3JR
Tel: 01539 722464 Fax: 01539 722494

Blackwell is the most important surviving example of work by the architect M H Baillie Scott. Opening in July 2001, Blackwell is a superb example of an Arts and Crafts Movement house. Completed in 1900, it sits in an elevated position with wonderful views of Lake Windermere and the mountains beyond. Changing exhibitions of the highest quality applied arts and crafts can be seen in the beautifully restored rooms. The interiors glow with fine examples of the decorative arts taken from nature including Lakeland birds, local wild flowers, trees and berries, as can be seen in the stained glass, oak panelling and plasterwork. These rooms were designed for relaxation and everywhere you turn you will find places to sit and enjoy the views. **Open:** 7 days a week 4 July–21 Dec 2001 10am–5pm (reduced hours in winter). **Admission:** Charge (concessions available). **E-mail:** info@blackwell.org.uk **Internet:** www.blackwell.org.uk

map 11 F6

Detail of Romney's 'Gower family' at Abbot Hall

'Windermere' by JMW Turner

Blackwell

Blackwell - Dining Room

Museum of Lakeland Life

MUSEUM OF LAKELAND LIFE

Abbot Hall, Kendal, Cumbria LA9 5AL
Tel: 01539 722464 Fax: 01539 722494

The Museum of Lakeland Life is housed in the stable block of Abbot Hall Art Gallery. It is a popular family attraction full of real objects that tell the story of how people lived, worked and entertained themselves in years gone by. Displays include a Victorian street scene, reconstructed farmhouse rooms and Arthur Ransome's recreated study. The museum also houses a fascinating collection of Arts and Crafts Movement furniture and fabrics which were made in the Lake District towards the end of the 19th century. **Location:** 10 minutes drive from junction 36 off the M6. Follow brown museum signs to South Kendal. **Open:** 7 days a week, 8 Feb–21 Dec 2001, 10.30am–5pm (reduced hours in winter). **Admission:** Adult £3, OAP £2.80, Child £1.50, Family £7.50. **E-mail:** info@lakelandmuseum.org.uk **Internet:** www.lakelandmuseum.org.uk

KENDAL MUSEUM

Station Road, Kendal, Cumbria LA9 6BT
Tel: 01539 721374 Fax: 01539 737976

Kendal Museum houses fascinating collections of archaeology, geology, natural history and local social history. Celebrating the life of the great fell walker and Honorary curator, Alfred Wainwright, is a display including a reconstruction of his office and many of his personal belongings. Visitors can travel back in time through the interactive Kendal Castle display with exhibits charting Kendal's history from Roman and Mediaeval times to the present day. **Location:** 10 minutes drive from junction 36 off the M6. Situated opposite Kendal railway station. **Open:** Mon–Sat 8 Feb–21 Dec 2001 10.30am–5pm (reduced hours in winter). **Admission:** Adult £3, OAP £2.80, Child £1.50, Family £7.50. **E-mail:** info@kendalmuseum.org.uk **Internet:** www.kendalmuseum.org.uk

map 11
F6

Museum of Lakeland Life

Hiberno - Norse Cross at Kendal Museum

Swallows and Amazons Forever at Museum of Lakeland Life

Wainwright Galleries at Kendal Museum

THE DOCK MUSEUM

North Road, Barrow-in-Furness, Cumbria LA14 2PW
Tel: 01229 894444 Fax: 01229 811361

The Dock Museum is a spectacular modern museum built over an original Victorian Graving Dock. Its fascinating displays follow the development of Barrow from a tiny nineteenth century hamlet to the biggest iron and steel centre in the world, and then to a major shipbuilding force, within 40 years. The story of the people who brought about such change is both unique and extraordinary. The Dock Museum has a landscaped coastal site with an adventure playground and walkways linking to Cumbria's coastal path. Facilities include a high tec filmshow 'Reflections in the Dock', a gallery for temporary exhibitions, coffee shop, museum shop, free car parking, and full wheelchair accessibility. **Open:** All year. Closed on Mondays. Also closed on Tuesdays in the winter. **Admission:** Free.

map 10 E7

HOLKER HALL AND GARDENS

Cark-in-Cartmel, nr Grange-over-Sands, Cumbria LA11 7PL
Tel: 015395 58328 Fax: 015395 58838 (Lord and Lady Cavendish)

Holker Hall is Cumbria's premier stately home. No ropes or barriers bar your way as you view the magnificent New Wing with its fine woodcarvings, furniture and paintings. The 25 acres of National Award winning gardens include water features, rare plants, trees and shrubs, 'World Class ... not to be missed by foreign visitors' (Good Gardens Guide). Also superb Lakeland Motor Museum, Exhibitions, 125 acre Deer Park, Adventure Playground, World's largest Slate Sundial. Home of the spectacular Holker Garden Festival 1-3 June. **Location:** S. of Cark-in-Cartmel on B5278 from Haverthwaite; 4 miles W. of Grange-over-Sands. **Station:** Cark-in-Cartmel. **Open:** 1 Apr–31 Oct every day excluding Sat, 10–6 last admission 4.30pm. **Admission:** Call for details. Reduction for groups of 20 or more. **Refreshments:** Home-made cakes, sandwiches, salads in the Stableyard Buttery. **Internet:** www.holker-hall.co.uk

map 10 E6

HUTTON-IN-THE-FOREST

Penrith, Cumbria
Tel: 017684 84449 Fax: 017684 84571 (Lord and Lady Inglewood)

The home of Lord Inglewood's family since 1605. Built around a medieval pele tower with 17th, 18th and 19th century additions. Fine English furniture, portraits, ceramics and tapestries. The lovely walled garden established in 1730 has an increasing collection of herbaceous plants, wall trained fruit trees and topiary. Also dovecote and woodland walk through magnificent specimen trees, identifiable from leaflet. **Location:** 6 miles NW of Penrith on B5305 Wigton Road (3 miles from M6 exit 41). **Stations:** Penrith. **Open:** House 12.30–4pm last entry, Thurs, Fri, Sun, and Bank Hols. 12 Apr–30 Sep. Gardens 11–5pm everyday except Sat. Groups by arrangement from Apr–Oct. **Admission:** House and Gardens: Adult £4.50, child £2.50, family £12. Gardens only: Adult £2.50, children free. **Refreshments:** Home-made light lunches & teas in Cloisters when house is open, 11–4.30pm.

map 10 E4

ISEL HALL

Cockermouth, Cumbria CA13 OQG
(The Administrator)

Isel Hall welcomes groups from 2 to 30 on Monday afternoons. 16 Apr–1 October 2001, 2-4pm. Other times by arrangement. Isel Hall demonstrates how a manor house coped with the danger of Scottish raids in the 14th and 15th centuries by the addition of a Pele Tower. Situated on the north bank of the River Derwent, 3.5 miles from Cockermouth (Map ref: NY158 337). From the formal gardens the ground drops down to the river and offers views of the 11th Century Norman Church and Skiddaw. **Admission:** £3. Dogs and photography in the house are not permitted. There is limited disabled access.

map 10 D4

LEVENS HALL

Kendal, Cumbria LA8 0PD
Tel: 015395 60321 Fax: 015395 60669 (C H Bagot Esq)

Elizabethan house and home of the Bagot family containing fine furniture, the earliest English patchwork (c.1708) and leather wall coverings. World famous award winning Topiary Gardens (c.1694). Location for BBC TV "Wives and Daughters". **Location:** 5 minutes drive from exit 36 of the M6. 5 miles south of Kendal on the A6. **Station:** Oxenholme. **Open:** 1 Apr–11 Oct, Sun–Thurs (including Bank Hol Mons). Garden & tearoom 10–5pm. House: noon–5pm. Last admissions 4.30pm. Closed Fri & Sat. **Admission:** House and Garden: Adults £6, Children £3. Gardens only: Adults £4.50, Children £2.20. **Refreshments:** Home-made light lunches and teas. We regret the house is not suitable for wheelchairs. **E-Mail:** email@levenshall.fsnet.co.uk **Internet:** http://www.levenshall.co.uk

map 10 E6

LANERCOST PRIORY
Tel: 01697 73030
(English Heritage)

Step back 800 years when you enter this stunning setting near Hadrian's Wall. Explore the ruins of a magnificent 12th-century Augustian priory. The church's nave contrasts with the ruined chancel, transepts and priory buildings. Take our fascinating free audio tour to learn more about the history of this beautiful priory. Free parking. **Location:** By car: Off minor road S of Lanercost, 2 miles NE of Brampton. By train: Brampton Station 3 miles away. By bus: Tel 01946 63222. **Open:** 1 Apr–30 Sept daily, 10am–6pm. 1–31 Oct daily, 10am–5pm. **Admission:** Adults £2.10, Concessions £1.60, Children £1.10, under 5 yrs free. 15% discount on groups of 11 or more. **Internet:** www.english-heritage.org.uk

map 11 F3

MIREHOUSE
Mirehouse, Keswick, Cumbria CA12 4QE
Tel: 017687 72287 Fax: 017687 72287 (James Spedding)

"The Best Property for Families in the U.K."1999 NPI Heritage Awards. This house maintains its three hundred year tradition of welcome and peaceful enjoyment. Our visitors particularly appreciate the extraordinary literary and artistic connections, varied gardens and walks, natural adventure playgrounds, live classical music and the personal attention of members of the family. The Old Sawmill Tearoom is known for generous Cumbrian cooking. **Location:** A591 3½ miles N of Keswick. Good bus service. **Open:** 1 Apr–31 Oct. Gardens and tearoom: daily 10–5.30pm. Please telephone for winter opening times. House: Sun, Wed (also Fri in Aug) 2–4.30pm last entry. Also throughout the year by appointment for groups. **E-mail:** info@mireho.freeserve.co.uk

map 10 E5

WINDERMERE STEAMBOAT MUSEUM
Rayrigg Road, Windermere, Cumbria LA23 1BN
Tel: 015394 45565 Fax: 015394 48769

A unique exhibition of Lake Windermere's nautical heritage. The Museum houses an historic collection of Victorian and Edwardian steam launches and classic motor boats both afloat and on display undercover (including 'Dolly', the world's oldest surviving mechanically powered boat). Spectacular lakeside setting, premier all-weather attraction. Guided tours of Museum and 'Esperance' (Ransome's inspiration for Captain Flint's houseboat). **Events/Exhibitions:** Swallows and Amazons, Model Boats – You Too Can Do It! Special events, cruises (weather permitting), shop, tea room, picnic area, model boat pond, free coach/car parking, toilets. Disabled facilities. **Open:** Daily 10am–5pm 17 Mar–28 Oct. **Admission:** Adult £3.40, Child £2.00, Family £8.50. Group discounts available. **Internet:** www.steamboat.co.uk

map 10 E6

TULLIE HOUSE MUSEUM & ART GALLERY
Castle Street, Carlisle, Cumbria CA3 8TP
Tel: 01228 534781 Fax: 01228 810249

Tullie House Museum is Carlisle's 'Jewel in the Crown'. With its use of audio-visual displays and exciting interactives, it truly illuminates the spellbinding history and legacies of Carlisle and the region. Old Tullie House is a fine town house, rebuilt in 1689 by Thomas Tullie. Its elegant frontage onto Abbey Street overlooks the herb garden. Older features still to be seen inside are the huge 1689 fireplace, a fine Jacobean oak staircase and panelled room. The house is used to display aspects of the museum's paintings collections. **Open:** All year except Christmas Day, Boxing Day & New Year's Day. **Facilities:** Contemporary Art Gallery, Border Galleries (main museum), Old Tullie House (Jacobean house with permanent displays of fine and decorative art), herb garden and family workshops and events. **E-mail:** tullie-house@carlisle.city.gov.uk

map 10 E4

WORDSWORTH HOUSE
Main Street, Cockermouth, Cumbria CA13 9RX
Tel/Fax: 01900 824805

Built in 1745, this fine Georgian town house was the birthplace of William Wordsworth, in 1770. His sister Dorothy was born here in 1771. The house is furnished in the Regency style, with some of the poet's personal effects on display. Many of the fittings, such as fireplaces, panelling, and plasterwork are the original. Walled garden, overlooking the river Derwent, described by Wordsworth in the 'Prelude'. Kitchen garden open to public. Video of 'Wordsworth's Lake District' showing in the old stables. Popular licensed tea room, in the Old Kitchen serves home-baking and local specialties. Gift shop open all year round(except Feb). **Open:** Apr–Oct, Mon–Fri 10.30-4.30pm (last entry to house 4pm); Jun–Aug & B.H.Mon open on Sat.

map 10 D5

🏛 MUNCASTER CASTLE, GARDENS & OWL CENTRE

Ravenglass, Cumbria CA18 1RQ
Tel: 01229 717 614 Fax: 01229 717 010 (Mrs P. Gordon-Duff-Pennington)

Situated on the wild and beautiful side of Cumbria, Muncaster Castle has been home to the Pennington family for over 800 years and is a genuine treasure trove of art and antiques. One can see statues, portraits and treasures, including a picture painted by Gainsborough as a bet and the 'Luck of Muncaster' bowl, presented by Henry V1 in 1461 whilst taking refuge during the War of the Roses. While appreciating the stunning view across the Lakeland Fells, one can marvel at the spectacle of over 70 acres of plants from all over the world - such as unique Tibetan species flourishing in Muncasters' mild climate. There is a 30 acre Sino-Himalayan trail for the energetic visitor. The World Owl centre at Muncaster features the first and finest collection of these thrilling birds in existence. Birds flown daily at 2.30pm (Weather Permitting). Watch the feeding of wild herons on the Canon Bank at Heron Happy Hour, every day at 4.30pm. Children can learn about environmentaland conservational issues at - the Meadow Vole Maze where you can imagine being a meadowvole living in meadowland. You can meet Max MeadowVole and his family and wonder at the secret world of wildlife where life is truly wild! Take a day on the wild side at the New Muncaster. Facilities: Gift shop, cafe, children's play area, disabled access, licensed for civil marriages. **Open:** Gardens, Owl Centre, Meadowvole Maze: daily all year 10.30 - 6.00pm (or dusk if earlier). Castle: 11 Mar - 4 Nov, Sunday to Friday 12 noon - 5.00pm (Castle closed Saturdays.) **E-mail:** info@muncastercastle.co.uk **Internet**: www.muncastercastle.co.uk

🌸 ☕ ✕ 🅰 🛋 🔔 ♿ 🚶 🦌 🪴 🎭 🐾 C 🎥 👥👥   map 9 D6

Derbyshire

Within the borders of Derbyshire, the English countryside passes from lowland to hill country. The county's principal attraction is the Peak District, which became Britain's first National Park in 1951. The area is popular with walkers, climbers and pot-holers, who congregate on the Pennine Way. The Tissington Trail is also popular, and winds round the charming old village of the same name. In the north of the county lies the former spa town of Buxton, whose elegant sweeping terraces echo those found in Bath. Matlock is another fine spa town, developed in the 18th century and home to some impressive buildings, including the former hydrotherapy centre, perched on a hill overlooking the town.

Viaduct in Monsdale

BUXTON MUSEUM & ART GALLERY

Terrace Road, Buxton, Derbyshire SK17 6DA
Tel: 01298 24658 Fax: 01298 79394

Set in the heart of this elegant spa town, the museum is a centre for local history. Explore the Wonders of the Peak, from the Big Bang to the Victorians, through geological and archaeological time, meeting wild animals, Neolithic man and the Romans on the way. Be amazed by the delicate inlays in Ashford Black Marble and turned Blue John. Step into the study of the eminent geologist Sir William Boyd Dawkins, author of 'Cave Hunting'. Or find relaxation through art, in our changing programme of paintings, photographs, sculpture and craft, and the highlight of the year, the Derbyshire Open in May and June. **Open:** Tues–Fri 9.30am–5.30pm, Sat 9.30am–5pm, Summer Sun & Bank Holidays 10.30am–5pm. **Admission:** Downstairs free; Gallery I and Wonders: Adult £1, Conc 50p, Family (2+2) £2.00.

map 8
D5

BLUEBELL NURSERY & WOODLAND GARDEN

Smisby, Derbyshire
Tel: 01530 413700

5 acre young Arboretum planted in the last 6 years including many specimens of rare trees and shrubs. Bring wellingtons in wet weather. **Location:** From the A511 Burton Trent to Ashby-de-la-Zouch Road, turn for Smisby by the Mother Hubbard Inn, 1 mile north-west of Ashby. Arboretum is on left after 1/2 mile Annwell Lane. Please call Tel: 01530 413700 for opening times and admission prices.

BOLSOVER CASTLE

Bolsover, Derbyshire S44 6PR
Tel: 01246 823349 (English Heritage)

Bolsover has the air of a romantic story book castle, but is an historic house with a fascinating story to tell. Visitors can explore the recently restored 17th century mansion and 'Little Castle' with its elaborate Jacobean fireplaces, panelling and wall paintings. Discover the mock-medieval fortifications, battlements, ruined staterooms (where Charles I was entertained) and indoor riding house, one of the oldest in Europe. An inclusive audio tour brings this magical castle to life. See the working Venus fountain and statuary, enjoy the Visitor and Discovery Centre Bolsover is now available for civil weddings, receptions and corporate hospitality. **Location:** Off M1 at junction 29, 6m from Mansfield. In Bolsover 6m E of Chesterfield on A632. **Open:** 1 Apr–31 Oct: daily 10am–6pm (5pm in Oct). 1 Nov–28 Mar: Wed–Sun 10am–4pm. Closed 24–26 Dec & 1 Jan. **Admission:** Adult £5, Conc £3.75, Child £2.50. 15% discount for groups of 11 or more.

map 8
D5

EYAM HALL

Eyam, Hope Valley, Derbyshire, S32 5QW
Tel: 01433 631976 Fax: 01433 631603 (Mr R H V Wright)

This small charming manor house in the famous plague village has been the home of the Wright family since 1671 and it retains the intimate atmosphere of a much-loved private home. A Jacobean staircase, fine tapestries, family portraits and costumes are among its interior treasures. **Location:** Eyam Hall is in the centre of the village of Eyam. **Open:** June, July, and August: Tues, Wed, Thur, Sun & BHol Mon, 11–4pm. Guided Tours. Victorian Christmas tours and Schools please phone for details. **Admission:** Adult £4.25, Child £3.25, Conc £3.75, Family (2+4) £13.50. Group rates with advance booking. Craft Centre, Gift Shop & Buttery in historic farmyard, with crafts people at work & local products for sale. Open daily except Mondays, all year, 10.30–5pm. **Events:** Indoor & outdoor concerts & plays -see Events Diary. **Weddings:** Eyam Hall is now licensed for civil weddings. **Internet:** www.eyamhall.co.uk

map 8
C4

CHATSWORTH

Chatsworth, Bakewell, Derbyshire, DE45 1PP
Tel: 01246 582204 Fax: 01246 583536 (Chatsworth House Trust)

Chatsworth, home of the Duke and Duchess of Devonshire, is one of the great treasure houses of England. Visitors see 26 richly decorated rooms furnished with the outstanding art collection. This year the special exhibition is devoted to modern art collected by the Duke and Duchess over the last 60 years, including work by Freud, Epstein, Sickert and Gwen John. 'Revelation', a new water sculpture, has recently been added to the unique assemblage of fountains, ponds and the Cascade in the 105 acre Garden. Children are thrilled by the woodland adventure playground and the farmyard, and there are award winning shops and a restaurant. The home of the Cavendish family for 450 years, and recently voted the country's favourite National Treasure, Chatsworth offers a day out that will entertain and astonish visitors of all ages. Guided tours and behind-the-scenes days are available by prior arrangement. **Open:** 21 Mar–28 Oct 2001, 11–4.30pm.
Events: International Horse Trials 12–13 May, Angling Fair 19–20 May, Country Fair 1–2 Sept.

map 8
C5

CALKE ABBEY

Ticknall, Derby DE73 1LE
Tel: 01332 863822 Fax: 01332 865272

A great house with a big difference! A baroque mansion, built 1701–3 for Sir John Harpur and set in a landscaped park. Little restored, Calke is preserved as a graphic illustration of the English country house in decline; contains the family's collection of natural history, a fine 18th century state bed and interiors that are virtually unchanged since the 1880s. Walled garden, pleasure ground and recently restored Orangery. Early 19th century church. Historic parkland with Portland sheep and deer. **Open:** 31 Mar–4 Nov, daily except Thurs & Fri. House & Church 1–5.30pm. Garden 11am–5.30pm (last entries 5pm). Ticket Office & Restaurant 11am–5pm. Shop 11am–5.30pm. Restaurant & Shop open weekends Nov–Mar 11am–4pm. Park: most days until 9pm or dusk if earlier. House, Church & Garden closed 11 August for concert. **Admission:** £5.20, Child £2.60, Family ticket £13. Gardens only £2.60. NT members free. **E-mail:** eckxxx@smtp.ntrust.org.uk

map 8
C6

HARDWICK HALL, GARDENS, PARK & MILL

The National Trust, Doe, Chesterfield, Derbyshire S44 5QJ
Tel: 01246 850430 Fax: 01246 854200 (The National Trust)

Set high on a hill in North-East Derbyshire, one of the greatest Elizabethan houses, which survives almost unchanged today. Completed 403 years ago and known to have "more glass than wall", the Hall contains one of Europe's best collections of embroideries and tapestries recorded in a 1601 inventory. A gardener's delight - the spectacular gardens, orchards and herb area are a relaxing place to spend an afternoon. The historic 300 acre parkland with woods and meadows has great walks and many attractive ponds and views. A new circular route around Miller's Pond offers mobility-impaired visitors good access. Stainsby Mill - a tranquil water powered corn mill. A mill has stood on this site since the 13th century, providing flour for the local villages and later for the Hardwick Estate. The Sixth Duke of Devonshire, owner of Hardwick, restored it in 1850. He spent the equivalent of £1,000,000 to put it into working order after years of neglect. The working mill is of advanced engineering design. **Location:** Follow brown tourist signs for Hardwick Hall from Junction 29 of the M1, 9½m southeast of Chesterfield and 7 miles northwest of Mansfield. **Open:** Hall: 31 Mar–4 Nov: Wed, Thurs, Sat, Sun & Bank Hol Mon, 12.30–5pm. Garden: 31 Mar–4 Nov: daily 12–5.30pm. Mill: 31 Mar–4 Nov: Wed, Thurs, Sat, Sun & Bank Hol Mondays, Good Friday, New Year's Day and Fridays during June, July, August and September 11am–4.30pm (last entry 4pm). Restaurant/Shop: 12noon to 5pm.

map 8
D5

KEDLESTON HALL AND PARK

Kedleston Hall, Derby DE22 5JH
Tel: 01332 842191 Fax: 01332 841972 (The National Trust)

Experience the age of elegance in this neoclassical house built between 1759 and 1765 for the Curzon Family. Set in 800 acres of parkland with an 18 C pleasure ground, garden and woodland walks. Parties welcome. Introductory talks can be arranged. **Location:** 5m NW of Derby, signposted from roundabout where A38 crosses A52. **Open:** House: 31 Mar–4 Nov daily except Thurs and Fri (closed Good Fri) 12–4.30pm last admissions 4pm.

Garden: same days as house 11–6pm. Park: 31 Mar–4 Nov daily 11–6pm; Nov–Dec: Sat & Sun only 12–4pm. Events: concerts and theatre. Details from Property Manager. **Admission:** Adult £5.10, Child £2.50, Family £12.70. £1 reduction for pre-booked parties of 15+. Park & Garden only: Adult £2.30, Child £1 (refundable against tickets for house); Thurs and Fri vehicle charge of £2 for park only.

map 8 C6

SUDBURY HALL & MUSEUM OF CHILDHOOD

Sudbury, Ashbourne, Derbyshire
Tel: 01283 585337 Fax: 01283 585139 (The National Trust)

The ideal family day out - an intriguing house and an entertaining museum. The Hall is one of England's most individual late 17th century houses. Look at the recently opened kitchen, which is featured in the current BBC2 drama series 'In a Land of Plenty'. The Museum contains fascinating displays about children from the 18th century onwards. Chimney climbs for adventurous youngsters plus Betty Cadbury's fine collection of toys and dolls. Parties

welcome, special 'Behind the Scenes/Roof top/Conservation tours tailored to suit your requirements. Contact Property Secretary for details. **Location:** 6 m E of Uttoxeter at Jct of A50 Derby–Stoke & A515 Ashbourne. **Open:** 31 Mar–4 Nov daily expect Mon & Tues, plus Bank Holiday Mondays from 1–5.30pm. Open Good Friday from 1–4pm. **Admission:** Adult £3.80, Child £1.90, Family £9.50.

map 8 C6

HADDON HALL

Bakewell, Derbyshire

Tel: 01629 812855 Fax: 01629 814379 (Haddon Hall Trust)

William the Conqueror's illegitimate son, Peverel and his descendants held Haddon for a hundred years before it passed into the hands of the Vernons. The following four centuries saw the development of the existing medieval and Tudor manor house from its Norman origins. In the late 16th century, it passed through marriage to the Manners family, later to become Dukes of Rutland, in whose possession it has remained ever since. Little has been added since the reign of Henry VIII, whose elder brother was a frequent guest and despite its time-worn steps, no other medieval house has so triumphantly withstood the passage of time. The terraced gardens, one of the chief glories of Haddon, were added during the 16th century. Now with roses, clematis and delphiniums in abundance, it is perhaps the most romantic garden in all England. A popular choice with film producers, Haddon Hall has recently appeared in: Elizabeth (1997); Jane Eyre (1996); The Prince and The Pauper (1996); Moll Flanders (1996). **Location:** On the A6, 2 miles S of Bakewell. **Open:** 1 Apr–30 Sept, everyday and Mon–Thurs in Oct. Closed Sun 15 July 2001. **Admission:** Adult £5.90, concession £5.00, child £3.00, family (2+3) £15.00. **Refreshments:** Licensed restaurant serving home-made food. **Events:** Partake Elizabethan Dancers Sun 29 April & Sun 23 September

map 8
C5

LEA GARDENS

Lea, Matlock, Derbys DE4 5GH

Tel: 01629 534380 Fax: 01629 534260 (Mr & Mrs Jonathan Tye)

Visit Lea Gardens where you can see our highly acclaimed unique collection of rhododendrons, azaleas, kalmias and other plants of interest introduced from the far corners of the world. The gardens are sited on the remains of a medieval millstone quarry and cover an area of approximately four acres amidst a wooded hillside. The excellent rock gardens contain a huge variety of alpines with acers, dwarf conifers, heathers and spring bulbs. The teashop on site offers light lunches and home baking. A plant sales area reflects the contents of the garden offering up to 200 varieties of rhododendrons and azaleas. **Special Event:** Music Day, 10 June. **Open:** Daily 10–5.30pm, 20 Mar–30 June. **Admission:** Adults £3, Children 50p, Season ticket £5.

map 8 C6

MELBOURNE HALL & GARDENS

Melbourne, DE73 1EN

Tel: 01332 862502 Fax: 01332 862263

This beautiful house of history is the home of Lord and Lady Ralph Kerr. Melbourne Hall was once the home of Victorian Prime Minister William Lamb who, as 2nd Viscount Melbourne, gave his name to the famous city in Australia. One of the most famous formal gardens in Britain featuring Robert Bakewell's wrought iron 'Birdcage'. **Location:** 7 m S of Derby off the A453 in village of Melbourne. **Open:** House open every day of Aug only (except first 3 Mons) 2pm–Last entry 4.15pm. Garden open Apr–Sept Weds, Sats and Suns, Bank Hols Mons 1:30-5:30pm. **Refreshments:** Melbourne Hall Tearooms and Visitor centre and shops open at various times throughout the year. Car parking limited. Suitable for disabled persons. All enquiries 01332 862502.

map 8 C6

THE NATIONAL TRAMWAY MUSEUM

Crich, Matlock, Derbyshire DE4 5DP

Tel: 01773 852565 Fax: 01773 852326

Nestling on the edge of the Peak District, this award-winning museum takes you on a mile-long scenic journey through a period street to open countryside with panoramic views over the Derwent Valley. Enjoy unlimited vintage tram rides and explore 30,000 sq ft of indoor attractions. The Exhibition Hall houses the largest collection of vintage electric trams in Britain. Ring for details of special events. **Location:** 8 miles from M1 junction 28. **Open:** Daily April–October. **Admission:** Adults £7, Children £3.50, Senior Citizens £6, Family £19. Special rates for groups of 10 or more.

map 8 C5

RENISHAW HALL

Near Sheffield, Derbyshire S21 3WB

Tel: 01246 432310 Fax: 01246 430760(Sir Reresby Sitwell)

Home of Sir Reresby and Lady Sitwell. Seven acres of Italian style formal gardens stand in 300 acres of mature parkland, encompassing statues, shaped yew hedges, a water garden and lakes. The Sitwell museum and art gallery are located in the Georgian stables alongside craft workshops and café, furnished with contemporary art. Located 3 miles from exit 30 of the M1, equidistant from Sheffield and Chesterfield. Tours of house and gardens can be arranged. Telephone for details. **Open:** Gardens and Georgian Stables: Thrusdays (Jul-Aug), 6 Apr-30 Sep; Fridays, Saturday, Sunday and Bank Holidays 10.30–4.30pm. Free car parking. **E-mail:** info@renishawhall.free-online.co.uk **Internet:** www.sitwell.co.uk

map 8 C4

ARKWRIGHT'S CROMFORD MILL

Mill Lane, Cromford,

Derbyshire DE4 3RQ

Tel & Fax: 01629 823256

The world's first successful Water Powered Cotton Spinning Mill – one of the great historic industrial monuments of the world Guided tours, exhibition, clothing at factory prices, cards and gifts, books, wholefood restaurant, free parking, friendly staff. There is an on-going restoration programme and a guide will explain the history and plans for the future. You will find us at Cromford, Derbyshire, just off the A6. Look out for the brown signs. **Opening Times**: Daily 9–5.00pm. **Admission:** Free. Guided tours: Adults £2.00, Concessions £1.50. The Arkwright Society is a Registered Charity. Reference No. 515526.

map 8 C5

Devon

South Pool

Unspoilt, uncrowded, and blessed with a temperate climate, Devon is the perfect holiday county. Inland, the visitor will find small villages nestling in a patchwork of lush greenery and stunning gardens. On the coast, the scenery is far more dramatic, and equally beautiful, ranging from the soaring chalk headlands at Beer and red cliffs at Sidmouth, to the gentle, golden beaches at Exmouth.

Much of East Devon is designated an Area of Outstanding Natural Beauty, and highlights include the heath, cliff-top grassland, estuaries and countryside such as Blackdown Hills and Woodbury Common. A huge number of sporting activities can be enjoyed, including golf, tennis, cycling and riding, although the less energetic can simply while away the hours watching fishing boats ply the crystal waters.

The streets of Ottery St Mary fan out from a central hub in an arrangement that dates back to Saxon times; today, over 80 marked footpaths allow for a splendid choice of walks. The surrounding area was described by naturalist W H Hudson to as "the greatest, most luxuriant in its vegetation and, perhaps, the hottest in England".

Ilfracombe sits against the rocky cliffs of the majestic Atlantic coast, and its amazing Torrs walks have been described as some of the finest in England. To the East, the beautiful cove of Hele Bay is the perfect place to unwind, with its quiet inlets and shady rock pools.

BARNSTAPLE HERITAGE CENTRE
Queen Anne's Walk, The Strand, Barnstaple, North Devon EX31 1EU
Tel & Fax: 01271 373003

Discover a wealth of fascinating history at Barnstaple Heritage Centre, situated on the picturesque quayside. Step inside the magnificent colonnaded Queen Anne's Walk building, which houses the Centre, and see the past come to life. The story of Barnstaple's rich past is revealed to visitors through an exciting combination of audio-visual displays, atmospheric exhibits and detailed information panels, with something to appeal to everyone. The Heritage Centre gift shop boasts a wide range of local heritage books, gifts and souvenirs. Full wheelchair access and toilet facilities are among the centre's excellent features. Generous concessions and group rates are always available. **Open:** All year. For further details call 01271 373003.

map 2 E3

MUSEUM OF BARNSTAPLE & NORTH DEVON
The Square, Barnstaple, Devon EX32 8LN
Tel: 01271 346747 Fax: 01271 346407

'The Story of North Devon' traces life from pre-history to the 1930s and includes geology and archaeology. A reconstruction of waterside life in 'Tarka Centre' and of marine life in the 'Undersea World', both with hands-on activities and special effects help to create a memorable visit. Other permanent displays of pottery, wartime and furniture. Changing exhibition programme, shop. Limited parking. **Open:** Tues–Sat 10am–4.30pm. Closed Sun and Bank Holidays. **Admission:** Adults £1, Concessions 50p. FREE Saturday mornings. **Internet:** www.northdevon.gov.uk

map 2 E3

BICKLEIGH CASTLE
Bickleigh, Nr. Tiverton, EX16 8RP, Devon.
Tel: 01884 855363 (M.J. Boxall)

A Royalist Stronghold with 900 years of history and still lived in. The 11th century detached Chapel, Armoury Guard Room with Tudor furniture and pictures, the Great Hall, Elizabethan bedroom, 17th century farmhouse. Picturesque moated garden, 'spooky' tower. Licensed French restaurant open from 12 noon. **Location:** 4 miles south of Tiverton, A396. **Open:** Easter Week (Easter Sun–Fri), then Wed, Sun, Bank Hol Mons to late May Bank Hol; then to early Oct daily (except Sat) 2–5pm. (Last admission 4.30pm). Parties of 20 or more by prior appointment. **Admission:** Adults £4, Children (5–15) £2, Family Ticket £10. Very popular for wedding receptions, civil wedding licence etc. For further details please telephone the Administrator.

map 3 F4

BICTON PARK BOTANICAL GARDENS

East Budleigh, Budleigh Salterton, Devon EX9 7BJ
Tel: 01395 568465 Fax: 01395 568374

Spanning three centuries of horticultural history, Bicton Park Botanical Gardens are set in the picturesque Otter Valley, near the coastal town of Budleigh Salterton, East Devon. The 63-acre park's oldest ornamental area is the Italian Garden, created in the axial style of Versailles landscaper André le Notre in c1735. By that time, formal designs were becoming unfashionable in England, which may explain why the garden was located out of view from the manor house. Today, the full grandeur of the Italian Garden can be seen from the spacious restaurant in the classically styled Orangery, built at the beginning of the 19th century. Bicton's high-domed Palm House, one of the world's most beautiful garden buildings, was the first of many developments between 1820 and 1850. Others included an important collection of conifers in the Pinetum, now the subject of a rare species conservation project, and St Mary's Church, where Queen Victoria once worshipped. A large museum reflects changes in agriculture and rural life generally over the past 200 years. The Grade I listed gardens, which are open all year, also feature a narrow-gauge railway, gift shop, garden centre and children's play hall. **Open:** The Gardens are open from 10 am–6 pm summer; 10 am–5 pm winter. **Admission:** Adults £4.75, Children £2.75, Families (2 adults and up to 4 children) £12.75, Concessions £3.75. **E-mail:** info@bictongardens.co.uk **Internet:** www.gardensatbictonpark.co.uk

map 3
G5

CADHAY

Ottery St Mary, EX11 1QT
Tel/Fax: 01404 812432 (Mr O William-Powlett)

The main part of the present house was built about 1550 by John Haydon, who retained the 'great hall' of the earlier house, of which the fine timber roof (1420–70) can be seen. An Elizabethan Long Gallery was added by John's great-nephew, Robert Haydon, thus forming a unique and lovely courtyard. Robert Haydon had married Joan, the eldest daughter of Sir Amias Poulett of Hinton St George. William Peere Williams acquired Cadhay in 1737 and made a number of alterations, providing some fine examples of Georgian architecture. Cadhay was restored in 1911 by W C Dampier Wetham. Wherever possible he restored the work of the 16th and 17th century, but where the work of Peere Williams was the dominant factor he restored that instead. In 1924 the William-Powlett family, descendants of the same family as Sir Amias Poulett, came to Cadhay and bought the property in 1935. Cadhay is approached by an avenue of limes and stands in a pleasant listed garden, with herbaceous borders and yew hedges, and looks out over the original medieval fish ponds, which may well have been used by the Warden and Canons of the lovely Collegiate Church of St Mary of Ottery. Conducted tours. **Location:** 1 mile NW of Ottery St Mary; from W on A30: exit Pattersons Cross, signs to Fairmile, then Cadhay; from E: exit Iron Bridge. **Open:** Late Spring & Summer Bank Hol Suns & Mons, also Tues, Weds, Thurs in July and Aug 2–6 (last adm. 5.30pm) **Admission:** Adults £4, Children £2. Groups by arrangement only. **Weddings:** The house is licenced for Civil Weddings and the gardens and grounds are available for receptions and corporate entertainment. **E-mail:** cadhay@east.cleron.net **Internet:** www.eastcleron.net/cadhay

map 3
F5

COLDHARBOUR MILL

Working Wool Museum

Coldharbour Mill, Uffculme, Cullompton, EX15 3EE
Tel: 01884 840960 Fax: 01884 840858

Discover the sights and sounds of a Victorian Mill! Guided tours enable visitors to see machinery working; feel the softness of newly spun wool and hear about the lives of the men, women and children who worked at Coldharbour Mill in Victorian times. One of Britain's best preserved industrial heritage sites, the museum provides an enthralling day out for all ages. The 'New World Tapistry' is also on permanent display at the mill, telling the story of English colonisation of the Americas in a lively, humorous way. The Mill runs a special events programme and discounted rates for groups. Call for opening times.
E-mail: info@coldharbourmill.org.uk **Internet:** www.coldharbourmill.org.uk or www.newworldtapestry.org.uk

map 3
G4

 HARTLAND ABBEY & GARDENS

Nr Bideford, North Devon EX39 6DT
Tel & Fax: 01237 441264/234 (Sir Hugh and Lady Stucley)

Built 1157 in beautiful valley leading to Atlantic cove. Given by Henry VIII to Keeper of his Wine Cellar whose descendants live here today. Remodelled in 18-19th C, contains spectacular architecture and murals, fascinating collections of paintings, furniture, porcelain. Documents & seals from 1160AD; Victorian & Edwardian photographs; Museum; Dairy. Paths by Gertrude Jekyll lead to Bog Garden, Victorian Fernery discovered in 1999, woodland gardens of camellias, rhododendrons etc, secret 18th C walled gardens. Walk to beach with abundant wildflowers and wildlife. Peacocks, donkeys, black sheep. Cream Teas. 1998 N.P.I. National Heritage Award Winner. **Location:** Off A39, between Hartland and Quay. **Open:** April 1–30 Sept: Weds, Thurs, Suns & BHs plus Tues in July & Aug 2-5.30p.m. Gardens only also open daily.(except Sats) to end of October. **Admission:** House, gardens & grounds: Adults £5.00, OAP's £4.50 Children £1.50. Reduction for gardens only & groups etc.

map 2
D3

DARTMOUTH CASTLE

Castle Road, Dartmouth, Devon TQ6 0JN
Tel: 01803 833588

Boldly guarding the narrow entrance to the Dart Estuary this castle was among the first in England to be built for artillery. Construction began in 1481 on the site of an earlier castle which was altered and added to over the following centuries. Victorian coastal defence battery with fully equipped guns, a site exhibition and magnificent views can all be seen at the castle. Partial disabled access. **Location:** 1m (1 ⅔ km) south east of Dartmouth, off B3205. **Open:** Apr–Sept 10–6pm daily. Oct 10-5pm daily; Nov-Mar, Wed-Sun 10-4pm. **Admission:** Adult £3.20, Conc £2.40, Child £1.60, Group discout 15% of 11 or more.

map 3
F6

THE MUSEUM OF DARTMOOR LIFE

3 West Street, Okehampton, Devon EX20 1HQ
Tel: 01837 52295 Fax: 01837 52295

The collection that forms the Museum of Dartmoor Life is displayed over three large galleries. It includes historical and educational artefacts, exhibits and reconstructions depicting man's close interaction with Dartmoor over the centuries. The Museum set in a medieval burgage plot, is situated in the centre of Okehampton. **Open:** Easter-October 6 days, June-Sept 7days 10am-5pm. Winter ring for details.

map 2
E4

FLETE

Ermington, Ivybridge, Plymouth, Devon, PL21 9NZ.
Tel: 01752 830 308 Fax: 01752 830 309
(Country Houses Association)

Built around an Elizabethan manor, with alterations in 1879 by Norman Shaw. Wonderful II drop waterfall garden, designed by Russell Page ably assisted by Laurance of Arabia in the 1920's. Location: 11 miles E of Plymouth, at junction of A379 and B3121. Station(s): Plymouth (12 miles), Totnes (14 miles). Bus Route: No. 93, Plymouth–Dartmouth. Open: May–Sept. House and Garden: Wed & Thurs, 2–5pm. (Latest admission time 4.30pm) Admission: Please call for further details.

map 2
E6

KILLERTON HOUSE

Broadclyst, Exeter, Devon
Tel: 01392 881345 Fax: 01392 883112

Just 6 miles from Exeter, Killerton is Devon's most popular National Trust property. Elegant 18th century house designed by John Johnson with later additions, home of the Acland family. Also on display is costume from the Killerton Dress collection in a special exhibition for Victorian laundry. 18 acre garden landscaped by Veitch with many original plantings of specimens collected by the plant hunters William and Thomas Lobb, Ernest 'Chinese' Wilson. Killerton also has a wonderful early 19th century rustic summer house and an ice house built in 1809. Excellent facilities for the less abled. Children quiz available.

map 3
F4

POWDERHAM CASTLE

Kenton, Exeter EX6 8JQ
Tel: 01626 890243 Fax: 01626 890729 (Earl & Countess of Devon)

Powderham Castle, the historic family home of the Earl of Devon, lies in an ancient and beautiful setting beside the Exe Estuary. There are regular guided tours of the magnificent State Rooms, beautiful gardens and grounds to explore, including the Children's Secret Garden, in the old Victorian walled garden. In springtime the Woodland Garden is full of colour and later in the summer The Rose Garden provides a fragrant home to Timothy Tortoise, at 155, the World's oldest pet! Powderham's Farm Shop and Plant Centre provide an excellent regional shopping centre. Courtyard Restaurant and Gift Shop. **New in 2001:** Powerham Steam Railway opens: Take a trip on the model steam train 'The Earl of Devon', which runs up to the Woodland Garden. By separate admission, 'The Knights of Powderham' joust daily except Saturday, 17 July–9 September. **Location:** Signposted on A379 Exeter to Dawlish Road. Tel 01626 890243 for all information. **Open:** Every day (except Sat). Castle and grounds from 2 April–29 Oct. Guided tours every half an hour, last admission 5pm. Farm Shop at Powderham Castle open seven days a week, 9am–6pm (Sunday 10am–4pm). **Admission:** Adult £5.85, Seniors £5.35, Child £2.95 (5–16), Family ticket £14.65 (2 adults & 2 children).

map 3
G5

TORRE ABBEY

The Kings Drive, Torquay TQ2 5JE
Tel: 01803 293593 Fax: 01803 215948 (Torbay Council)

For 800 years, Torre Abbey has been the home of Torquay's leading citizens. Founded as a monastery in 1196, the Abbey later became a country house and the Cary family's residence for nearly 300 years. As well as important monastic remains, you can see over twenty historic rooms, including the beautiful family chapel, a splendid collection of paintings and Torquay terracotta, colourful gardens and mementoes of crime writer Agatha Christie. Teas are served in the Victorian kitchen. **Open:** Daily, Easter to 1 Nov, 9.30–6pm. Last admission 5pm. **E-mail:** torre-abbey@torbay.gov.uk **Internet:** www.torre-abbey.org.uk

UGBROOKE PARK

Chudleigh, Devon, TQ13 0AD
Tel: 01626 852179 Fax: 01626 853322 (Lord Clifford)

Beautiful scenery and quiet parkland in the heart of Devon. Original House and Church built about 1200, redesigned by Robert Adam. Home of the Cliffords of Chudleigh. Ugbrooke contains fine furniture, paintings, beautiful embroideries, porcelain, rare family military collection. Capability Brown Park with lakes, majestic trees, views to Dartmoor. Guided tours relate stories of Clifford Castles, Shakespeare's 'Black Clifford', Henry II's 'Fair Rosamund, Lady Anne Clifford who defied Cromwell, The Secret Treaty, the Cardinal's daughter, Clifford of the CABAL and tales of intrigue, espionage and bravery. **Location:** Chudleigh, Devon. **Open:** 8 July–6 Sept, Sun, Tues, Wed & Thurs. Grounds open 1–5.30pm. Guided tours of House 2pm and 3.45pm. **Admission:** Adults £4.80. Children (5–16) £2. Groups (over 20) £4.50. Private party tours/functions by arrangement.

TOTNES CASTLE

Castle Street, Totnes TQ9 5NU
Tel: 01803 864406 (English Heritage)

By the North Gate of the hill town of Totnes you will find a superb motte and bailey castle, with splendid views across the roof tops and down to the River Dart. It is a symbol of lordly feudal life and a fine example of Norman fortification. **Location:** In Totnes, on the hill overlooking the town. Access in Castle Street off west end of High Street. **Open:** 1 Apr–end Sept: daily 10–6pm. Oct: daily 10–5pm. Nov–28 Mar: Wed–Sun 10–4pm. Closed 1–2pm in winter. Closed 24–26 Dec and 1 Jan. **Admission:** Adult £1.60, Concession £1.20, Child 80p.

YARDE

Yarde Farm, Malborough, Kingsbridge, Devon TQ7 3BY
Tel: 01548 842367 (John and Marilyn Ayre)

Grade I listed. An outstanding example of the Devon farmstead with a Tudor Bakehouse, Elizabethan farmhouse and Queen Anne mansion under restoration. Still a family farm. **Location:** On A381 ½ mile E of Malborough. 4 miles S of Kingsbridge. **Open:** Easter–30 Sept, Sun 2–5pm. **Admission:** Adults £2.50, children 50p, under 5s free.

Dorset

The countryside of Dorset is quietly charming, with its beautiful thatched flint-and-chalk cottages. Neither wild nor grand, just charming and a little quaint, it remains true to its portrait in Thomas Hardy's novels. The county town, Dorchester, has also changed little from its depiction as "Casterbridge"; here, visitors can wander along charming thoroughfares lined with elegant 18th century houses. Hardy was very much a man of the countryside, and the landscape around his cottage at Wimbourne Minster reveals the inspiration for his pastoral idylls. To the north of Wimbourne stands Cranborne, a beautiful village on the edge of what was once a royal forest: a charming site for country walks.

The landscape becomes markedly more dramatic along the coast, with impressive cliffs at Lyme Regis, Canford, and Hengistbury Head. The nearby Purbeck Hills were once part of a mighty range linking the headlands of Brittany to the coast of England, but millennia of erosion have reduced them to a craggy coastline.

Poole, the largest natural harbour in Europe, is a great spot for sailing and wind surfing, and the surrounding countryside is a haven for rare plants and wildlife.

Hardy's Cottage

ABBOTSBURY SUB TROPICAL GARDENS

Bullers Way, Abbotsbury, dt3 4la
Tel:01305 871387 Fax: 01305 871 092

One of England's most exotic and romantic gardens. This grade one listed garden was established in 1765 by the first countess of Ilchester. A mixture of formal and informal with a charming walled garden and spectacular woodland valley views. This 20-acre garden is world famous for its Camilla groves, Magnolias and noted for its Hydrangea and Rhododendron collections. A superb plant nursery and a splendid colonial style Tea House. Location: off the A35 on the B3157 between Weymouth and Bridport. **Open:** 10-6pm, last admission 5pm Mar-Oct. Winter 10am-dusk. **Admission:** Adult£4.70, Child£3, under 5 yrs free. Wedding receptions & private functions.

map 3 H5

CHIFFCHAFFS

Chaffeymoor, Bourton, Gillingham, SP8 5BY, Dorset.
Tel: 01747 840841 (Mr & Mrs K. R. Potts)

The garden surrounds a typical 400 year old stone Dorset cottage, with a very wide range of bulbs, alpines, herbaceous trees and shrubs, many of them unusual. It is planted for long periods of interest and divided into small individual gardens with many surprise views. In addition, a woodland garden with azaleas, camellias, rhododendrons, bog primulas and daffodils, unusual trees and shrubs. The bluebells are particularly beautiful in the spring. **Location:** 3 miles E of Wincanton, just off A303. **Open:** Every Wednesday and Thursdsay. 4 Mar–15 Oct, 2–5pm. Sundays 4 March, 1, 15, 22 7 29 Apr, 6, 20 & 27 May, 10 & 24 June, 8 July, 26 Aug, 9 Sept, 7 Oct. Also by appointment. Groups welcome. **Admission:** £2. **Refreshments:** By arrangement.

map 3 J3

Photo: Jerry Harpur

ATHELHAMPTON HOUSE & GARDENS
Athelhampton, Dorchester, Dorset DT2 7LG
Tel: 01305 848363 Fax: 01305 848135 (Patrick Cooke)

Athelhampton is one of the finest 15th century manor houses and is surrounded by one of the great architectural gardens of England. The house contains many magnificently furnished rooms. The Great Hall was built in 1485 by Sir William Martyn with permission from Henry VII. The Elizabethan West Wing includes The Great Chamber, Wine Cellar, King's Room and Library. The East Wing contains The State and Yellow Bedrooms as well as The Dining Room with a fine collection of Georgian furniture. The glorious Grade I gardens, dating from 1891, are full of vistas and gain much from the fountains and River Piddle flowing through. The walled gardens include the world famous topiary pyramids and two garden pavilions designed by Francis Inigo Thomas. Fine collections of tulips, magnolias, roses, clematis and lilies can be seen in season. A 15th century Dovecote and a 19th century Toll House are also situated in the grounds. Visited often by Thomas Hardy, Athelhampton is at the heart of Dorset's heritage. Recently used as a location for the BBC Antiques Roadshow. **Location:** Off the A35 at Northbrook Junction, 5 miles East of Dorchester. Ordnance Survey Grid Reference SY770942. **Open:** Mar–Oct daily (except Sat) 10.30–5pm. Nov–Feb, Sun 10.30–5pm. Also open Sat at Easter and Aug Bank Hol weekend. Restaurant serving lunches, cream teas and refreshments. Carvery on Sun. Gift shop and free car park. **Admission:** House & Gardens: Adult £5.50, OAPs £5.20, Children free. Pre-booked group rate (min 12) £4.20. Garden Only: Adults/OAPs £3.95. **Weddings:** Also available for Wedding Receptions and Private Functions. Licensed for civil ceremonies. **Internet:** www.athelhampton.co.uk

map 3 J4

CRANBORNE MANOR GARDEN
Cranborne, Wimborne, Dorset BH21 5PP
Tel: 01725 517248 Fax: 01725 517862
(The Viscount and Viscountess Cranborne)

Walled gardens, yew hedges and lawns; wild garden with spring bulbs, herb garden, Jacobean mount garden, flowering cherries and collection of old-fashioned and specie roses. Beautiful and historic garden laid out in the 17th century by John Tradescant and much embellished in the 20th century. **Location:** 18 miles N of Bournemouth B3078; 16 miles S of Salisbury A354, B3081. **Open:** Garden Centre open Mon–Sat 9–5pm, Sun 10–5pm. Something for every gardener, but specialising in old-fashioned and specie roses, herbs, ornamental pots and garden furniture. Garden only Mar–Sept, Wed 9–5pm. South Court occasionally closed. Free car park. **Internet:** www.cranborne.co.uk **E-mail:** gardencentre@cranborne.co.uk

map 3 K5

CORFE CASTLE
Wareham, Dorset, BH20 5EZ
Tel: 01929 481294

This castle, now in ruins, once controlled access to the Purbeck Hills, and was an important stronghold in Norman times. It also played a part in the Civil War, when it was defended by Lady Bankes. Today, many interesting Norman and early English architectural features remain. **Open:** Daily, all year round, 10am–6pm. Early closing in winter. **Admission:** Adult £4.20, Child £2.10.

DEANS COURT GARDEN
Deans Court, Wimborne, BH21 1EE, Dorset.
Wimborne Tourist Info: 01202 886116 (Sir Michael & Lady Hanham)

13 peaceful acres a few minutes walk south of the Minster. Free parking, specimen trees, lawns, borders, herb garden and kitchen garden with long serpentine wall. Chemical–free produce usually for sale also interesting herbaceous plants. Rose garden. Wholefood teas in garden or in Housekeeper's room (down steps). Lavatory for disabled. **Location:** OS Ref. SZ 010 997. **Open:** 15 Apr 2–6pm; 16 Apr 10–6pm; 6 May 2–6pm; 7 May 10–6pm; 27 May 2–6pm; 28 May 10–6pm; 10 June 2–6pm; 24 June 2–6pm; 22 July 2–6pm; 4&5 Aug. 2-6pm. Organic Gardening Weekend: 26 Aug 2–6pm, 27 Aug 10-6pm &16 Sept 2–6pm. Organic Gardening Weekend is open in aid of Henry Doubleday Research Association. All other openings in aid of National Gardens Scheme. **Admission:** Adults £2, Children (5–15) 50p, OAPs £1.50. Groups by arrangement. **House:** Open by prior written appointment but not on days when garden is open. Prices on request.

map 3 K4

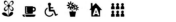

The Tutankhamun Exhibition

High West Street, Dorchester, Dorset DT1 1UW
Tel: 01305 269571 Fax: 01305 268885

Experience the magnificence and wonder of the world's greatest discovery of ancient treasure. Be there at the moment of discovery and walk through the ante-chamber filled with treasures. Smell the pleasant aromas of the funerary oils and listen to the excited voices of Howard Carter and Lord Carnarvon as they become the first people in 3000 years to look upon Tutankhamun's undisturbed tomb. Then enter the burial chamber, complete with its accurate wall paintings, to witness Carter and Callender raising the golden coffins from the quartzite sarcophagus.

In the 'Hall of Treasures' marvel at the beautiful facsimiles of some of Tutankhamun's greatest golden treasures, including the Harpooner and the famous Funerary Mask. Whilst the 'Jewels of Tutankhamun' shows some of the most intricate and exquisite jewellery from the tomb. Finally come face to face with

Tutankhamun's mummified body superbly recreated using new techniques. Featured in several major television documentaries, The Tutankhamun Exhibition is the only exhibition of its kind outside Egypt, and has recreated Tutankhamun's tomb, treasures, jewels and mummy in innovative and exiting ways. It's a complete experience spanning time itself.
Open: All year daily 9.30am–5.30pm. Nov–Mar weekdays 9.30am–5pm, weekends 10am–5pm.

E-mail: info@tutankhamun-exhibition.co.uk
Internet: www.tutankhamun-exhibition.co.uk

The Dorset Teddy Bear Museum

Teddy Bear House, Antelope Walk, Dorchester, Dorset DT1 1BE
Tel: 01305 263200 Fax: 01305 268885

The Dorset Teddy Bear Museum is a virtual treasure house of childhood wonders, tracing the history of the teddy bear from its birth, at the beginning of the last century, to the present day. The evocative and atmospheric displays include a panorama of old bears set in a 'curator's office'. The museum's oldest teddy bear is 'Michael', made from the original pattern of the first teddy bear by the Ideal Toy Co. in 1906. Further displays are of world-famous bears, record breakers and 'bearsonalities' of TV films and books such as Paddington, Winnie the Pooh and Rupert. The museum has an extensive display of modern artist bears which are highly prized and collectable. **Open:** All year daily 9.30am–5pm.

E-mail: info@teddybearhouse.co.uk
Internet: www. teddybearhouse.co.uk

The Dinosaur Museum

Icen Way, Dorchester, Dorset DT1 1EW
Tel: 01305 269880 Fax: 01305 268885

Recently voted Dorset's Family Attraction of the Year, the Dinosaur Museum is unique. It is Britain's only museum solely devoted to dinosaurs – actual fossils, skeletons and life-size reconstructions combined with audio-visual, hands on, computer and CD-ROM displays to excite and entertain. Among the most popular exhibits are the awesome life-size dinosaur reconstructions, which include Tyrannosaurus rex, Stegosaurus and Triceratops. They beg to be touched by little hands – and that's encouraged. The museum is great family fun and has twice been chosen as one of Britain's Top Ten Hands On Museums. The 'Dinosaur Discovery' Gallery is filled with all sorts of new interactive displays, and the Mary Anning Room of Time displays fossils through time. **Open:** All year daily 9.30am–5.30pm. Nov–Mar 10am–4.30pm.

E-mail: info@dinosaur-museum.org.uk
Internet: www.dinosaur-museum.org.uk

map 3 J5

FORDE ABBEY AND GARDENS
Forde Abbey, Chard, Somerset TA20 4LU
Tel: 01460 221290, Fax: 01460 220296 (Mr M Roper)

Dating back to 1146 Forde Abbey is the finest example of a Cistercian monastery still standing today. It was transformed into a family home by Sir Edmund Prideaux in 1650 and has remained as such ever since. The house contains a magnificent set of 17th century tapestries taken from the Raphael cartoons drawn for the Sistine Chapel in Rome. There are also many wonderfully intricate Cromwellian plaster ceilings throughout the house. The Abbey is surrounded by 30 acres of award winning gardens with many unusual plants and shrubs. In the spring the garden is awash with spring bulbs, and throughout the season there is always something of interest including azaleas, magnolias, herbaceous borders, rock garden, bog garden and fully functioning kitchen garden. **Location:** 1 mile E of Chard Junction, 4 miles SE of Chard signposted off A30. **Open:** Gardens open daily throughout the year 10–4.30pm (last admission). House open 1–4.30pm Tuesday, Wednesday, Thursday, Sunday & Bank Holiday afternoons 1 April–31 Oct. **Admission:** House and gardens: Please telephone for details. **Refreshments:** Undercroft open for light lunches and teas 11–4.30 daily 1 April–end Oct.

map 3
H4

MAPPERTON
Mapperton, Beaminster, Dorset DT8 3NR
Tel: 01308 862645 Fax: 01308 863348 (Earl & Countess of Sandwich)

Terraced valley gardens surround charming Tudor/Jacobean manor house, stable blocks, dovecote and All Saints' Church. Pevsner's Dorset guide says, "There can hardly be anywhere a more enchanting manorial group than Mapperton". Above, the Orangery and Italianate formal garden with fountain court and topiary. Below, a 17th century summer house and fishponds. Lower garden with specimen shrubs and trees. Magnificent walks and views. Shop with plants, pots and gift items. Featured in Country Life, Country Living, Daily Telegraph and used as film location. **Location:** 1 m off B3163, 2 m off B3066. **Station:** Crewkerne. **Open:** Mar–Oct daily 2–6pm. **Admission:** Adults £3.50, under 18s £1.50, under 5s free. House open to group tours by appointment, adults £3.50. **E-mail:** office@mapperton.com **Internet:** www.mapperton.com

map 3
H4

MINTERNE GARDENS
Minterne Magna, Nr Dorchester, Dorset, DT2 7AU
Tel: 01300 341 370 (The Lord Digby)

If you want a formal immaculate garden, do not come to Minterne, but if you want to wander peacefully through 20 wild woodland acres, where magnolias, rhododendrons, eucryphias, hydrangeas, water plants & water lilies, provide a new vista at each turn, and where ducks enhance the small lakes and cascades, then you will be welcome at Minterne, the home of the Churchill & Digby families for 350 years. The house is open for special interest groups only. **Location:** On A352 Dorchester/Sherborne Rd 2 miles N of Cerne Abbas. **Open:** Daily, 1 March–10 November 10–7pm. **Admission:** Adults £3 (Acc. children free).

map 3
J4

PORTLAND CASTLE
Castleton, Portland, Dorset DT5 1AZ
Tel: 01305 820539

Discover one of Henry VIII's finest coastal fortresses. Perfectly preserved in a waterfront location overlooking Portland harbour. You can try on armour, explore the Tudor kitchen and gun platform and see ghostly sculpted figures from the past. An excellent audio tour, included in the admission charge, brings the castle's history and characters to life, from Tudor times to both World Wars. Today features include the Captain's House and Gardens. Relax, enjoy the harbour views with refreshments from the tea room and come face to face with King Henry VIII in the Great Hall. Throughout the summer the castle plays host to an exciting programme of special events. Location: In Castleton, Isle of Portland (signposted). **Open:** Apr–Oct daily 10am – 6pm (5pm in Oct), Nov–Mar Fri–Sun 10am–4pm. **Admission:** Adult £3.00, Conc £2.30, Child £1.50. Group discount 15% (groups of 11 or more).

map 3
J5

LULWORTH CASTLE

The Lulworth Estate, East Lulworth, Wareham, Dorset BH20 5QS
Tel: 01929 400352 Fax: 01929 400563 (Mr & Mrs Weld)

A 17th century hunting lodge restored by English Heritage after the fire of 1929. Features include a gallery devoted to the Weld family, owners of the Castle and Estate since 1641. The kitchen and wine cellar have been furnished and the history of the building is brought to life through a video presentation. The Chapel of St Mary is the first free standing Roman Catholic Church to be built in England since the Reformation and contains an exhibition of 18th & 19th century vestments, church and recusant silver. A short walk from the Castle & Chapel is the Animal Farm, Play Area & Woodland Walk. The Stables have been converted to house the licensed Café and Courtyard Shop. **Open:** Sun-Fri plus Easter Saturday. Closed Saturdays, Christmas Eve and Day. 30 Oct 00–26 Mar 01, 10am-4pm or dusk if earlier, 27th Mar 01-26 Oct 01,10.30am-6pm, 28 Oct 01-24 Mar 02-10.30am-4pm or dusk if earlier. Lulworth Leisure reserve the right to close the Castle without notice. **Admission:** Lulworth Castle: Adults £5, concessions £4. Groups (10–200): Adults £4.50, concessions £3.60. Lulworth Castle House (Joint ticket with Lulworth Castle): Adult £7, concessions £5.50. **Events:** 15/16 Apr: Easter Bunny Hunt. 12/13 May: Country Gardening & Food Fair. 28/29 July: Lulworth Horse Trials & Country Fair. 14-16 Sept: International Floral Design Show. **Lulworth Castle House:** Modern house of the Weld family containing the Blundell collection of pictures and 18th century sculptures as well as portraits and furniture from Lulworth Castle. Walled gardens and grounds. **Open:** 30 May–26th Sept, Wed 2–5pm. Groups Mon–Fri by appointment only. **Admission:** Adult £4, Senior Citizen £3.50, Child (5–16 yrs) £1.50, Family (2 adults + 3 children) £10, Children under 5 free. 5 Holiday Cottages available on the Estate. Contact Mrs Weld 01929 400100.

map 3
J5

THE PRIEST'S HOUSE MUSEUM & GARDEN
23–27 High Street, Wimborne, Dorset BH21 1HR
Tel: 01202 882533

Award winning museum set in a historic town house. A series of period rooms takes the visitor back through the centuries. With hands-on activities in the Archaeology Childhood and East Dorset Villages Galleries and special events and exhibitions through the year, there is plenty to do. Our award-winning garden is a tranquil retreat and the Tea Room offers home made cakes (June to September). **Open:** 2 Apr–31 Oct: Mon–Sat, 10.30–5pm. Sundays: June to Sept and Bank Hols. **Admission:** Adult £2.40, Senior Citizens, Students £1.80 & Children £1, Family ticket £6.

map 3
K4

RUSSELL-COTES ART GALLERY & MUSEUM
East Cliff, Bournemouth, Dorset
Tel: 01202 451800 Fax: 01202 451851
(Bournemouth Borough Council)

Discover Annie and Merton Russell-Cotes' house, they loved travelling and collecting; it is full of interesting objects and artefacts from their travels and tells a story of the house being built and what their ideas were. Walk from the Victorian dining room into the light and airy modern part, enjoy the 'Café at the Russell-Cotes', which has commissioned work from local artists. Delight in our Stories, Myths and Journeys Gallery – travel by lift into the Japanese Gallery, and finally into our Temporary Exhibition Gallery. This part of the Russell-Cotes leads into our newly restored Garden, this has been taken back to its orignal Japanese theme as envisaged by Annie and Merton Russell-Cotes. **Open:** Tues–Sun 10am–5pm. Closed Christmas Day & Good Friday. **Admission:** Free. **E-mail:** dedge@russell-cotes-demon.co.uk **Internet:** www.russell-cotes.bournemouth.gov.uk

map 3
K5

SANDFORD ORCAS MANOR HOUSE
The Manor House, Sandford Orcas, Sherborne, Dorset DT9 4SB.
Tel: 01963 220206 (Sir Mervyn Medlycott, Bt.)

Tudor Manor House in remarkable original state of preservation, with gatehouse, spiral staircases and Tudor and Jacobean panelling. Fine collection of 14th–17th century stained glass, Queen Anne and Chippendale furniture, Elizabethan and Georgian needlework and 17th century Dutch paintings. Terraced gardens, with fine mature trees, topiary and herb garden. **Location:** 2 miles N or Sherborne, entrance next to church. **Open:** Easter Mon 10–6pm then May–Sept: Suns 2–6pm & Mons 10–6pm. **Admission:** £3, Children £1.50. Pre-booked parties (of 10 or more) at reduced rates on other days if preferred.

map 3
J4

SHERBORNE CASTLE
Sherborne DT9 3PY
Tel: 01935 813182 Fax: 01935 816727 (Sherborne Castle Estates)

Built by Sir Walter Raleigh in 1594, Sherborne Castle has been the home of the Digby family since 1617. Prince William of Orange was entertained here in 1688, and George III visited in 1789. Lancelot 'Capability Brown' created the lake in 1753 and gave Sherborne the very latest in landscape gardening. **Location:** 5 miles E of Yeovil off A30 to south, Station Sherborne. **Open:** From 1 Apr - 31 Oct. 2001. Garden; Everyday except Wed., from 10am-last entry 5pm. Tearoom and Shop; Everyday except Wed., from 12:30-last entry 5pm. Castle; Tue, Thur, Sun, B. H. Mon. from 12:30; Sat. from 2:30pm-last admission 4:30pm. **Admission:** Garden; Adult £2.75, Child (5-16) £1.30. No concession or party rate. Under 5yrs. free. Castle & Garden; £5.50, Seniors£5, Child (5-16)£2.75, Family(2+2)£13.75, Party rate(15+) Adult£4.75, Child(5-16)£2.30 under 5yrs. free. Private views(min. 15 people) Adult£8.50, Child£4.25. **E-mail:** enquiries@sherbornecastle.com **Internet:** www.sherbornecastle.com

map 3
J4

WOLFETON HOUSE
Dorchester, Dorset DT2 9QN
Tel: 01305 263 500 Fax: 01305 265090 (Capt. NTLL Thimbleby)

A fine medieaval and Elizabethan Manor House lying in the water-meadows near the confluence of the Rivers Cerne and Frome. It was much embellished around 1580 and has splendid plaster ceilings, fireplaces and panelling of that date. See the Great Hall, stairs and chamber; parlour, dining room, chapel and cyder house. The medieaval gatehouse has two unmatched and older towers. There are many fine works of art. **Location:** 1.5 miles from Dorchester on Yeovil road (A37); indicated by Historic House signs. **Station(s):** Dorchester South and West, 1.75 miles. **Open:** 15 July–15 Sept. Mon, Wed, Thurs. Groups at any time by appointment throughout the year. **Admission:** Adult £4, Child £2. **Refreshments:** Ploughman's lunches, teas, evening meals for groups by arrangement. Cyder for sale. Available for weddings, parties etc.

map 3
J4

TOLPUDDLE MARTYRS MUSEUM
Tolpuddle, Dorset
Tel: 01305 848237

The Tolpuddle Martyrs Museum traces the fascinating story of the Tolpuddle Martyrs and their cause, an important part of British social history. The exhibition is presented on three levels. Visitors may simply view the panels in four sections of the story – describing the horrendous conditions of agricultural workers in the early 19th century, the Martyrs' trial, their transportation overseas, their reprieve and homecoming. Or the visitor can delve deeper into detail, and hear vivid eye witness accounts by the principal characters in the drama. They can also find answers to a wide range of questions about people, events and background by using the touch-sensitive screens. **Open:** Daily Tuesday–Sunday and Bank Holidays. **Internet:** www.tolpuddlemartyrs.org.uk

map 3
J4

County Durham

A county of moors and rivers, County Durham is renowned for its fascinating heritage and magnificent scenery. Quiet roads lead to some of the highest, wildest and finest scenery in England. Much of the west of the County, the Durham Dales, is designated an Area of Outstanding Natural Beauty. From the famed long-distance Pennine Way to riverbank rambles and town trails, the county provides excellent opportunities for walking, and a superb network of public footpaths includes over 60 miles of former railways now reclaimed as attractive countryside paths. The Low Barnes Nature Reserve in Witton-le-Wear consists of over 100 acres of woodland, lakes, and meadows, and offers great opportunities to see the local wildlife.

Low Force Waterfall

County Durham's Roman heritage can be rediscovered on the Dere Street Trail. Built in about AD80, this was once a military supply route running from York to Hadrian's Wall. Dere Street remained in continuous use throughout the Roman period and a number of forts were built along its length. Durham City, built in AD995 on Dunholm ("Island hill"), is compact enough to be explored on foot, but is a site of international historical importance: its castle and cathedral are designated a World Heritage Site. The ancient centre of Durham is reached by a series of bridges that connect the older buildings to the modern town, and there are few sights more awe-inspiring than that of the mighty towers of the cathedral reflected in the waters of the River Wear.

AUCKLAND CASTLE
Bishop Auckland, Co Durham, DL14 7NR
Tel: 01388 601627 Fax: 01388 609323

The Prince Bishops' principle country residence since the 12th century, now home to the Bishops of Durham. The original Norman banqueting hall, now a unique private chapel, the State Rooms housing original works of art (including 17th century paintings by Francisco de Zurbaran) and the adjacent Deer Park and 18th century Deer House are all accessible to the public. **Open:** May– Sep: (please ring for exact times) with special openings for pre-arranged groups of +15. **Admission:** Adults £3.50, Concessions £2.50, Children under 12 free of charge. Exclusive venue for weddings, conferences private/corporate hospitality. **E-mail:** auckland.castle@zetnet.co.uk **Internet:** www.auckland.castle.co.uk

map 11 H5

BEAMISH, THE NORTH OF ENGLAND OPEN AIR MUSEUM
Beamish, Durham DH9 0RG
Tel: 01207 231811 Fax: 01207 290933
(Joint Committee of Local Authorities)

Beamish is unique. It's no ordinary museum but a living, working experience of life as it was in the Great North in the early 1900s and 1800s. This award-winning museum has something to delight and entertain visitors of all ages and interests. Discover the early 20th century Town, Colliery Village, Working Farm and Railway Station. An 1825 railway and small manor house represent life in the early 1800s. **Open:** Daily in summer (Apr–Oct) 10am–5pm. Winter closed Mon & Fri. Open 10am–4pm. Also closed Christmas & New Year. Reduced operation in winter. **Admission:** Charge. **Internet:** www.beamish.org.uk

map 11 H4

THE BOWES MUSEUM
Barnard Castle, County Durham DL12 8NP
Tel: 01833 690606 Fax: 01833 637163

Situated in Barnard Castle, an elegant Georgian town in rural Teesdale, The Bowes Museum houses more than 30 galleries of fine and decorative art and antiquities. Built on a grand scale in the style of a French château, it is the inspiration of John Bowes, the illegitimate son of the 10th Earl of Strathmore and his Parisian actress wife Josephine. The museum has an active programme of temporary exhibitions (including contemporary art) and events such as open air theatre, concerts, monthly craft markets and family fun days. **Location:** Barnard Castle, just off A66. Train: Darlington. Bus: Bishop Auckland, Darlington, Richmond. **Open:** Daily 11am–5pm. **Admission:** Adults £4, Concessions £3, Family £12. Parking and admission to grounds, café and shop free. **Internet:** www.bowesmuseum.org.uk

map 11 G5

BEDE'S WORLD

The Museum, Church Bank, Jarrow,
Tyne & Wear NE32 3DY
Tel: 0191 489 2106 Fax: 0191 428 2361

A stunning museum and exhibition celebrating the extraordinary life and achievemennts of the Venerable Bede who lived and worked in Jarrow over 1300 years ago. Walk round the 11 acre Anglo-Saxon farm, relax and have a meal in the attractive café/restaurant within historic Jarrow Hall and visit the ancient church of St Paul and ruins of the medieval monastery. **Open:** Apr-Oct, 10-5:30pm Mon-Sat & Sun12-5:30pm. Nov-Mar, 10-4pm Mon-Sat & Sun 12-4pm. Admission charges apply. **E-mail:**visitor.info@bedesworld.co.uk **Internet:** www.bedesworld.co.uk

map11 H4

DURHAM CASTLE

Durham, DH1 3RW
Tel: 01913 743 800 Fax: 01913 747 470 (The University of Durham)

Durham Castle, the former home of the Prince Bishop of Durham, was founded in the 1070s. Since 1832 it has been the foundation College of the University of Durham. With the Cathedral it is a World Heritage Site. Important features include the Norman Chapel (1072), the Great Hall (1284), the Norman Doorway (1540s). With its 14th century style Keep it is a fine example of a Motte and Bailey Castle. In vacations the Castle is a conference and holiday centre and prestige venue for banquets etc. **Location:** In the centre of the city (adjoining Cathedral). **Station(s):** Durham (1/2 mile) **Open:** Mar-Sep: 10-12 noon, 2-4.30pm. Oct-Mar 2-4pm. **Admission:** Adults £3, children £2.

map11 H4

THE ORIENTAL MUSEUM
UNIVERSITY OF DURHAM

Elvet Hill, (off South Road), Durham DH1 3TH
Tel & Fax: 0191 374 7911

The only museum in the North East devoted entirely to Oriental Art and Antiquities, with a new Chinese Gallery opening October 2000. Collections cover all major cultures and periods of the East from Ancient Egypt, to India, Tibet and Japan. Of interest to the specialist and non-specialist alike through imaginative displays. **Open:** weekdays 10-5pm. Weekends 12-5pm. **Admission:** £1.50, Conc £1. Group rate. **E-mail:** oriental.museum@durham.ca.uk **Internet:** www.dur.ac.uk/oriental.museum

map11 H4

MUSEUM OF ANTIQUITIES

University of Newcastle-upon-Tyne, Newcastle-upon-Tyne NE1 7RU
Tel: 0191 222 7849 Fax: 0191 222 8561

The largest archaeological collection in the North of England, where you can see prehistoric rock art, Stone Age axes, and Bronze Age pottery and tools. There is also an accurate scale model of Hadrian's Wall, a display of Roman jewellery and military equipment, and objects from three temples of Mithras. **Open:** All year, daily 10am–5pm, except Sun, 1 Jan, Good Friday, and Christmas period.

RABY CASTLE

Staindrop, Darlington, Co. Durham, DL2 3AY
Tel: 01833 660 202 Fax: 01833 660169 (The Lord Barnard, T.D.).

Raby is one of the most impressive lived-in castles in England. Built mainly in the 14th century by the Nevill family on the site of an earlier manor house, it remained in their ownership until 1569. Since 1626 to the present day it has been the home of the Vane family. Today, Raby Castle, home of the 11th Lord Barnard welcomes thousands of visitors each year. Every room from the mediaeval Kitchen, virtually unaltered since it was built in 1360 to the Baron's Hall where 700 knights plotted the Rising of the North brings history to life. Housing a fabulous art collection and sumptuous interior, treasures include a renowned collection of Meissen porcelain. The Castle is situated amidst a 200-acre Deer Park within the North Pennines. Beautiful walled gardens with formal lawns, rose gardens and ornamental pond frame picturesque views of the Castle. The 18th century stable block contains a horse drawn carriage collection & an Adventure Playground near the Stable Tearooms & Giftshop. **Location:** 1 mile N of Staindrop village, on the Barnard Castle-Bishop Auckland Road (A688) accessible from A1(M),M6,A66 & A68. **Station(s):** Bishop Auckland & Darlington. **Open:** B.H., Sat-Wed.; May-Sept. Wed-Sun; Jun-Aug. Daily except. Sat.Castle 1-5pm; Park & Garden 11-5:30pm. Private Groups(20+) by apt. on weekday mornings from Easter-Sept. **Admission:** Castle, Park & Gardens: Adults £5, Child (5–15) £2, OAP/NUS £4, Family (2 adults & 3 children) £12. **Park & Gardens:** Adults £3, Other £2. Park and Gardens Season Ticket: Adult £12, Other £10. Private Groups £7.50. **Refreshments:** Tea at the Stables. Picnic area. **E-mail:** rabyestate@rabycastle.com **Internet:** www.rabycastle.com

map 11 G5

Essex

Long the target of unkind jokes, Essex seems to have had the last laugh. This much-maligned county is the sunniest and most affluent in Britain, and boasts a wealth of heritage sites set in beautiful countryside.

Essex is famous for its ancient woodlands (including Epping and Hatfield forests) where wildlife abounds, and for the multitude of quiet villages it shelters. Four thousand miles of bridleways and footpaths allow the visitor to explore leafy glades and unspoilt grasslands; there are also many opportunities for cycling and hiking through the gently rolling landscape.

Dedham

The Sir Alfred Munnings Art Museum

Much of the Essex coastline remains blissfully undeveloped. The sheltered estuaries of Stour, Blackwater and Crouch are internationally renowned for their wildlife, and are ideal for sailing and other watersports. Sailing can also be enjoyed out at sea, and the bustling centres at Brightlingsea and Burnham-on-Crouch cater for novices and experts alike. Elsewhere, visitors can enjoy miles of clean, safe, and sandy beaches, or walk the cliffs at Walton's "Naze".

AUDLEY END HOUSE
Saffron Waldon, Essex CB11 4JF
Tel: 01799 522842 (English Heritage)

"Too large for a King but might do for a Lord Treasurer", was how King James I described Audley End, built by his own Lord Treasurer Thomas Howard first Earl of Suffolk. Come and see its wonderful palatial interiors and famous picture collection. Stroll in 'Capability' Brown's fine landscaped parkland with its enchanting follies and colourful Parterre Garden. Also visit the newly opened kitchen garden and purchase produce from its shop. **Location:** 1m W of Saffron Walden on B1383 (M1 exits 8, 9 Northbound only & 10) **Open:** House & Grounds: 1–31 Oct, Wed–Sun 10am–3pm. House closes at 4pm. House by pre-booked guided tour: 1 Apr–30 Sept, Wed–Fri 10am–noon. Grounds: 1 Apr–30 Sept, Wed–Sun 1–6pm (last admission 5pm). **Admission:** House & Grounds: Adult £6.75, Conc £5.10, Child £3.40, Family £16.90. Grounds only: Adult £4, Conc £3, Child £2, Family £10.

map 5 F2

THE GARDENS OF EASTON LODGE
Warwick House, Easton Lodge, Great Dunmow, Essex CM6 2BB
Tel: 01371 876979 Fax: 01371 876979 (Brian & Diana Creasey)

Beautiful gardens set in 23 acres. Visit the Italian gardens, designed by Harold Peto in 1902 for 'Daisy' Countess of Warwick (Edward VII's close friend), abandoned in 1950: restoration commenced 1993. Other features include - Peto Pavilion, herringbone and cobbled courtyard with fountain; Glade (formerly Japanese Garden); ruined Shelley Pavilion and tree house; Millennium Yew and Box sundial. World War 2 airfield. In the dovecote, study the history of the house, garden and owners over 400 years. Visitors comments (1999): "Magical", "Fascinating", "Riveting and so Romantic", "Superb", "Brilliant", "It's a dream we hope to often return to", "Merveilleux jardin pour rever". **Admission:** Adult £3.80, Conc £3.50, Child £1.50.

map 5 G3

RHS GARDEN HYDE HALL
Rettendon, Chelmsford, Essex CM3 8ET
Tel: 01245 400256 (Royal Horticultural Society)

A charming hilltop garden which extends to over 24 acres. Highlights include the spring bulbs, the modern all and intermediate bearded irises in late May and the rope walk of climbing roses and large beds ablaze with floribunda and hybrid tea roses in midsummer. There is also a small plant centre and delightful hot and cold meals are available in the Essex thatched barn when the garden is open. **Open:** 1 Apr–28 Oct. daily 11am-6pm Sept-Oct 11-5pm. **Admission:** Adults £3, children (6–16yrs) £1.

map 5 G3

HEDINGHAM CASTLE

Castle Hedingham, Nr. Halstead, Essex CO9 3DJ
Tel: 01787 460261 Fax: 01787 461473 (The Hon. Thomas Lindsay)

One of the finest and best preserved Norman keeps in England, it was built in 1140 by Aubrey de Vere. The keep walls are 12ft thick at the base, and is approached by a beautiful Tudor bridge which spans the dry moat surrounding the inner bailey. This was built in 1496 to replace the drawbridge, by the 13th Earl of Oxford, one of Henry VII's chief commanders at the battle of Bosworth. Visited by King Henry VII, King Henry VIII and Queen Elizabeth I and besieged by King John. Home of the de Veres, Earls of Oxford for 550 years, and still owned by their descendent, The Honourable Thomas Lindsay. The Banqueting Hall, reached from the first floor by a beautiful spiral staircase, 13ft wide in circumference and constructed round a central column, has a splendid Minstrels' Gallery and timbered ceiling supported by a magnificent central arch, 28ft wide, the finest Norman arch in England. Beautifully kept grounds with peaceful lakeside and woodland walks. Large picnic area. Light refreshments served inside the keep. Hog Roast on Bank Holiday weekends. **Location:** 40km (24 miles) SE of Cambridge, approached along the A1017. Within easy reach of A12, M11 and M25. (60 miles from London). **Open:** Week before Easter to the end of Oct, Daily 10–5pm. Open all year round for private parties. **Admission:** Adults £4, Children £3 (5–15), Family £11 (2 adults & 5 children). Except for special events, please telephone for prices. **Events:** Grounds open to the public in Feb/March to view the snowdrops (please telephone to confirm opening times). Admission price includes entrance to the keep and a free glass of mulled wine! Various events planned throughout the year such as, Jousting Tournaments, Medieval Displays, with music and dance, including Falconry and historical drama.

map 5
G2

INGATESTONE HALL
Hall Lane, Ingatestone, Essex CM4 9NR
Tel: 01277 353010, Fax: 01245 248979 (Lord Petre)

Tudor mansion in 11 acres of grounds, built by Sir William Petre, Secretary of State to four monarchs. The house continues to be the home of his descendants and contains furniture, pictures and memorabilia accumulated over the centuries. The house retains its original form and appearance including two priests' hiding places. **Location:** From London end of Ingatestone High Street, take Station Lane. House is half a mile beyond the level crossing. **Open:** Easter–end Sept. Sat, Sun and Bank Holidays. 1–6pm Plus (school hols only) Wed, Thurs and Fri 1–6pm. **Admission:** Adults £3.50 OAPs/Students £3, Children 5–16 £2 (under 5s free), Parties 20 or more 50p per head reduction. **Refreshments:** Tearoom. Car park adjacent to gates. 200m walk to house. Gift shop. No dogs (except guide dogs). The upper floor and some rooms downstairs are inaccessible to wheelchairs.

map 5 G3

LAYER MARNEY TOWER
Nr Colchester, Essex CO5 9US
Tel & Fax: 01206 330 784 (Mr Nicholas Charrington)

Lord Marney's 1520 masterpiece is the tallest Tudor gate house in the country. Visitors may climb the tower for excellent views of the Essex countryside. Explore the formal gardens and visit the Long Gallery, Corsellis Room and church. The Medieval Barn has rare breed farm animals and the deer are on the farm walk. Guided tours are available by arrangement (minimum cost of 25 people). The Long Gallery and Corsellis Rooms may be hired for corporate days, weddings, receptions, banquets or concerts. **Location:** 6 miles S of Colchester, signpost off the B1022 Colchester–Maldon Road. **Open** 1 Apr–7 Oct 2001: everyday except Saturday 12pm–5pm & 22 Jul-7 Sept. 11-5pm. Bank Holiday Sundays and Mondays 11–6pm. Groups anytime by arrangement. **Admission:** Adults £3.50, Children £2, Family ticket £10. **Refreshments:** Stable tearoom.

map 5 H3

THE SIR ALFRED MUNNINGS ART MUSEUM
Castle House, Dedham, Essex CO7 6AZ
Tel: 01206 322127 Fax: 01206 322127 (Castle House Trust)

Castle House and its collection is a fitting memorial to Sir Alfred Munnings who lived at Castle House from 1919 until his death. Castle House, a mixture of Tudor and Georgian periods, has been restored, with Munnings' original furniture, and stands in spacious well-maintained gardens. A collection representative of Munnings' life span of work. Each season there is a special exhibition. **Location:** ¾ mile from Dedham Village. **Station(s):** Colchester, Manningtree, Ipswich. **Open:** Easter Sunday–first Sunday in October, Wed, Sun & Bank Hol Mons. Also Thurs and Sats in Aug, 2–5pm. **Admission:** Adult £3, Conc £2, Child 50p. Private parties by arrangement. Free car park.

map 5 H2

TILBURY FORT
Tilbury, Essex, RM18 7NR
Tel: 01375 858489

The largest piece of seventeenth-century military engineering in England. Exhibitions show how the fort once protected London from seaborne attack. **Open:** 1 Apr–31 Oct, daily, 10am–6pm. 1 Nov–31 Mar, Wed–Sun, 10am–4pm **Admission:** Adult £2.75, Child £1.40.

SHALOM HALL
Layer Breton, Nr Colchester, Essex
Tel: 01206 330338 Fax: 0207 831 9607 (Lady Phoebe Hillingdon)

19th century house containing a collection of 17th and 18th century French furniture, porcelain and portraits by famous English artists including Thomas Gainsborough, Sir Joshua Reynolds etc. **Location:** 7 miles southwest of Colchester, 2 miles from A12. **Open:** August Mon–Fri 10–1pm, 2.30–5.30pm. **Admission:** Free.

map 5 H3

VALENCE HOUSE MUSEUM & ART GALLERY
Becontree Avenue, Dagenham, Essex
Tel: 020 8227 5293 Fax: 020 8227 5293 (Barking & Dagenham Council)

The only remaining manor house in Dagenham, partially surrounded by a moat. Dates from 15th century. There is an attractive herb garden to the west of the house. **Location:** On the south side of Becontree Avenue, ½ mile west of A1112 at Becontree Heath. **Open:** Tues–Fri, 9.30–1pm & 2–4.30pm. Sats 10–4pm. **Admission:** Free.

map 5 F4

Gloucestershire

The Cotswolds are the heart and soul of Gloucestershire, a timeless area of gentle hills and honey coloured cottages, where river valleys and rough-hewn stone walls frame the landscape. Many Cotswolds villages were established in the 12th century, with money from the burgeoning wool trade, but Roman roads and villas show that the area was commercially important long before. Towns such as Chipping Camden, Cirencester and Stow-on-the-Wold are charmingly undeveloped, but even the more busy cities of Gloucester and Cheltenham retain an air of old-world elegance. Gloucester is dominated by its imposing Norman cathedral, the scene of Henry III's coronation, and famous for its wonderful fan vaulting. Cheltenham established itself as a fashionable spa town in the 1700s, and much of its gracious Regency architecture remains.

Bibury

BERKELEY CASTLE
Gloucestershire, GL13 9BQ
Tel: 01453 810332 (Mr R J G Berkeley)

England's most Historic Home and Oldest Inhabited Castle. Completed in 1153 by Lord Maurice Berkeley at the command of Henry II and for nearly 850 years the home of the Berkeley family. 24 generations have gradually transformed a savage Norman fortress into a truly stately home. The castle is a home and not a museum. Enjoy the castle at leisure or join one of the regular one-hour guided tours covering the dungeon, the cell where Edward II was murdered, the medieval kitchens, the magnificent Great Hall and the State Apartments with their fine collections of pictures by primarily English and Dutch masters, tapestries, furniture of an interesting diversity, silver and porcelain. Splendid Elizabethan Terraced Gardens and sweeping lawns surround the castle, Tropical Butterfly House with hundreds of exotic butterflies in free flight – an oasis of colour and tranquillity. Facilities include free coach and parks, picnic lawn and two gift shops. Tearooms for refreshments, light lunches and afternoon teas. **Location:** Midway between Bristol and Gloucester, just off A38, M5 junctions 13 or 14. **Open:** April & May: Tues–Sun 2–5pm; June & Sept: Tues–Sat 11–5pm, Sun 2–5pm; July & Aug: Mon–Sat 11–5pm, Sun 2–5pm; Oct: Sun only 2–5pm; Bank Holiday Mondays 11–5pm. **Admission:** Castle & Gardens: Adult £5.50, Child £3, Senior Citizen £4.50. Pre-booked parties 25 or more: Adult £5, Child £2.70, Senior Citizen £4.20, Family Ticket £15 (2 adults & 2 children). Gardens only: Adult £2, Child £1. Butterfly Farm: Adult £2, Child/OAP £1, Family Ticket £5 (2 adults & 2 children), School Groups 80p.

map 3 J1

CHAVENAGE
Tetbury, Gloucestershire GL8 8XP
Tel: 01666 502329 Fax: 01453 836778 (David Lowsley-Williams, Esq.)

Elizabethan House (1576) set in the tranquil Cotswold countryside with Cromwellian associations. 16th and 17th century furniture and tapestries. Personally conducted tours, by the owner or his family. **Location:** 2 miles N of Tetbury, signposted off A46 (Bath–Stroud) or B4014. **Open:** Thurs, Sun and Bank Hols, 2–5pm. May – end Sept plus Easter Sun and Mon. **Admission:** Adults £4, Children half-price. Parties by appointment as shown or other dates and times to suit. **Refreshments:** Catering for parties by arrangement. **Conferences:** Wedding receptions, dinners, corporate hospitality, also available for film and photographic location. **Internet:** www.chavenage.com

map 4 A3

CHEDWORTH ROMAN VILLA
Yanworth, Cheltenham
Tel: 01242 890256 Fax: 01242 840544 (The National Trust)

Chedworth Roman Villa is one of the finest Roman-period sites in Britain. Nestling in a wooded combe in the Cotswolds, it contains the ruins of a large, opulent country house of the 4th century. There are some very special features surviving–fine mosaics, a water shrine with running spring, two bath-houses, several hypocaust systems (Roman central heating) and many artefacts in the site museum. There is a ten minute video introduction to the site and a new audio tour which guides the visitor around the villa. There are various events and open days during the year and archaeological work continues. Visit Chedworth for a flavour of life in 4th century Britain. **Open:** Mar–Apr, Weds–Sun 11–4pm, BHols & Event Days 10–5pm. May–Sept, Tues–Sun 10–5pm. Oct–19 Nov, Weds–Sun 11–4pm. **Admission:** Adult £3.40, Child £1.70, Family £8.50. **Location:** 20 mins from Cirencester.

map 4 B3

CHELTENHAM ART GALLERY & MUSEUM

Clarence Street, Cheltenham, Gloucestershire GL50 3JT
Tel: 01242 237431 Fax: 01242 262334

A world-renowned collection relating to the Arts & Crafts Movement, including fine furniture and exquisite metalwork, made by craftsmen inspired by William Morris. Rare Chinese and English pottery. 300 years of painting by Dutch and British artists. Also discover the town's history – Britain's most complete Regency town and archeological treasures from the neighbouring Cotswolds. **Exhibitions:** Special exhibitions throughout the year. **Open:** Mon–Sat 10–5.20pm. From April 2001, Sundays 2.00-4.20pm. Closed Bank Holidays and Easter Sunday. **Admission:** Free, donations welcome. **E-mail**: artgallery@cheltenham.gov.uk **Internet:** www.cheltenhammuseum.org.uk

```
map 4
A3
```

COTSWOLDS MOTORING MUSEUM

The Old Mill, Bourton on the Water, Gloucestershire, GL54 2BY
Tel: 01451 821255

Situated in the picturesque Cotswolds village of Bourton on the Water, this unique museum houses an amazing and varied collection of cars, motorcycles, pedal cars and motoring memorabilia. The museum is also home to Brum, the little yellow car from the BBC children's TV series. With teddy bears and one of the largest collections of metal motoring signs, there is something for everyone whatever their age. **Open:** 10am–6pm Mar–Oct. **Admission:** Adults £2.25, Children (over 5) £1.25, Family £6.50. Concession for CSMA members.

```
map 4
B3
```

FRAMPTON COURT

Frampton-on-Severn, Gloucester GL2 7EU
Tel: 01452 740267 Messages/Fax: 01452 740698 (Mrs H. Clifford)

Listed Grade I, by Vanbrugh. 1732. Stately family home of the Cliffords who have lived at Frampton since granted land by William the Conquerer, 1066. Fine collection of the original period furniture, tapestries, needlework and porcelain. Panelled throughout. Fine views over well kept parkland to extensive lake. A famous Gothic orangery, now self-catering holiday lets, stands in the garden reflected in a long Dutch ornamental canal similar to Westbury. Special bed and breakfast by appointment £45. Tel: Before 10.30am, between 1–2pm and after 7pm. The original well known floral water colours by the gifted 19th century great Aunts hang in the house. These inspired the book "The Frampton Flora". **Open:** All year by appointment £4.50. Tel: 01452 740267. **Location:** Near jct. 13 of M5 motorway. Signposted.

```
map 4
A3
```

GLOUCESTER CITY COUNCIL TOURISM & CULTURAL SERVICES

Herbert Warehouse, The Docks, Gloucester GL1 2EQ
Tel: 01452 396620 Fax: 01452 396622

Visit our splendid City Museum and Art Gallery in Brunswick Road, or the 'tardis-like' Folk Museum in Westgate Street. Interactive and stimulating exhibits for all the family. In the City Museum, alongside superb paintings and antiques, dinosaurs and natural history, see national treasures like the Norman 'Gloucester Tables Set' and the iron age 'Birdlip Mirror'. Enjoy nostalgia and curiosities in the Folk Museum, where Gloucester's more recent history is revealed through traditional and modern displays, including the new 'Portal' computer gallery. **Admission:** Small charge for adults. Concessions apply. Further information: 01452 396620. **E-mail:** culture@gloucester.gov.uk **Internet:** www.mylife.gloucester.gov.uk

```
map 4
A3
```

HARDWICKE COURT

Nr Gloucester, Glos
Tel: 01452 720212 (C G M Lloyd-Baker)

Late Georgian house designed by Robert Smirke, built in 1816–1817. Entrance Hall, Drawing Room, Library and Dining Room open. **Location:** 5 miles S of Gloucester on A38 (between M5 access 12 S only and 13). **Open:** Easter Mon-end Oct, Mon only 2–4pm other times by prior written agreement. **Admission:** £2, parking for cars only. Not suitable for disabled.

```
map 4
A3
```

KIFTSGATE COURT GARDENS

Chipping Campden, Gloucestershire GL55 6LW
Tel: 01386 438777 Fax: 01386 438777 (Mr & Mrs J G. Chambers)

Garden set on the edge of the Cotswold escarpment with fine views. Many unusual shrubs and plants including tree peonies, abutilous, specie and old fashioned roses. New water garden in the old tennis court. **Location:** 3 miles NE of Chipping Campden. **Open:** Apr–May & Aug–Sept; Wed, Thurs and Sun, 2–6pm. June–July; Wed, Thurs, Sat and Sun, 12noon–6pm. Bank Hols Mon 2–6pm. **Admission:** Adults £4, Children £1. **Refreshments:** Home-made teas throughout the season and light lunch in June and July. Coach by appointment only. Unusual plants for sale on open days.

```
map 4
B2
```

LITTLEDEAN HALL

Littledean, nr Cinderford, Gloucestershire GL14 3NR
Tel: 01594 824213 Fax: 01594 824213 (Sheila Anthony)

Littledean Hall is a fascinating historical document and is considered to be the oldest, continually lived-in house in England. The building's hidden features first came to light around twenty years ago when the cellar was excavated and found to be around 10th or 11th century. The grounds boast a Roman temple site; and when the drive was excavated, a Roman road was found and beneath that a neolithic road. Ancient horse chestnut trees, circa 5-700 years old, line the drive. **Open:** 1 Apr–31 Oct, 11am–5pm. **Admission:** Adults £3.50, Senior Citizens £2.50, Children £1.50, Family £8. Groups by arrangement.

```
map 3
J1
```

NATURE IN ART
Wallworth Hall, Twigworth, Gloucester GL2 9PA
Tel: 01452 731422 Fax: 01452 730937

The world's first museum dedicated exclusively to art inspired by nature. Twice specially commended in the National Heritage Museum of the Year Awards. In scope, appeal and stature, its collection spanning 1500 years from over 60 countries is unrivalled. From Picasso to Shepherd, Jan van Kessel to contemporary crafts, Audubon to Galle, Scott to Moore, there is something for everyone in this unique collection all housed in a fine Georgian mansion. **Events/Exhibitions:** Vibrant programme of temporary exhibitions from around the world. Watch artists demonstrating Feb–Nov (average of 70 artists each year working for a week). Regular monthly events. **Internet:** www.nature-in-art.org.uk

OWL HOUSE GARDENS

Lamberhurst, Kent TN3 8LY
Tel: 01892 891290 Fax: 01892 891222

This is the property of the late Maureen, Marchioness of Dufferin & Ava and the setting of her 16th Century half-timbered and tile-hung smuggler's cottage, once surrounded by a cabbage patch and ploughed fields when the property was purchased in 1952. It now comprises 16 acres of romantic gardens; in Spring the expansive lawns are filled with daffodils and the trees with apple and cherry blossom; the woodland gardens carpeted with bluebells and primroses. Rhododendrons, azaleas and camellias encircle the informal sunken water gardens, **Open:** Daily except Christmas Day and New Years Day. **Admission:** Adult £4, children £1. Coach parties welcome by appointment. Dogs welcome on leads.

map 5 G5

RODMARTON MANOR
Cirencester, Gloucestershire GL7 6PF
Tel: 01285 841253 Fax 01285 841298 (Mr & Mrs Simon Biddulph)

The house is a unique example of the Cotswold Arts and Crafts and was built and furnished with local materials entirely by hand. The garden is a series of outdoor rooms. There are hedges, topiary, a troughery, a rockery, lawns, magnificent herbaceous borders and kitchen garden all in a romantic setting. **Location:** Off A433 6m west of Cirencester. **Open:** House and Garden open Wed, Sat and Bank Hol Mons 9 May–29 Aug 2–5pm. Groups please book. Guided tours of house can be booked for groups of 20 or more people at other times. Groups of 20 or more are welcome to visit the garden by appointment at other times. Guided tours of garden can also be booked. **Admission:** House and Garden £6 (children under 14 £3). Minimum group charge for house £120. Garden only £3 (accompanied children under 14 free).

map 4 A3

SEZINCOTE

Moreton-in-Marsh, Gloucestershire GL56 9AW
(Mr & Mrs D Peake)

Oriental water garden by Repton and Daniell with trees of unusual size. House in Indian style, inspiration of Royal Pavilion, Brighton. **Location:** 1 mile W of Moreton-in-Marsh on A44 to Evesham; turn left by lodge before Bourton-on-the-Hill. **Station(s):** Moreton-in-Marsh **Open:** Garden Thurs, Fri & Bank Hol Mons 2–6pm (or dusk if earlier) throughout the year, except Dec. House May, June, July and Sept, Thurs and Fri 2.30–6pm parties by appointment. Open in aid of National Gardens Scheme Sun July 1st 2–6pm. **Admission:** House and Garden £5; Garden only £3.50, Children £1, under 5s free. **Refreshments:** Hotels and restaurants in Moreton-in-Marsh. No dogs except guide dogs for the blind.

map 4 B2

SNOWSHILL MANOR
Snowshill, Nr. Broadway, WR12 7JU.
Tel/Fax: 01386 852410

Snowshill is a Tudor House containing Charles Paget Wade's collection of craftsmanship. Visitors can admire a range of clocks, toys, bicycles and spinners' tools, or walk in the small formal gardens. **Open:** 31 Mar–4 Nov: daily Wed–Sun, 12–5pm. Also Mon in July and Aug. Entry to Manor by timed ticket. **Admission:** Adult £6, Child £3. **E-mail:** snowshill@smtp.ntrust.org.uk

SUDELEY CASTLE

Winchcombe, Cheltenham, Gloucestershire GL54 5JD
Tel: 01242 602 308 (Lord & Lady Ashcombe)

Surrounded by magnificent, award-winning gardens, Sudeley Castle is the romantic home of Lord and Lady Ashcombe and the Dent-Brocklehurst family. Henry VIII, Anne Boleyn, Lady Jane Grey and Elizabeth I stayed here. Charles I sought refuge here and Prince Rupert of the Rhine made it his headquarters during the Civil War. Former home of Queen Katherine Parr, her marble tomb can be seen in St. Mary's Church, in the gardens. The Castle houses an impressive collection of pictures and furniture and includes works by Van Dyck, Turner and Sir Joshua Reynolds. **Open:** 3 Mar–28 Oct: Gardens, Exhibition Centre, Plant Centre and Shop: 10.30–5.30pm. 31 Mar–28 Oct: Castle Apartments and Church: 11–5pm and Restaurant 10.30–5pm. Group and private tours out of season by arrangement. **Admission:** Castle and Gardens: Adults £6.20, Concessions £5.20, Children (5–15yrs) £3.20. Group rates (min. 20): Adults £5.20, Concessions £4.20, Children (5–15yrs) £3.20. Gardens and Exhibition only: Adults £4.70, Concessions £3.70, Children (5–15yrs) £2.50. Family ticket (2 adults and 2 children) £17. Guided Tours and Garden Tours available (pre-booking required). **Events:** Please call for the full events programme. **Accommodation:** Small, attractive complex of Cotswold stone holiday cottages within walking distance of the castle.

map 4
B2

Hampshire

Chawton Church

Curled in the semi circle formed by the Western Downs, the Hampshire Downs and the South Downs, and sheltered from the Channel winds by the pearl and emerald hills of the Isle of Wight, the county of Hampshire basks in as mellow a climate as any part of the British Isles. The unassuming county town of Winchester was the one time capital of England and is home to a beautiful cathedral and many points of historic interest.

Hampshire's New Forest, 145 square miles of heath and woodland, is the largest area of unenclosed land in southern England.

"New" at the time of William the Conqueror, the forest is one of the few remaining primeval oak woods in England, and is now home to over a thousand fallow deer. It was a popular hunting ground for the Norman kings, and it was here that William II was shot (the Rufus Stone marks the spot). The famous New Forest ponies roam the surrounding area, where the woodland opens out into gently rolling moorland.

The city of Southampton has a long naval history, influenced by the unique double high tide in its harbour. The age of the aeroplane inevitably led to a downtown in Southampton's fortunes, but the city has continued to prosper, and is a lively and interesting place to visit. Portsmouth is also an important site for naval heritage, where visitors can see the Mary Rose, raised from the seabed in 1982 after 450 years underwater.

The Sir Harold Hillier Gardens & Arboretum

AIRBORNE FORCES MUSEUM

The Parachute Regiment,
Browning Barracks, Aldershot, Hampshire GU11 2BU
Tel: 01252 349619

The Museum traces the history of the Parachute Regiment and British Airborne Forces since 1940. Using weapons, equipment, dioramas and briefing models the museum depicts the story of airborne actions e.g. the early raids, D Day, Arnhem, Rhine Crossing and post-war campaigns such as Suez, Falklands and Kosovo. **Location:** Located in Browning Barracks, Aldershot, just off the A325 Farnborough-Farnham Road. The museum is easily recognised by the Dakota aircraft at the entrance. **Open:** Mon–Fri 10am–4.30pm (last admission 3.45pm), Sat, Sun & BH 10am–4pm.

`map 4 D5`

AVINGTON PARK

Winchester, Hampshire SO21 1DB
Tel: 01962 779260 Fax: 01962 779864 (Mrs C P S Bullen)

Avington Park is a Palladian mansion, where both Charles II and George IV stayed at various times. It was enlarged in 1670 with the addition of two wings and a classical portico surmounted by three statues. The State Rooms on view include the magnificent silk and gilded Ballroom, hand painted Drawing Room, Library and Hall. In a delightful parkland and lakeside setting, it adjoins an exquisite Georgian church, which may be visited. **Open:** May to September 2.30–5pm, Sundays and Bank Holiday Monday. Last tour 5pm. **Admission:** Adults £3.50, Children £1.50. Coaches welcome by appointment all year. **E-mail:** sarah@avingtonpark.co.uk **Internet:** www.avingtonpark.co.uk

`map 4 D5`

BROADLANDS

Romsey, Hampshire SO51 9ZD
Tel: 01794 505010

One of the finest examples of mid–Georgian architecture in England, Broadlands stands serenely in Capability Brown parkland on the banks of the River Test. Country residence of the famous Victorian Prime Minister, Lord Palmerston, and later home of Queen Victoria's great grandson, Earl Mountbatten of Burma. Visitors may view the House with its countless mementoes of the Mountbatten and Palmerston eras and its fine collection of art, furniture, porcelain and sculpture. History is brought vividly to life by means of the Mountbatten Exhibition and the audiovisual presentation. **Open:** Daily 11 June–2 Sept, 12–5.30pm (last adm. 4pm). **Admission:** Adult £5.95, Senior Citizen £4.95, Student £4.95, Disabled £4.95, Child 12–16 £3.95 & Children under 12 free. For group rate please call the number detailed above. **E-mail:** admin@broadlands.net **Internet:** www.broadlands.net

`map 4 C6`

BEAULIEU

Beaulieu, Brockenhurst, Hampshire SO42 7ZN
Tel: 01590 612345 · Fax: 01590 612624

Beaulieu is set in the heart of the New Forest and is a place that gives enormous pleasure to people with an interest in seeing history of all kinds. Overlooking the Beaulieu River, Palace House has been Lord Montagu's ancestral home since 1538. The House was once the Great Gatehouse of Beaulieu Abbey and its monastic origins are reflected in such features as the fan vaulted ceilings. The House also contains many of the current Montagu family treasures, portraits and personal photographs. Beaulieu Abbey was founded in 1204 and although most of the buildings have been destroyed, much of beauty and interest remains. The Domus, which houses an exhibition of monastic life in the middle ages; is home to embroidered wall hangings designed and created by Belinda, Lady Montagu, depicting the story of the Abbey since its foundation. Beaulieu is also home of the world famous National Motor Museum which traces the story of motoring from 1894 to the present day. 250 vehicles are on display including legendary World Record breakers such as Bluebird and Golden Arrow plus Veteran, Vintage and Classic cars and motorcycles. When visiting Beaulieu arrangements can be made to view the Estate's own vineyards. Visits, which can be arranged between Apr–Oct, must be pre–booked at least one week in advance with the Beaulieu Estate office. Beaulieu also offers a comprehensive range of facilities for conferences and corporate hospitality functions. In addition, Beaulieu has a 4x4 track and facilities which are suitable for team building activities, company days out, exhibitions, outdoor events and product lauches. **Open:** Daily 10–5pm except May–Sept 10–6pm. Closed Christmas Day. **Location:** By car take M27 to junction 2 then follow the Brown Tourist Signs. **Admission:** Please phone for details on 01590 612345. **Internet:** www.beaulieu.co.uk

map 4
C6

EXBURY GARDENS
Nr Southampton SO45 1AZ, Tel: 01703 891203
Fax: 01703 243380 (E.L. de Rothschild, Esq.)

Described as 'Heaven with the gates open', this 200 acres garden, created by Lionel de Rothschild, contains magnificent displays of rhododendrons, azaleas and other woodland shrubs. Free 'Trail Guides' in Spring, Summer and Autumn to encourage the visitor to see newly planted areas, making this a beautiful day out any time. **Location**: Exbury village, south drive from Jct.2 M27 west of Southampton. Turn W off A326 at Didben Purlieu towards Beaulieu. **Open:** Daily, 24 Feb–25 Nov, 10–5.30pm (dusk if earlier). Free entry to Gift shop and Plant Centre. Please phone for admission charges.

JANE AUSTEN'S HOUSE
Chawton, Alton GU34 1SD
Tel/Fax: 01420 83262 (Jane Austin Memorial Fund)

17th century house where Jane Austen wrote or revised her six great novels. The house contains many items associated with her and her family, documents and letters, first editions of the novels, pictures, portraits and furniture. Pleasant garden, suitable for picnics, bakehouse with brick oven and wash tub, houses Jane's donkey carriage. **Location:** Just S of A31, 1 mile SW of Alton, signposted Chawton. **Open:** 1 Mar–1 Jan daily. 11–4.30pm. Jan & Feb: Sat & Sun. Closed Christmas Day and Boxing Day. **Admission:** Adult £3, child (8–18) 50p, concessions £2.50.

FAMILY TREES
Sandy Lane, Shedfield, Hampshire, SO32 2HQ
Tel: 01329 834 812
(Philip House)

Wide variety of fruit for the connoisseur. Trained tree specialists; standards, espaliers, cordons etc. Other trees, old-fashioned and climbing roses, and evergreens. Free catalogue from Family Trees (as above). **Location:** See map in free catalogue. **Station(s):** Botley (2.5 miles). **Open:** Mid Oct–end Apr, Wed & Sat, 9.30am–12.30. **Admission:** No charge. No minimum order. Courier dispatch for next day delivery.

`map 5 V20`

GILBERT WHITE'S HOUSE
& THE OATES MUSEUM
'The Wakes', Selborne, Nr. Alton, Hampshire, GU34 3JH
Tel: 01420 511275   Fax: 0140 511040

Charming 18th century house and glorious garden, home of famous naturalist Rev. Gilbert White. Furnished rooms and original manuscript. Also fascinating museum on Capt. Lawrence Oates, hero of Scott's ill-fated Antarctic Expedition & Frank Oates, Victorian explorer. Tea Parlour-fare based on 18th century recipes. Excellent shop. **Open:** 11–5 daily. 1 Jan–24 Dec. Groups welcome all year and summer evenings. **Admission:** Adults £4, OAPs £3.50, Children £1, group rates if booked in advance. **Events:** Unusual Plants Fair 16 & 17 June 2001. Picnic to 'Jazz in June', 16 June 2001. Mulled Wine & Christmas Shopping Day 25 November 2001. Plus other events, exhibitions & courses. Details on request. **E-mail:** gilbertwhite@btinternet.com

`map 4 D5`

GOSS & CRESTED CHINA CENTRE &
MUSEUM
62 Murray Road, Homdean, Waterlooville, Hampshire PO8 9JL
Tel: 02392 597440 Fax: 02392 591975

The Goss & Crested China Centre has over 5,000 pieces of heraldic souvenir ware porcelain for sale from the Victorian and Edwardian eras. There is a museum with free entry, and here is explained the story of how newly acquired paid holidays and improved wages for the workers in the 1870s began the seaside tourist industry and the need for souvenir china mementoes. The growing network of railways, charabancs and paddlesteamers enabled the growing army of holidaymakers to visit previously inaccessible places. The craze for crested china had begun.

`map 4 D6`

HALL FARM HOUSE
Bentworth, Alton, Hampshire GU34 5JU
Tel: 01420 564010 (A.C & M.C Brooking)

`map 4 D5`

HOUGHTON LODGE GARDENS
Stockbridge, Hampshire SO20 6LQ
Tel: 01264 810912 (Capt & Mrs M W Busk)

5 Acres of landscaped pleasure grounds and fine trees (Grade II*) surround unique 18th C 'Cottage Ornée' beside the River Test with lovely views over the tranquil and unspoilt valley. Featured in BBC TV's "David Copperfield". Chalkcob walls shelter the 1 acre kitchen garden with ancient espaliered fruit trees, glasshouses and newly established herb garden. The Hydroponicum shows how to garden easily at home without soil or pesticides. **Location:** 1½ miles south of A30 at Stockbridge on minor road to Houghton village. **Station(s):** Winchester, Andover. **Open:** Mar–Sept, Sat, Sun & Bank Holidays 10–5pm, Mon, Tues, Thurs and Fri 2–5pm or by appointment. House by appointment. **Admission:** £5 (Children free). Special group discounts. Visitor centre with hydroponics shop serves free tea/coffee. **E-mail:** info@hydroponicum.co.uk
Internet: www. hydroponicum.co.uk

`map 4 C5`

HIGHCLERE CASTLE
Newbury RG20 9RN
Tel: 01635 253210

Designed by Charles Barry in the 1830s at the same time as he was building the Houses of Parliament. This soaring pinnacled mansion provided a perfect setting for the 3rd Earl of Carnarvon, one of the great hosts of Queen Victoria's reign. Old master paintings mix with portraits by Van Dyck and 18th century painters. The 5th Earl of Carnarvon, discovered the Tomb of Tutankhamun with Howard Carter.

FOR FURTHER INFORMATION, OPENING TIMES AND DATES WITH PHOTOGRAPHY, SEE PAGES 28 & 29 UNDER THE COUNTY OF BERKSHIRE.

THE SIR HAROLD HILLIER GARDENS & ARBORETUM

Jermyns Lane Ampfield, Nr Romsey, Hampshire
Tel: 01794 368787 Fax: 01794 368027

Set in the rolling Hampshire countryside between Winchester and the market town of Romsey, The Sir Harold Hillier Gardens & Arboretum comprises the greatest collection of hardy trees and shrubs in the world. Established in 1953, by the late Sir Harold Hillier, the 180-acre Hampshire County Council managed public garden provides a stunning range of seasonal colour and interest and features 11 National Plant Collections, Champion Trees, the Ghurka Memorial Garden and the largest Winter Garden in Europe. A garden for all seasons. **Location:** 3 m NE of Romsey on A3090. **Open:** All year except Christmas BH, 10.30–6pm (or dusk if earlier) **Admission:** Adults £4.25, Conc (Seniors, Jobseekers/UB40, Students, Disabled) £3.75, under 16s free. Discount rate for groups of 10+ when booked in advance. Free car parking. Regret no dogs. **Internet:** www.hillier.hants.gov.uk

map 4 C6

LANGLEY BOXWOOD NURSERY

Rake, Nr Liss, Hampshire GU33 7JL
Tel: 01730 894467 Fax: 01730 894703 (Elizabeth Braimbridge)

This small nursery, in a beautiful setting, specialises in box-growing, offering a chance to see together a unique range of old and new varieties, hedging, topiary, specimens and rarities. Some taxus also. **National Collection – Buxus**. Descriptive list available (4 x 1st class stamps). **Location:** Off B2070 (old A3) 3 miles south of Liphook. Ring for directions. **Open:** Mon–Fri 9–4.30pm, Sat – 10-4. **E-mail:** langbox@msn.com **Internet:** www.boxwood.co.uk

map 4 D6

PYLEWELL PARK GARDENS

South Baddesley, Lymington, Hampshire
Tel: 01329 833130
(Arnolds Tilbury, Agents to Estate)

Rhododendrons and azaleas. **Open:** Weekends in May and June, 2pm–5.30pm. **Admission:** £3. Other months by appointment.

map 4 C6

MOTTISFONT ABBEY

Mottisfont, Nr Romsey, Hants, SO51 OLP
Tel: 01794 340757 Fax: 01794 341492 (The National Trust)

The abbey and garden form the central point of an 809 hectare estate which includes most of the village of Mottisfont, farmland and woods. It is possible to walk along a tributary of the River Test which flows through the garden, forming a superb and tranquil setting for a 12th century Augustinian priory, which, after the Dissolution, became a house. It contains the spring or 'font' from which the place-name is derived. The magnificent trees, walled garden and the national collection of old-fashioned roses combine to provide interest throughout the seasons. The abbey contains a drawing room decorated by Rex Whistler and the cellarium of the old priory. In 1996 the Trust acquired Derek Hill's 20th-century picture collection. **Open:** 17 Mar–4 Nov: Sat–Wed, 11am–6pm (or dusk if earlier). Special opening 9–24 June daily 11am–8.30pm.

map 4 C6

ST AGATHA'S CHURCH

Market Way, Portsmouth, Hants
Tel & Fax: 01329 230330

A grand Italianate basilica of 1894, built for the famous Anglo Catholic priest, Fr R Dolling. Interior enriched with marble, alabaster, polished granite, carved stone and coloured glass. The apse displays a magnificent sgraffito mural c.1901, by Heywood Sumner, described by the late Sir Nikolaus Pevsner as "one of Portsmouth's few major works of art". Fine furnishings, many rescued from redundant churches. Guides available. **Location:** By Cascades Shopping Centre. On route for Historic Ships. **Open:** Sat, Sun, Wed Jun–Sept 10–3pm. Sat, Sun Oct–May 10–2pm. Traditional High Mass every Sunday, 11am (B.C.P. & English Missal). Other times by arrangement. **Admission:** Free. Nave available for hire subject to availability.

map 4 C6

THE VYNE

Vyne Road, Sherborne St John, Basingstoke,
Hampshire RG24 9HL
Tel: 01256 881337 Fax: 01256 881720 (The National Trust)

Built in the early 16th century in beautiful diaper brickwork by William Sandys, Lord Chamberlain to Henry VIII. Passed to the Chute family in the mid-17th century resulting in extensive alterations. Tudor chapel contains extremely fine renaissance glass and majolica floor tiles. A wealth of tudor panelling and collections of furniture, ceramics and textiles. Herbaceous borders, lawns sloping down to lake and surrounded by parkland. Woodland walks. Refreshments. **Open:** House: 31 Mar-4 Nov, Sat-Wed 1-5pm. Gardens: Weekends in Feb & March, 11–4.30pm. 31 Mar-4 Nov, Sat-Wed 11-6pm. **Admission:** House & Grounds £5.50, Grounds only £3. **E-mail:** svygen@smtp.ntrust.org.uk

map 4 D5

STRATFIELD SAYE HOUSE
Stratfield Saye, Nr Reading, Hampshire RG27 0AS
Tel: 01256 882882 (The Duke of Wellington)

Home of the Dukes of Wellington since 1817. The house and exhibition pay tribute to Arthur Wellesley, the first and Great Duke – soldier and statesman. **House:** Contains a unique collection of paintings, furniture and personal effects of the Great Duke. **Wellington Exhibition:** Depicts the life and times of the Duke and features his magnificent funeral carriage. **Grounds:** Include gardens and the grave of Copenhagen, the Duke's favourite charger which carried him throughout the Battle of Waterloo. **Location:** 1 mile W of A33 between Basingstoke & Reading (turn off at Wellington Arms Hotel); signposted. **Open:** June, July & Aug, Wed–Sun. Grounds & Exhibition: 11.30–5pm. House 12–3pm. Last admission 3pm. Groups: by arrangement, June, July & Aug: Mon & Tues. Sept: Mon–Fri. **Admission:** Adult £5.50, Child £2.50, OAP £5.

map 4 D5

UPPARK
South Harting, Petersfield, Hampshire GU31 5QR
Tel: 01730 825415 Fax: 01730 825873 (The National Trust)

An extensive award-winning, exhibition shows the exciting work which restored this beautiful house and its treasures following the disastrous 1989 fire. The elegant, fully restored mid-18th century interior houses the rescued Grand Tour paintings, fine ceramics, textiles, furniture and famous dolls' house. Nostalgic servants rooms as they were in 1874 when H G Wells' mother was housekeeper. The restored garden, high on the South Downs with magnificent views, is in the Picturesque style - primarily foliage, with flowering shrubs, under-planted bulbs, perennials, herbaceous plants. **Location:** 5 miles SE of Petersfield (B2146). **Open:** 1 Apr–31 Nov; daily except Fri & Sat. Exhibition, Shop, Restaurant & Grounds 11.30–5.30pm. House: 1–5pm (Open 12_5 on Sunday in July & August). **Admission:** Adults £5.50, Family ticket £13.75. Groups must book.

map 4 D6

WHITCHURCH SILK MILL
28 Winchester Street, Whitchurch, Hampshire
Tel: 01256 892065

This picturesque Grade II★ watermill was built around 1800 and has been in continuous use as a silk weaving mill since the 1820s. Now a working museum, Whitchurch Silk Mill keeps alive the art of silk weaving in the south of England. The historic machinery which once wove taffeta linings for Burberry raincoats and ottoman for judges' gowns produces traditional silks for theatrical and film costume and for historic houses, including the National Trust. Waterwheel, delightful riverside garden, shop selling affordable silk gifts, tearoom serving home cooking. **Admission:** Adults £3, Children £1.50, Students/OAPs £2.50, Family ticket (2+3) £7.50. Discount for pre-booked groups (10+). **Open:** All year (except Christmas week), Tues–Sun & Bank Holiday Mondays, 10.30am–5pm. Enquiries: 01256 892065.

map 4 C5

WINCHESTER COLLEGE
College Street, Winchester SO23 9NA
Tel: 01962 621209 Fax: 01962 621215

This is one of the oldest public schools in the country. The college was founded by Bishop William of Wykeham in 1382. **Location:** In Winchester city centre, south of the Cathedral. **Open:** Year round, between 10am – 4pm. Closed on Sunday mornings and Tuesday and Thursday afternoons. **Admission:** Charges apply. Guided tours may be booked for groups of 10+. **E-mail:** mvh@bursary.wincoll.ac.uk. **Internet:** www.wincoll.ac.uk

map 4 C5/6

WINCHESTER MUSEUMS SERVICE
75 Hyde Street, Winchester, Hampshire
Tel: 01962 848269 Fax: 01962 848299

City Museum: New galleries tell story of Winchester, important Roman town, and principal city of Alfred, through to modern times. In the Square, near Cathedral. **Open:** Apr–Oct Mon–Sat 10–5pm, Sun 12-5pm; Nov–Mar Tues–Sat 10–4pm, Sun 12–4pm. **Westgate:** Medieval gateway, prisoners' graffiti, rooftop views. Close to Great Hall. **Open:** Apr–Oct Mon–Sat 10–5pm, Sun 12–5pm; Feb & Mar Tues–Sat 10–4pm, Sun 12–4pm. **Guildhall Gallery:** Programme of mainly contemporary art works, above TIC. **Open:** Apr–Oct Mon–Sat 10–5pm, Sun 12–5pm; Nov–Mar Tues–Sat 10–4pm, Sun 2–4pm. **Historic Resources Centre:** Museums Service HQ, near to former Hyde Abbey. Temporary exhibitions. **Open:** Office hours. Partial disabled access. **Admission:** Free to all sites (except Westgate: nominal charge). **E-mail:** museums@winchester.gov.uk. **Internet:** www.winchester.gov.uk/heritage/home.htm

map 8 B6

Herefordshire

The ancient county of Herefordshire lies up against the Welsh border, and its quiet and unspoilt countryside allows the visitor to step back in time. In the shelter of the spectacular Black Mountains, the rolling countryside of the Golden Valley is truly an oasis of rural calm, with peaceful hamlets housing small farming communities.

The relaxed pace of life evokes an almost forgotten rural Old England, and the many beautiful village churches tell the story of countless generations of simple country folk. Hereford's Norman cathedral towers over the fertile floodplain of the River Wye, and here visitors can marvel at England's oldest map, the Mappa Mundi.

Ross-on-Wye

BURTON COURT

Eardisland, Nr Leominster, Herefordshire HR6 9DN
Tel: 01544 388231 (Lt. Cmdr. & Mrs. R. M. Simpson)

A typical squire's house, built around the surprising survival of a 14th century hall. The East Front re-designed by Sir Clough Williams-Ellis in 1912. Some European and Oriental costume, natural history specimens and models including a children's working model fairground and model railway. Pick your soft fruit in season. **Location:** 5 miles W of Leominster signposted on A44. **Open:** Spring Bank Holiday to end September, Wed, Thur, Sat, Sun, Bank Holiday Mon 2.30–6pm. **Admission:** Adults £3.50, Children £2. Parties of twelve or more people: £3.00 per person. **Refreshments:** Teas by arrangement. **Conferences:** Subject to availability.

 ## CROFT CASTLE

Leominster, Herefordshire, HR6 9PW
Tel: 01568 780246

Occupied by the Croft family almost continuously since Domesday, with walls and towers dating from the fourteenth century. The interior dates mainly from the eighteenth century, and outside there is an avenue of 350 year old Spanish chestnuts. **Open:** 31 Mar–29 Apr, Weekends and Bank Hols. 2 May–30 Sept, daily Wed–Sun, 1–5pm. Also weekends in Oct. **Admission:** Adult £3.90, Child £1.95.

`map 7 F2`

HAMPTON COURT'S VAN KAMPEN GARDENS

Hampton Court Estate, Hope under Dinmore, Leominster, HR6 0PN
Tel: 01568 797777 Fax: 01568 797472

The Van Kampen Gardens at Hampton Court, Herefordshire, are extensive new gardens in the historic grounds of a medieval fortified manor house. There is a walled organic kitchen garden, flower gardens, canals, pavilions, a maze and a secret tunnel, a hermit's grotto, waterfalls and a flooded sunken garden. There are beautiful parkland views and river walks. An organic teashop serves light lunches, tea and cake from a conservatory designed by Joseph Paxton. **Location:** Off A417 near junction with the A49. **Admission:** Adult £4, Child (6-13) £2, Senior Citizens £3.50 (Groups by prior arrangement). **Open:** 13 April–28 October, Wednesday-Sunday & Bank Holiday Monday 11am–5pm. **Email:** vankampengardens@hamptoncourt.org.uk **Internet:** www.hamptoncourt.org.uk.

`map 7 F1`

Eastnor castle

Eastnor, Ledbury, Herefordshire HR8 1RL
Tel: 01531 633160 Fax: 01531 631776 (Mr J. Hervey–Bathurst)

Home of the Hervey-Bathurst family, this magnificent Georgian Castle was built by their ancestors in 1812. Eastnor is dramatically situated in a 5000 acre sporting estate in The Malvern Hills. The lavish Italianate and Gothic interiors have recently been restored to critical acclaim. Unique collection of medieval armour, tapestries, furniture and pictures by Van Dyck, Kneller, Romney & Watts. Castellated terraces descend to a beautiful lake and the castle is surrounded by a famous arboretum containing many rare mature trees and 300 acre Deer Park which is used successfully for large outdoor events and concerts.

Location: 5 miles from junction 2 of M50. 2 miles east of Ledbury on A438 Tewkesbury Road. **Open:** 15 Apr–7 Oct on Sun and Bank Holiday Mon plus every day in Jul and Aug, except Sat. **Admission:** Castle and Grounds: Adults: £5.00, Children £3.00. Reduced rates for groups, families and grounds only. Eastnor Castle is also available for exclusive corporate and private entertainment, activity and teambuilding days, product launches, private parties and dinners, wedding ceremonies, receptions and luxury accommodation for small groups. **E-mail:** enquiries@eastnorcastle.com. **Internet:** www.eastnorcastle.com.text

map 7
G1

 HERGEST CROFT GARDENS

Kington, Herefordshire HR5 3EG

Tel: 01544 230160 Fax: 01544 230160 (W.L. Banks, Esq.)

Spring bulbs to autumn colour, a garden for all seasons. Old-fashioned kitchen garden; spring and summer borders, roses. Over 59 champion trees and shrubs in one of the finest collections in the British Isles. National Collections of birches, maples and zelkovas. Rhododendrons up to 30ft. **Location:** On outskirts W of Kington off Rhayader Road (A44) (signposted to Hergest at W end of bypass). **Station(s):** Leominster–14 miles. **Open:** 1 Apr–31 Oct 1.30–6pm. **Admission:** Adult £4, Children under 16 free. Groups of 20+ by appointment anytime £3.50. Guided tours available (pre-booked and 20+) £5.50 . Season tickets £15, access Apr–Mar. **Refreshments:** Home-made light lunches (pre-booked for groups) and teas. **Events:** Mon 1 May Flower Fair: plant stalls, special events. (£5 admission). Gift shop: Attractive gifts. Plant sales: Rare, unusual trees and shrubs. **Internet:** www.hergest.co.uk

map 7 G2

 HOW CAPLE COURT GARDEN

How Caple, HR1 4SX, Hereford & Worcester.

Tel: 01989 740 612 Fax: 01989 740 611 (Mr & Mrs Roger Lee)

Discover 11.5 acres of delightful Edwardian gardens set high above the River Wye. The planting is formal and woodland with a unique atmosphere of peace and tranquillity. The nursery has a wide variety of rose shrubs and herbaceous plants. The stable shop offers a selection of dried and silk flowers and How Caple preserves and pickles. **Location:** B4224, Ross-on-Wye (4.5 miles), Hereford (9 miles). **Open:** Easter - end of September. Closed Oct–Easter. **Admission:** Adults £2.50, Children £1.25. Parties welcome by appointment. Dogs on leads welcome. **Refreshments:** Teashop open daily offering home made cakes.

map 7 G1

 KENTCHURCH COURT

Nr. Pontrilas, Hereford, Herefordshire, HR2 0DB

Tel: 01981 240 228 (Mr & Mrs John Lucas-Scudamore)

Fortified border manor house altered by Nash. Part of the original 14th century house still survives. Pictures and Grinling Gibbons carving. Owen Glendower's tower. Game shooting and shooting parties. Also wine appreciation weekends. **Location:** Off B4347, 3 miles SE of Pontrilas. Monmouth (12 miles). Hereford (14 miles). Abergavenny (14 miles). On left bank of River Monnow. **Open:** May–Sept. All visitors by appointment only. **Admission:** Adults £4, Children £4. **Refreshments:** At Kentchurch Court by appointment. **Accommodation:** By appointment.

map 7 G2

 LANGSTONE COURT

Llangarron, Ross on Wye, Herefordshire

Tel: 01989 770254 (R M C Jones Esq.)

Mostly late 17th century house with older parts. Interesting staircases, panelling and ceilings. **Location:** Ross on Wye 5 miles, Llangarron 1 miles. **Open:** Wednesdays & Thursdays 11–3pm between May 20– August 31, spring and summer bank holidays. **Admission:** Free.

map 7 H1

LONGTOWN CASTLE

Abbey Dore, Herefordshire

Tel: 0121 625 6820

Longtown Castle was built in 1180 by Walter de Lacy, a Norman Lord, on the site of an earthern enclosure dating back to Roman times. Its unusual cylindrical keep provides great views over the Black Mountains. **Open:** All year, any reasonable time. **Admission:** Free.

MOCCAS COURT

Moccas, Herefordshire, HR2 9LH

Tel: 01981 500 381 (Trustees of Baunton Trust)

Built by Anthony Keck in 1775 overlooking the River Wye, decoration including the round room and oval stair by Robert Adam. Scene of famous 17th century romance and destination of epic night ride from London. Set in 'Capability' Brown parkland with an attractive walk to The Scar Rapids. **Location:** 10 miles E of Hay on Wye. 13 miles W of Hereford on the River Wye. 1 mile off B4352. **Station(s):** Hereford. **Open:** House & Gardens: Apr–Sept, Thurs, 2–6pm. **Admission:** £2.00. **Refreshments:** Food and drink available at the Red Lion Hotel, Bredwardine, by pre-booking only. **Accommodation:** Available at the Red Lion Hotel, Bredwardine. Disabled access in the garden only.

map 7 G2

ROTHERWAS CHAPEL

Hereford, Herefordshire

Tel: 0121 625 6820

Interesting Roman Catholic chapel, parts of which date back to the fourteenth century. Once owned by the wealthy Bodenham family, it features a fascinating Victorian side chapel and altar. Located just south-east of the town. **Open:** On request, at any reasonable time. **Admission:** Free.

Hertfordshire

Capel Manor

Despite its location just outside the capital, Hertfordshire retains its own essentially rural identity – a few miles from its busy towns, the visitor will find only sleepy villages in a landscape of picturesque woodland, streams and open farmland. There are almost 2000 miles of public footpaths to explore, including the 11 mile Ver Colne Valley walk, which passes through a number of sites of historic interest. The Chiltern Hills to the west and north-west of the county, designated an Area of Outstanding Natural Beauty, are also excellent for walking. Hertfordshire's historic towns also merit a visit: St Albans, a thriving market town, has a beautiful mediaeval cathedral, Tring boasts picturesque Rothschild architecture and the Wren Mansion House, and any visit to Berkhamsted should include its castle, where Geoffrey Chaucer once worked as a Clerk.

ASHRIDGE
Berkhamsted, Hertfordshire HP4 1NS
Tel: 01442 843491 Fax: 01442 841209
(Governors of Ashridge)

150 acres of both parkland and intimate smaller gardens. The landscape influenced by Humphry Repton. Mature trees combined with unique features e.g. Beech Houses with windows and doors in a Pink and Grey Garden, Grotto – Ferns planted between Herts Pudding Stone. **Location:** 3½ miles N of Berkhamsted (A4251), 1 miles S of Little Gaddesden. **Station(s):** Berkhamsted. **Open:** Gardens open Easter, Apr–Sept Sat & Sun & B/Holidays 2–6pm. **Admission:** Gardens: Adults £2 Children/OAP £1. **Conferences:** For information please contact Carol Johnston, Conference Manager (01442 841027).

map 4 E3

CROMER WINDMILL
Ardeley, Stevenage, Hertfordshire SG2 7QA
Tel: 01279 843301 (Hertfordshire Building Preservation Trust)

Hertfordshire's last surviving Post Mill now fully restored, with grants from English Heritage and Heritage Lottery Fund. Short video for visitors showing method of working. ½ hour video available on loan, with brochure giving history of Mill. Disabled access, adequate parking, no lavatories, literature and tea towels on sale. **Open:** Sundays, Bank Holidays, 2 and 4 Saturday 2.30–5pm mid May–mid Sept. Special parties by arrangement. Cristina Harrison 01279 843301. **Admission:** Adults £1.50, Children 25p. **Location:** OSS TL304287. On the B1037 between Stevenage and Cottered.

map 4 E3

FIRST GARDEN CITY HERITAGE MUSEUM
296 Norton Way South, Letchworth, SG6 1SU
Tel: 01462 482710 Fax: 01462 486056

The museum tells the story of the world's first garden city and the foundation of the garden city and new town movement. Many interactive exhibits demonstrating the development of Letchworth, the world's first garden city, are displayed. The museum holds regular special exhibitions and events relating to the different aspects of the town's history. Talks and guided tours of the town are available for group visits. The museum is housed in the drawing offices of the town's original architect, Barry Parker. **Open:** Mon–Sat 10am–5pm, closed Christmas Day and Boxing Day. **Admission:** Residents £0.50, non-residents £1.00, under 16s free. **E-mail:** fgchm@letchworth.com

map 4 E2

GORHAMBURY
St Albans, Hertfordshire AL3 6AH
Tel: 01727 855000 Fax: 01727 843675 (The Earl of Verulam)

Mansion built 1777–84 in classical style by Sir Robert Taylor, 16th century enamelled glass and historic portraits. **Location:** 2 miles W of St Albans, entrance off A4147 at Roman Theatre. **Station(s):** St Albans. **Open:** May–Sept, Thurs 2–5pm. Last tour of house 4.30pm. Gardens open with the house. **Admission:** House and Gardens: Adults £6, Children £3, OAPs £4. Guided tours only. Parties by prior arrangement, Thurs £5, other days £6.

map 4 E3

THE GARDENS OF THE ROSE
Chiswell Green, St Albans, Herts AL2 3NR
Tel: 01727 850461, Fax: 01727 850360 (The Royal National Rose Society)

The Royal National Rose Society's Gardens provide a wonderful display of one of the best and most important collections of roses in the world. There are some 30,000 roses in 1800 different varieties. The Society has introduced many companion plants which harmonise with the roses including over 100 varieties of clematis. The garden, named for the Society's Patron HM The Queen Mother, contains a fascinating collection of old garden roses. Various cultivation trials show just how easy roses are to grow and new roses can be viewed in the International Trial Ground. **Open:** 1 Jun-30 Sept, Mon–Sats 9–5pm. Sun & Bank Hols. 10–6pm. **E-mail:** mail@rnrs.org.uk **Internet:** roses.co.uk

map 4 E3

HATFIELD HOUSE, PARK & GARDENS

Hatfield, Hertfordshire AL9 5NQ
Tel: 01707 287010, Fax: 01707 275719 (Contact – The Curator)

Hatfield House was built by Robert Cecil, 1st Earl of Salisbury and Chief Minister to King James I, in 1611. This celebrated Jacobean house, which stands in its own Great Park, has been in the Cecil family ever since and is the home of the Marquess of Salisbury. The State Rooms are rich in world-famous paintings, exquisite furniture, fine tapestries and historic armour. Superb examples of Jacobean craftsmanship can be found throughout the house. Within the delightful gardens stand the surviving wing of the Royal Palace of Hatfield (1485), were Elizabeth I spent much of her childhood. Today, the Marchioness of Salisbury continues to recreate and maintain the beautiful gardens in a style that reflects their Jacobean history. **Location:** 21 miles N of London - A1(M) Junction 4, 2m. Signed off A414 & A1000. Opposite Hatfield railway station (Kings Cross 25mins). **Open:** 24 March–23 September (closed Good Friday, but open BH Mondays). House: Tue–Fri: guided tours only, 12–4pm. Sat & Sun: no guided tours, 1–4.30pm. Bank Hols: no guided tours, 11–4.30pm. Park: Daily, except Fri, 10.30–8pm. Fri: 11–6pm. West Gardens: Tue–Sun: 11–6pm. East Gardens: Fri(Connoisseurs' Day): 11–6pm. Shop: Tue–Sat: 11–5.30pm. Sun: 1–5.30pm. Restaurant: Tue–Sun 10.30–5.30pm. **Admission:** (except at major events) House, Park & West Gardens (not Fri): Adult £6.60, Child £3.30, Booked Party (20+) £5.60. Park only (not Fri): Adult £2.00, Child £1.00. Connoisseurs'Day (Fri): Park & Gardens (East & West): £6.00. House Tour, Park & Gardens: £10.00. **Major Events:** Living Crafts: 10–13 May. Festival of Gardening: 23–24 June, Art in Clay, 3–5 Aug, Country Homes & Gardens Show, 7–9 Sept.

map 4
E/F 3

KNEBWORTH HOUSE

Knebworth, Hertfordshire
Tel: 01438 812661 (The Hon Henry Lytton Cobbold)

Home of the Lytton family since 1490 and still a lived-in family house. Transformed in early Victorian times by Edward Bulwer–Lytton, the author, poet, dramatist and statesman, into the unique High Gothic fantasy house of today, complete with turrets, griffins and gargoyles. Home of Constance Lytton, the Suffragette, and Robert Lytton, the Viceroy of India who proclaimed Queen Victoria Empress of India at the Great Delhi Durbar of 1877. Visited by Queen Elizabeth I, Charles Dickens and Sir Winston Churchill. The interior contains many different styles, including the Jacobean Banqueting Hall, the Regency elegance of Mrs Bulwer–Lytton's bedroom, the Victorian State Drawing Room and the Edwardian designs of Sir Edwin Lutyens in the Entrance Hall, Dining Parlour and Library. 25 acres of beautiful gardens, simplified by Lutyens, including pollarded lime avenues, formal rose garden, maze and Gertrude Jekyll herb garden. 250 acres of gracious parkland, with herds of red and sika deer, includes extensive children's adventure playground and miniature railway. Special events staged throughout the summer. World famous for its huge open-air rock concerts, and used as a film location for Batman, the Shooting Party, Wilde, Jane Eyre and the Canterville Ghost, amongst others. **Location:** Direct access off A1(M) junction 7 (Stevenage South A602). 28 miles N of London. 12 miles N of M25 junction 23. **Open:** Daily: 7–22 Apr, 26 May–3 June, 7 July–4 Sept. Weekends & Bank Hols only: 28 Apr–20 May, 9 June–1 July, 8–30 Sept. **Times:** Park, Gardens & Playground 11–5.30pm. House & Exhibition 12–5pm. (last admission 4.30pm). **E-mail:** info@knebworthhouse.com **Internet:** www.knebworthhouse.com

map 4
E3

MILL GREEN MUSEUM & MILL
Mill Green, Hatfield, Herts AL9 5PD
Tel: 01707 271362 Fax: 01707 272511 (Welwyn Hatfield Museum Service)

Fully restored 18th century watermill, producing organic wholemeal flour every week, and local history museum. **Exhibitions/Events:** There is a small temporary exhibitions gallery and a programme of craft demonstrations and special events at summer weekends. **Open:** Tuesday-Friday 10-5pm. Saturday, Sunday and Bank Holidays 2-5pm. Closed Monday except Bank Holidays. Milling Hours: Tuesday, Wednesday 10.30-12.30pm, 1.30-3.30pm. Sunday 2.30-4.30pm. Sales Point: Souvenirs, local history publications and freshly ground Mill Green Flour available. **Admission:** Free. Donations welcome.

map 4 E3

SCOTT'S GROTTO
Scott's Road, Ware, Herts SG12 9SQ
Tel: 01920 464131, 01992 584322 (East Hertfordshire District Council)

Grotto, summerhouse and garden built 1760–73 by Quaker poet John Scott. Described by English Heritage as 'one of the finest grottos in England.' Now extensively restored by The Ware Society. **Location:** Scott's Road, Ware (off A119 Hertford Road). **Station:** Ware/Liverpool Street line. **Open:** Every Sat beginning of Apr–Sept and Easter, Spring and Summer Bank Hol Mons 2–4.30pm. **Admission:** Free but donation of £1 requested. Please park in Amwell End car park by level crossing (300 yards away) and walk up Scott's Road. Advisable to wear flat shoes and bring a torch. Parties by prior arrangement.

map 4 D3

THE WALTER ROTHSCHILD ZOOLOGICAL MUSEUM
Akeman Street, Tring, Hertfordshire HP23 6AP
Tel: 020 7942 6171 Fax: 020 7942 6150

This museum was once the private collection of Lionel Walter, 2nd Baron Rothschild, and is now part of The Natural History Museum. It houses more than 4000 specimens in a unique Victorian setting. The displays comprise of mounted specimens of animals from all parts of the world - from whales to fleas, humming birds to tigers, even a large collection of domestic dogs. **Refreshments:** Light refreshments in the Zebra Café. Picnic area available in spring & summer. **Exhibitions:** Temporary exhibitions & events. Interactive centre, workshops & education service. **Open:** Mon–Sat 10am–5pm. Sun 2–5pm. **Admission:** A small charge for adults & concessions. Free entry for: children (0–16), over 60s, shop & café only & booked school parties.

map 4 D3

SHAW'S CORNER

Ayot St Lawrence, Nr Welwyn, Herts AL6 9BX
Tel: 01438 820307 (The National Trust)

The home of George Bernard Shaw from 1906 until his death in 1950. The rooms remain much as he left them, with many literary and personal effects evoking the individuality and genius of this great dramatist. The garden has richly planted borders and views over the Hertfordshire countryside. **Open:** 31 Mar–4 Nov: Wed-Sun & BH Mons, 1–5pm (closed Good Fri). **Admission:** £3.50, Family ticket £8.75. **Location:** At SW end of village, 2 miles NE of Wheathampstead: approx. 2 miles from B653. **E-mail:** www.tscgen@smtp.ntrust.org.uk

map 4 E3

WELWYN ROMAN BATHS
Welwyn By-pass, Welwyn Village, Herfordshire
Tel: 01707 271362 Fax: 01707 272511 (Welwyn Hatfield Museum Service)

All correspondence to Mill Green Museum & Mill

A 3rd century bathing suite, the one surviving feature of a villa, ingeniously preserved within the embankment of the A1(M). **Open:** January-November: Saturday, Sunday and Bank Holidays 2-5pm or dusk when earlier. School half terms and holidays Monday-Sunday 2-5pm or dusk when earlier. Closed December. Pre-booked parties any time. Small charge per head. Sales Point: Souvenirs and local archaeology publications on sale. **Admission:** Adults £1. Children free.

map 4 E3

Isle of Wight

Known as the Garden Isle, the Isle of Wight boasts a wide variety of scenery, from sheltered river valleys to wind-swept headlands, and from long golden beaches to forests. The climate is consistently warmer and sunnier than on the mainland, and sub-tropical plants grow in sheltered south-facing gardens. The island's history is as turbulent as its gardens are serene. Successive invasions of Romans, Danes, Normans and Spaniards have left a rich legacy of ancients churches, castles and forts. Carisbrooke Castle, royal fortress and prison to Charles I, is set dramatically on a sweeping ridge at the very heart of the island.

Carisbrooke Castle

DEACONS NURSERY (H.H)
Moor View, Godshill, PO38 3HW, Isle of Wight
Tel: 01983 840 750 or 01983 522 243 Fax: 01983 523 575 (G. D. Deacon & B. H. Deacon)

Specialist national fruit tree growers. Trees and bushes sent anywhere so send NOW for a FREE catalogue. Over 300 varieties of apples on various types of root stocks from M27 (4ft), M26 (8ft) to M25 (18ft). Plus Pears, Peaches, Nectarines, Plums, Gages, Cherries, Soft Fruits and an unusual selection of Family Trees. Many special offers. Catalogue always available (stamp appreciated). Many varieties of grapes; dessert and wine, plus Hybrid Hops and nuts of all types. **Location:** The picturesque village of Godshill. Deacons Nursery is in Moor View off School Crescent (behind the only school). **Open:** Winter – Mon–Fri, 8–4pm & Sat, 8–1pm. Summer – Mon–Fri, 8–5pm.

map 4 C7

MUSEUM OF ISLAND HISTORY
The Guildhall, High Street, Newport, Isle of Wight PO30 1TY
Tel: 01983 823366 Fax: 01983 823841

Discover the history of the Island from the time of the dinosaurs to the present day. Using the latest in touch screen computer technology, hands-on exhibits, microscopes, quizzes and games, the Guildhall is an experience for all the family. Displays show how the island was formed 8000 years ago, how its wild landscape was tamed by the first islanders and how it became the holiday isle so cherished by thousands of visitors each year. The museum also incorporates the island's principal Tourist Information centre. Facilities: Gift shop, toilets, disabled access. **Admission:** Entry change. There are special rates for groups of over 12.

map 4 C7

NEWPORT ROMAN VILLA
Cypress Road, Newport, Isle of Wight
Tel: 01983 529720 (Isle of Wight Council)

Discover the luxurious lifestyles of Romano-Britons among the extensive remains of a 3rd century farmhouse. Unearthed in 1926, Newport Roman Villa has one of the best preserved domestic bath suites in Britain. Cold and hot baths, steam room and underfloor heating system are visible reminders of Roman creature comforts. Reconstructed living rooms and kitchen show how important mod cons were to affluent Roman farm owners. An exhibition of archaeological finds from around the island tells the story of the Roman occupation of the Isle of Wight. Guided tours are available to group bookings of 12 and more, on request. Toilet. **Admission:** Entry charge.

map 4 C7

NUNWELL HOUSE & GARDENS
Coach Lane, Brading, Isle of Wight
Tel: 01983 407240 (Col. & Mrs J A Aylmer)

Nunwell House has been a family home for 5 centuries and reflects much island and architectural history. Finely furnished with Jacobean and Georgian wings. Lovely setting with Channel views and 5 acres of tranquil gardens. Special family military collections. **Location:** 1 mile from Brading turning off A3055 signed; 3 mile South of Ryde. **Station:** Brading. **Open:** 27/28 May then 2 July–5 Sept, Mon, Tues & Weds 1–5pm with House tours at 1.30, 2.30 and 3.30pm. **Admission:** £4 (includes guide book) – reductions for senior citizens, children and parties. Gardens only £2.50. **Refreshments:** Picnic areas: large parties may book catering in advance. Parties welcome out of season if booked. Large car park. Regret no dogs.

map 4 C7

OSBORNE HOUSE
East Cowes, Isle of Wight PO32 6JY
Tel: 01983 200022 (English Heritage)

Visit the magnificent Osborne House, the beloved seaside retreat of Queen Victoria, and gain insight into the private family life of Britain's longest reigning monarch. The Royal Apartments have been preserved almost unaltered since Victoria died here in 1901. The Swiss Cottage, a chalet built in the grounds for the children, gives a fascinating insight into the children's lives and there is an authentic Victorian carriage to take visitors between house and cottage. **Location:** 1m SE of East Cowes. **Open:** 1 Apr–30 Sept: House daily, 10–5pm. Grounds daily, 10–6pm. 1 Oct–31 Oct: House & Grounds daily, 10–5pm. Telephone for details of our winter guided tours, pre-booking essential. **Admission:** House & Grounds: Adults £7.20, Conc £5.40, Child £3.60, Family £18. Grounds only: Adults £3.80, Conc £2.90, Child £1.90. (15% discount for groups of 11 or more).

map 4 C7

Kent

Kent is both the Garden of England and the gateway to Europe, where the castles that once defended England from the French now welcome her tourists through the Channel Tunnel. The county boasts beautiful countryside, quiet villages and one of the most historic county towns in England. Canterbury possesses many fine buildings, but the jewel in its crown is undoubtedly the cathedral, whose stained glass dates back to the twelfth century.

The elegant spa town of Royal Tunbridge Wells is set in the rolling hills of the Weald of Kent, where oast-houses, orchards, and even vineyards testify to the county's agricultural importance.

Matfield Village Green

BELMONT

Belmont Park, Throwley, Faversham, Kent ME13 0HH
Tel: 01795 890202 (Harris (Belmont) Charity)

Charming late 18th century mansion by Samuel Wyatt set in fine parkland. Seat of the Harris family since 1801 when it was acquired by General George Harris, the victor of Seringapatam. The delightfully furnished house contains interesting mementoes of the family's connections with India and colonies, plus the fifth Lord Harris's fine clock collection. There is a walled garden and a pinetum containing some fine specimens of trees and a small grotto. In the spring the rhododendrons and azaleas give a blaze of colour and these are followed by the hydrangeas. There is also a charming pets' cemetery. Tearoom and gifts. **Location:** 4½ miles south-southwest of Faversham, off A251 (signed from Badlesmere). **Open:** 1 April–30 September 2001, Sat, Sun & Bank Hols from 2–5pm. (Last admission 4.30pm). Groups on Tue & Thur by appointment. **Admission:** House & garden: Adult £5.25, OAP £4.75, Child (2–16 yrs) £2.50. Garden: Adult £2.75, OAP £2.75, Child £1. Cream tea £2.95.

map 5
H5

DICKENS HOUSE MUSEUM
BROADSTAIRS
on the Main Seafront
Victoria Parade, Broadstairs, Kent CT10 1QS
Tel: 01843 862853

Once the home of Mary Strong, on whom Dickens based much of the character of Miss Betsey Trotwood, David Copperfield's aunt. It was here, while having tea with Miss Strong, that his son, Charles Jnr, watched what he called 'the famous donkey fights'. The donkey fights and the description of the parlour found their way into the novel. Dickens wrote much of David Copperfield during his last long holiday in Broadstairs. Miss Strong's parlour has been restored as described by Dickens and illustrated by 'Phiz'. Dickens' letters from Broadstairs, memorabilia, local and Dickensian prints, costume and Victoriana. **Open:** Daily Apr–mid Oct 2–5pm. Parties by arrangement with the Honorary Curator.

map 5
J4

CHARTWELL

Mapleton Road, Westerham, Kent
Tel: 01732 868381 Fax: 01732 868193

The family home of Sir Winston Churchill from 1924 until the end of his life. The house and extensive grounds have magnificent views over the Weald of Kent. The rooms are left as they were in Sir Winston and Lady Churchill's lifetime with daily papers, fresh flowers and his famous cigars. Museum and exhibition rooms contain displays and sound recordings, superb collections of memorabilia from his political career, including uniforms and a 'siren suit'. The garden studio contains Sir Winston's easel and paintbox as well as many of his paintings. Visitors can also see the garden walls that Churchill built with his own hands and enjoy the water gardens and lake. The Mulberry Room can be booked for conferences, private dinners and wedding receptions. **Events:** Concerts 18 & 19 August.

Garden parties 4 & 25 August. Phone Box office 01892 891001. **Location:** Signed from M25, A21 & A25. 2 m S of Westerham forking left off B2026. Chartwell Explorer green transport link from Sevenoaks (June–Sept). Metrobus 246 from Bromley (all year). **Open:** 31 Mar–4 Nov, Wed–Sun 11am–5pm (last entry 4.15pm). In addition, Tuesdays throughout July and August and Bank Holiday Mondays. **Restaurant:** 10.30am–5pm, hot lunches 12–2pm. **Shop:** 11am–5.30pm. **Admission:** Adults £5.60, Children £2.80, Family £14. Coaches and groups by appointment. NT members free. Private guided tours by arrangement. **E-mail:** kchxxx@smtp.ntrust.org.uk

map 5 F5

COBHAM HALL

Cobham, Nr Gravesend, Kent DA12 3BL
Tel: 01474 823371 Fax: 01474 825906/825904

'One of the largest, finest and most important houses in Kent', Cobham Hall is an outstandingly beautiful, red brick mansion in Elizabethan, Jacobean, Carolean and 18th century styles, set in 150 acres of parkland. It yields much of interest to the student of art, architecture and history. The Elizabethan wings were begun in 1584 whilst the central section contains the Gilt Hall, wonderfully decorated by John Webb, Inigo Jones' most celebrated pupil, in 1654. Further rooms were decorated by James Wyatt in the 18th century. Cobham Hall, now a girls' school, has been visited by several of the English monarchs from Elizabeth I to Edward VIII, later Duke of Windsor. Charles Dickens used to walk through the grounds from his house in Higham to the Leather Bottle public house in Cobham Village. In 1883, the Hon Ivo Bligh, later the 8th Earl of Darnley, led the victorious

English cricket team against Australia bringing home the 'Ashes' to Cobham. Gardens: Landscaped for the 4th Earl by Humphry Repton, the gardens are gradually being restored by the Cobham Hall Heritage Trust. The gardens are particularly delightful in spring, when they are resplendent with daffodils and a myriad of rare bulbs. **Location:** By A2/M2, between Gravesend & Rochester, 8 miles from Jct 2 on the M25. **Open** March, April, July & August, most Wednesdays & Sundays; Easter Weekend, 2-5pm each day. Please call to check dates & times. **Admission:** Adult £3.50, OAP/Child £2.75. **Events/Exhibitions:** 25 Mar & 15 July: National Garden Scheme Days. 23–26 Apr & 20–21 Oct Medway Craft Show. Many through year, please phone for details. **E-mail:** smithk@cobhamhall.com

map 5 G4

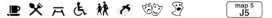

DOVER CASTLE
Dover, Kent CT16 1HU
Tel: 01304 211067 (English Heritage)

The special highlight of a visit to Dover Castle is the recently opened network of secret wartime underground tunnels which functioned as the nerve centre for the evacuation of Dunkirk. There is even a hospital where visitors can experience the sights, sounds and smells of life underground. However, there's as much to see above ground as there is below. Visitors will unlock over 2,000 years of history when they explore Henry II's Keep and new reconstruction of the Tudor Court preparing for the arrival of Henry VIII in 1539. Also explore the Royal Regiment Museum, Saxon Church and Roman lighthouse. **Location:** On East side of Dover. **Open:** 1 Apr–30 Sept: daily 10–6pm. 1 Oct–31 Oct: daily, 10–5pm, 1 Nov–28 Mar: 10–4pm. (closed 24–25 Dec & 1 Jan) **Admission:** Adult £7, Conc £5.30, Child £3.50, Family £17.50 (15% discount for groups of 11 or more).

map 5 J5

DOVER MUSEUM
Market Square, Dover, Kent CT16 1PB
Tel: 01304 201066   Fax: 01304 241186

A large and exciting museum devoted to the history of Dover from the Stone Age to World War II, and with a regularly changing Special Exhibitions gallery. The museum is also home to the Dover Bronze Age Boat, the world's oldest seagoing boat, displayed in a state-of-the-art gallery. As well as the boat and a large collection of other treasures from the Bronze Age, the gallery also includes a full-scale Bronze Age home, a film show and an interactive section, puzzles, games, video microscopes and multimedia computers. You can even build your own boat and see if it will cross the Channel or sink! **Internet:** www.dover.gov.uk/museum

map 5 J5

EMMETTS GARDEN
Ide Hill, Sevenoaks, Kent TN14 6AY
Tel: 01732 868381   Fax: 01732 868193

Enjoy spectacular views across the Weald of Kent from this peaceful garden designed and created in the 19th century by the Lubbock family. Follow the 'tree trail' and see rare trees and shrubs and the tallest tree top in Kent. Enchanting bluebell bank, wide variety of rhododendrons and azaleas, rock garden and rose garden. Parts of the garden accessible to disabled visitors, some steep paths. Volunteer driven 'buggy' available from car park to ticket hut. Adapted toilet. **Events:** Blues concert 28 July, various garden tours. Box office: 01892 891001. **Location:** 1.5 m S of the A25 on Sundridge to Ide Hill Road; 1.5 m N of ide Hill off B2042; M25/J5 - 4 miles. **Open:** Apr/May: Wed–Sun; June–Oct Wed, Sat & Sun, BH Mon 11am–5.30pm (last entry 4.30pm) **Tearoom & Shop:** 11.30am–4.30pm same days as garden. **Admission:** Adults £3.40, Children £1.70, Family £8.50. **E-mail:** kchxxx@smtp.ntrust.org.uk

map 5 F5

FINCHCOCKS
Goudhurst, Kent TN17 1HH
Tel: 01580 211702   Fax: 01580 211007 (Mr & Mrs Richard Burnett)

Georgian manor in beautiful garden, housing a magnificent collection of ninety historical keyboard instruments. Many of these are fully restored and played whenever the house is open in entertaining musical tours. Pictures, prints and exhibition 'The Lost Pleasure Gardens'. **Location:** Off A262 1½ west of Goudhurst, 10 miles from Tunbridge Wells. **Open:** Easter–end of Sept, Suns and BH Mons and Wed and Thurs in Aug: 2–6pm. **Admission:** Adults £7, Children £4, Family ticket £15. **Garden only:** £2. Free parking. **Refreshments:** Teas. **Reserved Visits:** Groups and individuals most days April–October. **Events:** Finchcocks Festival: weekends in September. Craft & Garden Fairs: end of May–October. **Civil Marriages and Receptions:** Available for functions.

map 5 G5

DOWN HOUSE: HOME OF CHARLES DARWIN
Downe, Kent BR6 7JT
Tel: 01689 859119 (English Heritage)

Explore the home of the 19th century's most influential scientist, Charles Darwin. It was in his study that he wrote the scientific works that first scandalised and then revolutionised the Victorian World in 1859; *On the Origin of Species by means of Natural Selection*. Today his study remains full of the notebooks and journals from his voyage of discovery, that took him most famously to the Galapagos Islands. **Location:** In Luxted Road, Downe off A21 near Biggin Hill. **Open:** 10 Apr–31 Oct: Wed–Sun, 10–6pm. 1 Nov–23 Dec: Wed–Sun, 10–4pm. 7 Feb–31 Mar: Wed–Sun, 10–4pm. **Admission:** Adults £5.50, concs £4.10, child £2.80. Groups over 11 pre-book please call 01689 859119. All visitors must pre-book at least one day in advance from 12 July–17 Sept.

map 5 F5

GAD'S HILL PLACE
Rochester, Kent ME3 7PA
Tel: 01474 822366 (Gad's Hill School Ltd)

Grade 1 listed building, built in 1780. Home of Charles Dickens from 1857 to 1870. **Location:** On A226; 3 miles from Rochester, 4 miles from Gravesend. **Station:** Higham (1½ m) **Open:** House and grounds, 1st Sun in month Easter–Oct and Bank Hol Sun (incl. Easter) 2–5pm. During Rochester Dickens Festivals (June and Dec) 11–4.30pm. At other times by arrangement. Parties welcome. Rooms, including newly restored conservatory, can be hired for weddings/parties (wedding licence). Free coach/car parking. **Admission:** £2.50, Child £1.50. Parties by arrangement. Proceeds to restoration fund. **Refreshments:** Sundays, cream teas; Dickens Weekends, Dickensian refreshments; other catering by arrangement.

map 5 G4

HALL PLACE
Bourne Road, Bexley, DA5 1PQ, Kent
Tel: 01322 526 574 Fax: 01322 522 921
(Bexley Council)

Historic house built in 1540, with additions c.1650, set in award-winning gardens. Magnificent Tudor Great Hall, now used extensively for weddings and other functions. Museum and changing exhibition programme. Outstanding rose, rock and herb gardens and topiary. Conservatories, parkland and floral bedding displays. **Location:** Near the junction of A2 and A223. **Station(s):** Bexley (half a mile). **Open:** House: Mon–Sat, 10–5pm (4.15pm in winter). British Summer Time only – Suns, 2–6pm. Park & Grounds: Daily during daylight all year. **Admission:** Free. **Refreshments:** At café & restaurant.

map 5 F4

IGHTHAM MOTE
Ivy Hatch, Sevenoaks, Kent TN15 ONT
Tel: 01732 810378 Fax: 01732 811029

Ightham Mote, a moated medieval manor house, originates from the 14th century. Grade I Listed building and a Scheduled Monument constructed largely from oak timbers and local ragstone. Bequeathed to the National Trust in 1985 by an American businessman, Charles Henry Robinson, and the focus of the largest conservation project ever undertaken by the Trust on a house of this age and fragility. Visitors are able to visit ' Conservation in Action' Exhibition in the Visitor Reception building. Free Introductory Talks and Garden Tours are normally available. Estate walks. Booked special guided tours for groups of 15 or more on open weekday mornings only. **Open:** 1 Apr–4 Nov, daily except Tues & Sat, 11–5.30pm (last entry 4.30pm) incl. Sun & BH. **Admission:** House & Gardens: Adult £5, Child £2.50, Family ticket £12.50. **Refreshments:** Tea Pavilion & Shop.

map 5 G5

KNOLE
Sevenoaks, Kent
Tel: 01732 462100 Fax: 01732 465528 (The National Trust)

Tour 13 magnificent state rooms in one of the great treasure houses of England – a 'calendar' house dating from the 15th century with 365 rooms, 52 staircases and 7 courtyards. Find the treasures of kings and queens; exquisite silver furniture, fragile tapestries, rare carpets and other unique furniture including the first 'Knole' settee, state beds and even an early royal loo! Enjoy the extensive deer park throughout the year by courtesy of Lord Sackville. **Location:** located off M25 at south end of Sevenoaks, Kent. **Open:** 31 Mar-4 Nov: Wed–Sat, 12–4pm (last entry 3.30pm). Sun & BH Mon & Good Fri, 11–5pm (last entry 4pm). **Admission:** Adult £5, Child £2.50, Family £12.50, Group £4.25. Car park £2.50 - members free.

map 5 F5

HEVER CASTLE AND GARDENS

Nr Edenbridge, Kent TN8 7NG
Tel: 01732 865224 Fax: 01732 866796 (Hever Castle Ltd)

Hever Castle is a romantic 13th century moated castle, once the childhood home of Anne Boleyn. In 1903, William Waldorf Astor bought the castle and created beautiful gardens. He filled the castle with wonderful furniture, paintings and tapestries which visitors can enjoy today. The spectacular award-winning gardens include topiary, Italian and Tudor gardens, a 110 metre herbaceous border and a lake. A yew maze (open May–Oct) and a unique water maze (open April–Oct) are also in the gardens. The Miniature Model Houses Exhibition must also be seen. **Location:** Hever Castle is 30 miles from London, 3 miles SE of Edenbridge. Exit M25 junctions 5 or 6. Stations: Edenbridge Town 3 miles (taxis available), Hever 1 mile (no taxis). **Open:** Daily 1 Mar–30 Nov. Gardens open 11am. Castle opens 12 noon. Last admission 5pm. Final exit 6pm. Mar & Nov 11–4pm. **Admission:** Castle and garden ticket, Gardens only ticket and family ticket. Group discounts also available (minimum 15). Pre-booked guided tours of the castle available for groups. **Refreshments:** Two licensed self-service restaurants serving hot and cold food throughout the day. Picnics welcome. **Events:** Special events include Merrie England Weekend: 26–28 May, Patchwork & Quilting Exhibition: 14–16 Sept and Rose Week: 22–28 June. **Conferences:** Exclusive luxury conference facilities available in the Tudor Village.

E-mail: mail@hevercastle.co.uk **Internet:** www.hevercastle.co.uk

map 5
F5

LEEDS CASTLE AND GARDENS

Maidstone, Kent ME17 1PL.
Tel: 01622 765400 Fax: 01622 735616 (Leeds Castle Foundation)

Standing majestically on two islands in the middle of a natural lake, Leeds Castle is one of England's oldest and most romantic stately homes. Known as "the loveliest Castle in the world", Leeds was home to six of the medieval Queens of England, and most famous of monarchs, King Henry VIII. It now contains a magnificent collection of furnishings, tapestries and paintings. Leeds Castle is surrounded by 500 acres of rolling parkland and superb gardens which include a Wood Garden with meandering streams and the Culpeper Garden – many people's idea of the perfect English country garden. Opened in May 1999, the terraced, Mediterranean-style Lady Baillie Garden has intimate suntraps and stunning views over the Great Water. Other attractions at the Castle include a unique Dog Collar Museum, a maze and secret underground grotto, greenhouses, a vineyard and an exotic bird aviary housing more than 100 species of rare and endangered birds. **Events:** An extensive programme of events include Open Air Concerts on 30 June and 7 July, the Festival of English Food & Wine on 12–13 May and the Balloon & Vintage Car Weekend on 8–9 Sept. **Location:** 4 miles east of Maidstone, M20/A20 Junction 8. **Open:** All year (except 30 June, 7 July and 25 Dec 2001). **Admission:** Please phone 01622 765400 for details. **Internet:** www.leeds–castle.co.uk

map 5
G5

MAIDSTONE MUSEUM & BENTLIF ART GALLERY
St Faith's Street, Maidstone, Kent, ME14 1LH
Tel: 01622 754497 Fax: 01622 685022

An exceptional regional museum housed in an Elizabethan manor house. Collections include fine art, Egyptology, archaeology, ethnography and the finest collection of Japanese art outside London. The museum offers a varied and exciting rage of children's activities and workshops and a colourful series of temporary exhibitions. New galleries include costume, local history, local ecology and the installation of two moving dinosaurs as well as a display on Maidstone's Iguanodon. Also incorporated is the Queen's Own Royal West Kent Regimental Museum, a general collection of Regimental Colours, medals, weapons, uniforms and militaria of the Queen's Own Royal West Kent Regiment and its forebears, the 50th Regiment, 97th Foot, West Kent Militia, West Kent Light Infantry Militia, the 20th London Regiment and Kent Cyclists Battalions. **Open:** Mon–Sat 10am–5pm. Sun 11am–4pm. **Admission:** Free.

map 5
G5

MUSEUM OF KENT LIFE
Cobtree, Loch Lane, Sandling, Maidstone, Kent ME14 3AU
Tel: 01622 763936 Fax: 01622 662024

Kent's open-air Museum boasts a collection of historic buildings housing exhibitions on life in Kent over the past 100 years. Including oast, granary, hoppers huts, farmhouse, village hall & cottages. With hop, herb & kitchen gardens, farmyard, adventure playground and boat trip. **Location:** M20, junction 6, A229 to Maidstone. **Open:** March–end October. **Admission:** Adults £4.70, Conc £3.20, Family £14. **E-mail:** enquiries@museum-kentlife.co.uk
Internet: www.museum-kentlife.co.uk

map 5
G5

THE NEW COLLEGE OF COBHAM
Cobhambury Road, Cobham, Nr Gravesend, Kent DA12 3BG
Tel: 01474 812503 (The New College of Cobham Trust)

Almshouses based on medieval chantry built 1362, part rebuilt 1598. Originally endowed by Sir John de Cobham and descendants. **Location:** 4 miles W of Rochester; 4 miles SE of Gravesend; 1½ miles from junction Shorne-Cobham (A2). In Cobham rear of Church of Mary Magdelene. **Station(s):** Sole St (1 mile). **Open:** Apr–Sept, daily 10–7pm. Oct–Mar, daily 10–4pm. **Refreshments:** Afternoon teas by prior arrangement. Guided tours and historical talk by prior arrangement.

map 5
G4

OWL HOUSE GARDENS
Lamberhurst, Kent TN3 8LY
Tel: 01892 891290 Fax: 01892 891222

This is the property of the late Maureen, Marchioness of Dufferin & Ava and the setting of her 16th Century half-timbered and tile-hung smuggler's cottage, once surrounded by a cabbage patch and ploughed fields when the property was purchased in 1952. It now comprises 16 acres of romantic gardens; in Spring the expansive lawns are filled with daffodils and the trees with apple and cherry blossom; the woodland gardens carpeted with bluebells and primroses. Rhododendrons, azaleas and camellias encircle the informal sunken water gardens, **Open:** Daily except Christmas Day and New Years Day. **Admission:** Adult £4, children £1. Coach parties welcome by appointment. Dogs welcome on leads.

map 5
G5

PORT LYMPNE WILD ANIMAL PARK, MANSION & GARDENS
Lympne, Hythe, nr Folkestone, Kent CT21 4PD
Tel: 01303 264647 Fax: 01303 264944 (the John Aspinall Foundation)

Described as "the last historic house built this century", the mansion was designed by Sir Herbert Baker for Sir Philip Sassoon, who spared no expense in its building. It played host to many important members of pre-war society including Edward and Mrs Simpson, Queen Mary, Winston Churchill, Mountbatten and Charlie Chaplin. Inside there are two magnificent mural rooms painted by Arthur Spencer Roberts and Martin Jordan, the Rex Whistler Tent Room and a wonderful Moorish patio. With 15 acres of terraced gardens, the 400-acre wild animal park is home to John Aspinall's gorillas, elephants, tigers, rhinos and many more. **Open:** Every day except Christmas. Please check that the mansion is open before visit as there are several booked functions.

map 5
H5

PENSHURST PLACE AND GARDENS

Penshurst, Nr Tonbridge, Kent TN11 8DG
Tel: 01892 870307 Fax: 01892 870866 (Viscount & Viscountess De L'Isle)

The Ancestral home of the Sidney Family since 1552, with a history going back six and a half centuries, Penshurst Place has been described as "the grandest and most perfectly preserved example of a fortified manor house in all England". See the awe-inspiring medieval Barons Hall with its 60ft high chestnut beamed roof, where Kings, Queens, noblemen, poets and great soldiers have all dined. The Staterooms contain fine collections of tapestries, furniture, portraits, porcelain and armour from the 15th, 16th, 17th and 18th centuries. They chart the history of the family whose forebears include the Elizabethan poet, courtier and soldier, Sir Philip Sidney. On his death in 1586 he was accorded the honour of a state funeral at St Pauls Cathedral, the first commoner to receive such a tribute and not to be repeated until the death of Nelson and later, Sir Winston Churchill. The Gardens, first laid out in the 16th century have remarkably remained virtually unaltered during 400 years. A network of trimmed yew hedges and flower terraces make up the 10 acre patchwork of individual garden rooms designed to give colour all year round. Other features include a toy museum, adventure playground, shop, plant centre, restaurant, 200 acre park with lakes and a nature trail. Penshurst Place offers an exquisite arena for corporate and private entertainment amidst beautiful Kent countryside. **Open:** Weekends from 3 Mar. Daily: 31 Mar–31 Oct. Grounds: 10.30–6pm. House: 12–5pm. Shop & Plant Centre: 10.30–6pm. **Admission:** House & Gardens: Adults £6, OAPs £5.50, Child (5–16) £4, Family Ticket £16. Adult Party (20+) £5.30. Gardens only: Adults £4.50, OAPs £4, Children (5–16) £3.50, Family Ticket £13. Garden season ticket £25. House Tours: Adults £6, Children £3.20. Garden Tours: Adults £6.50, Children £4. House & Garden Tours: Adults £8. **E-mail:** enquiries@penshurstplace.com **Internet:** www.penshurstplace.com

map 5 F5

SCOTNEY CASTLE GARDEN
Lamberhurst, Tunbridge Wells, Kent TN3 8JN
Tel: 01892 891081 Fax: 01892 890110 (The National Trust)

One of England's most romantic gardens designed in the picturesque style, surrounding the ruins of a 14th century moated castle. Rhododendrons, azaleas, roses, water-lilies and wisteria flower in profusion. Also renowned for its autumn colour. The surrounding estate, open all year, has many country walks. **Location:** located off A21 south of Lamberhurst village. **Open:** 17-25 Mar: weekends only 12–4pm. 31 Mar–4 Nov(Old Castle May–mid Sept): Wed–Fri, 11–6pm. Sat–Sun, 2–6pm. BH Sun & Mon, 12–6pm (closed Good Fri). Last admission 1hr before close. **Admission:** Adult £4.40, Child £2.20, Family £11. Pre-booked groups £3.80.

map5 G5

SMALLHYTHE PLACE
Smallhythe, Tenterden, Kent TN30 7NG
Tel/Fax: 01580 762334 (National Trust)

Beautiful half-timbered cottage, much-loved home of the legendary Shakespearean actress Dame Ellen Terry. Contains fascinating theatrical and personal mementoes including items belonging to Sir Henry Irving, Sarah Siddons, Oscar Wilde and Sarah Bernhardt. Central to the collection are the sumptuous stage costumes, dating from Dame Ellen's partnership with Henry Irving at the Lyceum Theatre. Pretty cottage garden and rose garden and in spring a lovely display of daffodils and Snake's Head fritillaria. Also the Barn Theatre is open most days by courtesy of the Barn Theatre Society. **Location:** OS Ref. TQ893 300. 2 miles South of Tenterden on East side of Rye road B2082. **Open:** 31 Mar–31 Oct 2001, 1.30–6pm. Last admission ½ hour before closing. **Admission:** Adult £3.20, Child £1.60, Family £8.

map 5 H6

RIVERHILL HOUSE GARDENS
Riverhill, Sevenoaks, Kent TN15 0RR
Tel 01732 458802/452557 Fax: 01732 458802 (The Rogers Family)

A lived in family home. Panelled rooms, portraits and interesting memorabilia. Historic hillside garden with sheltered terraces. Rhododendrons, azaleas and bluebells in natural woodland. Rare trees. **Location:** Close to Knole. 2 miles S of Sevenoaks on A225. **Station:** Sevenoaks. **Open:** April, May & June only. Gardens: Every Wed, Sun and all Bank Hol weekends during above period. 12–6pm. The house is also open but only to pre-booked groups of adults, 20 upwards, any day during above period. **Admission:** Gardens: Adults £3, Child 50p. House & Garden: £4. **Refreshments:** Home-made teas on open days, Ploughmans lunches, teas etc by arrangement for party bookings any day in April, May or June. No dogs. Unsuitable for disabled. Specialising year round in country house luncheon and dinner parties for from 12–24 visitors.

map 5 F5

SQUERRYES COURT
Manor House & Gardens, Westerham, Kent TN16 1SJ
Tel: 01959 562345/563118 Fax: 01959 565949 (Mr J St. A Warde)

Squerryes Court is a beautiful, privately owned Manor House built in 1681 in a parkland setting. The house was acquired by the Warde family in 1731 and is lived in by the same family today. The Old Master paintings, furniture, porcelain and tapestries were collected by the Wardes in the 18th century. The lovely gardens, landscaped in the 18th century, are interesting throughout the year with a lake, spring bulbs, borders, recently restored formal garden, topiary and 18th century dovecote. **Location:** Western outskirts of Westerham signposted from A25. Junctions 5 & 6 M25 10 mins. **Station(s):** Oxted or Sevenoaks. **Open:** 1 Apr–30 Sept. Wed, Sat, Sun & BH Mon. Garden: 12–5.30pm.. House 1.30–5.30pm (last entry 5pm).

Admission: House and Grounds: Adults £4.20, OAPs £3.80, Children (under 14) £2.50. Garden only: Adults £2.50, OAPs £2.20, Children (under 14) £1.50. Parties over 20 (any day) by arrangement House and Grounds £3.60. Garden only £2.20. Guided (small extra charge). Pre-booked lunches/teas. Restaurant licence. **Refreshments:** Home-made teas served in Old Library from 2–5pm on open days. **Conferences:** House and Grounds are available for private hire all year e.g. marquee wedding receptions, corporate conferences, luncheons, dinners, promotions, launches, clay pigeon shoots. Dogs on leads in grounds only. Free parking at house. **E-mail:** squerryescourt@pavilion.co.uk

map 5 F5

TONBRIDGE CASTLE
Tonbridge, Kent TN9 1BG
Tel: 01732 770929 Fax: 01732 770449 (Tonbridge & Malling Borough Council)

A fine example of the layout of a Norman Motte and Bailey Castle set in landscaped gardens overlooking the River Medway. The site is clearly interpreted. Tours are available from the Tourist Information Centre. **Location:** In town centre off High Street. **Station(s):** Tonbridge (Main line Charing Cross). **Open:** Apr–Sept Mon–Sat 9–5pm, Sun and BH 10.30–5pm; Oct–Mar, Mon–Fri 9–5pm, Sat 9–4pm, Sun 10.30–4pm. Last tours 1 hr before closing time. Self guided headset tours available from the Tourist Information Centre. Tours in English, French, Dutch and German. **Admission:** Adult £3.60, Child/OAP £1.80, Family (2+2) £8.50. **Refreshments:** Nearby. **Accommodation:** Nearby. **E-mail:** tonbridge.castle@tmbe.gov.uk

map 5
G5

TUNBRIDGE WELLS MUSEUM AND ART GALLERY
Civic Centre, Mount Pleasant, Royal Tunbridge Wells, TN1 1JN
Tel: 01892 554171

The museum has displays of local history, dolls and toys, archaeology, agricultural and domestic bygones and natural history. There is also an unrivalled collection of Tunbridge ware, a woodware made locally since the 1600s. In the art gallery there are frequently changing exhibitions which show a wide range of art and craft from modern art to miniatures and from Victorian oils to pottery. There are occasional displays from the museum's reserve collections, including the Ashton Bequest of Victorian oil paintings, photographs by Henry Peach Robinson and works by the Dodd family of Tunbridge Wells artists. **Open:** Daily 9.30am–5pm. Closed Sundays, Bank Holidays and Easter Sunday. **Admission:** Free. **Internet:** www.tunbridgewells.gov.uk/museum

map 5
G5

TYRWHITT-DRAKE MUSEUM OF CARRIAGES
Archbishops' Stables, Mill Street, Maidstone, Kent ME15 6YE
Tel: 01622 754497   Fax: 01622 685022

Housed in the historic 14th Century Archbishops' Stables, visitors can witness this remarkable collection of vehicles started by former Mayor of Maidstone, Sir Garrard Tyrwhitt-Drake. He set about collecting horse drawn vehicles as motor cars began to replace them. The collection varies from Queen Alexandra's rickshaw, to the Mayor of Maidstone's ceremonial landau, from a costermongers' barrow to an 18th Century sedan chair, and includes a stunning mail phaeton as well as a ceremonial state chariot. Ambitious plans for the future include the relocation and enlargement of this national collection to a specially designed park site. **E-mail:** evelynglover@tourism.gov.uk
Internet: www.maidstone.museum.gov.uk

map 5
G5

WALMER CASTLE & GARDENS
Kingsdown Road, Walmer, Deal, Kent CT14 7LJ
Tel: 01304 364288 (English Heritage)

Walmer Castle was originally built by Henry VIII to defend the south coast but has since been transformed into an elegant stately home. As the residence of the Lords Warden of the Cinque Ports, Walmer was used by the Duke of Wellington (don't miss the Duke's famous 'Wellington boots') and is still used today by HM the Queen Mother. Many of her rooms are open to view. Recently opened are the Queen Mother's Gardens that commemorate her 95th birthday. The gardens are stunning in summer and the herbaceous borders are exceptional. **Location:** On coast S of Walmer on A258. **Open:** 1 Apr–30 Sept: daily 10am–6pm. 1 Oct–31 Oct: daily 10am–5pm. 1 Nov–31 Dec & 1–28 Mar: Wed–Sun 10–4pm. Jan & Feb: Sat & Sun only, 10am–4pm. Closed 24–26 Dec, 1 Jan and when Lord Warden is in residence. **Admission:** Adult £4.80, Conc £3.60, Child £2.40. 15% discount for groups of 11 or more.

map 5
J5

GRAHAM CLARKE
UP THE GARDEN STUDIO
Green Lane, Boughton Monchelsea,
Maidstone, Kent ME 17 4LF
Tel:01622 743938 Fax: 01622 747229

A visit to Graham Clarke's studio offers an opportunity to view more than one hundred of his hand-coloured limited edition etchings, posters and greeting cards, depicting English rural life and history, the Bible and the Englishman's view of Europe. Also his books, including the recently published Graham Clarke's Cornwall - Bait Box Stew, a Cornish Sketchbook and Graham Clarke's Kent - a Kentish Sketchbook. Details of Studio Open Days are available on request, the Studio being open by appointment at other times. **Admission:** Free. Groups are welcome by prior arrangement. Wheelchair access. **E-mail:** info@grahamclarke.co.uk
Internet: www.grahamclarke.co.uk

map 5
G5

YALDING ORGANIC GARDENS
Benover Road, Yalding, Near Maidstone, Kent ME18 6EX
Tel & Fax: 01622 814650

Highly acclaimed gardens run by HDRA – the organic organisation. Set against a traditional Kentish backdrop of hop gardens and oast houses they illustrate beautifully gardening through the ages. Themed display gardens guide visitors from Medieval times through to the present day. These include an Apothecary's Garden, a Tudor Knot Garden, superb herbaceous borders, a stimulating Children's Garden and a Garden of the Future. There is a regular programme of events and tours and garden staff on hand to give organic gardening advice. An organic café offers morning coffee, home cooked lunches and afternoon teas. Freshly prepared dishes often use ingredients from the gardens. The shop stocks all the essentials the organic gardener might need plus quality gifts and books. We look forward to your visit! **Internet:** www.hdra.org.uk

map 5
G5

Lancashire

Ribble Valley

Lancashire is blessed with beauty, charm and even grandeur – and much maligned by the stereotypical image of dreary industrial mines, mills, ugly towns and smoke-blackened countryside.

In reality, the visitor will find farming land with great expanses of cornfields, meadows, pleasant vales and bare moorlands.

The north of the county has some of the finest mountain and lake scenery in Britain, and the Forest of Bowland and the Ribble Valley both offer fantastic views.

The historic county town of Lancaster is tiny when compared to Liverpool and Manchester, but it boasts a long history. Today, its university and cultural life still thrive and the Norman castle, Georgian streets, Lune Aqueduct and a smattering of museums will fascinate the traveller.

ASTLEY HALL MUSEUM & ART GALLERY
Astley Park, Chorley PR7 1NP
Tel: 01257 515555 Fax: 01257 515556

A charming house with a timber-framed courtyard dating back to the 1580s. Additions in the 1660s included rebuilding the front façade and the construction of sumptuous plaster ceilings. A new wing and a landscaped park added in about 1800 complete the story of the house. Interiors include fine oak furniture and tapestries. A programme of temporary exhibitions and special events supplements any visit to the house. **Open:** Easter–Oct: Tues–Sun 12–5pm, Nov–Mar: weekends only 12–4pm. **Admission:** Adult £2.90, Conc £1.90, Family £7. Special group and educational rates – enquire for details.
E-mail: astleyhall@lineone.net **Internet:** www.astleyhall.co.uk

map 6
B1

BROWSHOLME HALL
Nr Clitheroe, Lancashire BB7 3DE
Tel: 01254 826719 Fax: 01254 826739 (Robert Redmayne Parker)

Built in 1507 and set in a landscaped park, the Ancestral home of the Parker family, with an Elizabethan façade and Regency West Wing recast by Sir Jeffrey Wyatville. Portraits (incl. Devis & Romney), a major collection of furniture, arms, stained glass and other strange antiquities from stone age axes to fragment of a zepellin. **Location:** 5 miles NW of Clitheroe: off B6243; Bashall Eaves–Whitewell signposted. **Open:** 2–4pm May Spring Bank Hol Sun and Bank Hol Mon, 1–14 July (except Mondays) and 14 Aug–Aug Bank Hol Mon (except other Mondays). **Admission:** Adults £4, Children £1. Booked parties particularly welcome by appointment. **Internet:** www.browsholme.co.uk

map 11
F7

GAWTHORPE HALL
Padiham, Nr Burnley, Lancashire BB12 8UA
Tel: 01282 771004 Fax: 01282 770178

An Elizabethan gem in the heart of industrial Lancashire. The Rachel Kay-Shuttleworth textile collections exhibited. Portrait collection loaned by National Portrait Gallery. Events and exhibitions during high season. **Open:** Hall 1 Apr–31 Oct: daily except Mon and Fri, open Good Fri & BH Mondays. 1–5pm. Last admission 4.30pm. Garden: all year, daily 10–6pm. Tearoom open as Hall 12.30–5pm. **Admission:** Hall: Adults £3, Children £1.30, Family ticket £8, Concessions £1.50 (charges maybe subject to change). Garden: free. Parties by prior arrangement. Free parking 150m. Hall not suitable for baby-packs or pushchairs. **Location:** ¾ mile out of Padiham on A671 to Burnley. Bus services from Burnley (Barracks & Manchester Road Tel: 01282 423125.) Railway station 2m (Rose Grove). Managed by Lancashire County Council. Free to NT members.

map 8
B3

HARRIS MUSEUM AND ART GALLERY
Market Square, Preston, Lancashire PR1 2PP
Tel: 01772 258248 Fax: 01772 886764

The Harris is a Magnificent Grade I Greek Revival building holding collections of fine and decorative art, costume and social history as well as an acclaimed programme of temporary exhibitions. **Admission:** Free.
E-mail: harris@pbch.demon.co.uk **Internet:** www.preston.gov.uk

map 6
A1

STONYHURST COLLEGE
Stonyhurst, Clitheroe. Lancashire BB7 9PZ
Tel: 01254 826345 Fax: 01254 826732

The original house (situated close to the picturesque village of Hurst Green in the beautiful Ribble Valley) dates from the late 16th century. Set in extensive grounds which include ornamental gardens. The College is a co-educational Catholic boarding & day school, founded by the Society of Jesus in 1593. **Location:** Just off the B6243 (Longridge–Clitheroe) on the outskirts of Hurst Green. 10 miles from junction 31 on M6. **Station(s):** Preston. **Open:** House weekly 16 July–27 Aug, daily except Fri (incl. Aug Bank Hol Mon) 1–5pm. Grounds and Gardens weekly 1 July–28 Aug, daily except Fri (incl. Aug BHol Mon) 1–5pm. **Admission:** House and Grounds £4.50, Child (4–14) £3.50 (under 4 free), Senior Citizens £3.50. Grounds only £1. **Refreshments:** Refreshments/Gift shop: Limited facilities for disabled. Coach parties & evening groups by prior arrangement. No dogs permitted.

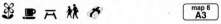

map 8
A3

RUFFORD OLD HALL
Rufford, Nr Ormskirk, L40 1SG
Tel: 01704 821254 Fax: 01704 821254 (The National Trust)

Come and enjoy the former ancestral home of the Lords of the Manor of Rufford, one of Lancashire's finest 16th century buildings. There's a glorious garden, kitchen restaurant and shop and within the House, a wide variety of tapestries, arms, armour and paintings. The Great Hall has an intricately carved movable wooden screen and dramatic hammerbeam roof. **Location:** 7 miles N of Ormskirk, in the village of Rufford on E side of A59. **Open:** 31 Mar–4 Nov, Sat–Wed 1–5pm. Garden open same days, 12-5.30pm **Admission:** House and garden £3.80, Children £1.90, Family ticket £9.50. Garden only: £2.

map 6
B2

TOWNHEAD HOUSE
Slaidburn, Clitheroe, Lancashire
Tel: 01772 421566

Notice is hereby given that part of Townhead House (unfurnished) a Grade II★ Listed Building at Slaidburn, near Clitheroe will be open to the Public for viewing on: 13–16 Apr, 4 May-7 May, 25–28 May, 29 June–2 July, 27–30 July, 24–27 Aug, 21–23 Sept 2001. On each occasion the House will be open between the hours of 2–5pm. A £1 charge will be made for entry. For further information, apply to: John Forrester, Chartered Surveyor and Land Agent, First Floor, 19/21 Chapel Brow, Leyland, Preston PR5 2NH Tel: 01772 421566

map 8
A2

TOWNELEY HALL ART GALLERY & MUSEUMS
Burnley, Lancashire, BB11 3RQ
Tel: 01282 424213 Fax: 01282 436138 (Burnley Borough Council)

The former home of the Towneley family, dating from the 14th century, has been an Art Gallery and Museum since 1903. Collections include oak furniture, 18th and 19th century paintings and decorative arts. Loan exhibitions. There is a Natural History Centre with aquarium and nature trails in the grounds. A separate museum of Local Crafts and Industries is housed in the former brew-house. **Location:** ½ mile SE of Burnley on the Burnley/Todmorden Road (A671). Station(s): Burnley Central (½ miles). **Open:** All the year Mon–Fri 10–5pm, Sun 12–5pm, closed Sat throughout year and Christmas–New Year. Guided tours available Tuesday, Wednesday and Thursday at 3pm (small charge). There maybe some restrictions due to redevelopment work late 2001 and 2002. **Admission:** Free. **Refreshments:** At cafe on grounds.

map 8
B3

WIGAN PIER
Trencherfield Mill, Wigan, Lancashire WN3 4EF
Tel: 01942 323 666 Fax: 01942 701 972 (Wigan Council)

The award-winning Wigan Pier Experience is set in an 8½-acre site beside the re-developed Leeds and Liverpool Canal. This family attraction offers hours of great fun and entertainment. You can capture the scene of yesteryear with a look at 'The Way We Were' Heritage Centre; here you can sit with back 'ram rod' straight in the Victorian schoolroom, visit the 'Palace of Varieties' Music Hall or follow a promenade play. Afterwards, hop on a waterbus and see our newest attraction, the £2.2m Opie's Museum of Memories. This unique attraction will take you on an extraordinary journey through the 20th century examining fashions, packaging, music and the events which will bring back your fondest memories. **Open:** All year except Christmas Day, Boxing Day and all day Friday. Mon–Thurs 10am–5pm, Sat & Sun 11am–5pm. **Admission:** Charge.

map 8
A4

Leicestershire

Within Leicestershire's borders, the Midlands meet the level stretches of East Anglia and merge into gentle, undulating countryside.

Leicester itself was founded by the Romans, and is home to one of the country's oldest buildings, the Old Town Hall. Here, under the magnificent oak-beamed roof, Shakespeare is reputed to have recited verses to Queen Elizabeth.

During Saxon times, the city was the seat of the East Mercian bishops, and possessed a royal castle during the reign of the House of Lancaster.

Town Hall Square, Leicester

The Manor House, Coalville

The countryside also has much to offer the visitor: Charnwood Forest and Martinshaw Woods are good spots for walking, as is the newly-opened National Forest Centre in the west of the county. The Beacon Hill stands 803 feet tall in the heart of Charnwood Forest, and affords marvellous views over the Trent and Soar Valleys. The rocks around the summit were formed by volcanoes some 700 million years ago, when the area lay under the sea.

BELVOIR CASTLE
Nr Grantham, Lincolnshire NG32 1PD
Tel: 01476 870262 (Duke of Rutland)

Seat of the Dukes of Rutland since Henry VIII's time and rebuilt by Wyatt in 1816. A castle in the grand style, commanding magnificent views over the Vale of Belvoir. The name dates back to the famous Norman Castle that stood on this site. Many notable art treasures, and interesting military relics. The Statue gardens contain many beautiful 17th century sculptures. Flowers in bloom throughout most of the season. Medieval Jousting Tournaments and other weekend events. Conference and filming facilities. Banquets, school visits, private parties. **Location:** 7 m WSW of Grantham, between A607 (to Melton Mowbray) and A52 (to Nottingham). **Open:** Daily 11am–5pm: 13–17 Apr inc, Sun 22 & 29

April, May–Sept daily, Oct Sundays only. Other times for groups by appointment. **Admission:** Adults £6, Children £3.50, Senior Citizens £5.50. Parties 20+: Adults £5.50, Seniors £5, Family Ticket £16.00 (2+2). School parties £3. Privilege Card holders – party rate. Ticket office and catering facilities in the Castle close approximately 30 mins before the Castle. Guide books are on sale at the ticket office or inside the Castle, or by post £3.50 include. post and packing. We regret that dogs are not permitted (except guide dogs). Leaflet sent free on application. **E-mail:** info@belvoircastle.com **Internet:** www.belvoircastle.com

map 8
E6

KAYES GARDEN NURSERY

1700 Melton Road, Rearsby, Leicester, Leicestershire LE7 4YR
Tel: 01664 424578 (Mrs Hazel Kaye)

Set in the lovely rural Wreake Valley, this all-year garden houses an extensive collection of interesting and unusual hardy plants. A long pergola leads the visitor into the garden and forms a backdrop to the double herbaceous borders. Mixed beds beyond are filled with a wide range of herbaceous plants, shrubs and shrub roses in subtle colour coordinated groups. A stream dissects the garden and ends in a large wild life pond alive with a myriad of dragonflies. Aromatic herbs surround a much favoured seat which looks out across one of the garden ponds towards flower beds shaded by old fruit trees, where hellebores, ferns and many other shade loving plants abound. **Open:** Mar–Oct incl. Tues–Sat 10–5pm Sun 10am–noon. Nov–Feb incl. Fri & Sat 10–4.30. Closed Dec 25–Jan 31 incl. **Admission:** Entrance to garden £2. Coach parties welcome by appointment.

map 8
D6

LEICESTER CITY MUSEUMS SERVICE

New Walk Museum, New Walk, Leicester LE1 7EA
Tel: 0116 255 4100

Leicester City Museums Service have some of the finest objects of local, national and international importance, covering social history, fine, modern and decorative art, technology, biology, geology and archaeology. In fact, something for everyone.... Discover ancient Egyptians, dinosaurs, rocks and fossils, German Expressionists, Modern, Decorative and European art, the Royal Leicestershire Regiment, the Iron Age, Romans, Saxons, Normans, Victorians, Social and Industrial History and Arts and Crafts from around the world. And all located within some of Leicester's finest buildings. For details of opening times, facilities, events and exhibitions, please contact Leicester City Museums Service, New Walk Museum, New Walk, Leicester LE1 7EA. Tel: 0116 255 4100, **E-mail:** hidem001@leicester.gov.uk **Internet:** www.leicestermuseums.co.uk

map 8
D7

COUGHTON GALLERIES

The Old Manor, Arthingworth,
Market Harborough, Leics. LE16 8JT
Tel: 01858 525 436 Fax: 01858 525 535

(Lady Isabel Throckmorton)

Coughton Galleries Ltd, previously at Coughton Court, Alcester, Warwickshire, for 25 years, moved to Arthingworth in 1992. The Gallery carries a large stock of 20th century British, Irish and Scottish oil paintings and watercolours, many by Royal Academicians. **Location:** Arthingworth lies 5 miles SE of Market Harborough and 1 mile off the A508 Market Harborough/Northampton Road with access to the A14 just 2 miles away. **Open:** All year round, 10.30am–5pm, Wed, Thurs, Sat, Sun, Bank Holidays & by appointment.

map 4
D7

STANFORD HALL

Lutterworth, Leicestershire, LE17 6DH
Tel: 01788 860250 Fax: 01788 860870 (The Lady Braye)

William and Mary house, fine pictures (including the Stuart Collection), furniture and family costumes. Replica 1898 flying machine, motorcycle museum, rose garden, nature trail. Craft centre (most Sundays). **Location:** M1 exit 18, M1 exit 19 (from/to North only); M6 exit at A14/M1(N) junction. **Open:** 7 April–end Sept, Sats, Suns, Bank Hol Mons and Tues following 1.30–5.30pm (last admission 5pm). Museum open Suns & BH Mons only. On Bank Hols and event days open 12 noon (house 1.30pm). **Admission:** House and grounds: Adult £4.20, Child £2. Grounds only: Adult £2.50, Child £1. Prices subject to increase on some event days. Parties (min 20): Adult £3.90, Child £1.80. Museum: Adult £1, Child 35p. **Refreshments:** Home-made teas. Light lunches most Sundays. Suppers, teas, lunches for pre-booked parties any day during season. **E-mail:** stanford.hall@virginnet.co.uk

map 4
C1

WARTNABY GARDENS

Melton Mowbray, Leicestershire LE14 3HY
Tel: 01664 822296 Fax: 01664 822900 (Lord & Lady King)

This garden has delightful little gardens within it, including a white garden, a sunken garden, a purple border of plants, shrubs and roses, and there are good herbaceous borders, climbers and old-fashioned roses. Large ponds have an adjacent box garden with primulas, ferns, astilbes and several varieties of willow. There is an Arboretum with a good collection of trees and shrubs. Alongside the drive is a beech hedge in a Grecian pattern. Greenhouses, a fruit and vegetable garden with rose arches and cordon fruit. **Location:** OS Ref. SK709 228, 4 miles northwest of Melton Mowbray. From A606 turn west in Ab Kettleby for Wartnaby. **Open:** June, Sundays 11–4pm. Parties by appointment, weekdays (except Wednesdays). Open days: Sun 30 April & Sun 25 June, 11–4pm. Plant sales: 25 June only. **Admission:** Adult £2.50, Children free.

map 8
D6

Lincolnshire

The view from Bluestone Heath Road

One of the most unspoilt parts of rural England, Lincolnshire is a county of contrasts. The southwest corner is a patchwork of country houses, ancient woods, winding lanes and charming villages where time stands still. From here, the Lincoln Edge runs the length of the county, and rewards travellers with fantastic views across the rolling hills of the Wolds. The landscape then flattens towards the east coast, where fens and sandy beaches stretch out to a distant horizon. Thousands of miles of public footpaths and "Green Lanes" make this an excellent county for walking, cycling or riding.

When the Domesday Book was complied, Boston was not sufficiently established to merit a mention, but by the Middle Ages, it had become the country's second port. Its importance declined after the silting up of the harbour, but it went on to play a role in the colonisation of the New World. Some of the Pilgrim Fathers were imprisoned in Boston's Guildhall, before eventually being allowed to leave for America, and a monument to the founders of Boston, Massachusetts, stands in St Botolph's Church. The church itself is magnificent, with a 270-foot tower known locally as the Boston Stump.

Lincoln, the county town, was founded by the Romans in AD48 on a cliff overlooking the River Witham. Today, the spires of its cathedral rise majestically out of the flat fens, and are visible for many miles around.

AYSCOUGHFEE HALL MUSEUM & GARDENS
Churchgate, Spalding, Lincolnshire.
Tel: 01775 725468 Fax: 01775 762715

Ayscoughfee Hall is a late-Medieval wool merchants house set in five acres of walled gardens. The Hall is on the east bank of the River Welland five minutes walk from Spalding town centre. The fully Registered 'Museum of South Holland Life' is housed within the Hall and has galleries on local villages, the history of Spalding, agriculture and horticulture. The Museum also includes a gallery dedicated to Matthew Flinders, the District's most famous son, and many specimens from the important Ashley Maples bird collection are on display. Wheelchair access to ground floor of the hall only. **Open:** Garden café open seasonally, Mar–Sept. Museum: Mon–Sat 10–5pm. Sun & BHols 11–5pm. Exhibitions of local artists' work in the Geest Gallery, change monthly. The Spalding Tourist Information Centre is also housed within Ayscoughfee Hall. Hall closed winter weekends (Nov–Feb).

`map 9 6F`

AUBOURN HALL
Aubourn, Nr. Lincoln, Lincolnshire, LN5 9DZ
Tel: 01522 788 270

Late 16th century house attributed to J. Smythson (Jnr). Important carved staircase and panelled rooms. Lovely garden with deep borders, roses, pond and lawns. **Open:** "Aubourn Hall will not be open on a regular basis during 2001 The garden will be open on occasional Sundays". **Admission:** £3, OAPs £2.50. Disabled access to gardens only.

`map 9 E5`

BELTON HOUSE
Grantham, Lincolnshire NG32 2LS.
Tel: 01476 566116 Fax: 01476 579071

A beautiful Restoration country house, built 1685-88, and set in landscaped gardens. Fine tapestries, portraits, furniture, and porcelain on display, together with carvings from the Grinling Gibbons school. **Open:** 31 Mar–4 Nov, Wed–Sun and BH Mon (closed Good Friday), 1–5.30pm. **Admission:** Adult £5.40, Child £2.70

THE GUILDHALL MUSEUM
South Street, Boston PE21 6HT
Tel: 01205 365954 Fax: 01205359401
(Boston Borough Council)

Boston Guildhall is a fascinating 'time capsule' of history from 1450 when the Hall was built. In 1546, it became the Town Hall and is now a fascinating museum. Today, visitors can see the Cells and Courtroom where the Pilgrim Fathers were imprisoned and tried in 1607. You can now see Boston as it was in the 16th century through a virtual reality simulation - Boston AD1536. **Open:** Tues–Sat 10am–5pm, all year round. Sun 1.30–5pm, April–end September. **Admission:** Small admission charge. Entry is free to all on Thursdays. For more information call 01205 365954.

`map 9 6F`

BURGHLEY HOUSE

Stamford, Lincolnshire PE9 3JY

Tel: 01780 752451 Fax: 01780 480125 (Burghley House Preservation Trust Ltd)

The finest example of later Elizabethan architecture in England, built (1565-1587) by William Cecil, the most able and trusted adviser to Queen Elizabeth I. Eighteen magnificent state rooms are open to visitors. Those painted by Antonio Verrio in the late 17th century form one of the greatest decorated suites in England. Burghley is a sumptuous Treasure House and contains one of the finest private collections of 17th century Italian paintings in the world. There are superb collections of English and continental tapestries and furniture, many of which have been recently conserved. Burghley also houses the earliest inventoried collection of Oriental porcelain in the West. Works of art, silver, marbles and wood carving fill the state rooms. The house is surrounded by a large and beautiful deer park, landscaped by 'Capability' Brown in the late 18th century. Car parking and entry to the park is free. **Special events 2001:** The Huge Rainbow Craft Fair: 25–28 May; enquiries 01529 414793. Classical Concert in the Park - 'an American Dream' with fireworks finale: 30 June; enquiries 01625 560000. Gala Concert in the Park - Symphony Orchestra with fireworks and light extravaganza: 28 July; enquiries 01625 560000. The Burghley House Trials: 30 Aug–2 Sept; enquiries 01780 752131. **Refreshments:** Snacks, lunches and teas in the 'Capability' Brown Orangery. **Location:** 1 m SE of Stamford, clearly signposted from the A1 and all approaches. **Station(s):** Stamford (1 m), Peterborough (10 m). **Open:** 1 Apr–28 Oct daily. Closed 1 Sept. **Admission:** Adults £6.80, OAPs £6.30, accompanied children free (1 per adult, otherwise £3.30 per child). Party rates available. Enquiries for bookings, party rates & menus, telephone: 01780 752451.

map 8
E7

DODDINGTON HALL
Doddington, Lincoln LN6 4RU
Tel: 01522 694308 Fax: 01522 685259 (F.Watson)

Doddington Hall is a superb Elizabethan Mansion surrounded by walled gardens and courtyards and entered through a Tudor Gate House. It stands today as it was built, and its fascinating contents reflect 400 years of unbroken family occupation with fine china, textiles, furniture and family portraits. The gardens contain magnificent box-edged parterres, sumptuous borders and a wonderful succession of spring flowering bulbs that give colour in all seasons. **Open:** Gardens only: Sundays 2–6pm, 4 Feb–30 Apr. House & Gardens: Weds, Suns and Bank Hol Mons 2–6pm May–Sept. Groups & school parties at other times by appointment. **Admission:** Adults: house & gardens £4.50, gardens only £3.00. Children: house & gardens £2.25, gardens only £1.50. Family ticket £12.00. **E-mail:** doddingtonhall@doddingtonhall.free-online.co.uk **Internet:** www.doddingtonhall.free-online.co.uk

map 8 E5

ELSHAM HALL COUNTRY AND WILDLIFE PARK AND ELSHAM HALL BARN THEATRE
Brigg, North Lincolnshire DN20 0QZ
Tel: 01652 688698 Fax: 01652 688240 (Park Manager: Robert Elwes)

Beautiful lakes and gardens; miniature zoo; giant carp; falconry centre; wild butterfly walkway; adventure playground; mini–beast talks; garden and working craft centre: Granary tearooms and restaurant; animal farm; museum and art gallery; caravan site; ten National Awards. Also excellent new theatre with indoor winter and new outdoor summer programme with various festivals. **Location:** Near Brigg M180 Jct 5, near Humberside Airport. **Station(s):** Barnetby. **Open:** Times and prices on application. Contact Manager. **Refreshments:** Granary Tearooms, ice cream shop, restaurant, banqueting. **Conferences:** Conference facility. Licensed for civil weddings, medieval banquets and corporate entertainments/paintballing. **Internet:** www.brigg.com/elsham.htm

map 8 E3

EPWORTH OLD RECTORY
Epworth, Doncaster, South Yorkshire DN9 1HX
Tel: 01427 872268 (Andrew Milson)

Epworth Old Rectory is the childhood home of John and Charles Wesley. It was burnt down in 1709 and rebuilt at a cost of £400 within twelve months and remains the same magnificent Queen Anne building. John Wesley proceeded to found the Methodist Church and his brother, Charles, became one of the greatest hymn writers. Epworth Old Rectory remained as the Rectory to St Andrew's Church until 1954 when it was purchased by the Methodist Church, and in 1957 it was opened as a museum/house for members of the public to visit. People visit the Old Rectory from all over the world, and it is regarded as the birthplace of Methodism. The Old Rectory contains many items related to the Wesley family which include period furniture, prints, paintings and Wesley memorabilia. Limited disabled access.

map 8 B4

MARSTON HALL
Grantham
Tel: 01400 250225 (The Rev Henry Thorold, FSA) or 01400 250167 (Mrs Ballaam)

Tudor manor house with Georgian interiors, held by Thorold family since 14th century. Interesting pictures and furniture. Romantic garden with long walks and avenues, high hedges enclosing herbaceous borders and vegetables. Gothick gazebo and ancient trees. **Open:** Suns, 13 & 20 June, 25 July 1999, 2–6pm and by appointment. **Admission:** House & garden £2.50. **Refreshments:** Home-made cream teas. In aid of local causes. **Location:** 6 miles NW of Grantham.

map 8 E6

NORMANBY HALL
Normanby, Scunthorpe, North Lincolnshire, DN15 9HU
Tel: 01724 720588 Fax: 01724 721248 (North Lincolnshire Council)

The restored working Victorian Walled Garden is growing produce for the 'big house', as it would have been done 100 years ago. Victorian varieties of fruit and vegetables are grown using organic and Victorian techniques. Set in 300 acres of park, visitors can also see the Regency Mansion, designed by Sir Robert Smirke, which the Garden was built to serve. The rooms of the Hall are displayed in styles depicting the Regency, Victorian and Edwardian eras. Costume galleries and farming museum. **Location:** OS Ref. SE886 166. 4 miles North of Scunthorpe off B1430. Tours by arrangement. **Open:** Hall & Farming Museum: 26 Mar–30 Sept daily, 1–5pm. Park: All year daily, 9am–dusk. Walled Garden: All year daily, 10.30am–5pm (4pm winter). **Admission:** Summer Season: Adult £2.90, Conc £1.90, Family ticket (2 adults, 3 children) £8, discount for North Lincolnshire residents. Winter Season £2.20 per car.

map 8 3E

London

London is a city with a thousand faces, where every visitor is guaranteed to find something to their taste, and perhaps a few things that are not. One of the world's financial powerhouses, London nevertheless remains one of the greenest of all capital cities, with acres of parkland and quiet squares offering respite from the hectic pace of city life.

Recent years have seen a revival in London's international standing, and a massive programme of investment has ensured that it remains at the forefront of culture. Hollywood stars are now a regular sight on London stages, and Saatchi's "Britart" protégés are numbered amongst the most important artists of the day.

London is a city that continues to evolve, and nowhere is this more evident than in its skyline. London Bridge affords views not only of St Paul's Cathedral and of The Tower, but also of the

Regents Park and Lake

Somerset House

skyscrapers on Canary Wharf and of Bankside power station, now the Tate Modern. The London Eye, a 435ft tall observation wheel, is the newest addition to this panorama, and has fared far better than its near-contemporary, the Dome.

Seasoned visitors to London will be pleased to find that the Inland Revenue has finally moved most of its operations away from Somerset House, allowing the magnificent courtyard to open to the public. Away from the bustle of the City and the West End, visitors will find a host of fascinating places to visit, from the parks and historic buildings of Greenwich in the East, to the canals of Little Venice in the North-West. Perhaps the best place to appreciate the beauty of London is from the top of Primrose Hill, a park overlooking Regent's Park and the whole panorama of the city beyond.

APSLEY HOUSE
Hyde Park Corner, London, W1J 7NT
Tel: 020 7499 5676 Fax: 020 7493 6576

Apsley House was designed by Robert Adam 1771–78 for Baron Apsley. Known as 'No. 1 London' because of its position just past the toll-gate into the Capital from the West, it was bought by the Duke of Wellington in 1817. The Duke enlarged the house, notably adding on the spectacular 90' long Waterloo Gallery. The lavish gilt and silk interiors, now restored to their former glory, house his magnificent collection: paintings (many from the Spanish Royal Collection and including works by Velazquez, Goya, Rubens, Brueghel, Lawrence, Wilkie, Dutch and Flemish masters), porcelain, silver, sculpture, furniture, medals and memorabilia. **Open:** Tue–Sun 11–5pm. **Admission:** Adults £4.50, over 60s free, Concessions £3, both including sound guide, Pre-booked groups £2.50/head, Children under 18 free.

map 5
J6

BURGH HOUSE
New End Square, Hampstead, London, NW3 1LT
Tel: 020 7431 0144 Fax: 020 7435 8817 (London Borough of Camden)

A Grade I listed building erected in 1703, in the heart of old Hampstead. Home to many notable professional people before the war. Re-opened in 1979, it houses the Hampstead Museum, an Art Gallery with regularly changing exhibitions and a panelled Music Room popular for weddings, (the house is licensed), wedding receptions, seminars and conferences. Also used for recitals, talks, local society meetings, book fairs and other events. Licensed basement Buttery and award-winning Gertrude Jekyll -inspired terrace garden. Buttery reservations on 020 7431 2516. **Station(s):** Hampstead or Hampstead Heath. **Buses:** 24, 46, 168, 210, 268, C11. **Open:** Wed–Sun 12–5pm. Saturdays by appointment only. Bank Hols 2–5pm. Buttery: 11–5.30pm. Closed Christmas/New Year, Good Friday & Easter Mon. **Admission:** Free to House/Museum. **Refreshments:** The Buttery.

map 5
J6

BROMLEY MUSEUM
The Priory, Church Hill, Orpington BR6 0HH
Tel: 01689 873826

Housed in an interesting medieval building situated in attractive gardens • Find out about the archaeology of the London Borough of Bromley from earliest times to Domesday • Learn about Sir John Lubbock, 1st Lord Avebury, the eminent Victorian responsible for giving this country its Bank Holidays • See how people lived before World War II **Exhibitions/ Events:** • Changing exhibitions throughout the year • Free school and adult education service. **Open:** All year: Monday–Friday 1–5pm. Saturday 10am–5pm. 1 April–31 October: Sundays and Bank Holidays 1–5pm. **Admission:** Free. **E-mail:** bromley.museum@bromley.gov.uk

map 5
F4

ADDINGTON PALACE

Gravel Hill, Addington Village, Croydon, Surrey CRO 5BB
Tel: 020 8662 5000   Fax: 020 8662 5001

Built in the 1770s for Barlow Trecothick, a Lord Mayor of London, and used as a country retreat by six Archbishops of Canterbury, Addington Palace was sold in 1898 to Frederick English, a South African diamond merchant, who engaged Richard Norman Shaw to restructure the house and create the magnificent Great Hall as it is seen to this day. A Grade II★ Palladian-style mansion, with a wealth of ornate marble fireplaces, hand carved wooden architraves, and magnificent crystal chandeliers, Addington Palace is now being transformed into a deluxe Hotel and Country Club with period furnishings and décor. Situated some ten miles from London, with excellent rail, road and air connections to London, Gatwick, Heathrow, and the coast, the Palace has ten individually designed function rooms, as well as a Grand Marquee in the grounds next to a 250-year-

old Cedar of Lebanon. The Palace can accommodate any style of private function or public reception, and any number of guests, from two to 1,000, day and evening, 7 days a week. The members-only Country Club with its state-of-the-art gym equipment also offers to non-members a wide range of health and beauty therapists and a variety of pamper days enabling anyone to experience the luxuriousness of this idyllic Palace. 2001 sees the planned opening of the Hotel and the addition of a swimming pool complex. **Open:** Throughout the year for functions and receptions (Tel: 020 8662 5000); Country Club (Tel: 020 8662 5050). **Admission:** 6 open days a year, with free admission (for dates of opening, please telephone 020 8662 5000). **Internet:** www.addington-palace.co.uk

map 5
F4/5

BUCKINGHAM PALACE

London SW1A 1AA

Tel: The Visitor Office 020 7839 1377 Fax: 020 7930 9625

Buckingham Palace, Windsor Castle and the Palace of Holyroodhouse are the Official residences of the Sovereign and are used by The Queen as both home and office. The Queen's personal standard flies when Her Majesty is in residence. Furnished with works of art from the Royal Collection, these buildings are used extensively by The Queen for State ceremonies and official entertaining. They are opened to the public as much as these commitments allow. **THE STATE ROOMS:** Are opened daily from 6 Aug–30 Sept 9.30–4.30pm. Tickets can be obtained during Aug–Sept from the Ticket Office in Green Park but are subject to availability. **Admission:** Adult £11, Children (under 17) £5.50, Senior Citizens (over 60) £9. To pre book your tickets telephone the Visitor Office 020 7839 1377. All tickets booked in advance are subject to a small transaction fee.

Disabled visitors are very welcome and should telephone in advance for information on access. **THE QUEEN'S GALLERY:** The Queen's Gallery is closed for refurbishment and will reopen in 2002, the Golden Jubilee year. **THE ROYAL MEWS:** Is one of the finest working stables in existence. It offers a unique opportunity for visitors to see a working department of the Royal Household. The Monarch's magnificent Carriages and Coaches including the Gold State Coach are housed here, together with their horses and State liveries. **Open:** All year Mon, Tues, Wed, Thurs 12–4pm. Last admission 3.30pm. Extra days and hours are added in the summer months. **Internet:** www.the-royal-collection.org.uk

The Gold State Coach
The Royal Collection © 2001, H. M. Queen Elizabeth II

The Throne Room
The Royal Collection © 2001, H. M. Queen Elizabeth II/Derry Moore

map 5 **J6**

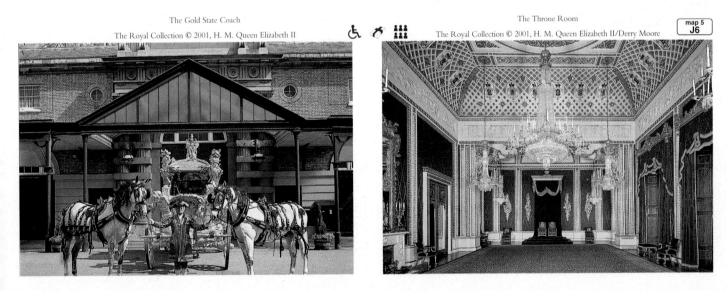

BANQUETING HOUSE

Whitehall Palace, London
Tel: 020 7930 4179

From the days of Henry VIII until its destruction by fire in 1698, the Palace of Whitehall was the Sovereign's main London residence. The only part to survive that fire was the Banqueting House. It is also the only building in Whitehall that is open to the public and it offers an oasis of peace and tranquillity amidst the bustle of Westminster. The Banqueting House was built in 1622 from a design by Inigo Jones, the leading architect of the time. The beautiful vaults beneath are known as the Undercroft–a favourite haunt of James I. When Charles I came to the throne, he further enhanced the building's interior by commissioning the Flemish painter, Rubens, to paint the ceiling. In 1635 Ruben's nine canvasses, including two measuring 28x20 feet and two measuring 40x10 feet, were finally put in place. These exquisite paintings are still intact and provide a spectacular sight for today's visitors. Just as the Banqueting House featured in Charles I's early career as King, so it was to feature at the end of his reign. On 30 January 1649 on a high platform outside the north end of the building, Charles I was beheaded, the only British Monarch ever to suffer such a fate. **Location:** London underground–Westminster (District/Circle line) Embankment (District/Circle, Northern & Bakerloo lines), Charing Cross (Northern, Bakerloo & Jubilee lines). BR–Charing Cross. **Open:** Mon–Sat 10–5pm. Closed Suns, 24–26 Dec, 1 Jan, Good Friday & other public holidays & at short notice for Government Functions. **Admission:** Adults £3.30, Senior Citizens/Students £3, Child under 16 yrs £2.30, under 5s free. From 1 April: Adults £3.90, Senior Citizens/Students £3.10, Children £2.30. **Internet:** www.hrp.org.uk

map 5
J6

CHELSEA PHYSIC GARDEN

66 Royal Hospital Road, London, SW3 4HS
Tel: 020 7352 5646 (The Chelsea Physic Garden Company)

The second oldest botanic garden in the country, founded in 1673 including notable collection of medicinal plants, comprises 4 acres densely packed with c. 6,500 plants, many rare and unusual. **Location:** Swan Walk, off Royal Hospital Road, Chelsea; near junction of Royal Hospital Road and Chelsea Embankment. **Station(s):** Sloane Square – underground. **Open:** Apr–end Oct, Suns, 2–6pm, Wed 12–5pm. Also 12–5pm in Chelsea Flower Show Week and Chelsea Festival Week. Open at other times for subscribing friends and groups by appointment. **Admission:** Adults £4, Children/Students/Unemployed £2. Garden accessible for disabled and wheelchairs via 66 Royal Hospital Road. Parking in street on Sun and on other days across Albert Bridge in Battersea Park. **Refreshments:** Home-made teas. No dogs (except guide dogs). **Internet:** www.cpgarden.demon.co.uk

map 5
J7

CHISWICK HOUSE

Burlington Lane, Chiswick, London, W4
Tel: 020 8995 0508 (English Heritage)

Lord Burlington's internationally celebrated villa never fails to inspire a sense of awe in all who visit. An exhibition on the ground floor reveals why this villa and its gardens are so important to the history of British architecture and an audio-tour will escort you through the fine interiors, including the lavish Blue Velvet Room. The Italianate grounds are equally impressive and have, at every turn, something to surprise and delight – including statues, temples, obelisks and urns. **Location:** Burlington Lane, W4. **Open:** 1 Nov–31 Mar: Wed–Sun, 10–4pm. 1 Apr–30 Sept: daily 10–6pm. 1–31 Oct: daily, 10–5pm. 1 Nov–31 Mar: Wed–Sun, 10–4pm. Closed 24–26 Dec & 1–18 Jan. **Admission:** Adults £3.30, Concs £2.50, Children £1.70 (15% discount for groups of 11 or more).

map 5
H7

CHURCH FARMHOUSE MUSEUM

Greyhound Hill, Hendon, London NW4 4JR
Tel: 020 8203 0130 Fax: 020 8359 2666 (London Borough of Barnet)

Set in a small public garden in a conservation area, Church Farmhouse, built c.1660, is London's oldest surviving dwelling. It has a Victorian dining room, kitchen and laundry room, and holds a continuous programme of temporary exhibitions on local and social history and the decorative arts. Forthcoming topics include: rag dolls, the Festival of Britain in 1951, masks, and Enid Blyton. The dining room is decorated for a Victorian Christmas in December. **Open:** Mon–Thurs 10am–12.30pm, 1.30–5pm. Sat 10am–1pm, 2–5.30pm. Sun 2–5.30pm. **Admission:** Free. Free audio-tape tour available.

map 4
E4

COLLEGE OF ARMS
Queen Victoria Street, London, EC4V 4BT
Tel: 020 7248 2762 Fax: 020 7248 6448 (College of Arms)

Mansion built in 1670s to house English Officers of Arms and panelled Earl Marshal's Court. Official repository of Armorial Bearings and Pedigrees of English, Welsh, Northern Ireland and Commonwealth families, with records covering 500 years. **Location:** S of St. Paul's Cathedral **Station(s):** Blackfriars or St Pauls. **Open:** Earl Marshal's Court: All year (except public holidays and State and special occasions), Mon–Fri, 10–4pm. Record Room: Open for tours (groups of up to 20) by special arrangement in advance with Officer in Waiting. (Fee by negotiation). **Admission:** Free. Officer in Waiting available to take enquiries concerning grants of Arms and genealogy.
Internet: www.college-of-arms.gov.uk

map 5 J6

CROFTON ROMAN VILLA
Crofton Road, Orpington BR6 8AD
(adj. Orpington BR Station)

• The only Roman Villa in Greater London which is open to the public
• Ten rooms of a villa-house protected inside a public viewing building
• Conducted tours • Schools service • Graphic displays • Access for people with disabilities. **Opening Times:** 1 April–31 October 2001. Wednesdays, Fridays and Bank Holiday Mondays 10am–1pm and 2–5pm, Sundays 2–5pm. Other days by arrangement with Bromley Museum. **Admission:** Adults £1, Children/Concessions 50p. Further Information: Bromley Museum, Orpington. Tel: 01689 873826. Kent Archaeological Rescue Unit. Tel & Fax: 020 8462 4737

DICKENS HOUSE MUSEUM
48 Doughty Street, London WC1N 2LX
Tel: 020 7405 2127 Fax: 020 7831 5175

The Dickens House Museum was first opened to the public in 1925. It houses the world's largest collection of Dickens-related material including manuscripts, paintings by well known 19th century artists, furniture, personal items and memorabilia. It was while at this address that Dickens finally gained recognition with the completion and publication of 'The Pickwick Papers', 'Oliver Twist' and 'Nicholas Nickleby'. This Georgian terraced house, built in 1801, was Dickens' home between 1837 and 1839. The museum consists of an exciting mixture of reconstructed rooms and information gallery space telling the story of Dickens' life and works. The house is the ideal destination for anyone who has ever enjoyed the rich characterisation of one of the world's best loved authors. **E-mail:** dhmuseum@rmplc.co.uk **Internet:** www.dickensmuseum.com

map 5 F4

THE DE MORGAN FOUNDATION
Old Battersea House, 30 Vicarage Crescent, Battersea, SW11 3LD
Tel/Fax: 020 7371 8385

A substantial part of The De Morgan Foundation collection of ceramics by William De Morgan and Pre Raphaelite paintings and drawings by Evelyn De Morgan (née Pickering), her uncle Roddam Spencer Stanhope, J. M. Strudwick and Cadogan Cowper are displayed on the ground floor of Old Battersea House – a Wren-style building which is privately occupied. **Location:** Battersea, London SW11. **Open:** Admission by appointment only, usually Wednesday mornings. All visits are guided. **Admission:** £2.50 (optional catalogue £1.50). Parties – max. 30 (split into two groups of 15). Apply to The De Morgan Foundation, 56 Bradbourne Street, London, SW6 3TE.

map 5 J7

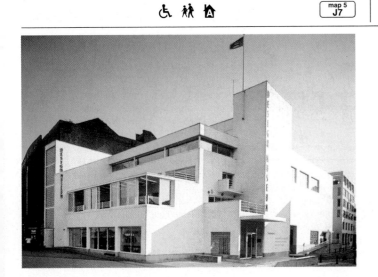

DESIGN MUSEUM
Butler's Wharf, 28 Shad Thames, London SE1 2YD
Tel: 020 7403 6933 Fax: 020 7378 6540

Discover the excitement of design evolution, ingenuity and inspiration at one of London's most inspiring attractions, dedicated to the study of contemporary design. A programme of highly acclaimed exhibitions encompasses interiors, fashion, furniture; architecture, engineering; technology, product and graphic design. For further information 020 7940 8790 or view www.designmuseum.org **Open:** Monday–Friday 11.30–6pm. Weekends 10.30–6pm. **Admission:** Adults £5.50, Students £4.50, Concessions £4, Family (2+2) £15. **Location:** Underground: Tower Hill, Bermondsey or London Bridge.
Internet: www.designmuseum.org

map 5 J6

DULWICH PICTURE GALLERY

Gallery Road, London SE21 7AD
Tel: 020 8693 5254 Fax: 020 8299 8700

"The most beautiful small gallery in the world"- Martin Gayford, *Sunday Telegraph* "On holiday in Umbria or Tuscany we would all travel bravely for a day to see much less" – Brian Sewell, *Evening Standard*

Dulwich Picture Gallery is England's oldest public gallery with an outstanding collection of 17th and 18th century Old Master paintings including works by Rembrandt, Poussin, Rubens, Van Dyck, Murillo, Hogarth, Gainsborough and Watteau. The building was designed for the collection by Sir John Soane in 1811 and is of great architectural interest. The founders are buried in the mausoleum which is lit through amber glass creating a mysterious and sombre mood. The Gallery is surrounded by parks and fields and lies in Dulwich Village which remains very much as it was in the eighteenth century. **Location:** Just off the South Circular, A205 (free parking). **Train:** Victoria/West Dulwich or London Bridge/North Dulwich. **Open:** Tuesday–Friday, 10–5pm Sat, Sun & B.H.Mon 11–5pm. **Admission:** Adults £4, Seniors £3, Children, Disabled, Students & Unemployed free. Guided Group rate £5 p.p. Group bookings: 020 8299 8711. **Internet:** www.dulwichpicturegallery.org.uk

map 5 F4

ELTHAM PALACE

Eltham, London SE9 5QE
Tel: 020 8294 2548 (English Heritage)

A master piece of *Moderne* design, Eltham Palace dramatically shows the glamour and allure of 1930's style. Bathe in the light flooding from a spectacular glazed dome in the Entrance Hall, as it highlights the beautiful blackbean veneer and figurative marquetry. Step into Virginia's magnificent gold-leaf and onyx bathroom, and wander throughout the house discovering the 'ocean liner' style veneered interior with custom designed furniture. A Chinese sliding screen is all that separated the chic '30s Art Deco from the Medieval Great Hall. **Open:** 1 April–30 Sept: Wed–Fri & Sun, 10am–6pm. 1–31 Oct: Wed–Fri & Sun, 10am–5pm. 1 Nov–28 Mar: Wed–Fri & Sun, 10am–4pm. Open BH Mondays. Closed 24–26 Dec & 1 Jan. **Admission:** House & Garden: Adult £6, Concession £4.50, Child £3. Gardens only: Adult £3.60, Concession £2.70, Child £1.80.

map 5 F4

THE FAN MUSEUM

12 Crooms Hill, Greenwich, London SE10 8ER
Tel: 020 8305 1441 Fax: 020 8293 1889

This unique and award-winning museum is the only museum in the world entirely dedicated to the history of fans. Housed in beautifully restored 18th century town houses in the centre of Historic Greenwich, The Fan Museum is home to an unsurpassed collection of over 3000 fans from around the world dating from the 11th century. Its own collections and fans lent from other collections are displayed in changing themed exhibitions. **Exhibitions/ Events:** Art Nouveau Fans (9 December-4 March); From the Land of the Fan (7 March-24 June). **Admission:** Adults: £3.50. Concs £2.50. Free on Tuesdays for Disabled and OAPs (except for groups) from 2pm. **Open:** Tues–Sat 11–5pm. Sun 12–5pm. Closed on Mondays (except Bank Holiday Mondays). **Internet**: www.fan-museum.org

map 5 J7

THE FLORENCE NIGHTINGALE MUSEUM
2 Lambeth Palace Road, London SE1 7EW
Tel: 020 7620 0374 Fax: 020 7928 1760

The 'Lady of the Lamp' is famous around the world for her remarkable career and influence on modern nursing. Visit this award-winning museum to discover the woman behind the fame; from a serious and solitary Victorian child to an internationally recognised role model, reformer and writer. Personal artefacts, reconstructions of period settings and an audio-visual presentation work together to reveal Florence Nightingale's inspirational life. **Open:** Mon–Fri 10am–5pm, Sat & Sun 11.30am–4.30pm (last admission one hour before closing). Closed: Good Friday, Easter Sunday, 24 December to 2 January. **Admission:** Adult £4.80, Concession £3.60, Family £10 (group rates also available). **Internet:** www.florence-nightingale.co.uk

map 5 J6

GUNNERSBURY PARK MUSEUM
Gunnersbury Park, London W3 8LQ
Tel: 020 8992 1612 Fax: 020 8752 0686

This lively community museum presents the heritage of Ealing and Hounslow through changing displays featuring plenty of hands-on activities for children. Its wide ranging collections include costume and toys, archaeology and carriages. The museum has fine interiors and its original kitchens are on show on summer weekends. It is surrounded by 183 acres of beautiful parkland. Changing exhibitions and regular events. **Activities:** Snakes & Ladders, Corset Corner, A Feel For The Past. **Location:** Acton Town Underground. Bus: E3. **Open:** Nov–Mar: Daily 1–4pm. Apr–Oct: Daily 1–5pm. (6pm weekends & Bank Hols). **Admission:** Free. Donation welcome. Café open daily.

map 5 J6

GUILDHALL ART GALLERY
Guildhall Yard, London EC2P 2EJ
Tel: 020 7332 3700 Fax: 020 7332 3342

Guildhall Art Gallery recently re-opened in a stunning new building in the heart of the City of London. Originally established in 1885, it is home to the Corporation of London's renowned art collection. Among the highlights are: Victorian paintings and sculpture, including famous Pre-Raphaelite works; fascinating views of London and Londoners from the 16th century to the present; John Singleton Copley's enormous painting, *The Siege of Gibraltar*, which spans two floors of the gallery. **Exhibitions:** There is a programme of changing exhibitions and the entire gallery is rehung annually. Open: Mon–Sat 10am–5pm, Sun 12–4pm. **Admission:** Adults £2.50, Concessions £1, Children under 16 free. Group rates available on request. **E-mail:** guildhall.artgallery@corpoflondon.gov.uk **Internet:** www.guildhall-art-gallery.org.uk

map 5 J6

GREENWICH – OBSERVATORY
National Maritime Museum, Romney Road, Greenwich, SE10 9NF
Tel: 020 8312 6565 (24hr infomation line) Fax: 020 8312 6632

Stand aside the famous Greenwich Meridian Line. See the Astronomer Royal's apartments. Charming Wren building. Watch the time ball fall at 1 o'clock. Harrison's amazing clocks. The nearby National Maritime Museum's modern new extension opened Easter 1999 with features on exploration, Nelson, trade and empire, passenger liners and the global garden. **Location:** Off A2. River boats from central London. **Station(s):** Greenwich (BR) Cutty Sark (DLR) **Open:** Daily (except 24–26 Dec) 10–5pm. **Admission:** Observatory: Adult £6, OAP free, Child free. National Maritime Museum: Adult £7.50, OAP free, Child free. **Internet:** www.nmm.ac.uk

map 5 J6

THE HORNIMAN MUSEUM & GARDENS
100 London Road, Forest Hill, London SE23 3PQ
Tel: 0208 6991872 Fax: 0208 291 5506

Set in 16 acres of gardens, this fascinating, free museum has unique exhibitions, events, and activities to delight adults and children alike. Housed in Townsend's wonderful Arts and Crafts building the museum has three permanent displays. Discover the African Worlds gallery featuring the largest African mask; experience the Natural History gallery with many original specimens from the Victorian age; explore marine ecology in the Living Waters Aquarium with tropical fish and seahorses. The museum is constructing a new extension and will be closed from 22nd January – 30th April 2001. **Location:** South Circular Road (A205) – Free parking opposite. Forest Hill BR – 13 mins London Bridge. **Admission:** Free. **Open:** Mon – Saturday 10.30 am – 5.30 pm, Sunday 2 – 5.30 pm

map 6 J6

HAMPTON COURT PALACE

East Molesey, Surrey KT8 9AU
Tel: 020 8781 9500

With its 500 years of royal history Hampton Court Palace has been home to some of Britain's most famous kings and queens and also the setting for many great historical events. When viewed from the west, Hampton Court is still the red brick Tudor palace of Henry VIII, yet from the east it represents the stately Baroque façade designed by Sir Christopher Wren for William III. The sumptuous interiors reflect the different tastes of its royal residents and are furnished with great works of art, many still in the positions for which they were originally intended. Discover the delights that this marvellous palace has to offer – the recently restored Privy Garden, the 16th century Tudor kitchens and the Mantegna's, a series of nine paintings that represent some of the most important Italian Renaissance works of art in the world. Costumed guides give lively and informative tours of the stunning interiors of the State Apartments, giving a unique insight into the daily lives of the kings and their courtiers. **Location:** Take Exit 12 & A308 from M25 or Exit 10 onto the A307. **Station:** Hampton Court 32 minutes from London Waterloo via Clapham Junction. **Open:** Mid Mar–Mid Oct, Tue–Sun 9.30–6pm, Mon 10.15–6pm. Mid Oct–Mid Mar, Tue–Sun 9.30–4.30pm, Mon 10.15–4.30pm. Closed 24–26 Dec inclusive. **Admission:** Adults £10.50, Senior Citizens/Students: £8, Child under 16yrs £7, Child under 5yrs free, Family Ticket (2 adults & 3 children) £31.40. **Events/ Exhibitions:** Special events throughout the year, including storytelling, family trails, special tours and hands-on demonstrations. Take a tour by Lantern light in the Autumn and celebrate Christmas Tudor style with entertainment, dancing and a feast fit for Henry VIII. **Internet:** www.hrp.org.uk

map 4
E4

HANDEL HOUSE MUSEUM

Until May 2001: 10 Stratford Place, London W1N 9AE
From May 2001: 25 Brook Street, London W1Y 1AJ
Tel: 020 7495 1685 Fax: 020 7495 1759

Located in the house where the composer George Frideric Handel lived from 1723–1759, and died, the museum includes refurbished interiors as well as fine and decorative arts from the early Georgian period. The displays illustrate the life, work and times of Handel. **Location:** 25 Brook Street (entrance at the rear in Lancashire Court). Tube: Bond Street. **Open:** Tues–Sat 10am–6pm (late opening until 8pm on Thursday), Sun & Bank Hol Mon 12–6pm. **Admission:** Adults £4.50, Concessions £3.50, Children £2. Enquiries to above addresses, museum opens late 2001.

map 5
J6

KEATS HOUSE

Keats Grove, Hampstead, London, NW3 2RR
Tel: 020 7435 2062 Fax: 020 7431 9293 (Corporation of London)

Keats House was built in 1815–1816. The poet John Keats lived here from 1818–1820 and wrote many of his best known poems, including 'Ode to a Nightingale', during this time. The house has letters, books and personal items belonging to the poet and his fiancée Fanny Browne. **Open:** 1 May–31Oct, Tues–Sat 10–12, admission only by advanced booking. Tues–Sun 12-5pm, open to general public. 1 Nov–Dec 2001 Tues–Sat 10–12, admission only by advanced booking. Tues–Sun 12–4pm, open to general public. **Location:** S end of Hampstead Heath, near South End Green. **Station(s):** BR: Hampstead Heath. Underground: Belsize Park/Hampstead. Bus: 24, 46, C11, C12, (alight South End Green), 268 (alight Downshire Hill). **Admission:** Adults £3, Concessions £1.50, Children 16 and under free. **Keats House may be closed for repairs from December 2001 - please ring before visiting at this time.**

map 5
F4

THE JEWISH MUSEUM

129-131 Albert Street, Camden Town, London NW1 7NB
Tel: 020 7284 1997 Fax: 020 7267 9008

Explores the history and religious life of the Jewish community in Britain from the Norman conquest until recent times. One of the world's finest collections of Jewish cermonial art, awarded Designated status in recognition of their outstanding national importance. Changing exhibitions and audio-visual programmes. **Open:** Mon–Thurs 10-4pm, Sun 10-5pm. Late opening first Tues of the month until 8pm. Closed Jewish Festivals and Public Holidays. **Admission:** Adults £3.50, OAPs £2.50, Students/Children £1.50. The museum also has social history displays, with reconstructions of tailoring and furniture workshops, hands-on activities for children, and a moving display on British-born Holocaust survivor, Leon Greenman, at The Jewish Museum, Finchley, 80 East End Road, London N3 2SY (Tel: 020 8349 1143). Group visits and education programmes by arrangement. **Internet:** www.jewmusm.ort.org

map 5
J6

THE ROYAL BOTANIC GARDENS, KEW

Kew, Richmond, Surrey TW9 3AB
Tel: 020 8332 5655 Fax: 020 8332 5610

Few attractions offer the variety and spectacle of Kew Gardens, 300 acres - four of them under glass - containing the largest collection of plant species in the world. The extensive, world famous glass houses ensure that even in winter a visit is full of fascination. The Palm House, 2248 square metres of Victorian ingenuity, houses tropical plants from around the globe, banana, coffee, breadfruit and paw-paw, to name but a few. Here also, you will find the fascinating Marine display. The Princess of Wales Conservatory contains ten climatic zones - from steamy rain forest to arid desert. The restored Japanese Gateway, Chokushi-Mon, is surrounded by an exciting landscape and the Evolution House takes you on a journey through four hundred million years of plant life. There is a visitor centre, two art galleries, various restaurant facilities and two gift shops. Tel 020 8940 1171. **Location:** Bus: London routes 65 and 391; underground: Kew Gardens station (District Line); rail: Kew Bridge station. **Open:** Daily from 9.30am, except Christmas Day and New Year's Day. **Internet:** www.kew.org

map 5
H6

THE IMPERIAL WAR MUSEUM
Lambeth Road, London SE1 6HZ
Tel: 020 7416 5320

The Imperial War Museum is a site that should not be missed. It covers 20th century conflict that involved Britain and the Commonwealth, both in the front line and on the Home Front. The museum offers a dramatic illuminated atrium which holds a wonderful collection of aircraft and large exhibits. There are permanent displays on the First and Second World Wars, Secret War and Conflicts since 1945. Special features incl: interactive videos, the walk through the Trench Experience, the dramatic Blitz experience, complete with sound, smell and other effects of London during a bombing raid. Special exhibitions and events throughout the year. Major new exhibition on the Holocaust. Café, shop, baby changing facilities. Nearest station: Waterloo or Lambeth North. **Open:** Daily 10-6pm. **Admission:** Charge.

map 5
J7

DUXFORD AIRFIELD
Duxford, Nr Cambridge CB2 4QR
Tel: 01223 835000

Situated off junction 10 of the M11 this famous RAF station which played a vital role in the Battle of Britain, is now home to Britain's finest collection of military and civil aircraft. The legendary Spitfire is one of over 140 aircraft on show and you can even climb aboard Concorde. Military vehicles, artillery, naval exhibits and supporting exhibitions complement the aviation collection. The preserved hangars, control tower and operation room retain their wartime atmosphere and historic aircraft regularly take to the air. Restaurant, picnic areas, souvenir shops, ample free parking. See the stunning new American Air Museum and experience history in the air at Duxford's airshows. **Open:** Daily 10–6pm. **Admission:** Charge.

map 5
F2

HMS BELFAST
Morgans Lane, Tooley Street, London SE1 2JH
Tel: 020 7940 6300

For a day out on the river, why not visit HMS Belfast? Once onboard, you can experience how sailors lived, worked and fought during the Second World War. Permanently moored in the Thames, close to Tower Bridge, HMS Belfast was commissioned into the Royal Navy in 1939. She last fired her guns in anger during the Korean War. A tour of the ship takes approximately two hours, giving visitors the opportunity to discover all nine decks, from the Captains Bridge all the way down to the massive Boiler and Engine rooms well below the waterline. Visitors can also explore the crew's messdecks, galley, operations room, six-inch-gun turrets and the punishment cells. **Nearest station:** London Bridge or Tower Hill Underground. **Open:** Daily. Please telephone for further details. **Admission:** Charge.

map 5
J7

CABINET WAR ROOMS
Clive Steps, King Charles Street, London SW1A
Tel: 020 7930 6961

In 1940, as the bombs fell on London, Winston Churchill, his Cabinet, his Chiefs of Staff and his Intelligence Chiefs met below ground in a fortified basement in Whitehall known as the Cabinet War Rooms. Today visitors can see it just as it looked during the war, with several of the most important rooms, including Churchill's bedroom, the Cabinet Room and the Map Room, undisturbed for over 50 years. The Rooms are situated on Horse Guards Road, opposite the beautifully landscaped St. James's Park. The Cabinet War Rooms welcomes groups and offers generous discounts to parties comprising 10 or more people. Complementary sound guides to the site are available in English, French, German and Spanish. **Nearest station:** St James's Park or Westminster Underground. **Open:** Daily 10-6pm. **Admission:** Charge.

map 5
J7

KENSINGTON PALACE STATE APARTMENTS

Kensington, London W8 4PX
Tel: 020 7937 9561

Situated in the peaceful surroundings of Kensington Gardens, Kensington Palace State Apartments are open to the public. The history of the Palace dates back to 1689 when the newly crowned William III and Mary II commissioned Sir Christopher Wren to convert the then Nottingham House into a Royal Palace. The palace was again altered when George I had the artist William Kent paint the magnificent trompe l'oeil ceilings and staircases which can still be enjoyed at this most intimate of Royal Palaces. Other highlights include the Cupola room where Queen Victoria was baptised and the recently restored King's Gallery. The State Apartments are home to 'Dressing for Royalty' – a stunning presentation of Royal Court and Ceremonial Dress dating from the 18th century, which allows visitors to experience the excitement of preparing for Court – from invitation to presentation. There is also a dazzling selection of 16 dresses owned and worn by HM Queen Elizabeth II. **Location:** On the edge of Hyde Park, just off Kensington High Street. **Open:** Open every day. Summer: 10am–last entry 5pm. Winter: 10am–last entry 4pm. **Admission:** Adults £8.50, Conc £6.70, Children £6.10, Family £26.10. **Refreshments:** Available all day in the Orangery. **Events/Exhibitions:** The Royal Ceremonial Dress Collection is complemented by special exhibitions throughout the year. **Internet:** www.hrp.org.uk

map 5
J6

LEIGHTON HOUSE MUSEUM & ART GALLERY

12 Holland Park Road, London, W14 8LZ
Tel: 020 7602 3316 Fax: 020 7371 2467

Leighton House was the first of the magnificent Studio Houses to have been built in the Holland Park area and today is open to the public as a museum of High Victorian Art. The home of the great classical painter and President of the Royal Academy, Frederic Lord Leighton, was designed by George Aitchison. The Arab Hall, is the centrepiece of Leighton House with dazzling gilt mosaics and authentic Isnik tiles. Temporary exhibitions are held throughout the year. **Nearest Underground:** High Street Kensington. **Buses:** 9, 9a, 10, 27, 28, 49. **Open:** All year, daily except Tues, 11–5.30pm. Open spring & summer BHols. **Admission:** Free. Donations welcome. The house may be booked for concerts, lectures, receptions and private functions.

map 5
J6

LONDON'S TRANSPORT MUSEUM

Covent Garden Piazza, London WC2E 7BB
Tel: 020 7379 6344 Fax: 020 7565 7254
24hr Recorded Info: 020 7565 7299

Uncover the story of 200 years of London's public transport, its impact on the growth of the capital and the lives of Londoners. Explore fascinating displays of trams, buses, trolleybuses and Tube trains and meet characters from the past. Clear and innovative interpretation including video, touchscreens, simulators, KidZones, interactive displays and changing exhibitions, and friendly and enthusiastic staff ensure a memorable experience for everybody. Situated in the heart of Covent Garden and housed in the atmospheric former Victorian flower market, the Transport Museum offers a fascinating day out for all ages. **Facilities:** Shop, café, baby changing room, full access and toilet facilities for disabled. **Open:** Daily 10am–6pm, Fri 11am–6pm; last admission 5.15pm. **Admission:** Adult £5.95, accompanied children under 16 free. **Internet:** www.ltmuseum.co.uk.

map 4
B2

LORD'S TOUR

Lord's Cricket Ground, London
Tel: 020 7432 1033 Fax: 020 7266 3825

The Lord's Tour provides a fully guided behind the scenes visit to the world famous 'home of cricket'. The tour includes the Pavilion with the Long Room and players' dressing rooms, the MCC Museum where the Ashes urn is on display, the Real Tennis Court, either of the Mound or Grand Stands, both with magnificent views of the playing area and the Nursery End home to the Indoor School, practice grounds and futuristic NatWest Media Centre. Lord's Cricket Ground is one of the most recognisable arenas in sport with a fine collection of period and contemporary architecture. You don't have to be a cricket lover to be thrilled by Lord's! **Open:** Tours normally at noon and 2pm (also 10am Apr–Sept). **Admission:** Adult £6.50, Student/OAP £5, Child £4.50.
E-mail: tours@mcc.org.uk **Internet:** www.lords.org

map 5
J6

KENWOOD HOUSE

Hampstead, London NW3 7JR
Tel: 020 8348 1286 (English Heritage)

Discover a true hidden gem amongst the multitude of attractions in London and visit Kenwood, a neoclassical house containing one of the finest private collections of paintings ever given to the nation. With important works by many world-famous artists, including Rembrandt, Vermeer, Turner, Reynolds and Gainsborough, a visit to Kenwood is a must for art lovers. In the 1760s the house was re-modelled by Robert Adam and the breathtaking library is one of his finest achievements. Outside, the sloping lawns and ornamental lake form a spectacular backdrop for our programme of hugely popular lakeside concerts with their dramatic firework finales. **Location:** Hampstead Lane NW3. **Open:** 1 Apr–30 Sept: daily, 10am–6pm. 1–31 Oct: daily, 10am–5pm. 1 Nov–28 Mar: daily, 10am–4pm. Closed 24–25 Dec. **Admission:** House & grounds free. Donations welcome.

map 5
J4

MALL GALLERIES

17 Carlton House Terrace, London SW1Y 5BD
Tel: 020 7930 6844 Fax: 020 7839 7830

The Mall Galleries stage a packed programme of varied exhibitions of work for sale together with artists' demonstrations, talks, and workshops. The galleries are run by the Federation of British Artists which is the umbrella organisation for nine of the country's leading art societies: Royal Institute of Painters in Water Colours; Royal Society of British Artists; Royal Society of Marine Artists; Royal Society of Portrait Painters; Royal Institute of Oil Painters; New English Art Club; Pastel Society; Society of Wildlife Artists; Hesketh Hubbard. **Open:** 10-5 daily (Including Sundays). **Admission:** usually £2.50, £1 concession.

map 8
B6

MERTON HERITAGE CENTRE

The Canons, Madeira Road, Mitcham, Surrey CR4 4HD
Tel: 020 8640 9387 Fax: 020 8640 7266

Based at The Canons, a beautiful historic house in Mitcham, the Centre tells the story of Merton and its people through a changing programme of exhibitions and events. Staff are committed to making history accessible for people of all ages and exhibitions frequently feature hands-on displays. Merton Heritage Centre has good adjacent parking and lies within easy reach of local bus, train and Tramlink networks. **Open:** Tues–Thurs 10am–4pm, Fri & Sat 10am–5pm (last admission 4.30pm), Sun 2–5pm. **Admission:** Free.

map 5
F4

THE MUSEUM OF GARDEN HISTORY

Lambeth Palace Road, London SE1 7LB
Tel: 020 7401 8865 Fax: 020 7401 8869

The Museum of Garden History is housed in the historic church of St. Mary-at-Lambeth. The Tradescant family tomb can be found in what was once the graveyard but is now the Museum's Garden. John Tradescant the elder (c 1570-1638) and his son, John (1608-1662), were both enthusiastic collectors of curiosities, adventurous plant hunters and also gardeners to Charles I and II. The Tradescant Trust was created in 1977 to save the church of St. Mary's from demolition and form the first Museum of Garden History. Years of hard work and intensive fundraising have resulted in a beautifully restored building and an extensive museum collection. The Trust now looks to the future growth of the Museum as an information resource and a visual history of gardening. The historic tool collection, artefacts and information panels provide an intriguing overview of garden history. Delve into the horticultural past and learn more about the Tradescants and other plant hunters. St. Mary-at-Lambeth has a fascinating history and many important memorials remain, including the tombs of Captain Bligh of the Bounty and the Sealy family of Coade stone fame. The 17th century style knot garden is a peaceful haven full of plants of the period. Fine topiary adds to the structure of the garden, rose plants of the time, herbaceous perennials, annuals and bulbs provide colour and scent in summer. The Museum also has a gift shop and coffee shop and runs courses, lectures and events throughout the year. **Open:** Seven days a week. **Admission:** £2.50 & £2, voluntary donation. **Registered Charity:** 273436. **E-mail:** info@museumgardenhistory.org **Internet:** www.museumgardenhistory.org

map 5 J6

THE MUSICAL MUSEUM

368 High Street, Brentford, Middlesex TW8 0BD
Tel: 020 8560 8108

Enjoy the sight and sounds of one of the country's finest collections of historic automatic musical instruments. Step back in time as sounds from the past fill the air - the sweet tones musical box - the grandeur of the Mighty Wurlitzer theatre organ - the subtle sounds of the concert pianist and the racy rhythms of ragtime. Experience this fascinating world during a visit including a continuous demonstration in which the instruments are explained and played. **Open:** Sat & Sun 2–5pm Apr–Oct and Wed 2–4pm in July & Aug, plus series of summer concerts. **Admission:** Adult £3.20, OAP/Child/UB40 £2.50. Party bookings by arrangement. Registered charity no: 802011.

map 5 H6

MUSEUM OF RUGBY

Twickenham Stadium, Rugby Road, Twickenham, Middlesex TW1 1DZ
Tel: 020 8892 8877 Fax: 020 8892 2817

From the moment you pass through the authentic Twickenham turnstile at the Museum of Rugby, you'll be immersed in a world of Rugby Union history. Enjoy the finest and most extensive collection of rugby memorabilia in the world. Let interactive touch-screen computers, video footage and period set pieces take you on a journey through the history of the game. Also operating from the Museum are tours of Twickenham Stadium. Expert tour guides will take you on an awe-inspiring journey through the home of England rugby. Walk alongside the hallowed turf, visit England's dressing room and experience the excitement of match day as you enter the stadium through the players' tunnel. Prepare to be inspired, spend a day in the life of rugby.

map 4 E4

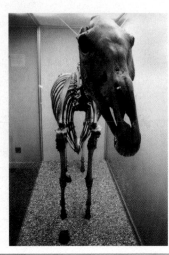

NATIONAL ARMY MUSEUM

Royal Hospital Road, Chelsea, London SW3 4HT
Tel: 020 7730 0717   Fax: 020 7823 6573

Discover the colourful story of the British Army and the people who have served in it, from Agincourt right up to the present day. Find out the facts behind some of the most remarkable episodes in Britain's history and the experiences of those involved. Interactive displays enable visitors to try on helmets and kit, feel the weight of a Tudor cannonball, survey a huge model of Waterloo, explore a reproduction WWI trench and test modern 'military' skills in exciting computer challenges. There are portraits by Reynolds and Gainsborough, a lamp used by Florence Nightingale, the frost-bitten fingers of Everest conqueror Major 'Bronco' Lane, and even the skeleton of Napoleon's horse! The ordinary soldier's story is brought vividly to life. **Open:** Daily 10am–5.30pm. **Admission:** Free. **E-mail:** pr@national-army-museum.ac.uk   **Internet:** www.national-army-museum.ac.uk

map 5 J6

NATIONAL PORTRAIT GALLERY

St Martin's Place, London WC2H 0HE
Tel: 020 7306 0055   Fax: 020 7306 0056

From Elizabeth I to Oscar Wilde, William Shakespeare to Florence Nightingale. With the largest collection of portraiture in the world, the National Portrait Gallery has over 10,000 works of famous British men and women who have created the history and culture of the nation from the Middle Ages until the present day. In addition to the main collection, the Gallery offers a varied programme of special exhibitions throughout the year. The recently completed Ondaatje Wing offers new public galleries, a roof-top Restaurant with views across London and an IT Gallery offering a touchscreen database of the Gallery's collection. The Gallery is open until 9pm on Thur & Fri evenings with special evening lectures and music every week. **Open:** Mon-Wed, Sat & Sun 10-6pm. Thurs & Fri 10-9pm. Closed Good Fri, 24-26 Dec & 1 Jan. **Admission:** Free. Charge for some temporary exhibitions. **Internet:** www.npg.org.uk

map 5 J6

THE NATURAL HISTORY MUSEUM

Cromwell Road, London SW7 5BD
Tel: 020 7942 5000

The world's finest museum of nature and one of London's most beautiful buildings, The Natural History Museum is home to a wide range of exhibitions certain to appeal to visitors of all ages. Highlights include the acclaimed *Dinosaurs* exhibition, an 'earthquake experience' in *The power within* and *Earth's treasury*, a beautifully designed exhibition displaying the Museum's unparalleled collections of gems and minerals. **Special Exhibitions for 2001** include the internationally respected *BG Wildlife Photographer of the Year* exhibition, featuring stunning images (closes end Feb 2001) and *Rhythms of Life*, a family exhibition, taking an intriguing look at the fascinating links between nature and time (closes 7 May 2001). At the end of May the Museum stages an exhibition of the artworks of influential 19th century wildlife artist Joseph Wolf (closes December 2001) and during the summer opens a dramatic new family exhibition investigating attack and defence, evolutionary 'arms races' and games strategies in the animal world (closes in 2002). **Open:** Mon–Sat 10am–5.50pm. Sunday 11am–5.50pm (last admission 5.30pm). **Admission:** Free to children up to and including 16 yrs, 60s and over; charge made for adults and concessions. **Location:** Nearest tube: South Kensington. **Internet:** www.nhm.ac.uk

map 5 J6

NATIONAL PORTRAIT GALLERY
St Martin's Place, London WC2H 0HE
Tel: 020 7306 0055 Fax: 020 7306 0056

From Elizabeth I to Oscar Wilde, William Shakespeare to Florence Nightingale. With the largest collection of portraiture in the world, the National Portrait Gallery has over 10,000 works of famous British men and women who have created the history and culture of the nation from the Middle Ages until the present day. In addition to the main collection, the Gallery offers a varied programme of special exhibitions throughout the year. The recently completed Ondaatje Wing offers new public galleries, a roof-top Restaurant with views across London and an IT Gallery offering a touchscreen database of the Gallery's collection. The Gallery is open until 9pm on Thur & Fri evenings with special evening lectures and music every week. **Open:** Mon-Wed, Sat & Sun 10-6pm. Thurs & Fri 10-9pm. Closed Good Fri, 24-26 Dec & 1 Jan. **Admission:** Free. Charge for some temporary exhibitions. **Internet:** www.npg.org.uk

`map 5 J6`

ORLEANS HOUSE GALLERY
Riverside, Twickenham, Middlesex TW1 3DJ
Tel: 020 8892 0221 Fax: 020 8744 0501

Sheltered within tranquil woodland overlooking the Thames stands Orleans House Gallery former home of Louis Philippe, Duc d'Orleans later King of France. The original house (1710) has vanished, but the stunning Gibbs baroque Octagon (c. 1720) is not to be missed. The main gallery and nearby stables gallery feature an innovative programme of contemporary and historical exhibitions. The permanent Borough Art Collection can be viewed by appointment. Call the gallery for further information. Situated near Marble Hill House and a short ferry ride away from Ham House, OHG is the perfect day out. Stations: St. Margarets station from Waterloo/Richmond, District Line. **Open:** Tues-Sat 1-5.30pm. Suns & Bank Holidays 2-5.30pm. The gallery closes at 4.30pm between October & March. **Admission:** Free. **Internet:** www.richmond.gov.uk/dept/opps/leisure/arts/orleanshouse.

`map 4 E4`

PITSHANGER MANOR & GALLERY
Mattock Lane, Ealing, London W5 5EQ
Tel: 020 8567 1227 Fax: 020 8567 0595

Pitshanger Manor and Gallery is set in the beautiful surroundings of Walpole Park, Ealing in West London. The Manor's most illustrious owner was the architect Sir John Soane (1753–1837), 'Architect and Surveyor' to the Bank of England. He rebuilt most of the house to create a Regency villa using highly individual ideas in design and decoration. The house has largely been restored and refurbished to its early 19th century style. A Victorian wing houses a large collection of Martinware pottery. Pitshanger Manor and Gallery is open to the public as a historic house and cultural centre. Adjacent to the manor is a newly refurbished contemporary art gallery, programming a wide range of changing exhibitions. Please phone for current exhibition programme. **Open:** Tues–Sat 10–5pm. Closed Sun and Mon. Also closed Christmas, Easter and New Year. **Admission:** FREE. Parties by arrangement. **Internet:** www.ealing.gov.uk/pitshanger

`map 5 H6`

PETRIE MUSEUM OF EGYPTIAN ARCHAEOLOGY
Malet Place, University College London, London WC1E 6BT
Tel: 020 7679 2884 Fax: 020 7679 2886

The Petrie Museum is one of the world's most inspiring collections of Egyptian archaeology. The displays illustrate life in the Nile Valley from prehistory to Islamic times. Most objects on display were excavated or bought in Egypt by William Flinders Petrie (1853-1942), often called "the father of scientific archaeology". The Museum is richest in personal items illustrating life and death in ancient Egypt. The collection includes the World's earliest dress (around 2800 BC), decorative art from Akhenaten's city at Amarna and a large collection of mummy portraits. **Admission:** Free. **E-mail:** petrie.museum@ucl.ac.uk **Internet:** petrie.ucl.ac.uk

`map 5 J6`

ROYAL INSTITUTION OF GREAT BRITAIN
21 Albemarle Street, London W1S 4BS
Tel: 020 7409 2992 Fax: 020 7629 3569

The Royal Institution was founded in 1799 to promote the application of science "to the common purpose of life", and continues to fulfil this goal with a world class laboratory and lecture programmes such as the televised Christmas lectures. The Institution is located in a modified 1720's town house. In its laboratories Davy, Faraday annd the Braggs made seminal scientific discoveries, including sodium, potassium, the electric motor and generator, and the underlying work leading to the structure of DNA. The Museum contains much of Faraday's original scientific apparatus, including the first electric transformer, and some of his personal belongings. The Museum is open during weekday office hours. **Admission:** £1, Conc £0.50. **E-mail:** ri@ri.ac.uk **Internet:** www.ri.ac.uk

`map 5 J6`

SOUTHSIDE HOUSE
3 Woodhayes Road, Wimbledon, SW19 4RJ
Tel: 0181 946 7643
(The Pennington Mellor Munthe Charity Trust)

Built by Robert Pennington in 1665 after the death of his first born in the Plague. Bedroom prepared for Prince of Wales in 1750 and gifts to John Pennington–family 'Scarlet Pimpernel'. Guided tours give reality and excitement to the old family histories. **Location:** On S. Side of Wimbledon Common (B281) Opposite Crooked Billet Inn. **Open:** 2 Jan–24 Jun, Wed, Sat, Sun & Bank Holiday Mons. Guided tours on the hour 2–5pm (last tour 5pm). Also open for private parties by arrangement with the Administrator from 1 Dec–24 Jun. **Admissions:** Adults £5, (child accompanied by adult £3).

`map 5 F4`

ROYAL SOCIETY OF ARTS
8 John Adam Street, London WC2N 6EZ
Tel: 020 7930 5115 Fax: 020 7321 0271

The house of the Royal Society of Arts was designed especially for the society by Robert Adam in the early 1770's. One of the few remaining buildings from the original Adelphi development its Georgian façade conceals many unexpected delights of both traditional and contemporary architecture. Designed as one of London's earliest debating chambers, the Great Room is one of the most spectacular theatres in the city. The Benjamin Franklin Room is spacious and elegant, featuring an antique chandelier and two Adam fireplaces. The Vaults were originally designed as river front warehouses. Now fully restored they offer a striking contrast to the splendour of the rooms above. All rooms maybe hired for meetings, receptions and weddings. **Internet:** www.rsa.org.uk

map 5 J6

SIR JOHN SOANE'S MUSEUM
13 Lincoln's Inn Fields, London WC2A 3BP
Tel: 020 7405 2107 Fax: 020 7831 3957
(Trustees of Sir John Soane's Museum)

Built by the leading architect Sir John Soane, RA, in 1812–1813, as his private residence. Contains his collection of antiquities and works of art. **Station(s):** London Underground – Holborn. **Open:** Tues–Sat, 10–5pm. Lecture tours, Sat 2.30pm, Max. 22 people. Tickets £3, on a first come, first served basis from 2pm, no groups. Groups welcome at other times by prior arrangement (Tel: 0171 405 2107). Late evening opening on first Tues of each month, 6–9pm. Also library and architectural drawings collection by appointment. Closed Bank Hols. **Admission:** Free but donations welcome. **Events/Exhibitions:** Changing exhibitions of drawings in the 'Soane Gallery'. **Internet:** www.soane.org

map 5 J6

SOUTHWARK CATHEDRAL
Monague Close, London SE1 9DA
Tel: 020 7367 6700 Fax: 020 7367 6725

The history of the site records a progression from Roman building to Saxon minster, from Augustinian priory (1106) to parish church of St. Saviour (1540) in the Winchester Diocese and, finally to Cathedral(1905).The present building dates back from 13th century. It has literary connections with Gower, Chaucer, Shakespeare, and Dickens. The benefactor of the USA's oldest university, John Harvard was baptised here. The oldest gothic church building in London housing many interesting monuments, new visitors centre opening in early 2001. **Open:** Daily 8:30-6pm, Sun service 9am, 11 am &3pm. Wed service 8am, 12:30pm &5:30pm. Sat service 9am & 4pm. **Admission:** Individuals by donation (suggested£2.50p.p.). Groups should pre-book on 020 7367 6734. **E-mail:** cathedral@dswark.org.uk **Internet:** www.dswark.org.uk

map 5 J6

THE MUSEUM OF THE ORDER OF ST. JOHN AT ST. JOHN'S GATE
St. John's Lane, Clerkenwell, London EC1M 4DA
Tel: 020 7253 6644 Fax: 020 7336 0587

Discover the rich history of the Knights Hospitaller, a monastic order dedicated to serving the sick, dating back to the Crusades. Tours take visitors round their ancient Priory's Tudor Gate house, 16th century Church and Norman Crypt. Armour, silver and a 15th century Flemish altarpiece are among the treasures in the Museum. Shakespeare, Hogarth and Dr Johnson all have connections with the Gate, and in 1877, St. John Ambulance was founded here, inspired by the Knights' medical traditions. A new interactive gallery tells its story. **Station:** Farringdon Underground. **Open:** Museum: Mon–Fri, 10–5pm. Sat, 10–4pm. Tours: 11am & 2.30pm, Tues, Fri & Sat. **Admission:** Free to Museum, donations of £4 (£3 OAP) requested for tours. Charity Reg No: 1077265. **Internet:** www.sja.org.uk

map 5 J6

SHAKESPEARE'S GLOBE EXHIBITION AND THEATRE TOUR
21 New Globe Walk, Bankside, Southwark, London SE1 9DT
Tel: 020 7902 1500 Fax: 020 7902 1515

The biggest exhibition of its kind devoted to the world of Shakespeare from Elizabethan times to the present day - situated beneath the Globe Theatre itself. Explore Bankside, the Soho of Elizabethan London, follow Sam Wanamaker's struggle to recreate an authentic Globe for the twentieth century and beyond and take a fascinating guided tour of today's working theatre. Theatre Performances: May–September. Education: Globe Education Workshops, lectures, courses and evening classes are available for students of all ages and nationalities. Tel: 020 7902 1433. Shop: open daily 10-5pm selling books and souvenirs. **Open:** Oct-Apr, daily 10am–5pm. Closed 24 and 25 December. May–Sept, daily 9am–12noon with theatre tour, 1–4pm with virtual tour. **Admission:** Adults £7.50, Students & Seniors £6, Children £5. Advanced booking essential for groups of 15+, discounts available. Tel: 020 7902 1500 Fax: 020 7902 1515

map 5 J6

SPENCER HOUSE

27 St James's Place, London SW1A 1NR
Tel: 020 7514 1964 Fax: 020 7409 2952

Spencer House, built 1756–1766, for the first Earl Spencer, an ancestor of Diana, Princess of Wales (1961–97) is London's finest surviving 18th century private palace. The construction of the House involved some of the greatest artists and craftsmen of the day, including the Palladian architect John Vardy and James 'Athenian' Stuart. The House has now regained the full splendour of its 18th century appearance after a ten year programme of restoration undertaken by RIT Capital Partners plc, under the Chairmanship of Lord Rothschild. Spencer House is now partly used as offices and as a place where entertainments can be held in the historic setting of the state rooms, where the remarkable restoration is complemented by a magnificent collection of paintings and furniture. The House is open to the public on Sun and is available for private and corporate entertaining during the rest of the week. **Station(s):** Green Park. **Open:** Every Sun, except during Jan & Aug, 10:30am–5:30pm. Tours last approx. 1 hour (Last tour 4.45pm). Tickets available at door from 10:30 on day. Monday mornings, for pre-booked groups only. Enquiry Line: 020 7499 8620. **Admission:** Adults £6, Concessions £5 (Students/Friends of the Royal Academy, Tate and V&A, all with cards/children 10–16; under 10 not admitted) **Internet:** www.spencerhouse.co.uk

map 5
J6

Somerset House with Courtauld Gallery, Gilbert Collection & Hermitage Rooms

Strand, London WC2R 1LA

Courtauld Gallery Tel: 020 7848 2526 Gilbert Collection Tel: 020 7420 9400 Somerset House Tel: 020 7845 4600 Hermitage Rooms Tel 020 7845 4630

Somerset House, Sir William Chambers' masterpiece, is open to the public for the first time. Situated between Covent Garden and the South Bank, it takes its place as one of Europe's great centres for art and culture, where visitors can also enjoy long-hidden classical interiors and architectural vistas. The **Gilbert Collection** is London's newest museum of the decorative arts. Given to the nation by Sir Arthur Gilbert, the magnificent collections of European silver, gold snuffboxes and Italian mosaics are pre-eminent in the world. The **Courtauld Gallery** has one of the greatest small collections of paintings in the world, including the finest Impressionist paintings in Britain. The **Hermitage Rooms** at Somerset House recreate, in miniature, the imperial splendour of the Winter Palace and its various wings, which now make up The State Hermitage Museum in St Petersburg. The inaugural exhibition 'Treasures of Catherine the Great' presents a dazzling mix of jewels, silver, antiquities and paintings. **Location:** Entrances Strand or Victoria Embankment. **Open:** Mon–Sat 10am–6pm, Sun & Public Holidays 12–6pm. Closed 24–26 Dec and 1 Jan. **Admission:** Somerset House free except special events; Gilbert and Courtauld: Adult £4 separate entry (£3 concessions or pre-booked groups) or £7 joint ticket (£6 concessions or pre-booked groups, Under 18 and UK full-time students free. Hermitage Rooms: Adult £6. Concessions and pre-booked groups £4 each.

map 5
J6

Vigilius Eriksen: Portrait of Catherine II (Hermitage Rooms)

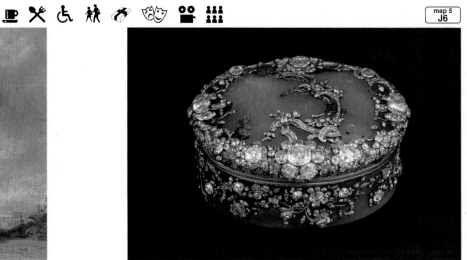

Jewelled Box: c.1755 (Gilbert Colllection)

Edouard Manet: A Bar at the Folies-Bergère *(Courtauld Gallery)*

Photo credit: Richard Bryant/ Arcaid

View of the West Façade at Somerset House

STRAWBERRY HILL HOUSE

Waldegrave Road, Strawberry Hill, Twickenham, Middlesex
Tel: 020 8240 4114 Fax: 020 8255 6174 (St. Mary's College)

Horace Walpole converted a modest house into a fantasy villa. It is widely regarded as the first substantial building of the Gothic Revival, and as such internationally known and admired. A century later Lady Waldegrave added a magnificent wing to Walpole's original structure. Guided tours take approximately 75 minutes and it is worth coming to see this unique house. These magnificent rooms can also be hired for corporate events, wedding receptions and conferences both day and residential. **Open:** Advance group bookings by appointment only are taken throughout the year and the House is open to the general public on Suns from Easter to Mid October, between 2pm and 3.30pm. This information was correct at the time of going to print, please phone 020 8240 4224 for up to the minute information. **Admission:** The ticket price is £5; concessions for OAPs, a maximum of 20 people per tour. The house is not suitable for disabled or children under 14 years of age. For information regarding advance group bookings or functions, please call the conference office on 020 8240 4114/4311.

map 4 E4

SYON PARK

Syon House & Gardens, Syon Park, Brentford, Middlesex TW8 8JF
Tel: 0208 560 0881/2 Fax: 0208 568 0936

Sir John Betjeman described Syon House as "The Grand Architectural Walk". Syon House is the London home of the Duke of Northumberland, whose family have lived here since the late 16th century. The present house is Tudor in origin, having been built by Lord Protector Somerset on the site of a medieval Abbey. It was in the Long Gallery that Lady Jane Grey was offered the Crown and at Syon where some of Charles 1st's children were imprisoned during the Civil War. The first Duke of Northumberland commissioned Robert Adam in 1761 to remodel the interior into the magnificent suite of State rooms on view today. The magnificent 200 acres of parkland beside the Thames, was landscaped by Capability Brown. Within it there are 40 acres of gardens which incorporate 'The Great Conservatory', (shown above) designed by Charles Fowler in the 1820s, the Rose Garden and over 200 species of rare trees. Syon House and the Great Conservatory can be hired for civil wedding ceremonies, receptions and corporate/private functions. All wedding receptions are held in the Great Conservatory but marquees can be erected for larger corporate/private functions for example, balls or fashion shows, for up to 1000 guests. Please call 020 8758 1777 for corporate functions or 020 8758 1888 for Wedding enquires. **Open:** House 11–5pm, Wed, Thurs, Suns and Bank Hols, 14 Mar–31 Oct. Gardens open daily 10–5.30pm or dusk except 25–26 Dec. Group rates, audio tour and optional guide service available. **Internet:** www.syonpark.co.uk

map 4 E4

TATE BRITAIN
Millbank, London SW1P 4RG
Tel: 020 7887 8008   Fax: 020 7887 8007

The Tate Gallery at Millbank has been relaunched as Tate Britain, showing the greatest collection of British art in the world. A dynamic series of themed displays spanning five centuries, from the 16th century to the present day, includes masterpieces by artists such as Turner, Hogarth, Gainsborough, Stubbs, Blake, Constable, the Pre-Raphaelites, Hepworth and Moore. **Open:** Daily 10am–6pm. **Admission:** Free, with a charge for major temporary exhibitions.

TATE MODERN
Bankside, London SE1 9TG
Tel: 020 7887 8008   Fax: 020 7887 8007

In May 2000, Tate Modern opened in the transformed Bankside Power Station. Standing at the heart of London, Tate Modern is a symbol of London in the 21st century. The new gallery displays the celebrated Tate collection of international 20th century art including artists such as Picasso, Matisse, Mondrian, Duchamp, Dalí, Bacon, Giacometti, Pollock, Rothko and Warhol. It also shows new and contemporary art as it is created. **Open:** Sun–Thurs 10am–6pm. Fri & Sat 10am–10pm. **Admission:** Free, with a charge for major temporary exhibitions.

TOWER OF LONDON
London, EC3N 4AB
Tel: 020 7709 0765

Begun by William the Conqueror in 1078, the Tower of London has served as a royal residence, fortress, mint, armory and more infamously as a place of execution. Since the 17th century, the Crown Jewels have been on public display and you can still see them in all their glory. Explore the White Tower, the original Tower of London, which houses the stunning collections of the Royal Armories Museum. Above the notorious Traitor's Gate within the Tower's walls, costumed guides evoke life at the court of King Edward I in the recently restored chambers of the medieval palace. **Location:** Underground to Tower Hill or Bus 15, 25, 42, 78, 100 or D1. Included on all major sightseeing tours. **Admission:** Call for rates. **Open:** Mar-Oct, Mon-Sat 9-5pm, Sun 10-5pm. Nov-Feb, Tues-Sat 9-4pm, Sun–Mon 10-4pm. Tower closes 1 h after last admission. Closed 24-26 Dec & 1 Jan. **Internet:** www.hrp.org.uk

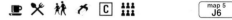

map 5 J6

THE TRAVELLERS CLUB
106 Pall Mall, London, SW1Y 5EP
Tel: 020 7930 8688 Fax: 020 7930 2019

The Club House was designed by 34 yr. old Charles Barry. His design broke architectural precedent, the Pall Mall façade being derived from the Palazzo Pandolfino in Florence, causing considerable comment in its day. Barry went on to design the Houses of Parliament. **Location:** 106 Pall Mall. **Station(s):** London Underground: Piccadilly Circus, Charing Cross. **Open:** By prior appointment only, Mon–Fri, 10–12noon. Closed Bank Hols, August and Christmas. **Admission:** Adults £9 by prior appointment. **Refreshments:** Included.

map 5 J6

WIMBLEDON LAWN TENNIS MUSEUM
Centre Court, The All England Club, Church Road, London SW19 5AE
Tel: 020 8946 6131   Fax: 020 8944 6497

The Museum, located within Centre Court, tells the story of lawn tennis and explains many of the quintessentially English traditions associated with the game. Highlights include a view of the world-famous Centre Court, the original Championship trophies, and film and video footage of great players in action. The extensive collection of tennis memorabilia, equipment and paintings tells how the once gentle game of lawn tennis has grown to become a multi-million dollar professional sport, played all over the world. Guided tours of the grounds are also available, in a variety of languages, for pre-booked groups of 15 or more. The Museum Shop and Café Centre Court are open all year. **Open:** Throughout the year, 10.30am–5pm, open only to tournament visitors during The Championships. **Internet:** www.wimbledon.org

map 4 E4

OSTERLEY PARK
Jersey Road, Isleworth, Middlesex, London TW7 4RB
Tel: 020 8568 7714 (The National Trust)
Recorded Visitor Information 01494 755566

Although originally a Tudor house, Osterley was transformed into what we see today by Robert Adam in 1761. The spectacular interiors contain one of Britain's most complete examples of his work and include exceptional plasterwork, carpets and furniture. The house also has an interesting kitchen. The house is set in extensive park and farmlands. **Open:** House: 31 Mar–4 Nov; Wed to Sun 1–4.30pm but open Bank Hol Mon. Closed Good Fri. Last admission 4.30. Park and Pleasure grounds open all year 9–7.30pm or sunset if earlier. **Admission:** Adult £4.30, Child £2.15. Car Park £2.50; family ticket £10.50.

2 WILLOW ROAD
2 Willow Road, Hampstead, London NW3 1TH
Tel: 020 7435 6166 (The National Trust)

The former home of Erno Goldfinger, designed and built by him in 1939. One of Britain's most important examples of modernist architecture, the house is filled with furniture also designed by Goldfinger. The interesting art collection includes work by Henry Moore and Max Ernst. **Open:** 4–24 Mar: Sat only 12–5pm. 30 Mar–3 Nov: Thurs–Sat 12–5pm. **Admission:** Adults £4.30, Children £2.15. No parking at house. Limited on-street parking.
E-mail: twlgen@smtp.ntrust.org.uk

VICTORIA AND ALBERT MUSEUM
Cromwell Road, London SW7 2RL
Tel: 020 7942 2000 Fax: 020 7942 2266

The V&A is the world's greatest museum of art and design. Highlights for any visit should include: the largest collection of Italian Renaissance sculpture outside Italy; paintings and drawings by John Constable; the sparkling Glass Gallery; the fashion court and the superb Canon Photography Gallery. **Exhibitions/Events:** The exhibitions and events programme includes: 5 Apr–29 July 2001: *Inventing New Britain: The Victorian Vision.* 5 Apr–27 Aug 2001: *Rural England through a Victorian Lens: Benjamin Brecknell Turner* (Canon Photography Gallery). **Admission:** Full £5. Free for senior citizens, under 18s, full time students and pre-booked educational groups. A separate charge in addition to standard museum entry may be made for exhibitions. **Open:** Daily 10am–5.45pm (10am–10pm Weds and selected Fridays) except 24, 25 & 26 Dec. **Internet:** www.vam.ac.uk

map 5 J6

THE WALLACE COLLECTION
Hertford House, Manchester Square, London W1M 6BN
Tel: 020 7563 9500 Fax: 020 7224 2155

The Wallace Collection is both a national museum and the finest private collection of art ever assembled by one family. It was acquired during the nineteenth century and bequeathed to the nation by Sir Richard Wallace's widow in 1897. It is displayed against the opulent backdrop of Hertford House, the family's main London residence. The magnificent collection of 18th century French paintings, furniture and porcelain is one of the finest in the world. There are also old master paintings including masterpieces by Titian, Rembrandt and Rubens, princely arms and armour, and opulent displays of gold boxes, sculpture and Renaissance works of art. **Open:** Monday-Saturday 10-5pm, Sunday 12-5pm. Closed 24, 25, 26, 31 December, 1 January, Good Friday and May Day Bank Holiday. **Exhibitions:** 22 Jan-29 Apr: 'Queen Victoria and Thomas Sully: an American Painter at Buckingham Palace'. 4 Oct–30 Dec: 'Marquetry in French Furniture'. **Internet:** www.wallace-collection.co.uk

map 5 J6

Greater Manchester

The city was founded by the Romans as Mancunium, and later became a thriving centre for commerce with the arrival of weavers from Belgium. In the 19th century, Manchester found itself at the heart of the Industrial Revolution, and the city became one of the most important in the British Empire. The subsequent decline in Britain's manufacturing industries hit Manchester hard, but in recent years it has undergone something of a rejuvenation. Derelict buildings have been replaced by new ones, the canals have been cleaned up, and the city is now a vibrant centre for culture and entertainment.

BURY ART GALLERY & MUSEUM

Moss Street, Bury, Lancashire BL9 0DR
Tel: 0161 253 5878 (Bury MBC)

Discover the charm of Victorian paintings and the challenges of contemporary art in a delightful Edwardian building. Bury Art Gallery & Museum was built in the grand style - mosaic floors, stained glass and brass turnstiles - to house the renowned Wrigley Collection of Victorian paintings. Highlights of the collection include Turner, Landseer and Constable. Works by Lamorna Birch, Lowry and Burra feature in the 20th century collection and a lively programme of contemporary art exhibitions completes the picture. 'Paradise Street' in the museum recreates Bury life with shops and homes, as well as a working model railway of the town. **Internet:** www.bury.gov.uk/culture.htm

map 8
A3

HEATON HALL

Heaton Park, Prestwich, Manchester, Lancashire, M25 2SW
Tel: 0161 773 1231/234 1456 Fax: 0161 236 7369
(Manchester City Art Galleries)

Set in 650 acres of rolling parkland, Heaton Hall is a magnificent Grade I listed building described as 'the finest house of its period in Lancashire and one of the finest in the country'. Designed by James Wyatt in 1772, the building's beautifully restored 18th century interiors are furnished with fine paintings and furniture of the period. A superb collection of Wyatt furniture from Heveningham Hall in Suffolk is also a highlight. The unique circular Pompeiian Room and elegant Music Room are also not to be missed. **Open:** Easter–Oct. **Admission:** Free. Please call for details.

map 8
B4

MANCHESTER JEWISH MUSEUM

190 Cheetham Hill Road, Manchester M8 8LW
Tel: 0161 834 9879 Fax: 0161 834 9801

Opened as a synagogue in 1874, this Grade II★ Listed Building has housed the Museum (Registered Charity 508278) since 1984. A permanent first floor display charts the history of the Jewish community in the region. The Museum's Education and Outreach programme won the 1998 Sandford Award. The Shop sells educational materials, books and gifts. **Exhibition:** Until 29 July 2001: '100 Years of Cheetham and Broughton'. An exhibition hosted for the local Millennium Partnership Project Committee, recording the area's ethnic minorities and community groups during the 20th century in sound, vision, photographs and artefacts. **Open:** Mon–Thurs 10.30–4pm, Sun 10.30–5pm. Closed Fri (except for educational parties, by arrangement), Sat and Jewish Holidays. **Admission:** Adult £3.50, Conc £2.60, Family £8.50. **E-mail:** info@manchesterjewishmuseum.com **Internet:** www.manchesterjewishmuseum.com

map 8
B4

SALFORD MUSEUM & ART GALLERY

Peel Park, Salford M5 4WU Tel: 0161 736 2649

Hundreds of objects, original shop fronts and authentic sounds make Lark Hill Place a wonderful recreation of a typical northern street c.1900. There is also a Victorian Gallery, temporary exhibitions and family activities throughout the year. Parkland adjacent. **Open:** Monday–Friday 10–4.45pm. Saturday & Sunday 1–5pm. **Admission:** Free. **E-mail:** salford.museum@salford.gov.uk

ORDSALL HALL MUSEUM

322 Ordsall Lane, Salford M5 3EX Tel: 0161 872 0251

This 600 year old building is one of the finest examples of Tudor architecture in the region. Tudor Great Hall, medieval Star Chamber bedroom and Victorian kitchen. Temporary exhibitions and events throughout the year. **Open:** Monday–Friday 10–4pm. Sunday 1–4pm. Closed Saturdays. Limited disabled access. **Admission:** Free. **Internet:** www.ordsallhall.org.uk. Free parking at both sites.

map 8
B4

Merseyside

The Mersey Estuary has an auspicious and fascinating history as one of the most significant ports in the world. It was here, during the nineteenth century, that millions of hopeful emigrants began their journeys to the countries of the New World; America, Canada and Australia. Industries such as the wealthy Lever Brothers soap manufacturers have grown up in this area, and merchants and smugglers alike have made their fortunes. This heritage is reflected in the museums and galleries that stand today along the waterfront and in the surrounding area, collectively housing over 1.2m objects relating to art, history and science, and many exciting exhibitions.

The proud seafaring heritage of Liverpool and the Merchant Navy is celebrated in the Merseyside Maritime Museum where visitors can experience the opulent surroundings and dramatic stories of the Edwardian floating palaces; The Titanic and The Lusitania. The movement of people both in and out of England is relived in moving exhibitions in reconstructed ships. These tell the stories of the slaves who were brought on transatlantic ships to England, and the emigrants who left to through the same port to seek their fortunes in far-off lands.

The Walker Art Gallery

Lady Lever Art Gallery

Liverpool is home to a large number of famous artworks, both historic and contemporary. Many of these are lovingly preserved in the Walker, Sudley House and Lady Lever art galleries. The latter was built as a public service to the people of Port Sunlight by its founder William Lever, in memory of his wife. It still stands on its original site in a picturesque village, accessible from Merseyside by a short ferry ride. Port Sunlight was built in 1913 to house the workers of the thriving Lever Brothers factory. It epitomised the innovative vision of William Lever, who believed that the housing standards of his workers were of great importance, and who took pains to ensure that they lived in attractive surroundings. These buildings remain today, as examples of superb architecture and the well-conceived planning that contributed to this famous village.

Many well-known celebrities and sporting phenomena originate in Liverpool, and these are celebrated in attractions throughout the city. The Museum of Liverpool offers a unique insight to the city and its people in the 'Mersey Culture' exhibition where The Beatles, the Grand National and many football legends are featured.

Liverpool and the Mersey Estuary continue to be busy, exciting places to visit today, proud of a heritage of industry, culture and seafaring legend.

Sudley House

NATIONAL MUSEUMS & GALLERIES ON MERSEYSIDE

P.O. Box 33, 127 Dale Street, Liverpool, L69 3LA
Tel: 0151 207 0001

The eight National Museums and Galleries on Merseyside represent a wealth of historic and contemporary culture. **Liverpool Museum**, William Brown Street, is an encyclopaedia brought to life where you can discover all under one roof the wonders of space, Egyptian mummies, dinosaurs and rain forest creatures. **The Conservation Centre**, Whitechapel, allows visitors a behind-the-scenes look at how the experts preserve everything from birds to fine art. At the Albert Dock, the **Merseyside Maritime Museum** tells the story of one of the world's greatest ports. You can discover the opulence of the floating palaces and the tragic stories of The Titanic and The Lusitania, investigate the moving history of transatlantic slavery and explore the new Lifelines Gallery, a story of merchant ships and seafarers. Incorporated within the museum is the **Customs and Excise National Museum**: discover the exciting world of smugglers and customs officers. **Liverpool Life**, Pier Head, provides a unique insight into a great city and its people. **Walker Art Gallery**, William Brown Street, brings visitors face to face with a fine collection of paintings and sculpture. **Sudley House**, Mossley Hill Road, is preserved in all its Victorian luxury including a magnificent collection of paintings by British masters. Across the River Mersey in Port Sunlight Village, **Lady Lever Art Gallery** houses a collection of exquisite 18th-century furniture, fine porcelain and Pre-Raphaelite masterpieces. **<u>Open:</u>** All venues are open every day of the year, except 23–26 Dec and New Year's Day. Albert Dock and Pier Head venues: 10am–5pm. Other venues: Mon–Sat 10am–5pm, Sun noon–5pm. **<u>Admission:</u>** The NMGM Eight Pass gives unlimited free access for 12 months to all sites, and costs just £3 (Concessions £1.50, Senior Citizens and Children FREE).

Norfolk

Norfolk remains one of England's most peaceful counties, from the tranquil backwaters of the Broads National Park to the glorious coastline. Norwich itself is remarkably unspoilt, and the layout of its streets has changed very little since the Middle Ages. The remaining sections of the ancient city walls enclose a number of historic buildings, including the honey-coloured Norman Cathedral and Castle, and the medieval Guildhall. Norwich contains more medieval churches than any other city in Europe, and the relatively small city centre makes it a great place to explore on foot. At one time, the city was reputed to have a church for every week of the year, and a pub for every day. Indeed, brewing has been an important industry here for over two hundred years.

Kings Lynn

BICKLING HALL

Blickling, Norwich, Norfolk NR11 6NF
Tel: 01263 738030 Fax: 01263 731660

One of England's great Jacobean Houses, built in the early 17th century, Blickling houses a spectacular long gallery and collections of pictures and tapestries. **Open:** 7 Apr–28 Oct: Wed–Sun 1–4.30pm (Closes at 3.30pm in October). **Admission:** Hall & Gardens £6.70, Garden only £3.80.

FELBRIGG HALL

Felbrigg, Norwich, Norfolk NR11 8PR
Tel: 01263 837444 Fax: 01263 837032

One of the finest 17th century houses in the region, Felbrigg still houses its original furniture and Grand Tour paintings. The restored walled garden features a small orchard and dovecote. **Open:** 31 Mar–4 Nov: daily except Thurs and Fri, 1–5pm. **Admission:** House and Gardens: Adult £5.80, Child £2.90.

HOLKHAM HALL

Wells-next-the-Sea, Norfolk NR23 1AB
Tel: 01328 710227, Fax: 01328 711707 (The Earl of Leicester)

One of Britain's most majestic stately homes, situated in a 3,000 acre deer park, on the beautiful north Norfolk coast. This celebrated Palladian style mansion, based on designs by William Kent, was built between 1734 and 1764 by Thomas Coke, 1st Earl of Leicester. The magnificent alabaster entrance hall rises the full height of the building and in the richly and splendidly decorated Staterooms are Greek and Roman statues, brought back by the 1st Earl from his Grand Tour of Europe, fine furniture by William Kent and paintings by Rubens, Van Dyck, Claude, Poussin and Gainsborough. In addition to the Hall there is a Bygones Museum in the original stable block, History of Farming Exhibition in the porters' lodge and Holkham Nursery Gardens in the 18th century walled kitchen garden. **Location:** 2 miles W of Wells-next-the-Sea. S off the A149. **Open:** Suns–Thurs (incl.) 27 May–30 Sept 1–5pm. Plus Easter, May, Spring & Summer Bank Hols. Sun & Mon 11.30–5pm. (last admission 4.45pm). Restaurant, Shop & Nursery Gardens open from 10 am. **Admission:** Hall: Adults £5, children £2.50. Bygones: Adults £5, children £2.50. Combined ticket: Adults £8, children £4. Reduction on parties of 20 or more. Private tours of the Hall by arrangement. **Refreshments:** Restaurant. **Events:** Holkham Country Fair Sat 21 & Sun 22. July. NB: Hall & Museum closed.

map 9
H6

HOUGHTON HALL

Kings Lynn

Tel: 01485 528569 (The Marquess of Cholmondeley)

The Home of the Marquess of Cholmondeley, Houghton Hall was built in the 18th century for Sir Robert Walpole by Colen Campbell and Thomas Ripley, with interior decoration by William Kent and is regarded as one of the finest examples of Palladian architecture in England. Houghton was later inherited by the 1st Marquess of Cholmondeley through his grandmother, Sir Robert's daughter. Situated in beautiful parkland, the house contains magnificent furniture, pictures and china. Pleasure grounds. A private collection of 20,000 model soldiers and militaria. 5-acre walled garden. **Location:** 13 miles E of King's Lynn; 10 miles W of Fakenham off A148. **Open:** Thurs, Sun and Bank Hol. Mon from 15 April–30 September. Park and grounds, soldier museum, walled garden, tearoom and shop: 1–5.30pm. House: 2–5.30pm. Last admission 5pm. **Admission:** Adult £6, Child £3. Excluding House Adult £3.50, Child £2.

map 9 H6

HOVETON HALL GARDENS

Hoveton Hall, Norwich, Norfolk, NR12 8RJ

Tel: 01603 782798 Fax. 01603 784564

Hoveton Hall Gardens – 15 acres of rhododendron and azalea filled woodland, laced with streams leading to a lake. Daffodils galore in Spring. Formal walled herbaceous and vegetable gardens. Morning coffee, light lunches and delicious home-made teas. **Open:** Easter Sun to mid Sept, Wed, Fri, Sun and Bank Hol Mons 11–5.30pm also Thursdays in May. Coaches welcome by appointment.

map 9 J6

MANNINGTON HALL

Saxthorpe, Norfolk

Tel: 01263 584175, Fax: 01263 761214 (Lord and Lady Walpole)

15th century moated house and Saxon church ruins set in attractive gardens. Outstanding rose collections. Extensive walks and trails around the estate. **Location:** 2 miles N of Saxthorpe, near B1149; 18 miles NW of Norwich; 9 miles from coast. **Open:** Walks daily all year; Garden May–Sept Sun 12–5pm. Also June–Aug Wed, Thurs and Fri 11–5. **Admission:** Adults £3, Children (accompanied children under 16) free OAPs/Students £2.50. House open by prior appointment only. **Refreshments:** Coffee, salad lunches and home-made teas.

map 9 J6

SANDRINGHAM HOUSE, MUSEUM & GROUNDS

Estate Office, Sandringham, Norfolk PE35 6EN

Tel: 01553 772675 (Her Majesty The Queen)

Sandringham is the charming country retreat of Her Majesty The Queen hidden in the heart of sixty acres of beautiful wooded grounds. All the main ground floor rooms used by The Royal Family, full of their treasured ornaments, portraits and furniture, are open to the public. More Royal possessions dating back more than a century are displayed in the Museum housed in the old stable and coach houses. Glades, dells, lakes and lawns are surrounded by magnificent trees and bordered by colourful shrubs and flowers. Location: 8 m NE of King's Lynn (off A148). **Open:** House: from 1 April–20 July 1999 daily 11–4.45pm (Grounds and Museum 24 July), reopens 5 August–3 October, daily 10.30 (Museum 11am) to 5pm. Grounds and Museums open weekends in October. **Admission:** Charges apply.

WOLTERTON PARK

Erpingham, Norfolk

Tel: 01263 584175, Fax: 01263 761214 (Lord and Lady Walpole)

Extensive historic park with lake and 18th century Mansion house. **Location:** Near Erpingham, signposted from A140 Norwich to Cromer Road. **Station(s):** Gunton. **Open:** Park open all year, daily 9–5pm or dusk if earlier. 2001 Hall: Fridays from April 27, 2–5pm (last entry 4pm). For Sundays and events see local press. **Admission:** Park £2 per car. Hall: £5. **Refreshments:** Pub at drive gate. **Events/Exhibitions:** Yes. **Accommodation:** Limited. **Conferences:** Yes.

map 9 J6

Northamptonshire

A gently undulating county, where church spires and grand estates nestle in a beautiful landscape of waterways, meadow and ancient woodlands. Here, one can take time to appreciate the simple rural pleasures of a bygone age, far from the hubbub of modern life. Northampton houses the Holy Sepulchre, one of only four surviving round Norman churches in England, which was fortunate not to be destroyed in the great fire that ravaged the town in the 17th century. A fine display of works of art by Henry Moore and Graham Sutherland may be viewed at St Matthew's church in nearby Kingsley. Further east, St James' church in Thrapston bears the family coat of arms of Sir John Washington, a relative of the first president of America.

Oundle

BOUGHTON HOUSE

Boughton House, Kettering, Northamptonshire.
Tel: 01536 515731 Fax: 01536 417255 E-mail: llt@boughtonhouse.org.uk (Duke of Buccleuch)

Northamptonshire home of the Duke of Buccleuch and his Montagu ancestors since 1528. A 500-year-old Tudor Monastic building, gradually enlarged until French style addition of 1695 led to the sobriquet "The English Versailles". Outstanding collection of fine arts from the world renowned Buccleuch Collection including 16th century carpets, 17th, 18th century French and English furniture, tapestries, porcelain and painted ceilings and notable works of art including works by El Greco, Murillo, Caracci and over 40 Van Dyck paintings. There is an incomparable Armoury and Ceremonial Coach. Extensive parkland with historic avenues of trees, woodlands, lakes and riverside walks. There is a Plant Centre in attractive old walled garden and tearooms in the refurbished Stable Block adjacent to the House, which together with the Adventure Woodland Play area (open subject to weather conditions) and Gift Shop are open weekends and daily throughout August. **Internet:** Award winning site gives full information, a 'virtual' tour of House and details of group visits and educational facilities (Heritage Education Trust, Sandford Award Winner 1988, 1993 and 1998) www.boughtonhouse.org.uk. **Open: House and Park:** Daily (incl Fri) 1 Aug–1 Sept. Park 1pm, House 2pm, last entry 4.30pm. Staterooms strictly by pre-booked appointment, tel 01536 515731 for details. **Park:** Daily (except Fri) 1 May–1 Sept, 1–5pm Plant Centre, Adventure Play area, tearoom open daily in Aug and weekends during park opening. Educational groups throughout the year, by prior appointment. **Admission:** House and Park: Adults £6, OAP/Child £5. Park only: Adults £1.50, OAP/Child £1. Wheelchair visitors free.

map 4 D1

ALTHORP

Althorp, Northamptonshire NN7 4HQ
Tel: 01604 770107 Fax: 01604 770042

Althorp has been the Spencer family home for nearly five centuries and twenty generations. Since the death of Diana, Princess of Wales, the house has become known all around the world. The honey-coloured stable block is now the setting for an exhibition celebrating her life. **Open:** 1Jul–31Aug. Daily 9am-5pm. Last admission 4pm. At the time of booking, visitors will be asked to state a preference for a morning or an afternoon visit. Pre-booking is strongly recommended. **Admission:** (Pre-booked) Adult £10, Child £5, Conc £8. All profits from visitor activity are donated to the Diana, Princess of Wales Memorial Fund. Dedicated booking line (24hrs): 0870 1679000. **Internet:** www.althorp.com

COTON MANOR GARDEN

Nr Guilsborough, Northamptonshire NN6 8RQ
Tel: 01604 740219 Fax: 01604 740838 (Mr & Mrs Ian Pasley-Tyler)

Traditional old English garden set in unspoilt countryside, with yew and holly hedges, extensive herbaceous borders, rose garden, water garden, herb garden, woodland garden, famous bluebell wood (early May) and recently established wild flower meadow. **Location:** 10 miles N of Northampton and 11 miles SE of Rugby. Follow tourist signs on A428 and A5199 (formerly A50). **Station(s):** Northampton, Long Buckby. **Open:** 1 Apr-30 Sept daily Wed-Sun and Bank Hol Mons 12–5.30pm. **Admission:** Adults £3.50, Senior Citizens £3, Children £2. **Refreshments:** Tearoom serving light lunches and teas. **Events/Exhibitions:** Unusual plants propagated from the garden for sale during season.
E-mail: pasleytyler@cotonmanor.fsnet.co.uk **Internet:** www.cotonmanor.co.uk

map 4 D1

NORTHAMPTON CENTRAL MUSEUM & ART GALLERY

Guildhall Road, Northampton, Northamptonshire NN1 1DP
Tel: 01604 238548 Fax: 01604 238720

The largest collection of boots & shoes in the world. Northampton's history. Fine and Decorative Arts. Leathercraft. **Open:** Mon–Sat 10–5pm. Sun 2–5pm. **Admission:** Free.

ABINGTON MUSEUM

Abington Park, Northampton, Northamptonshire

A 15th century manor house. Northampton life from cradle to grave. Northamptonshire's military history at home and abroad. **Open:** Mar–Oct Tues–Sun & BH Mon 1–5pm. Nov–Feb Tues–Sun 1–4pm. **Admission:** Free. **Internet:** www.northampton.gov.uk/museums

map 4 D1

COTTESBROOKE HALL AND GARDENS

Nr Northampton, Northamptonshire NN6 8PF
Tel: 01604 505808 Fax: 01604 505619 (Captain & Mrs John Macdonald-Buchanan)

Architecturally magnificent Queen Anne house commenced in 1702. Renowned picture collection, particularly of sporting and equestrian subjects. Fine English and Continental furniture and porcelain. House reputed to be the pattern for Jane Austen's 'Mansfield Park'. Celebrated gardens of great variety including herbaceous borders, water and wild gardens, fine old cedars and specimen trees. **Location:** 10 miles N of Northampton (A14–A1/M1 Link Road), near Creaton on A5199, near Brixworth on A508. **Open:** Easter to the end of September. House and Gardens: Thursdays, Bank Holiday Sunday and Monday afternoons, plus the first Sunday of each month May–Sept, 2-5:30pm. Last Admission 5pm. Gardens Only: 1st June to the end of Sept.–Tues, Wed, and Friday afternoons 2-5:30pm. Last admission 5pm. **Refreshments:** Tearoom open 2.30–5pm.

Gardens, but not house, suitable for disabled. Car park. Plants for sale. No dogs. **PRIVATE BOOKINGS:** Available for group visits to the house and gardens, or gardens only, on any other day during the season, except weekends, by prior appointment. **Lunches/refreshments** Available for groups by prior arrangement. Please telephone for information. **Functions and Banquets:** Evening and lunchtime functions, outdoor events, company days and lectures, details upon request. **Admission:** House & Gardens Adult £4.50. Gardens only Adult £3. Children half price.
E-mail: hall@cottesbrooke.co.uk **Internet:** www.cottesbrookehall.co.uk

map 4 D1

HOLDENBY HOUSE GARDENS & FALCONRY CENTRE

Holdenby, Northampton, Northamptonshire NN6 8DJ
Tel: 01604 770074 Fax: 01604 770962
(Mr & Mrs James Lowther. Administrator: Sarah Maughan)

On a hill across the fields from Althorp stands Holdenby. Once the largest house in England, it was a palace to entertain Queen Elizabeth I, then prison to her successor Charles I. Now this family home provides a splendid backdrop to the beautiful gardens by Rosemary Verey and Rupert Golby, the Falconry Centre, historical attractions and children's activities. Shop. Teas. **Location:** 7 m NW of Northampton off A428 & A5199. M1 exit 15a or 18. **Open:** Gardens & Falconry (G) Apr–end Sept, Sun 1–5pm. Daily in July & Aug (exc Sat) 1–5pm. House (H) 16 Apr, 28 May, 27 Aug & by appointment. Events (E) all BH 1–6pm. **Admission:** Adult (G) £3, (H) £5, (E) £4. Discounts for children & OAP.

map 4 D1

HADDONSTONE SHOW GARDEN

The Forge House, Church Lane, East Haddon, Northampton, NN6 8DB
Tel: 01604 770711 Fax: 01604 770027 (Haddonstone Limited)

See Haddonstone's classic garden ornaments in the beautiful setting of the walled manor gardens – including urns, troughs, fountains, statuary, bird baths, sundials, obelisks, columns and balustrading. Featured on BBC Gardeners' World, the garden is on different levels with shrub roses, ground cover plants, conifers, clematis and climbers. In 1998 the new Jubilee Garden opened, complete with temple, pavilion and Gothic Grotto. **Location:** 7 miles NW of Northampton off A428. **Open:** Mon–Fri 9–5.30pm closed weekends, Bank Hols and Christmas period. **Admission:** Free. Groups must apply in writing for permission to visit.

map 4 D1

KELMARSH HALL

Kelmarsh, Northampton, Northants NN6 9LU
Tel & Fax: 01604 686543 (The Kelmarsh Trust)

Built in 1732 to a James Gibbs design, Kelmarsh Hall is surrounded by its working estate, grazed parkland & beautiful gardens. In 1928 the Palladian house was occupied and decorated by Nancy Lancaster, and the Great Hall, Chinese Room & other rooms still bear her creative touch that has become known as the English Country House style. The gardens, with schemes & designs also by Geoffrey Jellicoe & Norah Lindsay, now have a unique place in garden history. **Location:** 12 miles N of Northampton; 5 miles S of Market Harborough on A508/A14 (J2). **Open:** Suns & B.H.Mons from 15 Apr-26 Aug, 2:30-5pm. Garden: Tue,Thur, Sun & B.H.Mons from 15 Apr-27 Sep, 2:30-5pm. **Admission:** Adults £3.50, OAPs £3, Children/garden only £2. Group bookings by arrangement. Welcome all year round. **Refreshments:** Home-made teas.

map 4 D1

LAMPORT HALL & GARDENS

Lamport, Northamptonshire, NN6 9HD
Tel: 01604 686 272 Fax: 01604 686 224
(Lamport Hall Preservation Trust Ltd)

Built for the Isham family. The South West front is a rare example of John Webb, pupil of Inigo Jones and was built in 1655 with wings added in 1732 and 1740. The Hall contains a wealth of outstanding books, paintings, furniture and china. Set in spacious wooded parkland with tranquil gardens, including a remarkable rock garden. **Location:** 8 miles north of Northampton on A508. **Open:** Easter to 7th Oct, Sun & Bank Hol Mons, 2.15–5.15pm. 20 & 21 Oct, 2.15–5.15pm. Last tour/admission 4.00pm. Aug, Mon–Sat for one tour only at 2.30pm. **Group Visits:** Welcome at anytime by prior arrangement. **Admission:** Adults £4, senior citizens £3.50, children £2. **Refreshments:** Home-made teas in Victorian Dining Room. **Events:** Please telephone for a free brochure. **Conferences:** Available for conferences/corporate hospitality.

map 4 D1

THE PREBENDAL MANOR HOUSE

Nassington, Nr. Peterborough, Northamptonshire, PE8 0QG
Tel: 01780 782 575 (Mrs J. Baile)

Grade 1 listed and dating from the early 13th century the Prebendal Manor is the oldest house in Northamptonshire, steeped in history and still retaining many architectural features. Unique to the region are the 14th century re-created medieval gardens which include a rose arbour, herber, flowery mead, and medieval fish ponds. Also included are the 15th century dovecote and tithe barn museum. Home-made teas. Lunches to order. Location: 6 miles N of Oundle, 7 miles S of Stamford, 8 miles W of Peterborough. **Open:** May, Jun, & Sept: Suns, Weds & BH Mons. Jul-Aug: Suns, Weds & Thurs 1-5.30pm. **Admission:** Adults £4, Child £1.20.

SULGRAVE MANOR

Manor Road, Sulgrave, Banbury, Oxon OX17 2SD
Tel: 01295 760205 (Sulgrage Manor Board)

The home of George Washington's Ancestors. A delightful 16th Century Manor House presenting a typical walthy man's home and gardens in Elizabethan times. "A perfect illustration of how a house should be shown to the public" – Nigel Nicholson, Great Houses of Britain. Location: Sulgrave Village is off Banbury/Northampton Road (B4525); 5 m from Banbury junction of M40, 12m from Northampton junction of M1; 7 m NE of Banbury. **Open:** 1 Apr–31 Oct daily except Weds week days 2–5.30pm. Weekends 10.30–1pm and 2-5.30pm. Nov, Dec, Mar: weekends only 10.30–1pm and 2–4.30pm. **Admission:** Adult £4, Children £2. Gardens only £2.

SOUTHWICK HALL

(Christopher Capron)
Southwick, Peterborough, Northants PE8 5BL
Tel: 01832 274064 (W.J. Richardson)Manager

A family home since 1300, retaining medieval building dating from 1300, with Tudor rebuilding and 18th century additions. Exhibitions: Victorian and Edwardian life; collections of agricultural and carpentry tools, named bricks and local archeological finds and fossils. **Location:** 3 miles N of Oundle; 4 miles E of Bulwick. **Open:** Bank Holidays (Sunday & Monday) Apr 15–16, May 6–7 & 27–28, Aug 26–27 and Weds May–Aug, 2–5pm (last admission 4.30pm). Parties at other times (Easter–Aug) by arrangement with the Manager. **Admission:** Adults £3.50, OAPs £3, Children £2 (all inclusive). **Refreshments:** Teas available.

map 8 E7

Northumberland

Lindisfarne Castle

Situated at the northernmost point of England, Northumberland is blessed not only with tremendous natural beauty, but also with a fascinating history. The border between England and Scotland in the north of the county was the scene of a four hundred year territorial conflict that ended in 1707 with the Union of Parliament. From the reign of Edward I onwards, feuding families, known as Reivers, fought endless and bitter battles across the border hills. As a result, there are now more castles and fortified buildings in Northumberland than in any other English county.

Testimony to Northumberland's outstanding beauty is the fact that a large area of its countryside has been designated National Parkland. Northumberland National Park stretches between two sites of historic importance – the round Cheviot Hills, which today form the border between England and Scotland, and Hadrian's Wall, which lies 60 miles to the south. Its 398 square miles take in glorious wooded valleys and dramatic stretches of open moorland.

To the east, Northumberland is edged by dramatic coastline, historically the scene of invasion by the Vikings. The Holy Island of Lindisfarne, one of the first areas to be invaded, is now a tranquil nature reserve for seals and seabirds. Northumberland's small population (it remains the least densely populated county in England) is the key to its consistently beautiful and unspoilt scenery. Small picturesque villages sit proudly in their deep valleys, many centred on an ancient landmark such as a stone cross or runic inscription.

Human activity within Northumberland dates back at least 8,000 years, and the nomadic tribes that followed herds of deer across the county have left artefacts crafted from bones, stone and flint. Haltwhistle, the gateway to Hadrian's Wall and Blanchland, lying in a vast dale of the Pennines, are worth a visit, as are Corbridge, on the banks of the River Tyne, Bellingham and Allendale.

BELSAY HALL, CASTLE & GARDENS

Belsay, Northumberland NE20 0DX
Tel: 01661 881636 (English Heritage)

Explore a ruined castle, manor house and neoclassical hall all set amidst 30 acres of magnificent landscaped grounds – a great and varied day out for all who visit. The beautiful honey-coloured stone from which the Belsay Hall is built came from its own quarries which have since become the unusual setting for one of the series of spectacular gardens, deservedly listed Grade I in the Register of Gardens. Enjoy the mix of formal and informal; rhododendrons, magnolias, ornate terraces and even a winter garden are among Belsay's special features. **Location:** In Belsay, 14m NW of Newcastle on A696. **Open:** 1 Apr–30 Sept: daily, 10am-6pm. 1 Oct–31 Oct: daily, 10–5pm. 1 Nov–28 Mar: daily 10–4pm. (Closed 24–26 Dec). Open 1 Jan. **Admission:** Adult £3.90, Conc £2.90, Child £2 (15% discount for groups of 11 or more).

map 11
G3

BAMBURGH CASTLE

Bamburgh ME69 7DF
Tel: 01669 620314

Bamburgh Castle is the home of Lady Armstrong and her family. The earliest reference to Bamburgh shows the craggy citadel to have been a royal centre by AD 547. The public rooms contain many exhibits, including the collections of armoury on loan from HM Tower of London. Porcelain, china , jade, furniture from many periods, oils, water – colours and a host of interesting items are all contained within one of the most important buildings of Britain's national heritage. Location: 42m N of Newcastle–upon–Tyne. 6m E of Belford by B1342 from A1 at Belford. Open: April–October daily 11–5pm. Last entry 4.30pm. Admission: Adult £4.50, child £1.50, OAP £3.50. Groups: Adult £3, child £1, OAPs £2. Groups up to 16 – min. payment £30.

CHIPCHASE CASTLE & GARDENS

Wark on Tyne, Hexham, Northumberland
Tel: 01434 230203, Fax: 01434 230740 (Mrs P J Torday)

An imposing Grade I listed 17th and 18th Century Castle, set in formal and informal gardens including a lake and two walled gardens, one of which is now run as a nursery specialising in the sale of unusual perennials. Grade I listed chapel stands in the park. Holiday cottages and salmon fishing also available on weekly basis on the Estate. **Location:** 2 miles South of Wark on the Barrasford Road **Open:** Castle: 1-28 June, daily 2-5pm. Tours by arrangement at other times. Gardens and Nursery: Easter-31 July, Thurs to Sun and Bank Hols 10-5. **Admission:** Castle £4, Gardens £1.50, Nursery free.

map 11
G3

CHESTERS ROMAN FORT
Tel: 01434 681379 (English Heritage)

Chesters, located between the 27th and 28th milecastles, is one of the best-preserved examples of a cavalry fort. Many parts are still visible, including the barracks and a finely preserved bath house. So much is known about this early fort because of the pioneering archaeological work of John Clayton, who inherited the local estate in 1832. The museum, which was built in 1896 soon after his death, houses the important Clayton Collection of altars and sculptures from all along Hadrian's Wall. **Location:** ¼ m W of Chollerford on B6318 (OS Map 87; ref NY 913701). **Open:** 1 Apr–30 Sept, daily 9.30am–6pm. 1-31 Oct, daily 10am–5pm. 1 Nov–31 Mar, daily 10am–4pm. Closed 24–26 Dec & 1 Jan. **Admission:** Adults £2.90, Concessions £2.20, Children £1.50. 15% discount for groups of 11+.

map 11
G3

CORBRIDGE ROMAN SITE AND MUSEUM
Tel: 01434 632349 (English Heritage)

Originally the site of a fort on the former patrol road, Corbridge evolved into a principal town of the Roman era, flourishing until the 5th century. The large granaries, with their ingenious ventilation system, are among its most impressive remains. Corbridge is an excellent starting point to explore the Wall. Its museum contains fascinating finds and remarkable sculptures. **Location:** ½ m NW of Corbridge on minor road, signed Corbridge Roman Site (OS Map 87; ref NY 983649). **Open:** 1 Apr–30 Sept, daily 10am–6pm. 1-31 Oct, daily 10am–5pm. 1 Nov–31 Mar, Wed–Sun 10am–1pm, 2–4pm. Closed 24–26 Dec & 1 Jan. **Admission:** Adults £2.90, Concessions £2.20, Children £1.50. 15% discount for groups of 11+.

map 11
G3

HOUSESTEADS ROMAN FORT
Tel: 01434 344363 (English Heritage)

Housesteads occupies a commanding position on the cliffs of the Whin Sill. One of 17 permanent forts built by Hadrian c. AD124, it is the most complete example of a Roman fort in Britain. Its visible remains include 4 gates with towers between them, as well as the principal buildings from within an auxiliary fort. There are also remains of the civilian settlement that clustered at its gates. From the archaeological record of Housesteads, we can glimpse the people who lived at the edge of the Empire. Children's Activity Book available. A volunteer guide may be provided if requested in advance. **Location:** 2¾ m NE of Bardon Mill on B6318 (OS Map 87; ref NY 790687). Parking charge payable to the National Trust. **Open:** 1 Apr–30 Sept, daily 10am–6pm. 1-31 Oct, daily 10am–5pm. 1 Nov–31 Mar, daily 10am–4pm. Closed 24–26 Dec & 1 Jan. **Admission:** Adults £2.90, Concessions £2.20, Children £1.50. 15% discount for groups of 11+.

map 11
F3

Local Tourist Information: Hexham Tel: 01434 605225 Haltwhistle Tel: 01434 322002
English Heritage (NE Region): Tel: 0191 269 1200
Public Transport: Journey Planner Tel: 08706 082608 Rail Enquiries Tel: 08457 484950
Websites: www.hadrians-wall.org/www.english-heritage.org.uk

ALNWICK CASTLE

Alnwick, Northumberland NE66 1NQ

Tel: 01665 510777 24 hour Information Line: 01665 511100 Fax: 01665 510876 (His Grace the Duke of Northumberland)

Set in stunning landscape, designed by Capability Brown, Alnwick Castle is the home of the Duke of Northumberland. Owned by his family since 1309. This beautiful and awe-inspiring Castle was a major defence against invading Scottish armies in the Middle Ages. Visitors arriving through the massive and imposing Medieval Barbican are then treated to views of one of the finest Castles in England. Beautifully kept grounds are the wonderful setting for the Keep, which was restored by the first Duke in the 18th century to create a Fortress on the outside and a luxurious stately home on the inside. The grounds also contain the Museum of Northumberland Fusiliers, telling the story from 1674 to the present day. The Postern Tower displays one of the finest archeological collections in private hands and the Constable's Tower an exhibition on the Percy Tenantry Volunteers, who were formed in response to the threat from Napoleon's France.

Furnishings and decoration were of the highest quality with paintings by Canaletto, Van Dyck and Titian hanging on the walls. **Guest Hall:** Alnwick Castle Guest Hall is one of the chief buildings of Anthony Salvin's 19th century restoration. Built as a magnificent coach house, it has throughout its history served as a venue for entertainment. This splendid Guest Hall is available for conferences, corporate entertaining, wedding receptions, concerts, dinner dances and theatre productions. Please note that the Guest Hall is not open to Castle visitors. **Location:** 35 miles from Newcastle on the A1. Accessible by public transport. **Open:** Daily 11–5pm (last admission 4.15pm). 1 April-26 October **Education:** Service provides programmes of activities for schools and colleges. **Parking:** Free for cars and coaches. **E-mail:** enquiries@alnwickcastle.com

map 11
H2

CHILLINGHAM CASTLE & GARDENS

Chillingham, Northumberland NE66 5NJ
Tel: 01668 215359 Fax: 01668 215463 (Sir Humphry Wakefield Bt)

Situated in a spectacular setting, Chillingham Castle is the finest surviving example of fortified domestic architecture in the County. The same family line has owned the castle since the mid 1200s. 13th and 14th century monarchs rested here on their way to Scottish campaigns. There are fortifications, courtyards, a Minstrel's Hall, even dungeons and torture chambers. We have hidden passages through which castle defenders escaped. The Avenues and Gardens were laid out by Sir Jeffrey de Wyatville fresh from his Royal Windsor triumphs. The best specimen trees in Northumberland form a backdrop to the formal topiary gardens and England's longest herbaceous border. Astonishing drifts of snowdrops, daffodils and bluebells give way to rhododendrons and then the glory of the summer gardens. Near to hand the famous Chillingham Wild Cattle have their own

separate venture and with luck, you may see red squirrels and fallow deer as well as badger and even otter up by the lake. **Location:** 12 miles N of Alnwick, signposted from A1 and A697. **Open:** Easter, 1 May–30 Sept, 12–5pm. Open 7 days a week July & Aug. Closed Tue May, Jun & Sept. All year for groups by arrangement. **Admission:** Adults £4.50, OAPs £4, Children 3-13 50p, Parties (10+) £3.80. Coaches welcome. Free parking. **Refreshments:** Tearoom. Full meals for groups by arrangement. **Accommodation:** 7 self-contained apartments. The castle is a wonderful base for visits to the sea, fishing resorts, mountainous walks and several golf courses. **Conferences:** It is a unique venue for weddings, seminars and small conferences. **E-mail:** enquiries@chillingham-castle.com **Internet:** www.chillingham-castle.com

map 11
G2

LINDISFARNE PRIORY
Tel: 01289 389200 (English Heritage)

You cross the causeway to Holy Island and journey into spiritual heritage. When the corpse of St Cuthbert was discovered undecayed in 698AD, Lindisfarne became one of the holiest shrines in Christendom. Learn about the monastery's fantastic wealth and walk in the grounds where brutal Viking raiders plundered the priory. Visit the award-winning, lively and atmospheric museum; it explains what life was like more than a millennium ago and illustrates the drama of Lindisfarne. **Location:** On Holy Island, only reached at low tide across causeway (tide tables at each end or details from Berwick Tourist Information Centre, Tel 01289 330733). Train: Berwick-upon-Tweed 14m. Bus: Tel 01670 533128. **Open:** All year: 1 Apr–30 Sept daily, 10am–6pm. 1–31 Oct daily, 10am–5pm. 1 Nov–28 Mar daily, 10am–4pm. Closed 24–26 Dec & 1 Jan. **Admission:** Adult £2.90, Conc £2.20, Child £1.50, under 5 yrs free. 15% discount on groups of 11 or more. **Internet:** www.english-heritage.org.uk

map 11 H1

SEATON DELAVAL HALL
S eaton Sluice, Whitley Bay, Northumberland NE26 4QR
Tel: 0191 237 0786/1493 (The Lord Hastings)

The home of Lord and Lady Hastings, a ½ mile from Seaton Sluice, is the last and most sensational mansion designed by Sir John Vanbrugh, builder of Blenheim Palace and Castle Howard. It was erected between 1718 and 1728 and comprises a high turreted block flanked by arcaded wings which form a vast forecourt. The centre block was gutted by fire in 1822, but was partly restored in 1862 and again in 1959–62 and 1999–2000. The remarkable staircases are a visual delight, and the two surviving rooms are filled with family pictures and photographs and royal seals spanning three centuries as well as various archives. This building is used frequently for concerts and charitable functions. The east wing contains immense stables in ashlar stone of breathtaking proportions. Nearby are the Coach House with farm and passenger vehicles, fully documented, and the restored ice house with explanatory sketch and description. There are beautiful gardens with herbaceous borders, rose garden, rhododendrons, azaleas, laburnum walks, statues, and a spectacular parterre by internationally famous JIm Russel, and also a unique Norman Church. **Open:** May & August BH Mondays, June–30 Sept Wed & Sun 2–6pm. **Admission:** Adult £3, Concessions £2.50, Children £1. **Refreshments:** Tearoom. Free car park.

map 11 H2

WARKWORTH CASTLE
Tel: 01665 711423 (English Heritage)

Let the audio tour bring you all the magic of this mighty fortress. Regional court, military stronghold, massive aristocratic home - Warkworth was all of these. Home to the all-powerful Percy family who at times wielded more power than the King himself. Most famous of them all was Harry Hotspur, immortalised in Shakespeare's 'Henry IV'. There is so much to explore - the chambers and a maze of passageways and staircases. **Open:** All year, 1 Apr–30 Sept daily, 10am–6pm. 1–31 Oct daily, 10am–5pm. 1 Nov–28 Mar daily, 10am–4pm. Closed 24–26 Dec & 1 Jan. **Admission:** Adults £2.50, concessions £1.90, children £1.30, under 5 yrs free. 15% discount on groups of 11 or more. **Warkworth Hermitage:** This curious chapel is cut deep into the rock of the river cliff. Visit the castle, then stroll upstream and the ferryman will row you across the river. **Open:** 1 Apr–30 Sept, Wed, Sun & BH 11am–5pm. **Admission:** Adult £1.70, Conc £1.30, Child 90p. **Internet:** www.english-heritage.org.uk

map 11 H3

Nottinghamshire

Nottinghamshire is perhaps best known as the home of Robin Hood, who once poached the King's deer in the royal hunting forest of Sherwood. Whether Robin was real or imaginary, we will probably never know, but the legend surrounding him has continued to grow since early mediaeval times. Visitors to Sherwood can still see the mighty Major Oak, one of the largest oak trees in England, whose hollow trunk is said to have concealed Robin and his men from the Sheriff of Nottingham.

To the south of the forest lies Nottingham itself, a thriving city famous for its lace and textiles. The grand civic buildings of its centre contrast strongly with the humble cottages that dot the floodplain of the River Trent just beyond.

The countryside of Nottinghamshire has been the inspiration for a number of writers, including the Romantic poet Lord Byron, and D.H. Lawrence, who referred to it as "the country of my heart". The quiet pastoral landscape remains undisturbed and largely undeveloped, and sleepy villages are often the only sign of man's presence. Particularly worth a visit are Wellow, near Rufford Abbey, and Maplebeck, near Newark, home to one of the smallest pubs in England.

Nottingham

CARLTON HALL

Carlton-on-Trent, Nottinghamshire NG23 6LP
Tel: 01636 821421 Fax: 01636 821554

Mid 18th century house by Joseph Pocklington of Newark. Stables attributed to Carr of York. Family home occupied by the same family since 1832. Magnificent drawing room. **Location:** 7 miles north of Newark off A1. Opposite the church. **Open:** By appointment only. **Admission:** Hall and Garden: £3.50. Minimum charge for a group £35.

map 8 D6

NEWARK TOWN HALL

Market Place, Newark, Nottinghamshire
Tel: 01636 680 333 Fax: 01636 640 967 (Newark Town Council)

One of the finest Georgian Town Halls in the country, the building has recently been refurbished in sympathy with John Carr's original concept. On display is the Town's collection of Civic Plate, silver dating generally from the 17th and 18th century, including the 'Newark Monteith' and the Newark 'Siege Pieces'. Other items of interest are some early historical records and various paintings including a collection by the artist Joseph Paul. Location: Market Place, Newark. Located on A1 and A46. Station(s): Newark Castle. Northgate (1/2 mile). **Open:** All year, Mon–Fri, 10.30–1pm & 2–4.30pm; Sat 2–4.30pm (Apr–Oct). Open at other times for groups by appointment. Closed: Sun, Bank Hol Mons & Tue following and Christmas week.

NORWOOD PARK

Norwood Park, Southwell, Nottinghamshire NG25 0PF
Tel: 01636 815649 Fax: 01636 815702 (Sir John and Lady Starkey)

Delightful Georgian country house and stables, set in a medieval deer Park with ancient oaks, fishponds and eyecatcher Temple overlooking apple orchards and the cricket ground, Norwood Park is the ideal venue for events of all kinds. The charming reception rooms of the house are perfect for weddings, meetings and dinners, while the Stables Gallery complex is a unique and spacious setting for events such as dances and conferences. The grounds are varied and ideal for filming, shows and activity days. The USA designed golf course and practice area is a recent bonus to the facilities offered at Norwood Park. **Contact:** Sarah Dodd Events Manager.

PAPPLEWICK HALL

Nr. Nottingham, NG15 8FE, Nottinghamshire
Tel: 0115 963 3491 Fax: 0115 964 2767 (Dr R. Godwin-Austen)

Fine Adam house built 1784 with lovely plasterwork ceilings. Park and woodland garden, particularly known for its rhododendrons. **Location:** 6 miles N of Nottingham, off A69. 2 miles from Junction 27, M1. **Open:** 1st, 3rd & 5th Weds in the month and by appointment. **Refreshments:** By arrangement. **Events/Exhibitions:** 3rd Sat in June – annual fête and maypole dancing. **Conferences:** Up to 30 people. **Admission:** £5.

map 8 D5

Oxfordshire

Oxford Botanic Garden

Oxfordshire is a county of contrasts: famous for its beautiful, unspoilt countryside and enviable heritage, it is also home to some of the most advanced research and industry in the country. With much of its population based in Oxford and Banbury, the county is, for the most part, a patchwork of small villages and open land, where riverside walks are a popular pastime.

The centre of Oxford itself is a blend of ancient buildings and modern amenities, where quiet quadrangles lie just behind the busy streets. The University dominates the city, and is made up of over thirty separate colleges, the earliest of which dates back to the 13th century. Visitors are normally drawn to the traditional architectural charms of Balliol, Christchurch and Magdalen, but an interesting contrast can be seen in the controversial work of Danish architect Arne Jacobsen in St Catherine's. Oxford is also home to a number of historic pubs, including The Turf Tavern, The Eagle and Child (a regular haunt of C.S. Lewis), and the Bear. The Trout Inn, which lies just beyond Portmeadow, is a popular spot for riverside lunches, and is well worth a visit.

ARDINGTON HOUSE

Ardington House, Wantage, Oxfordshire
Tel: 01235 821566 Fax: 01235 821151 (The Baring Family)

Home of the Baring family. This early 18th century beautifully symmetrical house with exceptionally fine brickwork is surrounded by well-kept lawns, terraced gardens and peaceful paddocks. To the south, the house looks across the garden to the river, well known to enthusiastic fly fishermen. The entrance of the house is dominated by the Imperial Staircase – two flights of stairs coming back into one. These are very rare, and the Ardington Staircase is a magnificent example. The Hall and Dining Room have original panelling. Cornices and woodwork in the Hall are beautiful, and the Dining Room has a plasterwork ceiling. The perfect venue for weddings, dinner parties and small conferences. In the past two years

Ardington House has been enjoyed as a venue by many businesses including Land Rover, The CLA Gamefair & Hampton's International. "I have no doubt that the food, wine and service which you provided played a major role in selling some additional shares in the horses." Nick Robinson, Chairman - Kennet Valley Thoroughbreds. **Location:** 12 miles S of Oxford, 12 miles N of Newbury, 2½ miles E of Wantage. **Open:** 1–4, 7–11, 14–16, 18, 21 May, 1–3, 6–7, 9–10, 13–16 Aug & Bank Holiday Mondays 2.30–4.30pm. **Admission:** House & Gardens: Adult £3.50.

map 4 C4

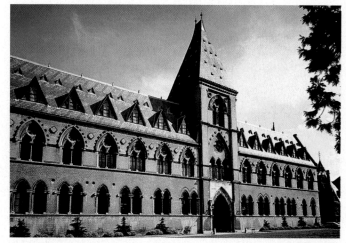

THE ASHMOLEAN MUSEUM OF ART & ARCHAEOLOGY

Beaumont Street, Oxford OX1 2PH
Tel: 01865 278000. Fax: 01865 278018

Archaeology, European paintings and ceramics; sculpture and bronzes; silver; coins and medals; Eastern porcelain, painting and applied arts. **Open:** Tues–Sat 10–5pm. Sun 2–5pm. Closed St Giles Fair in Sept, Christmas, New Year & Easter. Café, Shop & Guided tours. School & adult parties welcome (tel: 01865 278015 for information and booking). **Admission:** Free. **Internet:** www.ashmol.ox.ac.uk

OXFORD UNIVERSITY MUSEUM OF NATURAL HISTORY

Parks Road, Oxford OX1 3PW.
Tel: 01865 272950. Fax: 01865 272970. Information Line: 01865 270949

Displays the fossil dinosaur material and the historic collections donated by Darwin, Burchall and Hope. The glass-roofed museum court shows the influence of John Ruskin. **Open:** Everyday (incl. Sun) 12–5pm. Check at Easter and Christmas. **Admission:** Free. **Internet**: www.oum.ox.ac.uk

THE PITT RIVERS MUSEUM

South Parks Road, Oxford OX1 3PP
(entrance through University Museum of Natural History)
Tel: 01865 270927. Fax: 01865 270943

One of the world's great ethnographic museums. Collections of masks, jewellery, weaponry, textiles, toys, tools and much more in a setting now famous for its period atmosphere. Special Exhibition: 'Transformations: The Art of Recycling'. The Balfour Galleries, 60 Banbury Road: archaeology, hunter gatherer societies, and musical instruments. Groups bookings tel: 01865 270931. **Open:** Mon–Sat 1–4.30pm. Sun 2–4.30pm (not Balfour Galleries). Check at Christmas and Easter. **Admission:** Free. **Internet:** www.prm.ox.ac.uk

  map 4 C3

BROUGHTON CASTLE

Banbury, Oxfordshire OX15 5EB
Tel & Fax: 01295 276070/722547 (the Lord Saye and Sele)

The home of the family of Lord and Lady Saye & Sele for 600 years. Surrounded by a moat, it was built in 1300 and greatly enlarged in 1550. It contains fine panelling and fireplaces, splendid plaster ceilings and good period furniture. Civil War Parliamentarian connections. Beautiful walled gardens, with old roses, shrubs and herbaceous borders. **Location:** 2 miles W of Banbury on the B4035 Shipston-on-Stour Road. **Open:** Weds and Suns 20 May–12 Sept. Also Thurs in July and August. Bank Hol Suns and Bank Hol Mons (including Easter) 2–5pm. Groups welcome on any day and at any time during the year, by appointment. . **Admission:** Adult £4.50, Senior Citizens £4, Students £4, Children £2. Groups reduced rates. Tearoom and shop. **E-mail:** admin@broughton castle.demon.co.uk **Internet:** www.broughtoncastle.demon.co.uk

  map 4 C2

BUSCOT PARK

Faringdon, Oxfordshire SN7 8BU
Tel: 01367 240786 Fax: 01367 241794 (Lord Faringdon)

The late 18th century neoclassical house contains the Faringdon Collection of paintings and furniture. The park features a water garden, designed in the early 20th century by Harold Peto. **Open:** House & grounds: 3 Apr–29 Sept, Wed–Fri 2–6pm (incl. Good Fri and also open Easter Sat & Sun). Also open every 2nd & 4th Sat and immediately following Sun in each month 2–6pm. Last admission to house 5.30pm. Grounds only: 1 Apr–end Sept: open as house but also Mon (but not Bank Hol. Mon) & Tue 2–6pm. **Admission:** House & Grounds £4.40. Grounds only £3.30. Children half price. Parties must book in writing or by fax. Unsuitable for wheelchair users due to gradients, gravel paths and steps to house. Tearoom open same days as house 2.30–5.30pm. No dogs allowed. **Location:** Between Lechlade and Faringdon, on A417. **E-mail:** estbuscot@aol.com **Internet:** www.faringdon–coll.com

map 4 B4

CHRIST CHURCH PICTURE GALLERY

Canterbury Quadrangle, Christ Church, Oxford OX1 1DP
Tel: 01865 276172 Fax: 01865 202429

Christ Church Picture Gallery houses an internationally important collection of old master paintings and drawings. The paintings include works by the Carracci, Tintoretto, Filippino Lippi, Van Dyck and Frans Hals. A selection of drawings is usuallly exhibited, including works by Leonardo, Raphael, Michelangelo and Rubens. Displays of 18th century glass, Russian icons and old master prints, along with exhibitions of work by contemporary artists from Oxfordshire also feature in the Gallery's programme. The building, which was opened in 1968, is an award-winning example of modernist architecture. **Open:** Mon-Sat; 10:30-1pm & 2-4:30pm. Sun; 2-4:30. Easter to end Sept. open until 5:30 every day. **Admission:** Free on Mondays; Adult £2, Student, OAP/UB40 £1. Free to children under 12 & members of the Oxford Universities. **E-mail:** dennis.harrington@christ-church.ox.ac.uk **Internet:** www.chch.ox.ac.uk

map 4 C3

DITCHLEY PARK

Enstone, Chipping Norton, Oxfordshire OX7 4ER
Tel: 01608 677346, Fax: 01608 677399 (Ditchley Foundation)

Third in size and date of the great 18th century houses of Oxfordshire, Ditchley is famous for its splendid interior decorations (William Kent and Henry Flitcroft). For three and a half centuries the home of the Lee family and their descendants – Ditchley was frequently visited at weekends by Sir Winston Churchill during World War II. It has now been restored, furnished and equipped as a conference centre devoted to the study of issues of concern to the people on both sides of the Atlantic. **Location:** 1½ miles W of A44 at Kiddington; 2 miles from Charlbury (B4437). **Station(s):** Charlbury (2 miles) **Open:** Group visits by prior arrangement with the Bursar, Mon to Thurs afternoons only. Closed July-mid Sept. **Admission:** Entry fee £5 per person, minimum charge £40. **Internet:** www.ditchley.co.uk

map 4 C3

BLENHEIM PALACE

Woodstock, Oxfordshire OX20 1PX

Tel: 01993 811325 (24hrs information) Fax: 01993 813527 (His Grace the Duke of Marlborough)

Blenheim Palace, home of the 11th Duke of Marlborough and birthplace of Sir Winston Churchill, is an English baroque masterpiece designed by Sir John Vanbrugh for John Churchill, 1st Duke of Marlborough. It contains fine collections set in magnificent gilded state rooms overlooking sweeping lawns, formal parterres and water gardens. It is a World Heritage site, reflecting the importance of both the house and the 2,100-acre park, landscaped by "Capability" Brown. The park provides a matchless setting, framing the Palace against the skyline and overlooking the lake and Vanbrugh's Grand Bridge. The Palace admission ticket also includes rides on the miniature train and entry to the lavender and herb gardens and the butterfly house. Optional extras for the more energetic are the adventure playground next to the Pleasure Gardens, and the Marlborough Maze - the world's largest symbolic hedge maze. Licensed restaurant and self-service cafés. **Events:** Craft Fairs May Day and August Bank Holiday weekends; Blenheim Palace Flower Show 21–24 June; Fireworks Concert 24 August; Blenheim International Horse Trials 6–9 September. **Conferences and Entertaining:** The Palace Great Hall, Saloon and Library make stunning venues for private or corporate entertaining. Contact the Functions Manager for further details. The Orangery and Spencer Churchill Conference Room are also available for conferences and banqueting. **Education:** Sandford Award holders since 1982; support is offered on a wide range of National Curriculum subjects. **Location:** 8 miles NW of Oxford, at Woodstock, on A44. **Open:** 12 March–31 Oct 10.30am–4.45pm (last admission). **Admission:** Please phone for details. **E-mail:** administration@blenheimpalace.com **Internet:** www.blenheimpalace.com

map 4
C3

Oxfordshire

ASHDOWN HOUSE
Lambourn, Newbury RG16 7RE
Tel: 01488 72584

Dutch-style 17th century house famous for its association with the Winter Queen (Elizabeth of Bohemia), to whom the house was consecrated by Charles I. Impressive staircase and important collection of paintings, as well as spectacular views from roof. **Open:** Apr to end Oct, Weds and Sats, guided tours only at 2.15pm, 3.15pm, and 4.15pm. **Admission:** Adult £2.10

CHASTLETON HOUSE
Chastleton, Moreton-in-Marsh, Gloucestershire, GL56 0SU
Tel: 01608 674355

One of the finest and most complete Jacobean houses in England, dating from 1612. Continuously occupied for over four hundred years by a single family. The gardens saw the laying-down of the rules of modern croquet. **Open:** 4 Apr–29 Sept: Wed–Sat 1–5pm. 3 Oct–3 Nov, Wed–Sat, 1–4pm. **Admission:** By timed ticket, booked in advance on 01494 755585: Adult £5.20, Child £2.60.

GREYS COURT
Rotherfield Greys, Henley-on-Thames, Oxfordshire RG9 4PG
Tel: 01491 628529

A sixteenth-century house built within the walls and towers of a ruined fourteenth-century fortified house. The garden contains Archbishop's Maze, inspired by Runcie's enthronement speech in 1980. **Open:** 3 Apr–end Sept, Wed–Fri and Bank Holidays, 2–6pm. Closed on Good Friday. **Admission:** Adult £4.60, Child £2.30.

KINGSTON BAGPUIZE HOUSE
Nr Abingdon, Oxfordshire OX13 5AX
Tel: 01865 820259 Fax: 01865 821659 (Mr and Mrs Francis Grant)

Beautiful 1660's manor house remodelled in early 1700's in red brick with stone facings. Cantilevered staircase and finely proportioned panelled rooms. Set in mature parkland, the gardens contain a notable collection of plants including rare trees, shrubs, perennials and bulbs. Available for functions. **Location:** In Kingston Bagpuize village, S of A420/A415 intersection. Abingdon 5 miles, Oxford 9 miles. **Station(s):** Oxford or Didcot. **Open:** Feb 18,Mar 4, 18; Apr 1, 14, 15, 16, 29; May 5, 6, 7, 26, 27, 28; Jun 10, 24; Jul 1, 21, 22; Aug 11, 12, 15, 25, 26, 27; Sept 8, 9, 12, 22, 23, 30; Oct 14; Nov 11. 2–5.30pm (tours of house 2.30pm to 4.45pm). Garden: Last entry 5pm. **Admission:** House & Garden: Adult £3.50, OAP £3, child £2.50. Garden only £1.50 (under 5s not admitted to house but free to garden). Groups welcome by appointment. Wheelchairs garden only. No dogs. **Refreshments:** Home-made teas.

`map 4 D4`

FAWLEY COURT
Henley-on-Thames, Oxon RG9 3AE
Tel: 01491 574917 Fax: 01491 411587 (Congregation of Marian Fathers)

Designed by Sir Christopher Wren, built in 1684 for Col W Freeman, decorated by Grinling Gibbons and by James Wyatt. The Museum consists of a library, various documents of the Polish kings, a very well preserved collection of historical sabres and many memorable military objects of the Polish army. Paintings, early books, numistmatic collections, arms and armour. **Location:** 1 mile north of Henley-on-Thames east to A4155 to Marlow. **Open:** May–Oct Wed, Thurs & Sun, 2–5pm. Other dates by arrangement. Closed Easter and Whitsuntide weeks and Nov–Feb. **Admission:** House, museum and grounds: Adults £4, OAPs £3, Children £1.50, Groups (min 12) £3.

`map 4 D4`

KELMSCOTT MANOR
Kelmscott, Nr. Lechlade, Oxfordshire,GL7 3HJ.
Tel: 01367 252 486 Fax: 01367 253 754 (Society of Antiquaries)

Kelmscott Manor was the country home of William Morris – poet, craftsman and socialist – from 1871 until his death in 1896. It is the most evocative of all his houses and continues to delight with the charm of its architecture, the fascination of its contents and the charm of its garden, which has recently undergone extensive restoration and now contains many fine examples of plants and flowers which would have been an inspiration to Morris. **Location:** 2 miles SE of Lechlade, on the Lechlade/Faringdon Road. **Open:** Apr–Sept, Wed 11am–1pm, 2–5pm. The 3rd Sat in Apr, May, June and Sept, 2–5pm. The 1st and 3rd Sat in July & Aug, 2–5pm. Thurs & Fri – private group visits. **Admission:** Adults £7, Children £3.50, Students £3.50. **Events/Exhibitions:** Centenary exhibition "William Morris at Kelmscott". Gift shop and bookshop. **E-mail:** admin@kelmscottmanor.co.uk **Internet:** www.kelmscottmanor.co.uk

`map 4 B3`

NUFFIELD PLACE
Huntercombe, Henley-on-Thames, Oxon RG9 5RY
Tel: 01491 641224(Nuffield College/Friends of Nuffield Place)

Home from 1933–63 of William Morris, Lord Nuffield, car manufacturer and philanthropist. A rare survival of a complete upper-middle class home of the 1930's, retaining majority of furniture and contents acquired on taking up residence. Fine quality rugs, clocks, tapestries and custom-made furniture. Four acre gardens, laid out around 1914 when house was built, contain mature trees, yew hedges, rose pergola, rockery and pond. **Location:** Approximately 7 miles Henley-on-Thames just off A4130 to Oxford. Coach service X39 Oxford/Henley. **Open:** Apr–Sept every 2nd and 4th Sun 2–5pm. **Admission:** Please call for details. Parties by arrangement. **Refreshments:** Home-made teas. Ground floor and gardens suitable for disabled. No disabled lavatory.

MAPLEDURHAM HOUSE & WATERMILL
Nr. Reading, Berkshire, RG4 7TR Tel: 01189 723 350
Fax: 01189 724 016 (The Mapledurham Trust)

Late 16th century Elizabethan home of the Blount family. Original plaster ceiling, great oak staircase, fine collection of paintings and private chapel in Strawberry Hill Gothick added in 1797. The 15th century Watermill is fully restored and producing flour and bran which are sold in the gift shop. **E-mail:** mtrust1997@aol.com **Internet:** www.mapledurham.co.uk

FOR FULL ILLUSTRATED ENTRY INCLUDING OPENING TIMES AND ADMISSION PRICES, SEE ENTRY UNDER BERKSHIRE, PAGE 27.

THE MUSEUM OF MODERN ART OXFORD
30 Pembroke Street, Oxford OX1 1BP
Tel: 01865 722733 Fax: 01865 722573
Recorded information: 01865 813830

Since it opened in 1965 MOMA has established an international reputation for the high quality of its pioneering exhibition programme, which covers 20th century painting, sculpture, photography, film, video, architecture, design and performance from all over the world. There is no permanent collection. Orginally built as a brewery in the 1880s, the premises now offer 5 large exhibition galleries, a café and bookshop. Visitors of all ages can take advantage of a comprehensive education and public access programme which includes evening talks, debates, workshops, holiday activities and guided tours. **Open:** Tues–Sun 11am–6pm, Thurs 11am–9pm, closed Mon. **Admission:** Adults £2.50, Conc £1.50 (people over 60, registered disabled, unwaged & students), Children under 16 free. Admission free: Wed 11am–1pm, Thurs 6–9pm. **Internet:** www.moma.org.uk

map 4 C3

THE OXFORDSHIRE MUSEUM
Fletcher's House, Park Street, Woodstock, Oxfordshire OX20 1SN
Tel: 01993 811456 Fax: 01993 813239

The Oxfordshire Museum has recently undergone extensive refurbishment, and the new permanent displays depicting aspects of the County and its history are now open to the public. As well as these galleries the museum hosts a variety of temporary exhibitions in the Garden Gallery. **Garden Gallery Exhibitions:** 18 Jan–25 Feb *Abingdon Before the Abbey*; 3 Mar–1 Apr *Oxford Printmakers*; 7 Apr–6 May *Sounding the Heart* - Roma Tearne; 10 May–11 June *Crafts at Woodstock* - Oxfordshire Crafts Guild; 23 June–19 Aug *Shake Rattle & Roll*; 1 Sept–14 Oct *Bonnets, Birds & Twopenny Baubles: Embroidery as a protection against evil spirits* - Sheila Paine; 19 Oct–18 Nov *If all the World Were Paper* - Paperweight; 23 Nov–23 Dec *Christmas Crafts* - Oxfordshire Crafts Guild. **Open:** Tues–Sat 10am–5pm, Sun 2–5pm (last adm to Garden Gallery 4.30pm, last adm to permanent displays 4.45pm). Closed Mon. **E-mail:** oxon.museum@oxfordshire.gov.uk **Internet:** www.oxfordshire.gov.uk

Also visit: **Swalcliffe Barn**, Swalcliffe, Tel: 01295 788278: One of the finest barns in Britain, built by New College between 1400 and 1409 for the Rectorial Manor of Swalcliffe. It houses an exhibition about the village and the County Museums Service's collection of horse-drawn trade vehicles. **Open:** Easter–end Sept, Sun & BH 2–5pm. **Admission:** Free. **The Oxfordshire Museums Store**, Standlake, Tel: 01865 300972: A purpose-built store housing the County's reference collections and museums' support services. Identification and enquiry services are provided and group visits welcomed for behind-the-scenes tours. **Open:** Public open days and by appointment. **Admission:** Free.

map 4 C3

ROUSHAM HOUSE

Rousham, Steeple Aston, Oxfordshire OX6 3QX
Tel: 01869 347110 or 0860 360407 (C Cottrell-Dormer Esq.)

Rousham House was built by Sir Robert Dormer in 1635 and the shooting holes were put in the doors while it was a Royalist garrison in the Civil War. Sir Robert's successors were Masters of Ceremonies at Court during eight reigns and employed Court artists and architects to embellish Rousham. The house stands above the River Cherwell one mile from Hopcrofts Holt, near the road from Chipping Norton to Bicester. It contains 150 portraits and other pictures and much fine contemporary furniture. Rooms were decorated by William Kent (1738) and Roberts of Oxford (1765). The garden is Kent's only surviving landscape design with classic buildings, cascades, statues and vistas in thirty acres of hanging woods above the Cherwell. Wonderful herbaceous borders, pigeon house and small parterre. Fine herd of rare Long-Horn cattle in the park. Wear sensible shoes and bring a picnic and Rousham is yours for the day. **Location:** 12 miles N of Oxford; E of A4260; S of B4030. **Station:** Heyford (1 mile). **Open:** Apr–Sept inclusive Wed, Sun & Bank Hols 2–4.30pm. Gardens only every day all year 10–4.30pm. No children under 15. No dogs. Groups by arrangement on other days. **Admission:** House: Adults £3. Garden £3.

map 4
C3

STONOR PARK

Nr Henley-on-Thames, Oxfordshire RG9 6HF
Tel: 01491 638587, Fax: 01491 639348 (Lord and Lady Camoys)

Ancient home of Lord and Lady Camoys and the Stonor family for over 800 years and centre of Catholicism throughout the Recusancy Period, with its own medieval Chapel where mass is still celebrated today. Sanctuary for St. Edmund Campion in 1581. An exhibition features his life and work. The house is of considerable architectural interest, built over many centuries from c.1190 and the site of prehistoric stone circle, now recreated within the grounds. A family home containing fine family portraits and rare items of furniture, paintings, drawings, tapestries, sculptures and bronzes from Britain, Europe and America. Peaceful hillside gardens with magnificent roses and ornamental ponds. Souvenir gift shop and afternoon tearoom serving home-made cakes. Parties welcome, lunches available by prior arrangement. John Steane says of Stonor " If I had to suggest to a visitor who has only one day to sample the beauties of Oxfordshire I would suggest a visit to Stonor and a walk through its delectable park". **Location:** On B480; 5 miles N of Henley-on-Thames, 5 miles S of Watlington. **Station(s):** Henley-on-Thames. **Open:** Sun; 2-5:30pm, 1 Apr-30 Sept. Mon; 2-5:30pm, B.H. Mons only. Wed; 2-5:30pm, Jul-Aug. only. Groups welcome by appointment on Tues- Thurs, Apr- Sept. **Admission:** House & Gardens: Adult £4.50, Child (under 14 with adult) free. Adults (Group) £4 subject to group payment on arrival. Private tours £5 per person subject to group payment. Gardens only: Adults £2.50. **Refreshments:** Tearoom. Group lunches and suppers by arrangement.

map 4
D4

RIVER & ROWING MUSEUM

Mill Meadows, Henley-on-Thames, Oxfordshire OX9 1BF
Tel: 01491 415600 Fax: 01491 415601

The River & Rowing Museum, winner of numerous awards, has three permanent galleries dedicated to Rowing and the 'Quest for Speed', from the Greek Trireme to modern Olympic rowing boats; the River Thames from source to sea with its rich history and varied wildlife; and the riverside town of Henley featuring the Royal Regatta. Special temporary exhibitions run throughout the year. Free visitor parking. Coach & tour parties welcome. Group bookings. Functions, conferences, education centre, private parties. Full details available on request. **Open:** Museum and Riverside Café are open daily 10am (Mon–Fri), 10.30am (Sat, Sun). Closes 5 pm (Sept 1st - Apr 3rd) 5.30pm (May 1st - Aug 31st) **E-mail:** museum@rrm.co.uk **Internet:** www.rrm.co.uk

map 4 D4

ST PETER'S COLLEGE

New Inn Hall Street, Oxford OX1 2DL
Tel: 01865 278900

St Peter's occupies the site of two of Oxford's oldest Inns (mediaeval hostels), and is made up of a number of buildings from different periods grouped around quiet quadrangles and lawns. The main entrance to the college is Linton House, a handsome Georgian rectory that holds the library and the Porters' Lodge. A peaceful quad lies just beyond the entrance, to the left of which stands the imposing tower of the college chapel (1874), which enjoys splendid views over the city centre. Canal House, built in the early 19th century, serves as the Master's Lodge and has a beautiful garden. The college's newer buildings are also notable: the New Block, designed by Frank Woods, is an exciting example of modern architecture, and whilst the Matthew's Block is not the most beautiful of buildings, it was used to host the reception for Liz Taylor and Richard Burton's second wedding. Visitors to the college should report to the Porter's Lodge.

UNIVERSITY OF OXFORD BOTANIC GARDEN

Rose Lane, Oxford, Oxfordshire
Tel: 01865 286690 Fax: 01865 286693 (University of Oxford)

The University of Oxford Botanic Garden is the oldest botanic garden in Britain. For more than 375 years this Walled Garden, built before the English Civil War, has stood on the bank of the River Cherwell in the centre of Oxford. It has evolved from a seventeenth century collection of medical herbs to the most compact yet diverse collection of plants in the world. In addition to the botanical family beds and the National Collection of Euphorbias, there is a range of glasshouses including a Tropical Lily House, Palm House and Arid House. Outside the original Walled Garden there are herbaceous borders, a newly restored bog garden and a rock garden. **Open:** Open all year (except Good Fri and Christmas Day). Apr–Sept 9–5pm. Oct–Mar 9–4.30pm. Last admission 4.15pm. **Admission:** £2, Apr–Aug. **E-mail:** postmaster@botanic–garden.ox.ac.uk

map 4 C3

VALE & DOWNLAND MUSEUM

Church Street, Wantage, Oxfordshire OX12 8BL
Tel: 01235 771447 Fax: 01235 764316

An ideal place to begin your exploration of the Vale of the White Horse with exhibits covering the geology, archaeology and history of the Vale from earliest times to the latest technology. The exhibits range from an Anglo-Saxon skeleton to a Williams Formula 1 racing car. Facilities include a tourist information centre, bookshop, art gallery and award-winning café serving a range of delicious snacks and drinks. The museum provides a warm and welcoming atmosphere for visitors of all ages. There are activities for children from four years of age and baby changing facilities. **Open:** Mon–Sat 10am–4.30pm, Sun 2.30–5.30pm. Check Bank Holidays. **Admission:** Adult £1.50, Child (6–16) £1, Family £4. Tickets are valid for 12 months. **Internet:** www.wantage.com/museum

map 4 C4

WALLINGFORD CASTLE GARDENS

Castle Street, Wallingford, Oxfordshire
Tel: 01491 835 373 Fax: 01491 826 550 (Wallingford Town Council)

These gardens are situated on part of the site of Wallingford Castle, which was built by William the Conqueror and demolished by Oliver Cromwell in 1652. The remains of St. Nicholas Priory are a feature of the Gardens, which is a haven of beauty and tranquillity and has a well-established wildlife area. **Location:** Bear Lane, Castle Street, Wallingford, Oxfordshire. **Open:** Apr–Oct, 10–6pm. Nov–Mar, 10–3pm. **Admission:** Free. **Events/Exhibitions:** Band concerts some Sundays in summer. Telephone for details. "Thames & Chilterns Country in Bloom" winner 1993, 1996, 1997, 1998 and 2000. Car parking in the town. **Tourist Information Office:** 01491 826 972.

map 4 C4

WATERPERRY GARDENS

Nr Wheatley, Oxfordshire OX33 1JZ
Tel: 01844 339226/254 Fax:01844 339883

The peaceful gardens at Waterperry feature a magnificent herbaceous border, shrub and heather borders, alpine and rock gardens, a formal garden and a new rose garden. Together with stately trees, a river to walk by and a quiet Saxon Church to visit – all set in 83 acres of unspoilt Oxfordshire. The long established herbaceous and alpine nurseries provide year round interest. For the experienced gardener, the novice, or those who have no garden of their own, here is a chance to share, enjoy and admire the order and beauty of careful cultivation. Garden Shop and Plant Centre with exceptionally wide range of plants, shrubs etc produced in the nurseries for sale. Main agents for Haddonstone, Pots and Pithoi and Whichford Pottery. The Pear Tree Teashop provides a delicious selection of freshly prepared food made on the premises. Serving hot and cold light lunches, morning coffee, cream teas etc. Wine licence. The Art in Action Gallery exhibits and sells quality ceramics, wood, glass, paintings, jewellery, textiles, etchings and engravings. **Location:** 9 miles from Oxford, 50 miles from London (M40 Junction 8), 42 miles from Birmingham (M40 Junction 8a). Well signposted locally with Tourist Board symbol. **Station(s):** Oxford & Thame Parkway. **Open:** Gardens & Shop: Apr–Oct 9–5.30pm, Nov–Mar 9–5pm. Pear Tree Teashop: Apr–Oct 10–5pm, Nov–Mar 10–4pm. Art in Action Gallery: Apr–Oct 9–5pm, Nov–Mar 9–4.30pm. **Open daily** except Christmas and New Year Holidays. Open only to Art in Action visitors (enquiries 020 7381 3192) 19–22 July. The Pear Tree Teashop will close from 18 July–23 July incl. **Admission:** Apr–Oct Adults £3.40, Senior Citizens £2.90, Parties (20+) £2.90. Nov–Mar £1.60 all categories. Coaches by appointment. **Internet:** www.waterperry.co.uk

map 4
D3

Shropshire

This county is a hidden treasure, a land of contrasts where England meets Wales. Shrewsbury sits in a loop of the River Severn, which made it a prime defensive bastion during the frontier battles. Visitors to the town will now find a wealth of mediaeval buildings and monuments, along with a number of timber-framed Tudor buildings and a beautiful old market square. Ludlow also boasts many fine buildings in its narrow streets, but Shropshire's charms are not limited to its ancient towns. To the north, a network of lakes provides wonderful opportunities for walking and bird watching.

BOSCOBEL HOUSE & THE ROYAL OAK

Shifnal, Shropshire ST19 9AR
Tel: 01902 850244 (English Heritage)

Discover the fascinating history of the fully restored and refurbished lodge and famous 'Royal Oak' tree where the future King Charles II hid from Cromwell's troops in 1651. 2001 will be the 350th anniversary of this event. The panelled rooms, secret hiding places and pretty gardens lend a truly romantic character. A fascinating guided tour and an award winning exhibition also cover the later additions to the site - a Victorian farmhouse, dairy, smithy and farmyard complete with resident ducks and geese. **Location:** On classified road between A41 and A5, 8m NW of Wolverhampton. **Open:** 1 Apr–30 Sept: daily 10am–6pm; 1–31 Oct: daily 10am–6pm; 1–30 Nov: Wed–Sun 10am–4pm; 1–31 Dec: Sat–Sun 10am–4pm. Closed 1 Jan–31 Mar. Last admission 45 minutes before closing. **Admission:** Adult £4.40, Conc £3.30, Child £2.20. 15% discount for groups of 11 or more.

map 8
B7

BURFORD HOUSE GARDENS

Tenbury Wells, Worcestershire, WR15, 8HQ
Tel: 01584 810 777 Fax: 01584 810 673 (C. Chesshire)

The sweeping lawns and plantsman's paradise of Burford House Gardens are set in the picturesque valleys of the River Teme and Ledwyche Brook. The late Georgian bridge over the Ledwyche has been restored, leading to a new wildflower garden down to the heavenly spot where the two rivers meet. The grass garden has been redesigned, a bamboo collection planted and the National Collection of Clematis of over 200 varieties continues to grow. Also on site is **Treasures Garden Centre/Nursery** growing over 300 varieties of clematis and many of the unusual plants that can be seen in the gardens; specialising in quality plants for sale, pots, tools and friendly practical advice; **Burford House Gallery:** contemporary and one botanical art show annually; **Gift Shop:** decorative and functional gifts, books and cards; **Mulu** exotic plants; **Jungle Giants** bamboos. **Refreshments:** Treasure's Cafe-Bar, serving a wide selection of home-made cakes, pastries, hot and cold meals, teas and coffees. Seating 120 inside (including Marquee), 40 outside. Evening Bistro, Thurs–Sat. **Location:** Tenbury Wells, Worcestershire, WR15 8HQ (off A456, 1 mile west of Tenbury Wells, 8 miles from Ludlow). **Car Parking:** Free parking for 120 cars, 10 coaches. **Open:** All year daily 10–6pm (last entry into gardens 5pm); evenings by arrangement. **Admission:** Adults £3.50, Children £1.00; Groups of 10+ £3. **E-mail:** treasures@burford.co.uk

map 7
F1

HODNET HALL GARDENS

Hodnet, Market Drayton, Shropshire TF9 3NN
Tel: 01630 685202 Fax: 01630 685853 (Mr & Mrs A.E.H. Heber-Percy)

60+ acres of landscaped gardens, renowned to be amongst the finest in the country. Woodland walks amidst forest trees, shrubs and flowers alongside a daisy chain of ornamental pools. Light lunch or afternoon tea in the 17th century tearooms, adjacent to which is a gift shop. The walled Kitchen Garden grows a wide range of flowers and produce which are available for sale during the appropriate season. Disabled visitors are especially welcome. Guided tours and evening parties by appointment. **Location:** A53 (Shrewsbury–Market Drayton): A442 (Telford–Whitchurch): M6 exits 12 & 15: M54 exit 3. **Open:** 1 April–30 Sept. Tues–Sun & Bank Holiday Mons 12–5pm. **Admission:** Adult £3.25, OAPs £2.75, Child £1.20. Special rates for parties (prebook please).

map 6
D1

HAWKSTONE HISTORIC PARK & FOLLIES

Weston-under-Redcastle, Nr Shrewsbury, Shropshire SY4 5UY
Tel: 01939 200 611 Fax: 01939 200 311

Few places in the world can claim to be truly unique. However, Hawkstone Park with its well hidden pathways, concealed grotto, secret tunnels and magical collection of follies earns that right. A giant theatre in landscape - it was originally one of the most visited landscapes in Britain and is the only Grade I landscape in Shropshire. Work to restore the Park to its former glory began in April 1991 after a 100 year closure. Visitors are once more privileged to enter the Hawkstone Labyrinth. Folly buildings, it has been said 'indulge a natural urge to express eccentricity with the resources of wealth and imagination". It is a description which sits perfectly on the shoulders of the hills of Hawkstone. Sir Roland Hill started it all in the 18th century with his son Richard "The Great Hill", not only taking over but also increasing the tempo and arranged for some 15 miles of paths and some of the best collections of follies in the world to be constructed in the grounds of their ancestral home.

At the turn of the 19th century the Hills could no longer accommodate the growing number of sightseers to the Hall. As a result an inn, now the Hawkstone Park Hotel, was opened and guided tours were organised. Hawkstone, according to one top writer, became "the inspiration for Longleat, Wombourne and other stately homes which attract visitors". Little has changed since then. The Park is full of attractions, surprises and features. Even the Duke of Wellington was a regular visitor. It takes about 3 hours to complete the whole tour of the Park. **Location:** 12 m N of Shrewsbury, off A49. **Open:** 6 Jan-29 Mar (weekends); 30 Mar-30 Jun (Wed-Sun & Bank Holidays); 1Jul-2 Sept (daily); 3 Sept-28 Oct (Wed-Sun) **Admission:** Adult £4.50, Child £2.50, Senior Citizen £3.50, Family £12. Small additional charges on Bank Holidays and special events. Special reduced rates for groups. Hotel & golf course adjacent. Please wear sensible shoes. Guided tours by arrangement.

map 6 D1

IRONBRIDGE GORGE MUSEUMS

Ironbridge, Telford, Shropshire TF8 7AW

Tel: 01952 433522 or 432166 (w/ends) Fax: 01952 432204 (Independent Museum Trust)

Scene of pioneering events which led to the Industrial Revolution. The Ironbridge Gorge is home to 9 unique museums set in 6 square miles of stunning scenery. These include Jackfield Tile Museum, Coalport China Museum and a recreated Victorian Town where you can chat to the locals as they go about their daily business. You'll need 2 days here. **Location:** OS Ref. SJ666 037. Telford, Shropshire via M6/M54. **Open:** All Year: daily from 10am (closed 24/25 Dec & 1 Jan) Please telephone for winter details before visit. **Admission:** Passport tickets which allows admission to all museums; Adult £10, Child/Student £6, 60+yrs. £9, Family £30. Prices valid until Easter 2001, Group discounts also available. Freephone: 0800 590258 for a free colour guide.

Internet: www.ironbridge.org.uk

map 6 E1

ROYAL AIR FORCE MUSEUM

Cosford, Shifnal, Shropshire TF11 8UP

Tel: 01902 376200 Fax: 01902 376211

The Royal Air Force Museum is located at Cosford on the A41, one mile from junction 3 of the M54. This is one of the largest aviation collections in the UK. Exhibits include the Victor and Vulcan bombers, the Hastings, York and British Airways airliners, the Belfast freighter and the last airworthy Britannia. World War II aircraft, including the Spitfire, Mosquito and Hurricane. The Research & Development Collection includes the notable TSR2, Fairy Delta, Bristol 188 and many more important aircraft. Shop, restaurant, picnic area, large car park. Events: June: RAF Cosford Air Show. July: International Large Model Aircraft Rally. **Admission:** Adult £5.90, Unemployed & Students £3.75. Senior Citizens & Children free of Charge Reduced rates for groups and educational visits. **E-mail:** cosford@rafmuseum.com **Internet:** www.rafmuseum.com

map 8 B7

SHREWSBURY MUSEUM AND ART GALLERY

Rowley's House Barker Street, Shrewsbury, Shropshire

Tel: 01743 361196 Fax: 01743 358411 (Shrewsbury and Atcham Borough Council)

Major regional museum displaying varied collections in timber-framed 16th century warehouse and adjoining 17th century brick mansion. Archaeology, including Roman Wroxeter; geology; costume; natural and local history; special exhibitions including contemporary arts and crafts. **Open:** Easter–end Sept Tues–Sat 10am–5pm, Sundays and Bank Holiday Mondays 10am–4pm; Oct–Easter Tues–Sat 10am–4pm. Closed Christmas/New Year period. **Admission:** Free.

map 6 E1

SHIPTON HALL

Much Wenlock, Shropshire, TF13 6JZ.

Tel: 01746 785 225 Fax: 01746 785 125 (J. N. R. N. Bishop)

Delightful Elizabethan stone manor house c.1587 with Georgian additions. Interesting Rococo and Gothic plaster work by T. F. Pritchard. Stone walled garden, medieval dovecote and parish church dating from late Saxon period. Family home. **Location:** In Shipton, 6 miles SW of Much Wenlock near junction B4378 & B4368. **Station(s):** Craven Arms (10 miles), Telford (14 miles), Ludlow (14 miles). **Open:** Easter–end Sept, Thurs. Bank Hol Suns & Mons (except Christmas & New Year) 2.30–5.30pm. Also by appointment throughout the year for parties of 20+. **Admission:** House & Garden: Adults £4, Children £2, Parties of 20+ less 10%. **Refreshments:** Teas/buffets by prior arrangement.

map 6 E1

SHREWSBURY CASTLE & SHROPSHIRE REGIMENTAL MUSEUM

Castle Street, Shrewsbury, Shropshire

Tel: 01743 358516 Fax:01743 358411

Norman castle with 18th century work by Thomas Telford. The Great Hall now houses the collections of the Shropshire Regimental Museum plus graphic displays on the history of the castle. **Open:** Museum: Easter–end Sept Tues–Sat 10am–5pm, Sundays & Bank Holiday Mondays 10am–4pm. Oct–Dec & Feb–Easter Wed–Sat 10am–4pm. Grounds: Open Mon–Sat all year and Sundays as above. **Admission:** Free to the attractive floral grounds Mon–Sat (and summer Suns). Small charge to the Main Hall. **E-mail:**museums@shrewsbury-atcham.gov.uk

Internet:www.shrewsburymuseums.com or www.shropshireregimental.co.uk

map 6 E1

WESTON PARK

Weston-under-Lizard, Nr Shifnal, Shropshire TF11 8LE
Tel.: 01952 852100 Fax.: 01952 850430

Set in spectacular Staffordshire/Shropshire countryside, Weston Park is a magnificent Stately Home resting in 1,000 acres of Parkland. The ancestral seat of the Earls of Bradford it is now held in trust for the nation by The Weston Park Foundation. Royalty, politics, drama and tragedy all feature throughout Weston's rich history, and indeed it was chosen as the retreat day for the G8 Summit of World Leaders. Built in 1671 by Lady Wilbraham, the house boasts a superb collection of paintings, furniture and objets d'art, including a number of works by Van Dyck. Outside the glorious Parkland includes formal gardens, woodland and wildlife walks, all landscaped by the famous 'Capability' Brown in the 18th century. Visitors can also enjoy the adventure playground, miniature railway and pets corner before relaxing in The Stables Restaurant and Bar, or browsing in the gift shop. Weston Park has a well-established reputation for staging outstanding events. The House and Park are also available on an exclusive basis and with 28 bedroom of individual character, the House provides the perfect backdrop to any private event. **Location:** Situated on the A5 near to the M54 (jct 3) and M6 (jct 12), Weston Park is only a 30-minute drive from the centre of Birmingham. **Open:** Easter, then every weekend until 30 June. Every day until 2 Sept then every weekend until 16 Sept (Closed 6 May, 14 July, 4 Aug, 17–20 Aug). House 1–4.30pm; Park 11am–7pm. Please note admission charges and times may vary on special events days. **Admission:** Park & Gardens: Adults £2.50, OAPs £2, Children £1.50, Family £6. House: Adults £2, OAPs £1.50, Children £1. **E-mail:** enquiries@weston-park.com **Internet:** www.weston-park.com

map 8
B7

Somerset

The scenery in Somerset is wonderfully diverse: from the long sandy beaches at Minehead to the dramatic rocky coastline of Exmoor, and from the rolling Mendips and Quantocks to the flat expanses of the moors, this is truly a county with something for everyone. Nestling in the Mendip Hills is Wells, England's smallest city, which boasts a beautiful cathedral. Somerset's County Town, Taunton, has a busy but friendly centre with great opportunities for shopping; more peaceful surroundings can be found further south, around Yeovil.

The county has long been associated with the legend of King Arthur, and the curious can visit 'Camelot' at South Cadbury, or Glastonbury Abbey, where monks claimed to have discovered the remains of this warrior King and his Queen, Guinevere.

Glencot House

Glastonbury Tor

Dotted around the countryside are many splendid old churches, and visitors should also try to experience some of the county's ancient rural traditions, such as the 'Wassailing' of apple orchards to ensure a good crop.

Exmoor sits on a high plateau where the River Exe rises, and offers almost 700 miles of well-kept footpaths and bridleways. An unusually high area of southern England, it supports a great variety of flora and fauna, including the famous wild red deer and Exmoor ponies.

THE BISHOP'S PALACE

The fortified and moated medieval palace unites the early 13th century first floor hall (known as The Henderson Rooms), the late 13th century Chapel and the now ruined Great Hall, also the 15th century wing which is today the private residence of the Bishop of Bath and Wells. The extensive grounds, where rise the springs that give Wells its name, are a beautiful setting for borders of herbaceous plants, roses, shrubs, mature trees and the Jubilee Arboretum. The Moat is home to a collection of waterfowl and swans. **Location:** City of Wells: enter from the Market Place through the Bishop's Eye or from the Cathedral Cloisters, over the Drawbridge. **Station(s):** Bath and Bristol. **Open:** The Henderson Rooms, Bishop's Chapel and Grounds: 1 Apr–31 Oct, Tues, Wed, Thurs, Fri 10.30–6pm and Sun 2–6pm and most days in Aug, 10.30–6pm. As this is a private house, the Trustees reserve the right to alter these times on rare occasions. **Admission:** As advertised – Guided and educational tours by arrangement with the Manager. **Refreshments:** A restaurant service is available in the Undercroft using fresh produce from the Palace gardens, unless prior bookings are made. **Events/Exhibitions:** Wedding receptions a speciality. Open air theatre. **Conferences:** Conferences, training courses and seminars by arrangement with the manager.

map 3
H3

ADMIRAL BLAKE MUSEUM
Blake Street, Bridgwater, Somerset TA6 3NB
Tel: 01278 456127 Fax: 01278 444076

The birthplace of Robert Blake (1598–1657), 17th century soldier, sailor and statesman, the house is now home to a fascinating local museum with collections that show off the colourful and dramatic past and present of Bridgwater and the surrounding area. From the earliest inhabitants to the drama of the last battle fought on English soil – the Battle of Sedgemoor in 1685 – the Museum has plenty to see and do. Temporary exhibitions, events and education service. **Opening Times:** The Museum is open Tues–Sat, 10am–4pm. **Admission:** Free. **E-mail:** museums@sedgemoor.gov.uk

map 3
H3

BARFORD PARK
Enmore TA5 1AG
Tel: 01278 671269

Set in a large garden and looking out across a ha-ha to a park dotted with fine trees, it presents a scene of peaceful domesticity, a miniature country seat on a scale appropriate today. The well-proportioned rooms, with contemporary furniture, are all in daily family use. The walled flower garden is in full view from the house, and the woodland and water gardens and archery glade with their handsome trees form a perfect setting for the stone and red-brick Queen Anne building. **Location:** 5m W of Bridgwater. **Open:** May–Sept by appointment. **Admission:** Charges not available at the time of going to press. **Refreshments:** Teas for groups, by appointment.

map 3
G3

BATH POSTAL MUSEUM
8 Broad Street, Bath BA1 5LJ
Tel & Fax: 01225 460333

The Bath Postal Museum tells the exciting story of 4,000 years of written communication from clay mail to E-mail, from the Babylonians to the Romans, Victorians and present day. See the re-creation of an 1840s post office, celebrating the sending of the first ever stamp - the Penny Black from the museum's building 160 years ago. Visit the children's activity and education room, see the story unfold of Bath's pioneers who revolutionised the postal systems internationally. New exhibitions include the Victorians, Bath entrepreneur Ralph Allen and the Romans. **Open:** Mon–Sat 11am–5pm. **Admission:** £2.90. Concessions for party bookings available. **E-mail:** info@bathpostalmuseum.co.uk

Internet: www.bathpostalmuseum.org

map 3
H3

CROWE HALL
Widcombe Hill, Bath, Somerset, BA2 6AR
Tel: 01225 310322 (John Barratt)

Elegant George V classical Bath villa, retaining grandiose mid-Victorian portico and great hall. Fine 18th century and Regency furniture: interesting old paintings and china. 10 acres of romantic gardens cascading down hillside. Terraces, Victorian grotto, ancient trees. **Location:** Approx. ¼ mile on right up Widcombe Hill, 1 mile from Guildhall. **Open:** Garden: 18 March, 22 April, 13 May, 10 June, 15 July and groups by appointment. House: By appointment only, £2. **Admission:** House or Garden only £2; House and Garden £4. **Refreshments:** Teas on opening days and by appointment. Dogs welcome.

map 3
V16

DODINGTON HALL
Nr. Nether Stowey, Bridgwater, Somerset
Tel: 01278 741 400
(Lady Gass, Occupier: P.Quinn)

Small Tudor manor house on the lower slopes of the Quantock Hills. Great hall with oak roof. Carved stone fireplace. Semi-formal garden with roses and shrubs. **Location:** ½ mile from A39, 11 miles from Bridgwater. 7 miles from Williton. **Open:** Sat 19 May–Mon 28 May inclusive, 2–5pm. **Admission:** Donations for charity. Parking for 15 cars. Regret unsuitable for disabled.

map 3
J2

DUNSTER CASTLE
Dunster, nr. Minehead, Somerset TA24 6SL
Tel: 01643 821314 Fax: 01643 823000

For 600 years the residence of the Lutrell family, Dunster has evolved from a Norman motte-and-bailey to a distinguished country seat. The house and ruins are set amongst beautiful sub-tropical plants.

For details of opening times and admission prices, please contact the property.

EAST LAMBROOK MANOR GARDEN
South Petherton, Somerset Tel: 01460 240 328
Fax: 01460 242 344 (Mr & Mrs Robert Williams)

This Grade I listed garden is one of the best loved in Britain. It was the home of the late Margery Fish. It is also the subject of many books, articles and television and radio programmes. The 17th century malthouse has been developed to provide modern facilities for visitors retaining its unique character. During the summer months, as well as cream teas there are also exhibitions by well known local artists. The garden contains the National Collection of Geraniums. **Location:** Off A303. 2 miles N of South Petherton. **Open:** All year round, daily 10–5pm. **E-mail:** elambrook@aol.com **Internet:** www.margeryfish.com

map 3
H4

FAIRFIELD
Stogursey, Bridgwater, Somerset
Tel: 01278 732251 Fax: 01278 732277 (Lady Gass)

Elizabethan House of medieval origin, undergoing extensive repairs. Woodland garden. Location: 11 miles W of Bridgwater, 8 miles E of Williton. From A39 Bridgwater/Minehead turn N; house 1 mile W of Stogursey. **Open:** House open in summer (when repairs allow) for groups by appointment only. Other openings may be advertised. Garden open for NGS and other charities on dates advertised in spring. **Admission:** Donations for charity. Disabled access. No dogs, except guide dogs. Parking for 30 cars. Unsuitable for coaches.

map 3
G3

FLEET AIR ARM MUSEUM
RNAS Yeovilton, Ilchester, Somerset BA22 8HT
Tel: 01935 840565 Fax: 01935 842630

The Fleet Air Arm Museum is one of the world's largest aviation museums with over 50 historic aircraft on display. Experience the development of Britain's flying Navy, in a succession of superb exhibits. 'NEW' Leading Edge Exhibition 'NOW OPEN'. Free car park, adventure playground, restaurant, excellent disabled facilities, extensive gift shop, book and model shop. Open all 362 days a year, 10–5:30pm in summer, and 10-4:30pm in winter. Located just off the A303, on the B3151 at RNAS Yeovilton, Somerset. **E-mail:** info@fleetairarm.com **Internet:** www.fleetairarm.com

map 3 H4

GAULDEN MANOR
Tolland, Lydeard St Lawrence, Nr Taunton, Somerset TA4 3PN
Tel: 01984 667213 (James Le Gendre Starkie)

Small historic red sandstone Manor House of great charm. A real home lived in and shown by the owners. Past seat of the Turberville family immortalised by Thomas Hardy. Great Hall has magnificent plaster ceiling and oak screen to room known as the chapel. Fine antique furniture and many hand embroideries worked by the wife of owner. Interesting grounds include rose gardens, bog garden with primulas and moisture loving plants, butterfly and herb garden. Visitors return year after year to enjoy this oasis of peace and quiet set amid superb countryside. **Location:** 9 miles NW of Taunton signposted from A358 and B3224. **Open:** Garden: June 3–Aug 27 on, Sun & Bank Hols Thurs, 2–5pm. House open for Groups of 15+ on any days. Morning, afternoon or evening. **Admission:** Adults: house and garden £4.20. Garden only £3, Children £1.

map 3 G3

GLASTONBURY ABBEY
Abbey Gatehouse, Magdalene Street, Glastonbury, Somerset
Tel: 01458 832267 Fax: 01458 832267 (Glastonbury Abbey Estate)

Traditionally the oldest Christian sanctuary in Britain and legendary burial place of King Arthur. Magnificent Abbey ruins set in 36 acres of glorious Somerset parkland. Visit our Award winning museum to see model of pre-reformation abbey and the Othery Cope. From April to October meet Brother Cleeve (actor) who will tell you how the monks used to live and feed. **Open:** Daily 9.30–6pm or dusk if earlier (except Christmas Day). June, July and Aug: open 9am. Dec, Jan and Feb: open 10am. Car and coach park adjoins our entrance. Audio tape guide specially produced for blind or partially sighted visitors is now available. Refreshments in Summer only. **Admission:** Adults £3, Children (5–15yrs inc) £1. **E-mail:** glastonbury.abbey@dial.pipex.com **Internet:** www.glastonburyabbey.com

map 3 H3

HESTERCOMBE GARDENS
Hestercombe, Cheddon Fitzpaine, Taunton, Somerset TA2 8LG
Tel: 01823 413923 Fax: 01823 413747

Over three centuries of garden history are encompassed in Hestercombe's fifty acres of formal gardens and parkland near Cheddon Fitzpaine, Taunton. The unique Edwardian gardens, designed by Sir Edwin Lutyens and planted by Gertrude Jekyll, were completed in 1906. With terraces, pools and an orangery, they are the supreme example of their famous partnership. These gardens are now reunited with Hestercombe's secret Landscape Garden, which opened in the Spring of 1997 for the first time in 125 years. Created by Coplestone Warre Bampfyide in 1750s, these Georgian pleasure grounds comprise forty acres of lakes, temples and delightful woodland walks. **Location:** 4 m NE of Taunton off A361. **Open:** Daily 10–last admission 5pm. **Admission:** Adults £4, OAPs £3.80, Children (5–15) £1. Groups and coaches by prior arrangement only.

map 3 G3

THE HOLBURNE MUSEUM OF ART
Great Pulteney Street, Bath BA2 4DB
Tel: 01225 466669 Fax: 01225 333121

This jewel in Bath's crown, once the Georgian Sydney Hotel, is opposite Jane Austen's former home. It displays the treasures collected by Sir William Holburne: superb English and continental silver, porcelain, maiolica, glass and Renaissance bronzes. The Picture Gallery contains works by Turner, Guardi, Stubbs and others, plus portraits of Bath society by Thomas Gainsborough. Licensed Tea House in garden setting. Free car park. Book shop. Guided tours by arrangement. Lift. **Exhibitions for 2001:** 14 Feb-11 Apr 'LOVE'S PROSPECT' - Gainsborough's Byam Family and the 18th century marriage portrait; 18 May–2 Sept 'MOTHER AND CHILD'; 21 Sept–2 Dec 'IN RUINS'. **Open:** Tues-Sat 10am-5pm (including Bank Holidays). Sun 2.30-5.30pm. Open mid Feb-mid Dec; closed Mondays except for group bookings by appointment. **Internet:** www.bath.ac.uk/holburne

map4 A4

GREAT HOUSE FARM
Wells Rd, Theale, Wedmore, BS28 4SJ
Tel: 01934 713133

A 17th Century Farm House with carved staircase and murals. We regret that it is unsuitable for the disabled. No coaches or dogs. Open: From May-August, Tuesdays and Thursdays 2-5pm. By appointment only. **Admission:** £2.

 map 3 H3

KING JOHN'S HUNTING LODGE
The Square, Axbridge, Somerset
Tel: 01934 732012 Fax: 01278 444076

This mediaeval merchant's house at the heart of this small town is a clear reminder of Axbridge's position as a Royal Borough for 1000 years. The building, which belongs to the National Trust, now houses a remarkable local museum. With fascinating collections of archaeology and local history from Axbridge and the wider area, the museum provides a keen insight into this community's past. **Open:** Easter–end Sept daily 2–5pm. **Admission:** Free.

map 3 H3

HUNSTRETE HOUSE HOTEL
Hunstrete, nr Bath, Somerset BS39 4NS
Tel: 01761 490490 Fax: 01761 490732

Hunstrete House stands in a classical English landscape on the edge of the Mendip Hills, surrounded by lovely gardens and woodlands. It is largely 18th century, although the history of the estate goes back to 963AD. The Terrace dining room looks out on to an Italianate, flower filled courtyard. A highly skilled head chef offers light, elegant dishes using produce from the extensive garden, including substantial use of organic meat and vegetables. The menu changes regularly and the hotel has an excellent reputation for the quality and interest of its wine list. In a sheltered corner of the walled garden there is a heated swimming pool for guests to enjoy. For the energetic, the all weather tennis court provides another diversion and there are riding stables in Hunstrete village, a 5-minute walk away. **Location:** From Bath take the A4 towards Bristol and then the A368 to Wells. **Open:** Open for resident and non-resident guests.

map 3 H3

MAUNSEL HOUSE
North Newton, Nr Bridgwater, Somerset TA7 0BU
Tel: 01278 661076

This imposing 13th century manor house was partly built before the Norman Conquest, but latterly around a Great Hall erected in 1420. Geoffrey Chaucer wrote part of The Canterbury Tales whilst staying at the house. Maunsel House is the ancestral seat of the Slade family and is now the home of the 7th baronet, Sir Benjamin Slade. Wedding receptions, private and garden parties, conferences, functions, filming, fashion shows, archery, clay pigeon shooting, equestrian events. **Location:** OS Ref: ST302 303, Bridgwater 4m, Bristol 20 miles, Taunton 7 m, M5/J24, turn left North Petherton 2½ m SE of A38 at North Petherton. **Open:** Coach and group parties welcomed by appointment. **Admission:** For further information, please tel: 01278 661076. **Internet:** www.sirbenslade.co.uk

map 3 G3

MILTON LODGE GARDENS
Old Bristol Road, Wells, Somerset
Tel: 01749 672168 (Mr D C Tudway Quilter)

Grade II listed terraced garden dating from 1906, with outstanding views of Wells Cathedral and Vale of Avalon. Mixed borders, roses, fine trees. Separate 8 acre early XIX century arboretum. **Location:** ½m N of Wells. From A39 Bristol-Wells turn N up Old Bristol Road; free car park first gate on left. **Open:** Garden and arboretum only Easter–end Oct: Tuesday, Wednesday, Sunday and Bank Holidays 2–5pm. Parties and coaches by prior arrangement. **Admission:** Adults £2.50, Children (under 14) free. Open on certain Suns in aid of National Gardens Scheme. **Refreshments:** Teas available Suns and Bank Hols Apr–Sept. No dogs.

  map 3 H3

MONTACUTE HOUSE
Montacute, Somerset, TA15 6XP
Tel/Fax: 01935 823289

A magnificent H-plan Elizabethan house set in formal gardens. Contains a collection of seventeenth-century furniture and samplers, along with a number of paintings from the National Portrait Gallery. **Open:** 31 Mar-4 Nov, daily except Tues, 12–5.30pm. **Admission:** Adult £6, Child £3.

MUSEUM OF COSTUME & ASSEMBLY ROOMS
Bennett Street, Bath, Somerset
Tel: 01225 477789/477785 Fax: 01225 477743

The Museum of Costume (admission charge) is one of the finest collections of fashionable dress in the country. Its extensive displays of original dress cover the history of fashion from the late 16th century to the present day, interpreted by hand-held audio guides at no extra charge. The shop sells noted publications and gifts. The Assembly Rooms are open to the public daily when not in use for functions (admission free) and every day in August. They are also popular for dinners, dances, concerts and conferences. The magnificent interior consists of a splendid Ball Room, Tea Room and Card Room, connected by two fine octagonal rooms. They are managed by Bath and North East Somerset Council, which runs a full conference service. **Open:** All year, 10–5pm. Closed 25/26 Dec. Last admission ½ hr before closing. **Internet:** www.museumofcostume.co.uk

map 3 J2

PEPPERPOT CASTLE
Exmoor National Park (near Wimbleball Lake & Dulverton), Somerset
Tel: 01398 341 615

Beautiful accommodation in Georgian Gothic Folly, believed to have been built by the Earl of Carnarvon for his bride. Set in glorious countryside, with a large garden, it is ideal for romantic weekends and holidays. The self-catering accommodation is suitable for up to five people. Also available as a film or photographic location.

ORCHARD WYNDHAM
Williton, Taunton, Somerset TA4 4HH
Tel: 01984 632309 Fax: 01984 633526 (Wyndham Est Office)

English Manor House. Family home for 700 years encapsulating continuous building and alteration from 14th to 20th centuries. **Location:** 1 mile from A39 at Williton. **Open:** August, thurs.Fri. 2–5pm. B.H.11am–5pm Guided tours only, last tour 4pm. Limited showing space within the house: to avoid disappointment please advance book places on tour by telephone or fax. Narrow road suitable for cars only. **Admission:** Adults £5, Children under 12 £1.

map 3 G3

NUMBER 1, ROYAL CRESCENT
Bath, Avon.
Tel: 01225 428 126 Fax: 01225 481 850 (Bath Preservation Trust)

Number 1 was the first house built in the Royal Crescent in 1767 and is a fine example of John Wood the Younger's Palladian architecture. Visitors can see a grand town house of the late 18th century with authentic furniture, paintings and carpets. There is a study, dining room, lady's bedroom, drawing room, kitchen and museum shop. **Location:** Bath, upper town, close to the Assembly Rooms. **Open:** Mid Feb–end Oct, Tues–Sun, 10.30–5pm. Nov, Tue–Sun, 10.30–4pm. Last admission 30 mins before closing. Private tours out of hours if required by arrangement with the Administrator. Open Bank Hols and Bath Festival Mon. Closed Good Fri. **Admission:** Adults £4, Children/Students/OAPs £3, all groups £2.50, Family ticket £10.
Internet: www.bath–preservation–trust.org.uk

map 4 A4

ROMAN BATHS AND PUMP ROOM
Abbey Church Yard, Bath, Somerset
Tel: 01225 477785 Fax: 01225 477743

The first stop for any visitor to Bath is the Roman Baths surrounding the hot springs where the city began. Here you'll see one of the country's finest ancient monuments - the great Roman temple and bathing complex built almost 2000 years ago. A host of new interpretative methods bring these spectacular buildings vividly to life. The Grand Pump Room, overlooking the Spring, is the social heart of Bath. Enjoy a glass of spa water drawn from the fountain, a traditional Pump Room tea, morning coffee or lunch. The Pump Room Trio and resident pianists provide live music daily. The Roman Baths shop sells publications and gifts. The Pump Room is available for banquets, dances and concerts. **Open:** All year, Jan/Feb 9.30am–5.30pm, Mar–June 9am–6pm, July/Aug 9am–10pm, Sept/Oct 9am–6pm, Nov/Dec 9.30am–5.30pm. Last adm. 1 h before closing. Closed 25&26 Dec. **Internet:** www.romanbaths.co.uk

map 3 J2

Staffordshire

Staffordshire is a treasure trove of undiscovered beauty set in the undulating Midlands landscape. Famous for the exquisite pottery that is produced here, the scenery surrounding its industrial centres is equally beautiful.

The winding thread of the River Dove, which flows though Staffordshire, is strung with market towns and hamlets, gems of unspoiled England, such as picturesque Ellastone, the setting of George Elliot's 'Adam Bede'. Nearby, the Weaver Hills contain fabulous parkland and several noteworthy properties.

There are ancient sites to explore, such as the iron hill fort remains at Cannock Chase, which itself is a historic royal hunting site, and now part of a superb country park.

North Staffordshire is home to Stoke-on-Trent, where internationally famed fine porcelain is produced, and the town celebrates its craftsmanship with several interesting museums.

Lichfield, the birthplace of Dr. Samuel Johnson, is famous for its distinctive 13th century three-spired cathedral, which houses some magnificent Belgian stained glass.

Chillington Hall

Elsewhere in the county, there are numerous castles and country houses to explore.

ANCIENT HIGH HOUSE
Greengate Street, Stafford, Staffordshire, ST16 2JA
Tel: 01785 619131 Fax: 01785 619132 (Stafford Borough Council)

The Ancient High House is the largest timber-framed town house in England. It was built in 1595 by the Dorrington family. Its most famous visitor was King Charles 1, who stayed here in 1642. Now a registered museum, the fascinating history of the house is described in a series of displays. The top floor contains the Museum of the Staffordshire Yeomanry. An attractive gift and souvenir shop is on the ground floor. A temporary art exhibitions programme runs throughout the year. **Location:** Town centre. **Admission:** Phone for prices. **E-mail:** ahh@staffordbc.gov.uk

`map 8 B6`

BARLASTON HALL
Barlaston, Staffs ST12 9AT
Tel: 01782 372749 Fax: 01782 372391 (Mr and Mrs James Hall)

Barlaston Hall is a mid-eighteenth century palladian villa, attributed to the architect Sir Robert Taylor, extensively restored during the 1990s with the support of English Heritage. The four public rooms, open to visitors, contain some fine examples of eighteenth century plaster work. **Open:** By appointment to groups of 10–30. **Admission:** £3.50 per head including refreshments. If you wish to visit the hall, please write or fax giving details of your group including numbers, range or possible dates and a telephone contact. Recorded message with other opening times on above number.

CHILLINGTON HALL
Nr Wolverhampton, Staffordshire WV8 1RE
Tel: 01902 850236 (Mr & Mrs John Giffard)

Georgian house. Part 1724 (Francis Smith); part 1785 (Sir John Soane). Fine saloon. The lake in the park was created by 'Capability' Brown. The bridges by Brown and Paine and the Grecian and Roman Temples, together with the eye-catching Sham House, as well as many fine trees add great interest to the four mile walk around the lake. Dogs welcome in grounds if kept on lead. **Location:** 4 miles SW of A5 at Gailey; 2 miles Brewood. Best approach is from A449 (Jct 12, M6 Jct 2, M54) through Coven (no entry at Codsall Wood). **Open:** June–31 Aug Thurs (also Suns in Aug) 2–5pm open Easter Sun & Suns preceding May and late Spring Bank Holidays 2–5pm. Parties of at least 15 other days by arrangement. **Admission:** Adults £3 (grounds only £1.50), Children half-price.

THE DOROTHY CLIVE GARDEN

Willoughbridge, Market Drayton, Shropshire, TF9 4EU
Tel: 01630 647237 Fax: 01630 647902 (Willoughbridge Garden Trust)

The garden is known for its woodland plantings, established in a disused gravel quarry. A spectacular waterfall cascades between mature rhododendrons, azaleas and choice woodland plants. A south facing hillside garden provides views of surrounding countryside. A scree garden, water features and colourful summer borders are among the many delights. **Location:** A51, midway between Nantwich and Stone, 2 miles south of Woore. **Open:** Garden only: 1 Apr–31 Oct, daily 10–5.30pm. **Admission:** Adults: £3.20, Senior Citizens £2.70, Children up to 11 yrs. free, 11-16 yrs. £1. Free car park. **Refreshments:** Tearoom open daily. Beverages, home baking and light snacks.

map 8
A6

DUNSTALL HALL

Dunstall, Burton-on-Trent, Staffordshire DE13 8BE
Tel: 01283 711123 Fax: 01283 711333

Dunstall Hall is an unbelievable gem. Set in its own outstanding parkland with rolling meadows, mature woodlands, discrete lakes and a stunning cricket pitch, this truly magnificent setting positions the hall perfectly for entertaining in glorious style. In 1145 the Earl of Derby held the estate, and today Sir Stanley and Lady Clarke have chosen this beautiful venue to establish a much loved home that will be enjoyed by their family for future generations. In 2001 Dunstall Hall will be available for special occasions and private hire. A small dinner party for ten guests or a wedding for several hundred will be equally well entertained in rooms that have been built at the very pinnacle of extravagance. The catering is provided in house to the highest standard and this quality complemented by a professional team allows clients to be guaranteed a privileged, enjoyable and outstanding experience. **Location:** The Hall is situated N of Lichfield and 4 miles S of Burton-upon-Trent off the A38. The village of Dunstall and its estate is between Barton under Needwood and Tattenhill. The M1, M42 and M6 are all in close proximity

map 8
C6

DUNWOOD HALL

Longsdon, Nr Leek, Staffordshire ST9 9AR
Tel: 01538 385071

Dunwood Hall is a private country home in the Staffordshire Moorlands, a few miles from the Peak District National Park. Built of stone in 1871 by the Pugin-influenced architect Robert Scrivener, it is an unspoilt example of Victorian neo-Gothic, featuring a richly-carved doorway rising to a tower bearing four grotesques and, inside, a high–galleried hall over an original Minton-tile floor. The secluded gardens include a romantic stable block with archway and spire. Groups interested in Gothic Revival in particular or old houses in general are welcome to a fascinating venue, located 3 miles West of Leek, on the A53 to Stoke-on-Trent. **Open:** By arrangement. **Accommodation:** B&B available. **Admission:** From £5. Home–made refreshments.

map 8
B5

FORD GREEN HALL

Ford Green Road, Smallthorne, Stoke-on-Trent, Staffordshire.
Tel: 01782 233 195 Fax: 01782 233 194
(Stoke-on-Trent City Council)

A 17th century house, home of the Ford family for almost two centuries. Designated a museum with an outstanding collection, the rooms are furnished with original and reproduction textiles, ceramics and furniture according to 17th century inventories. Outside, a garden has been reconstructed with Tudor and Stuart features including knot garden, raised herb beds and viewing mount. The museum has an award-winning education service offering Key Stage 1-3 and GNVQ provision. Light refreshments are served in the shop and tearoom. Regular events include childrens' activities every school holiday. **Location:** NE of Stoke-on-Trent on B551. Signposted from A500. Situated next to Nature Reserve. **Open:** Sunday–Thursday 1–5pm. Closed 25 Dec–1 Jan. **Admission:** Adults £1.50, Conc £1. **Internet:** www.stoke.gov.uk/fordgreenhall

map 8
B5

Staffordshire

IZAAK WALTON'S COTTAGE
Worston Lane, Shallowford, Nr. Great Bridgeford,
Stafford, Staffordshire ST15 0PA
Tel: 01785 760 278 (Stafford Borough Council)

Izaak Walton's Cottage was bequeathed to Stafford by this famous author of the 'Compleat Angler'. It is a delightful timber-framed, thatched cottage and registered museum. It has a series of angling displays showing how the equipment for this sport developed over the years. The events programme takes place each summer, both in the cottage and within its' beautiful garden. It has facilities for disabled visitors, although gravel paths can make access difficult. There are refreshment facilities. **Open:** Apr – Oct. Now licenced for weddings.

map 8 B6

THE POTTERIES MUSEUM & ART GALLERY
Bethesda Street, Hanley, Stoke-on-Trent, Staffordshire ST1 3DE
Tel: 01782 232323 Fax: 01782 232500

Home of the world's finest collection of Staffordshire ceramics. BBC expert Eric Knowles descibes it as, 'the definitive collection; unrivalled on both national and international levels'. Paintings and prints, dazzling decorative arts and a lively programme of changing exhibitions. Discover people, products and landscapes and Stoke-on-Trent's Mark XVI Spitfire. New 'You're History' the look of a lifetime, a hands-on gallery for family fun, 'Our Secret Garden' with plants to smell and touch, Fingerprints and Thumbnails a hands-on virtual art exhibition. Winner of the 1999 Railtrack ADAPT Award for 'Excellence in Access'. This prestigious Museum & Art Gallery has something for everyone. **Opening Times:** 1 Mar-31 Oct: Mon-Sat 10-5pm. Sun 2-5pm. 1 Nov-28 Feb: Mon-Sat 10-4pm. Sun 1-4pm. Closed 25 Dec-1 Jan incl. **Admission:** Free.

map 8 B6

THE SHUGBOROUGH ESTATE
Milford, Nr. Stafford, Staffordshire ST17 0XB
Tel: 01889 881388 Fax: 01889 881323 (Staffordshire County Council)

Shugborough is the magnificent 900 acre ancestral home of the 5th Earl of Lichfield, known world-wide as Patrick Lichfield the leading photographer. The 18th century mansion house contains a fine collection of ceramics, silver, paintings and French furniture. Part of the house is still lived in by the Earl. Visitors can enjoy the 18 acre Grade 1 Historic garden with its Edwardian styly Rose Garden and terraces. A unique collection of neo-classical monuments by James Stuart can be found in the parkland. Other attractions include the County Museum, housed in the original servants' quarters. The working laundry, kitchens and brewhouse have all been lovingly restored and are staffed by costumed guides. Shugborough Park Farm is a Georgian working farm which features an agricultural museum, restored working corn mill and a rare breeds centre. In the kitchen visitors can see

bread baked in brick ovens and cheese and butter being made in the dairy. A lively collection of themed tours are in operation for the coach market and an award-winning educational programme for schools. From April to December an exciting events programme is in operation. Shugborough is an ideal venue for weddings, meetings, conferences, corporate activity days and product launches. **Location:** 6 miles E of Stafford on A513. 10 mins from M6, Jct 13. **Station:** Stafford. **Open:** 31 Mar–30 Sep (daily except Mon but open BH Mon) 11–5pm. Oct Sun only. All year to booked parties. **Admission:** Adult £4.50, Conc £3, Voyager ticket (all 3 sites) Adult £9, Conc £6, Family £22. Site entry £2 per vehicle. **Conferences:** Facilities available. Please contact Mrs Anne Wood. **E-mail:** shugborough. promotions@staffordshire.gov.uk **Internet:** www.staffordshire.gov.uk

map 8 B5

STAFFORD CASTLE & VISITOR CENTRE
Newport Road, Stafford, Staffordshire, ST16 1DJ
Tel: 01785 257 698 (Stafford Borough Council)

Stafford Castle is the impressive site of a Norman motte and bailey fortress. A later stone castle was destroyed during the Civil War, after being defended by Lady Isabel Stafford. It was partly rebuilt in the early 19th century and although now a ruin, is an important example of Gothic Revival architecture. A series of trail boards tell the story of the site. The Visitor Centre displays artefacts from a series of archaeological excavations. An audiovisual presentation narrated by Robert Hardy sets the scene. A collection of chain mail and other objects are fun to try on. A herb garden and attractive gift shop complete this interesting corner of Staffordshire. Picnic area, disabled access and guided tours available.

map 8 B6

TAMWORTH CASTLE
The Holloway, Tamworth, Staffordshire B79 7LR
Tel: 01827 709626 Fax: 01827 709630
(Tamworth Borough Council)

Dramatic Norman castle with 15 rooms open to the public, set in attractive town centre park noted for its floral terraces. Includes Great Hall, Dungeon and Haunted Bedroom featuring *Living Images*. "The Tamworth Story" – interactive exhibition telling the town's history from Roman times to the present day. Wheelchair users restricted to the ground floor. **Location:** Town centre, in Castle Pleasure Grounds; 15 miles NE of Birmingham. **Station:** Tamworth. **Open:** Mon–Sat 10am–5.30pm and Sun 2–5.30pm (last admission 4.30pm). Please check opening times after 1 November. **Admission:** Charge. **Events:** Approx 20 special events are held annually. Many are on Bank Holidays. **Internet:** www.tamworthcastle.co.uk

map 8 C7

WHITMORE HALL
Whitmore, Nr Newcastle-under-Lyme, Staffordshire ST5 5HW.
Tel: 01782 680478 Fax: 01782 680906 (Guy Cavenagh-Mainwaring Esq)

Whitmore Hall is a fine example of a small Carolinian Manor House, although parts of the Hall date back to a much earlier period. It has been the owner's family home for over 900 years and has continuous family portraits dating back to 1624. A special feature of Whitmore is the extremely rare example of a late Elizabethan stable block. The exterior grounds include a beautiful home park with a lime avenue leading to the house. **Location:** 4 miles from Newcastle-under-Lyme, on A53 to Market Drayton. **Open:** 1 May–31 August, Tues & Wed. Parties of +15 by arrangement outside normal opening days (between 1 April–31 Aug) Teas arranged for parties over 15. 2-5pm. **Admission:** Adult £3, Child 50p.

map 8 A6

TUTBURY CASTLE
Tutbury, Staffordshire
Tel: 01283 812129

A ruined motte and bailey castle, set in beautiful countryside overlooking the Dove Valley. Visitors can see a recreated Tudor garden, and there are often costumed guides. **Open:** Apr–Oct, Wed–Sun, 11am–5pm. **Admission:** Adult £3, Child £1.50.

WATLING STREET ROMAN WALL (LETOCETUM)
Watling Street, nr Lichfield, Staffordshire, WS14 0AW
Tel: 01543 480768

Formerly a staging post on Watling Street, where a range of archaeological finds can be viewed. Also on site: foundations of a bath-house and an inn. **Open:** 1 Apr–31 Oct, daily 10am–6pm. Closes one hour earlier in Oct. **Admission:** Please phone for prices.

Suffolk

Snape Maltings

real love was landscape painting, and many of his portraits contain recognisable local scenes in the background.

Suffolk is blessed with a largely unspoilt coastline of shingle, sand, heathland and cliffs, where the visitor can enjoy bracing walks under the ever-changing canvas of the sky. Charming seaside villages nestle here and there, offering good seafood and locally-brewed ale to the hungry walker.

Inland are some of Britain's best-preserved small towns, a re-constructed Anglo-Saxon village, and a range of historical re-enactments throughout the year.

The wide, open spaces of Suffolk create an atmosphere quite unlike that of any other county. Its gently rolling countryside has a static charm, as if lifted directly from a painting. Indeed, many views may seem familiar to art lovers, for Suffolk was the birth place of two of England's greatest painters, Constable and Gainsborough. The English lowlands had a marked effect on Constable, whose landscapes continued to be inspired by childhood memories of the Stour Valley long after he had left the area. Whilst Gainsborough is better known for his portrait work, it seems from his writings that his

Christchurch Mansion

THE ANCIENT HOUSE
Clare, Suffolk CO10 8NY
Tel: The Landmark Trust: 01628 825920
(Leased to the Landmark Trust by Clare Parish Council)

A 14th century house extended in the 15th and 17th centuries, decorated with high relief pargeting. Half of the building is managed by the Landmark Trust, which lets buildings for self-catering holidays. **Open:** By appointment only, and for Clare Arts Festival, w/c 16th June 2001. The other half is run as a Museum. **Open:** Contact Clare Museum Tel: 01787 277662 for details. **Accommodation:** Available for up to two people for self-catering holidays. Telephone: 01628 825925 for Bookings. Full details of the Ancient House and 170 other historic buildings are featured in the Landmark Handbook (price £9.50, refundable against a booking) from the Landmark Trust, Shottesbrooke, Maidenhead, Berkshire SL6 3SW. **Internet:** www.landmarktrust.co.uk

`map 5 G2`

CHRISTCHURCH MANSION
Christchurch Park, Ipswich, Suffolk
Tel: 01473 433544 Fax: 01473 433564 (Ipswich Borough Council)

A fine tudor house set in beautiful parkland. Period rooms furnished in styles from 16th to 19th centuries. Outstanding collections of china, clocks and furniture. Paintings by Gainsborough, Constable and other Suffolk artists. Attached, the Wolsey Art Gallery shows a lively temporary exhibition programme. Location: Christchurch Park, near centre of Ipswich. **Station(s):** Ipswich (1.25 miles). **Open:** Tues–Sat, 10–5pm (dusk in winter). Sun 2.30–4.30pm (dusk in winter). Also open Bank Hol Mons. Closed 24–26 Dec, 1 Jan & Good Fri. **Admission:** Free.

`map 5 H2`

HENGRAVE HALL CENTRE
Hengrave Hall, Bury St Edmunds, Suffolk
Tel: 01284 701561 Fax: 01284 702950 (Religious of the Assumption)

Hengrave Hall is a Tudor mansion of stone and brick built between 1525 and 1538. Former home to the Kytson and Gage families, it was visited by Elizabeth I on her Suffolk Progress. Set in 45 acres of cultivated grounds, the Hall is now run as a Conference and Retreat Centre by the Hengrave Community of Reconciliation. The ancient church with Saxon tower adjoins the Hall and continues to be used for daily prayer. **Location:** 3.5 miles NW of Bury St Edmunds on the A1101. Enquire: The Warden for: tours (by appointment); conference facilities (day/ residential); retreats, programme of events; schools' programme. **E-mail:** co-ordinator@hengravehallcentre.org.uk
Internet: www.hengravehallcentre.org.uk

`map 5 G1`

HELMINGHAM HALL GARDENS

The Estate Office, Helmingham Hall, Stowmarket, Suffolk IP14 6EF
Tel: 01473 890363 Fax: 01473 890776

Completed in 1510, the Hall has been the home of the Tollemache family continuously to the present day. There are two superb gardens that extend to several acres set in 400 acres of ancient parkland containing herds of Red and Fallow deer and Highland cattle. The main garden is surrounded by its own Saxon moat and 1740 wall, with wide herbaceous borders and planted tunnels intersecting an immaculate kitchen garden; the second is a very special rose garden enclosed within high yew hedges with a herb and knot garden containing plants grown in England before 1750. Listed Grade I by English Heritage. **Open:** 29 Apr–9 Sept, Sun only 2–6pm. Also by appointment only for groups, Wed 2–5pm. **Admission:** Adults £3.75, Children £2, Groups 30+ £3.25 (£3.75 on Wed). Please call 01473 890363 to make appt. **Internet:** www.helmingham.com

map 5 H2

HAUGHLEY PARK

Nr Stowmarket, Suffolk IP14 3JY
Tel: 01359 240701 (Mr & Mrs R J Williams)

Imposing red-brick Jacobean manor house of 1620, set in gardens, park and woodland. Unaltered three storey east front with five gables topped with crow steps and finials. North end rebuilt in Georgian style, 1820. Six acres of well-tended gardens including walled kitchen garden. Nearby 17th century brick and timber barn restored as meeting rooms. Three woodland walks (1.5 to 2.5 miles) through old broadleaf and pine woodland with bluebells, lily of the valley, rhododendron, azaleas and camellias. **Location:** 4 miles West of Stowmarket signed off A14 (Haughley Park, not Haughley). **Open:** Gardens: May–Sept, Tues and 'Bluebell Sundays' 29 Apr and 6 May 2–5.30pm. House: by appointment (01359 240701) May–Sept, Tues 2–5.30pm. **Admission:** Adults £2, Children £1. Plants for sale on Sundays only. Barn converted for meeting rooms.

map 5 H1

IPSWICH MUSEUM

Ipswich, Suffolk IP1 3QH.
Tel: 01473 433550 (Ipswich Borough Council)

Geology and natural history of Suffolk; Mankind galleries covering Africa, Asia, America and the Pacific. 'Romans in Suffolk' and 'Anglo-Saxons in Ipswich' exhibitions. **Location:** High Street in Ipswich town centre. **Station(s):** Ipswich. **Open:** Tues–Sat, 10–5pm. Closed Dec 24, 25 & 26, Jan 1 & Good Friday. Closed Bank Holidays. Temporary exhibition programme. **Admission:** Free.

map 5 H2

KENTWELL HALL

Long Melford, Suffolk CO10 9BA,
Tel:01787 310207. Fax: 01787 379318 (Mrs Phillips)

A mellow redbrick moated Tudor Mansion. Exterior little changed from when it was built. Interior shows changes of successive family occupiers. Fine service buildings; Moat House with dairy, bakehouse and brewhouse. Moated Walled Garden with potager and herb garden. Lived in family home. Famous for RECREATIONS OF DOMESTIC TUDOR LIFE AND WWII on selected weekends throughout season. Also Rare Breeds Farm. **Open:** Gardens & farm only: 4 Mar–8 Apr. House, gardens & farm: 22 Apr–10 Jun, Suns only. 17-20 Apr daily, Half Term 29 May–1 Jun. 11 Jul–21 Sept daily, Suns only. 30 Sept–28 Oct and daily 21–25 Oct, usually 12–5pm. Great Annual Re-creation: 17 Jun–8 Jul (Sats & Suns only & Fri 6 Jul); **Mini Re-creations:** 13–16 Apr, 5/6, 19/20 & 26–28 May, 4/5 & 24–27 Aug, 22/23 Sept, 27/28 Oct. Phone for opening times.

map 5 G2

OTLEY HALL

Otley, Nr Ipswich, Suffolk IP6 9PA
Tel: 01473 890264 Fax: 01473 890803 (Mr Nicholas & Mrs Ann Hagger)

A stunning medieval moated hall, grade 1 listed and a family home. Rich in history and architectural detail: ornately carved beams, superb linenfold panelling and 16 C wall paintings. Home of the Gosnold family for some 300 years from 1401. Bartholomew Gosnold voyaged to the New World in 1602 and named Cape Cod and Martha's Vineyard. He returned in 1606/7 to found the Jamestown colony, the first English-speaking settlement in the US, 13 years before the *Mayflower* landed. He is also linked to Shakespeare. The house is set in 10 acres of gardens. They include parts of a design by Francis Inigo Thomas (1866–1950): an H-canal, nutteries, croquet lawn, rose garden and moat walk. There are also historically accurate medieval/Tudor recreations designed by Sylvia Landsberg,

author of *The Medieval Garden*, including a knot garden that symbolises the Universe, 25 beds representing 25 civilisations. Care has been taken to encourage growth of wild flowers and hedges, and preserve the habitats of native wildlife. There are newly constructed woodland walks with over 60 varieties of holly; collections of hostas, grasses and asters; and some surprises. **Open:** Bank Hol Suns and Mons, 12.30–6pm; Gardens only Mons & Weds from 23 Apr–24 Sept, 2–5pm. **Admission:** Adult £4.50, Child £2.50. Garden Days: Adult £3, OAP £2.60, Child £1. Coach parties welcome by appointment for private guided tours. Also available for Conferences and Seminars, Corporate Entertainment, Concerts and Theatrical Productions. Pre-booked meals available.

map 5 H2

ICKWORTH HOUSE, PARK AND GARDEN

The Rotunda, Horringer, Bury St Edmunds, IP29 5QE
Tel: 01284 735270 Fax: 01284 735175

An eighteenth-century Italianate house with an enormous Rotunda, making it perhaps the most unusual and intriguing property in the region. Holds collections of Regency furniture, Georgian silver, and Old Masters. **Open:** 24 Mar–28 Oct: daily except Mon and Thurs, 1–5pm. **Admission:** Adult £5.70, Child £2.50.

LAVENHAM – THE GUILDHALL OF CORPUS CHRISTI

Market Place, Lavenham, Sudbury, CO10 9QZ
Tel: 01787 247646

A wonderful sixteenth-century timber-framed building, containing exhibitions on local farming and industry, and on the mediaeval wool trade. **Open:** Apr – end Oct: daily (except Good Friday), 11am–5pm. Weekends in Mar and Nov, 11am–4pm. May be closed on occasions for community use. **Admission:** Adult £3, accompanied child free.

SOMERLEYTON HALL & GARDENS

Somerleyton, Lowestoft, Suffolk NR32 5QQ
Tel: 01502 730224 Fax: 01502 732143 (The Rt. Hon. Lord Somerleyton GCVO)

Home of Lord and Lady Somerleyton, Somerleyton Hall is a splendid early Victorian mansion built in Anglo-Italian style with lavish architectural features, magnificent carved stonework and fine state rooms. Paintings by Landseer, Wright of Derby and Stanfield, wood carvings by Willcox of Warwick and Grinling Gibbons. The justly renowned 12 acre gardens feature an 1846 yew hedge maze, glasshouses by Paxton, fine statuary, pergola, walled garden, Vulliamy tower clock, magnificent specimen trees and beautiful borders. Also Loggia Tea Rooms. **Location:** 5 miles NW Lowestoft B1074. **Open:** Easter Sunday–end Sept, Thursdays, Sundays and Bank Holidays plus Tuesdays and Wednesdays during July and August. Gardens 12.30–5.30pm, Hall 1– 5pm. Coach parties welcome, private tours and functions by arrangement. **Internet:** www.somerleyton.co.uk

MECHANICAL MUSIC MUSEUM & BYGONES

Blacksmith Road, Cotton, Nr Stowmarket, Suffolk IP14 4QN
Tel: 01449 613876

Unique collection of music-boxes, gramophones, polyphons, street-pianos, barrel-organs, fair-organs, Wurlitzer Theatre pipe organ, many unusual items, all played, plus memorabilia. **Open:** Sundays 27 May–30 September: 2–5.30pm. **Admission:** Adults £3, Children £1. Parking free. Evening tours weekdays by arrangement. Fair Organ Enthusiasts' Day: 7 October 10–5pm.

map 5
H1

SHRUBLAND PARK GARDENS

Shrubland Park, Coddenham, Ipswich, Suffolk
Tel: 01473 830221 Fax: 01473 832202 (Lord De Saumarez)

The extensive formal garden of Shrubland Park is one of the finest examples of an Italianate garden in England. Much use is made of evergreens clipped into architectural shapes to complement the hard landscaping of the masonry. Pines, cedars, holly and holm oak soften this formal structure and add to the Italian flavour. Sir Charles Barry exploited the chalk escarpment overlooking the Gipping Valley to create one of his famous achievements, the magnificent 'Grand Descent' which links the Hall to the lower gardens through a series of terraces. **Location:** 6 miles north of Ipswich to the east of A14/A140 Beacon Hill junction. **Open:** Suns 2–5pm from 15 Apr–23 Sept 2001 inclusive, plus Bank Hol Mons. **Admission:** Adults £3, Children and Seniors £2. Guided tours by arrangement. Toilet facilities but no refreshments. Limited suitability for wheelchairs.

map 5
H2

WINGFIELD OLD COLLEGE & GARDENS

Wingfield, Nr Stradbroke, Suffolk IP21 5RA
Tel: 01379 384888 Fax: 01379 388082 (Mr & Mrs Ian Chance)

This delightful medieval house with walled gardens offers a unique Arts and Heritage experience. Spectacular medieval Great Hall. Exhibitions of contemporary art in the new College Yard galleries plus permanent collections of textiles, ceramics and garden sculpture. Some of history's colourful characters associated with the Old College are the Black Prince, William de la Pole and Mary Tudor. Summer 2000 - 17th century walled garden restoration project. **Location:** Signposted off B1118 (Off the A140 Ipswich/Norwich trunk road) and the B1116 (Harleston–Fressingfield). **Open:** Easter Sat–end Sept Sats, Suns, Bank Hol Mons 2–6pm. **Admission:** Adults £3.80, Seniors £3, Children/Students £1.50, Family ticket £9. **Refreshments:** Cream teas and homemade cakes.

map 5
H1

WYKEN HALL

Stanton, Bury St.Edmunds, Suffolk IP31 2DW
Tel: 01359 250287 Fax: 01359 252256

The garden, vineyard, country store and vineyard restaurant at Wyken are at the heart of an old Suffolk manor that dates back to Domesday. The garden, set among old flint walls and fine trees, embraces herb and knot gardens, an old-fashioned rose garden, maze, nuttery and gazebo set in a wild garden with spring bulbs. The Leaping Hare Vineyard Restaurant in the 400 year old barn serves Wyken's award-winning wines and is the 1998 Good Food Guide's 'Vineyard Restaurant of the Year'. It is a BIB Gourmand in the Michelin Guide. The Country Store offers an unique collection of textiles, pottery and other country goods. A walk through ancient woodland leads to the vineyard. **Location:** Follow brown tourist signs to Wyken Vineyards from the A134 at Ixworth. **Open:** Wed–Sun 10am–6pm and for dinner Fri–Sat. Garden closed on Saturdays.

map 5
H1

Surrey

Surrey's sleepy and charming countryside saw the birth of English democracy, with the signing of the Magna Carta at Runnymede in 1215. Over the succeeding centuries, a number of great houses and royal palaces have been constructed here, including one of Henry VIII's residences, Hampton Court, but Surrey's peaceful villages seem oblivious to the tides of history. Likewise, the bustle of nearby London has not affected the pace of life in the rural backwaters of the county. The sandy heaths that stretch across much of its landscape attract walkers from all around, but the less-energetic may prefer to enjoy the spectacular view from the Hog's Back, a long ridge running over the North Downs past Guildford, the county's Georgian capital.

River Wey, Guildford

CLANDON PARK

West Clandon, Guildford, Surrey, GU4 7RQ
Tel: 01483 222482 Fax: 01483 223176 (The National Trust)

An outstanding Palladian country house of dramatic contrasts; from the magnificent neoclassical Marble Hall to the Maori Meeting House in the garden and the opulent Speaker's Parlour. The house is rightly acclaimed for housing the famous Gubbay Collection of porcelain, furniture and needlework, as well as Onslow family pictures and furniture, the Mortlake tapestries and the Ivo Forde collection of Meissen Italian comedy figures. The garden has a grotto and parterre and there is a gift shop and licensed restaurant. **Location:** At West Clandon on the A247, 3 miles E of Guildford. B Rail Clandon 1 mile. **Open:** 1 Apr–4 Nov., Tue, Wed, Thur, Sun plus Bank Hols & Easter 11.00–5pm. Events: Programme of concerts in the Marble Hall throughout the year. Tel: 01483 225804.

map 4 E5

CLAREMONT HOUSE

Claremont Drive, Esher, Surrey
Tel: 01372 467 841 Fax: 01372 471 109

Excellent example of Palladian style. Built in 1772 by Capability Brown for Clive of India. Henry Holland and John Soane were responsible for the interior decoration. It is now an independent co-educational school. **Location:** 1/2 m SW of Esher on A307, Esher-Cobham Road. **Open:** Apr–Oct, first complete weekend (Sat & Sun) each month (except first Sat in Jul), 2–5pm. Last tour 4.30pm. **Admission:** Adult £3, Child/OAP £2. Reduced rates for parties. Guided tours and souvenirs. **E-mail:** sthomas@claremont.surrey.sch.uk. **Internet:** www.claremont-school.co.uk

map 4 E5

CLAREMONT LANDSCAPE GARDEN

Portsmouth Road, Esher, Surrey KT10 9JG
TEL: 01372 467 806 FAX: 01372 464 394

Claremont's creation and development involved some of the great names in garden history. The first Garden was begun in 1715 and later that century, their delights were famed throughout Europe. The many features include a lake, island with pavilion, grotto, turf amphitheatre, with ever changing view points and vistas. A safe haven and green oasis. Level pathways provide easy access around the lake. There are 50+ species of waterfowl. Guided walks at 2pm on 1&3 Sat, 2 Wed & last Sun each month from Apr–Oct. Light lunches, home-made cakes and scones served at tea-room, 12–2pm. **Location:** S of Esher on E side of A307. Access: 2 wheelchairs-booking advisable. **Open:** Garden: Jan-end Dec, daily 10-5pm; 10-7pm weekends (or sunset if earlier). Closed Mons Nov-Mar & 10-11 Jul and from 2pm 13-15 Jul & 25 Dec. **Admission:** NT free. Adult £3.50.

map 4 E5

CROYDON PALACE

Old Palace School, Old Palace Road, Croydon, Surrey, CR0 1AX
Tel: 020 8680 0467/020 8688 2027 Fax: 020 8680 5877
(The Whitgift Foundation)

Seat of the Archbishops of Canterbury since 871 AD. 15th century Banqueting Hall, Guardroom and Chapel. Norman Undercroft. **Location:** In Croydon Old Town, adjacent to the Parish Church. **Station(s):** East Croydon or West Croydon. **Open:** Conducted Tours only. Doors open 1:45pm. Tours at 2pm. 17–21 Apr & 28 May–1 June & 16–21 July & 23–28 July. **Admission:** Adults £4.00, Children/OAPs £3, Family £10. Includes tea served in the Undercroft. Parties catered for by prior arrangement (Tel: 020 8680 0467). Souvenir shop. Unsuitable for wheelchairs.

map 5 F4

HAMPTON COURT

East Molesey, KT8 9AY
Tel: 020 8781 9500

The Splendour of Cardinal Wolsey's house, begun in 1514, surpasses that of many a Royal Palace, so it was not surprising that Henry VIII obtained it prior to Wolsey's fall from power. Henry VIII enlarged it; Charles I lived in it as a prisoner; Charles I repaired it; William III and Mary I rebuilt it to a design by Sir Christopher Wren and Queen Victoria opened it to the public.

FOR FULL DETAILS, OPENING TIMES, AND COLOUR PHOTOGRAPHS, PLEASE SEE ENTRY UNDER LONDON SECTION, PAGE 120.

FARNHAM CASTLE

Farnham, Surrey GU4 0AG

Tel: 01252 721194 Fax: 01252 711283 (Church Commissioners)

Bishop's Palace built in Norman times by Henry of Blois, with Tudor and Jacobean additions. Formerly the seat of the Bishops of Winchester. Fine Great Hall re-modelled at the Restoration. Features include the Renaissance brickwork of Wayneflete's tower and the 17th century chapel. **Location:** ½ miles N of Town Centre on A287. **Station(s):** Farnham. **Open:** All year round, Weds 2–4pm; parties at other times by arrangement. All visitors given guided tours. Centrally heated in winter. **Admission:** Adults £1.50, OAPs/Children/Students 80p, reductions for parties. **Conferences:** Please contact Conference Organiser. Centrally heated in winter. Not readily accessible by wheelchair.

map 4
D5

GODDARDS

Abinger Common, Dorking, Surrey, RH5 6TH

Tel: The Landmark Trust: 01628 825920

(Leased to the Landmark Trust by the Lutyens Trust)

Built by Sir Edwin Lutyens in 1898–1900. Garden by Gertrude Jekyll. Managed and maintained by the Landmark Trust, which lets buildings for self-catering holidays. **Open:** By appointment only. Must be booked in advance, including parking, which is very limited. Visits booked for Wed afternoons from the Wed after Easter until last Wed of Oct between 2–6pm. **Admission:** Tickets £3, obtainable from Mrs Baker on 01306 730871, Mon–Fri, 9–6pm. Visitors will have access to part of the house and garden only. **Accommodation:** Available for up to 12 people. Tel: 01628 825925 for bookings. Full details of Goddards and 170 other historic buildings are featured in The Landmark Handbook (price £9.50 refundable against a booking) from The Landmark Trust, Shottesbrooke, Maidenhead, Berkshire, SL6 3SW. **Internet:** www.landmarktrust.co.uk

map 4
E5

 ## GREAT FOSTERS

Stroude Road, Egham, Surrey

Tel: 01784 433822 Fax: 01784 472455

Probably built as a Royal Hunting lodge in Windsor Forest, very much a stately home since the 16th century, today Great Fosters is a prestigious hotel. It is evident in the mullioned windows, tall chimneys and brick finials, while the Saxon moat – crossed by a Japanese bridge – surrounds three sides of the formal gardens complete with topiary, statuary and a charming rose garden. Within are fine oak beams and panelling, Jacobean chimney pieces, superb tapestries and a rare oakwell staircase leading to the Tower. Some guest bedrooms are particularly magnificent – one Italian styled with gilt furnishings and damask walls, others with moulded ceilings, beautiful antiques and Persian rugs. **Location:** Close to M25, Heathrow and M3. London 40 minutes by rail. **E-mail:** enquiries@greatfosters.co.uk **Internet:** www.greatfosters.co.uk

map 4
E4

GUILDFORD HOUSE GALLERY

155 High Street, Guildford, Surrey, GU1 3AJ

Tel: 01483 444740, Fax: 01483 444742 (Guildford Borough Council)

A beautifully restored 17th century town house with a number of original features including a finely carved staircase, panelled rooms and decorative plaster ceilings. A varied temporary exhibition programme including paintings, photography and craft work. Exhibition and events leaflet available. Lecture and workshop programme. Details on application. **Location:** Central Guildford on High Street. Public car parks nearby off pedestrianised High Street. **Open:** Tues–Sat 10–4.45pm **Admission:** Free. **Refreshments:** Old kitchen tearoom. **Gallery Shop:** with attractive selection of cards, craftwork and other publications. **E-mail:** guildfordhouse@remote.guildford.gov.uk **Internet:** www.guildfordhouse.co.uk

map 4
E5

HATCHLANDS PARK

East Clandon, Guildford, Surrey GU4 7RT

Tel: 01483 222482 Fax: 01483 223176

Built in 1758 for Admiral Boscawen and set in a beautiful Repton park offering a variety of park and woodland way-marked walks, Hatchlands contains splendid interiors by Robert Adam, his first commission in a country house in England. It houses the Cobbe Collection, the world's largest group of early keyboard instruments associated with famous composers, e.g. Purcell, JC Bach, Chopin, Mahler, Elgar, and also Marie Antoinette. Small garden by Gertrude Jekyll, gift shop, licensed restaurant and tearoom. Audio Guide. Lunchtime recitals most Wednesdays. **Location:** 5 miles E of Guildford, on A246 Guildford–Leatherhead Road. **Open:** 1 Apr–31 Oct. Walks: daily 11–6pm. House: Tues, Wed, Thurs, Sun plus BH Mons and all Fris in Aug 2–5.30pm. **Events:** Second weekend in July 2001, Hatchlands Hat Trick Open Air Concerts Tel: 01483 2225804.

map 4
E5

LOSELEY PARK
Guildford, Surrey, GU3 1HS
Tel: 01483 304 440 (Mr & Mrs Michael More-Molyneux)

Loseley House was built in 1562 by Sir William More, a direct ancestor of the present owner. It is a fine example of Elizabethan architecture, dignified and beautiful, set amid magnificent parkland. Inside are many fine works of art, including panelling from Henry VIII's Nonsuch Palace, paintings and tapestries. The glorious 2.5 acre Walled Garden features an award-winning Rose Garden a Herb Garden a Flower Garden, a Vegetable Garden, a Fountain Garden and also Moat Walk. **Location:** 2 miles south of Guildford. (Take B3000 off A3 through Compton). **Open: Garden, Shop & Tea Room:** 1 May–30 Sept, Wed–Sun & Bank Hol, 11–5pm. **House:** 29 May–27 Aug, Wed–Sun & Bank Hol, 1–5pm (last tour 4pm). Internet: www.loseley-park.com

map 4 E5

PAINSHILL LANDSCAPE GARDEN
Portsmouth Road, Cobham, Surrey KT11 1JE
Tel: 01932 868113 Fax: 01932 868001 (Painshill Park Trust)

Painshill, contemporary with Stourhead and Stowe, is one of Europe's finest 18th century landscape gardens. Europa Nostra Medal winner for "exemplary restoration". The 14 acre lake, filled by a massive waterwheel, gives a perfect setting for a Gothic temple, ruined abbey, Turkish tent, Chinese bridge, crystal grotto and much, much more. **Location:** W of Cobham of A245; 200 metres E of A307 roundabout. Visitor entrance: Between Streets, Cobham. **Open:** April–Oct daily except Mon (open Bank Hols). 10.30–6.00pm (last entry 4.30pm). Nov–Mar daily except Mon & Fri, Christmas Day & Boxing Day. 11–4pm dusk if earlier. (Last entry 3pm) **Admission:** Adults £4.20, Concessions £3.70, Children 5–16 £1.70. Adult groups of 10+ £3.30 (**must pre-book phone 01932 868113**). No dogs please.

map 4 E5

RHS GARDEN WISLEY
Wisley, Woking, Surrey GU23 6QB
Tel: 01483 224234 (Royal Horticultural Society)

Voted Visitor Attraction of the year 1999, Wisely demonstrates British gardening at its best in all aspects. Covering over 240 acres, highlights include the Alpine Meadow carpeted with daffodils in Spring, Battleston Hill, brilliant with rhododendrons in early Summer, the heathers and Autumnal tints. All this together with the Glasshouses, Trials and Model Gardens are features for which the Garden is renowned. Facilities include Restaurant and Cafeteria, The Wisley Shop containing the finest collection of horticultural books in the world as well as other gifts and The Wisely Plant Centre with over 10,000 varieties of plant for sale. **Location:** Wisely is just off the M25 Jet 10, on the A3. **Open:** Daily, all year, except Christmass Day though please note, Sundays are open for RHS **members only.** **Internet:** www.rhs.org.uk

map 4 E5

RURAL LIFE CENTRE
Reeds Road, Tilford, Farnham
Tel/Fax: 01252 79 5571

The Rural Life Centre is a museum of past village life covering the years from 1750 to 1960. It is set in over ten acres of garden and woodland and housed in purpose-built and reconstructed buildings including a chapel, village hall and cricket pavillion. Displays show village crafts and trades such as wheelwrighting of which the centre's collection is probably the finest in the country. An historic village playground provides entertainment for children as does a preserved narrow gauge light railway which operates on Sundays. There is also an arboretum with over 100 species of trees from around the world. **Open:** April to September, Wed–Sun & B.H. Mons 11–6pm. **E-mail:** rural.life@argonet.co.uk **Internet:** www.surreyweb.org.uk/rural-life

map 4 D5

HAM HOUSE
Ham Street, Richmond, Surrey TW10 7RS
Tel: 020 8940 1950 Fax: 020 8332 6903 (The National Trust)

Set in beautiful gardens by the Thames, Ham House is one of the finest 17th century houses in Europe, with exquisite furniture, textiles and paintings. **Location:** South bank of River Thames. West of A307 at Petersham. **Station(s):** BR/London Underground – Richmond (2m by road). BR - Kingston (2m by road). **Buses:** 65, 371 (both passing Richmond & Kingston stns.). **Open:** 31 Mar-1 Nov: daily except Thurs & Fri 1–5pm. Last admission ½ hr before closing. Garden: all year daily except Thurs & Fri 11am–6pm or dusk if earlier. Closed 25–26 Dec & 1 Jan. **Admission:** Adults £6, Child £3, Family £15. Pre-booked parties on application. **Refreshments:** Orangery Restaurant – self-service (Tel: 020 8940 0735). Open Sat–Wed, 11am–5.30pm. Disabled visitors may park near entrance. Disabled toilet.

map 4 E4

Sussex

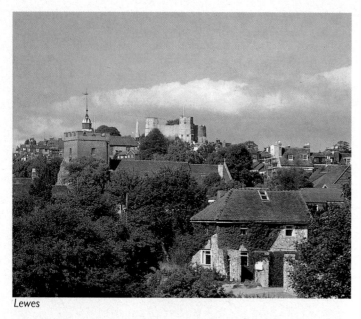

Lewes

Sussex is a county of great natural beauty, from the chalk grassland of the Downs to the tranquil valleys of the Weald, and from the woodland trails of Bewl Water to the vast chalk cliffs outside Eastbourne. The county's historical importance can be seen in the array of monuments, castles and country houses still standing within its boundaries. Towns such as Arundel and Lewes once defended England against attack, and visitors can still see their fine castles and fortifications.

Beachy Head is the highest chalk sea cliff in Britain, rising 530 feet above the sea, and offering wonderful panoramic views of up to 70 miles on a clear day. The cliffs along this part of the coast remain white thanks to constant erosion by the sea. Local heritage policy is to allow this natural process to continue, and in 1999 Belle Toute lighthouse had to be moved back from the cliff face to stop it from collapsing into the sea. The chalk was formed over a period of 30 million years from the shells of billions of microscopic sea-creatures, which gradually hardened into layers a thousand feet thick. Movements of the earth's crust forced the cliffs up to form the Downs, now home to a rich variety of plants, insects and birds. Stretching for over 100 miles, the chalk and flint South Downs provide fantastic opportunities for walking, with a network of well-maintained footpaths and bridleways.

Close to the border between East and West Sussex stands the famous resort of Brighton, which houses a vibrant cultural scene and nightlife second only to London.

ARCHITECTURAL PLANTS

Cooks Farm, Nuthurst, Nr Horsham, West Sussex RH13 6LH
Tel: 01403 891772 Fax: 01403 891056 (Angus White)

Specialising in unusual and hardy exotics from around the world, Architectural Plants is a unique nursery that grows and provides spectacular plants for adventurous gardeners. Set up by owner Angus White in the spring of 1990, the nursery has a well deserved reputation for supplying excellent quality plants, backed up by sound practical help and advice. The range of plants offered concentrate first and foremost on strong shapes, bold outlines and are mostly evergreen. Included amongst the rare and not so rare you will find bananas, bamboos, red-barked strawberry trees, giant Japanese pom-poms, green olive trees, topiary, spiky plants, Chinese cloud trees, hardy jungle plants and Lord knows what else.... **Open:** Horsham Nursery open Monday to Saturday 9am to 5pm; Chichester Nursery open from Sunday to Friday 10am to 4pm. Phone for free catalogue. **Internet**: www.architecturalplants.com

map 4
E 5/6

ARUNDEL CASTLE

Arundel, West Sussex, BN18 9AB
Tel: 01903 883136 Fax: 01903 884581

Magnificent castle overlooking the beautiful town of Arundel.
FOR FULL DETAILS, OPENING TIMES, AND COLOUR PHOTOGRAPHS, PLEASE SEE PAGES 182 & 183.

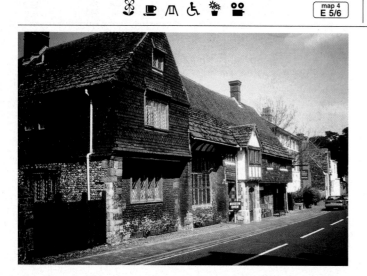

ANNE OF CLEVES HOUSE

52 Southover High Street, Lewes, Sussex BN7 1JA
Tel: 01273 474 610 Fax: 01273 486 990 (Sussex Past)

This beautiful 16th century timber-framed Wealden hall-house contains wide-ranging collections of Sussex interest. Furnished rooms give an impression of life in the 17th and 18th centuries. Exhibits include artefacts from nearby Lewes Priory, Sussex pottery, Wealden ironwork and kitchen equipment. **Station(s):** Lewes (10 mins walk). **Bus route:** Adjacent. Bus station 15 mins walk away. **Open:** 2 Jan–17 Feb: Tues, Thurs & Sat 10–5pm. 19 Feb–4 Nov: Mon–Sat 10–5pm; Sun 12–5pm. 6 Nov–23 Dec; Tues–Sat, 10–5pm; Sun 12–5pm. **Admission:** Adults £2.60, Children £1.30, OAP/Student £2.40, Family (2+2) £6.80; 1 Adult + 4 Children £5.20. Combined ticket with Lewes Castle available. No dogs. **E-mail:** castle@sussexpast.co.uk
Internet: www.sussexpast.co.uk

map 5
F6

BATTLE ABBEY AND THE 1066 BATTLEFIELD

Battle, Sussex, TN33 0AD
Tel: 01424 773792 Fax: 01424 775059

Visitors can explore the stunning ruins of the Abbey, near to the site of the Battle of Hastings. There are free audio tours to guide you round the battlefield, and a themed children's play area. **Open:** All year round, except Christmas period and New Year's Day. Times: 1 Apr–30 Sept, daily, 10am–6pm. 1–31 Oct, 10am–5pm. Otherwise, daily 10am–4pm. **Admission:** Adult £4.30, Child £2.20.

CHICHESTER DISTRICT MUSEUM

29 Little London, Chichester, West Sussex PO19 1PB
Tel: 01243 784683 Fax: 01243 776766

This is the idael place to explore the history of Chichester and District. Look out for displays on geology and pre-history including Boxgrove Man, Roman Chichester, Saxon and Medieval life. Find out about Chichester during the Civil War and changes which have taken place from the eighteenth century onwards. There are hands-on activities around the galleries to accompany the displays. Look out for changing exhibitions and an exciting programme of events for all ages. **Open**: Tuesday–Saturday, 10am–5.30pm. Closed Sundays, Mondays & all public holidays. **Admission:** Free.

map 4 D6

BODIAM CASTLE

Bodiam, nr. Robertsbridge, E. Sussex, TN32 5UA
Tel: 01580 830436 Fax: 01580 830398

Built in 1385 against a French invasion that never came and as a comfortable dwelling for a rich nobleman, Bodiam Castle is one of the finest examples of medieval military architecture. The virtual completeness of its exterior makes it a popular filming location. Inside, although a ruin, floors have been replaced in some of the towers and visitors can climb the spiral staircase to enjoy superb views from the battlements. Audio-visual presentations of life in a castle and museum room. **Location:** OS Ref: TQ782 256. 3 m S of Hawkhurst, 2 m E of A21 Hurst Green. **Open:** 17 Feb–31 Oct daily 10am–6pm. Last entry 5pm or dusk, 3 Nov–mid Feb 2002 Sat & Sun 10am–4pm. **Admission:** Adult £3.70, Child £1.85, Family £9.25 & Group (min 15 people) £3.15. Car park £1.50.

map 5 G6

BENTLEY HOUSE & GARDENS

Halland, Nr. Lewes, East Sussex, BN8 5AF
Tel: 01825 840573 (East Sussex County Council) Fax: 01825 841322

Bentley House dates back to early 18th century times and was built on land granted to James Gage by the Archbishop of Canterbury, with the permission of Henry VIII. The family of Lord Gage was linked with Bentley from that time until 1904. The estate was purchased by Gerald Askew in 1937 and during the 1960s he and his wife, Mary, added two Palladian rooms to the original farmhouse. The architect was Raymond Erith, who had worked on 10 Downing Street. The drawing room contains mid 18th century Chinese wallpaper and gilt furniture. The Bird Room contains a collection of wildfowl paintings by Philip Rickman. The gardens at Bentley have been created as a series of 'rooms' divided by Yew hedges, specialising in many old-fashioned roses including the Bourbons, the Gallicas and the Damask. Nearby 6 stone sphinxes stand along a broad grass walk where daffodils bloom in spring. **Location:** 7 miles northeast of Lewes, signposted on A22, A26 & B2192. **Open:** 19 Mar–31 Oct, daily 10.30–4.30pm (last admissions). House opens 12noon daily 1 Apr–31 Oct. **Admission:** 2000 prices: Adult £4.80, Senior/Student £3.80, Child (4–15) £3, Family (2A+4C) £14.50, 10% discount for groups 11+. Special rates for disabled (wheelchairs available). Admission price allows entry to House, Gardens, Grounds, Wildfowl Reserve, Motor Museum, History of Bentley Exhibition, Woodland Walk, Children's Adventure Play Area. Picnic area, Gift shop complimented by resident crafts people, Education Centre. **Refreshments:** Licensed tearooms. **Conferences:** Civil wedding ceremonies. Ample free parking. Dogs allowed in this area only.
E-mail: barrysutherland@pavilion.co.uk **Internet:** www.bentley.org.uk

map 5 F6

ARUNDEL CASTLE

Arundel, West Sussex BN18 9AB.
Tel: 01903 883136 Fax: 01903 884581(Arundel Castle Trustees Ltd)

A Castle has overlooked the picturesque South Downs town of Arundel and River Arun for almost 1000 years. The Castle is set in spacious and beautiful landscaped grounds and features a fully restored Victorian kitchen garden. The original Castle suffered some destruction by Cromwell's troops during the Civil War. With restoration and later additions, the Arundel Castle of today is quite magnificent and houses a very fine collection of furniture dating from the 16th century, tapestries, clocks and paintings by Canaletto, Gainsborough, Van Dyck and many other masters. There is such a wealth of treasures to see – the Library with its spectacular carved and vaulted ceiling, the Bedrooms including the suite refurbished for Queen Victoria and Prince Albert with its sumptuous gilt state bed, the Dining Room, the Picture Gallery and much, much more. **Open:** From 1 April until the 31 October, 12–5pm, the last admission on any day is at 4pm. The Castle is closed on Good Friday and Saturdays. Delicious home-made lunches and afternoon teas are served daily in the restaurant. Pre-booked parties are welcome and menus are available on request. Gifts and mementoes, chosen especially by the Countess of Arundel, can be purchased in the shop which is open at the same time as the Castle. For further information please contact: The Comptroller, Arundel Castle, West Sussex BN18 9AB. Tel: 01903 883136/882173. Fax: 01903 884581.

map 4
E6

CHARLESTON

Firle, Nr Lewes, East Sussex

Tel: 01323 811265 (Visitor Information) Fax: 01323 811628

Charleston was the home of Vanessa Bell, the sister of Virginia Woolf, and Duncan Grant from 1916 until Grant's death in 1978. The house became a 'Bloomsbury' outpost, full of intellectuals, artists and writers; walls, furniture and ceramics were decorated by the artists with their own designs, strongly influenced by post impressionism and interior decoration styles in France and Italy. The walled garden displays a vivid collection of contrasting plants and flowers **Location:** Signposted off the A27, 6 miles E of Lewes, between the villages of Firle and Selmeston. **Open:** 1 Apr–31 Oct, Weds to Sun & Bank Holiday Mons 2–5pm. Jul & Aug Wed–Sat 11.30–5pm, Sun & Bank Holiday Mons 2–5pm. Guided tours Weds–Sats; unguided Suns & Bank Holiday Mons. Connoisseur Fridays; in-depth tour of the house including Vanessa Bell's studio and the kitchen, not July and Aug. **Admission:** House/Garden: Adult £5.50, Children £4, Connoisseur Fridays £6.50, Concessions £4 Wed & Thurs only. Organised groups should telephone 01323 811626 for rates and information. **Refreshments:** Tea and cakes available Wed to Sun. **Events/Exhibitions:** The Charleston Festival 24–28 May. Literature, art and theatre. The Charleston Gallery; explores Charleston's history and influence on contemporary art. The shop is Craft's Council selected; applied art and books. No disabled access beyond ground floor. Disabled toilet. No dogs. No film, video or photography in the house. **Internet:** www.charleston.org.uk

map 5
F6

COBBLERS GARDEN

Mount Pleasant, Crowborough, East Sussex TN6 2ND

Tel: 01892 655969 (Mr & Mrs Furniss)

This two-acre garden shows as an enlarged and more intricate cottage garden. It is in the shape of a large quadrant whose focal point is the 16th century house and 15th century barn. The fascinating pattern of the garden is formed by lawns, 16 mixed borders and roses, two beautifully planted natural pools, bound together by intriguing brick and stone paths. There is colour and interesting planking everywhere from May to September. This naturally formed and planted garden would, no doubt, be approved of by the father of modern English gardening, William Robinson, and his disciple, Gertrude Jekyll, whose book has a dust cover illustrating this garden. Elderly visitors will find eleven owner designed individual seats placed at strategic points.

map 5
F6

CHICHESTER DISTRICT MUSEUM

29 Little London, Chichester, West Sussex PO19 1PB

Tel: 01243 784683 Fax: 01243 776766

This is the idael place to explore the history of Chichester and District. Look out for displays on geology and pre-history including Boxgrove Man, Roman Chichester, Saxon and Medieval life. Find out about Chichester during the Civil War and changes which have taken place from the eighteenth century onwards. There are hands–on activities around the galleries to accompany the displays. Look out for changing exhibitions and an exciting programme of events for all ages. **Open**: Tuesday–Saturday, 10am–5.30pm. Closed Sundays, Mondays & all public holidays. **Admission:** Free.

map 4
D6

DENMANS GARDEN

Denmans Lane, Fontwell, Nr Arundel, West Sussex BN18 0SU

Tel: 01243 542808 Fax: 01243 544064 (Mr John Brookes)

Unique 20th century garden artistically planted with emphasis on colour, shape and texture. Individual plantings within the garden are allowed to self-seed and ramble, often in gravel. A remarkable and unique collection of plants - glass areas for tender species. **Location:** Between Arundel and Chichester, turn off A27 into Denmans Lane (W of Fontwell racecourse). **Station(s):** Barnham (2 miles). **Open:** Daily from 1 March–31 October including Bank Hols 9–5pm. Coaches by appointment. **Admission:** Adults £2.90, Children £1.60, Senior Citizens £2.60. Groups of 15 or more £2.40 (2000 prices). **Refreshments:** Restaurant open 11–5pm. Plant centre. No dogs.

map 4
E6

FISHBOURNE ROMAN PALACE

Salthill Road, Fishbourne, Chichester, Sussex PO19 3QR
Tel: 01243 785 859 Fax: 01243 539 266 (Sussex Past)

First occupied as a military base in AD43, Fishbourne's sumptuous palace was built around AD75. Remains include 20 spectacular mosaics and its story is told in the museum and by an audio-visual programme. The Roman garden has been replanted to its original plan and now features a Roman gardening museum. There is also an Education Centre and shop. **Station(s):** Fishbourne (5 mins walk). **Bus route:** 5 mins walk away. **Open:** 6Jan–4 Feb & 15–30 Dec: Sat & Sun 10–4pm. 5 Feb–14 Dec: daily 10–5pm (Mar–Jul & Sept–Oct) 10–6pm (Aug) 10–4pm (Feb, Nov–Dec). **Admission:** Adults £4.50, Children (5–15) £2.40. Students/OAP £3.90, Disabled £3.70, Family (2+2) £11.70. **Refreshments:** Cafeteria. Picnic area. Suitable for disabled. Parking and toilets. No dogs. **E-mail:** adminfish@sussexpast.co.uk **Internet:** www.sussexpast.co.uk

map 4 D6

FIRLE PLACE

Nr Lewes, East Sussex BN8 6LP
Tel: Enquiries 01273 858307, Information 01273 858335, Events 01273 858567   Fax: 01273 858188 (The Rt. Hon. Viscount Gage)

House: Firle Place is the home of the Gage family, and has been for over 500 years. Set at the foot of the Sussex Downs within its own parkland, this unique House, originally Tudor, was built of Caen stone, possibly from a monastery dissolved by Sir John Gage, friend of Henry Vlll. Remodelled in the 18th century, it is similar in appearance to that of a French Château. The House contains a magnificent collection of Old Master paintings, fine English and European furniture and an impressive collection of Sevres Porcelain collected mainly by the Third Earl Cowper from Panshanger House, Hertfordshire. **Events:** The Great Tudor Hall can, on occasion, be used for private dinners, with drinks on the Terrace or in the Billard Room. A private tour of the house can be arranged. The paddock area is an ideal site for a marquee. The park can be used for larger events using the house as a backdrop. **Restaurant:** Enjoy the licensed restaurant and tea terrace with views over the gardens for luncheon and cream teas. Tel: 01273 858307. **Location:** OS Ref: 473 071 4 miles South of Lewes on the A27 Brighton to Eastbourne Road. **Open:** 15 & 16 April, 6 & 7 May. Then 23 May–27 Sept: Wed, Thurs, Sun & Bank Holiday Mon 2–4.30pm. Guided tours. **Admission:** Adults £4.50, Conc £4, Children £2; Connoisseur's Day £5, on first Thursday of each month, June–Sept. **E-mail:** gage@firleplace.co.uk

map 5 F6

GOODWOOD HOUSE

Goodwood, Chichester, West Sussex PO18 0PX
Tel: 01243 755048 Fax: 01243 755005 (The Duke of Richmond)

Richly refurbished ancestral home of the Dukes of Richmond. Of note is the newly restored tapestry drawing room. The unparalleled collection includes commissioned works by Canaletto and Stubbs, French furniture, and the unique Sèvres Bird Service. **Location:** 3½ miles NE of Chichester. **Open:** Most Sundays and Mondays from 1Apr.–1Oct; Sun-Thur. from 5 Aug.-6 Sept. 1-5pm. **Some special closures: please check Recorded Information:** 01243 755040. Groups welcome on Open Days. All groups must book. Guided tours for groups on Mon mornings by arrangement and on Connoisseurs' Days. **Admission:** Adult £6.50, Child (12–18) £3. Groups (20–200) Connoisseurs £8.50, Economy £5.50. **Refreshments** and teas. Free coach/car park.

map 4 D6

GLYNDE PLACE

Glynde, Lewes, East Sussex BN8 6SX

Tel: 01273 858 224 Fax: 01273 858 224 (Viscount & Viscountess Hampden)

Set below the ancient hill fort of Mount Caburn, Glynde Place is a magnificent example of Elizabethan architecture and is the manor house of an estate which has been in the same family since the 12th century. Built in 1569 of Sussex flint and Caen stone round a courtyard, the house commands exceptionally fine views of the South Downs. Amongst the collections of 17th and 18th century portraits of the Trevor family, a collection of Italian old masters brought back by Thomas Brand on his Grand Tour and a room dedicated to Sir Henry Brand, Speaker of the House of Commons 1872–1884. The house is still the family home of the Brands and can be enjoyed as such. **Location:** In Glynde village, 4 miles SE of Lewes, on A27. **Station(s):** Within easy walking distance of Glynde station, with hourly services to Lewes, Brighton and Eastbourne. **Open:** Jun & Sept: Sun & Wed. July & Aug: Sun, Wed, Thurs & Bank Holiday. Guided tours for parties (25 or more) can be booked on a regular open day (£3 per person) or on a non-open day (£5 per person). Contact Lord Hampden on 01273 858 224. House open 2pm. Last admission 4.45pm. **Admission:** Adults £5, Children £2.50. Free parking. **Refreshments:** Sussex cream teas in Georgian Stable block. Parties to book in advance as above. Exhibition of watercolours and prints by local artists and shop. **Exhibitions:** 'Harbert Morley and the Great Rebellion 1638–1660', the story of the part played by the owner of Glynde Place during the Civil War. **Weddings:** Glynde Place can be hired for a civil wedding. **E-mail:** hampden@glyndeplace.co.uk

map 5 F6

GREAT DIXTER HOUSE AND GARDENS

Northiam, Nr Rye, East Sussex TN31 6PH.

Tel: 01797 252 878 Fax. 01797 252 879 (Mr Christopher Lloyd)

Great Dixter, birthplace and home of gardening writer Christopher Lloyd, was built c1450 and boasts one of the largest surviving timber–framed halls in the country. Lutyens was employed to restore both the house and gardens in 1910. The gardens are now the hallmark of Christopher Lloyd with an exciting combination of meadows, ponds, topiary and the famous Long Border and Exotic Garden. **Location:** Signposted off the A28 in Northiam. **Open:** 1 Apr–28 Oct; Tues–Sun 2–5.30pm (last admission 5pm); open Bank Hol Mon. **Admission:** House & Gardens: Adult £6, Child £1.50. Gardens only: Adult £4.50, Child £1. **Refreshments & facilities:** Pre–packed refreshments, free parking, plant nursery. All enquiries to Elaine Francis, Business Manager. **E-mail:** greatdixter@compuserve.com

map 5 G6

HAMMERWOOD PARK

Nr East Grinstead, RH19 3QE

Tel: 01342 850 594 Fax:01342 850 864

Benjamin Latrobe designed Hammerwood Park in 1792 as a grand hunting lodge with porticos dedicated to Apollo. Latrobe's porticos of the White House, Washington DC derive from his Hammerwood designs. The 18th century parkland incorporates subsequent gardens around the house. Visitors like Hammerwood because it is still a home where tours are given by a member of the family. **Open:** Wed, Sat & BH Mon afternoons, Easter Monday to end of Sept. The Guided Tour begins at 2.05pm and an excellent tea is available afterwards. **Admission:** Adults £5, Children £2. **E-mail:** latrobe@mistral.co.uk **Internet:** www.name.is/hammerwood

map 5 F5

HERSTMONCEUX CASTLE

Hailsham, East-Sussex

Tel: 01323 833816 Fax: 01323 834499

This breathtaking 15th Century Moated Castle is set in beautiful Parkland and superb Elizabethan Gardens. Ideal for pic-nics and woodland walks. Your experience begins with your first sight of the castle as it breaks into view. **Open:** 13 April-28 October; daily 10-6pm (last admission 5pm). Closes at 5pm from Oct. **Admission:** Gardens & Grounds: Adult £3.50, Child under 5 yrs. free, Cons £2.70. Castle tours: Adult £ 2.50, Child £1. (Group rates available-please call 01323 834457) **E-mail:** c_cullip@isc.queensu.ac.uk **Internet:** seetb.org.uk/herstmonceux

map 5 G6

HIGH BEECHES GARDENS
Handcross, West Sussex RH17 6HQ
Tel: 01444 400589 Fax: 01444 401543

Help us to preserve these twenty acres of enchanting landscaped woodland and water gardens, with Magnolias, Rhododendrons and Azaleas, in Spring. In Autumn, one of the most brilliant gardens for leaf colour. Gentians and Primulas are naturalised. Many rare plants. Tree trail. Four acres of natural wildflower meadows recommended by Christopher Lloyd. Location: 1 mile east of A23 at Handcross, on B2110.Open: Gardens only: 1–5pm, 17 Mar–30 June & 1 Sept–31 Oct. Daily except Weds; Sun to Tues in July & August. **Admission:** Adults £4. Accompanied children free.£3.50pp for groups of 30 or more. Refreshments: Hot and cold drinks, ice cream and biscuits in Gate Lodge. Sadly, gardens not suitable for wheelchairs. Please enquire for Event Days, plant sales and Group bookings. Regret no dogs. **E-mail:** office@highbeeches.com **Internet:** www.highbeeches.com

map 5 F6

LEWES CASTLE
Barbican House, 169 High Street, Lewes, Sussex, BN7 1YE
Tel: 01273 486 290 Fax: 01273 486 990 (Sussex Past)

Lewes' imposing Norman castle provides an invigorating climb rewarded by magnificent views. Adjacent Barbican House Museum follows the progress of Sussex people from their earliest beginnings. ' The Story of Lewes Town' is a superb scale model of Victorian Lewes and an audio-visual presentation. There is also an Education Centre and shop. **Station(s):** Lewes (7 mins walk). **Bus route:** Adjacent. Bus station 10 mins walk away. **Open:** Daily (except Christmas & Boxing Day and 8 Jan 2001), 10–5.30pm. (Sun & Bank Hols 11–5.30pm). **Admission:** Adult £4, Child (5–15) £2, OAP/Student £3.50, Family (2+2) £10.90, 1 Adult and 4 Children £8. Joint ticket with 'Anne of Cleves House' available: Adult £5.50, Child £2.70. No dogs. **E-mail:** castle@sussexpast.co.uk **Internet:** www.sussexpast.co.uk.

MERRIMENTS GARDENS
Hawkhurst Road, Hurst Green, East Sussex TN19 7RA
Tel: 01580 860666 Fax: 01580 860324 (Weeks Family with Mark Buchele)

"A unique experiment in colour composition." Set in 4 acres of gently sloping Wealden farmland, a naturalistic garden which never fails to delight. Deep curved borders richly planted and colour themed. An abundance of rare plants will startle the visitor with sheer originally. **Admission:** Adults £3.50; Children £2 **Open:** 2 April–end October. Daily 10–5pm. **E-mail:** info@merriments.co.uk **Internet:** www.merriments.co.uk

map 5 F6

LAMB HOUSE
3 Chapel Hill, Lewes
Tel: 01273 475657

The coromandel lacquer panels at Lamb House, Lewes, are an unusual surviving example of imported late 17th Century incised chinese lacquer-work that remain in their original position as decorative wall panelling. This is because the panels were hidden behind layers of local newspapers in 1796, and only discovered again 200 years later, in 1967. A recent grant from English Heritage has allowed them to be restored to their full glory. **Open:** Weekends only, by appointment.

map 4 D6

MARLIPINS MUSEUM
High Street, Shoreham-by-Sea, Sussex BN43 5DA
Tel: 01273 462994

Shoreham's local and especially its maritime history are explored at Marlipins, itself an important historic Norman building believed to have once been used as a Customs House. It has a beautiful chequer-work facade of Caen Stone and inside, much of the original timberwork of the building is open to view. The maritime gallery contains many superb nautical models and fine paintings, while the rest of the museum houses exhibits dating back to Man's earliest occupation of the area. The development of Shoreham's airport and life in the town during the war years feature prominently in the displays. **Open:** 1 May–30 Sept: Tues–Sat, 10.30–4.30pm. Sun 2.30–4.30pm. Please note that due to the construction of a new Millenium Gallery during 2001, opening times and dates may change. Please ring in advance to check. **Admission:** Adults £1.50, Children 75p, Senior Citizens/Students £1. **Internet:** www.sussexpast.co.uk

LEONARDSLEE GARDENS

Lower Beeding, Nr Horsham RH13 6PP
Tel: 01403 891212 Fax: 01403 891305 (Mr Robin Loder)

Leonardslee Gardens, created and maintained by the Loder family since 1889, are set in a peaceful 240-acre valley. There are delightful walks around seven beautiful lakes, which provide breath-taking views and reflections. Camellias, magnolias and the early rhododendrons provide colour in April, while in May - the best time to visit – it becomes a veritable paradise, with banks of sumptuous rhododendrons and azaleas overhanging the paths which are fringed with bluebells. Also in May, the Rock Garden becomes a Kaleidoscope of colour with Japanese evergreen azaleas and ancient dwarf conifers. During the summer months, the Superb flowering trees and interesting wild-flowers enhance the tranquillity of the valley and the mellow seasonal tints of autumn, complete the season. The fascinating Bonsai collection shows this oriental living art-form to perfection. Wildlife abounds! Many visitors are surprised to see the wallabies, which have been used as environmentally–friendly mowing machines for over 100 years! Axis Fallow and Sika Deer roam in the parks and wildfowl are seen on the lakes. The Loder family collection of Victorian Motor Cars (1895–1900) has some fine examples–all in running order–from the dawn of motoring! The new "Behind the Dolls House" exhibition shows a country estate of 100 years ago, all in miniature 1/12th scale. There is a licensed restaurant and a café for refreshments, as well as a gift shop and a wide selection of plants for sale. **Open:** Daily 1 Apr–31 Oct, 9.30–6pm. **Admission:** May (weekends & bank hols) £7, May (weekdays) £6 all other times £5. Children (age 5–15) £3
Internet: www.leonardslee.com

map 4
E6

PASHLEY MANOR GARDENS

Pashley Manor, Ticehurst, Nr Wadhurst, E. Sussex TN5 7HE
Tel: 01580 200888 Fax: 01580 200102 (Mr and Mrs J. Sellick)

The Gardens offer a sumptuous blend of romantic landscaping imaginative plantings and fine old trees, fountains, springs and large ponds. This is a quintessentially English Garden of a very individual character with exceptional views to the surrounding valleyed fields. Many eras of English history are reflected here, typifying the tradition of the English Country House and its garden. Mr and Mrs James Sellick, who opened the gardens to the public in 1992, have brought them two there present splendour, with the assistance of the eminent landscape architect, Anthony du Gard Pasley. An exciting programme of events has been devised for the discerning garden-lover; the Tulip Festival in May (a unique fixture in the garden calendar); and an Exhibition of Sculptures lasting throughout the season. Pashley prides itself on itself on its delicious food. Home-made soups, ploughman's lunches with pickle and patés, fresh salads from the garden (whenever possible), home-made scones and delicious cakes, filter coffee, specialist teas, soft drinks, fine wines, beers and ciders - served at the Terrace Restaurant or in the Old Stables Tearoom. The gift shop caters for every taste... from postcards and local honey to traditional hand-painted ceramics and tapestry cushions. A wide selection of plants and shrubs, many of which grow at Pashley, are available for purchase. **Admission:** £5, Concessions/Groups £4.50. **Open:** Tues, Wed, Thurs, Sat & Bank Hol Mons. 7 Apr–29 Sept 2001. **Location:** On B2099 between A21 and Ticehurst village. **Events:** Tulip Festival: 3rd-7th May. Spring Plant Fair: 20th May. Summer Flower Festival: 14–17 June. Summer Plant Fair: 19 Aug. St. Michael's Hospice: 28th July.

map 5
G6

MICHELHAM PRIORY

Upper Dicker, Hailsham, Sussex, BN27 3QS
Tel: 01323 844 224 Fax: 01323 844 030 (Sussex Past)

Enclosed by a medieval moat, the remains of this beautiful Augustinian Priory are incorporated into a splendid Tudor mansion featuring a fascinating array of exhibits. Superb gardens are enhanced by a 14th century gatehouse, watermill, physic herb and cloister gardens, smithy, rope museum and dramatic Elizabethan Great Barn. **Location:** O.S. map ref: OS 198 TQ 558093. **Station(s):** Polegate (3 miles). Berwick (2 miles). **Buses:** Bus route (1.5 miles). **Open:** Wed–Sun. 14 Mar–28 Oct. Mar & Oct, 10.30–4pm. Apr–July & Sept, 10.30–5pm. Daily in Aug, 10.30–5.30pm. Open all B. H. Mondays. **Admission:** Adult £4.70, Child £2.30, OAP/Students £4, Family (2+2 or 1+4)£11.50. Disabled/Carer £2.35. **Refreshments:** Tearoom/restaurant. Picnic area. Museum, education centre and shop. Dogs are admitted in car park only. **E-mail:** adminmich@sussexpast.co.uk **Internet:** www.sussexpast.co.uk

map 5 F6

PALLANT HOUSE GALLERY

9, North Pallant, Chichester, West Sussex, PO19 1TJ
Tel: 01243 774557 Fax: 01243 536038

Meticulously restored Queen Anne town house with eight rooms decorated and furnished in styles from early Georgian to late Victorian. Also Georgian style gardens and important displays of Bow Porcelain (1747–1775) and Modern British Art (1920–1980). **Location:** Chichester City centre. **Open:** All year Tues–Sat 10–5pm, also open Sun & Bank Hols: 12.30–5pm. **Admission:** Adults £4, over 60s £3, Students/UB40 £2.50. **Refreshments:** Victorian Kitchen Café. **Events/Exhibitions:** Major exhibitions held throughout the year, please call for details. **E-mail:** pallant@pallant.co.uk

Internet: www.pallanthousegallery.com

map 4 D6

THE PRIEST HOUSE

North Lane, West Hoathly, Sussex RH19 4PP
Tel: 01342 810479

The Priest House nestles in the picturesque village of West Hoathly, on the edge of Ashdown Forest. Originally a 15th century timber-framed farmhouse with central open hall, it was modernised in Elizabethan times with stone chimneys and a ceiling in the hall. Later additions created a substantial yeoman's dwelling. Standing in the beautiful surroundings of a traditional cottage garden, the house has a dramatic roof of Horsham stone. Its furnished rooms, including a kitchen, contain a fascinating array of 17th and 18th century domestic furniture, needlework and household items. In the formal herb garden, there are over 150 herbs used in medicine and folklore. **Open:** 1 March–31 Oct, Mon–Sat, 11–5.30pm, Sun 2–5.30pm. **Admission:** Adults £2.50, Children £1.20, OAP/Student £2.30. **Internet:** www.sussexpast.co.uk

map 5 F5

PARHAM HOUSE & GARDENS

Parham Park, near Pulborough, West Sussex.
Tel: 01903 742021 Fax: 01903 746557 (Parham Park Ltd)

A much-loved family home open from April–October on Wednesdays, Thursdays, Sundays and Bank Holiday Mondays (with private guided visits on Tuesday or Friday afternoons, and Wednesday or Thursday mornings.) Our Big Kitchen opens from 12 noon for light lunches and delicious cream teas. Complementing the panelled rooms containing beautiful furniture, paintings and needlework are fresh flower arrangements. Spend a peaceful afternoon strolling through our award-winning gardens, with walled garden containing greenhouse, orchard, potager and herbiary, try your hand at the brick and turf maze! **Open:** Gardens from 12pm, House from 2pm, Last entry 5pm. **Events:** Annual Garden Weekend: 14/15 July; Needlework Exhibition 19/20 May; Autumn Flowers at Parham House 1/2 Sept. **Info Line:** 01903 744888. **E-mail:** parham@dial.pipex.com. **Internet:** www.parhaminsussex.co.uk

map 4 E6

THE ROYAL PAVILION

Brighton, East Sussex, BN1 1EE
Tel: 01273 290900 Fax: 01273 292871

A distinctive Indian-style exterior makes this one of the most exotically beautiful buildings in the country. FOR FULL DETAILS, OPENING TIMES AND COLOUR PHOTOGRAPHS, PLEASE SEE PAGE 193.

SAINT HILL MANOR

Saint Hill Road, East Grinstead, West Sussex RH19 4JY

A handsome sandstone manor house, beautifully restored throughout, where visitors can admire a 100ft mural by John Spencer Churchill. FOR FULL DETAILS, OPENING TIMES, AND COLOUR PHOTOGRAPHS, PLEASE SEE PAGES 194 & 195.

SHEFFIELD PARK GARDEN
Sheffield Park, East Sussex TN22 3QX
Tel: 01825 790231 Fax: 01825 791264

A magnificent 120 acre landscaped garden, laid out in the 18th century and extended with the advice of the famous landscape designers 'Capability' Brown and Humphrey Repton. There are four lakes and the garden is renowned for stunning displays of daffodils, bluebells, rhododendrons and azaleas in Spring, and in Autumn the garden is transformed by a blaze of colour. The North American trees and shrubs produce a display of gold, orange and crimson reflected in the lakes. The garden was further developed early this century by its owner, Arthur G. Soames, who planted on an ambitious scale much of what the visitor sees today including rare and exotic trees and shrubs. **Open:** Jan–Feb: Sat & Sun 10.30–4pm. March–end of Oct: Daily 10.30–6pm (except Mons, but open BH Mons). Nov–Dec: Daily 10.30–4pm (except Mon).

map 5 F6

THE WEALD & DOWNLAND OPEN AIR MUSEUM
Singleton, Nr Chichester, West Sussex
Tel: 01243 811348

Over 40 historic buildings in one beautiful Downland park vividly demonstrate the homes and workplaces of the past. Buildings, furnished interiors and complete work environments bring the past to life. Bayleaf medieval farmstead is complete with furnishings, animals, fields and gardens, the Victorian school is intact and the working 17th century watermill produces flour daily. Constantly evolving this museum is the only one to be Designated as outstanding in West Sussex. Summer open-air theatre programme. **Location:** 6 miles N of Chichester on A286 just S of Singleton. **Open:** 1 Mar–31 Oct daily 10.30am–6pm, 1 Nov–28 Feb, Wed, Sat and Sun only 10.30am–4pm, 26 Dec–1 Jan daily 10.30am–4pm. **Admission:** Adult £7.00, OAP £6.50, Child £4.00, Family £17.00. Parties by arrangement (group rates available). **Refreshments:** Light refreshments. **Internet:** www.wealddown.co.uk

map 4 D6

WEST DEAN GARDENS
The Edward James Foundation, Estate Office,
West Dean, Chichester, West Sussex PO18 0QZ
Tel: 01243 818210 Fax: 01243 811342

Extensive downland garden with 300ft pergola, herbaceous borders and bedding displays. Victorian Walled Kitchen Garden with unusual vegetables, herbs, cut flowers, fruit collection and 16 original glasshouses and frames. Included are vineries, fig and peach houses and an outstanding collection of chilli peppers together with extensive floral display houses. Park Walk (2.4 miles) through landscaped parkland and the 45-acre St Roche's Arboretum. Visitor Centre (free entry). Call for group bookings/guided tours. **Location:** 6 m N of Chichester on A286. **Open:** Daily, Mar–Oct. Mar, Apr & Oct 11–5pm; May–Sept 10.30–5pm. Last admission 4.30pm. **Admission:** Adult £4.50, over 60s £4, Child £2. Group rates: same. **Events:** Garden Event: 23–24 June; Chilli Fiesta: 11–12 Aug; Totally Tomato Show: 8 & 9 Sept; Apple Day: 21 Oct. Coach/car parking. No dogs. **E-mail:** gardens@westdean.org.uk **Internet:** http//www.westdean.org.uk

map 4 D6

WILMINGTON PRIORY
Wilmington, Nr Eastbourne, East Sussex BN26 5SW
Tel: The Landmark Trust: 01628 825920
(Leased to the Landmark Trust by Sussex Archaelogical Society)

Founded by the Benedictines in the 11th century, the surviving, much altered buildings date largely from the 14th century. Managed and maintained by the Landmark Trust, which lets buildings for self-catering holidays. **Open:** The grounds, ruins, porch and crypt on 30 days between April and October. The whole property including interiors on 8 of these days: 22–25 May and 7–10 Sept 2001. Telephone: 01628 825920 for details. **Accommodation:** Available for up to six people for self-catering holidays. Tel: 01628 825925 for Bookings. Full details of Wilmington Priory and 170 other historic buildings are featured in The Landmark Handbook (price £9.50 refundable against a booking) from The Landmark Trust, Shottesbrooke, Maidenhead, Berkshire, SL6 3SW. **Internet:** www.landmarktrust.co.uk

map 4 E5

WORTHING MUSEUM & ART GALLERY
Chapel Road, Worthing, West Sussex BN11 1HP
Tel: 01903 239999 ext 2528 (01903 204229 Sats)

Full of hidden treats, Worthing Museum delights and entertains visitors of all ages. More than simply a good local museum, it has some of the best toys, dolls and costume displays in the country and an award-winning archaeology gallery. **Exhibitions:** A varied programme of temporary exhibitions draws visitors back time and time again. **Open:** Monday–Saturday 10–5pm. All year. **Admission:** Free.

map 8 D3

BRIGHTON MUSEUM & ART GALLERY
Church Street, Brighton BN1 1EE

Closed Until Autumn 2001 due to major redevelopment work. The exhibition galleries will temporarily re-open in May for the Brighton Festival. The museum is famous for its collection of 20th Century furniture, glass, textiles and jewellery, including examples by this century's leading designers. The extensive ceramics collection includes the famous Willett Gallery, exploring 18th & 19th Century British social history through earthenware. The museum's spectacular collection of non-western art is of national importance and it also boasts a treasury of archaeological exhibits, a stunning fashion gallery and a fascinating local history collection. The museum has an extensive collection of fine art, ranging from the 15th to the 20th Century. **Telephone:** (01273) 290 900 for details of specific opening times, admission fees, exhibitions, events and guided tours.

map 5 F6

HOVE MUSEUM & ART GALLERY
19 New Church Road, Hove BN3 4AB

Hove museum's highlights include the South East Arts and Crafts Collection, a celebration of Hove's history as the home of early filmmakers, and the magical toy-filled childhood room. The museum houses fascinating local history archives and an impressive collection of 20th Century paintings, and it organises an exciting programme of contemporary exhibitions and events for adults, children and schools. **Admission:** Free. **Telephone:** (01273) 290 900 for details of specific opening times, exhibitions, events and guided tours.

map 5 F6

BOOTH MUSEUM
194 Dyke Road, Brighton BN1 5AA

Over half a million specimens, natural history literature and data extending back over three centuries are housed in this fascinating museum, including hundreds of British birds displayed in recreated natural settings. Plus butterflies, skeletons, a whale and dinosaur bones. Children and families can explore the museum's collections through a variety of interactive displays in the 'hands on' Discovery Lab. The museum also organises an exciting programme of temporary exhibitions and events for adults, children and schools. **Admission:** Free. **Telephone:** (01273) 290 900 for details of specific opening times, exhibitions, events and guided tours.

map 5 F6

PRESTON MANOR
Preston Drove, Brighton BN1 6SD
Tel: 01273 292770 Fax: 01273 292771 (Brighton & Hove Council)

Experience the charms of this delightful Manor House which powerfully evokes the atmosphere of an Edwardian gentry home both 'Upstairs' and 'Downstairs'. There are more than twenty rooms to explore over four floors, from the superbly renovated servants' quarters and butler's pantry in the basement to the day nursery and attic bedrooms on the top floor. Situated adjacent to Preston Park, the Manor also comprises picturesque walled gardens and a pets' cemetery. Guided tours can be pre-booked for groups. Manor is avail. for corp. & priv. hire. **Location:** 2 miles north of Brighton on the A23 London Road. **Open:** Daily Tues–Sat 10–5pm, Sun 2–5pm, Mon 1–5pm (Bank Holidays 10–5pm). Closed 25 & 26 Dec and Good Friday. **Admission:** Adults £3.20, Children £2, Conc £2.70. Please call for details of family & group tickets, . (Prices valid until 31.3.2001) **Internet:** www.museums.brighton-hove.gov.uk

map 5 F6

FOREDOWN TOWER
Portslade BN41 2EW

Appealing to everyone with an interest in science, nature and the environment, Foredown Tower offers breathtaking views across the beautiful Sussex Downs, as well as interactive displays and exhibitions, countryside research and scientific data. It is the home of the only operational camera obscura in the South East, an unusual optical device that is used to observe the landscape, sun and sky (weather permitting). The building, an Edwardian water tower built in 1909, is of architectural interest and has been converted with considerable care to preserve many original features. Foredown Tower organises a regular programme of activities for children and families, from pond dipping to nature events, plus astronomy talks and lectures. The Tower is also a popular starting point for walks on the South Downs. **Telephone:** (01273) 290 900 for details of specific opening times, admission fees, exhibitions, events and guided tours.

map 5 F6

WEST BLATCHINGTON WINDMILL
Hove BN3 7LE

This regency 'Smock' Mill is a grade II listed building, retaining the original mill workings over five floors. Climb the five flights of steps and follow the course of the grain as it descends into the grindstones and subsequently to the ground floor as flour. Discover how a traditional Windmill operates and explore a fascinating display of historical milling and agricultural exhibits. **Telephone:** (01273) 290 900 for details of specific opening times, admission fees, exhibitions, events and guided tours.

map 5 F6

THE ROYAL PAVILION

Brighton, East Sussex BN1 1EE
01273 290900, Fax: 01273 292871 (Brighton & Hove Council)

The Royal Pavilion, the famous seaside palace of King George IV, is one of the most exotically beautiful buildings in the British Isles. Originally a simple farmhouse, in 1787 architect Henry Holland created a neoclassical villa on the site. From 1815–1822, the Pavilion was transformed by John Nash into its current distinctive Indian style complete with Chinese-inspired interiors. Magnificent decorations and fantastic furnishings have been re-created in an extensive restoration programme. From the opulence of the main State Rooms to the charm of the first floor bedroom suites, the Royal Pavilion is filled with astonishing colours and superb craftsmanship. Witness the magnificence of the Music Room with its domed ceiling of gilded shell shapes, and the dramatic Banqueting Room lit by a huge crystal chandelier held by a silvered dragon. Visitors can discover more about life behind the scenes at the Palace during the last 200 years with a new interactive multimedia visitor interpretation programme and join public guided tours daily at 11:30am and 2:30pm (for a small extra charge). The Royal Pavilion is an ideal location for filming and photography, from fashion shoots to corporate videos. Rooms are also available for hire for corporate and private functions and civil wedding ceremonies. **Location:** In centre of Brighton (Old Steine). **Station(s):** Brighton (^{1}/2 mile). **Open:** Daily (except 25 & 26 Dec) June–Sept 10–6pm, Oct–May 10–5pm. **Admission:** Adults £4.90, Children £3, Conc £3.55. Please call for details of family and group tickets. (Prices valid until 31.3.2000). **Refreshments:** Regency teas and light lunches in Queen Adelaide tearooms with balcony providing sweeping views over the Regency gardens.. **Events/Exhibitions:** A popular winter programme of events.

Internet: www.royalpavilion.brighton.co.uk

map 5
F6

SAINT HILL MANOR

Saint Hill Road, East Grinstead, West Sussex RH19 4JY
Tel: 01342 326711 (contact Liz Nyegaard)

Fine Sussex sandstone house built in 1792 and situated near the breathtaking Ashdown Forest. Previous owners of Saint Hill include Gibbs Crawfurd of Scottish origin, archaeologist Edgar March Crookshank, Mrs Drexel Biddle, the wife of the American Ambassador, and the Maharajah of Jaipur. Saint Hill Manor's final owner, acclaimed author and humanitarian, L. Ron Hubbard, lived here for many years with his family. Under his direction extensive renovations were carried out uncovering exquisite period features hidden for over a century. Fine wood panelling, marble fireplaces, Georgian windows and plasterwork ceilings have been expertly restored to their original beauty. Outstanding features of this lovely house include a complete library of Mr. Hubbard's work, the elegant Winter Garden and the delightful Monkey Room, housing John Spencer Churchill's 100ft mural depicting many famous characters as monkeys, including his uncle Sir Winston Churchill. 59 acres of landscaped gardens, lake and woodlands are open before and during house tour times. **Location:** Just off A22. At Felbridge, turn down Imberhorne Lane. Straight over crossroads into Saint Hill Road, 300 yds on right. Stations: East Grinstead. Owner: Church of Scientology. **Open:** All year, daily. Tours on the hour: 2, 3, 4 and 5pm. Tours outside these hours can be booked by appointment. Group parties welcome. Parking for coaches and cars. **Admission:** Free. **Events/Exhibitions:** Outdoor production of Sheridan's "The School for Scandal", Sunday afternoon, 24th June. Telephone for details. Summer concerts on the terrace, musical evenings throughout the year. Business conference and wedding reception facilities available in Saint Hill Castle in the Great Hall, which seats up to 600 theatre style and 300 for dinner. Also available as a film location.

map 5
F5

Warwickshire

Kenilworth Castle

This most charming of English counties has managed to retain its air of genteel tranquillity in spite of the neighbouring industrial powerhouses that are Birmingham and Coventry. Warwick, the county town, was partly destroyed by fire in the late seventeenth century, but can still boast some fine mediaeval buildings. Royal Leamington Spa is a beautifully preserved town of wide avenues and quiet parks, whose springs were visited by Queen Victoria in 1838. Nearby Kenilworth Castle once hosted huge tournaments on the flooded plain that surrounded it in the Middle Ages. However, the county is perhaps best known for its association with William Shakespeare, whose birthplace can be visited at Stratford-upon-Avon.

BADDESLEY CLINTON HALL

Rising Lane, Baddesley Clinton Village, Knowle, Solihull, West Midlands
Tel: 01564 783294 Fax: 01564 782706 (The National Trust)

A romantic and atmospheric moated manor house dating from the 15th century and little changed since 1634. The interiors reflect the house's heyday in the Elizabethan era, when it was a haven for persecuted Catholics – there are no fewer than 3 priest-holes. There is a delightful garden, ponds, lake walk and nature trail. **Open: House:** 28 Feb–28 Oct, open Wed-Sun & BH. Mons (Closed good Fri.); Feb, Mar, Apr & Oct 1.30-5pm; May-end Sept. 1.30–5.30pm. **Grounds:** 28 Feb–16 Dec, open Wed-Sun, Good Fri & B.H.Mons. Times: Feb, Mar, Apr & Oct 12-5pm; May-end Sept 12-5.30pm; Nov-16 Dec 12-4.30pm. **Events**: Tel. or send s.a.e. for details. **Admission:** House & Grounds: Adult £5.60, Child £2.80, Family £14, Party rate £4.50, Guided tour (outside hours)£9; Garden only: Adult £2.80, Child £1.40. **Internet:** www.ntrustsevern.org.uk

map 4
B1

BOSWORTH BATTLEFIELD VISITOR CENTRE & COUNTRY PARK

Sutton Cheney, Nr Nuneaton, Warwickshire CV13 0AD
Tel: 01455 290429

Historic site of the Battle of Bosworth Field 1485, where King Richard III lost his crown and his life to the future Henry VII. •Battle Trail (open all year) •Visitor Centre •Film Theatre •Book and gift shop •Picnic areas •Summer events. Medieval Spectacular 18-19 Aug 2001 (incl. battle re-enactment) •Parking: cars £1, coaches £7 •Disabled Visitors: visitor centre and battle trail accessible. Wheelchair available on request •Catering: Battlefield Buttery. **Open:** Visitor Centre 1 Apr-31 Oct: Mon-Sat 1-5pm. Sun and BHols 11-6pm. **Admission:** Visitor Centre: Adults £3, Children (under 16) and Senior Citizens £1.90. Family Ticket £7.95.

map 8
C7

CHARLECOTE PARK

Warwick CV35 9ER
Tel: 01789 470 277, Fax: 01789 470 544

Home of the Lucy family since 1247. Present house built in 1550's. Queen Elizabeth I visited. Victorian interiors; objects from Fonthill Abbey. Park landscaped by Capability Brown. Jacob sheep. Red and fallow deer, reputedly poached by Shakespeare. **Open:** 24 Mar–4 Nov, Fri–Tues, grounds 11–6pm, house 12–5pm. Park, garden, restaurant & shop: 3 Feb–18th Mar Sat/Sun 11am–4pm. **Admission:** Adult £5.60, Child £2.80. Family £14. Parties £4.60 by arrangement. Park & garden: Adult £3, Child £1.50. Evening guided tours for booked parties: May–Sept (Tues 7.30–9.30) £6.50 (incl NT members; min. charge £150). Wheelchair facilities: All ground floor rooms accessible including Orangery and shop. Parking. Lavatories. **Refreshments:** Morning coffee, lunch, afternoon tea in restaurant (licensed). Picnic in deer park only. Changing and feeding room. No dogs allowed. **E-mail:** charlecote@smtp.ntrust.org.uk.

map 4
B2

ARBURY HALL
Nuneaton, Warwickshire CV10 7PT
Tel: 02476 382804, Fax: 02476 641147 (The Rt. Hon. The Viscount Daventry)

Arbury Hall has been the seat of the Newdegate family for over 400 years and is the ancestral home of Viscount and Viscountess Daventry. This Tudor/Elizabethan House was Gothicised by Sir Roger Newdigate in the 18th century and is regarded as the 'Gothic Gem' of the Midlands. The Hall contains a fine collection of both Oriental and Chelsea porcelain, portraits by Lely, Reynolds, Devis and Romney and furniture by Chippendale and Hepplewhite. The principal rooms, with their soaring fan vaulted ceilings and plunging pendants and filigree tracery, stand as a most breathtaking and complete example of early Gothic Revival architecture and provide a most unique and fascinating venue for Corporate entertaining, Product Launches, Receptions, Fashion Shoots and Activity days. Exclusive use of this historic Hall, it's Gardens and Parkland is offered to clients. The Hall stands in the middle of beautiful Parkland with landscaped gardens of rolling lawns, lakes and winding wooded walks. **Location:** 2 miles SW of Nuneaton off B4102. **Station(s):** Nuneaton. **Open:** All the year round on Tuesdays, Wednesdays and Thursdays only for Corporate Functions and Events. Pre–booked parties for 25 and over on Tuesdays, Wednesdays and Thursdays (until 4pm) only, from Easter–end Sept. Hall and Gardens open on Bank Holiday Weekends only (Sun & Mon) from Easter–Sept. Hall: 2–5pm. Bank Holiday Sun & Mon., Easter-Sept. **Admission:** Hall & Garden: Adult £5, Child £3; Gardens only: Adult £4, Child £3, Family ticket £12; Groups/Parties (25+adults) £4.50pp. **Events:** Special Party Rates and Corporate Events by arrangement with the Administrator; Tel: 02476 382804 Fax: 02476 641147. Wheelchair access ground floor only. Gravel paths. Free car park.

map 8 C7

THE HILLER GARDEN

Dunnington Heath Farm, Nr. Alcester, Warwickshire B49 5PD
Tel: 01789 490991 Fax: 01789 490439 (A. H. Hiller & Son Ltd)

Among gravelled walks, large beds display an extensive range of unusual herbaceous perennials providing colour and interest throughout the year in this two acre garden near Ragley Hall. The Rose Gardens, at the peak of their beauty from the end of June, hold a collection of some 200 old-fashioned, species, modern shrub, rugosa and English roses in settings appropriate to their characters. There is a well-stocked plant sales area, a garden gift shop, farm shop and licensed tearooms. **Location:** 2 miles south of Ragley Hall on B4088 (formerly A435/A441 junction). **Open:** Daily (except Christmas and New Year), 10–5pm. **Admission:** Free.

map 4 B2

HONINGTON HALL

Shipston-on-Stour, Warwickshire CV36 5AA
Tel: 01608 661434, Fax: 01608 663717 (Benjamin Wiggin Esq)

This fine Caroline manor house was built in the early 1680s for the Parker family. It was modified in the mid 18th century with the introduction within of exceptional and lavish plasterwork and the insertion of an octagonal saloon. It is set in 15 acres of grounds. **Location:** 10 miles S of Stratford-on-Avon; ½ mile E of A3400. **Open:** June, July, Aug, Weds & Bank Hol Mons 2.30–5pm. Parties at other times by appointment. **Admission:** Adults £3.50, Children £1.75.

map 4 B2

KENILWORTH CASTLE

Kenilworth, Warks CV8 1NE
Tel 01926 852078 (English Heritage)

Explore England's finest and most extensive castle ruins. Wander through rooms used to lavishly entertain Queen Elizabeth I. Learn of the building's links with Henry V, who retired here return from his victorious expedition to Agincourt. Today you can view the marvellous Norman keep and John of Gaunt's Great Hall, once rivalling London's Westminster Hall in palatial grandeur. An audio tour, and interactive model of the Castle, provide a fascinating insight into the development of the Castle through the centuries. **Location:** Off A46. Follow A452 to Kenilworth town centre. **Open:** 1 Apr–31 Oct: daily, 10am–6pm (5pm in October). 1 Nov–28 Mar: daily, 10am–4pm. Closed 24–26 Dec & 1 Jan. **Admission:** Adult £4, Conc £3, Child £2, Family ticket £10. 15% discount for groups of 11 or more. **Refreshments:** Tea room: open Apr–Oct daily.

map 4 B1

LORD LEYCESTER HOSPITAL

High Street, Warwick, Warwickshire
Tel/Fax: 01926 491422 (The Governors of Lord Leycester Hospital)

In 1571, Robert Dudley, Earl of Leycester, founded his hospital for 12 old soldiers in the buildings of the Guilds, which had been dispersed in 1546. The buildings have been restored to their original condition: the Great Hall of King James, the Guildhall, the Chaplain's Hall (Queen's Own Hussars Regimental Museum), the Brethren's Kitchen and the Chapel. A new Knot Garden has been created to celebrate the Millennium. The recently restored historic Master's Garden is now open to the public (Apr–30 Sept £1 donation please). The Hospital, with its medieval galleried courtyard, featured in the TV series 'Pride and Prejudice', 'Tom Jones', 'Moll Flanders' and 'Dangerfield'. **Location:** West Gate of Warwick (A429). Station(s): Warwick (¾m). **Open:** All year, Tues–Sun, 10–5pm (summer) and 10–4pm (winter). Open BH Mons, closed Good Fri & Christmas Day. **Admission:** Adult £3, Child (under 14) £2, OAP/Student £2.50. Free car park.

map 4 B1

PACKWOOD HOUSE

Lapworth, Solihull, B94 6AT
Tel: 01564 783294 Fax: 01564 782706 (The National Trust)

The house, originally 16th-century, is a fascinating 20th-century evocation of domestic Tudor architecture. Created by Graham Baron Ash, its interiors reflect the period between the world wars and contain a fine collection of 16th-century textiles and furniture. The gardens have renowned herbaceous borders and a famous collection of yews. **Open:** House: 28 Mar–28 Oct: Wed–Sun, Good Fri and BH Mons, 12–4.30pm. Note: on busy days entry may be by timed ticket. Garden: 3 Mar–25 Mar: Sat & Sun. 28 Mar–28 Oct: Wed–Sun, Good Fri and BH Mons. Times: March, April & Oct 11am–4.30pm; May–end Sept 11am–5.30pm. Park and woodland walks: all year, daily. **Admission:** Whole property: Adult £5, Child £2.50, Family £12.50. Garden: Adult £2.50, Child £1.25, Party £4. Guided Tours (out of hours) £8. **E-mail:** baddesley@smtp.ntrust.org.uk **Internet:** www.ntrustsevern.org.uk

map 4 B1

RAGLEY HALL

Alcester, Warwickshire B49 5NJ
Tel: 01789 762090 Fax: 01789 764791 (Marquess of Hertford)

Ragley Hall, a byword for splendour and elegance and the Warwickshire home of The Marquess and Marchioness of Hertford and their family is one of the great English houses displaying unmissable beauty at every turn. The grandeur of its facades are only surpassed by the breathtaking beauty of its Great Hall and rooms. The Hall was designed by Robert Hooke in 1680 and is one of the earliest and loveliest of England's great Palladian Houses. It contains some of the finest Baroque plasterwork by James Gibb, and Graham Rust's stunning mural 'The Temptation'. On show are some of the finest antique porcelain and furniture. Ragley is a working estate with more than 6000 acres of land. The House is situated in 27 acres of gardens which were designed by Capability Brown and include the beautiful Rose Garden. Near to the Hall are working stables housing a carriage collection dating back to 1760 and a display of harnesses and assorted historical equestrian equipment. There is a lake and picnic area, and for the children an Adventure Wood, Woodland Walk, 3D Maze and for the younger children an additional playground. **Location:** 8 miles South of Stratford-upon-Avon. **Open:** 9 Apr–30 Sept. House: Thurs, Fri, Sun 12.30–5pm (last entry 4.30pm). Sat 11am–3.30pm (last entry 3pm). Bank Holiday Mons 11am–5pm (last entry 4.30pm). The Park, Gardens and Adventure Wood open Thurs–Sun 10am–6pm (last entry 4.45pm) and every day between 9 Apr.-22 Apr, 24 May-3 Jun. and 19 Jul-2 Sept. **Admission:** House, Park, Gardens and Adventure Wood: Adults £5.50, Senior Citizens and Disabled Badge Holders £5.00, Children £4, Family Ticket £20. Season Tickets for the Park, Gardens, and Adventure Wood also available. **E-mail:** ragley.hall@virginnet.co.uk

map 4 B2

Anne Hathaway's Cottage

THE SHAKESPEARE HOUSES IN AND AROUND STRATFORD-UPON-AVON

The Shakespeare Centre, Henley Street, Stratford-upon-Avon, Warks CV37 6QW.
Tel: 01789 204016 Fax: 01789 296083 E-mail: _info@shakespeare.org.uk

Five beautifully preserved Tudor houses, all associated with William Shakespeare and his family. In Town: **Shakespeare's Birthplace**, Henley Street. Half-timbered house where William Shakespeare was born in 1564. Visitor's centre showing highly acclaimed exhibition **William Shakespeare, His Life and Background**. **Nash's House and New Place**, Chapel Street. Nash's House was the home of Shakespeare's grand-daughter, Elizabeth Hall and contains exceptional furnishings. Upstairs there are displays about the history of Stratford. Also site and gardens of **New Place** (including Elizabethan style Knott Garden and Shakespeare's Great Garden), where Shakespeare lived in retirement. Discover why the house was demolished and see the foundations and grounds of his final Stratford home. **Hall's Croft**, Old Town. Impressive 16th century house and garden, with Jacobean additions. Owned by Dr John Hall who married Shakespeare's eldest daughter, Susanna. Includes exhibitions about medicine in Shakespeare's time and beautiful walled garden with mulberry tree and herb garden. Out of Town: **Anne Hathaway's Cottage**, Shottery. Picturesque thatched farmhouse cottage which belonged to the family of Shakespeare's wife. Contains the famous Hathaway bed and the other original furniture. Outside lies a beautiful English cottage garden, orchard and the Shakespeare Tree Garden. **Mary Arden's House** and the **Shakespeare Countryside Museum**, Wilmcote. The site of Shakespeare's mother's family home offers a fascinating insight into rural farm life in the Tudor period. See also falconry display, working blacksmith and prize-winning livestock. <u>Open:</u> Daily all year round except 23–26 Dec. Inclusive tickets available to three in-town, or all five houses. The Shakespeare Birthplace Trust is a Registered Charity, No. 209302.

map 4
B2

Shakespeare's Birthplace

Mary Arden's House

Nash's House and New Place

Hall Croft

RYTON ORGANIC GARDENS

Ryton-on-Dunsmore, Coventry, Warwickshire CV8 3LG
Tel: 024 7630 3517 Fax: 024 7663 9229 (HDRA - the organic organisation)

Home of HDRA - the organic organisation and set in Warwickshire countryside. Ten acres of beautifully landscaped grounds highlight the benefits and delights of organic gardening. 35 individually themed gardens for visitors to enjoy. These include stunning herbaceous borders, herbs, roses, wildlife areas, unusual fruit and vegetables and a cook's garden. New attractions are added each year like the Paradise Garden in memory of Geoff Hamilton. Guided tours and a very full programme of courses and special events throughout the year. Conference facilities on site. The shop has the widest selection of organic food and wine in the Midlands, and also stocks books, beautiful gifts, plants and gardening sundries. The organic restaurant offers morning coffee, lunches and afternoon tea. Waitress service in welcoming surroundings.**Internet:** www.hdra.org.uk

STONELEIGH ABBEY

Estate Office, Kenilworth, Warwickshire CV8 2LF
Tel: 01926 858585 Fax: 01926 850724 (Stoneleigh Abbey Ltd)

Stoneleigh Abbey has been the subject of a major restoration programme funded by the Heritage Lottery Fund, English Heritage and the European Regional Development Fund. Visitors will experience a wealth of architectural styles spanning more than 600 years: the magnificent state rooms and chapel of the 18th century Baroque West Wing designed by Francis Smith of Warwick; the medieval Gatehouse, one of very few complete monastic gatehouses left; the Gothic Revival style Regency Stables; 690 acres of grounds and parkland with the River Avon flowing through, displaying the design influences of Humphry Repton and other major landscape designers. Other attractions include a visitor centre and a riverside conservatory serving light refreshments. A series of special events will be staged throughout the season. **E-mail:** enquire@stoneleighabbey.org

WARWICK CASTLE

Warwick, Warwickshire, CV34 4QU
Tel: 0870 442 2000 Fax: 01926 401 692

Never in a thousand years will you believe what's happened over the last ten centuries. From the days of William the Conqueror to the reign of Queen Victoria, Warwick Castle has provided a backdrop for a world of treason, treachery and murder. With a thousand years waiting to unfold before your eyes, come and discover the secret life of England for yourself. In our Kingmaker attraction, join a mediaeval household and see a 15th century army prepare for the Earl of Warwick's final battle. Or enter the Ghost Tower, where it is said that the unquiet spirit of Sir Fulke Greville roams. A ghostly reminder of his brutal murder at the hands of a once loyal manservant. Descend the narrow steps into the dungeon and discover the cruel secrets of the torture chamber. Step forward in time and marvel at the grandeur of the State Rooms, including the Great Hall which houses some of history's most stunning artefacts. Move a few hundred years on to witness the perfect manners and hidden indiscretions of Daisy, Countess of Warwick and friends at the Royal Weekend Party 1898. Then stroll around 60 acres of grounds, beautifully landscaped by Capability Brown. Warwick Castle has seen it all. Now it's your turn. **Internet:** www.warwick–castle.co.uk

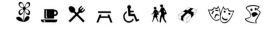

West Midlands

The West Midlands was at the very heart of the Industrial Revolution, but the fast-paced development left much of its heritage untouched. The bustling city of Birmingham has established itself as a city of culture, with a thriving arts scene: The City of Birmingham Symphony Orchestra enjoys a worldwide reputation for excellence, and the City Museum and Art Gallery houses a number of important pre-Raphaelite works. Britain's first modern cathedral rose out of the ruins of the bombed city centre of Coventry, and its controversial architecture is still a talking point today.

Meriden

BARBER INSTITUTE OF FINE ARTS

University of Birmingham, Edgbaston, Birmingham B15 2TS
Tel: 0121 414 7333 Fax: 0121 414 3370

One of the finest small picture galleries in the world housing an outstanding permanent collection of Old Master and modern paintings, drawings and sculpture including masterpieces by Bellini, Rubens, Poussin, Murillo, Gainsborough, Rossetti, Whistler, Monet, Degas and Margritte. Changing displays in the Education Gallery. Events include lectures, gallery talks, study days, children's holiday workshops and annual Open Day (9 June 2001). For details about activities for schools, please contact the Education Officer on 0121 414 7335. For details about the gallery shop, guided tours for groups and disabled access, please call the Visitors Services Officer on 0121 414 6985. **Open:** Mon-Sat, 10-5pm, Sun 2-5pm. Closed 1 Jan, Good Friday and 24-26 Dec. **Admission:** Free. **E-mail:** info@barber.org.uk **Internet:** www.barber.org.uk

map 8
B7

BIRMINGHAM BOTANICAL GARDENS & GLASSHOUSES

Westbourne Road, Edgbaston, Birmingham, West Midlands B15 3TR
Tel: 0121 454 1860 Fax: 0121 454 7835

The Gardens are a 15 acre 'Oasis of Delight' with the finest collection of plants in the Midlands. The Tropical House, full of rainforest vegetation, includes many economic plants. Palms, tree ferns and orchids are displayed in the Palm House. The Orangery features citrus fruits and conservatory plants while the Cactus House conveys a desert scene. There is colourful bedding on the Terrace plus Rhododendron, Rose, Rock, Herb and Cottage Gardens, Trials Ground, Historic Gardens and the National Bonsai Collection. Children's Playgrounds and Aviaries. Gallery. The 'Shop at the Gardens' has a wide range of gifts, souvenirs and plants. Refreshments in the Pavilion. Bands play summer Sun. afternoons. **Open:** Daily.

E-mail: admin@bham-bot-gdns.demon.co.uk **Internet:** www.bham-bot-gdns.demom.co.uk

map 4
B1

CASTLE BROMWICH HALL GARDENS

Chester Road, Castle Bromwich, Birmingham, West Midlands
Tel/Fax: 0121 749 4100

Set within 10 acres these historic gardens have been restored to their former 18th Century glory, offering as oasis of tranquillity within their walls. They contain a large collection of unusual period plants, and a 19th Century Holly Maze. The elegant Summer House and Green House stand at each end of the Holly Walk. In the formal vegetable garden many historic vegetables and herbs are grown, along with unusual varieties like the black 'Congo' potato and white carrot. Trained fruit trees include apple, pear, apricot, fig and cherry. Guided tours available. **Open:** pm, April–end October. Closed Mon, Fri. and Good Friday. Open Bank Holiday Mondays. **E-mail:** enq@cbhgt.swinternet.co.uk **Internet:** www.cbhgt.swinternet.co.uk

map 8
C7

HAGLEY HALL

Hagley, Worcestershire DY9 9LG
Tel: 01562 882408 Fax: 01562 882632 (The Viscount Cobham)

The last of the great Palladian Houses, designed by Sanderson Miller and completed in 1760. The house contains the finest example of Rococo plasterwork by Francesco Vassali and a unique collection of 18th century furniture and family portraits including works by Van Dyck, Reynolds and Lely. **Location:** Just off A456 Birmingham to Kidderminster, 12 m from Birmingham within easy reach M5 (exit 3 or 4), M6 or M42. **Station(s):** Hagley (1 m) (not Suns); Stourbridge Junction (2 m). **Open:** 3 Jan–25 Jan (excluding Sats); 29 Jan–2 Feb (excluding Sats);5 Feb-16 Feb(excluding Sats)–19 Feb-29 Feb(excluding Sats); 13-20 Apr inclusive; 27 May 1 June (excluding Sats) 26-31 Aug(excluding Sats). Please telephone to ensure the house is open. **Admission:** Charges apply. **Refreshments:** Tea available in the house. **Conferences:** Specialists in corporate entertaining and conferences throughout the year.

map 4
A1

Wiltshire

Castle Combe

Wiltshire is just two hours away from central London, and allows the visitor to step back 6,000 years in time. There are hundreds of ancient burial mounds and earthworks on the chalk downlands, but Stonehenge remains the main attraction, and is widely considered the finest neolithic structure in the world. Much of the south of the county is officially an area of outstanding natural beauty, and a network of bridleways and footpaths allows the visitor to explore unspoilt villages and quiet river valleys. Just west of Salisbury is Wilton, the ancient capital of Wessex, a traditional English market town with a history spanning more than 2000 years. Salisbury's magnificent cathedral, perhaps Britain's finest example of mediaeval architecture, was built between 1220 and 1258, and has the tallest spire in England.

BOWOOD HOUSE AND GARDENS

The Estate Office, Bowood, Calne, Wiltshire SN11 0LZ
Tel: 01249 812102 Fax: 01249 821757

Bowood House is the magnificent family home of the Marquis and Marchioness of Lansdowne and was designed by Robert Adam in the 18th century. On display in the rooms upstairs is a remarkable collection of family heirlooms built up over 250 years. Part of the house was demolished in 1955, leaving a perfectly proportioned Georgian home, much of which is open to visitors. Robert Adam's magnificent Diocletian wing contains a splendid library, the laboratory where Joseph Priestley discovered oxygen gas in 1774, the orangery, now a picture gallery, the Chapel and a sculpture gallery. Over 2,000 acres of gardens and grounds landscaped by 'Capability' Brown. **Admission:** Adults £5.90, senior citizens £4.90, children £3.70. **Open:** daily from 1 April–28 October. **Internet:** www.bowood-estate.co.uk

CHARLTON PARK HOUSE

Malmesbury, Wiltshire SN16 9DG
(The Earl of Suffolk and Berkshire)

Jacobean/Georgian mansion, built for the Earls of Suffolk, 1607, altered by Matthew Brettingham the Younger, c.1770. **Location:** 11/2 miles NE Malmesbury. Entry only by signed entrance on A429, Malmesbury/Cirencester road. No access from Charlton village. **Open:** 1 May–30 Sept: Mon 2–4pm. Viewing of Great Hall. Staircase and saloon. **Admission:** Adults £1, Children/OAP 50p. Car parking limited. Unsuitable for wheelchairs. No dogs. No picnicking.

map 3
K1

CORSHAM COURT

Corsham, Wiltshire SN13 0BZ
Tel/Fax: 01249 701610 (J Methuen-Campbell Esq)

Home of the Methuen family since 1745, Corsham Court displays one of the most distinguished collections of Old Master paintings in the country. The surviving collection includes works by Van Dyck and Carlo Dolci which hang alongside family portraits by Reynolds. Georgian State Rooms furnished by Thomas Chippendale and others during late 19th century. The Gardens have magnificent views, particularly East, providing a tranquil aspect over the Park. The grounds comprise sweeping lawns and formal areas with a rose garden, lily pond and herbaceous borders. There are beautiful specimen trees including the Great Plane, cedars, beeches and oaks dating back to the original 18th century plantings by 'Capability' Brown and Repton. **Location:** Signposted 4 miles West of Chippenham from the A4 Bath Road. **Open:** Throughout the year by appointment to groups of 15 or more. Otherwise, open 20 March-30 Sept daily except Mondays (but including Bank Hols) from 2-5.30pm. From 1 Oct-19 Mar open weekends, 2-4.30pm. Closed December. Last entry 30 minutes before close. **Admission:** Adult £5, OAP £4.50, Child £2.50, Group rates £4.50. **Refreshments:** Available at Johnson's Bakery nearby. **E-mail:** chris@corsham-court.co.uk

map 3
J2

HAMPTWORTH LODGE

Landford, Nr Salisbury, Wiltshire SP5 2EA
Tel: 01794 390215 (Mr N Anderson)

Rebuilt Jacobean Manor, with period furniture, including clocks. **Location:** 10 miles SE of Salisbury on the C44 road linking Downton on A338, Salisbury-Bournemouth to Landford on A36, Salisbury-Southampton. **Open:** House and garden daily, except Sundays. 30 March – 30 April. Conducted parties only 2.30 and 3.45. Coaches by appointment only Apr 1–Sept 30. By appointment all year, 18 hole golf course 01794 390155. **Admission:** £3.50, under 11s free. No special arrangement for parties, but about 15 is the maximum. **Refreshments:** Downtown, Salisbury; nil in house. Car parking; disabled ground floor only.

map 4 **B6**

HEALE GARDEN & PLANT CENTRE

Middle Woodford, Salisbury SP4 6NT
Tel: 01722 782504 (Mr & Mrs Guy Rasch)

1st Winner of Christie's/HHA Garden of the Year award. Early Carolean manor house where King Charles II hid during his escape. The garden provides a wonderfully varied collection of plants, shrub, musk and other roses, growing in the formal setting of clipped hedges and mellow stonework, at their best in June and July. Particularly lovely in Spring and Autumn is the water garden, planted with magnificent Magnolia and Acers, surrounding an authentic Japanese Tea House and Nikko Bridge which create an exciting focus in this part of the garden. Stunning winter aconites and snowdrops. **Location:** 4 m N of Salisbury on the Woodford Valley road between A345 and A360. Midway between Salisbury, Wilton and Stonehenge. No dogs. **Open:** Garden, Plant Centre and shop open year round 10–5pm. **Admission:** Adults £3.25, Children under 15 £1.50, under 5 free.

map 4 **B5**

LACOCK ABBEY

Lacock, Nr. Chippenham, Wiltshire SN15 2LG
Tel: 01249 730227

Converted to a country house in the mid-sixteenth century, the cloisters, sacristy and chapter house of this mediaeval abbey have survived almost intact. The building, now set in a beautiful Victorian woodland garden, houses a museum commemorating the life of William Fox Talbot, one of the pioneers of photography. **Open:** Museum: 3 Mar–4 Nov, daily (except Good Friday), 11am–5.30pm. Abbey: 31 Mar–4 Nov, daily (except Tues and Good Friday), 1–5.30pm. **Admission:** Combined ticket: Adult £6, Child £3.30.

LUCKINGTON COURT

Luckington, Chippenham, Wiltshire SN14 6PQ
Tel: 01666 840205 (The Hon Mrs Trevor Horn)

Mainly Queen Anne with magnificent group of ancient buildings. Beautiful mainly formal garden with fine collection of ornamental trees and shrubs. Home of the Bennet family in the BBC TV adaptation 'Pride and Prejudice'. **Location:** 6 miles W of Malmesbury on B4040 Bristol Road. **Open:** All through the year Weds 2–5pm, garden only. Open Sunday 13 May 2001, 2.30–5pm. Collection box for National Gardens' Scheme. Inside view by appointment 3 weeks in advance. **Admission:** Outside gardens only £1, house £2. **Refreshments:** Teas in garden or house (in aid of Luckington Parish Church) on Sun 13 May only.

map 3 **J2**

THE PETO GARDEN AT IFORD MANOR

Bradford-on-Avon, Wiltshire, BA15 2BA
Tel: 01225 863 146 Fax: 01225 862 364 (Mrs Cartwright-Hignett)

This Grade 1 Italian-style award winning garden was the home of Harold A Peto, the well known Edwardian architect and landscape designer. Situated beside the River Frome, this unique and romantic hillside garden is characterised by steps, terraces, sculpture and magnificent rural views. **Location:** 7 miles S of Bath via A36. **Open:** Easter Sun–Mon, Apr & Oct, Sun only. May–Sept, Sat–Sun & Tue–Thur & Bank Hol Mon, 2–5pm. **Admission:** Adults £3, Children (10+) and OAPs £2.50. Children under 10 not admitted at weekends. **Refreshments:** Saturdays and Sundays, May–Aug only, 2–5pm.

map 3 **J2**

PHILIPPS HOUSE & DINTON PARK

Dinton, Salisbury, Wiltshire, SP3 5HJ
Tel: 01985 843600

Set in beautiful parkland, this nineteenth-century neo-Grecian house was designed by Jeffry Wyattville. The main ground floor rooms contain a selection of excellently-preserved Regency furniture. **Open:** House: 31 May–29 Oct, Mon 1–5pm & Sat 10am–1pm. Park open daily all year round. **Admission:** House £3.

LONGLEAT

Warminster, Wiltshire, BA12 7NW

Tel: 01985 844400 Fax: 01985 844885 (The Marquess of Bath)

Nestling within magnificent 'Capability' Brown landscaped grounds in the heart of Wiltshire, Longleat House is widely regarded as one of the finest examples of high Elizabethan architecture in Britain and one of the most beautiful stately homes open to the public. This magnificent Elizabethan property, built by Sir John Thynne and substantially completed by 1580, has been the home of the same family ever since. The House contains many treasures including paintings by Tintoretto and Wootton, exquisite Flemish tapestries, fine French furniture, as well as elaborate ceilings by John Dibblee Crace incorporating paintings from the 'School of Titian'. The Murals in the family apartments in the West Wing were painted by Alexander Thynn, the present Marquess, and are fascinating and remarkable additions to the collections. Apart from the ancestral home, Longleat is also renowned for its Safari Park, the first of its kind outside Africa. Discover the famous pride of lions, giraffe, elephants and tigers before exploring the other attractions at Longleat.... the 'World's Longest Hedge Maze', Safari Boats, Longleat Railway and much much more. In fact, there is so much to see that we recommend the Passport Ticket (5★ Value for money, Which? Guide to Tourist Attractions) to enjoy all 12 of these amazing attractions! Visit Longleat in a day or come back at any time before the end of the season to see those attractions previously missed, the choice is yours. Each attraction can be visited only once. **Open:** Longleat House is open 24 Mar–31 Dec (excl. Christmas Day) 1st Jan–23 Mar 2001 weekends only (groups visits available daily, pre-booking essential). All other attractions are open 24 Mar–4 Nov 2001. Please telephone or contact our website for opening times & further information. **Internet:** www.longleat.co.uk

map 3 J3

SALISBURY CATHEDRAL
The Close, Salisbury SP1 2EJ
Tel: 01722 555120 Fax: 01722 555116

Salisbury Cathedral is probably the finest medieval building in Britain, with the highest spire, the best preserved Magna Carta, the unique 13th century frieze of bible stories in the Chapter House and Europe's oldest working clock. Boy and girl choristers sing daily services, continuing a tradition of worship that goes back over 750 years. Volunteer guides conduct tours of the Cathedral most days. Special tours for pre-booked parties include the roof and tower. **Location:** In The Close, just south of the city centre. **Open:** 7.15am every day of the year. Closing time: Jan–May & Sept–Dec: 6.15pm. June, July & Aug: 8.15pm. Every Sun: 6.15pm. Times subject to change for services and concerts.
E-mail: visitors@salcath.co.uk **Internet:** www.salisburycathedral.org.uk

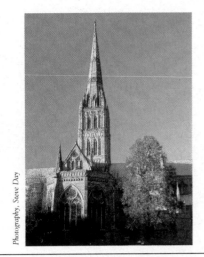

Photography, Steve Day

 map 3 K3

STOURHEAD
Stourton, Warminster, BA12 6QD
Tel: 01747 841 152 Fax: 01747 841 152

Beautiful Palladian mansion set in one of Britain's finest landscape gardens. FOR FULL DETAILS AND OPENING TIMES, PLEASE SEE THE ILLUSTRATED ENTRY ON PAGE 208.

WESTWOOD MANOR
Bradford-on-Avon, Wiltshire, BA15 2AF
Tel: 01225 863374

A stone manor house dating back to the 15th century, with some 17th-century alterations. Features of interest include Jacobean windows and a topiary garden. **Open:** 1 Apr–30 Sept; Sun, Tues & Wed 2–5pm. **Admission:** £3.80.

WILTON HOUSE
The Estate Office, Wilton, Salisbury, Wiltshire SP2 0BJ
Tel: 01722 746720 Fax: 01722 744447 (The Earl of Pembroke)

Wilton House stands on the site of the 9th century nunnery founded by King Alfred. This in turn was replaced by a 12th century Benedictine abbey which, including its surrounding lands, was surrendered during the Dissolution of the monasteries. Now home to the 17th Earl of Pembroke, Wilton House provides a fascinating insight on British history. Marvel at Inigo Jones' magnificent state rooms and admire the world famous art collection. Perhaps the most striking room in the house is the Double Cube, sixty feet long by thirty feet wide and thirty feet high. This room, among others, has offered film-makers the perfect setting for many major movies amongst which are, *The Madness of King George, Sense and*

Sensibility and *Mrs Brown*. Created within the atmospheric setting of the old indoor riding school, the Visitor Centre provides the starting point for your tour of Wilton House. The modern interpretative displays, including the Tudor kitchen, Victorian laundry and award-winning introductory film bring history to life. All set in 21 acres of landscaped parkland, water and rose gardens beside the River Nadder and Palladian Bridge. **Open:** Daily from 4 Apr–28 Oct 2001. 10.30am–5.30pm (last admission 4.30pm). **E-mail:** tourism@wiltonhouse.com **Internet:** www.wiltonhouse.com

map 4 B5

STOURHEAD

Stourton, Warminster, Wiltshire BA12 6QD
Tel: 01747 841152 Fax: 01747 841152 (The National Trust)

Stourhead combines Britain's foremost landscape garden with a fine Palladian mansion. Stourhead Garden is one of the most famous examples of the early 18th century English landscape movement. Planned in the belief that it was "Tiresome for the foot to travel, to where the eye had already been", the garden continually surprises the visitor with fresh glimpses of its enchanting lakes and temples. The House was designed in 1721 for Henry Hoare by Colen Campbell. Its contents include a collection of furniture designed by the younger Chippendale and many fine works of art. Interesting features of the estate include two Iron Age hill forts and King Alfred's Tower, a 160 ft high red brick folly. This tower offers magnificent views across the three counties of Wiltshire, Somerset and Dorset. **Location:** Stourton, off B3092, 3 miles NW of A303 (Mere). 2hrs from London,

1.5 hrs from Exeter. **Open:** Garden: All Year Daily, 9–7pm (or dusk if earlier). House: 31 Mar–4 Nov, Sat–Wed, 12–5.30pm or dusk if earlier (last admission 30 mins before closing). King Alfred's Tower: 31 Mar–4 Nov: Tues–Fri 2–5.30pm. Sat, Sun, Good Friday & Bank Holiday Mondays 11.30–5.30pm (or dusk if earlier). Plant Centre: Open Apr–Sept, 12–6pm. 01747 840894. **Admission:** Garden or House: Adult £4.80, Child £2.60, Group (15 or more by appointment) £4.30, Family £12 (2 adults & up to 3 children). Combined Garden and House: Adult £8.50, Child £4, Group £8, Family £20. Large coach and car park. King Alfred's Tower: Adult £1.60, Child 80p, Family £4. **Events:** Held throughout the year. Please phone for leaflet.

map 3
J3

Worcestershire

Worcestershire is a beautiful rural county with stunning landscape and a rich heritage. The peaceful valleys of The River Teme, which rises in the Shropshire Hills and runs down to join the Severn near Worcester, are still famous for hop growing and fruit production.

The birthplace of Sir Edward Elgar, Worcester boasts an impressive history of cultural and musical events, and hosts the internationally acclaimed Three Choirs Festival every three years. The next Festival will take place in 2002. Amongst its many beautiful buildings, visitors should ensure that they see the magnificent Guildhall and the cathedral, which faces the medieval chapter meadows. Traditionally a grazing place for cattle, the meadows are now a wetland haven for butterflies, dragonflies and birds, where beautiful wildflowers grow in their natural environment. Riverside walks can be enjoyed along the banks of the Severn, which runs through the heart of Worcester. The unspoilt banks are home to a variety of wildlife, and there is a special sanctuary for swans.

Harvington Hall

The Malvern Hills, which rise to the south of Worcester, offer great opportunities for walking, with splendid views to reward the tired climber. On a clear day, seven different counties can be seen from the summit of the Worcestershire Beacon, the mightiest of all the hills at 1,395 feet above sea-level.

AVONCROFT MUSEUM OF HISTORIC BUILDINGS

Stoke Heath, Bromsgrove, Worcestershire B60 4JR
Tel: 01527 831363/831886 Fax: 01527 876934 (Council of Management)

25 buildings of historic, architectural and social value authentically restored and re-erected on 15-acre rural site. Covering 7 centuries, it ranges from the magnificently carved timber roof of the Priory of Worcester Cathedral, now gracing a fine new Guesten Hall, to a 1946 Pre-Fab, authentically furnished. English life over the centuries is illustrated – early agriculture by a range of timber-framed buildings, including a working windmill; the local 19th century industries of nail and chain-making; and many aspects of domestic social life. We also house the National Telephone Kiosk Collection. **Location:** At Stoke Heath 2 miles south of Bromsgrove. **Open:** March–Nov from 10.30am. Some days closed. **Admission:** Adult £5.00, Senior Citizen £4.00, Child £2.50. Group Rates: Adult £4.00, Senior Citizen £3.50, Child £1.85. Under fives are free. **Internet:** www.avoncroft.org.uk

BEWDLEY MUSEUM

Load Street, Bewdley, Worcestershire DY12 2AE
Tel: 01299 403573 Fax: 01299 404740

Situated in the picturesque riverside town of Bewdley, the museum provides a fascinating insight into the past trades of the Wyre Forest area and the lives of its people. Displays feature woodland industries, brass founding and pewtering with daily demonstrations of clay pipe and rope making. **Exhibitions:** Annual programmes of special events and exhibitions. **Facilities:** Education service, group bookings welcome, museum shop, delightful herb garden and picnic area. Incorporated T.I.C. **Open:** 1 Apr-30 Sept: Daily 11-5pm. 1-31 Oct: Daily 11-4pm. Inclusive of BHols. **Admission:** Adults £2, Senior Citizens, Unemployed, Unaccompanied Children £1. Accompanied Children free. **Location:** Bewdley is situated on the edge of the Wyre Forest, 4 miles to the west of Kidderminster off the A456 Leominster Road, on the B4190.

BROADWAY TOWER

Broadway, Worcestershire, WR12 7LB
Tel: 01386 852390 Fax: 01386 858038

A fascinating building standing on top of the Cotswold ridge, with wonderful views for miles around. Set in 35 acres of beautiful parkland, with plenty to do and see for all the family. **Open:** 27 Mar–31 Oct, daily 10am–5pm. Rest of year, weekends 11am–3pm. **Admission:** Adult £4, Child £2.30. Season tickets also available.

THE COMMANDERY
Sidbury, Worcester WR1 2HU
Tel: 01905 361821 Fax: 01905 361822 (Worcester City Council)

The first view of the Commandery is deceptive for behind the small timber-framed entrance is a stunning complex of buildings dating from the medieval to the Georgian periods. Originally founded in 1085 as a monastic hospital, the Commandery later became the family home of the Wyldes whose Stuart lifestyle is reflected along with other periods from the building's history in the Commandery Chronicle exhibition. In 1651 the Commandery assumed national importance when it became the headquarters of the Royalists at the Battle of Worcester. The Civil War exhibition takes visitors back to the turbulent days of the English Civil war. The Commandery plays host to a varied events programme with living history, lectures, family days and theatre, and 2001 marks the 350th anniversary of the Battle of Worcester with special events being held throughout the year.

map 4 A2

THE ELGAR BIRTHPLACE MUSEUM
Crown East Lane, Lower Broadheath, WR2 6RH
Tel/Fax: 01905 333 224

Sir Edward Elgar, one of England's greatest composers, was born in 1857 in a Worcestershire country cottage with views of the Malvern Hills which inspired much of his music. On display inside is his desk, and a wealth of photographs, family scrapbooks, and personal possessions illustrating his life, work, family, friends, and interests. The new Elgar Centre shows further treasures from this unique collection of manuscripts, music scores, concert programmes, photographs, letters, press cuttings and memorabilia. Here you can explore Elgar's musical life and inspirations, and discover how he composed'Enigma Variations' and other much-loved works. **Open:** Every day 11am-5pm (last adm. 4.15pm). Closed four weeks in winter. Call for details. **Admission:** Adult £3.50, Child £1.50, Seniors £2.60, Student £1.75, Family £8.50 Call for group rates. **Internet:** www.elgar.org

map 4 A2

HARVINGTON HALL
Harvington, Kidderminster, Worcestershire DY10 4LR
Tel: 01562 777846 (the Roman Catholic Archdiocese of Birmingham)

Moated medieval and Elizabethan manor house containing secret hiding places and rare wall paintings. Georgian Chapel in garden with 18th century altar, rails and organ. **Location:** 3 miles SE of Kidderminster, ½ mile from the junction of A448 and A450 at Mustow Green. **Station(s):** Nearest Kidderminster. **Open:** Mar and Oct, Sat & Sun, Apr to Sept, Wed–Sun. Bank Holiday Mondays. The Hall is available every day for pre-booked schools or groups and for meetings, conferences or wedding breakfasts. **Admission:** Adults £3.80, OAPs £2.50, Children £2.50, Family ticket £10.50. Garden only £1. Free car parking. **Events:** Outdoor play – July. Craft Fair – Mar and Nov. Pilgrimage – early Sept. Wassail – December. Other events and reconstructions to be arranged. Occasionally the Hall may be closed for a private function, up to date information available by phone.

map 4 A1

HARTLEBURY CASTLE
Nr Kidderminster, Worcester, Hereford & Worcester DT11 7XX
Tel: 01299 250410 (State Rooms Secretary) 01299 250416 (Museum)

Home of the Bishops of Worcester for over 1,000 years. Fortified in 13th century, rebuilt after sacking in Civil War and gothicised in 18th century. State Rooms include medieval Great Hall, Hurd Library and Saloon. Fine plaster work and collection of episcopal portraits. Also County Museum in North Wing. **Location:** In village of Hartlebury, 5 mile south of Kidderminster, 10 miles N of Worcester off A449. **Station:** Kidderminster 4 miles. **Open:** County Museum: Mar–Nov, Mon–Thurs 10–5pm, Fri & Sun 2–5pm. Closed Good Friday. State rooms: Open Tuesday, Wednesday and Thursday please contact the museum for details. **Admission:** County Museum: Adults £2.20, Concessions £1.10, Family tickets £6.

map 4 A1

HOPTON COURT

Hopton Court, Cleobury Mortimer, Kidderminister, DY14 0EF
Tel: 01299 270734 Fax: 01299 271132 (C. R. D Woodward)

Substantial changes were made to the house and grounds from 1798 to 1803. The works were supervised by John Nash and Humphrey Repton. Around 1820, a conservatory (graded II★ in 1995) of cast-iron and glass was built. To the northeast of the house lies the stable block incorporating the Coach House. Both the Conservatory and the Coach House were renovated in 1997. Three rooms in the house and the Conservatory are licensed for civil ceremonies. The Conservatory is open four days a year without appointment, at other times by prior appointment. **Admission:** £3.50. The Coach House is available for receptions.

map 7
F1

LITTLE MALVERN COURT

Nr Malvern, Hereford & Worcester, WR14 4JN
Tel: 01684 892988 Fax: 01684 893057 (Mrs Berington)

14th century Prior's Hall once attached to 12th century Benedictine Priory, with Victorian addition by Hansom. Family and European paintings and furniture. Collection of 18th and 19th century needlework. Home of the Berington family by descent since the Dissolution. 10 acres of former monastic grounds. Magnificent views, lake, garden rooms, terrace. Wide variety of spring bulbs, old fashioned roses, shrubs and trees. **Location:** 3 m S of Great Malvern on Upton-on-Severn Road (A4104). **Open:** 18 April–19 July, Wed and Thurs 2.15–5pm, parties by prior arrangement. Guided tours – last admission 4.30pm. **Admission:** Adults: house and garden £4.60; house or garden only £3.60. Children: house and garden £2.50; house or garden only £1.50. **Refreshments:** Home-made teas only available for parties by arrangement. Partially suitable for wheelchairs in garden.

map 4
A2

SPETCHLEY PARK GARDEN

Spetchley Park, Hereford & Worcester WR5 1RS
Tel: 01905 345224 (Spetchley Gardens Charitable Trust)

This lovely 30 acre garden is a plantsman's delight, with a large collection of trees, shrubs and plants, many of which are rare or unusual. The park contains red and fallow deer. This is truly a garden for seasons. April and May produce a wonderful display of daffodils and other bulbs, and are also the months of flowering trees and shrubs, many rare or unusual. The large collection of roses come into their own in June and July, whilst July, August and September reveal the great herbaceous borders in all their glory. Late September sees the start of the Autumn tints. **Location:** 3 miles E of Worcester on Stratford-upon-Avon Road (A422). **Open:** Gardens: 1 Apr–30 Sept. Tues–Fri 11–5pm. Suns 2–5pm. Bank Hols 11–5pm. Closed all Sats & all other Mons. **Admission:** Adults £3.40, Children £1.70, Concessions for pre-booked parties. **Refreshments:** Tea in the garden. Regret no dogs. House not open.

map 4
A2

WORCESTER CATHEDRAL

College Green, Worcester, Worcestershire, WR1 2LA
Tel: 01905 28854 Fax: 01905 611139 (Dean & Chapter)

Beside the River Severn, facing the Malvern Hills. Built between 1084 and 1375. Norman Crypt and Chapter House. Early English Quire, Perpendicular Tower. Monastic buildings include the Refectory (now College Hall and open on request during August), Cloisters, remains of Guesten Hall and Dormitories. Tombs of King John and Prince Arthur. Elgar memorial window. Misericords. **Location:** Centre of Worcester. Main roads Oxford and Stratford to Wales. 3 miles M5, Junction 7. **Station(s):** Foregate Street (easier). Shrub Hill (taxi). **Open:** Every day, 7.30–6pm. Choral Evensong daily (except Thurs and school hols). **Admission:** FREE. Suggested donation £2. **Guided tours:** Visits Officer 01905 28854. **E-mail:** worcestercathedral@compuserve.com

map 4
A2

WITLEY COURT

Great Witley, Worcester WR6 6JT
Tel: 01299 896636

One of the largest and most spectacular ruins in the country, Witley Court stands in lansdcaped gardens with huge fountains. Originally the site of a Jacobean house, it was converted into an Italian-style mansion in the nineteenth century, with porticos designed by Nash. **Open:** 1 Apr–31 Oct, daily 10am–6pm. Rest of year: Wed–Sun, 10am–4pm. **Admission:** Adult £3.80, Child £1.90.

Yorkshire

Yorkshire is the largest county in England, and its landscape is correspondingly varied, with unspoilt coastline to the east, the Wolds to the south, the Dales to the west, and moorland to the north.

The North York Moors are a beautiful wilderness, where deep valleys shelter red-roofed villages amidst endless ridges of purple-hued heather moorland. The landscape of the Dales is similarly wild, and includes some of the finest upland scenery in the country, still divided into fields by ancient dry stone walls.

The Wolds are more hospitable, and no less scenic, with historic market towns and charming village greens set in an undulating landscape. Along the coast at Filey, the bay holds rows of Victorian houses interspersed amongst the fishermen's cottages, whilst at Whitby visitors can admire the abbey of St Hilda.

The city of York was founded by the Romans in 71AD as "Eboracum", "a place of yew trees", and the remains of a Roman bath can still be seen in St Samson's Square. It was then occupied successively by the Saxons and the Vikings, who renamed it Jorvik. They remained for only a

Aske Hall

Rievaulx Abbey

Thorp Perrow

century, but many of York's street names can be traced back to this period. The city has retained a great deal of its mediaeval architecture, the best example of which is the 800-year-old York Minster, whose Gothic Cathedral is the largest in Northern Europe, housing a huge collection of stained glass windows.

Also in the area are 18 mediaeval churches, the two-mile-long city walls, and a variety of Jacobean and Georgian buildings.

BOLTON CASTLE
Leyburn, North Yorkshire, DL8 4ET
Tel: 01969 623 981 Fax: 01969 623 332
(Hon. Mr & Mrs Harry Orde-Powlett)

Completed in 1399, Bolton Castle celebrated its 600th anniversary last year. Originally the stronghold of the Scrope family, the castle has a wealth of history. Mary, Queen of Scots was imprisoned here for 6 months shortly after her arrival in England. Medieval garden and vineyard also open to the public. Also tearoom and gift shop. **Location:** Just off A684, 6 miles W of Leyburn. **Open:** Daily throughout year 10–5pm or dusk if earlier. **Admission:** Guided tour by arrangement for groups of 15+. Adults £4, OAP/Children £3, Family Ticket £10 (2 adults & 2 children). **Refreshments:** Tearoom – meals available, picnic area. Wedding licence. **E-mail:** harry@boltoncastle.co.uk **Internet:** www .boltoncastle.co.uk

map 8 / B1

BRAMHAM PARK
Wetherby, West Yorkshire, LS23 6ND
Tel: 01937 846005 Fax: 01937 846006 (G. F. Lane Fox)

The Queen Anne house is 5 miles S of Wetherby on the A1, 10 miles from Leeds and 15 miles from York. The grand design of the gardens (66 acres) and pleasure grounds (100 acres) are the only example of a formal, early 18th century landscape in the British Isles. Unexpected views and grand vistas, framed by monumental hedges and trees, delight the visitor, while temples, ornamental ponds and cascades focus the attention. The profusion of spring and summer wild flowers give a constant variety of colour and include many rare species. **Location:** 5 miles S of Wetherby, on A1. **Open:** Every day 1 Apr-30 Sep, 10.30–5.30pm (closed for Bramham Horse Trials 4-10 June). Gardens: open every day. House: open by appointment only for parties 6+. **Admission:** Adult £4, Senior Citizen/Child under 16 £2. Under 5's free. Call for more info. 01937 846 005. **Refreshments:** Picnics in grounds permitted.

map 11 / H7

✤ BRODSWORTH HALL
Brodsworth, Nr. Doncaster, South Yorkshire DN5 7XY
Tel: 01302 722598 Fax: 01302 337165 (English Heritage)

Brodsworth Hall is an outstanding example of a Victorian country house. Within its grand Italianate exterior, visitors can glimpse a vanished way of life viewing over 30 rooms ranging from the sumptuous family reception to the plain but functional servants' wing. A pervasive sense of faded grandeur and of time past adds an element of enchantment to the Hall. The restored Victorian gardens form the ideal setting. **Location:** 5 m NW of Doncaster, A635 from Junction 37, A1(M). **Open:** 31 Mar-4 Nov: Tues–Sun & BH 1–6pm (last admission 5pm). Gardens, tearoom & shop from noon. Guided tours from 10am for pre-booked groups only. 10 Nov–25 Mar: weekends only, garden & servants wing 11am–4pm. Closed 24–26 Dec & 1 Jan. **Admission:** House: Adult £5, Conc £3.80, Child £2.50. Gardens: Adult £2.60, Conc £2, Child £1.30. **Winter:** Adult £1.60, Conc £1.20, Child 80p.

map 8 / B3

🏛 BROCKFIELD HALL
Warthill, York, North Yorkshire YO19 5XJ
Tel: 01904 489298 (Lord and Lady Martin Fitzalan Howard)

A fine late Georgian house designed by Peter Atkinson, whose father had been assistant to John Carr of York, for Benjamin Agar Esq. Begun in 1804, its outstanding feature is an oval entrance hall with a fine cantilevered stone staircase curving past an impressive Venetian window. It is the happy family home of Lord and Lady Martin Fitzalan Howard. He is the brother of the 17th Duke of Norfolk and son of the late Baroness Beaumont of Carlton Towers, Selby. There are some interesting portraits of her old Roman catholic family, the Stapletons, and some good furniture. **Location:** 5 miles east of York, off A166 or A64. **Open:** 1–31 August 2001, 1–4pm except Mondays, other times by appointment. **Admission:** Adults £3.50, Children £1.

map 11 / J7

BRONTË PARSONAGE MUSEUM
Haworth, Nr Keighley, West Yorkshire BD22 8DR
Tel: 01535 642323 Fax: 01535 647131

Manuscripts, personal effects, furniture and drawings belonging to the Brontë family housed in this small Georgian parsonage which is furnished as in the Brontës' day. **Admission:** Adult £4.80, Conc £3.50, Child £1.50, Family £10.50. Reduced entry for booked groups of 20+. Contact the museum for details. **Open:** 1 Apr–30 Sept 10am–5pm, 1 Oct–31 Mar 11am–4.30pm. Closed 8 Jan–2 Feb 2001 & 24–27 Dec 2001. **E-mail:** bronte@bronte.prestel.co.uk **Internet:** www.bronte.org.uk

map 8 / B3

BURNBY HALL GARDENS
The Balk, Pocklingston, East Riding of Yorkshire
Tel: 01759 302068 Fax: 01759 388272

Burnby Hall Gardens and The Stewart Collection Museum is maintained by The Stewart's Burnby Hall Gardens & Museum Trust, which was established in 1964 and is a registered charity, relying on income primarily from entrance fees to maintain the facilities for the benefit of the visitor's enjoyment. The Gardens comprise eight acres and include two large lakes which hold the National Collection of Hardy Water Lilies. There is an excellent Tea Room as well as a gift shop where plants and other commodities are on sale throughout the season. The Gardens have received an Age Concern Award for facilities for the disabled. **Open:** Daily Apr–Sept 10am–6pm. **Admission:** Adults £2.50, Senior Citizens £2, Parties (20+) £1.50, Children (5-15 yrs) £1, under 5 yrs free.

map 8 E2

 # BURTON AGNES HALL
Burton Agnes, Diffield, East Yorks YO25 0ND
Tel: 01262 490 324 Fax: 01262 490 513 (Burton Agnes Hall Preservation Trust Ltd).

The Hall is a magnificent example of late Elizabethan architecture - still lived in by descendants of the family who built it in 1598. There are wonderful carvings, lovely furniture and a fine collection of modern French and English paintings of the Impressionist Schools. The walled garden contains a potager, maze, herbaceous borders, campanula collection, jungle garden and giant games set in coloured gardens. Also woodland gardens and walk, children's corner, Norman manor house, donkey wheel and gift shop. **Location:** 6 miles SW of Bridlington on Driffield/Bridlington Rd (A166). **Open:** Apr 1–Oct 31 daily 11–5pm. **Admission:** Adults £4.80, OAPs £4.30, Children £2.40. **Gardens only:** Adults £2.40, OAPs £2.15, Children £1. **Refreshments:** Licensed cafeteria. Teas, light lunches & refreshments.

map 9 F2

 # CASTLE HOWARD
Nr York, North Yorkshire YO60 7DA
Tel: 01653 648444 Fax: 01653 648501 (The Hon. Simon Howard)

Magnificent palace designed by Vanbrugh in 1699. One of Britain's most spectacular stately homes. Impressive Great Hall and beautiful rooms are filled with fine furniture, paintings and objets d'art. Extensive grounds with lakes and colourful woodland. Rose garden, plant centre, adventure playground. **Location:** 15 m NE of York; 3 m off A64; 6 m W of Malton; 22 m from Scarborough. **Open:** Daily 16 Mar–4 Nov. Grounds from 10am, house from 11am. Last admission 4.30pm. **Admission:** Adult £7.50, Child £4.50, OAP £6.75. Groups (min. 12 people): Adult £6.50, Child £4, OAP £6. Grounds only: Adult £4.50, Child £2.50 **Refreshments:** Licensed cafeteria in House, Lakeside Café. Café and shops facilities in Stable Courtyard. **E-mail:** house@castlehoward.co.uk **Internet:** www.castlehoward.co.uk

map 8 D2

CONSTABLE BURTON HALL
Constable Burton, Leyburn, North Yorkshire DL8 5LJ
Tel: 01677 450428 Fax: 01677 450622 (Mr Charles Wyvill)

Situated 3 miles east of Leyburn on the A684 and 6 miles west of the A1. A large romantic garden surrounded by 18th century parkland with a superb John Carr house (not open). Fine trees, woodland walks, garden trails, rockery with an interesting collection of alpines and extensive shrubs and roses. Set in beautiful countryside at the entrance to Wensleydale. **Open:** Gardens: Mar 24–Oct 14, daily 9–6pm. **Admission:** Please phone for details. Group tours of the house and gardens available by Phil Robinson, The Dales Plantsman. Tel: 01677 460225. **Events:** Special Event - Tulip Festival 6 & 7 May.

map 8 G1

DUNCOMBE PARK

Helmsley, Ryedale, York, North Yorks YO62 5EB
Tel: 01439 770213 Fax: 01439 771114

Visit Lord and Lady Feversham's restored family home in the North York Moors National Park. Built on a virgin plateau in 1713 overlooking both Norman Castle and river Valley it is surrounded by 35 acres of 'spectacularly beautiful' 18th century landscaped gardens and 400 acres of rolling, Arcadian parkland with National Nature Reserve and veteran trees. **Location:** Just off Helmsley Market Place, along A170 (Scarborough–Thirsk road). **Open:** 13 Apr–28 Oct, Apr/Oct: Sun–Thurs. House & Garden: 10.30–6pm. Tearoom, shop and walks 10.30–5.30pm. **Admission:** House & Garden: Adult £6, Conc £5, Child (10–16) £3, Family (2+2) £13.50, Groups £4.50. Gardens & Parkland: Adult £4, Child £2. Parkland: Adult £2, Child £1. Season ticket (2+2) £20. Duncombe Park is available for weddings and corporate entertainment. **Internet:** www.duncombepark.com

map 8
D1

DALES COUNTRYSIDE MUSEUM

Station Yard, Hawes, North Yorkshire DL8 3NT
Tel: 01969 667494 Fax: 01969 667165

Tells the story of the Yorkshire Dales landscape and people over the last 10,000 years. Stroll through the Time Tunnel to see unique exhibits from the Stone Age to Victorian times. Climb aboard our static train and find out how family life has changed in the Dales. Take a walk down the 'lead mine' and discover how the industries of the Dales, together with farming, have helped to shape this treasured landscape. Events, demonstrations of traditional crafts and changing exhibitions help bring the museum alive. Hands-on, interactive exhibits make it fun for children.

map 8
B1

RIEVAULX ABBEY

Helmsley, North Yorkshire Y06 5LB
Tel: 01439 798228 (English Heritage)

Visit the spectacular remains of the first Cistercian monastery in Northern England and experience the unrivalled peace and serenity of its setting in the beautiful wooded valley of the River Rye. Imaginations will be fired as you listen to our audio tour while exploring the extensive remains; the soaring graceful arches silhouetted against the sky will take the breath away. Also, new interactive exhibition. **Location:** In Rievaulx, 2¼ m W of Helmsley on minor road off B1257. **Open:** 1 Apr–30 Sept: daily, 10–6pm. Open 9.30–7pm, July–Aug. 1 Oct–31 Oct: daily, 10–5pm, 1 Nov–28 Mar: daily, 10–4pm. Closed 24–26 Dec. **Admission:** Adults £3.60, Conc £2.70, Child £1.80. (15% discount for groups of 11 or more).

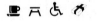

map 8
D1

THE FORBIDDEN CORNER

Tupgill Park Estate, Coverham, nr. Middleham, North Yorkshire DL8 4TJ
Tel: 01969 640638/640687

Now officially open to the public, after the successful appeal ended a two-year planning battle with the Yorkshire Dales National Park. The Forbidden Corner has been described as "The Best European Folly of the 20th Century". It is a four acre garden with a maze of underground passages leading to the grotto. Superb views and surprises at every turn. Voted the best children's attraction in Yorkshire (1998), but there is something for every age. From 2001 it is a required planning condition that entrance is by prior appointment, with a restriction of 120 visitors per hour. Please call us. **Open:** Good Friday (or 1st April) until 31st October, every day. Sundays through until Christmas. Mon-Sat: 12pm-6pm. Suns and Bank Hols, 10am-6pm.

map 8
B1

GREEN HOWARDS REGIMENTAL MUSEUM

Trinity Church Square, Richmond, North Yorkshire DL10 4QN
Tel: 01748 822133 Fax: 01748 826561

Take an audio-guided tour around this award-winning museum in a unique setting: the medieval church in the centre of Richmond's cobble market place. Interactive video on WW1 and WW2, CD-Rom on the Green Howards Today and realistic displays with simple informative labels tell the story and traditions of this 312 year old infantry regiment from North Yorkshire. There are exhibitions for female visitors - such as 'Ladies of the Regiment' - and for children - such as the 'Richmond Drummer Boy Legend' - with hands-on displays, linked to the National Curriculum, for school party visits which are free. There are also Stannah chair lifts on all three stairs for the aged or infirm. **Admission:** Adults £2, OAPs £1.50, Children £1. Booked school parties free. **Internet:** www.greenhowards.org.uk

map 8
C1

FAIRFAX HOUSE

Castlegate, York, North Yorkshire YO1 9RN
Tel: 01904 655 543 Fax: 01904 652 262 (York Civic Trust)

An 18th century house designed by John Carr of York, and described as a class architectural masterpiece of its age. Certainly one of the finest town houses in England and saved from near collapse by the York Civic Trust who restored it to its former glory during 1982/84. In addition to the superbly decorated plaster work, wood and wrought iron, the house is now home for an outstanding collection of 18th century furniture and clocks, formed by the late Noel Terry. Described by Christie's as one of the finest private collections of this century, it enhances and complements the house and helps to create a very special 'lived in' feeling. Their regular set-piece exhibitions bring the House to life in a very tangible way. Special displays for the coming year. **Location:** Centre of York, follow signs for Castle Area and Jorvik Centre. **Station(s):** York (10 mins walk). **Open:** 17 Feb–6 Jan, Mon–Thurs & Sat, 11am–5pm, Sun 1.30–5pm. Last admission 4.30pm. Fri, guided tours only 11am and 2pm. Special evening tours, connoisseur visits and private dinners welcomed by arrangement with the Director. **Admission:** Adults £4, Children £1.50, OAPs/Students £3.50. Adult parties (pre-booked 15+) £3, Children £1.25. **Events/Exhibitions:** The Keeping of Christmas: 2 Dec–6 Jan 2001. Obession: The Collector & their Collections 1 Mar–1 June 2001. Cutting Edge: The Evolution of Cutlery and Place Settings 1 Sept–20 Nov 2001. **Conferences:** By arrangement with the Director. Public car park within 50 yards. Suitable for disabled persons only with assistance (by telephoning beforehand, staff can be available to help). A small gift shop offers selected antiques, publications and gifts. Opening times are the same as the house. **Internet:** www.fairfaxhouse.co.uk

map 8
D2

HARLOW CARR BOTANICAL GARDENS
Crag Lane, Harrogate, North Yorkshire HG3 1QB
Tel: 01423 565418 Fax: 01423 530663 (Northern Horticultural Society)

Sixty-eight acre headquarters of the Northern Horticultural Society. Vegetable, fruit and flower trials. Rock, foliage, scented, winter and heather gardens. Alpines, herbaceous beds, display houses, streamside, woodland and arboretum. National collections, Museum of Gardening, Model Village, library, childrens' play area. Fully licensed cafe bar, restaurant, plant and gift centre. Picnic area. Courses, exhibitions, displays, walks and talks held on a regular basis throughout the year. Ample free coach parking, shelters, seating and hard surface pathways. Driver facilities vouchers. **Location:** 1½ miles W of town centre on B6162 Otley road. **Open:** Daily from 9.30am–6pm. **Admission:** Adults £4.50, OAPs and groups of 20+ £3.50, Children 11–16 £1.00, Children under 11 free. **Internet:** www.harlowcarr.fsnet.co.uk

map 8 C2

HORNSEA MUSEUM
11 Newbegin, Hornsea, East Yorkshire HU18 1AB
Tel: 01964 533443

Charming folk museum housed in listed Georgian farmhouse and outbuildings in the middle of small seaside town. Period rooms and comprehensive displays capture Victorian village life. Fifties and Sixties nostalgia evoked by the large collection of Hornsea Pottery. Craft days every Thursday in August. Large garden, souvenir shop. **Open:** Easter–October, Mon-Sat 11am–5pm, Sun 2–5pm. **Admission:** Small charge. Group bookings welcome all year.

HAREWOOD HOUSE
The Harewood Estate, Leeds, West Yorkshire, LS17 9LQ
Tel: 0113 218 1010 Fax: 0113 218 1002 (Earl & Countess of Harewood)

Yorkshire home of the Queen's cousin, the Earl of Harewood. Stunning architecture; exquisite Adam interiors; outstanding collections of Chippendale furniture including the newly restored State Bed on permanent display; Renaissance masterpieces; Turner watercolours and fine porcelain; beautiful gardens and 'Capability' Brown landscape; popular lakeside Bird Garden. **Location:** A61, between Leeds and Harrogate. **Open:** 14 March- 4 November, daily. Grounds & Bird Garden: 10am. House: 11am, last admissions 4pm. **Admission:** Adult £7.50, OAP £6.75, Children £5, Family £26. **Events/Exhibitions:** Guided tours, wide variety of outdoor and inside events. Telephone for details. **E-mail:** business@harewood.org **Internet:** www.harewood.org

map 8 C2

HOVINGHAM HALL

Hovingham, York, North Yorkshire YO62 4LU
Tel: 01653 628206 Fax: 01653 628668 (Sir Marcus Worsley)

Palladian House built c.1760 by Thomas Worsley to his own design. Unique entry by huge riding school. Visitors see family portraits and rooms in everyday use; also the extensive garden with magnificent yew hedges and dove-cot and the private cricket ground, said to be the oldest in England. **Location:** 18 miles N of York on Malton/Helmsley Road (B1257). **Open:** Open for parties of 15 or more **by written appointment only** Apr–end Sept 2001. Tues, Wed and Thurs 11–7pm. **Admission:** £4, Children £2. **Refreshments:** At the Hall by arrangement. Meals at the Worsley Arms Hotel, Hovingham. **E-mail:** office@hovingham.co.uk

map 8 D1

KIRKLEATHAM MUSEUM
Kirkleatham, Redcar, TS10 5NW
Tel: 01642 479500, Fax: 01642 474199

In 2001 the Museums Service for Redcar & Cleveland Borough celebrates the 20th Birthday of its accommodation in the early 18th century Old Hall. Collections include: natural history; archaeology: domestic and working life (ironstone mining; iron and steel making; ship building; sea rescue; fishing and shipping) photographs; paintings and drawing; costume and textiles. 'Permanent' displays plus temporary exhibitions. Associated activities and events, including "Meccano" & "Tudors" (Jan-Apr); "Our Century" (from July); "Sir James Knott" Lifeboat (Jun-Aug); Kirkleatham Rally (11-12 Aug) .Full programme upon request. Also responsible for Margrove Heritage Centre. **Admission:** Free. **Open:** Apr-Sep Tues-Sun 10am-5pm. Jan-Mar & Oct-Dec Tues-Sun 10am-4pm. (Closed Mon except Bank Holidays)

map 11 J5

LEDSTON HALL

Hall Lane, Ledston, Castleford, WF10 2BB, West Yorkshire
Tel: 01423 523 423 Fax: 01423 521 373 (G. H. H. Wheler)

17th century mansion with some earlier work. **Location:** 2 miles N of Castleford, off A656. **Station(s):** Castleford (2 ¾ miles). **Open:** Exterior only: May–Aug, Mon–Fri, 9–4pm. Other days by appointment. **Refreshments:** Chequers Inn, Ledsham (1 mile).

map 8 D3

LEEDS MUSEUMS AND GALLERIES
The vibrant city of Leeds and its surrounding countryside are home to a number of exciting attractions which reflect a long cultural and industrial heritage:

Armley Mills Museum

Kirkstall Abbey

Abbey House Museum

Leeds City Art Gallery

Thwaite Mills

The Leeds Museum Resource Centre

Temple Newsam

Lotherton Hall

For further information, please phone 0113 2477241.
FOR FULL DETAILS, PLEASE SEE PAGES 218-219.

LEEDS MUSEUMS AND GALLERIES

For further information, please phone 0113 2477241.

The vibrant city of Leeds and its surrounding countryside are home to a number of exciting attractions which reflect a long cultural and industrial heritage. **Armley Mills Museum** *Canal Road, Armley* is one of the world's largest woollen mills, once powered by the River Aire, which flows around the island upon which it stands. **Kirkstall Abbey** *Kirkstall Road, Leeds* is a fine monastic ruin, dating back to 1152. At the adjoining **Abbey House Museum**, visitors can experience life in the 1880s along its three traditional shopping streets and newly refurbished galleries. **Leeds City Art Gallery** *The Headrow, Leeds* houses a fine collection of Victorian paintings, early English watercolours and 20th century British paintings and sculpture. At **Thwaite Mills'** *Thwaite Lane, Stourton Leeds* working watermill, visitors can witness the power of the River Aire whose waters drive its massive wheel. **The Leeds Museum Resource Centre** *1 Moorfield Rd, Yeadon* is a multi-media resource centre, providing exciting ways to access the extensive museum collections. **Temple Newsam** *Leeds.* House is a magnificent Tudor-Jacobean House where Old-Master paintings, antique furniture silver and ceramics are part of its exquisite décor. **Lotherton Hall** *Aberford,* is a beautiful Edwardian country house, whose interior features impressive collections of period furniture, silverware, pottery, fine porcelain, paintings and sculpture, as well as examples of period costume. All attractions are open from Tuesday to Saturday 10-5 and on Sundays 1-5pm, except Leeds City Art Gallery which is also open on Mondays, and until 8pm on Wednesdays, and the Leeds Museum Resource Centre, which is open Mon-Fri 10-4 by appointment.

map 8
C3

MIDDLEHAM CASTLE
Tel: 01969 623899
(English Heritage)

Climb the battlements to admire the magnificent views once enjoyed by Richard III. Middleham was his home, but the castle dates back to 400 years before his time to a Norman earthwork castle - some of the ruins can still be seen. The existing castle was built in the 12th century, but Middleham reached its heyday in the 15th century when it was home to some of the greatest lords of the day. Admire the massive keep, one of the biggest in England. **Location:** By car: In Middleham, 2 miles S of Leyburn on A6108. By bus: Tel 0345 124125. **Open:** All year, 1 Apr–30 Sept daily, 10am–6pm. 1–31 Oct daily, 10am–5pm. 1 Nov–28 Mar Wed–Sun, 10am–4pm. Closed 24–26 Dec & 1 Jan. Closed 1–2pm in winter. Tel 01969 623899. **Admission:** Adults £2.40, Concessions £1.80, Children £1.20, under 5 yrs free. 15% discount on groups of 11 or more. **Internet:** www.english-heritage.org.uk

map 8
B1

MILLENNIUM GALLERIES
101 Norfolk Street, Sheffield, South Yorkshire
Tel: 0114 2782610 Fax: 0114 2782604 (Sheffield Galleries & Museums Trust)

Opening in April 2001, the Millennium Galleries will be a major cultural attraction for visitors to Sheffield. See major touring exhibitions from Britain and abroad of visual art, craft and design alongside displays from the city's own collections. Reflect on art and nature in the Ruskin Gallery, which displays an original collection gathered by John Ruskin of paintings, drawings, architectural artefacts, rocks and minerals. Find out how Sheffield became the international centre for metalwork and see an amazing range of beautiful and unusual pieces made in Sheffield in the metalwork gallery. **Open:** From April 2001, 7 days a week, throughout the year. Extensive facilities for visitors include a café, gallery shop, an educational centre and facilities for corporate events and seminars. More information on exhibitions and opening times: **Tel:** 0114 2782610 **E-mail:** info@sheffieldgalleries.org.uk **Internet:** www. sheffieldgalleries.org.uk

map 8
C4

NEWBURGH PRIORY
Coxwold, York, North Yorkshire, YO6 4AS
Tel: 01347 868 435 (Sir George Wombwell, Bt.)

One of the North's most interesting historic houses. Originally built in 1145 with alterations in 1568 and 1720–1760, the Priory has been the home of one family and its descendants since 1538. The house contains the tomb of Oliver Cromwell (his third daughter, Mary, was married to Viscount Fauconberg, the owner from 1647–1700). In the grounds there is a really beautiful water garden full of rare alpines, other plants and rhododendrons. **Location:** 5 miles from Easingwold, off A19, 9 miles from Thirsk. **Open: House & Grounds:** 1 Apr–27 June, Sun & Wed & Bank Hol Mons Easter and May Bank Hol, Mons. House open 2.30–4.45pm. Grounds open 2–6pm. Open at other times for parties of 25+ by appointment with the Administrator. **Admission:** House & Grounds: Adults £4, Children £1. Grounds only: Adults £2, Children free. **Refreshments:** Afternoon tea is served in the original Old Priory Kitchens.

map 8
D1

NATIONAL RAILWAY MUSEUM
Leeman Road, York, YO26 4XJ
Tel: 01904 621 261 Fax: 01904 611 112

There's only one place that contains enough amazing facts, sights, sounds and experiences for a great day out. It's the world's biggest railway museum – now with a new £4 million wing. From Royal carriages and giant steam engines to Eurostar and miniature railway rides, rail travel is brought dramatically to life with interactive displays and lavish exhibitions. Discover it all in one fun-packed family day. Nowwhere tells the story of the train better than the National Railway Museum. Open: Mon-Sun, 10am-6pm, Closed 24-26 Dec. **Admission:** Adult £6.50, Conc £4, Children (16 and under) and over 60s free.
Internet: www.nrm.org.uk

NUNNINGTON HALL
Nunnington, York, North Yorkshire YO62 5UY
Tel: 01439 748283 Fax: 01439 748284

The sheltered walled garden on the bank of the River Rye with its delightful mixed borders, orchards of traditional Ryedale fruit varieties and spring flowering meadows complements this mellow 17th-century manor house. From the magnificent oak-panelled hall, follow three staircases to discover family rooms, the nursery, the haunted room and the attics with their fascinating Carlisle collection of miniature rooms fully furnished to reflect different periods. **Open:** 31 Mar–4 Nov: daily except Mon and Tues (but open BH); 1 Jun–31 Aug: daily except Mon (but open BH); Times: Apr & Oct 1–4.30pm; 1 May–end Sept 1.30–5pm. **Admission:** Adult £4.50, Child £2, Family £11 (2 adults and up to 3 children). Garden: Adult £2, Children free. Group Rate: £4 per person (minimum 15 paying). **Tearooms:** Seating 72, plus 60 in the Tea Garden. Not licensed. Open 12.30–5pm.

NORMANBY HALL
Normanby, Scunthorpe, North Lincolnshire, DN15 9HU
Tel: 01724 720588 Fax: 01724 721248 (North Lincolnshire Council)

The restored working Victorian Walled Garden is growing produce for the 'big house', as it would have been done 100 years ago. Victorian varieties of fruit and vegetables are grown using organic and Victorian techniques. Set in 300 acres of park, visitors can also see the Regency Mansion, designed by Sir Robert Smirke, which the Garden was built to serve. The rooms of the Hall are displayed in styles depicting the Regency, Victorian and Edwardian eras. Costume galleries and farming museum. **Location:** OS Ref. SE886 166. 4 miles North of Scunthorpe off B1430. Tours by arrangement. **Open:** Hall & Farming Museum: 26 Mar–30 Sept daily, 1–5pm. Park: All year daily, 9am–dusk. Walled Garden: All year daily, 10.30am–5pm (4pm winter). **Admission:** Summer Season: Adult £2.90, Conc £1.90, Family ticket (2 adults, 3 children) £8, discount for North Lincolnshire residents. Winter Season £2.20 per car.

NOSTELL PRIORY
Wakefield, West Yorkshire, WF4 1QE
Tel: 01924 863892Fax: 01924 865282

Welcome to Nostell Priory, one of Yorkshire's finest jewels. Built in 1733, the house is by James Paine. The State Rooms were later completed by Robert Adam, and are magnificent examples of 18th century interior style. See the internationally renowned collection of Chippendale furniture, designed and made exclusively for Nostell. Other treasures include an outstanding art collection. The grounds are delightful, with a stunning collection of rhododendrons and azaleas in late spring. **Open:** 31 Mar–4 Nov Wed–Sun & BH Mon 1–5.30pm. 10 Nov–9 Dec Sat & Sun 12–4.30pm. Grounds open same days as house 11am–6pm. **Admission:** House & Gardens: Adult £4.50, Child £2.20, Family £11. Grounds only: Adult £2.50, Child £1.20, no family garden ticket available. Guided tours for booked parties outside normal hours, minimum charge £250.

NORTON CONYERS

Ripon, North Yorkshire, HG4 5EQ

Tel & Fax: 01765 640333 E-mail: norton.conyers@ripon.org (Sir James and Lady Graham)

Visited by Charlotte Brontë, Norton Conyers is an original of 'Thornfield Hall' in 'Jane Eyre' and a family legend was an inspiration for the mad Mrs Rochester. Another visitor was James II when Duke of York, in 1679. The room and the bed he and his wife traditionally used are still to be seen. 377 years of occupation by the Grahams (they bought it in 1624) have given the house a noticeably friendly atmosphere. Family portraits, furniture, ceramics and costumes. The paintings in the Great Hall include a celebrated John Ferneley, 'The Quorn Hunt', painted in 1822. The 18th century walled garden, with Orangery and herbaceous borders, includes a plant sales area, specialising in unusual hardy plants. Pick your own fruit in season; please check beforehand. **Location:** Near Wath, 4 miles N of Ripon, 3 miles from A1. **Open:** House and garden: Easter Sunday and Monday:Bank Hol Suns and Mons: Suns 13 May–9 Sept: daily 9-14 July. The house is open 2–5pm, the garden 11.30–5pm. **Admission:** Adults £4, Children (10–16) and OAPs £3: reduced rate for 2 or more children. Prices for parties on application. Garden is free (donations welcome); a charge is, however, made at charity openings. **Refreshments:** Teas are available at garden charity openings. Dogs (except guide dogs) in grounds and garden only and must be on a lead. Photography by owners' written permission only. No high-heeled shoes in house, please. Wheelchair access ground floor only.

map 8
C1

PLUMPTON ROCKS

Plumpton, Knaresborough, North Yorkshire HG5 8NA

Tel: 01423 863950 (Edward de Plumpton Hunter)

Owned by the Plumpton Family for over 750 years. This Grade 2★ listed garden extends to over 30 acres and includes an idyllic lake, dramatic Millstone Grit rock formations, romantic woodland walks winding through bluebells and rhododendrons. Declared by English Heritage to be of outstanding interest. Painted by Turner, Girtin and Hodges. Used in numerous television productions including Emmerdale Farm, Heartbeat and the Muppet Show. Described by Queen Mary as 'Heaven on Earth'. **Location:** Situated midway between Harrogate and Wetherby on the A661 one mile south east of that road's junction with the Harrogate Southern Bypass A658. **Open:** March–Oct: Sat, Sun and Bank Holidays 11–6pm. **Admission:** Adults £1.50, Children and Senior Citizens £1.

map 8
C2

RIEVAULX TERRACE & TEMPLE

Rievaulx, Helmsley, York, YO6 5LJ

Tel: 01439 748283 Fax: 01439 748284

A ½-mile-long grass-covered terrace and adjoining woodlands with vistas over Rievaulx Abbey (English Heritage) and Rye Valley to Ryedale and the Hambleton Hills. There are two mid-18th-century temples: the Ionic Temples has elaborate ceiling paintings and fine 18th-century furniture. **Note:** No access to Rievaulx Abbey from Terrace. No access to property Nov–end of March. **Open:** 31 Mar–4 Nov. Apr & Oct: daily 10.30am–4pm. Mar–Sept: daily 10.30am–5pm. Open Good Friday and Bank Holiday Mondays. **Admission:** Adult £3.30, Child £1.50, Family £8 (2 adults and up to 3 children). Group Rate: £2 per person (minimum of 15 paying). **Refreshments:** Ice cream only. Teas at Nunnington Hall 8m (see entry for Nunnington Hall).

map 8
D1

RICHMOND CASTLE

Tel: 01748 822493

(English Heritage)

Overlooking the River Swale and market town of Richmond, the views from the 30-metre high keep are simply stunning. Imagine the power of those who held this great stronghold and once palatial residence. Built by William the Conqueror to subdue the rebellious North, it is a delight to explore. Discover this dramatic history first hand. Take the pretty riverside walk to Easby Abbey, where romantic ruins cast an atmospheric spell. Look out for the new gift shop and exciting new exhibition 'Richmond: Castle, Commerce and Conscience'. **Open:** All year, 1 Apr–30 Sept daily, 10am–6pm. 1–31 Oct daily, 10am–5pm. 1 Nov–31 Mar daily, 10am–4pm. Closed 24–26 Dec & 1 Jan. Closed 1–2pm in winter. **Admission:** Adults £2.70, Concessions £2, Children £1.40, under 5 yrs free. 15% discount on groups of 11 or more. **Internet:** www.english-heritage.org.uk

map 8
C1

ROTHERHAM MUSEUMS AND ARTS SERVICE
YORK & LANCASTER REGIMENTAL MUSEUM

Central Library & Arts Centre, Walker Place, Rotherham S65 1JH
Tel: 01709 823635 Fax: 01709 823631

The displays cover the story of the Regiment and of the men who served during its 200 year history. The extensive Regimental archive is housed at the Museum and can be viewed by appointment. **Open:** Mon–Sat 9.30–5pm. Closed Sun & Bank Holidays. **Admission:** Free to all.

CLIFTON PARK MUSEUM

Clifton Lane, Rotherham S65 2AA
Tel: 01709 823635 Fax: 01709 823631

The Museum, set in a delightful 18th century house, once the home of the iron magnate, Joshua Walker, displays the UK's finest collection of Rockingham porcelain. There are also displays of glass, furniture, local and social history. There is a programme of temporary exhibitions throughout the year and special events for children during the school holidays. Please telephone for further details. **Open:** Mon–Thurs & Sat 10–5pm. Apr–Sept: Sun 1.30–5pm. Oct–Mar: Sun 1.30–4.30pm. Closed Fri. **Admission:** Free to all.

ROTHERHAM ART GALLERY

Central Library & Arts Centre, Walker Place,
Rotherham S65 1JH
Tel: 01709 382121 Fax: 01709 823653

Exhibitions: A continuous programme of temporary exhibitions of contemporary arts and crafts by nationally and regionally known artists. Also education and holiday activities for schools and young people. **Open:** Mon–Sat 9.30–5pm. Closed Sun & BHols. **Admission:** Free to all.

map 8
C4

RIPLEY CASTLE

Ripley Castle Estate, Harrogate, North Yorkshire
Tel: 01423 770152   Fax: 01423 771745 (Sir Thomas and Lady Ingilby)

Ripley Castle has been home to the Ingilby family for twenty-six generations and Sir Thomas and Lady Ingilby together with their five children continue the tradition. The guided tours are amusing and informative, following the lives and loves of one family for over 670 years. The historic Gatehouse, 550 years old in 2000 still bears bullet marks from Cromwell's Army after the Battle of Marston Moor. The Old Tower houses splendid armour, books, panelling and a Priest's Hiding Hole. The Knight's Chamber is a remarkable Tudor room that was completed in 1555 and the original oak ceiling and wall panelling create a wonderful atmosphere of antiquity. In the Georgian wing you can appreciate the fine paintings, china, furnishings and chandeliers collected by the family over the Centuries. The extensive Victorian Walled Gardens have been transformed and are a colourful delight through every Season. In the Kitchen Gardens you can see an extensive selection of rare vegetables from the Henry Doubleday Research Association. The restored Victorian Hot Houses are home to a tropical plant collection with cacti, ferns and exotic fruits. In the Spring you can enjoy 15,000 flowering bulbs which create a blaze of colour and the National Hyacinth Collection whose scent is breathtaking. The Castle and Gardens lie at the heart of the Ripley Estate with an extensive deer park and panoramic lakes. **Open:** 10.30–3pm (Last Tour 3pm). June, July & Aug: open daily. Sept–May: Tues, Thurs, Sat & Sun. Gardens open daily 10–5pm. Groups welcome all year round by prior arrangement. **Admission:** Adults £5.50, Senior Citizens £4.50, Children (up to 16 yrs) £3, Children under 5 yrs free. **E-mail:** enquiries@riplaycastle.co.uk

map 8
C2

ROYAL ARMOURIES MUSEUM

Armouries Drive, Leeds, Yorkshire LS10 1LT
Tel: 0113 220 1916 Fax: 0113 220 1955

8000 spectacular exhibits spanning over 3000 years, in stunning surroundings, make this world famous collection of arms and armour a must-see attraction. Experience an exciting combination of breathtaking displays, costumed demonstrations, live action events, entertaining films, interactive technology and thrilling exhibitions. There really is something for everybody with five magnificent themed galleries. You'll marvel at priceless displays including Henry VIII's magnificent tournament armour and the awesome 16th century Mughal elephant armour. With authentic demonstrations of jousting, falconry and pollaxe combat, you are guaranteed an unforgettable day out from start to finish. **Open:** Daily from 10.30am. Closed Christmas Eve and Christmas Day. **Admission:** Adult £4.90, Child/Conc £3.90, Family £14.90. **E-mail:** enquiries@armouries.org.uk **Internet:** www.armouries.org.uk

map 8 C3

SCARBOROUGH CASTLE

Tel: 01829 260464 (English Heritage)

Steep yourself in thousands of years of history, surrounded by a dramatically beautiful coastline. The castle was built in the 12th century and came to house many important figures in history. Come and see the panoramic view from the buttressed walls of this vast stonework castle. King Richard III admired the same view. He made the port his supply base for all his warships. Admire the remains of the great rectangular keep which still stand over three storeys high. Take the free audio tour and discover the dramatic history of the castle. **Location:** East of town centre on Castle Road. Train: Scarborough Station 1 m away. Bus: Tel 01723 375463. **Open:** All year, 1 Apr–30 Sept daily, 10am–6pm (Aug 9.30am–7pm). 1–31 Oct daily, 10am–5pm. 1 Nov–28 Mar Wed–Sun, 10am–4pm. Closed 24–26 Dec & 1 Jan. Closed 1–2pm in winter. **Admission:** Adult £2.50, Conc £1.80, Child £1.20, Family Ticket £6.20, under 5 yrs free. 15% discount on groups of 11+. **Internet:** www.english-heritage.org.uk

map 11 K6

SCARBOROUGH MUSEUMS & GALLERY

c/o Londesborough Lodge, The Crescent,
Scarborough, Yorkshire YO11 2PW
Tel: Wood End Museum 01723 367326, Scarborough Art Gallery 01723 374753, Rotunda Museum 01723 374839

3 historical buildings, including the Rotunda Museum, one the finest purpose-built museums of its age. Collections feature paintings from the Victorian and Edwardian periods depicting seascapes and the town of Scarborough including works by A.Grimshaw, E.Dade, F.Mason, and H.B.Carter; archaeological finds from the world famous Star Carr; fossil and wildlife from the Heritage Coast. The programme includes temporary shows, talks and holiday activities. Spring/summer 2001: exhibitions of railway posters and paintings celebrating the North York Moors National Park. Tel. for details. **Open:** 1 Jun–30 Sept: Tues–Sun 10–5pm. 1 Oct–31 May: Hours reduced; tel. for details. **Admission:** 'S' Pass to 3 sites, Adult £3, Conc £1.50, Family £7.

map 11 K6

SHIBDEN HALL

Lister's Road, Halifax, HX3 6XG, West Yorkshire
Tel: 01422 352 246 Fax: 01422 348 440 (Calderdale M.B.C. Leisure Services)

Allow yourself to drift into 600 years of history ... a world without electricity ... where craftsmen worked in wood and iron ... a house where you sense the family has just gone out ... allowing you to enjoy a sense of the past at Shibden Hall, Halifax's Historic Home. Set in 90 acres of park, Shibden Hall provides a whole day of entertainment. **Location:** 2 km outside Halifax, on A58 Leeds Road. **Buses:** 548/549 Brighouse, 508 Leeds, 681/682 Bradford. **Open:** Mar–Nov, Mon–Sat, 10–5pm. Sun, 12–5pm. Last admission 4.30pm. Contact for winter opening hours. **Admission:** (From April 1999) Adults £2, Children £1, OAPs £1, Family Ticket £5. Group rate for pre-booked party. **Refreshments:** Tearoom. Shop, amusements, toilets, car park, disabled access.

map 8 B3

SHANDY HALL

Coxwold, York, North Yorkshire, YO61 4AD
Tel: 01347 868 465 (The Laurence Sterne Trust)

Here in 1760–1767 the witty and eccentric parson Laurence Sterne wrote 'Tristram Shandy' and 'A Sentimental Journey'. Shandy Hall was built as a timber-framed open-hall in the mid-15th century and added to by Sterne in the 18th century. Not a museum but a lived-in house where you are sure of a personal welcome. Surrounded by a walled garden full of old-fashioned roses and cottage-garden plants. Also one acre of wild garden in an old quarry. **Location:** 20 miles north of York. **Open:** 31 May–30 Sept. Wed 2–4.30pm. Sun 2.30–4.30pm. Other times by appointment. Gardens open every day 1 May–30 Sept, except Sat, 11–4.30pm. **Admission:** Adults £3.50. Garden only £2.50. Children half price. **Refreshments:** In village. **Exhibitions:** May–Sept, paintings and pots, by local artists. Unusual plants for sale.

map 8 D1

SEWERBY HALL & GARDENS

Church Lane, Sewerby, Bridlington, YO15 1EA
Tel: Estate Office:01262 673 769 Hall: 01262 677 874
(East Riding of Yorkshire Council)

Sewerby Hall and Gardens, set in 50 acres of parkland overlooking Bridlington Bay, dates back to 1715. The Georgian House, with its 19th century Orangery, is now the Museum of East Yorkshire and contains history/archaeology displays, art galleries and an Amy Johnson Room with a collection of her trophies and mementos. The grounds include the magnificent walled Old English and Rose gardens and host many events all year round. Activities for all the family include a children's zoo and play areas, golf, putting, bowls, plus woodland and clifftop walks. **Location:** Bridlington, 2m NE. **Station:** Bridlington (2.5 miles). **Open:** Hall: 17 Feb–27 Mar, Sat–Tue 11-4pm;31 Mar–28 Oct, Daily 10-6pm; 29 Oct–23 Dec, Sat–Tue 11-4pm. Gardens and zoo open throughout the year. **Refreshments:** Traditional tearooms.

map 9 F2

SKIDBY WINDMILL

The Museum of East Riding Rural Life, Skidby, Cottingham
HU16 5TF
Tel: 01482 848405 Fax: 848432

Built in 1821, Skidby Windmill has been grinding grain almost continuously for nearly two centuries! The Wolds were the "bread basket" of Yorkshire, and in the 19th Century, over 200 windmills dominated the landscape. By 1900, most of these had fallen into decay ... now only Skidby remains, still producing its own wholemeal flour. The mill buildings house the recently redisplayed Museum of East Riding Rural Life. The new galleries bring the farming and village communities of the last hundred years evocatively to life, telling the story of the rural East Riding through the voices of the people themselves. **Open:** 10-5pm at weekends & B.H.(except Christmas and New Year); Wed-Sun during summer holidays. **Admission:** Adult £1.50, Child £0.50, Conc £0.80.

map 8 E3

SKIPTON CASTLE

Skipton, North Yorkshire BD23 1AQ
Tel: 01756 792442 Fax 01756 796100

For over 900 years Skipton Castle has survived wars and sieges. Once home of the famous Clifford Lords, it is one of the best preserved and most complete medieval castles in England. Fully roofed, it is a fascinating and delightful place to explore - from the atmospheric Dungeon to the great Watch Tower, from the beautiful Conduit Court to the ancient Chapel. **Location:** Centre of Skipton. **Open:** Daily, 10am (Sun 12noon). Last admission at 6pm (Oct-Feb, 4pm). Closed Christmas Day. **Admission:** Adults £4.40, Children (5–17) £2.20, Children (under 5) free, OAPs and Students £3.80. Family ticket: 2 adults & up to 3 children £11.90. Free tour sheets available in 8 languages. Guides are provided for pre-booked parties at no extra charge. Large car & coach park off nearby High Street. **Internet:** www.skiptoncastle.co.uk

map 8 B2

SION HILL HALL

Kirby Wiske, Nr Thirsk, North Yorkshire YO7 4EU
Tel: 01845 587206 Fax: 01845 587486 (H.W. Mawer Trust)

Sion Hill Hall was designed in 1912 by the renowned York architect Walter H Brierley, 'The Lutyens of the North'. With its fine lines, unique character and superb layout, the house was designated by the Royal Institue of British Architects as being of 'Outstanding Architectural Merit'. This accolade was given to Sion Hill as one of the best houses to be constructed before the Great War. The Hall contains the HW Mawer collection of fine antique furniture, porcelain, paintings and clocks all in superb room settings. **Guided Tours:** Min group size 20. Apr–Sept: £5.75 per person. **Open:** 13, 15, 16, 22 & 29 Apr, May–end Sept: Wed, Thurs & Sun 1–5pm. Last entry 4pm. Open BH Mons. **Admission:** Adult £4.50, Conc £4, Child (12–16) £2, accomp child under 12 free. **E-mail:** enquiries.sionhall@virgin.net **Internet:** www.sionhillhall.co.uk

map 8 C1

SWALEDALE FOLK MUSEUM

The Green, Reeth, Near Richmond,
North Yorkshire DL11 6QT
Tel: 01748 884373

Depicts how leadmining and sheep farming shaped family and social life in this remote and beautiful Dale. **Opening Times:** Easter–31 October: Daily 10.30-5pm and other months by arrangement. **Admission:** Fee charged. **Location:** Reeth Green (Parking available). **Refreshments:** Available on Reeth Green.

map 8 B1

SUTTON PARK
Sutton–on–the–Forest, York YO61 1DP
Tel: 01347 810249/811239 Fax: 01347 811251 (Sir Reginald & Lady Sheffield)

The prettiest house & gardens in Yorkshire. Sutton Park is a charming example of early Georgian architecture with a warm lived-in feeling. Plasterwork by Cortese, fine paintings, lovely 18th century furniture, important collection of porcelain. Award–winning GARDENS. Herbaceous and rose borders full of interesting plants. Georgian Ice House, and Nature Trail. **Open:** House: Every Sun & Weds 1 Apr–30 Sep; 1:30-5pm.Good Fri–Easter Mon 13–16 Apr & all BH Mons 1.30–5pm. Coach Parties to book please. Private parties by appt. Gardens: Daily 1 Apr–end Sep. 11–5pm. **Admission:** House & Garden: Adults £5, OAPs/Students £4, Children £2.50, Coaches £4.50pp. Garden only: Adults £2.50, OAPs £2, Children 50p. Private parties £5.50pp. Tearooms open on House open days & Booked Parties 12–5pm. Disabled access grounds only. **E-mail:** suttonpark@fsbdial.co.uk **Internet:** www.statelyhome.co.uk

map 11 J7

THE SUE RYDER HOME, HICKLETON HALL
Hickleton, Doncaster DN5 7BB
Tel: 01709 892070

The Home cares for 20 elderly residents and 33 disabled patients (from 40 years and above). This fine Georgian Mansion built in the 1740's, to a design by James Paine, is set in 12 acres of formal garden. The present garden design is by Inigo Thomas c 1866–1950 and laid out in the early 1900's. **Location:** 6 miles west of Doncaster on the A635 Doncaster/Barnsley Road. **Open:** Individuals wishing to visit Hickleton Hall and Gardens may do so, Mon–Fri 2–4pm with prior arrangement. **Refreshments:** Hotels and restaurants in Doncaster.

map 8 D7

ST WILLIAM'S COLLEGE
5 College Street, York, Yorkshire YO1 2JF
Tel: 01904 557233

A timbered fifteenth-century building, originally the home of the chantry priests of York Minster. After the dissolution of the monasteries the college was sold and allowed to fall into disrepair, but its former glory was restored in the early part of this century. Three mediaeval halls are open to the public, and can also be hired for functions. Please call for further information.

TREASURER'S HOUSE
Minster Yard, York, YO1 7JH
Tel: 01904 624247 Fax: 01904 647372

The peaceful surrounds of Minster Close are the setting for this fine house, which contains a collection of furniture and paintings. **Open:** 31 Mar-31 Oct, daily except Fridays, 11am-5pm. **Admission:** Adult £3.70, Child £2, Family £9.50.

STUDLEY ROYAL WATER GARDEN & FOUNTAINS ABBEY
Fountains, Ripon, HG4 3DY
Tel: 01765 608888

A UNESCO World Heritage site, with the ruins of a twelfth-century abbey, an Elizabethan mansion, and a beautiful Georgian water garden set in a mediaeval deer park. **Open:** All year round. Apr-Sept, daily 10am-7pm. Closes at 5pm during remaining months. Also closed 24-25 Dec, and Fridays Nov-Jan. **Admission:** Adult £4.50, Child £2.30, Family £11.00

TEMPLE NEWSAM HOUSE
Temple Newsam, Leeds, West Yorkshire LS15 0AE
Tel: 01132 647321 Fax: 01132 602285

A splendid Tudor-Jacobean house set in over one thousand acres of parkland. Thirty rooms are open to the public, and contain a number of important paintings, along with Chippendale furniture and de Lamarie silverware. **Open:** 1 Apr-31 Oct, Tues-Sat 10am-5pm. Sun 1pm-5pm, 1 Nov-31 Dec & Mar, Tues-Sat 10am-4pm. Sun 1-4pm. **Admission:** Adult £2, Child 50p, Conc £1.

THACKRAY MEDICAL MUSEUM
Beckett Street, Leeds, West Yorkshire LS9 7LN
Tel: 0113 244 4343 Fax: 0113 247 0219

This award-winning museum, offers interest and excitement for all. Experience the drama of life and medicine through the ages with interactive exhibitions that will literally have you in stitches. Walk through the slums of Victorian Leeds and see for yourself why life expectancy was only 40 years. Choose a character and discover how they lived and how they treated their ailments, help Mrs Hirst with her 12th child and try changing a nappy. How does your body work? In 'Bodyworks' we'll pull you to pieces and show you how! With help from Sherlock Bones, our body detective, see how the skin keeps you in and explore the giant gut. Finish off in the café and see how a drink goes down. **Open:** Tuesday-Sunday and Holiday Mondays 10-5pm. Last admission 3pm. **Admission:** Tel: 0113 245 7084 for charges.

map 8 C3

THORP PERROW ARBORETUM
Bedale, North Yorkshire DL8 2PR
Tel: 01677 425 323 Fax: 01677 425 323 (Sir John Ropner, Bt.)

The 85-acre Arboretum contains one of the largest and rarest collection of trees and shrubs in England. This peaceful haven is a treasure trove of specimen trees and woodland walks embracing a 16c Pinetum and a medieval 16c Spring Wood, and holds 3 National Collections – ash, lime and walnut. Spring sees thousands of naturalised daffodils and spring flowering plants, followed with blossom, bluebells and wild flowers. Autumn foliage provides dramatic effects and stunning colours. **The Falcons of Thorp Perrow** is a captive breeding and conservation centre giving visitors the opportunity to learn more about birds of prey. **Open:** Arboretum: All year, dawn to dusk. **Falcons:** Mar–end Nov 10.30am–5.30pm. **Admission:** (Groups of 20+) Please contact Arboretum Office. **E-mail:** louise@thorpperrow.freeserve.co.uk **Internet:** www.thorpperrow.com

map 8 C1

WAKEFIELD ART GALLERY
Wentworth Terrace, Wakefield, West Yorkshire WF1 3QW
Tel: 01924 305796 Fax: 01924 305770

Large and significant collection of works by locally born sculptors and international artists Henry Moore and Barbara Hepworth. Many of their most famous works reside in the gallery and outside in the gardens. There is also a good collection of other artists from the 20th century including Hitchens, Gore and Spencer Roberts. Set in a Victorian house in a leafy suburb of Wakefield, the Gallery provides a relaxing setting to view and enjoy these art works. Regular talks and activities take place. **Open:** Tues–Sat 10.30–4.30, Sun 2–4.30, closed Mondays. **Admission:** Free. Gift shop. Sorry we regret no wheelchair access. Closed Mondays. **Internet:** www.wakefield.gov.uk/community/museums&arts

map 8 C3

WAKEFIELD MUSEUM
Wood Street, Wakefield, West Yorkshire WF1 2EW
Tel: 01924 305351 Fax: 01924 305353

Refurbished early in 2000, features include a Charles Waterton collection. Waterton was an explorer, naturalist and eccentric who turned the grounds of his home into the worlds 1st nature reserve. Interactive displays help you discover the journey through the rainforest and the exotic species he brought back and preserved. Also The Story of Wakefield: from the earliest settlers through to the Romans, the battles of the Civil War and Sandal Castle. Life in Victorian Times is explored, and the story concludes around the 1980's miner strikes and teletubbies. There are over 8,000 digitised photos to view. **Open** Monday-Saturday 10.30-4.30pm. Sunday 2-4.30pm. **Admission:** Free. **Facilities:** Gift shop, fully accessible. **Internet:** www.wakefield.gov.uk

 map 8 C3

YORKSHIRE GARDEN WORLD
Main Road, West Haddlesey, Nr. Selby
N.Yorkshire Yo8 8QA
Tel/Fax: 01757 228279

Set in a 6 acre site, YGW is an organic plants & gardens centre specialising in herbs, wild flowers, heathers, conifers, cottage garden plants and evergreens. Over 17 different and unusual gardens: santolina & rose, lover's garden, knot garden, zodiac wheel, pygmy pinetum, owl maze, perennial, aromatherapy, open-air herb museum, winter garden, water garden and many others. See website for more info. Tea-room with home-baking, pets corner, and gift shop. Location: 6 miles S of Selby, off A19 turning off at Chapel Haddlesey/West Haddlesey crossroads. **Open:** Tues–Sat 9.30am–5.30pm, Sun & B.H.Mons 10am–5pm. **Admission:** Adult £2, Child, OAP & Conc, £1, Family ticket £5. **E-mail:** carole@yorkshiregardenw.f9.co.uk **Internet:** www.yorkshiregardenw.f9.co.uk

map 8 D3

Yorkshire's Great Houses, Castles & Gardens

Explore Yorkshire's Heritage

Yorkshire's Great Houses, Castles & Gardens are a consortium of over 40 fine houses, castles, abbeys and gardens in Yorkshire that are open to the public.

Discover the wonderfully rich and varied heritage of this rewarding area. Grand stately homes, elegant country houses, majestic castles, stunning abbeys and exquisite gardens all of which lie waiting to be explored. Many of the properties house unrivalled collections of art and furniture that were often gathered during their

owners' Grand Tour of Europe. These enchanting objects are still a source of wonder for the modern day visitor and will continue to delight for generations to come.

The architecture of these great buildings is complemented further by the beauty of Yorkshire's famous gardens and landscapes. Those seeking peace and tranquillity will surely find it here.

Below is a list of Yorkshire's Great Houses, Castles & Gardens, some of which are featured in this guide.

1 Whitby Abbey (EH)
2 Scarborough Castle (EH)
3 Sewerby Hall & Gardens
4 Burton Agnes Hall & Gardens
5 Wilberforce House
6 Brodsworth Hall & Gardens (EH)
7 Red House
8 Oakwell Hall & Country Park
9 Temple Newsam House
10 Lotherton Hall
11 Shibden Hall
12 Kirkstall Abbey (EH)
13 Harewood House
14 Brontë Parsonage Museum
15 East Riddlesden Hall (NT)
16 Harlow Carr Botanical Gardens
17 Skipton Castle
18 Ripley Castle
19 Newby Hall
20 Fountains Abbey & Studley Royal (NT)
21 Middleham Castle (EH)
22 Bolton Castle

23 Constable Burton Hall Gardens
24 Richmond Castle(EH)
25 Ormesby Hall (NT)
26 Mount Grace Priory (EH)
27 Rievaulx Terrace & Temples (NT)
27 Rievaulx Abbey (EH)
28 Helmsley Castle (EH)
28 Helmsley Walled Garden
28 Duncombe Park
29 Byland Abbey (EH)
30 Nunnington Hall (NT)
31 Pickering Castle (EH)
32 Kirkham Priory (EH)
33 Castle Howard
34 Sledmere House
35 Beningbrough Hall & Gardens (NT)
36 Cliffords Tower (EH)
36 Treasurer's House (NT)
37 Nostell Priory (NT)
38 Burton Constable Hall
39 Bolton Abbey
40 Thorp Perrow Arboretum

For your free guide, or Group Organisers Manual, to Yorkshire's Great Houses, Castles & Gardens, please telephone 01423 770152, fax 01423 771745 or e-mail: enquiries@castlesandgardens.co.uk or visit our web-site at: www.castlesandgardens.co.uk

Wales

The rugged natural beauty of the Welsh landscape continues to inspire the inhabitant and the visitor alike, and although the country is becoming an ever more popular tourist destination, it is still easy to find oneself entirely alone in unspoilt countryside.

The northern coastline is understandably popular: crystal-clear waters lap the dramatic rocky shoreline, along which are numerous pretty fishing villages. The mighty castle at Caernarfon bears witness to a tempestuous past, which has now given way to an air of tranquillity in the quiet towns of Criccieth and Porthmadog.

The mountains of Snowdonia stand just inlandm, and reward energetic walkers with incredible views over their mist-shrouded valleys. Further south, the moors are studded with limpid mountain lakes, and rocky streams tumble through the thickly wooded valleys.

Above: Marloes. Left: Harlech Castle. Bottom: Nant Gwynant

The south of Wales is more heavily populated, but here too the countryside is splendid. The area was hit particularly hard by the recent decline in coal-mining, but a programme of investment has seen a rejuvenation of Swansea and Cardiff. The Welsh have always been proud of their rich heritage of castles and national parkland, but have only recently become aware of the need to conserve their most prized possession: their language. Welsh is now firmly in fashion, and is popular with a new generation trying to re-establish their national identity in the wake of devolution. This resurgent national spirit makes Wales all the more interesting to visit.

CADW

WELSH HISTORIC MONUMENTS

The National Assembly for Wales,
Cathays Park, Cardiff CF10 3NQ
Tel: 029 2050 0200 **Fax:** 029 2082 6375
E-mail: Cadw@Wales.GSI.Gov.UK

Cadw is the executive agency within the **National Assembly for Wales** that carries out the Assembly's statutory responsibilities to protect, conserve and promote an appreciation of the historic environment of Wales.

Cadw gives grant aid for the repair or restoration of outstanding historic buildings. Usually it is a condition of grant that the owner or occupier should allow some degree of public access to the property. Conditions of grant remain in force for ten years.

Details of properties grant aided by Cadw and to which the public currently enjoys a right of access can be found on Cadw's website **www.cadw.wales.gov.uk**

This contains a wide range of information, including details of buildings and monuments in its care and, where appropriate, related public access.

Cadw encourages you to visit these properties, as well as buildings and monuments in its care.

 ## BEAUMARIS CASTLE
Beaumaris, Anglesey, Gwynedd, LL58 8AP
Enquiries Tel: 01248 810361
(Cadw: Welsh Historic Monuments)

This lovely castle overlooks the Menai Straits between Anglesey and the North Wales mainland, guarding an important medieval trade route. It was built by Edward I to complete his chain of coastal fortresses and served as Anglesey's garrison, protecting the island and its precious grain stores against invaders. The castle was ingeniously designed to use the straits' tides to both fill the defensive moat and to enable large ships to sail right up to the castle gate at high tide. The castle's picturesque setting and unusual design have drawn visitors for centuries, including Princess Victoria, later to be Queen, who visited for a Royal Eisteddfod in 1832.

map 6 C4

 ## BODNANT GARDEN
Tal Y Cafn, Nr Colwyn Bay, Conwy LL28 5RE
Tel: 01492 650460 Fax: 01492 650448 (The National Trust)

Eighty acres of magnificent garden in the beautiful Conwy Valley comprising formal lawns and borders, Italianate terraces and The Dell which contains the Wild Garden and Pinetum. Daffodils and spring bulbs in March and April; Rhododendrons, camellias and magnolias in April and May with the famous original Laburnum Arch and azaleas flowering mid May-mid June. The summer months give a colourful show of herbaceous borders, roses, hydrangeas, water lilies and climbers, which is followed by the superb autumn colours in October. **Open:** 17 Mar–4 Nov, daily 10–5pm (last adm. 4.30pm). **Admission:** Adult £5, Child £2.50. **Refreshments:** Morning coffee, light lunches and afternoon teas available from the Pavilion. Ample car and coach parking facilities.
Internet: www.oxalis.co.uk/bodnant.htm

map 6 C4

CHIRK CASTLE
Chirk, Wrexham
Tel: 01691 777701 Fax: 01691 774706 (The National Trust)

Chirk Castle is a magnificent marcher fortress close to the Welsh border, which has been lived in continuously since it was built in 1295. A dramatic dungeon was hollowed out of the rock and circular towers provide defensive viewpoints over the surrounding countryside. Chirk has elegant state rooms containing Adam style furniture, tapestries and portraits as well as excellent examples of Pugin's work. The castle gardens were voted National Trust Garden of the Year in 1999, a fragrant stroll amongst the roses, yews, flowering trees and shrubs will allow the visitor to appreciate the fine views over the surrounding countryside.

map 6 D2

  ## CAERNARFON CASTLE
Caernarfon, Gwynedd, LL55 2AY
Enquiries Tel: 01286 677617
(Cadw: Welsh Historic Monuments)

This most impressive of Edward I's Welsh defences was built near the Roman fort of Segontium, mentioned in the ancient tales of the Mabinogion. Its unique polygonal towers with decorative coloured stone bands echo the walls of the great city of Constantinople and marked the castle as a special place. Indeed, it was intended to be the official residence of the King's chief representative in the Principality and is inextricably linked with the Princes of Wales since it is the birthplace of Edward's heir, Edward Caernarfon, first English Prince of Wales. The twentieth century saw it rise again to prominence as the site of the Investiture of both this century's Princes of Wales.

map 6 C5

 ## CONWY CASTLE
Conwy, Gwynedd, LL32 8AY
Enquiries Tel: 01492 592358
(Cadw: Welsh Historic Monuments)

This finest and most complete example of a fortified town and castle was constructed after the second Welsh war of independence by Edward I, whose apartments are in the castle's Inner Ward. Edward believed in building walled towns alongside his castles to create small pockets of English dominance in Wales. The town not only housed the community needed to supply the castle, but increased local prosperity and acted as the focal point of local government. Conwy is a classic example of this philosophy, cleverly designed to have 21 "circuit-breaker" towers along the town walls which enabled defenders to isolate an attacking force and ward them off effectively.

map 6 C4

CRICCIETH CASTLE
Criccieth, Gwynedd LL52 0DP
Enquiries Tel: 01766 522227
(Cadw: Welsh Historic Monuments)

Set high on a rocky headland overlooking Cardigan Bay, this is the most striking of the castles built by the native Welsh Princes. Llewelyn the Great built the first castle here, during his long campaign against the English annexation of Wales. When his grandson, Llewelyn the Last continued the struggle, he extended and strengthened Criccieth's defences. Over a century later, during the revolt of Owain Glyn Dŵr, the rebel army was besieged in the castle, but were able to hold out due to the castle's position overlooking the sea, since provisions could be brought in by boat.

map 6 D5

CYMER ABBEY
Dolgellau, Gwynedd LL40 2HE
Enquiries Tel: 01341 422854
(Cadw: Welsh Historic Monuments)

The serene ruins stand in a lovely setting beside the River Mawddach. Even by the austere standards of the Cistercians, life must have been hard at Cymer – the abbey suffered badly during the troubled 13th century, the wars between England and Wales probably accounting for the failure to complete the original plan of the church. Cymer rewards visitors with a telling insight into the way of life of this enterprising order of monks. Particularly impressive are its great windows, arches and an unusual tower.

map 6 E4

DENBIGH CASTLE
Denbigh, Clwyd
Enquiries Tel: 01745 813385
(Cadw: Welsh Historic Monuments)

Encircling a rocky outcrop overlooking the Vale of Clwyd, Denbigh Castle is built on the site of a traditional Welsh court. At the end of Llewelyn the Last's wars of Welsh independence against Edward I, the English king gave Denbigh to his campaign commander, Henry de Lacy. Together they planned a castle and walled town similar to Edward's own fortresses along the north Welsh coast. Sadly, Henry never finished building the finely decorated gatehouse, the castle's final crowning glory, due to the death of his son in the castle well. In later years, as Denbigh passed into the hands of several powerful owners, the castle saw many famous visitors, including King Charles I.

map 6 C3

DOLWYDDELAN CASTLE
Dolwyddelan, Gwynedd
Enquiries Tel: 01690 750366
(Cadw: Welsh Historic Monuments)

Tradition claims Dolwyddelan as the birthplace of Llewelyn ap Iorwerth, Llewelyn the Great; the Prince who united Wales. However, the stone keep that now stands was probably re-built by Llewelyn to guard the road into the heart of the stronghold of Snowdonia and Gwynedd through the strategically important Lledyr Valley. The castle would also have watched over Llewelyn's precious cattle pastures, since this was a time of war when cattle were essential battle supplies that were easily moved to support hungry armies. When Edward I took the castle during the Welsh wars for independence under Llewelyn the Last, he outfitted the garrison in white snow camouflage and made some additions to the existing structure.

map 6 D4

GWYDIR CASTLE
Gwydir Castle, Llanrwst, Gwynedd.
Tel: 01492 641687 Fax: 01492 641687 (Mr and Mrs Welford)

Gwydir Castle is situated in the beautiful Conwy Valley and is set within a Grade 1 listed, 10 acre garden. Built by the illustrious Wynn family c.1500, Gwydir is a fine example of a Tudor courtyard house, incorporating re-used medieval material from the dissolved Abbey of Maenan. Further additions date from c.1600 and c.1826. The important 1640's panelled Dining Room has now been reinstated, following its repatriation from the New York Metropolitan Museum. **Location:** ½ mile W Of Llanrwst on A5106. **Open:** 1 Mar–31 Oct, daily 10–5pm. Occasional weddings on Saturdays. Limited opening at other times. **Admission:** Adults £3, Children £1.50. Guided tours & refreshments by arrangement. Group discount 10%.

map 6 C4

HARLECH CASTLE
Harlech, Gwynedd LL46 2YH
Enquiries Tel: 01766 780552
(Cadw: Welsh Historic Monuments)

Famed in song and story, Harlech is enshrined in the history of Wales. This is the "castle of lost causes" where a handful of defenders could hold off an army; a fortress which has been the last refuge for defiant, valiant men and women who have refused to compromise their principles. Built by Edward I, it had a clever channel connecting it to the sea, with a water gate and protected walkway to the castle allowing supplies to be brought in by boat. The castle was besieged in the 15th century when it was the headquarters and court of rebel leader, Owain Glyn Dŵr; and again during the Wars of the Roses when it was the last Lancastrian stronghold in Wales to fall to the Yorkists.

map 6 D4

 # ORIEL PLAS GLYN-Y-WEDDW ART GALLERY
Llanbedrog, Pwllheli, Gwynedd, North Wales, LL53 7TT
Tel: 01758 740 763 Fax: 01758 740232

Plas Glyn-y-Weddw Art Gallery is a thriving Art centre, with its own picture and print collection, and an important display of Swansea and Nantgarw porcelain. It is housed in a splendid Victorian mansion, with stained glass and hammer-beam roof, and has superb views over Cardigan Bay to Snowdonia. It also houses two celebrated sepulchral monuments of Welsh saints on the Llŷn mediaeval pilgrimage route and a historical display about the gallery. There are changing exhibitions of contemporary art throughout the year. The Gallery has full access for the disabled, and offers a popular and lively restaurant serving local food cooked on the premises. Within 5 minutes walk is a fine National Trust beach. The Arts Centre also provides residental courses throughout the year in the arts and related disciplines; courses take up to 16 residents. A brochure is available at the gallery. The gallery stages concerts and also has a civil wedding licence. **Admission:** Call for details. **Open:** Daily except Tuesdays, 11-5pm and in July and August every day. **Directions:** As you enter Llanbedrog on the A499, from Pwllheli, tourist signs direct you to bear left, past a garage, for 500 metres down a narrow road. Turn left at the end past St. Pedrog's Church towards the beach (Traeth), then right for 150 metres to the Art Gallery. Car parking is available.

E-mail: enquiry@oriel.org.net **Internet:** www.oriel.org.uk

map 6
D5

PENRHYN CASTLE
Bangor LL57 4HN
Tel: 01248 353084

Built between 1820 and 1845 for the Pennant family, this is a beautiful neo-Norman castle containing a number of museums and exhibitions. In the grounds, visitors can stroll in parkland and visit a Victorian walled garden. The Victorian kitchens have been fully restored and are now open to the public for the first time. **Open:** 28 Mar–2 Nov, daily (except Tues), 12–5pm (opens one hour earlier in Jul & Aug). **Admission:** Adult £6, Child £3.

PLAS BRONDANW GARDENS
Llanfrothen, Nr. Penrhyndeudraeth, Gwynedd, Wales.
Tel: 01766 771 136 (The Second Portmeirion Foundation)

Created by Sir Clough Williams-Ellis, architect of Portmeirion, below his ancestral home. Italian inspired gardens with spectacular mountain views, topiary and folly tower. **Location:** 2 miles north of Penrhyndeudraeth. ¼ mile off the A4085 on Croesor Road. **Open:** All year, daily, 9–5pm. **Admission:** Adults £2, Children £1.

map 6
D4

POWIS CASTLE & GARDEN
Nr Welshpool, SY21 8RF
Tel: 01938 554338 Fax: 01938 554336

Mediaeval castle overlooking a world famous garden containing rare plants and sculpted yew trees. Part Italianate and part French, the garden still houses its original lead statues, and an orangery on the terrace. **Open:** 31 Mar–4 Nov, Wed–Sun (also Tues in July & Aug). Also Bank Hol Mons 1–5pm, and 9 Nov–16 Dec, Fri–Sun, 11am–4pm. **Admission:** Adult £7.50, Child £3.75.

PLAS NEWYDD
Llanfairpwll, Anglesey, LL61 6DQ
Tel: 01248 714795 Fax: 01248 713673

An elegant 18th-century house, set in beautiful landscape with stunning views over Snowdonia. Woodland walks, Rhododendron Garden, and Australasian arboretum. **Open:** 31 Mar–31 Oct, Sat–Wed, 12–5pm. **Admission:** (Combined ticket) Adult £4.50, Child £2.25.

PLAS MAWR, CONWY
Conwy, Gwynedd LL32 8DE
Tel: 01492 580167 (Cadw: Welsh Historic Monuments)

Within the town of Conwy, best-known for its great medieval fortifications of castle and walls, hides a perfect Elizabethan jewel. Plas Mawr is the best-preserved Elizabethan town house in Britain, famous for the quality and quantity of its plasterwork decoration. Plas Mawr is a fascinating and unique place which gives visitors a chance to peek into the lives of the Tudor gentry and their servants. This was the fast moving time, when the creation of increased wealth among merchants and the gentry meant that private homes such as Plas Mawr could be decorated and furnished lavishly. Cadw gives visitors the opportunity to enjoy all of this through an audio tour which also explains the amazing process of restoration the house has been through.

map 6
C4

PORTMEIRION VILLAGE
Portmeirion, Gwynedd, Wales LL48 6ET
Tel: 01766 770000 Fax: 01766 771331

Sir Clough Williams-Ellis aimed to show at Porteirion that one could *"…develop even a very beautiful place without defiling it."* Located on the shores of Cardigan Bay in North Wales, Portmeirion has seven shops inlcuding one selling Portmeirion Pottery seconds, plus restuarants, gardens and miles of beaches. Surrounding the village are the Gwyllt woodland and gardens containing rare Himalayan flowering trees. All the houses in the village are let as part of the Portmeirion Hotel. In May 2001 Castell Deudraeth opens as a brasserie and bar surrounded by restored Victorian gardens. **Open:** The village is open every day all year round. **Location:** It is located off the A487 at Minffordd between Penrhyndeudraeth and Porthmadog. **Admission:** Adults £5, Children £2.50, Senior Citizens £4.

E-mail: info@portmeirion–village.com **Internet:** www.portmeirion.com

map 6
D4

RHUDDLAN CASTLE
Rhuddlan, Clwyd
Tel: 01745 590777
(Cadw: Welsh Historic Monuments)

One of the first castles built by Edward I in his programme to fortify the North Wales coast, a man-made channel three miles long linked Rhuddlan to the sea, giving supply ships access to the castle. This was reputed to be Queen Eleanor's favourite castle and indeed, it seems that she and King Edward spent a large amount of time here. It was in Rhuddlan that Edward made a treaty with the Welsh Lords and persuaded them to accept his baby son, recently born in Caernarfon Castle, as the Prince of Wales by promising them that their new Lord would be born in Wales, with an unblemished character and unable to speak a word of English.

map 6
C3

RUG CHAPEL & LLANGAR CHURCH
C/o Coronation Cottage, Rug, Corwen LL21 9BT
Enquiries Tel: 01490 412025
(Cadw: Welsh Historic Monuments)

Rug is a rare example of a little altered 17th century private chapel. Carved angels appear as part of an elaborate roof, decorated from end to end. The skills of local artists and wood carvers can even be seen in the bench ends, which are decorated with fantastic carvings. Nearby Llangar Church is even older. The small, idyllically located medieval building retains many ancient features, including extensive 15th century wall paintings, a 18th century figure of death, old beams, box pews, pulpit and minstrels gallery.

map 6
D3

SEGONTIUM ROMAN FORT
Beddgelert Road, Caernarfon LL55 2LN
Tel: 01286 675625

Overlooking the Menai Strait, Segontium Roman Fort can be dated back to AD77, when Cnaeus Julius Agricola completed the Roman conquest of Wales by capturing the Isle of Anglesey. Named after the nearby river of Seiont (Saint), it was without doubt one of the most important Roman garrisons at the edge of the Roman empire, and during its active lifetime was the military and administrative centre of north-west Wales. Textbook Roman military in location and layout, it was designed to accommodate a regiment of infantry up to 1000 strong. Coins recovered show that Segontium was garrisoned until about AD394. The site also has a well laid out museum run by the National Museums and Galleries of Wales, exhibiting finds made during excavation. **Open:** Apr–end Oct 10am–5pm (Mon–Sat), 2–5pm (Sun). Nov–end Mar 10am–4pm (Mon–Sat), 2–4pm (Sun). Closed 24, 25 & 26 Dec, 1 Jan. **Admission:** Small admission charge. No dogs allowed.

map 6
C5

SCHOOL OF ART GALLERY AND MUSEUM
University of Wales, Buarth Mawr, Aberystwyth, Wales SY23 1NG
Tel: 01970 622460 Fax: 01970 622461

Teaching and research collection of fine and decorative art: watercolours, drawings and European prints from 15th century to present; art in Wales since 1945; contemporary Welsh and post-war Italian photography. Changing exhibitions from the collection, touring shows and exhibitions by invited artists. Study collection by appointment. Housed in magnificent Edwardian building overlooking Cardigan Bay, just minutes walk from town centre and railway station. Contemporary British, European, American and Japanese studio pottery; 18th & 19th century Welsh and English slip ware; Swansea and Nantgarw porcelain; Art Pottery and Oriental ceramics; outstanding collection of early 20th century British pioneer studio pottery displayed in the University's Arts Centre. **Open:** Mon–Fri 10am–5.30pm. **Admission:** Free. **E-mail:** neh@aber.ac.uk. **Internet:** www.aber.ac.uk/museum

map 7
F4

VALLE CRUCIS ABBEY
Llangollen
Enquiries Tel: 01978 860326
(Cadw: Welsh Historic Monuments)

The Cistercian abbey founded in the 13th century, lies in green fields beneath Llangollen's deep sided mountains. Many original features remain including the glorious west front complete with richly carved doorway and a beautiful rose window. Other well preserved features include the east end of the abbey (which still overlooks the monks' original fishpond) and lovely chapter house with its striking rib-vaulted roof. Valle Crucis, the "Abbey of the Cross", is named after Eliseg's Pillar, a nearby 9th century Christian memorial cross.

map 6
D2

ABERGLASNEY GARDENS

Llangathen SA32 8QH

Tel & Fax: 01558 668998 (Aberglasney Restoration Trust)

Aberglasney is a 'garden lost in time'. Set in the beautiful Tywi Valley, Aberglasney has been an inspiration for poetry since 1477. The gardens, which are steeped in history, are destined to become one of the most enchanting in the UK. At its heart is a unique and fully restored Elizabethan and Jacobean cloister and parapet walk, giving wonderful views over the garden. Although its restoration is not yet complete, the many varied areas of the garden already contain a rich and diverse collection of plants. **Location:** Situated between Carmarthen and Llandeilo (4 miles). **Open:** Daily 1 April–31 October 2001, 10am–6pm (last entry 5pm). November 2001 –April 2002 10.30am–3pm Mon–Fri & 1st Sunday of the month.**Admission:** Adults £3.95 OAP's £3.45 Children £1.95 Under 5's Free Family (2+2) £9.85 Disabled £1.45 Season Ticket (Unlimited admission for 2 adults for 1 year) £35.00 Family Season Ticket (Unlimited admission for a family, 2+2 for 1 year) £48.00. Groups (10+) Adults £3.45 OAP's £2.95 Children £1.45 Under 5's 95p.**E-mail:** info@aberglasney.org.uk **Internet:** www.aberglasney.org

map 7
H4

BIG PIT MINING MUSEUM

Blaenafon, Torfaen

Tel: 01495 790311 Fax: 01495 7922618

At Big Pit you can visit the world beneath the hills and valleys-the disappearing world of the coal miner. At the colliery, where millions of tons of prime steam coal were mined between 1880 and 1980, you can go underground to see for yourself how generations of men and horses spent their working lives. You will be provided with helmets and caplamp. An experienced miner will escort you down the 300ft shaft by cage and guide you around the underground roadways, coalface, and stables. On the surface you can visit the original winding enginehouse, workshops and pithead baths, which now house exhibitions. Have a meal in the miners canteen and browse in a well-stocked gift shop. Hour-long underground tours run throughout the day, from 10-3:30pm. **Admission:** Call for charges and group rates.N.B. Children need to be at least 5yrs or 1 metre tall to join underground tour.

map 7
H2

 # BLAENAVON IRONWORKS

North Street, Blaenavon

Enquiries Tel: 01495 792615

(Cadw: Welsh Historic Monuments)

This site is not only one of Europe's best-preserved 18th-century ironworks, but a milestone in the history of the Industrial Revolution. Built in the 1780s, the ironworks were at the cutting edge of new technology. Visitors can still trace the entire process of production, which involved the harnessing of steam power to blow the blast furnaces, and the movement by water balance tower. The human side is represented at Stack Square, a community of small terrace dwellings built for pioneer ironworkers.

map 3
G1

 # CAERLEON ROMAN BATHS & AMPHITHEATRE

High Street, Caerleon NP6 1AE

Enquiries Tel: 01633 422518

(Cadw: Welsh Historic Monuments)

Caerleon is Britain's most fascinating and revealing Roman site. It was founded in AD75 as one of only three bases in Britain for the Roman's legionary troops. These elite soldiers enjoyed the conveniences of an entire township, complete with amphitheatre and bath house. The excavated remains of their barrack blocks – the only examples currently visible in Europe – stand in green fields near the fortress baths, a giant leisure complex equivalent to today's sports and leisure centre. The well-preserved amphitheatre, with seating for 6,000 was the setting for bloody combat involving wild beasts and gladiators.

map 7
J2

CAERPHILLY CASTLE
Caerphilly, Mid Glamorgan CF83 1JD
Enquiries Tel: 029 2088 3143
(Cadw: Welsh Historic Monuments)

The largest castle in Wales, with extensive water defences and a famous leaning tower, was built by the De Clare family to defend their territory against the armies of Llewelyn, the last Welsh Prince of Wales. The effectiveness of the finished work is proved by the fact that throughout its long and colourful history, the castle has never been taken by attackers. Due to conservation work in 1776, a large amount of the castle remains undamaged, giving visitors a fascinating insight into medieval life. During the summer reconstructions of warfare, including working replica siege engines, provide an exhilarating and entertaining day out for all the family.

map 7 J3

CAREW CASTLE & TIDAL MILL
Carew, Nr. Tenby, Pembrokeshire
Tel/Fax: 01646 651 782
(Pembrokeshire Coast National Park)

A magnificent Norman castle and later an Elizabethan residence. Royal links with Henry Tudor, setting for Great Tournament of 1507. The Mill is the only restored tidal mill in Wales. Automatic talking points explaining milling process. Special exhibition 'The Story of Milling'. **Location:** 4 miles E of Pembroke. **Station(s):** Pembroke. **Open:** April-end Oct, daily. **Admission:** Please phone for details. **E-mail:** tracy@carewcastle.pembrokeshirecoast.org.uk
Internet: www.carewcastle.pembrokeshirecoast.org.uk

map 7 H6

CARREG CENNEN CASTLE
Trapp, Dyfed SA19 6TS
Enquiries Tel: 01558 822291
(Cadw: Welsh Historic Monuments)

Spectacularly situated on a remote crag 300 feet above the River Cennen, this castle has for centuries been sought out by visitors who enjoy mystery and the dramatically picturesque. The site's origins are lost in ancient obscurity, but in the cave under the castle, which can be explored with torches, prehistoric human remains have been discovered. Other finds at the castle include Roman coins and it is believed that the existing castle is built on top of an Iron Age hill fort. The stone fortress we see today was started by a Norman knight, on top of a Welsh castle constructed by The Lord Rhys, the most famous Prince of South Wales.

map 7 H4

CASTELL COCH
Tongwynlais, Nr Cardiff, South Glamorgan CF4 7JS
Enquiries Tel: 029 2081 0101
(Cadw: Welsh Historic Monuments)

One of the most distinctive and memorable castles in Wales, this spectacular building peeks out from the treetops of a cliff towering over the Taff valley near Cardiff. The original medieval castle was rebuilt by the third Lord Bute, who spared no expense on its reconstruction and decoration. From the exterior's re-creation of a medieval fortress complete with conical-roofed towers, the amazed visitor enters the breathtaking apartments of Lord and Lady Bute. Although the castle was intended only for occasional use as a country retreat, the interior is richly and exquisitely carved and painted with scenes from fables and fantasies, all of which are immaculately preserved.

map 7 J3

CHEPSTOW CASTLE
Chepstow, Gwent NP6 5EZ
Enquiries Tel: 01291 624065
(Cadw: Welsh Historic Monuments)

It comes as quite a surprise to find a great castle in the pretty border town of Chepstow. But on a cliff overlooking the river Wye stands the earliest datable stone fortification in Britain; the great stone keep built by William the Conqueror's most trusted general. Since guarding the border was always an important task, Chepstow castle was developed and enlarged over the centuries in a series of modernisations and gives visitors the opportunity to trace centuries of history in its imposing stones. It was in use up to the Civil War and afterwards was used to keep Henry Marten under house arrest for signing the death warrant of Charles I.

map 7 J4

CRESSELLY
Kilgetty, Pembrokeshire SA68 0SP, Wales
Fax: 01646 687045 (HDR Harrison-Allen Esq.)

Home of the Allen family for 250 years. The house dates to 1770 with matching wings from 1869 and contains good plasterwork and fittings of both periods. The Allens are of particular interest for their close association to the Wedgwood family. **Location:** In the Pembrokeshire National Park, off the A4075. OS Ref SN0 606. **Open:** 28 days between May and September. Please write or fax 01646 687045 for details. **Admission:** Adults £3.50. No children under 12. Wedding receptions and functions in house or marquee for 20 to 300 persons. Dinners, private or corporate events in historic dining room. Guided tours only. Ample parking for cars (coaches by arrangement only). No dogs. Bed and breakfast and dinner by arrangement. Two double en suite with four-poster bed, single, twin and children by arrangement.

CILGERRAN CASTLE

Cilgerran, Dyfed SA13 2SF
Enquiries Tel: 01239 615007 (Cadw: Welsh Historic Monuments)

Sitting on a high, rocky crag above the meeting-point of two rivers, Cilgerran Castle has the perfect defensive position and is so spectacular that it became a popular subject for romantic artists such as Turner. The earliest castle on this site was built by a Norman lord who married Princess Nest, a famous Welsh beauty. When raiders came to assassinate her husband in his bed, Nest helped him to escape, although she and her children were kidnapped. The castle has had a long and chequered history, passing from English to Welsh hands and back again many times during the long wars for the conquest of Wales. The Castle we see today was the work of the English Marshal family, who extended and strengthened the fortress over a period of two hundred years.

map 7
G5

KIDWELLY CASTLE

Kidwelly, Dyfed SA17 5BQ
Enquiries Tel: 01554 890104
(Cadw: Welsh Historic Monuments)

Perched high above the river Gwendraeth, looking out towards Laugharne across the Taf estuary, Kidwelly's early Norman earth and timber castle could be reached by boat, making it difficult to besiege. However, The Lord Rhys, Prince of South Wales, captured and burned the castle, which did not return to Norman hands until 1244 when the construction of a stone fortress was started. Over the following centuries, the castle and its walled town passed into different hands and was added to and modernised by the Dukes of Lancaster and then by the most powerful man in early Tudor Wales, Sir Rhys ap Thomas.

map 7
H5

LAUGHARNE CASTLE

Laugharne, Dyfed
Enquiries Tel: 01994 427906 (Cadw: Welsh Historic Monuments)

Looking out over the estuary that Dylan Thomas was to make famous for its beauty, is Laugharne's "castle, brown as owls". Like its neighbours at Kidwelly and Llansteffan, Laugharne is built on the site of an early Norman earth and timber fort, and was rebuilt in stone during the Middle Ages by the local Lord, Guy de Brian. As the castle passed down through succeeding generations of the family, it was added to and strengthened. By the reign of Elizabeth I, the castle had fallen into disrepair, and it was modernised in the Tudor style by Sir John Perrot, who was tried for treason. In this century, the castle was rented out to author Richard Hughes who wrote his novel "In Hazard" in the castle's gazebo, where Dylan Thomas later wrote "Portrait of the Artist as a Young Dog".

map 7
H5

THE JUDGES LODGING

Broad Street, Presteigne, Powys
Mid Wales, LD8 2AD
Tel: 01544 260650 Fax: 01544 260652

Explore gaslit world of the Victorian judges, their servants, and felonious guests at this award-winning historic house. From the stunningly restored judge's apartments to the dingy servants' quarters below, you can wander through their gaslit world, aided by an 'eavesdropping' audiotour of voices from the past. Hear their tale, from hardworking maid, to Chairman of the Magistrates (portrayed by actor Robert Hardy). Damp cells and vast courtroom echo to the 1860's trial of a local duck thief. Totally 'hands-on' with special activities for children during holidays. **Open:** 1 Mar-31 Oct 10-6pm daily. 1 Nov-22 Dec 10-4pm, Wed-Sun. By appt. other times. **Admission:** Adult £3.75, Child/Conc £2.75, Family £11. Group rates (10+) Adult £3, Child/Conc £2.25. **Internet:** www.judgeslodging.org.uk

map 7
F2

LAMPHEY BISHOP'S PALACE

Lamphey, Nr Pembroke SA71 5NT
Enquiries Tel: 01646 672224
(Cadw: Welsh Historic Monuments)

The medieval bishops of St David's built themselves a magnificent retreat away from the worries of Church and State. Here, amongst fish ponds, fruit orchards, vegetable gardens and sweeping parklands, they could enjoy the life of country gentlemen. The palace was improved over two centuries, though it is mainly the work of Henry De Gower, bishop of St Davids from 1328 to 1347, who built the splendid Great Hall. Later additions include a Tudor chapel with a fine, five-light east window.

map 7
H6

LLANVIHANGEL COURT

Nr Abergavenny, Monmouthshire, NP7 8DH
Tel: 01873 890 217 (Mrs Julia Johnson)

A Grade 1 listed Tudor Manor of 15th century origins. Beautiful early 17th century plaster ceilings and panelling and magnificent yew staircase, leading to a bedroom where Charles I is reputed to have stayed during the Civil War. Remodelled during the 1650s by John Arnold. The main entrance overlooks 17th century terraces and steps. Unusual stables from the same period with turned wood pillars. **Location:** 4 miles north of Abergavenny on A465. **Open:** As advertised, or by appointment. **Admission:** Adults £4, Children (5–15) and OAPs £2.50.

map 7
H2

PENCARROW

Washaway, Bodmin PL30 3AG
Tel: 01208 841369 Fax: 01208 841722 (The Molesworth-St Aubyn Family)

Georgian house and listed gardens, still owned and lived in by the family. A superb collection of 18th century pictures, furniture and porcelain. Mile long drive and Ancient British Encampment. Marked walks through beautiful woodland gardens, past the great granite Victorian Rockery, Italian and American gardens, Lake and Ice House. Approximately 50 acres in all. Over 700 different rhododendrons, also an internationally known specimen conifer collection. **Open: House:** 1 Apr–14 Oct, 1.30–4.30pm (last entry), 11am from 28 May through to 27 Aug, Sun –Thurs. **Gardens:** 1 Mar–31 Oct daily, dawn to dusk. **Admission:** Adults – House & Gardens £5, Gardens only £2.50. Children – House £2.50, Gardens: children and dogs very welcome and free. Group rate 20% off. NPI National Heritage Award Winner 1997, 1998 & 1999. **E-mail:** pencarrow@aol.com **Internet:** www.pencarrow.co.uk

map 2
D5

MARGAM STONES MUSEUM
Margam Abbey, Port Talbot SA13 2TA
Tel: 029 2050 0200

Housed in a charming little building which formerly served as a school house, the collection includes examples of Christian memorials from the sub-Roman era right through to the hugely impressive 'cart wheel' crosses of the late 10th and 11th centuries. The finest monument here is the great Cross of Conbelin, an elaborately and extensively decorated disc-headed cross of the 10t century. Other notable exhibits include the 9th century Cross of Einion and a 6th century memorial with both Latin and Irish ogham inscriptions. The collection also includes a number of grave slabs from the medieval Cistercian abbey at Margam. **Open:** Last admission half an hour before closing. 1 April 30 - Sept 10am-4pm (Tues-Sun) 1 Oct - 31 March 10am-4pm (Wed-Sun). **Admission:** Adults £2, reduced rates £1.50, family £5.50 (2 adults + up to 3 children under 16). Children under 12 must be accompanied by an adult. Children under 5 free. No dogs allowed.

map 7
J4

OXWICH CASTLE
Oxwich, Nr Swansea, West Glamorgan
Enquiries Tel: 01792 390359 (Cadw: Welsh Historic Monuments)

On a headland overlooking Oxwich Bay in the beautiful Gower peninsula, stands Oxwich Castle. A Tudor mansion, rather than a medieval fortress, its impressive gatehouse emblazoned with the Mansel family's coat of arms was added more as a show of pride than for military purposes. Like many successful gentlemen, Sir Rice Mansel remodelled his ancestral home in the modern Tudor style, with his son continuing the building programme by adding a stupendous multi-storey wing during Queen Elizabeth's reign. During conservation work on the castle, a magnificent gold and jewelled brooch was discovered, which may once have been part of King Edward II's lost royal treasure. How it came to be at Oxwich remains an intriguing mystery.

map 7
J4

NATIONAL MUSEUM & GALLERY OF WALES

Cathays Park, Cardiff, Wales CF10 3NP
Tel: 029 2039 7951 Fax: 029 2037 3219

No other British museum claims such a dazzling range of displays on art, natural history and science. Visit the spectacular exhibition on the creation of Wales, complete with animated Ice Age creatures and simulated Big Bang; discover the world-class art galleries with works from Canaletto to Cezanne; experience the natural history galleries, with woodland and wildlife displays to enthrall all ages. Exhibitions/Events: A constantly changing programme of exhibitions, theatre, events and workshops. Call for details. **Open:** Tuesdays–Sundays 10–5pm. Closed Mondays except Bank Holidays, 24–25 December. **Admission:** Charge. Other Branches: South Wales: Museum of a Welsh Life St Fagans, Turner House Gallery Penarth, Roman Legionary Museum Caerleon. West & North Wales: Museum of the Welsh Woollen Industry Llandysul, Welsh Slate Museum Llanberis, Segontium Roman Museum Caernarfon.

Internet: www.nmgw.ac.uk

map 3
G2

THE NATIONAL BOTANIC GARDEN OF WALES
Middleton Hall, Llanarthne, Carmarthenshire, Wales SA32 8HG
Tel: 01558 668768 Fax: 01558 668933

The National Botanic Garden of Wales is the first national botanic garden to be created in the United Kingdom for more than two hundred years. Set in the eighteenth century parkland of the former Middleton Hall, on the edge of the Towy Valley, the Garden of Wales commands spectacular views over the surrounding Carmarthenshire countryside. This is an area rich in history and culture, famed for its gentle beauty. The Garden's creation is dedicated to horticulture, science, education and leisure driven by the vision of a twenty first century centre of international botanical significance. The centrepiece is the Great Glasshouse, designed by Norman Foster and Partners, which houses plants from the mediterranean ecosystems of the world

map 7
H4

PONTYPOOL MUSEUM
Park Buildings, Pontypool, Torfaen NP4 6JH
Tel: 01495 752036 Fax: 01495 752043 (Torfaen Museum Trust)

Pontypool Museum is housed in the Georgian stable block of Pontypool Park House, home of the Hanbury ironmasters. The industrial history of the Valley provides a trail for visitors to link with Blaenavon Ironworks and Big Pit. School visits are invited covering Key Stage 1 & 11 topics. **Open:** Daily, weekdays 10am–5pm, Sun 2pm–5pm. **Admission:** Charged. Group discounts. Free car/coach parking. Disabled facilities. Coffee & gift shop. **Location:** 20 minutes drive from M4 (J25/J26) along A4042.

map 3
G1

PENYCLAWDD COURT

Llanfihangel Crucorney, Abergavenny, Monmouthshire, NP7 7LB
Tel: 01873 890719 Fax: 01873 890848 (Julia Horton-Evans)

This Grade I listed Medieval Manor House dates from 1350 with an imposing Jacobean extension. The authentic restoration of the property has won a number of prestigious awards. The gardens, while compact, contain some fascinating features; herb and knot gardens and a maze of unique design. Abutting the gardens is a Norman Motte and Bailey, a scheduled Ancient Monument, dating from about 1070. **Location:** Approximately 4 miles north of Abergavenny, ¼ mile west of A465. **Open:** Easter–end Sept: Thur, Fri, Sat, Sun and Bank Holidays from 2pm, last entry 4pm. **Admission:** Adults £4, Concessions £3. Accommodation available. Researched Tudor Feasts (20 people). Groups and school parties by arrangement. Schools programmes based upon National Curriculum Tudor/Stuart period. No dogs at any time.

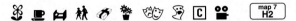
map 7 H2

PICTON CASTLE & WOODLAND GARDENS

Haverfordwest, Pembrokeshire, Wales, SA62 4AS
Tel/Fax: 01437 751 326

Built in the 13th century, home of the Philipps family, the Castle retains it external appearance but was remodelled inside, above the undercroft in the 1750's and extended around 1800. The woodland and walled gardens cover 40 acres and are part of The Royal Horticultural Society access scheme for beautiful gardens. Events include art exhibitions and spring and autumn plant sales. **Location:** OS Ref. SN011 135. 4 m E of Haverfordwest just off A40. **Open: Castle:** April–Sept. Closed Mon & Sat except Bank Hol, open all other afternoons for guided tours. **Garden & Gallery:** April–Oct. Tues–Sun inclusive. 10.30–5pm. **Admission: Castle, Garden & Gallery:** Adults £4.95, OAPs £4.75, Children £1.95. **Garden & Gallery:** Adults £3.95, OAPs £3.75, Children £1.95. Reduced prices for groups of 20 or more by prior appointment. **Internet:** www.pictoncastle.co.uk

map 7 H6

RAGLAN CASTLE

Raglan, Gwent, NP5 2BT
Enquiries Tel: 01291 690228
(Cadw: Welsh Historic Monuments)

A monument to medieval family pride, this imposing fortress-palace was built by the Herbert family. The water-moated Great Yellow Tower was built by Sir William, "The Blue Knight of Gwent", a veteran of Agincourt. His son, William Herbert continued the construction of the majority of the existing castle, using profits he made by importing French wine. William was one of the leading Yorkist supporters in the Wars of the Roses and was so well trusted by King Edward IV that he was given custody of young Henry Tudor, later King Henry VII, who was brought up at Raglan. William's loyalty as the King's right-hand man in Wales brought a string of titles and estates, but Raglan remained the family's stronghold.

map 7 H2

ST DAVIDS BISHOP'S PALACE

St Davids SA62 6PE
Enquiries Tel: 01437 720517
(Cadw: Welsh Historic Monuments)

Even in ruin, this imposing palace, standing next to St Davids Cathedral, still conveys the affluence and power of the medieval church. Largely the work of Bishop De Gower, no expense was spared in creating a grand residence fit for a major figure of both Church and State. De Gower's palace boasted two sets of state rooms ranged around a courtyard, one for his own use, the other for ceremonious entertainment. The palace is richly embellished with lavish stone carvings. Particularly fine are its arcaded parapets, decorated with chequered stonework.

map 7 G7

ST. DAVIDS CATHEDRAL

The Deanery, The Close, St. Davids, Pembrokeshire, Wales
Tel: 01437 720 199 Fax: 01437 721 885 (The Dean and Chapter)

This cathedral, begun in 1181, is at least the fourth church to have been built on a site reputed to be that on which St. David himself founded a monastic settlement in the 6th century. The outstanding features of the building are the magnificent ceilings – oak in the Nave, painted in the Choir and Presbytery – and the sloping floor. The stalls of the Chapter of the cathedral contain medieval misericords and the Chapter is unique in having the reigning Sovereign as a member. The cathedral has been an important place of pilgrimage for nearly fourteen centuries. In 1124, Pope Calixtus II declared that two pilgrimages to St. Davids were equal to one to Rome and that three were equal to one to Jerusalem itself.

map 7 G7

THE SOUTH WALES BORDERERS AND MONMOUTHSHIRE REGIMENTAL MUSEUM

The Barracks, Brecon, Powys LD3 7EB
Tel: 01874 613310 Fax: 01874 613275

Houses over 300 years of regimental history of the 24th Regiment of Foot, The South Wales Borderers and The Royal Regiment of Wales (24th/41st Foot), including the militia and volunteer units of Brecknock and Monmouthshire. The leading authority in the UK on the Zulu Wars of 1877–1879. On permanent display are guns, uniforms, equipment, paintings and war mementoes plus a large medal collection including 16 Victoria Crosses.

map 7 G3

STRATA FLORIDA ABBEY
Ystrad Meurig, Pontrhydfendigaid SY25 6BT
Enquiries Tel: 01974 831261
(Cadw: Welsh Historic Monuments)

None of the Cistercians' Welsh abbeys preserves that original spirit of remoteness more strongly than Strata Florida. There is much to captivate the visitor at this evocative, historically important site. The abbey, founded in the 12th century, grew to become a powerhouse of Welsh culture, patronised by princes and poets. Although in ruin, Strata Florida displays much evidence of its former status, including a wonderful carved doorway and beautiful medieval tiles.

map 7
F4

TECHNIQUEST
Stuart Street, Cardiff Bay, Cardiff CF10 5BW
Tel: 02920 475475 Fax: 02920 482517

Techniquest is the UK's leading Science Discovery Centre, located in spectacular waterfront premises overlooking Cardiff Bay. With 160 interactive exhibits, a Planetarium and Science Theatre, Techniquest provides a fun, but educational experience for visitors of all ages. Visit our web page for up-to-date information about special events. **E-mail:** info@techniquest.org **Internet:** www.techniquest.org

map 3
G2

TINTERN ABBEY
Tintern NP6 6SE
Enquiries Tel: 01291 689251
(Cadw: Welsh Historic Monuments)

Founded by Cistercian monks in 1131 and largely rebuilt by Roger Bigod, Lord of nearby Chepstow Castle in the 13th century, Tintern Abbey encompasses grand design and architectural detail of great finesse. The shell stands open almost to its full height, an outstanding example of the elaborate 'decorated' style of Gothic architecture. Visitors are captivated by the vast windows, with their delicate tracery and the wealth of detail on the walls, doorways and soaring archways. Tintern has inspired artists and poets like JMW Turner and William Wordsworth.

map 7
H1

TRETOWER COURT AND CASTLE
Crickhowell, Powys NP8 2RF
Enquiries Tel: 01874 730279
(Cadw: Welsh Historic Monuments)

In the quiet foothills of the Black Mountains stands a unique example of a family's building through the centuries. Alongside the castle which had protected them for 300 years, the Vaughan family built a manor house which was later extended and enlarged into a medieval mansion with elaborately timbered roofs and a galleried courtyard. During the Wars of the Roses, the house was fortified to enable the family to live there in safety. They continued to do so until the seventeenth century, when the great poet Henry Vaughan drew inspiration from his wonderfully well-preserved family home and its beautiful surroundings. Now visitors can also enjoy the re-created medieval garden that was featured in the television programme "Geoff Hamilton's Paradise Gardens."

map 7
H2

USK CASTLE
The Castle House, Usk, Monmouthshire NP15 1SD
Tel: 01291 672563 (J.H.L. Humphreys)

Romantic, ruined Norman castle overlooking the picturesque town of Usk. Inner and outer baileys, towers and earthwork defences. Surrounded by enchanting gardens (open under NGS and Usk Gardens open days) incorporating the Castle House, the former medieval gatehouse, as lived in by the current owner. **Location:** OS Ref SO 376 011, off Monmouth Road in Usk, opposite Fire Station. **Open:** Castle ruins: daily 11–5pm. Group bookings by arrangement. Gardens & House: Bank Holidays & June 2–5pm. Guided tours only. **Admission:** Castle ruins: Adults £2, Children free. House & Garden: Adults £5, Children £2.

map 3
H1

WEOBLEY CASTLE
Llanrhidian, Nr Swansea, West Glamorgan SA3 1HB
Enquiries Tel: 01792 390012
(Cadw: Welsh Historic Monuments)

This fortified manor house perches above the wild northern coast of the beautiful Gower peninsula, looking over the marshes towards the Loughor estuary. It dates from the medieval thirteenth and fourteenth centuries, a rare survivor from those wild and often troubled times. Weobley was designed to be a comfortable home for the knightly de la Bere family, but its defensive tower and turrets provided a safe shelter in times of trouble. In Tudor times, Sir Rhys ap Thomas, the most powerful man in Wales added the two-storey porch block, providing a more stately entrance to the hall and private apartments.

map 7
J5

WHITE CASTLE
Llantilio Crossenny, Gwent NP7 8UD
Enquiries Tel: 01600 780380
(Cadw: Welsh Historic Monuments)

One of a trio of castles built by the Normans to protect the route into Wales from Hereford, White Castle is the classic medieval castle. Standing on a low hill, its six towers and curtain wall are surrounded by a water-filled moat with drawbridge. It was built to house a garrison which, along with troops from Grosmont and Skenfrith castles, was responsible for the defence of the border against the rebellious Welsh. During Llewelyn the Last's attacks into the established Marcher lands of South Wales, the Three Castles were repaired and readied for war, but never saw action. After Henry Bolingbroke became King Henry IV, the castles, which were part of his Duchy of Lancaster, became the property of the Crown.

map 7
H2

TREDEGAR HOUSE & PARK

Newport, South Wales NP10 8YW
Tel: 01633 815880 Fax: 01633 815895 (Newport County Borough Council)

Set in 90 acres of award winning gardens and parkland, Tredegar House is one of the architectural wonders of Wales. For more than five hundred years it was the ancestral home of the Morgans, later Lords Tredegar. The medieval stone house, of which one wing survives, was rebuilt in brick by William Morgan between 1664 and 1672. Tredegar with its lavish interiors would be a symbol of the Morgan family wealth for the next 250 years, during which time they were a dominant influence on the political, social and economic life of the counties of Brecon, Glamorgan and Monmouth. The lavish lifestyle of the family in the 1930s and 40s saw the House sold together with its contents and the surrounding estate in 1951. For the twenty-three years it would be home to a girls' boarding school, until it was purchased in 1974 by Newport Borough Council, who embarked on an ambitious programme of restoration. Visitors to Tredegar can now discover what life was like for the Morgans 'above' stairs and their army of servants 'below' stairs in more than thirty restored rooms. **Location:** SW of Newport, signposted from M4, junction 28, A48. **Open:** From Good Friday–end Sept, Wed–Sun. Also open for special Halloween tours and leading up to Christmas. **Admission:** Adult £4.75, Concession £3.65, Child £2.25, Family (2 adults & 3 children) £12.95. Party Rates: Adult £4.50, Concession £3.25 (pre-booked only). Special Victorian tours for school parties. **Refreshments:** Available in the Brewhouse Tearoom.

Scotland

From the wild coast of the Highlands to the elegant streets of Edinburgh, and from the glassy lochs of Stirling to the majestic heights of Glen Coe, Scotland truly has something for everyone.

It is a pity that many visitors pass straight through the border counties on their way to Glasgow, Edinburgh, and the Highlands beyond, because they too boast beautiful scenery and heritage sites.

Much of Scotland's population is concentrated in the narrow strip of land running from the Firth of Clyde in the east to the Firth of Forth in the west, but the area is by no means crowded. It is still easy to find quiet little villages in forgotten

Above: Isle of Skye. Below: River Tweed. Bottom left: Culloden House Hotel. Bottom right: Mellerstain House.

corners of the countryside, where the pace of life has changed little since the nineteenth century.

The Highlands remain largely untouched by man, and are perhaps the most consistently beautiful part of the British Isles, a place where the peace of the ancient landscape is broken only by the cry of birds and the soft breath of the wind.

Borders

Borders runs from the imposing Cheviot Hills in the south to the outskirts of Edinburgh in the north, and marks the eastern boundary between England and Scotland. The peaceful Southern Uplands were not always so: a four hundred year territorial war raged here until the Union of Parliament in 1707, and a number of castles and fortified buildings tell the story of this conflict. The picturesque River Tweed rises in the south west of the county, flowing through Kelso and Coldstream on its way to the sea at Berwick. This area is famously associated with Sir Walter Scott, and it is easy to understand the inspirational effect it had on the author, for it contains some of Scotland's most attractive scenery. The verdant landscape shelters castles, abbeys, stately homes, woollen mills and a host of pretty villages. There is good fishing to be had in the Tweed and its tributaries, and the quiet country roads are ideal for cycling.

Abbotsford

AYTON CASTLE

Eyemouth, Berwickshire, Scotland, , TD14 5RD.
Tel: 018907 81212 Fax: 018907 81550
(D Liddell-Grainger of Ayton)

A Victorian castle built in red sandstone in 1846, which has been fully restored and is now lived in by the family owners. **Open:** 6 May–30 Sept: Sun, 2–5pm. At other times by appointment. **Admission:** £3, Children (under 15) free. **Events/Exhibitions:** Occasionally.

map 13 J6

BOWHILL

Selkirk, Borders TD7 5ET
Tel: 01750 22204 Fax: 01750 22204 (Buccleuch Heritage Trust)

Scottish Borders home of the Scotts of Buccleuch. Paintings by Guardi, Canaletto, Claude, Gainsborough, Reynolds and Raeburn. Superb furniture, porcelain. Monmouth, Sir Walter Scott, Queen Victoria relics. Victorian kitchen. Audiovisual. Theatre. Adventure Woodland. Nature trails. **Location:** 3 miles west of Selkirk on A708. Edinburgh, Carlisle & Newcastle approx 1.5 hrs by road. **Open:** House: 1–31 Jul, daily 1–4.30pm. Open by appointment at additional times for educational groups. Country park: 14 Apr–27 Aug daily except Fri, 12–5pm. Open on Fri in July with House. Last entry 45 mins before closing. (Heritage Education Trust, Sandford Award Winner 1993, 1998.) **Admission:** House & Country Park: Adults £4.50, Children £2, OAP & Groups £4. Wheelchair users & Children under 5 free. Country Park £2. **Refreshments:** Gift shop, tearoom. **E-mail:** bht@buccleuch.com

map 13 H6

FLOORS CASTLE
Kelso, TD5 7SF
Tel: 01573 223333 Fax: 01573 226056

Scotland's largest inhabited castle is the home of the 10th Duke & Duchess of Roxburghe and their family. It was built for the 1st Duke of Roxburghe in 1721 by the renowned William Adam and later remodelled by the Scottish architect William Playfair. Sir Walter Scott described Floors as 'a Kingdom for Oberon and Titania to dwell in'. The castle stands on a natural terrace overlooking the market town of Kelso, the River Tweed and the English Cheviot Hills. First opened to the public in 1977, it has since become one of the leading tourist attractions in the Scottish Borders receiving over 50,000 visitors each year. Floors Castle houses a magnificent collection of European and Oriental furnishings, tapestries, paintings, porcelain and a unique collection of Victorian birds. It is perhaps best known as the film location for 'Tarzan, Earl of Greystoke', starring Sir Ralph Richardson,

Andie McDowell and Christopher Lambert. The castle gardens with their colourful floral borders displays and Millennium Parterre are particularly attractive to visitors during the summer months. **Location:** N of Kelso. **Station(s):** Berwick-upon-Tweed. **Open:** 13 April–28 October daily except 1 May, 10am–4.30pm. **Admission:** Please contact for admission prices. Party rates on request. **Refreshments:** Restaurant and Café Terrace and Castle Kitchen Produce Shop. **Events/Exhibitions:** Family Fun Day with massed pipe bands on 26 Aug. **Accommodation:** At nearby Roxburghe Hotel & Golf Course. **Conferences:** Facilities available including dinners, receptions, product launches and outdoor events. Free parking, walled garden, woodland & river walks and garden centre.

map 13 J6

MANDERSTON
Duns, TD11 3PP, Berwickshire
Tel: 01361 883 450 Fax: 01361 882 010 (Lord & Lady Palmer)

Manderston, the home of Lord and Lady Palmer is an Edwardian mansion set in 56 acres of formal gardens (Scottish Borders).The only silver staircase in the world, insights into life at the turn of the century both 'upstairs' and 'downstairs'. Formal and woodland gardens, stables, Racing Room, Biscuit Tin Museum, Marble Dairy, lakeside walks. Tearoom serving cream teas on open days and gift shop. **Location:** 12 miles W of Berwick-upon-Tweed. **Open:** 10 May–30 Sept: Thurs & Sun, 2–5pm. Also Mons 28 May & 27 Aug 2–5pm. Group visits any time of year by appointment. **Admission:** Please phone 01361 883450 for details. **Refreshments:** Tearoom serving cream teas on open days. **Conferences:** Available as a corporate and location venue. **E-mail:** palmer@manderston.co.uk **Internet:** http://www.manderston.co.uk

map 13 J5/6

PAXTON HOUSE & COUNTRY PARK
Paxton, Nr Berwick upon Tweed, Scottish Borders TD15 1SZ
Tel: 01289 386291 Fax: 01289 386660 (The Paxton Trust)

Award-winning 18th century Palladian Country House built in 1758 to the design of John and James Adam for Patrick Home. The largest Picture Gallery in a Scottish Country House, an outstation for the National Galleries of Scotland plus the greatest collection of Chippendale Furniture in Scotland. 80 acres of woodland, parkland, gardens and riverside walks include picnic areas, adventure playground, croquet, children's 'nature detective trails', highland cattle, shetland ponies and an observation hide from which you can watch the red squirrels. **Location:** Just 4 miles from the A1 Berwick upon Tweed bypass. **Open:** Daily 1 Apr–31 Oct, House 11.15–5pm, last tour 4.15pm. Shops, Tearoom and Exhibitions, 10–5pm, Grounds 10–Sunset. **Admission:** Adults £5, Children £2.50. **E-mail:** info@paxtonhouse.com **Internet:** www.paxtonhouse.com

map 13 K6

PRIORWOOD GARDEN
Melrose, Borders TD6 9PX
Tel: (Melrose) 01896 822493 Shop: Tel: (Melrose) 01896 822965

Overlooked by the impressive ruins of Melrose Abbey, this is a specialist garden where most of the plants grown are suitable for drying. The colourful and imaginative selection ensures variety for the dried flower arrangements made on the premises. Visitors can enjoy a stroll through the orchard which includes historic varieties of apples that are organically grown. Priorwood is a short walk away from Harmony Garden, also in the care of The National Trust for Scotland. **Open:** 1 Apr-30 Sept, Mon-Sat 10am-5.30pm, Sun 1.30-5.30pm; 1 Oct-24 Dec, Mon-Sat 10am-4pm, Sun 1.30-4pm. NTS shop: 9 Jan-31 Mar, Mon-Sat 12-4pm; 1 Apr-24 Dec, Mon-Sat 10am-5.30pm, Sun 1.30-5.30pm. **Admission:** Adult £2, Concession £1 (honesty box). **Groups:** Please book in advance.

map 13 H6

ROBERT SMAIL'S PRINTING WORKS
High Street, Innerleithen, Perthshire, EH44 6HA
Tel: 01896 830206

Completely restored Victorian printing works, where visitors can see the presses in action. The buildings also house a Victorian office with acid-etched windows, a reconstructed waterwheel, and other items of historical interest. **Open:** 1 Mar-30 Sept, Mon-Sat 10am-1pm & 2-5pm. Sun 2-5pm. Also open at weekends in October. **Admission:** Adult £2.50, Child £1.70.

THIRLESTANE CASTLE
Lauder, Berwickshire, Scottish Borders TD2 6RU
Tel: 01578 722 430 Fax: 01578 722 761 (Thirlestane Castle Trust)

One of the seven 'Great Houses of Scotland', Thirlestane was the seat of the Earls and Duke of Lauderdale. It has unsurpassed 17th century ceilings, a restored picture collection, Maitland family treasures, historic toys and a country life exhibition. Woodland picnic tables, new adventure playground, tearoom and gift shop. **Location:** Off A68 at Lauder, 28 miles south of Edinburgh. **Open:** 1 Apr-31 Oct Daily except Sat 10.30-5pm. Last admission 4.15pm each open day. **Admission:** Adults £5.20. Family (parents and own school age children) £13. Grounds only £1.50. Party discounts available, also booked tours at other times by arrangement. Free parking. **E-mail:** admin@thirlestanecastle.co.uk. **Internet:** www.thirlestanecastle.co.uk

map 13 H6

 ## TRAQUAIR HOUSE
Innerleithen, Peeblesshire, Scotland EH44 6PW
Tel: 01896 830 323 Fax: 01896 830 639 (Ms Catherine Maxwell Stuart)

Traquair is Scotland's oldest inhabited and most romantic house, spanning over 1000 years of Scottish history. Once a pleasure ground for Scottish kings in times of peace, then a refuge for Catholic priests in times of terror, the Stuarts of Traquair supported Mary, Queen of Scots and the Jacobite cause without counting the cost. Imprisoned, tried and isolated for their beliefs, their home, untouched by time, reflects the tranquillity of their family life. In one of the 'modern' wings (completed in 1680) visitors can also see an 18th century working brewery, which was resurrected by the 20th Laird and now produces the world renowned Traquair House Ale. In the grounds there is also a brewery museum with shop, maze, craft workshops, 1745 Cottage Restaurant and extensive woodland walks. **Open:** Daily 14 April-31 Oct, 12.30-5.30pm. Jun-Aug 10.30am-5.30pm (last adm 5pm). Grounds open daily, Easter-end Oct. **Admission:** House & grounds: Adults £5.30, Children £2.80, Senior Citizens £5, Family (2 adults & 3 children) £15. Grounds only: Adults £2, Children £1. Group rate house & grounds (minimum of 20 people): Adults £4.80, Children £2.20. **E-mail:** enquiries@traquair.co.uk **Internet:** www.traquair.co.uk

map 13 H6

Dumfries & Galloway

Logan Botanic Garden, Galloway

Dumfries & Galloway is a special place - off the beaten track yet easy to reach. With over 200 miles of superb coastline and contrasting landscapes of unspooilt beauty, it's a haven for every lover of the outdoors.

The Gulf Stream sweeping across the west makes the climate milder, allowing one to enjoy the outdoors to the full. It also accounts for the profusion of glorious gardens and nurseries, filled with tropical plants and ablaze with colour all year round.

If you're a golfer, there are 32 courses to test your skills. If fishing is your fancy, there are five major salmon rivers and dozens of burns and lochs with sea trout, native brown trout or stocked rainbow trout. You can walk through wild mountains and along coasts, or pedal along some of the dozens of interesting cycle routes. Around the coast or on the many lochs one can windsurf, sail, canoe, scuba dive or just lie on a quiet beach.

Even the heavens are full of the unexpected. Rare golden eagles and peregrine falcons soar majestically over the rugged hills, while barnacle geese and waders sail over the skies of the Solway Firth. Dumfries & Galloway really is the natural place to holiday in Scotland.

ARDWELL GARDENS

Ardwell House, Ardwell, Stranraer DG9 9LY
Tel: (01776) 860 227 Fax: (01776) 860 288

The gardens surround an 18th Century country house (not open for the public) with the formal layout round the house blending into the informality of the woods and the shrubberies. In the spring, daffodils round the house and bluebells in the woods provide carpets of colour. These are fine Azaleas, camellias, rhododendrons and a walled garden with a good range of home grown plants for sale. The walk around the largest of the three ponds (approx. half an hour) gives good views over Luce Bay. **Admission:** £2, Children and Pensioners £1. There is ample free car parking. **Open:** Daily 1st April – 30th September 10 am – 5 pm. Off A 716, 10 miles south of Stranraer.

map 10
A4

BROUGHTON HOUSE AND GARDEN

12 High Street, Kirkcudbright, Dumfries & Galloway DG6 4JX
Tel/Fax: 01557 330437

This 18th-century town house was bought in 1901 by E A Hornel, the renowned artist and member of 'The Glasgow Boys'. Between 1901 and 1933 he added an art gallery and a studio overlooking the fascinating garden with Japanese influences, which leads down to the estuary of the Dee. The House still contains many of Hornel's works, paintings by other artists, an extensive collection of Scottish books and local history material. **Open:** House and garden, 1–12 Apr, 17 Apr–30 Jun and 1 Sep–31 Oct, daily 1–5.30pm; 13–16 Apr and 1 Jul–31 Aug, daily 11am–5.30pm. Last admission 4.45pm. Garden only, 24/25 Feb and 1–30 Nov, Mon–Fri 11am–4pm. **Admission:** Adult £3.50, Concession £2.50, Adult Group £3, Child/School Group £1, Family £9.50.

map 10
C4

CLACHANMORE GALLERY & TEAROOM

Ardwell, Stranraer DG9 9PQ
Tel & Fax: (01776) 860 200

The Gallery at Clachanmore near Ardwell Village is well signposted on the roads between Stranraer Drummore and Portpatrick. It is in a former Victorian school at the crossroads 1½ miles from Ardwell and Sandhead. The Playground provides a safe large car park and is also home to a number of amusing metal sculptures. There are at least four exhibitions of contemporary art in the gallery between Easter and October along with ceramics, prints and photographs all of which are for sale. Good quality tea, coffee home-baking, soups and snacks, are served in the gallery, or in the walled garden in summer. **Open:** Wed–Sun 11am – 5pm.

map 10
A4

DRUMLANRIG CASTLE

Nr. Thornhill, Dumfries & Galloway, Scotland, DG3 4AQ
Tel: 01848 330248 Fax: 01848 331682

Exquisite sandstone castle with a renowned art collection, set in beautiful landscaped gardens.

PLEASE SEE PAGE 250 FOR FULL DETAILS OF OPENING TIMES AND ADMISSION.

DUMFRIES AND GALLOWAY TOURIST BOARD

64 Whitesands, Dumfries, DG1 2RS
Tel: 01387 253862 Fax: 01387 245555

Enjoy the traditional taste of Dumfries and Galloway while in the region. Take a guided tour and enjoy a dram at Bladnoch Distillery, the most southerly in Scotland, founded in 1818, mothballed in 1994 and now distilling again in 2001. Or taste the local ales - Criffel and Knockendoch - at Sulwath Brewery, Castle Douglas, and view the brewing process in miniature. Dine at one of the award-winning restaurants on menus created by celebrity chefs from local produce. Try Solway scallops, Galloway beef or Annandale lamb, trout or salmon from the local rivers, followed by your choice of Galloway cheeses or the local recipe for Ecclefechan tart. And in the background? Coastline, wild mountains and moorlands, pretty towns and charming villages. Dumfries & Galloway is the natural place to get away from it all, to unwind, discover and explore at your own pace. Contact Dumfries & Galloway Tourist Information Centre on 01387 253862 for an information pack. **Internet:** www.dumfriesandgalloway.co.uk

GALLOWAY COUNTRY STYLE LTD

High Street, Gatehouse of Fleet, Galloway DG7 2HP
Tel: 01557 814001 Fax: 01557 814055

Under the original roof trusses of an 18th century tannery, this charming B listed building now includes a traditional kilt making business and exhibition, a very relaxed coffee shop (where the coffee beans really are ground!) and a gift shop and boutique with more than a little touch of class. Comfort is ensured with air conditioning - and no smoke! Located next to a large car park, this is just the best place to stop. **Location:** The Conservation Area of Gatehouse of Fleet is to be found halfway between Dumfries and Stranraer, just off the A75. **Open:** 10am (Sun 11am) –5pm, every day except 2 days at Christmas and 2 at New Year.

map 10
C4

RAMMERSCALES

Lockerbie, Dumfriesshire, Scotland, DG11 1LD
Tel: 01387 811 988 Fax: 01387 810 940
(M. A. Bell Macdonald)

Georgian manor house dated 1760 set on high ground with fine views over Annandale. Pleasant policies and a typical walled garden of the period. There are Jacobite relics and links with Flora Macdonald retained in the family. There is also a collection of works by modern artists. **Location:** 5 miles W of Lockerbie (M6/A74). 2.5 miles S of Lochmaben on B7020. **Open:** Last week of July–first 3 weeks of August (except Sats) 2–5pm. **Admission:** £5. Coach Parties by appointment.

map 10
D3

SHAMBELLIE HOUSE MUSEUM OF COSTUME

New Abbey, Dumfries,
Scotland DG2 8HQ
Tel: 01387 850375 Fax: 01387 850461

Shambellie House was designed by the celebrated Scottish architect David Bryce and built for the Stewart family in 1856. In 1977, Charles Stewart, the great grandson of the original owner, gave the house and his unique costume collection to National Museums of Scotland. Each room shows a different social event between 1860 and 1950. Costumes from film and television dramas on display at certain times phone for details **Open:** 1 April–31 October: 7 days a week 11–5pm. **Admission:** Adult £2.50, Concessions £1.50, Children free.

map 8
B6

THE WATERLOO GALLERY

Wellington House, Princes Street, Stranraer DG9 7RQ
Tel: 01776 702888

The Waterloo Gallery hosts exhibitions of professional artists' work throughout the year, and there is also a picture framing workshop on-site. The artists themselves are predominantly from the local regions of Dumfries, Galloway, and Ayrshire.**Open:** Tues to Sun 12pm-5pm. Closed on Mons (except Bank Holidays) To view works of art outside these hours, please phone 01776 702888. **E-mail:** amat@watartgall.fsnet.co.uk

map 10
A4

DRUMLANRIG CASTLE, GARDENS & COUNTRY PARK
Nr Thornhill, Dumfries & Galloway, Scotland DG3 4AQ
Tel: 01848 330248 Fax: 01848 331682 (His Grace The Duke of Buccleuch & Queensberry K.T.)

Exquisite pink sandstone castle built by William Douglas, 1st Duke of Queensberry. 1679–91. Renowned art collection, including work by Holbein, Leonardo and Rembrandt. Versailles furniture, relics of Bonnie Prince Charlie. Douglas family historical exhibition. Working forge. Extensive gardens and woodlands superbly landscaped. Craft centre. Cycle museum. **Open:** Castle Open:. April 14th, 15th 16th, then April 28th to August 12th and then August 25th to August 31st. inclusive. Weekdays 11–4pm, Sun 12–4pm. 1–30 Sept.

Groups by appointment. Grounds Open: April 14th to September 30th inclusive. For further details telephone: 01848 330248. Countryside Service: 01848 331555. **Admission:** Adults: Castle and country park £6, country park £3. Children: Castle and country park £2. Senior citizens: Castle and country park £4, country park £3. Family (2 adults, 4 children) £14. Pre-booked parties (minimum 20) Normal time £4, outwith normal time £8. Wheelchairs free.
E-mail: bre@drumlanrigcastle.org.uk

map 13
F7

THREAVE GARDEN AND ESTATE

Castle Douglas, Dumfries & Galloway DG7 1RX
Tel: 01556 502575 Fax: 01556 502683

Threave Garden is delightful in all seasons. At 26 ha (64 a), it is best known for its spectacular springtime daffodils (nearly 200 varieties), but herbaceous beds are colourful in summer and trees and heather garden are striking in autumn. The Victorian house (not open to the public) is home to the Trust's School of Practical Gardening, offering a one year training course for students who already possess some horticultural experience. Guided walks and amateur gardening classes available. Visitor Centre with exhibition. New Plant Centre. Threave Estate provides a good example of integrated management of the land, taking account of agriculture, forestry and nature conservation. Marked walks include a 2.5km estate trail which guides the visitor through this variety of landscapes. The Estate is wildfowl refuge and the wetland is important for its plants, breeding wading birds and wintering wildfowl. Bird hides provide good cover to enjoy the activity of this wildlife. New this year is the Countryside Centre in the old stables, highlighting nature conservation, horticulture, forestry and agriculture at Threave. The Centre offers an integrated interpretation of the property and will clearly illustrate the work of the ranger service. **Open:** Estate and garden: all year, daily 9.30am-sunset. Walled garden and glasshouses: all year, daily 9.30am-5pm. Visitor Centre, Countryside Centre, exhibition, licensed restaurant and shop, 1–31 Mar and 1 Nov–23 Dec, Wed-Sun 10am-4pm; 1 Apr–31 Oct, daily 9.30am-5.30pm. **Admission:** Adult £4.50, Concession £3.50, Adult Group £3.60, Child/School Group £1, Family £12.50.

map 10
C4

THE WHITHORN TRUST

45–47 George Street, Whithorn, Newton Stewart,
Dumfries and Galloway DG8 8NS
Tel: 01988 500508 (The Whithorn Trust)

Whithorn is the cradle of Christianity in Scotland. It is the home of the earliest known Christian community in Scotland, which has long been remembered by tradition but now revealed by archaeological excavation. The centre tells the story of Whithorn through the ages from its early beginnings with St Ninian, Scotland's first Saint, through periods of Northumbrian and Hiberno-Norse control to the golden years of medieval pilgrimage, the Reformation and the present day. **Location:** Follow road signs S off A75 to the 'Whithorn Dig' and the building is in the centre of the main street of Whithorn. **Open:** Daily from 1 Apr–31 Oct, 10.30am–5pm. **Admission:** Adults £2.70, Concessions £1.50, Family £7.50. **Internet:** www.whithorn.com

map 10
B4

THE WORLD FAMOUS OLD BLACKSMITH'S SHOP CENTRE

Gretna Green, Dumfries & Galloway
Tel: 01461 338441 Fax: 01461 338442 (Mr A Houston)

The Old Blacksmith's Shop was built in 1712. The building is famous for the countless thousands of young couples who ran away from England to marry here. Now a top visitor attraction, features include the Gretna Green Story Exhibition. An internationally renowned shopping feature adds to the experience. A showcase for UK manufacturing, The Tartan Shop extends in front of you from the cottage style frontage. An Arts and Crafts Centre offers unusual products, some made on site and others from local crafts people. The Old Smithy Restaurant and Café Ecosse offer a choice of snacks and meals. **Open:** All year round, 7 days a week. **Admission:** Entry to Gretna Green Story Exhibition: Adults £2, Concessions £1.50. **E-mail:** info@gretnagreen.com **Internet:**

map 10
E3

Edinburgh

Winton House

The city of Edinburgh and the surrounding regions of Lothian and Fife together form a relatively compact area, but the range of activities and places to visit they offer means that their charm is almost inexhaustible.

West Lothian's rich agricultural land is the setting for the ancient Royal Burgh of Linlithgow. Mary Queen of Scots was born here in the now-ruined royal palace, which stands on a grassy knoll overlooking a pretty loch. The narrow, high-hedged lanes of East Lothian radiate out through farmland to the grassy dunes of the coastline, where fishing villages still thrive. The scenery is altogether more dramatic at St. Abb's Head, where the towering 300-foot cliffs afford marvellous views of the sea. East Lothian is sometimes called "The Holy Land of Golf", and the game has been played here for over four hundred years.

Edinburgh is one of the world's great cities. It stands with one foot in the past and one in the future, proud of a long history rich in tradition, yet always at the cutting-edge of culture, unwilling to stand still and become just a museum. The centre is an area of broad plateaux, steep cliffs and deep canyons dominated by the magnificent castle, which rears up over the city on a gigantic craggy rock. The view from the Princes Street Gardens below is truly awe-inspiring. The shape of the city was determined by its turbulent history: a defeat at the hands of the English led to the hasty construction of the Flodden Wall in 1513. Edinburgh's inhabitants were afraid to build beyond it, and so the city grew upwards in tenements – buildings of nine to fourteen stories where people of all classes were thrown together in a maze of courts and closes. The modern city retains all the charm of its mediaeval counterpart, but thankfully none of the squalor, as the broad thoroughfare of Princes Street and the Georgian splendour of Charlotte Square will prove.

Hopetoun House

 THE GEORGIAN HOUSE

7 Charlotte Square, Edinburgh, EH2 4DR
Tel/Fax: 0131 226 3318

The Georgian House is located in Robert Adam's masterpiece of urban design, Charlotte Square, part of Edinburgh's New Town and now part of a World Heritage Site. The house's beautiful china, shining silver, paintings, furniture and fascinating kitchen all reflect the domestic surroundings and social conditions of the times and the three floors open to visitors give a good impression of life in 1796. Also open at No. 28, Charlotte Square, is The National Trust for Scotland's Head Office with a gallery, coffee house, shop and restaurant open to visitors all year. **Open:** 1 Mar–31 Oct, Mon–Sat 10am–5pm, Sun 2–5pm (last admission 4.30pm); 1 Nov–24 Dec, Mon–Sat 11am–4pm, Sun 2–4pm. **Admission:** (including audio-visual) Adult £5, Concession £4, Family £14. Limited access for wheelchairs. **E-mail:** thegeorgianhouse@nts.org.uk

map 13
G5

HILL OF TARVIT MANSION HOUSE

Cupar, Fife, KY15 5PB
Tel/Fax: Cupar 01334 653127

This fine house was rebuilt in 1906 by the renowned Scottish architect Sir Robert Lorimer for a Dundee industrialist, whose superb collection of French Chippendale-style and Scottish furniture is also preserved here. Fine paintings by Raeburn and Ramsay and eminent Dutch artists are on view together with Chinese porcelain and bronzes. The interior is very much in the Edwardian fashion. The formal gardens to the south were also designed by Lorimer to form an appropriate setting for the house. Restored Edwardian laundry behind the house. **Open:** House: 13-16 Apr, 1 May-30 Jun and 1-30 Sept, daily 1.30-5.30pm; 1 Jul-31 Aug, daily 11am-5.30pm; weekends in Oct, 1.30-5.30pm. **Admission:** House and Garden: Adult £5, Concession £4, Adult Group £4, Child/School Group £1, Family £14. Garden and Grounds only: Adult £2, Concession £1 (honesty box).

map 13
H4

THE PALACE OF HOLYROODHOUSE

Edinburgh EH8 8DX
Tel: 0131 556 7371 Information Line (24 hours): 0131 556 1096 Fax: 0131 557 5256

Holyroodhouse has evolved from a medieval fortress into a baroque residence. The Royal Apartments epitomise the elegance and grandeur of this ancient and noble house.

HOPETOUN

South Queensferry, West Lothian EH30 9SL
Tel: 0131 331 2451 Fax: 0131 319 1885

Hopetoun House is a unique gem of Europe's architectural heritage and undoubtedly 'Scotland's Finest Stately Home'.

FOR FULL DETAILS, PLEASE SEE PAGES 256 AND 257.

KELLIE CASTLE AND GARDEN

Pittenweem, Fife KY10 2RF
Tel: (Arncroach) 01333 720271 Fax: 01333 720326

Kellie Castle is a superb example of the domestic architecture of lowland Scotland believed to date back to the 14th century. The castle was sympathetically restored by the Lorimer family in the late 19th century and contains magnificent plaster ceilings, painted panelling and furniture designed by Sir Robert Lorimer. The late Victorian garden has a fine selection of old-fashioned roses, fruit trees and herbaceous plants, all grown organically. **Open:** Castle, shop and tearoom, 13 Apr–30 Sep, daily 1.30-5.30pm; weekends in Oct, 1.30-5.30pm. Last admission 4.45pm. Garden and grounds, all year, daily 9.30am-sunset. **Admission:** Castle and Garden: Adult £5, Concession £4, Adult Group £4, Child/School Group £1, Family £14. Garden and Grounds only: Adult £2, Concession £1 (honesty box).

map 13
H4

NATIONAL MUSEUMS & GALLERIES OF SCOTLAND

Edinburgh

The historic city of Edinburgh is home to a range of renowned museums and galleries.

FOR FULL ILLUSTRATED ENTRIES INCLUDING OPENING TIMES AND ADMISSION PRICES, TURN TO PAGES 258 AND 259.

KELLIE CASTLE AND GARDEN

Pittenweem, Fife KY10 2RF
Tel: (Arncroach) 01333 720271 Fax: 01333 720326

Kellie Castle is a superb example of the domestic architecture of lowland Scotland believed to date back to the 14th century. The castle was sympathetically restored by the Lorimer family in the late 19th century and contains magnificent plaster ceilings, painted panelling and furniture designed by Sir Robert Lorimer. The late Victorian garden has a fine selection of old-fashioned roses, fruit trees and herbaceous plants, all grown organically. **Open:** Castle, shop and tearoom, 13 Apr–30 Sep, daily 1.30-5.30pm; weekends in Oct, 1.30-5.30pm. Last admission 4.45pm. Garden and grounds, all year, daily 9.30am-sunset. **Admission:** Castle and Garden: Adult £5, Concession £4, Adult Group £4, Child/School Group £1, Family £14. Garden and Grounds only: Adult £2, Concession £1 (honesty box).

map 13
H4

YESTER HOUSE

Gifford, East Lothian EH41 4JH
Tel: 01620 810241 Fax: 01620 810650 (Francis Menotti)

Splendid neoclassical House designed by James Smith, set on the edge of the Lammermuir Hills. For centuries the seat of the Marquesses of Tweedale. Fine 18th century interiors by William and Robert Adam, including the Great Saloon which is a perfect example of their style. Formal gardens were laid out in the 17th century and provide a beautiful natural setting to this day. The House has been extensively restored and sumptuously furnished by the current owner. **Open:** House and Chapel: 29 & 30 Oct 2001, 2–5pm. **Admission:** House & Garden: Adults £4, Children £1.50, OAPs £2.50. Garden only £1. Chapel only £1.

map 13
H5

The Palace of Holyroodhouse. The Royal Collection © 2000, H. M. Queen Elizabeth II/John Freeman

THE PALACE OF HOLYROODHOUSE

Edinburgh EH8 8DX

Tel: 0131 556 7371 Information Line (24 hours): 0131 556 1096 Fax: 0131 557 5256

The Palace of Holyroodhouse, Buckingham Palace and Windsor Castle are the Official residences of the Sovereign and are used by The Queen as both home and office. The Queen's personal standard flies when Her Majesty is in residence. Furnished with works of art from the Royal Collection, these buildings are used extensively by The Queen for State ceremonies, and official entertaining. They are opened to the public as much as these commitments allow. At the end of the Royal Mile stands the Palace of Holyroodhouse. Set against the spectacular backdrop of Arthur's Seat, Holyroodhouse has evolved from a medieval fortress into a baroque residence. The Royal Apartments, an extensive suite of rooms,

epitomise the elegance and grandeur of this ancient and noble house, and contrast with the historic tower apartments of Mary, Queen of Scots which are steeped in intrigue and sorrow. These intimate rooms where she lived on her return from France in 1561, witnessed the murder of David Rizzio, her favourite secretary, by her jealous husband, Lord Darnley and his accomplices. **Open:** Every day, except Good Friday, Christmas Day, Boxing Day and during Royal Visits. 9.30–5.15pm Apr–Oct, 9.30–3.45pm Nov–Mar. **Admission:** Adults £6.50, Senior Citizens (over 60) £5 and Children (under 17) £3.30. Family Ticket (2 adults and 2 under 17) £16.30. **Internet:** www. the-royal-collection.org.uk

map 13
G5

Mary, Queen of Scots Bedchamber. The Royal Collection © 2000, H. M. Queen Elizabeth II/Antonia Reeve

Mary, Queen of Scots. The Royal Collection © 2000, H. M. Queen Elizabeth II

HOPETOUN HOUSE

South Queensferry, West Lothian EH30, 9SL
Tel: 0131 331 2451 Fax: 0131 319 1885 (Hopetoun House Preservation Trust)

Hopetoun House is a unique gem of Europe's architectural heritage and undoubtedly 'Scotland's Finest Stately Home'. Situated on the shores of the Firth of Forth, it is one of the most splendid examples of the work of Scottish architects Sir William Bruce and William Adam. The Bruce House has fine carving, wainscoting and ceiling painting, while in contrast the Adam interior, with opulent gilding and classical motifs reflect the aristocratic grandeur of the early 18th century. The House is set in 100 acres of rolling parkland including woodland walks, the Red Deer Park, the Spring Garden with a profusion of wild flowers, and numerous picturesque picnic spots. Panoramic views can be seen from the rooftop platform. **Location:** 2 miles from Forth Road Bridge. 10 miles from Edinburgh. **Open:** Daily 1 Apr–30 Sept, 10–5.30pm. Last admission 4.30pm. Winter by appointment only for groups of 15+. **Admission:** Adults £5.30, Children (5–16yrs) £2.70, OAP/Students £4.70, Groups £4.50, Family £15. Under 5s free. **Refreshments:** Delicious meals and snacks served in the recently converted Stables Restaurant.

map 13
G5

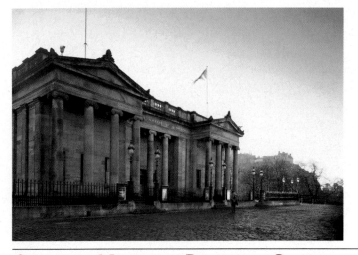

NATIONAL GALLERY OF SCOTLAND
The Mound, Edinburgh EH2 2EL
Tel: 0131 624 6200 Fax: 0131 343 3250

Home to Scotland's greatest collection of European paintings, drawings and prints dating from the early Renaissance to the late 19th century. This includes works by Raphael, Titian, Velázquez, Vermeer, El Greco, Poussin, Rembrandt, Rubens, Turner and the Impressionists. Also housed here is the national collection of Scottish art with works by Ramsay, Raeburn, Wilkie and McTaggart. The Gallery was designed by William Henry Playfair in the 1850s and stands on the Mound, adjacent to the Royal Scottish Academy. **Open:** Mon–Sat 10–5pm. Sun 12–5pm. **Admission:** Free, though entrance charges are made for special exhibitions. **Internet:** www.natgalscot.ac.uk.

map 13 G5

SCOTTISH NATIONAL PORTRAIT GALLERY
1 Queen Street, Edinburgh EH2 1JD
Tel: 0131 624 6200 Fax: 0131 343 3250

A visual history of Scotland from the 16th century to the present day, told through portraits of the people who shaped it: royals and rebels, poets and philosophers, heroes and villains. The gallery also houses the national photography collection, the core of which is its vast holding of work by Hill and Adamson, the Scottish pioneers of photography. Most of the best known figures of Scottish history are represented, including such luminaries as Mary, Queen of Scots, Bonnie Prince Charlie and Robert Burns. Contemporaries include the novelist Irvine Welsh, actor Sean Connery and the footballer Danny McGrain. **Open:** Mon–Sat 10–5pm. Sun 12–5pm. **Admission:** Free, though entrance charges are made for special exhibitions. **Internet:** www.natgalscot.ac.uk.

map 13 G5

SCOTTISH NATIONAL GALLERY OF MODERN ART
75 Belford Road, Edinburgh EH4 3DR
Tel: 0131 624 6200 Fax: 0131 343 3250

Scotland's finest collection of modern and contemporary art opened in 1960. It has since grown to include 5000 items, ranging from paintings, sculptures, prints and drawings of the 1890's right up to contemporary video installations of the 1990's. Highlights include works by Matisse, Picasso and Henry Moore; a superb selection of paintings by Scottish artists such as Peploe, Fergusson, Gillies and Redpath; post-war work by Bacon, Freud, Hockney and Léger; and more recent work by Baselitz, Antony Gormley and Damien Hirst. **Open:** Mon–Sat 10–5pm. Sun 12–5pm. **Admission:** Free, though entrance charges are made for special exhibitions. **Internet:** www.natgalscot.ac.uk

map 13 G5

DEAN GALLERY
73 Belford Road, Edinburgh EH4 3DS
Tel: 0131 624 6200 Fax: 0131 343 3250

Opposite the Gallery of Modern Art is this extensive collection of Dada and Surrealist art including many celebrated works by Dali, Duchamp, Ernst, Giacometti, Magritte, Man Ray and Miró. The Gallery is also home to a large collection of work by Sir Eduardo Paolozzi, including a substantial number of plaster sculptures, prints and drawings, as well as books, toys, machine parts and other items which have inspired his work over the years. Using these various artworks and objects, the gallery has recreated the artist's densely crowded London studio. **Open:** Mon–Sat 10–5pm. Sun 12–5pm. **Admission:** Free, though entrance charges are made for special exhibitions. **Internet:** www.natgalscot.ac.uk.

map 13 G5

NATIONAL MUSEUMS OF SCOTLAND

MUSEUM OF SCOTLAND
Chambers Street, Edinburgh EH1 1JF
Tel: 0131 247 4422 Fax: 0131 220 4819

The Museum of Scotland presents the history of Scotland, its land and people, through the rich national collections in this magnificent new building. Opening with Scotland's geological formation, the galleries travel through time to the 20th century.

ROYAL MUSEUM
Chambers Street, Edinburgh EH1 1JF
Tel: 0131 247 4219 Fax: 0131 220 4819

The Royal Museum houses outstanding international collections in an impressive Victorian building distinguished by its soaring, glass topped hall. There are galleries devoted to the Decorative Arts, Science and the Natural World.

Open: Mon–Sat 10am–5pm, Tues 10am–8pm, Sun 12 noon–5pm. Closed Christmas Day. **Admission:** Adult £3, Concession £1.50, Visitors 18 and under free. Museum Pass (which offers unlimited access to 12 museums in Scotland for 12 months, except special events): Adult £8, Concession £5, Family £15. **Accessibility:** All parts of the museums are accessible. Public lifts to all floors. Adapted toilets. **National Museums of Scotland also comprise:** Museum of Flight; East Fortune Airfield; East Lothian, Tel: 01620 880308; Shambellie House Museum of Costume, Dumfriesshire, Tel: 01387 850375; Museum of Scottish Country Life, Kittochside, East Kilbride (opening summer 2001); National War Museum of Scotland, Edinburgh Castle, Tel: 0131 225 7534. **Internet:** www.nms.ac.uk

map 13
G5

Mid Scotland

View of Kilmartin House

Whilst there is no official "Mid Scotland" area, for ease of reference we have grouped together properties in Ayrshire, Lanarkshire, Glasgow and the Clyde, the southern portion of Stirling, and the Isle of Arran.

Ayrshire is Robert Burns country, where visitors will be enchanted by the lochs and lochans, set in rolling green countryside, and by the craggy upland vistas of Leadhills.

The coastline facing Arran remains sparsely populated, and is a great place to get away from it all.

To the north is the city of Glasgow, which has blossomed into one of Europe's most vibrant cultural centers, whilst also remaining true to its industrial roots. A good number of art galleries and museums are hidden away amongst the beautiful Victorian municipal buildings.

The region's industrial heritage can be explored in New Lanark, South Lanarkshire, where Robert Owen's social reforms were pioneered. The site is on the UNESCO World Heritage register, and its award-winning Visitors Centre features a number of interesting and innovative attractions.

BLAIRQUHAN CASTLE & GARDENS

Straiton, Maybole, KA19 7LZ, Ayrshire, Scotland
Tel: 016557 70239 Fax: 016557 70278 (James Hunter Blair)

Magnificent Regency Castle approached by a 3 mile long private drive beside the River Girvan. Walled gardens and pinetum. Picture gallery. Shop. Tree Trail. **Location:** 14 miles S of Ayr, off A77. Entrance Lodge is on B7045, 1/2 mile S of Kirkmichael. **Open:** Sat.14th July–Sun.12th Aug daily except Mons, 1.30–4.15pm. **Admission:** Adults £5, Children £3, OAPs £4. Last admission to house 4:15pm. Parties by arrangement any time of the year. **Refreshments:** Tearoom. Car parking. Wheelchair access – around gardens and principal floors of the Castle. **E-mail:** enquiries@blairquhan.co.uk
Internet: www.blairquhan.co.uk

map 10 B2

CLYDEBUILT – SCOTTISH MARITIME MUSEUM AT BRAEHEAD

Kings Inch Road, Glasgow G51 4RN
Tel: 0141 886 1013 Fax: 0141 886 1015

Clydebuilt tells the fascinating story of the river Clyde, its ships and its people over the last 300 years. Situated on the south bank of the river, it blends film and sound with dramatic stage sets, hands-on activities, working engines and vessels moored on the river to create a unique experience. At Clydebuilt you can climb aboard the oldest Clydebuilt ship still afloat in the UK, steer a virtual ship up the Clyde, make a fortune as a Victorian merchant and enjoy the video spectacular on 100 years of Clyde shipbuilding, special exhibition programme, gift shop and maritime play park. **Open:** Mon–Sat 10am–6pm, Sun 11am–5pm. Closed Christmas Day and New Year's Day. **Admission:** Adult £3.50, Conc £1.75, Family £8. Group rates available.

map 12 E5

BRODICK CASTLE

Brodick, Isle of Arran, KA27 8HY
Tel: 01770 302202 Fax: 01770 302312
Tel: 01770 302462 (Countryside walks and events)

The site of this ancient seat of the Dukes of Hamilton was a fortress even in Viking times. Today the castle contains fine furniture, some dating from the 17th century, superb paintings, porcelain and stunning silver collected by the Hamiltons and by William Beckford. The woodland garden is now home to an internationally acclaimed rhododendron collection and the walled garden has been restored as a Victorian garden. The country park has waymarked trails, woodlands, gorges, waterfalls and a wildlife garden. **Open:** Castle: 1 Apr–30 Jun and 1 Sep–31 Oct, daily 11am-4.30pm, 1 Jul–31 Aug, daily 11am-5pm. Walled Garden: all year, daily, 9.30am–5pm; Country Park: all year, daily 9.30am-sunset. **Admission:** Castle & Garden: Adult £6, Conc £4.50, Family £16.50. Garden & Country Park only: Adult £2.50, Conc £1.70, Family £7.

map 12 C/D6

CULZEAN CASTLE

Maybole, South Ayrshire KA19 8LE
Tel: (Kirkoswald) 01655 884455 Fax: 01655 884503

Robert Adam converted a fortified tower house into this beautiful residence between 1777 and 1792. The castle contains a fine collection of paintings and furniture and a display of weapons in the Armoury. The circular saloon has a superb panoramic view over the Firth of Clyde and the wonderful oval staircase is Robert Adam's final masterpiece of interior design. Surrounding the castle are the garden areas including the terraced Fountain Court and Walled Garden and an extensive country park with woodland walks, swan pond and deer park. **Open:** Castle: 1 Apr-31 Oct, daily 11am-5.30pm. Weekends in Mar, Nov and Dec (castle guided tours every half-hour, 12-2.30pm). Country Park, all year, daily 9.30am-sunset. **Admission:** Castle and country park: Adult £8, Concession £6, Family £20. Country Park only: Adult £4, Concession £3, Family £10. **E-mail:** culzean@nts.org.uk

map 12
D7

DAVID LIVINGSTONE CENTRE

165 Station Road, Blantyre
Tel: 01698 823140

Scotland's most famous explorer and missionary was born here in 1813. Today the 18th century tenement commemorates David Livingstone's life and work. His childhood home remains much as it would have been in his day and gives visitors an insight into the living conditions endured by industrial workers in the 19th century. The rest of the museum tells the story of Livingstone's explorations in Africa and is home to a wide range of his personal belongings and travel aids, including diaries and even the famous red shirt he was wearing when he met the journalist H M Stanley. **Open:** 8 Jan-31 Mar and 1 Nov-23 Dec, Mon-Sat 10.30-4.30, Sun 12.30-4.30; 1 Apr to 31 Oct, Mon-Sat 10-5.30, Sun 12.30-5.30. **Admission:** Adult £3, Concession £2, Adult Group £2.50, Child/School Group £1, Family £8.

map 13
F5

DENNY SHIP MODEL EXPERIMENT TANK

Castle Street, Dumbarton G82 1QS
Tel: 01389 763444 Fax: 01389 7430093 (Scottish Maritime Museum)

Built in 1882, the Denny Tank was the world's first commercial ship model testing tank. Restored to working condition by the Scottish Maritime Museum, it retains many original features - a water tank as long as a football pitch, clay moulding beds for casting wax model ship hulls and Victorian machinery used for shaping models. The water tank is still used for testing ship designs. The Denny Tank is the last surviving part of the William Denny and Brothers shipyard, who built every type of vessel from sailing ships, such as the 'Cutty Sark', to modern liners. **Location:** Close to Dumbarton Central Rail Station. **Open:** Mon–Sat 10am–4pm (except Christmas and New Year). **Admission:** Adult £1.50, Conc £0.75, Family £3. Group rates available.

map 12
E5

VENNEL GALLERY

10 Glasgow Vennel, Irvine KA12 0BD
Tel/Fax: 01294 275059 (North Ayrshire Council)

Hidden away at the end of a cobbled street is the Vennel Gallery. It is housed in two restored 18th century cottages where Robert Burns once lived and worked. **Exhibitions:** As well as displays on Burns there is also a programme of changing exhibitions of contemporary art and crafts. **E-mail:** vennel@globalnet.co.uk **Internet:** www.northayrshiremuseums.org.uk

map 10
B1

GREENBANK GARDEN

Flenders Road, Clarkston, Glasgow G76 8RB
Tel: 0141 639 3281

A one-hectare (2.5 a) walled garden surrounding an elegant Georgian House (not open to visitors) built in 1764 for a Glasgow merchant. This attractive garden demonstrates how wide a range of ornamental plants, annuals, perennials, shrubs and trees can be grown in this area and is of particular interest to owners of smaller gardens. There is a special area for disabled visitors. **Open:** all year, daily 9.30am-sunset. Shop and tearoom, 1 Apr-31 Oct, daily 11am-5pm; 1 Nov-31 Mar, Sat/Sun 2-4pm. No dogs in garden, please. **Admission:** Adult £3.50, Concession £2.50, Adult Group £3, Child/School Group £1, Family £9.50. **Groups:** Please book in advance.

map 12
E5

HOLMWOOD HOUSE

61-63 Netherlee Road, Cathcart, Glasgow G44 3YG
Tel: 0141 637 2129 Fax: 0141 571 0184

Holmwood has been described as the finest domestic design by Alexander 'Greek' Thomson. It was built in 1857-8 for a small family and the architectural style is a picturesque adaptation of classical Greek. Many rooms are richly ornamented in wood, plaster and marble and, through ongoing conservation work, much of Thomson's original rich decoration, based on themes from the classical world, is beginning to emerge. The small kitchen garden is planted with a range of Victorian herbs, fruit and vegetables. **Open:** 1 Apr-31 Oct, daily 1.30-5.30pm. Groups MUST pre-book. **Admission:** Adult £3.50, Concession £2.50, Adult Group £3, Child/School Group £1, Family £9.50.

map 12
E5

HUTCHESONS' HALL

158 Ingram Street, Glasgow G1 1EJ
Tel: 0141 552 8591 Fax: 0141 552 7031

One of the most elegant buildings in Glasgow's city centre, Hutchesons' Hall was built in 1802-5 to a design by David Hamilton and reconstructed in 1876 by John Baird. It incorporates on its frontage the statues of the founders of Hutchesons' Hospital, built on this site in 1639-41 as a home for elderly tradesmen and orphaned boys. The impressive interior now houses an exciting multi media exhibition, The Glasgow Style, which includes a gallery showing and selling work by young Glasgow designers and an audio trail of the Merchant City. **Open:** Gallery, shop and function hall, all year, Mon-Sat 10am-5pm (except public holidays and 24 Dec-8 Jan). Hall on view subject to functions in progress. **Admission:** free.

map 12
E5

KELBURN CASTLE AND COUNTRY CENTRE

Kelburn, Fairlie, Nr Largs, Ayrshire KA29 0BE
Tel: 01475 568685 Fax: 01475 568121

Home of the Earls of Glasgow, Kelburn is famous for its castle, historic gardens, unique trees and romantic glen. Waterfalls, deep gorges, attractive woodland and spectacular views over the Firth of Clyde make it a place of great natural beauty. The park includes a riding school, adventure playgrounds, exhibitions, craft shop, licensed café and Scotland's most unusual attraction - 'The Secret Forest'. **Open: Castle:** Open for guided tours in July, August and first week in September, when not booked for a conference or function. **Park:** Easter–October 10am–6pm daily. **Admission:** Adults £4.50, Concessions £3, Family £13. **Internet:** www.kelburncountrycentre.com

map 8 B6

MAYBOLE CASTLE

High Street, Maybole, Ayrshire KA19 7BX
Tel: 01655 883765 (The Trustees of The Seventh Marquess of Ailsa)

Historic 16th century town house of the Kennedy family. **Location:** High Street, Maybole on A77. **Open:** May–Sept. Sun, 3–4pm. At other times by appointment. **Admission:** Adult £2, Concession £1.

map 10 B2

McLEAN MUSEUM & ART GALLERY

15 Kelly Street, Greenock, Inverclyde PA16 8JX
Tel: 01475 715624 Fax: 01475 715626

The displays feature James Watt, the engineer, exhibits on local, maritime and social history themes, ethnography, Egyptology and natural history. Fine art collection and temporary exhibition programme. **Open:** Monday–Saturday 10–5pm, except local and national public holidays. **Admission:** Free. **Facilities:** Ramped entrance and toilet for disabled. Gift shop.

NORTH AYRSHIRE MUSEUM

Manse Street, Saltcoats KA21 5AA
Tel/Fax: 01294 464174 (North Ayrshire Council)

The North Ayrshire Museum shows the history of North Ayrshire with displays on archaeology, costume, transport and popular culture. The museum also includes a section showing the maritime history of the port of Ardrossan and a reconstruction of an Ayrshire cottage interior. Accompanied children can play in the children's activity area. **E-mail:** namuseum@globalnet.co.uk **Internet:** www.northayrshiremuseums.org.uk

map 10 B1

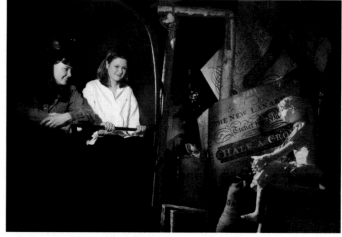

NEW LANARK WORLD HERITAGE VILLAGE

New Lanark Conservation Trust, New Lanark, South Lanarkshire ML11 9DB
Tel: 01555 661345 Fax: 01555 665738

Surrounded by native woodlands and close to the Falls of Clyde, this nominated World Heritage Site was once Britain's largest cotton manufacturing centre. Founded in 1785 by industrialists David Dale and Richard Arkwright, the village rose to fame in the early 19th century as the site of Robert Owen's radical social and educational reforms. Now beautifully restored as both a living community and visitor attraction, the fascinating history of the village is interpreted in an award-winning Visitor Centre which includes a brand new ride called the 'New Millennium Experience'. Accommodation is available in the New Lanark Mill Hotel and self-catering cottages called the Waterhouses. The hotel is a stunning conversion from the original Mill Number One, built by Dale in 1785. **E-mail:** development@newlanark.org **Internet:** www.newlanark.org

map 10 D1

POLLOK HOUSE

Pollok Country Park, 2060 Pollokshaws Road, Glasgow G43 1AT
Tel: 0141 616 6410 Fax: 0141 616 6521

Pollok House was built around 1750 after consultation with William Adam, replacing three earlier structures, and was extended in 1890 by Sir John Stirling Maxwell. The house contains an internationally important collection of paintings, including works by El Greco and Blake, silver and ceramics and is set in the extensive Pollok Country Park, also home to the Burrell Collection. Pollok House is managed by The National Trust for Scotland on behalf of Glasgow City Council. **Open**:1 Apr-31 Oct, daily 10am-5pm; 1 Nov-31 Mar (except 25/26 Dec & 1/2 Jan) daily 11am-4pm. **Admission:** Adult £4, Concession £3, Family £11. Free 1 Nov–31 Mar.

map 12
E5

ROZELLE HOUSE GALLERIES

Rozelle Park, Monument Road, Ayr KA7 4NQ
Tel: 01292 445447 Fax: 01292 442065

Set within beautiful woodland and park; Rozelle House Galleries house South Ayrshire Council's Art Collections, selections of which are carefully chosen and displayed throughout the year. In addition the galleries host a range of touring exhibitions; with the adjacent Maclaurin Galleries renowned for displays of contemporary art. Crafts at Rozelle feature unique, individual items for sale by local craftspeople. Coffee shop/restaurant; free car parking. Events: Varied programme of events & workshops throughout the year. Call for details. **Location:** From A77 Glasgow–Stranraer: follow signs for Burns Cottage then continue approx. 1/2 a mile past the cottage to Rozelle Park. Rozelle House Galleries is owned and operated by South Ayrshire Council. **Admission:** Free. **Open:** Mon–Sat 10–5pm. (Suns during Summer period 2–5pm.).

map 10
B2

SCOTTISH MARITIME MUSEUM

Harbourside, Irvine KA12 8QE
Tel: 01294 278283 Fax: 01294 313211

The Scottish Maritime Museum in Irvine is for everyone who likes messing about in boats, who has a love of the history of the sea and ships, who has worked at sea, is interested in the history of Scotland as a seafaring and great shipbuilding nation, or just likes a good day out at the seaside. The Linthouse Engine Shop, originally built in 1872, is being developed and holds a substantial part of the museum's collection in 'Open Store'. The Shipyard Workers' Tenement Flat and historic vessels moored at pontoons in the Harbour can be visited during a guided tour. Wheelchair access to exhibition, coffee shop and toilets. Limited access to pontoons. **Location:** Close to Irvine Railway Station. Telephone 01294 278283. **Open:** 10am–5pm daily from Easter. **Admission:** Adult £2.50, Concession £1.75, Family £5. Group rates available.

map 10
B1

STIRLING SMITH ART GALLERY & MUSEUM

Dumbarton Road, Stirling, Stirlingshire FK8 2RQ
Tel: 01786 471917 Fax: 01786 449523

Opening in 1874 with a bequest from artist and collector T S Smith (c1815-1869), the Stirling Smith Art Gallery and Museum is the focus for the history and material culture of the Stirling area. Scottish history collections, fine art and archaeology are used in the main display called 'The Stirling Story', which explores the history of the town over the past millennium. A changing programme of temporary exhibitions on a range of subjects and media together with lunchtime talks and other events contribute to make the Smith a lively and welcoming visitor attraction. Other facilities include a café serving lunches and light refreshments, shop, lecture and conference room and car park. **Admission:** Free. **E-mail:** museum@smithartgallery.demon.co.uk **Internet:** smithartgallery.demon.co.uk

map 13
F4

SORN CASTLE

Sorn, Mauchline, Ayrshire.
Tel: Cluttons 01505 612 124 (R. G. McIntyre's Trust)

Dating from 14th century, the Castle stands on a cliff on the River Ayr. The 18th and 19th century additions are of the same pink sandstone quarried from the river banks. The woodlands and grounds were laid out in the 18th century with fine hardwood trees, rhododendrons and azaleas. The Castle is essentially a family home with fine examples of Scottish paintings and artefacts. **Location:** 4 miles E of Mauchline, on B743. **Open:** Castle: Sat 14 July–11 Aug, 2–4pm or by appointment. Grounds: 1 Apr–30 Oct. **Admission:** Adults £3.50.

map 12
E6

THE TOWER OF HALLBAR

Braidwood Road, Braidwood, Lanarkshire, Scotland
Tel: 020 7930 8030 Fax: 020 7930 2295 (The Vivat Trust)

A sixteenth-century defensive tower and Bothy built in response to the 1535 Act of Parliament, advising landlords to construct a tower, 30 foot square to protect themselves from the lawlessness of the Border reivers. Converted into self-catering holiday accommodation and decorated in keeping with its history, by The Vivat Trust, Hallbar sleeps up to seven people, including facilities for a disabled person and their carer. **Location:** 45 minutes outside Glasgow, on B7056 in Braidwood. **Open:** Every Saturday afternoon 2–3pm year round, by appointment, and for four Open Days a year. **Admission:** Free.

map 10
C1

Highlands & North Scotland

The Highlands have a very small population, and yet to the outside world they represent the very essence of all things Scottish. From the deep and beautiful lochs in the east, to the inhospitable coastline of the north, the natural features here seem to embody all aspects of the Scottish character, at once poetic and warlike.

Any visit to the Highlands should include Skye, an island of lush green hills and stunning coastal scenery. The wildlife is plentiful and varied, and a number of boat trips visit the seal colonies on nearby islands. The myth of the Loch Ness monster has led many to overlook the simple beauty of the loch itself, and it certainly merits a visit on that basis alone.

To the south west is Britain's highest mountain, Ben Nevis, towering 1344 metres above nearby Fort William, the wettest town in Britain.

The majestic Grampian Mountains divide the highland villages of Aberdeenshire from the rugged lochs and valleys of Argyll, and the view across to the Cairngorm Mountains is truly awe-inspiring.

Dunrobin Castle

Craigston Castle

To the north east lies Moray, an unspoilt area where whisky distilleries nestle in picturesque valleys. The Spey Bay is dotted with traditional fishing villages such as Buckie, Cullen and Lossiemouth, which are all worth a visit.

ABERDEEN ART GALLERY

Schoolhill, Aberdeen, Grampian AB10 1FQ
Tel: 01224 523700 Fax: 01224 632133

One of the city's most popular tourist attractions, Aberdeen's splendid Art Gallery has, over the last 115 years, succeeded in acquiring an impressive collection of 18th, 19th and 20th century works of art. Visitors can see works by J M W Turner, William Dyce, Claude Monet, Sir John Lavery, Paul Nash, Henry Moore, Sir Francis Bacon and many others. In addition to paintings, drawings and sculpture, the Gallery also has an extensive collection of silver and glassware, jewellery, textiles and ceramics, as well as a busy programme of special exhibitions, ensuring there is always something new for visitors to see. **Open:** Mon–Sat 10am–5pm, Sun 2–5pm. **Admission:** Free. **E-mail:** info@aagm.co.uk **Internet:** www.aagm.co.uk

map 15 J6

ABERDEEN MARITIME MUSEUM

Shiprow, Aberdeen, Grampian AB11 5BY
Tel: 01224 337700 Fax: 01224 213066

Aberdeen Maritime Museum combines the historic 16th century Provost Ross's House with the award-winning 1997 link building to tell the story of the North Sea. The museum offers spectacular views of the harbour and interactive displays on the ships and people that made Aberdeen a successful shipbuilding, fishing and offshore port. Historic artworks and ship models of the 19th century together with a massive model of the *Murchison* oil platform make for a fascinating experience of Aberdeen's maritime heritage. Complemented by a full programme of events, exhibitions and young persons' activities. **Open:** Mon–Sat 10am–5pm, Sun 12 noon–3pm. **Admission:** Free.

map 15 J6

ALLOA TOWER

Alloa Park, Alloa, Clackmannanshire FK10 1PP
Tel: 01259 211 701 Fax: 01259 218 744

Alloa Tower is one of Scotland's largest surviving medieval keeps and from its defensive origins in the 1300s, successive generations of the Erskine family, Earls of Mar, transformed it into an inspiring 18th century home. Now fully restored, it is furnished with 18th century interiors, including a superb collection of family portraits. Rare medieval features, including the dungeon, internal well and original oak roof-beams can be seen, together with impressive 18th century additions inspired by the grand palaces of Italy, such as the Italianate staircase leading to the Great Hall. **Open:** 1 Apr–30 Sept, daily 1.30–5.30pm; weekends in October, 1.30–5.30pm (last admission 5pm). **Admission:** Adult £3, Concession £2, Adult Group £2.50, Child/School Group £1, Family £8 (25% discount to Clackmannanshire residents).

map 13 F4

ARDUAINE GARDEN

Arduaine, Oban, Argyll, PA34 4XQ
Tel/Fax: 01852 200366

A green oasis of tranquility nestling on the west coast, Arduaine will surprise and delight visitors all year round. This 20 acre garden benefits from the North Atlantic Drift and boasts spectacular rhododendrons, azaleas and magnolias which fill the garden with scent and colour. From the tall trees of the woodland garden to the water lilies in the ponds, Arduaine takes visitors on a horticultural journey across the temperate world. **Open:** All year, daily 9.30-sunset. **Admission:** Adult £3, Concession £2, Adult Group £2.50, Child/School Group £1, Family £8. **Groups:** Please book in advance.

map 12 C4

ARMADALE CASTLE GARDENS & MUSEUM OF THE ISLES

Armadale Castle, Sleat, Isle of Skye, Highland Region IV45 8RS
Tel: 01471 844305 Fax: 01471 844275 (Clan Donald Lands Trust)

The Clan Donald Lands Trust are the custodians of the beautiful 20,000 acre Armadale Estate on the South peninsular of Skye opposite Knoydart and half an hour by car ferry from Mallaig. The 40 acre gardens, surrounded by sea on three sides, are set around the sculptured ruins of Armadale Castle. They are remarkable, due to the warm generally frost-free climate of the West Highlands, with the Gulf Stream allowing these sheltered gardens to flourish with exotic trees, shrubs and flowers. Enjoy a complete experience to Armadale by visiting the Museum of the Isles within the grounds. Our Head Gardener would be delighted to guide small groups on request. **Internet:** www.cland.demon.co.uk

map 15 G5

BLAIR CASTLE

Blair Atholl, Pitlochry, Perthshire, Scotland PH18 5TI
Tel: 01796 481 207 Fax: 01796 481 487

Scotland's most visited historic house is home of the Atholl Highlanders, Britain's only private army. The Castle boasts 30 fascinating rooms containing a unique collection of beautiful furniture, fine paintings, arms and armour, china, costumes, lace and other treasures. Explore extensive grounds with walks, nature trails, deer park and enjoy the rare wildlife that exists in its natural habitat. 18th century walled garden restoration project. **Location:** 8 miles NW of Pitlochry, off A9. **Station:** Blair Atholl (half a mile). **Open:** Castle & Grounds: 1 Apr–26 Oct, daily 10–6pm. Last admission 5pm. **Admission:** Castle: Adults £6.25, Children £4, Senior Citizens £5.25. Grounds £2, Children £1. Family tickets. Reduced rates and guided tours for parties by prior arrangements.

map 13 F2

BRODIE CASTLE

Brodie, Forres, Moray IV36 2TE
Tel: 01309 641371 Fax: 01309 641600

Set in parkland, Brodie Castle is a 16th century Z-plan tower house with 17th- and 19th century additions. The house contains fine French furniture, English, Continental and Chinese porcelain and a major collection of paintings, including 17th-century Dutch art, 19th century English watercolours, Scottish Colourists and early 20th-century works. The house and its collections demonstrate the continuity of the Brodie family over many centuries. The grounds contain woodland walks, shrubbery garden and a unique daffodil collection. **Open:** Castle: 1 Apr-30 Sep, Mon-Sat 11am-5.30pm, Sun 1.30-5.30pm; weekends in Oct, Sat 11am-5.30pm, Sun 1.30-5.30pm. Grounds: all year, daily 9.30am-sunset. **Admission:** Adult £6, Concession £4.50, Adult Group £4.80, Child/School Group £1, Family £16.50. Grounds only £1 (honesty box). **Groups:** Please book in advance.

map 15 G5

CASTLE FRASER

Sauchen, Inverurie, Aberdeenshire AB51 7LD
Tel: 01330 833463

The most elaborate Z-plan castle in Scotland, and one of the grandest Castles of Mar. The castle was completed in 1636 and was the masterpiece of two great families of master masons, Bell and Leiper. The striking simplicity of the Great Hall and the stout walls evoke the atmosphere of past centuries, and today the castle houses many Fraser family portraits, including one by Raeburn, fine 18th and 19th century carpets, curtains and bed hangings. An ornamental garden has been developed in the historic walled garden. **Open:** Castle: 13 Apr-31 May and 1-30 Sep, daily 1.30-5.30pm; 1 Jun-31 Aug, daily 11am-5.30pm; weekends in Oct, 1.30-5.30pm. Garden: all year, daily 9.30am-6pm. Grounds: all year, daily 9.30am–sunset. **Admission:** Castle, Garden & Grounds: Adult £6, Concession £4.50, Family £16.50. Garden & Grounds only: Adult £2, Concession £1.30, Family £6. Car park, all year, £1.

map 13 J1

BRANKLYN GARDEN
116 Dundee Road, Perth, PH2 7BB
Tel: 01738 625535

This attractive garden in Perth was once described as 'the finest two acres of private garden in the country'. First established in 1922 on the site of a former orchard, it contains an outstanding collection of plants, particularly rhododendrons, alpines, herbaceous and peat-garden plants, which attract gardeners and botanists from all over the world. **Open:** 1 Mar-31 Oct, daily 9.30-sunset. **Admission:** Adult £3, Concession £2, Adult Group £2.50, Child/School Group £1, Family £8. **Groups**: Please book in advance.

map 13 G3

CASTLE MENZIES
Weem, Aberfeldy, PH15 2JD, Perthshire, Scotland.
Tel: 01887 820 982 (Menzies Charitable Trust)

Magnificent example of a 16th century 'Z' plan fortified house, seat of Chiefs of Clan Menzies for over 400 years and now nearing completion of its restoration from an empty ruin. It was involved in the turbulent history of the Central Highlands. 'Bonnie Prince Charlie' was given hospitality here on his way north to Culloden in 1746. Visitors can explore the whole of the 16th century building, together with part of the 19th century addition. Small clan museum and gift shop. **Location:** 1.5 miles from Aberfeldy, on B846. **Open:** 31 March-13 October, Mon-Sat, 10.30-5pm. Sun, 2-5pm. Last admission 4.30pm. **Admission:** Adults £3.50, OAPs £3, Children £2 (reduction for groups). **Refreshments:** Tearoom.

map 13 F3

CAWDOR CASTLE
Nairn, Scotland, IV12 5RD (The Dowager Countess Cawdor)
Tel: 01667 404615 Fax: 01667 404674

The most romantic castle in the Highlands. The 14th century keep, fortified in the 15th century and impressive additions, mainly 17th century, form a massive fortress. Gardens, nature trails and splendid grounds. Shakespearean memories of Macbeth. **Location:** S of Nairn on B9090 between Inverness and Nairn. **Station(s):** Nairn (5m) and Inverness (14m). **Open:** 1 May-14 Oct, daily, 10-5.30pm. Last admission 5pm. **Admission:** Adults £5.90, Children (5-15) £3, OAPs & Disabled £4.90. Groups: Adults (20+) £5.10, Children (5-15, 20+) £2.60, Family (2 adults & up to 5 children) £17. Blind people free. Gardens, grounds & nature trails only: £3. **Refreshments:** Licensed restaurant, snack bar. Gift shop, bookshop and wool shop. Picnic area, 9-hole golf course and nature trails. No dogs allowed in Castle or Grounds.
E-mail: info@cawdorcastle.com **Internet:** www.cawdorcastle.com

map 15 F5

CRATHES CASTLE
Banchory, Aberdeenshire AB31 5QJ
Tel: (Crathes) 01330 844525 Fax: 01330 844797

Crathes Castle, built in the second half of the 16th century, is a superb example of a tower house of the period. Some of the rooms contain their magnificent original painted ceilings and collections of family portraits and furniture. A visit is enhanced by the 3.75 a of walled garden, which incorporates herbaceous borders and many unusual plants - the garden provides a stunning display at all times of the year. The great yew hedges, fascinating examples of the art of topiary, date from as early as 1702. **Open:** Castle, Visitor Centre and Shop: 1 Apr-30 Sep, daily 10.30-5.30; 1-31 Oct, daily 10.30-4.30. Admission to the castle is by timed ticket (limited number available each day: entry may be delayed). Garden and grounds, all year, daily 9am-sunset. **Admission:** Castle only/Walled Garden only: Adult £4.50, Conc £3. Combined ticket (castle & garden): Adult £7, Conc £5, Adult Group £5.20, Child/School Group £1, Family £19. Car park, all year £1.

map 13 J1

CULLODEN
Culloden Moor, Inverness IV2 5EU
Tel: 01463 790607 Fax: (01463) 794294

Culloden is the scene of the last major battle fought on mainland Britain. The final Jacobite uprising ended here in 1746 when the army of Prince Charles Edward Stuart was crushed by the Government forces led by the Duke of Cumberland. Turf and stone dykes, which played a crucial part in the battle, have been reconstructed on their original site as part of the National Trust for Scotland's vision to restore the field to its state at the time of the battle. The visitor centre houses a Jacobite exhibition, shop and restaurant. **Open:** Site, all year, daily. Visitor Centre and shop, 15 Jan-31 Mar and 1 Nov-31 Dec (except 24-26 Dec), daily 10am-4pm; 1 Apr-31 Oct, daily 9am-6pm. **Admission:** Visitor Centre, including audio-visual presentation and Old Leanach Cottage: Adult £4, Concession £3, Adult Group £3.20, Child/School Group £1, Family £11.

map 15 F5

CULLODEN HOUSE HOTEL

Inverness, Inverness-shire, Scotland IV2 7BZ
Tel: 01463 790461 Fax: 01463 792181 (Stephen & Patricia Davies)

As capital of the Highlands, Inverness increasingly provided metropolitan sophistication and diversion as the town attracted wealthy families from all over the Highlands to settle. The finest of the country houses near Inverness still survives, Culloden House, an exquisite Georgian mansion. It was originally a Jacobean castle, where in 1746 Bonnie Prince Charlie requisitioned the building for his headquarters just prior to the tragic battle, which is forever etched into the history books of England and Scotland. The imposing Palladian mansion is set in 40 acres of parkland and gardens on the edge of Inverness, the capital of the Highlands, perfectly positioned for your headquarters of conquest and discovery. 28 charming bedrooms each uniquely decorated in understated comfort. **E-mail:** info@cullodenhouse.co.uk **Internet:** www.cullodenhouse.co.uk

map 15 F5

DELGATIE CASTLE

Delgatie, Turriff, Aberdeenshire, Scotland
Tel: 01888 563479 Fax: 01888 563479 (Delgatie Castle Trust)

Delgatie Castle dating from approx. 1030 has been lovingly restored over the last 50 years by the late Capt. and Mrs Hay of Delgatie and is not a museum, but a well loved home. Paintings, armoury and Victorian clothes are on display. It is reputed to have the widest turnpike stair of 97 steps and the original painted ceilings dating 1592/1597 are considered some of the finest in Scotland. Mary Queen of Scots stayed here after the Battle of Corrichie in 1562. The Castle is the official Clan Hay Centre. Pretty tearoom in the old Castle kitchen offers the best in homebaking and meals. **Open:** Daily from the 2 Apr–25 Oct, 10–5pm. **Admission:** Adults £3, OAPs and Children £2. Open all year for prebooked tours. **E-mail:** jjohnson@delgatie-castle.freeserve.co.uk

map 15 J5

DRUM CASTLE AND GARDEN

By Banchory, Aberdeenshire, AB31 5EY
Tel: (Drumoak) 01330 811204 Fax: 01330 811962

The combination of a 13th-century square tower, a fine Jacobean mansion house and the additions of Victorian lairds makes Drum Castle - owned for 653 years by the Irvine family - unique among Scottish castles. It contains superb furniture and paintings, and in the 16th-century chapel are a beautiful stained glass window and the Ausburg silver Madonna. In the walled garden, the Trust has created a fascinating Garden of Historic Roses. There are two trails to enjoy, one through the Old Wood of Drum, a children's playground, and shop and tearoom. **Open:** Castle: 13 Apr-31 May & 1-30 Sept, daily 1.30-5.30pm; 1 Jun-31Aug, daily 11-5.30pm; weekends in Oct, 1.30-5.30pm. Last admission 4.45pm. Garden: same dates, daily 10-6pm. Grounds: all year, daily 9.30-sunset. **Admission:** Castle, Garden & Grounds: Adult £6, Conc £4.50, Adult Group £4.80, Child/School Group £1, Family £16.50. Garden & Grounds only: £1 (honesty box).

map 15 J7

DRUMMOND CASTLE GARDENS

Muthill Crieff, Tayside, Scotland, PH5 2AA
Tel: 01764 681 257/433 Fax: 01764 681 550

The gardens of Drummond Castle, first laid out in the early 17th century by John Drummond, 2nd Earl of Perth, are said to be among the finest formal gardens in Europe. A spectacular view can be obtained from the upper terrace, overlooking a magnificent example of an early Victorian parterre in the form of a St. Andrew's Cross. The gardens you see today were renewed by Phyllis Astor in the early 1950's, preserving features such as the ancient yew hedges and the copper beech trees planted by Queen Victoria to commemorate her visit in 1842. The multi-faceted sundial by John Mylne, Master Mason to Charles I, has been the centrepiece since 1630. The gardens recently featured in United Artists 'Rob Roy'. **Location:** Entrance 2 miles S of Crieff, on A822 Muthill Road. **Open:** May–Oct & Easter Weekend, daily, 2–6pm. (Last admission 5pm). **Admission:** Adults £3.50, Children £1.50, OAPs £2.50. 10% discount for groups over 20. **E-mail:** thegardens@drummondcastle.sol.co.uk

map 13 F4

DUNROBIN CASTLE

Golspie, Sutherland KW10 6SF Scotland
Tel: 01408 633177 Fax: 01408 634081 (The Sutherland Trust)

Dunrobin Castle is the most northerly of Scotland's Great Houses and the seat of the Earls of Sutherland. The keep dates from c1300 and there are additions from the 17–19th centuries. Dunrobin Castle was remodelled in 1845 by Sir Charles Barry, who had just completed the Houses of Parliament. After a serious fire in 1915, Sir Robert Lorimer re-designed and re-decorated all the major rooms. The Castle is filled with fine furniture, china, superb paintings, family memorabilia and outstanding family silver. The beautiful gardens were laid out by Sir Charles Barry and are of French formal design. There are regular **falconry displays** in the garden. Museum, gift shop and tea room. **Location:** OS Ref: NC850 010. 50 miles N of Inverness on A9. **Open:** 1 Apr–31 May, 1–15 Oct: Mon–Sat 10.30am–4.30pm, Sun 12–4.30pm. 1 Jun–30 Sept: Mon–Sat 10.30am–5.30pm, Sun 12–5.30pm. **Admission:** Adults £6, Senior Citizens £4.50, Family ticket £17. **E-mail:** dunrobin.est@btinternet.com

map 13 F3

HOUSE OF DUN

Montrose, Angus DD10 9LQ
Tel: (Bridge of Dun) 01674 810264 Fax 01674 810722

This Georgian house, overlooking the Montrose basin, was designed and built by William Adam in 1730 for David Erskine, Lord Dun. It has superb contemporary plasterwork by Joseph Enzer, a family collection of portraits, furniture and porcelain. The house was also home to Lady Augusta Kennedy-Erskine, the daughter of William IV and the actress Mrs Jordan, and there is a collection of royal mementos of that period. The small walled garden has been restored to a late Victorian period and contains many plants typical of the 1880s. **Open:** 13-16 Apr, 1 May-30 Jun and 1–30 Sep, daily 1.30-5.30pm; 1 Jul-31 Aug, daily 11am-5.30pm; weekends in Oct, 1.30-5.30pm. Garden and grounds: all year, daily 9.30am-sunset. **Admission:** House & Garden: Adult £6, Concession £4.50, Family £16.50. Garden and grounds only: £1 (honesty box).

map 13 J2

FASQUE

Fettercairn, Laurencekirk, AB30 1DN, Kincardineshire,
Tel: 01561 340 202/ 340 569 Fax: 01561 340 569(Charles Gladstone)

Fasque is a spectacular example of a Victorian 'Upstairs-Downstairs' stately home. Bought by Sir John Gladstone in 1829, it was home to William Gladstone, four times Prime Minister, for much of his life. In front of the house red deer roam in the park and behind the hills dramatically towards the Highlands. Inside, very little has changed since Sir John's days. Fasque is not a museum, bur rather an unspoilt old family home. Visit the kitchen, laundry, bakery, knives hall and buttery. You'll find a wealth of domestic articles from a bygone age. Climb the famous double cantilever staircase and wander through the magnificent drawing room, library and bedrooms. Explore a Victorian gamekeeper's hut, complete with man trap, or discover our exhibition of William Gladstone memorabilia. Groups and Coach Parties welcome.

map 13 J2

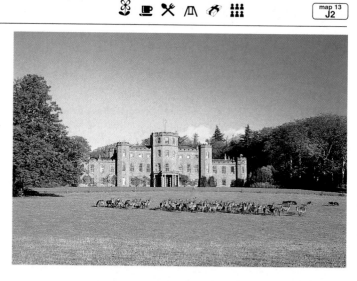

GLAMIS CASTLE
Glamis, Angus, Scotland DD8 1RJ
Tel: 01307 840 393 Fax: 01307 840 733

Family home of the Earls of Strathmore and Kinghorne and a royal residence since 1372. Childhood home of HM Queen Elizabeth, The Queen Mother, and the legendary setting of Shakespeare's play 'Macbeth'. **Location:** Glamis, 6 m W of Forfar, A94. **Open:** 31 Mar-28 Oct, daily 10.30–5.30pm (July & Aug from 10am). Last admission 4.45pm. **Admission:** Adult £6.20, Child (5–16) £3.10, OAP £4.70, Family £17.00. Grounds only: Adult £3.10, Child/OAP £1.60. Party (min 20): Adult £5.20, OAP £4.20, Child £2.60. **Facilities:** Licensed self-service restaurant, seating for 96. Picnic area, four shops, magnificent grounds, garden, pinetum and nature trail. Ample parking. **E-mail:** glamis@great–houses–scotland.co.uk. **Internet:** www.great-houses-scotland.co.uk/glamis

Online Shop: www.glamis-castle.co.uk

map 13
H3

GLENFINNAN MONUMENT
Glenfinnan, Highlands PH37 4LT
Tel/Fax: 01397 722250

Glenfinnan Monument, set amid superb Highland scenery at the head of Loch Shiel, was erected in 1815 in tribute to the clansmen who fought and died in the Jacobite cause. Prince Charles Edward Stuart's standard was raised near here in 1745 in the last attempt to reinstate the exiled Stuarts on the throne of Great Britain and Ireland. In the visitor centre, there are interpretive displays and an audio programme about the Prince's campaign from Glenfinnan to Derby and back to the final defeat at Culloden. **Open:** Site, all year, daily. Monument, Visitor Centre, shop and snack-bar, 1 Apr-18 May and 1 Sep-31 Oct, daily 10-5pm; 19 May-31 Aug, daily 9.30-6pm. Glenfinnan Games, 18 August. **Admission:** including parking, Adult £1.50, Concession £1.

map 12
C2

LEITH HALL AND GARDEN
Huntly, Aberdeenshire AB54 4NQ
Tel: (Kennethmont) 01464 831216 Fax: 01464 831594

Built around a courtyard, this mansion house was the home for almost 300 years of the Leith family and the elegantly furnished rooms reflect their lifestyle. Their long tradition of military service is reflected in the exhibition 'For Crown and Country'. The house is set in a 2.4 ha (6 a) garden with extensive herbaceous borders and a fine collection of alpines and primulas in the rock garden. The wider estate has ponds, trails, a bird observation hide and unusual semi-circular 18th century stables. **Open:** House and Tearoom, 13-16 Apr and 1 May-30 Sep, daily 1.30-5.30pm; weekends in Oct, 1.30-5.30pm. Last admission 4.45pm. **Admission:** Adult £6, Concession £4.50, Adult Group £4.80, Child/School Group £1, Family £16.50. Garden and Grounds only: Adult £2, Concession £1.30, Adult Group £1.60, Child/School Group £1, Family £6.

map 15
H6

HADDO HOUSE
Ellon, Aberdeenshire, AB41 7EQ
Tel: (Tarves) 01651 851440 Fax: 01651 851888

Haddo House is proud to be the most homely of the north-east of Scotland's great houses open to visitors. Designed by William Adam and refurbished in the 1880s, the house elegantly blends crisp Georgian architecture with late Victorian interiors by Wright and Mansfield. Haddo contains fine furniture and paintings and its personal portraits and memorabilia build up a fascinating account of the Gordon family who have lived here for over 400 years. Outside is a delightful terraced garden with geometric rosebeds and fountain, a lavish herbaceous border and secluded glades and knolls. **Open:** House: 13 Apr-30 Sep, daily 1.30-5.30pm; weekends in Oct, 1.30-5.30pm. Generally guided tours, Mon-Sat. Garden: 1 Mar-31 Oct, daily 9.30am-6pm; 1 Nov-28 Feb, daily 9.30am-4pm (closed 25/26 Dec and 1/2 Jan). Country Park, all year, daily 9.30am-sunset. **Admission:** Adult £6, Concession £4.50, Family £16.50.

map 15
J5/6

THE HILL HOUSE
Upper Colquhoun Street, Helensburgh G84 9AJ
Tel: 01436 673900 Fax: 01436 674685

The finest of Charles Rennie Mackintosh's domestic designs, the Hill House, sits high above the Clyde commanding fine views over the river estuary. The house was commissioned by Walter Blackie, a Glasgow publisher, and Mackintosh not only designed the house but also much of the furniture and all the interior fittings and decorative schemes. An exhibition in the upper east wing presents the work of new designers. The gardens have been restored to their former glory and reflect features common to Mackintosh's architectural designs. **Open:** 1 Apr-31 Oct, daily 1.30-5.30pm. **Admission:** Adult £6, Concession £4.50, Family £16.50. **Groups:** Must pre-book and are accepted only prior to 1pm.

map 12
D5

INVERARAY CASTLE
Cherry Park, Inveraray, Argyll, Scotland, PA32 8XE
Tel: 01499 302 203 Fax: 01499 302 421
(Home of the Duke and Duchess of Argyll)

Since the early 15th century Inveraray Castle has been the Headquarters of the Clan Campbell. The present Castle was built in the third quarter of the 18th century by Roger Morris and Robert Mylne. The Great Hall and Armoury, the State Rooms, tapestries, pictures and the 18th century furniture and Old Kitchen are shown. Those interested in Campbell Genealogy and History will find a visit to The Campbell Room especially enjoyable. **Location:** ¾ mile NE of Inveraray by Loch Fyne. 61 miles NW of Glasgow. **Open:** 7 Apr–14 Oct.

E-mail: enquiries@inveraray-castle.com

`map 12 D4`

INVEREWE GARDEN
Poolewe, Ross-shire IV22 2LG
Tel: 01445 781200 Fax: 01445 781497

This internationally renowned 50 acre garden is impressively set on a peninsula on the shores of Loch Ewe. The warm currents of the North Atlantic Drift help to create an outstanding oasis of colour and fertility where exotic plants from many countries flourish on a latitude more northerly than Moscow, giving an almost continual display of colour throughout the year. Osgood Mackenzie's Victorian dreams have now produced a glorious mecca for garden lovers, not to be missed. **Open:** Garden: 15 Mar–31 Oct, daily 9.30am-9pm; 1 Nov-14 Mar, daily 9.30am-5pm. Visitor Centre and shop, 15 Mar–31 Oct, daily 9.30am-5.30pm. Guided garden walks, 15 Apr-15 Sept, Mon-Fri at 1.30pm. No dogs in garden. **Admission**: Adult £5, Concession £4, Family £14.

`map 14 C4`

MOUNT STUART
Isle of Bute, Scotland, PA20 9LR
Tel: 01700 503877 Fax: 01700 505313 Internet: www.mountstuart.com

Award winning Mount Stuart, one of Britain's most spectacular High Victorian Gothic houses, is the magnificent architectural fantasy of the 3rd Marquess of Bute (1847–1900) and the Scottish architect Robert Rowand Anderson. The scale and ambition of Mount Stuart is equalled only by Bute's collaboration with William Burges to restore Cardiff Castle and Castell Coch. The profusion of astrological designs, stained glass and marble is breathtaking, and all combine to envelop the visitor in the mystique and history of the house. Fabulous interiors and architectural detail. Set in 300 acres of stunning woodlands,

mature Victorian pinetum, arboretum and exotic gardens. Facilities include shop, restaurant, adventure play and picnic areas, audio-visual, assisted wheelchair access, guided tours of house and gardens. Mount Stuart is easily accessible and can be reached by frequent ferry service from Wemyss Bay, Renfrewshire or Colintraive in Argyll. Regular bus service from Rothesay to Mount Stuart. **Open:** May–Sept, daily except Tue & Thurs. Gardens: 10–6pm, House: 11–5pm. **Admission:** (2000 prices) Adult £6, Child £2.50, Family £15. Season £15. Senior Citizen/Student/Group rates given.

`map 12 D6`

PROVOST SKENE'S HOUSE

Guestrow (off Broad Street), Aberdeen, Grampian AB10 1AS
Tel: 01224 641086

Dating from 1545, Provost Skene's House is one of Aberdeen's few remaining examples of early burgh architecture. It now houses an attractive series of period room settings, recalling the elegant furnishings of the 17th, 18th and 19th centuries. Visitors can see one of the most important and intriguing series of religious paintings in Scotland in the Painted Gallery, changing fashions in the Costume Gallery and enjoy a light snack in Provost Skene's Kitchen. An exciting programme of special displays of local interest, coins and archaeology from the city's collections are also on show. **Open:** Mon–Sat 10am–5pm, Sun 1–4pm. **Admission:** Free.

map 13
K1

STOBHALL

Guildtown, Perthshire, Scotland, (Earl of Perth)
Tel: 01738 451111

Gardens and policies. Chapel with 17th century painted ceiling. **Location:** 8 miles N of Perth on A93. **Open:** Mid May–mid June, 1–5pm. **Admission:** Adults £2, Children £1.

map 13
G3

SCONE PALACE

Scone, Perth, PH2 6BD, Perthshire
Tel: 01738 552300 (The Earl of Mansfield) Fax: 01738 552588

Situated 2 miles outside Perth, Scone was the ancient crowning place of the Kings of Scotland and the home of the Stone of Destiny. The present Palace was remodelled in the early nineteenth century, using the structure of the 1580 Palace and remains the home of the Earl and Countess of Mansfield. The State Rooms house unique collections of ivories, paintings, clocks, furniture, porcelain and Vernis Martin. The grounds contain magnificent collections of shrubs, the Murray Star Tartan Maze and woodland walks through the famed pinetum; many species were first introduced by David Douglas (of Douglas Fir fame). The magnificence of the Palace and its contents are complemented by an attractive gift shop, restaurants and adventure playground. Scone is ideal for any family visit and can also provide a exciting venue for corporate and incentive hospitality, both in the Palace or outside in the grounds or Parklands running down to the River Tay. **Open:** 1 Apr–31 Oct, 9.30–5.15pm (last admission 4.45pm). **Admission:** Adults £5.90, Children £3.40, OAP/Students £5.10. Groups: Adults £5.10, Children £2.80, OAP/Students £4.40. **E-mail:** visits@scone–palace.co.uk **Internet:** www.scone–palace.co.uk

map 13
G3

ULLAPOOL MUSEUM & VISITOR CENTRE

7 & 8 West Argyle Street, Ullapool, Scotland IV26 2TY
Tel & Fax: 01854 612987

Award-winning Highland museum. Housed within a unique former Telford Parliamentary Church, providing a stimulating insight into the life of a Highland Parish. Large screen audio-visual presentation of Lochbroom. Local archives, records, genealogy and photos. Touchscreens. Exhibitions. Tape Tour. Six European languages. Disabled access. **Admission:** Accompanied children free. **Open:** April-Oct inclusive, 9.30-5.30pm, Mon-Sat. Nov-Feb inclusive, 11-3pm, Wed, Thur & Sat. March, 11-3pm, Mon- Sat. **E-mail:** ulmuseum@waverider.co.uk

map 14
D4

URQUHART CASTLE

Drumnadrochit, Loch Ness, Highlands
Tel: 01456 450551

Sixteenth-century buildings on the ruins of one of the largest castles ever built in Scotland. The castle stands on a rock overlooking Loch Ness, and is managed by Historic Scotland. **Open:** 1 Apr-30 Sept, daily, 9.30am-6.30pm. 1 Oct-31 Mar, daily, 9.30am-4.30pm. **Admission:** Adult £3.80, Child £1.20, Conc £2.80.

Ireland

Top: Glin Castle. Left: Mount Usher. Below: Powerscourt

Ireland provides the warmest of welcomes to visitors, and the peace and quiet of its rural landscape will surprise those who have only seen the country presented in a negative light on news bulletins. In reality, it is a breathtakingly beautiful and friendly country, where the sleepy pace of life in rural communities is evidence of the inhabitants' relaxed outlook.

From the stark craggy cliffs on the west coast of Galway to the gentle flow of the River Liffey in Dublin, Ireland's scenery is dramatic and serene in equal measure. The barren lands of Connemara seem a world away from the ordered beauty of the landscaped gardens at Powerscourt, and the incredible geometric rock formations at the Devil's Causeway reinforce Ireland's claim to having some of the most varied scenery in Europe.

Irish hospitality can now be enjoyed all over the world, but devotees of Guinness should note that the best is kept within these borders. The pubs of Dublin are the perfect place to sample a pint or two, and the city is enjoying a boom in tourism. Airfares have never been cheaper, making this the perfect year to try Ireland for yourself.

ARDGILLAN VICTORIAN GARDEN
Balbriggan, Co Dublin, Ireland
Tel: 00 353 1 849 2212 Fax: 00 353 1 849 2786

The park consists of 82ha of rolling pasture land, mixed woodland and gardens. The Walled Garden of 1ha is unique in being sub-divided by two free standing walls, one of which has the unusual feature of a series of 20 alcoves for the growing of tender fruits. Each section has a specific theme including a Herb garden, Vegetable Potager, an Irish cottage garden and fruit garden. There is a magnificent Victorian conservatory overlooking the Rose Garden with its wide selection of old and new varieties. **Location:** 30km north of Dublin city. **Open:** All year 10–5pm. Guided tour each Thursday at 3pm during June, July and August. **Admission:** Guided Tours £3.

map 16
D4

BANTRY HOUSE
Bantry, Co. Cork, Ireland
Tel: 00 353 2 750 047 Fax: 00 353 2 750 795 (Mr Egerton Shelswell-White)

Partly Georgian mansion standing at edge of Bantry Bay, with beautiful views. Seat of family of White, formerly Earls of Bantry. Unique collection of tapestries, furniture, etc. Terraces and statuary in the Italian style in the grounds. Restoration work in progress. **Location:** In outskirts of Bantry (1/2 mile). 56 miles SW of Cork. **Open:** Daily, 9–6pm, 1 March–31 Oct. **Admission: House & Grounds:** Adults £6, Children (up to 14) accompanied by parents free, OAPs/Students £4.50. **Grounds only:** £2. **Groups (20+) House & Grounds:** £4. **Refreshments:** Tearoom, Bed & Breakfast and dinner. **Events/Exhibitions:** 1796 Bantry French Armada (permanent exhibition). West Cork Chamber Music Festival 26 June for ten days. **Accommodation:** B&B and dinner. Nine rooms en suite. **Conferences:** Facilities available. Shop.

map 16
B6

BENVARDEN
Benvarden, Denvock, Ballymoney
Tel: 028 20741331 Fax: 028 20741955

Benvarden Garden and grounds, near Balleymoney in Co.Antrim are situated on the banks of the river BUSH. The curved walled garden dates from 1788 and features espalier-trained apple and pear trees, roses box hedged gravel paths aparterre, lawns and a pergola hung with Wisteria, Honeysuckle and Ivy. The adjacent kitchen garden is in the traditional style, with melon houses, fruit trees, vegetables & paths edged with box and herbs. There is a tearoom in the cobbled stable yard. The wooden grounds extend to the banks of the river and there is a small woodland lake surrounded by old Irish Yews, Rhododendrums and many Azalias and wild flowers. **Open:** Tues-Sun. 1.30-5.30, 1 June–31 Aug. **Admission:** Adults £2.50, Children free.

BIRR CASTLE DEMESNE & IRELAND'S HISTORIC SCIENCE CENTRE
Birr, Co Offaly, Ireland
Tel: 00 353 509 20336 Fax: 00 353 509 21583

Ireland's Historic Science Centre includes demesne, telescope and galleries of discovery. **Admission:** Adult IR£5 or Euros5.70, Child IR£2.50 or Euros3.20, Senior Citizen IR£3.50 or Euros4.45, Student IR£3.50 or Euros4.45, Family (2 adults & 2 children) IR£12 or Euros15.20. Guided tours (must be pre-booked) IR£25 or 32. Groups (20+): Adult IR£4 or Euros5, Child IR£2.20 or Euros2.80, Senior Citizen IR£3 or Euros3.80, Student IR£2.50 or Euros3.20. **Open:** 9.30–6pm or dusk if earlier. **E-mail:** info@birrcastle.com **Internet:** www.birrcastle.com

map 16
C4

CARRIGGLAS MANOR

Longford, Ireland
Tel: +353 (0)43 45165 Fax: +353 (0)43 41026 (contact: Tricia Flynn)

A rare opportunity to visit an Irish country house which is still lived in by the family that commissioned it. Visitors can enjoy meeting the family, a guided tour, woodland walks, formal and wildflower gardens, a tea shop and gift shop. This beautiful Tudor-Gothic style Manor House has been the seat of the French Huguenot Lefroy family since Baron Thomas Lefroy commissioned it in 1837. Thomas was the youthful love of Jane Austen and she based the character of Mr Darcy, hero of Pride and Prejudice, on him. Visitors can enjoy a guided tour of the elegant Victorian interiors, which contain family pictures, period furniture and artefacts collected over the past five centuries. The graceful stableyards were built by James Gandon whose other work included The Customs House, The Four Courts and The Bank of Ireland in Dublin. **Location:** 80 miles E of Dublin off the N4; signed from Longford by-pass. **Open:** from 11am–3pm, May–September. Closed Wed, Thurs & Sun. **Admission:** IRP4, house tour additional IRp3. Both house and grounds are available for special interest groups, garden lunches etc. Groups are welcome by appointment. Details concerning corporate hospitality and functions are also available. **E-mail:** info@carrigglas.com **Internet:** www.carrigglas.com

map 16
C4

CASTLE COOLE

Enniskillen, Co Fermanagh, BT74 6JY
Tel: 028 6632 2690 Fax: 028 6632 5665

The finest neo-Classical house in all of Ireland, Castle Coole is set in acres of rolling landscaped park. Beautifully decorated, with fine Regency furniture and ornate state bedroom prepared for George IV. **Open:** 13-17 Apr, daily. Apr, May, Sept, weekends and Bank Hols. Jun & Aug: daily (except Thurs) 1–6pm. **Admission:** (includes guided tour) Adult £3, Child £1.50. Park free.

DUBLIN WRITERS MUSEUM

18 Parnell Square, Dublin 1, Ireland
Tel: 00 353 1 872 2077 Fax: 00 353 1 872 2231

The Dublin Writers Museum is located in a splendidly restored 18th century house. It uniquely represents that great body of Irish writers – in prose, poetry and drama – which has contributed so much to the world of literature over the years. **Location:** Dublin city centre – 5 mins. walk from O'Connell St. **Open:** All year except 24/25/26 Dec. Mon–Sat 10–5pm. Sun & Public Hols 11–5pm. Late opening Jun–Aug, Mon–Fri 10–6pm. **Admission:** Adults £4, Children £2, Concessions £3, Family £11. Group rates (20+): Adults £2.60, Children £1.20, Concessions £2.20. **E-mail:** writers@dublintourism.ie **Internet:** www.visitdublin.com

map 16
D4

HOTEL DUNLOE CASTLE

Beaufort, killarney, Kerry
Tel: 064 44111 Fax: 064 44583

You can walk around the world in an hour in the Castle Gardens. The voyage starts with Chilean fir trees and leads on to Australian gums, South African Lilies, American dogwoods, South American fuschias and back to the Killarney strawberry tree. The gardens surrounding the shell of MacThomas' medieval keep have a dramatic setting looking towards the mountains girdled by the RIng of Kerry. Camellias, magnolias, roses and rhododendrons flourish in the sheltered grounds together with rare specimens like the aromatic-leaved 'Headache' tree and Chinese swamp cypress. For further information and appointment. **Internet:** www.iol.ie/khl

map 16
B6

FERNHILL GARDEN

Sandyford, Co. Dublin, Ireland
Tel: 00 353 12 956 000 (Mrs Sally Walker)

A garden for all seasons, 200 years old in Robinsonion style with over 4,000 species and varieties of trees, shrubs and plants. Dogs not allowed. Location: Sandyford, Co. Dublin. **Open:** 1 Mar–30 Sept, Tue–Sat & BH Mons, 11am–5pm. Sun 2–6pm. Admission: Adults £3, Children £1, OAPs £2.

JAPANESE GARDENS & ST FIACHRA'S GARDEN
Tully, Co. Kildare, Ireland
Tel: 00 353 45 521617 Fax: 00 353 45 522964 (Irish National Stud)

(Both gardens are situated in the grounds of The Irish National Stud Farm). The Japanese Gardens were designed between 1906-1910, they symbolise the 'Life of Man' from the Cradle to the Grave. Now almost 100 years later, The Irish National Stud have created an Irish garden to celebrate the Millennium - St Fiachra's Garden. This garden seeks to capture the power of the Irish landscape in its rawest state, that of rock & water. **Location:** 1 mile outside Kildare town. 30 miles from Dublin off the M/N7. Easy access by rail and bus. **Open:** 12 Feb–12 Nov (Thereafter by booking only). **Admission:** which incl. all 3 attractions: Adults £6, Students/OAPs £4.50, Children (under 12) £3, Family (2 adults & 4 children under 12) £14. **Refreshments:** Yum Yum's Restaurant & Craft shop. Recently restored coach & car park.

 map 16 D4

THE JAMES JOYCE MUSEUM
The Joyce Tower, Sandycove, Co. Dublin, Ireland
Tel: 00 353 1 280 9265 Fax: 00 353 1 280 9265

The Joyce Tower is one of a series of Martello Towers built to withstand an invasion by Napoleon. James Joyce's brief stay here inspired the opening of his great masterpiece, Ulysses, whose first chapter is set in this very tower. The gun platform and living room are much as he described them in his book. It now houses the James Joyce Museum, a modern exhibition devoted to the life and works of the famous writer. **Location:** Sandycove Point on sea front, 1 mile from Dun Laoghaire. **Station(s):** DART to Sandycove. **Buses:** 8 (to Sandycove). **Open:** Apr–Oct, Mon–Sat, 10–1pm & 2–5pm. Suns and public hols, 2–6pm. **Admission:** Adults £4.00, Children £2.00, Concessions £3.00, Family £11.00. Groups prices (20+): Adults £3.50, Children £1.50, Concessions £2.30, by prior arrangement. **E-mail:** joycetower@dublintourism.ie **Internet:** www.visitdublin.com

 map 16 D4

KYLEMORE ABBEY & GARDENS
Connemara, Co Galway, Ireland
Tel: 00 353 95 41146 Fax: 00 353 95 41145

Set in the heart of the Connemara mountains is the renowned kylemore abbey estate. Its fame to date is derived from its status as a premier tourist attraction, international girls' boarding school, magnificent Gothic church, tranquil surrounds, superb restaurant and one of the finest craft shops in Ireland. The six acre Victorian Walled Garden opened to the public in Spring 1999, while under restoration.

FOR FURTHER DETAILS, OPENING TIMES AND PHOTOGRAPHY, PLEASE TURN TO PAGE 276.

LISMORE CASTLE GARDENS
Lismore, Co. Waterford, Ireland
Tel: 00 353 58 54424 Fax: 00 353 58 54896 (Lismore Estates)

Lismore Castle has been the Irish home of the Dukes of Devonshire since 1753 and at one time belonged to Sir Walter Raleigh. The gardens are set in seven acres within the 17th century outer defensive walls and have spectacular views of the castle. There is also a fine collection of specimen magnolias, camellias, rhododendrons and a remarkable yew walk where Edmund Spenser is said to have written the "Faerie Queen". Throughout the open season there is always plenty to see in this fascinating and beautiful garden. **Location:** Lismore, 45 miles W of Waterford. 35 miles NE of Cork (1 hour). **Open:** 14 Apr–14 Oct. **Admission:** Adults £3, Children (under 16) £1.50. Reduced rates for groups of 20+: Adults £2.50, Children £1.30. **E-mail:** lismoreestates@eircom.net

 map 16 C6

MALAHIDE CASTLE
Malahide, Co Dublin
Tel: 00 353 1 846 2184 Fax: 00 353 1 846 2537

Malahide Castle, set on 250 acres of parkland in the pretty seaside town of Malahide, was both a fortress and a private home for nearly 800 years and is an interesting mix of architectural styles. The house is furnished with beautiful period furniture together with an extensive collection of Irish portrait paintings, mainly from the National Gallery. **Open:** Apr–Oct: Mon–Sat 10–5pm, Sun & Public Hols 11–6pm. Nov–Mar: Mon–Fri 10–5pm, Sat, Sun & Public Hols 2–5pm. Closed for tours daily 12.45–2pm. **Admission:** Adults £4, Children £2, Concs £3, Family £11. Group (20+): Adults £2.65, Children £1.55, Concs £2.20. **E-mail:** malahidecastle@dublintourism.ie **Internet:** www.visitdublin.com

 map 16 D4

MOUNT USHER GARDENS
Ashford, Co Wicklow
Tel: 00 353 404 40205/40116 Fax: 00 353 404 40205 (Mrs Madelaine Jay)

Laid out along the banks of the river Vartry, Mount Usher represents the Robinsonian style, i.e. informality and natural design. Trees and shrubs introduced from many parts of the world are planted in harmony with woodland and shade loving plants. The river, with its weirs and waterfalls, is enhanced by attractive suspension bridges from which spectacular views may be enjoyed. The Gardens cover 20 acres and comprise over 5000 different species of plants, most serving as host to a variety of birds and other wildlife. To the professional gardener, the lover of nature or the casual tourist, a visit to Mount Usher is sure to be a memorable one. **Location:** Ashford, on the main Dublin to Rosslare Road N11, 50km from Dublin. 115km from Rosslare. **Open:** Mid Mar–end Oct. **Admission:** Adults £4, OAPs, Students, Children £3 (Special group rates for 20+). Guided tours booked in advance.

 map 16 D5

NEWMAN HOUSE
85–86 St Stephen's Green, Dublin 2
Tel: 00 353 706 7422 Fax: 00 353 706 7211 (University College Dublin)

Numbers 85 and 86 St Stephen's Green are two of the finest Georgian houses in the city of Dublin. Each house contains a series of spectacular 18th century stucco interiors. By good fortune these remarkable buildings were united in common ownership in the 19th century when they were acquired by the Catholic University of Ireland, the precursor of modern University College Dublin. The building was named in honour of John Henry Newman, the University's first rector. The great English poet Gerard Manley Hopkins spent the last years of his life at Newman House and James Joyce was a student here from 1899–1902. Recently restored to its former grandeur, Newman House offers the visitor a unique combination of visual splendour and evocative literary associations. **Open:** June, July & Aug only, Tues–Fri 12–5pm, Sat 2–5pm, Sun 11–2pm. The rest of the year tours by appointment only.

 map 16 D4

KYLEMORE ABBEY & GARDENS

Connemara, Co Galway, Ireland
Tel: 00 353 95 41146 Fax: 00 353 95 41145

Set in the heart of the Connemara mountains is the renowned **Kylemore Abbey Estate**. Its fame to date is derived from its status as a premier tourist attraction, international girls' boarding school, magnificent Gothic church, tranquil surrounds, superb restaurant and one of the finest craft shops in Ireland. The six acre Victorian Walled Garden opened to the public in Spring 1999, while under restoration. This garden was the most impressive in Ireland. The walls stretch for over half a mile to enclose: the kitchen garden, the flower garden, gardener's cottage, bothy and the impressive glass (hot) house complex. All of these features and more are being restored in phases over the next few years. The Benedictine

Nuns at Kylemore continue to work tirelessly at restoring the estate and opening it to the education and enjoyment of all who visit, carrying on the unique Benedictine tradition, spanning over 1,500 years of warmth and hospitality. **A visit to the west of Ireland is not complete without visiting Kylemore Abbey and Garden.** <u>Open:</u> Abbey, Grounds & Gothic Church: All year (Closed Good Friday & Christmas Week). Shop and Restaurant: Mar–Nov (Closed Good Friday). Garden: Easter–Oct.
E-mail: enquiries@kylemoreabbey.ie **Internet:** www.kylemoreabbey.com

map 16
B4

MUCKROSS HOUSE, GARDENS & TRADITIONAL FARMS
INCORPORATING MUCROS CRAFTS CENTRE

National Park, Killarney, Kerry
Tel: 00 353 64 31440 Fax: 00 353 64 33926 (Trustees of Muckross House)

Muckross House is a magnificent Victorian mansion, situated on the shores of Muckross Lake and set amidst the splendid and spectacular landscape of Killarney National Park. The exquisitely furnished rooms portray the lifestyles of the gentry, including Queen Victoria's boudoir and bedroom as it was when she visited in 1861. The Gardens of Muckross are famed for their beauty worldwide. Muckross Traditional Farms is an exciting outdoor representation of the lifestyles and farming traditions of a rural community of the 1930s. Three separate working farms, complete with animals, poultry and traditional farm machinery will help you relive the past when all work was carried out using traditional methods. Muckross Vintage Coach, visitors to the Farms can enjoy a Free trip around the site on a beautiful Vintage Coach. Visit the magnificent newly opened 'Mucros Crafts Centre', with full Restaurant and Craft Shop. **Location:** 3.5m from Killarney, on the Kenmare road. **Open:** Daily, all year. 9–5.30pm, 9–7pm Jul/Aug (Farms Mar–Oct) **Admission:** Adult Ir£4, Students Ir£1.60. Group rate for 20+ Ir£3. Family Ir£10. Ditto for Muckross Traditional Farms. Substantial savings on joint tickets. Gardens free. **Internet:** www.muckross–house.ie

map 16 B6

NEWBRIDGE HOUSE

Donabate, Co. Dublin, Ireland
Tel: 00 353 1 8436534 Fax: 00 353 1 8462537

This delightful 18th century mansion is set on 350 acres of parkland, 12 miles north of the city centre and boasts one of the finest Georgian interiors in Ireland. The house appears more or less as it did 150 years ago. It was built in 1737, to a design by Richard Castle, for the Archbishop of Dublin and contains elaborate stucco plasterwork by Robert West. The grounds contain a 29 acre traditional farm complete with farmyard animals, a delight to any young visitor and perfect for school tours and large groups. **Open:** Apr–Sept: Tues–Sat 10–5pm, Sun & Public Hols 2–6pm, closed Mons. Oct–Mar: Sat, Sun, Public Hols 2–5pm. Closed for tours daily 1–2pm. Coffee shop remains open **Admission:** Adult £3, Children £1.65, Conc £2.60, Family £8.25. Group (20+): Adult £2.60, Children £1.40, Conc £2.20. **Internet:** www.visitdublin.com

map 16 D4

NORTH DOWN HERITAGE CENTRE

Town Hall, Bangor Castle, Bangor, Co Down BT20 4BT
Tel: 91 271200 Fax: 91 271370

North Down Heritage Centre is situated in beautiful wooded surroundings at the rear of Bangor Castle. Its free exhibitions include Early Christian times, nostalgia for seaside holidays and the unique new Percy French Room. An observation beehive is in place in summer. There is no finer setting for a museum restaurant than the Castle Garden Room. **Open:** Open daily except Mondays.

E-mail: bangor_heritage_centre@yahoo.com

Internet: www.north–down.gov.uk/heritage/

map 16 E2

PALM HOUSE BOTANIC GARDENS

Belfast City
Tel: 028 9032 4902

Located between Stranmillis Road and Botanic Avenue in southern Belfast, these fine botanic gardens were built by Richard Turner, who went on to build the Great Palm House at Kew Gardens. **Open:** All year round. Apr–Sept: Mon–Fri, 10am–12pm and 1–5pm; weekends, 1–5pm. Closes one hour earlier in winter. **Admission:** Free.

POWERSCOURT GARDENS & WATERFALL

Enniskerry, Co. Wicklow, Ireland
Tel: 00 353 204 6000 Fax: 00 353 204 6900

Just 12 miles south of Dublin, in the foothills of the Wicklow Mountains, lies Powerscourt Estate. Its 20 hectares of gardens are famous the world over. It is a sublime blend of formal gardens, sweeping terraces, statuary and ornamental lakes, together with secret hollows, rambling walks, walled gardens and over 200 variations of trees and shrubs. The shell of the 18th century house gutted by fire in 1974 has an innovative new use: incorporating a terrace restaurant overlooking the spectacular gardens, speciality shops and an exhibition on the Estate and Gardens. Powerscourt Waterfall (5km from Gardens) is Ireland's highest. **E-mail:** gardens@powerscourt.ie **Internet:** www.powerscourt.ie

`map 16 D4`

SEAFORDE GARDENS

Seaforde, Downpatrick, Co. Down, BT30 8PG, Northern Ireland Tel: (028) 4481 1225 Fax: (028) 4481 1370 (Patrick Forde)

Over 600 trees and shrubs, container grown. Many camellias and rhododendrons. National collection of Eucryphius. Tropical butterfly house with hundreds of free flying butterflies. The 18th century walled gardens and pleasure grounds contain a vast collection of trees and shrubs. Many very rare. Huge rhododendrons. The Hornbeam maze is the oldest in Ireland. **Location:** On A24, Ballynahinch–Newcastle road. **Open:** Easter–end Sept, Mon–Sat 10–5pm. Sun 1–6pm.

`map 16 E3`

STROKESTOWN PARK HOUSE & GARDENS

Strokestown, Co Roscommon, Ireland
Tel: 00 353 78 33013 Fax: 00 353 78 33712

Strokestown Park was the home of the Pakenham Mahon family from the 1660's to 1979. The house retains most its original furnishings and is viewed by guided tour. The Famine Museum uses original documents and letters relating to the time of the Famine on the Strokestown Park Estate to explain the history of The Great Irish Famine and to draw parallels with the occurrence of famine in the Developing World today. The 4½ acre walled pleasure garden has been faithfully restored to its original splendour. Home of the longest herbaceous border in Ireland & UK. Open: House, gardens & Famine Museum 1 Apr–31 Oct, every day, 11–5.30pm (flexible for groups). **Admission:** Charges apply. Reduced rates for families, senior citizens, unemployed and groups. Parking. Wheelchair access to museum and garden. **E-mail:** info@strokestownpark.ie

TALBOT BOTANIC GARDEN

Malahide Castle Demesne, Malahide, Co Dublin, Ireland
Tel: 00 353 1 872 7777 Fax: 00 353 1 872 7530

Botanical Garden located within Malahide Demesne, containing over 4,000 species of non ericaceous plants with a comprehensive collection of Southern Hemisphere plants, many rare and unusual. The gardens were largely created by Lord Milo Talbot from 1948 to 1973 and cover an area of 9ha including the Walled Garden of 1.6ha. It includes many tender shrub borders, alpine yard, pond and 7 glasshouses including a most elegant Victorian Conservatory. The collection continues to expand with the addition of new species and varieties. **Location:** 16km north of Dublin city. **Open:** 1 May–30 Sept: Daily 2–5pm. Guided tour Wed at 2pm. Groups by appointment. **Admission:** Adults. £2 **Internet:** www.visitdublin.com.

`map 16 D4`

TULLYNALLY CASTLE & GARDENS

Castlepollard, Co. Westmeath, Ireland.
Tel: 00 353 44 61159/61289 Fax: 00 353 44 61856
(Thomas & Valerie Pakenham)

Home of the Pakenhams (later Earls of Longford) since the 17th century. The original house is now incorporated in a huge rambling gothic revival castle. 30 acres of romantic woodland and walled gardens are also open to the public. **Location:** 1.5 miles outside Castlepollard on Granard Road. **Station(s):** Mullingar. **House open:** 15 June–30 July, 2–6pm. Pre-booked groups admitted at other times. **Gardens:** May–August, 2–6pm. **Admission:** House & Gardens: Adults £5, Children £2.50, Groups £4. Gardens only: Adults £3, Children £1. **Refreshments:** Tearoom open mid June–August daily 2–6pm. **E-mail:** tpakenham@tinet.ie

`map 16 C4`

ULSTER MUSEUM

Botanic Gardens, Belfast, BT9 5AB
Tel: (028) 9038 3000 Fax: (028) 9038 3003

Visitors can browse through the permanent galleries to enjoy fine collections of Irish art, watercolours and drawings, Old Masters and Modern international art. Archaeology displays include Early Ireland and Midieval Ireland and the dazzling gold of Spanish Armada wrecks, as well as selections from the ethnography collections. The province's history can be followed through the local history galleries, including Making Irish Linen and Made in Belfast. Among the natural history displays, The Living Sea is a 'sight and sound' voyage of discovery and Treasures of the Earth offers a glimpse into the marvellous world of minerals and precious gems. **Open:** All year Mon-Fri 10-5pm, Sat 1-5pm, Sun 2-5pm. **Admission:** Free. 24-hour information line: 028 9038 3001.

`map 16 D3`

Channel Islands

With a wealth of wonderful scenery, magnificent coastline, historic buildings, natural and man-made attractions, and mouthwatering local produce, the Channel Islands provide a memorable destination that is charmingly different.

The island of Guernsey and its neighbours are the last remnants of the medieval Dukedom of Normandy, which held sway both in France and in England. The islands were the only British soil to be occupied in World War II, and were liberated on May 9, 1945. The capital of Guernsey is Saint Peter Port, which boasts a large deepwater harbour, providing excellent facilities for the numerous boats than crowd its quaysides. Inland, the visitor may be surprised to find that there are still some speakers of the islands Norman French dialect. Guernsey hosts a number of cultural events throughout the year, including the Floral Festival Week, 3rd-11th June, which offers a range of activities for gardening enthusiasts and horticulturists.

St. Aubins Harbour, Jersey

The island of Jersey will also hold various musical events between the 5th and 8th April when the Jazz Festival takes place, now celebrating its 21st year. The Jersey International Food Festival, held between 12th and 20th May 2001, gives visitors the chance to taste the finest local produce and experience the skills of top Jersey Chefs. The Battle of Flowers parade is held on 9th August 2001 and features floats covered in flowers, musicians, dancers and carnival queens. The evening of the 10th August will feature a spectacular Moonlight Parade, culminating in a firework display over St Aubins Bay.

A fine destination for all the family, the island offers a plethora of fun activities and attractions such as Jersey Zoo. The zoo was founded in 1959 by the celebrated author and naturalist, Gerald Durrell. With over one hundred species including Andean bears, ring-tailed coatis and short-clawed otters, visitors are both treated to an exciting experience and reminded of the diversity of the animal kingdom.

A view of the Bay in Jersey

SAUSMAREZ MANOR - HISTORIC HOUSE, SCULPTURE PARK & SUBTROPICAL GARDEN

St Martin, Guernsey GY4 6SG
Tel: 01481 235571 Fax: 01481 235572 (Peter de Sausmarez)

Regarded as the finest example of Queen Anne Colonial Architecture in Europe and the first example of American cultural influence in Britain. Built at the bequest of Sir Edmund Andros 1st Governor of New York, 1714 (also Governor of North Carolina, Massachusetts, Virginia, New Jersey and New England etc). Still the seat of the Seigneurs de Sausmarez since C1220. One of only 21 houses in Britain recommended by the Courvoisier Book of the Best in the world and in the top 20 houses as judged by the AA and NPI in '95. Also in the grounds are a lush subtropical woodland garden, a 9 hole par 3 pitch and putt course, petland, an art gallery and the 3rd largest dedicated Dolls House collection in Britain. Regularly used for celebrations, receptions and special horticultural, architectural and artistic visits and conventions. The remarkable Sculpture Park and Path is set in the

Formal Gardens and in and around the small lakes and the subtropical woodland amongst the bamboo groves, Tree Ferns, Lilies, Hibiscus, Magnolias, 320 Camellias, Rhododendrons, Fuchsias, Giant Echiums, Cyclamen and Banana Trees. The Sculpture Park is regarded by the 90 or so exhibitors as the most beautiful setting they have seen, where the 200 pieces in a constantly changing permanent exhibition sit so happily. The work that is bought is sent all over the world and are constantly having to be replaced. The Sculptors are members of the Royal Society of British Sculptors and the Society of Portrait Sculptors augmented by French, German, Italian, Irish and Channel Island artists.

Internet: www.guernsey.org/sausmarez

map 3 H6

Belgium

Belgium has, on balance, been somewhat unfortunate to find itself at the political centre of Europe. Many people consider the country to be the spiritual home of bureaucracy, red tape and the dreaded metric system, but whilst it may be true that the EC has annexed much of the centre of Brussels, the rest of Belgium is as varied and interesting as France.

The country's coastline does not consist solely of ferry ports, but also of long sandy beaches overlooked by elegant promenades, such as those at Knokke-Heist. Just inland stands the perfectly preserved mediaeval city of Bruges, with its wonderful bell tower and leafy towpath walks. Nearby Antwerp is a decidedly more modern city, built on the profits of the worldwide diamond trade, but it retains some interesting old buildings.

Brussels itself is a small, clean and friendly city, with delightful restaurants crammed into the narrow streets that radiate out from the magnificent Grand' Place. The city is reckoned to have more Michelin-starred restaurants per head of population than Paris, but the food is excellent even in the tiny

pavement cafés. Brussels is not particularly rich in historic buildings, but the Palais de Justice is well worth a visit, as are the numerous art-nouveau houses in the inner suburbs.

The road south from Brussels passes through a number of charming provincial towns, including Dinant, whose mighty fort stands on a cliff, towering over the river below. The flat landscape of the north then gives way to the forested hills of the Ardennes, where quiet villages have remained unchanged for hundreds of years. The area is rich in wildlife, and you may even chance upon a stag or a wild boar on one of the woodland trails. In winter, the same trails can be explored on cross-country skis.

Castles of the Ardennes Region

Château de Warfusee

Less than an hour's journey from Brussels, take a day or two to discover some superb historic properties in a beautiful region on the edge of the Ardennes. The Royal Association of Historic Houses in Belgium organises various guided tours for groups only, with accommodation in Liège, Huy or Brussels.

Tours can be tailored to your exact requirements, but the following will give an idea of the range available. One tour begins at the magnificent castle of **Warfusée**, once the residence of a bishop prince of Liège. His family still live there, and the rooms remain much as they were in the eighteenth century, with tapestries, beautiful furniture and an impressive portrait gallery. This is followed by a visit to the church of **Saint Séverin**, a former Benedictine priory built in the twelfth century from honey-coloured Condroz stone. The nearby **Donceel** manor house is set in a landscaped park, and features a number of murals and stucco walls. A visit to the **Château de Bois Seigneur Isaac** includes coffee with the owners, followed by a tour of the fine collections of painting and furniture. Next to the house is the famous **Chapelle du Saint-Sang**, which is the last stop before lunch near Nivelles. The afternoon tour takes in the **Château de la Follie**, with its superb gothic chapel, 16th-century courtyard, and 17th-century tapestries.

For information on booking, please contact Madame A. Renard-Ortmans, 82 rue de la Forière, 4100 Seraing, Belgium.
Tel: 00 32 4 336 16 87 Fax: 00 32 4 337 08 01 E-mail: anne.renard.ortmans@skynet.be

CASTLES OF WARFUSÉE & CORROY

Warfusée – 4470 St Georges s/Meuse   **Corroy** – 5032 Gembloux, Namur
Tel: 00 32 (0)4 336 1687 Fax: 00 32 (0)4 337 0801 (Mme Renard-Ortmans)

Château De Warfusée is a major part of Wallonie's heritage. One of the most beautiful buildings in the Mosane region, built in 1754 by the architect Jean Gilles Jacob. Former residence of the prince-bishop Charles Nicolas d'Oultremont, the rooms at Warfusée remain decorated as they were at the time. Magnificent rooms decorated with tapestries. Also features a collection of furniture, paintings, porcelain, silverware, bookshelves and family treasures. The house is still occupied by the same family to this day. A superb park surrounds the house. After your visit, it is possible to have lunch in the rooms at Aigremont house. **Location:** Between Liège and Huy, on the E42 motorway. **Open:** Throughout the year by prior arrangement only for groups (min 25 people). Guided tours. Closed on Sundays.

Château de Corroy-le-Château represents the most impressive 13th century open-country stronghold in Belgium. It was built by the Counts of Vianden to defend the south of the Duchy of Brabant. This fortress has passed down by succession, from the Sponheim, Bavarian and Nassau families, to the Marquesses of Trazegnies who currently live there. The interior has been perfectly restored, and contains a spectacular neo-gothic hall, a chapel dating from 1270, salons featuring canvas paintings and numerous family belongings. **Location:** 5km west of Gembloux, N29. **Open:** Weekends and holidays from 29 Apr–1 Oct, from 10–12pm, and from 2–6pm. **Admission:** Adults 150BF, Children (aged 6–10) 80BF, OAPs (groups) 100BF. Events: Music festival and summer theatre.

map 281
1

map 281
2

CHÂTEAU DE HEX
Kasteel Hex, B-3870 Heers-Heks
Tel: 00 32 12 74 73 41 Fax: 00 32 12 74 49 87 (Count & Countess G. d'Ursel)

The Château de Hex was built in the 18th century on a beautiful natural site. It was then surrounded by 12 acres of formal gardens set in a 150 acre English-style park. A collection of old and botanical roses - is of particular interest. This collection is the fruit of the never-ending efforts and joy of the late Countess Michel d'Ursel. The vegetable garden, where a wide variety of fruit and vegetables are still grown, includes a vegetable storage-cellar which is still operated using traditional methods. Every year the gardens are open to the public. **Open:** 2nd w/e in June: Festival of Roses 10am–5pm (8, 9, 10 June). 3rd w/e in Sept: Festival of Autumn and Kitchen Gardens 10am–5pm (15, 16 Sept). Guided tours, from Apr–Sept, except in Aug, upon written request, weekdays only, min 20 people. **Admission:** BF300. **E-mail:** gardens@hex.be **Internet:** www.hex.be

map 281
3

CHÂTEAU FORT ECAUSSINNES LALAING
1, rue de Seneffe–B7191 Ecaussinnes Lalaing, Belgium
Tel & Fax: 00 32 67 44 24 90

From the 11th and 12th century, transformed into a residence in the 15th century, this castle preserves the memory of the family of the counts van der Burch, who lived there from 1624 to 1854. Furnished rooms: grand salon, bedroom, oratory. Medieval part: armoury, ancient kitchen, chapel, dungeon. Collections: portraits of the counts van der Burch; paintings, sculptures, glasses, porcelain, furniture, ancient weapons. **Location:** 7km from exit 20 on E19 (direction Ronquieres). **Open:** 10–12pm, 2–6pm. 1 Apr–1 Nov–weekends and holidays. Jul–Aug, everyday except Tues and Weds. Groups by appointment 1 Apr–2 Nov (guided tours on request).

map 281
4

CHATEAU DE MODAVE
B–4577 Modave
Tel: 00 32 85 411 369 Fax: 00 32 85 412 676

Dating back to 13C, the castle owes its architectural appearance to the restoration by Count de Marchin from 1652–1673. Modave had many distinguished owners, before it was bought in 1941 by the 'Compagnie Intercommunale Bruxelloise des Eaux', in order to protect the impounded water. Twenty richly decorated and furnished rooms are open to the public and include remarkable ceilings, stucco works by Jean-Christian Hansche, sculptures, paintings, Brussels tapestries and 18C furniture. In 1667 Rennequin Sualem built the hydraulic wheel that was used as a pattern for the machine at Marly, bringing the water from the Seine to Versailles Palace. This technical achievement is illustrated in one of the rooms with several documents, plans and an accurate replica of the wheel, made to scale. **Open:** 1 Apr–15 Nov, 9–6pm. 16 Nov–31 Mar, by appointment. **Internet:** www.modave-castle.be

map 281
5

MONCEAU-SUR-SAMBRE
Charleroi
Tel: 00 32 71 32 11 23 (Ville de Charleroi)

Although its origins go back a long way, the château of Monceau is essentially the work of two families: the counts of Hamal, who built the main building in the early 17th century and their heirs, the princes of Gavre, who added a wing to it in the late 18th century, during the last years of Austrian rule. It was in 1795 that the prince of Gavre was given the duty of receiving at Bâle the unfortunate Marie-Thérèse of France, the orphan of the Temple, the only member of Louis XVI's family to escape the Terror. During the 19th century, the house passed first to the Eggers, then to the Houtarts, a family of industrialists who redecorated it at the end of the century, before bequeathing it to the local authorities. The town of Charleroi is courageously restoring the house. **Open:** All year from sunrise to sunset. **Admission:** Free.

map 281
6

MONTAIGLE
Falaën (Onhaye), Belgium
Tel: 00 32 82 69 95 85 or 00 32 81 22 37 98 (Patrick et Geoffroy del Marmol)

This impressive fortress, the ruins of which stand at the junction of two wild valleys, was built by Guy of Flanders. He was one of the heroes of the Battle of Courtrai in 1302 when the Flemish militias crushed the army of Philip the Fair, King of France. It became the residence of the dowager countesses of Namur and still harbours the shades of Marguerite of Lorraine and Jeanne d'Harcourt. It was in 1554 that Henri II of France reduced this imposing fortress to ruin once and for all. The Friends of Montaigle have made a tremendous effort to revive the site, which must be one of the most romantic places in the whole of Belgium. Telephone for prices and opening times.

map 281
7

NATIONAL BOTANIC GARDEN OF BELGIUM

Domein Van Bouchout, B-1860 Meise
Tel: 00 32 2 260 09 70 Fax: 00 32 2 260 09 45

At only a stones throw from Brussels, the centre of European activity, lies the National Botanic Garden of Belgium in the domain of Bouchout, Meise. The domain is closely interwoven with Belgian history. The earliest remains of the castle date back to the 12th century. In more recent times it was the refuge of the former Empress of Mexico, Charlotte, sister of King Leopold II. She died in 1927. Apart from the castle there are various smaller features. There are ice cellars, small ornamental buildings, an exquisite greenhouse by Alphonse Balat, ancient trees and wide sweeping lawns. The Botanic Garden was located to the site in 1939 and added extensive living collections. The immense Plant-Palace houses the tropical and subtropical collections and covers more than 1 hectare. The temperate collections are grouped in several locations in the park. During summer the old Orangery functions as a restaurant and the castle houses a small shop. **Open:** Every day, closed on 25 Dec and 1 Jan. Closing times vary according to season and weather conditions. Call: +32 (0) 2 260 09 70 for details. **Admission:** Adult BF160, Child/Student BF120. **Internet:** www.BR.fgov.be

map 281
8

OOIDONK CASTLE

Ooidonkdreef 9, B9800 Deinze, Belgium
Tel: 00 32 9 282 35 70 Fax: 00 32 9 282 52 82 (Count t'Kint de Roodenbeke)

Overlooking one of the bends of the Lys river, the castle proves to be the focal point of the surrounding countryside which sports lush green meadows and centuries old oak trees that shelter a colony of celebrated herons. What an imposing sight - austere and sumptuous as well! Dated from the 14th century, its massive towers and walls bear witness to its past, ravaged by war yet withstanding the fire and destruction that it brings. Although modernised in the 19th century, it stands almost intact as it was in 1595. Several generations can be traced back to its interior decoration, highlighted by its elegant white-stone staircase, its historical architecture, furniture and art collections. Please telephone for opening times and prices.

map 281
9

POEKE

Poeke, Belgium
Tel: 00 32 51 68 83 00 (Gemeente Aalter)

In former times, a powerful fortress stood on this spot, defending the town of Ghent. It was here that Jacques de Lalaing, known as the Good Knight perished in 1453. Charles-Florent de Preudhomme d'Hailly built a colossal château on the site in the Baroque style, incorporating four towers from the old fortications. The style is a reflection of the wealth of its builders but also of the Flemish style of the 18th century, less concerned with the grace of French influence than with a long tradition of pomp and opulence inspired by Rubens. Poeke later became a Catholic school, but it has lost none of its majesty, standing still in a beautiful park of fifty-three hectares. **Open:** All year, from sunrise to sunset. **Admission:** Free.

map 281
10

RAEREN

Raeren, Belgium
Tel: 00 32 87 85 09 03 Fax: 00 32 87 85 09 32 (Commune de Raeren)

Built by the Rhineland Schwarzenbergs in the 14th century, this water-castle has retained its medieval and austere appearance despite minor alterations made during the 16th and 17th centuries. However, the crenellated towers at the entrance of the castle have recently been built. The castle house an attractive museum of Raeren stoneware, the success of which dates back to the 16th century. **Open:** Daily 10–5pm (except Mondays). **Admission:** Please telephone for prices.

map 281
11

BURG REULAND

4790 Burg Reuland, Belgium
Tel: 00 32 80 32 97 12 Fax: 00 32 80 42 00 46 (Ministère des Travaux Publics)

This solid fortress, the impressive ruins of which dominate the village of the same name, was undoubtedly the work of one of the great heroes of the Middle Ages, John the Blind, count of Luxembourg and King of Bohemia, who died in the Battle of Crécy in 1346, giving his three-feathered crest and motto to the prince of Wales, who bears it to this day. Numerous Rhenish families inherited the property until the local authorities acquired it; it stood in ruins, after it had been damaged in successive wars and had been used as a stone quarry in the 19th century. Today, the castle has regained its former dignity. Open: July, Aug and Sept: daily 11–6pm. Open other school holidays and bank holidays 11–5pm. Admission: Free.

map 281
12

PROVINCIAAL MUSEUM STERCKSHOF – SILVER CENTRE

Hooftvunderlei 160, B-2100 Antwerp (Deurne)
Tel: 00 32 3 360 5250   Fax: 00 32 3 360 5253

The Provinciaal Museum Sterckshof –Silver Centre is a museum in a park on the edge of the city of Antwerp. It is a journey of discovery that leads through a picturesque castle to the treasures of Belgian silver production from the 16th to the 20th centuries inclusive. At the end of the 18th century little remained of the castle built in the 16th century. On the basis of the original foundation and iconographic material, a reconstruction emerged during the thirties. The library with public reading room (Internet: www.cipal.be/digibib/home.htm), many exhibitions and the museum workshop throw further light on the art of the silversmith. The garden was relaid in 1994. The Sterckshof Museum is situated in the Provinciaal Domain Rivierenhof (Castle Rivierenhof, now a restaurant).

Location: Provinciaal Domein Rivierenhof, entrance Cornelissenlaan, Antwerp (Deurne). Antwerp expressway (E 19) exit 3 and motorway Antwerp-Liège (E 313) exit 18. **Stations:** Antwerpen-Centraal and bus 18 (Collegelaan), 41 (Cogelsplein) or tram 10 (Cogelsplein), 24 (Waterbaan). Antwerpen-Berchem and bus 18 (Collegelaan). **Open:** 10–5.30pm. Closed on Mon and 25 Dec–2 Jan. **Admission:** Museum and garden free. Exhibition hall: BF200–120. **Events/Exhibitions:** 2001 - 'Royal Silver for People and King', 1 May–22 July. **E-mail:** info@sterckshof.provant.be **Internet:** www.provant.be/sterckshof

map 281
13

www.historichouses.co.uk

France

Top: Château de Chenonceau
Bottom left: Château de Cheverny   Bottom right: Château & Jardins de Villandry

In geographical terms, France is perhaps the most interesting and varied country in continental Europe. The flat coastal plains of the north give way to gentle hills and wooded valleys in the centre of the country, before rising to meet the magnificent peaks of the Alps in the south-east. The long sandy beaches and natural harbours of the south-west run inland to the "landes", an area of sandy pine forest unique to this part of the world, and south of here are the arid foothills of the Pyrenees. The south-east side of the hexagon basks in the Mediterranean climate, and its deep harbours and sheltered coves have proved attractive to the glamorous yacht-dweller.

However, it is probably the cultural and gastronomic delights of France that have made it one of the leading tourist destinations in the world, and the British are indeed fortunate to have such a magnificent country on their very doorstep. Brittany was once very closely linked to Cornwall, and their ancient language and Arthurian legends are inextricably linked. Famed for its quirky place names and the Breton traditions of cider and galettes (buckwheat pancakes), Brittany is also home to a number of splendid parks and gardens, many of which are featured in the guide for the first time this year.

Normandy is the entry point for most British visitors to France, and recent years have seen the construction of a number of unsightly hypermarkets and wine shops to cater to the bargain-hunting day-tripper. Thankfully, the landscape beyond remains typically French, with orange-roofed houses clustered round square-towered churches on the flat plains. The region is also strongly linked to Britain, and the Norman conquest of the eleventh century had a profound influence on our language and culture.

Paris stands in the Ile de France, the most prosperous area in Europe, where charming old towns conceal a thriving world of business and industry. The city itself possesses a wealth of famous landmarks, including the Eiffel Tower, the Sacré-Cœur and the cathedral of Notre-Dame, and a host of less-famous gems such as the Pantheon, the Sorbonne and the original Statue of Liberty.

The ancient church of St Julien-le-Pauvre still stands in a maze of winding cobbled streets just off the rue du Petit Pont in the Quartier Latin (so named because Latin was the spoken here throughout the Middle Ages), and the rue Mouffetard to the south-east has been crowded with restaurants for hundreds of years. Other lesser-known sights include the elegant Place des Vosges in the Marais, just to the north of rue de Rivoli, and the wonderful Parc André Citroën to the west of the Eiffel Tower, a intriguing modern park with themed gardens radiating out from the fountains and canals at the centre.

The Loire valley is within easy reach of Paris, and is home to France's greatest châteaux. The modern motorway is the most efficient way to travel, but the old Routes Nationales are a far better way to see the beautiful landscape along the river. The major towns along its length – Orléans, Blois, and Tours – all boast beautiful churches, castles and stone bridges, and the view south-west across the river at Saumur is breathtakingly beautiful, taking in the lofty castle and cathedral, the ancient stone bridge, and the broad, stately sweep of the Loire below.

The southern regions of France are home to some of its greatest wines, and charming country châteaux abound. The Dordogne is fast becoming the new Provence, where Francophile Britons are buying up pretty country retreats in a land of vineyards and quiet villages.

This year, we have reordered the French properties geographically, in order to facilitate the planning of itineraries. Properties in the northern part of France and the region around Paris come first, followed by the north-west (Brittany), the Loire valley, and finally the properties in the eastern and southern parts of the country.

A second map on page 295 shows a close-up of the Brittany and Loire Regions (properties 21–59).

NACQUEVILLE CHÂTEAU & GARDENS
50460 Urville-Nacqueville
Tel: 00 33 02 33 03 56 03 (Count & Countess Thierry d'Harcourt)

Construction of the château began in 1510 as a fortified manor. Partly modified during the 18th and 19th centuries, it displays granite walls and stone roofs and is, therefore, characteristic of the finest Cotentin manors. The park, created in the 1830s by an English landscape gardener, is romantic and most delightful. A stream runs down to an enchanting lake in which the château is reflected. Many varieties of rhododendrons, azaleas, hydrangeas and ornamental trees are spread over the large lawns. **Open:** Easter–30 Sept, every day except Tuesday & Friday. Guided visits at 2, 3, 4 & 5pm only. **Admission:** Adults FF30, Children FF10. **Location:** On North Cotentin coastal road, 5km West of Cherbourg.

map 287
1

CHÂTEAU ET PARC FLORAL DE MARTINVAST
Domaine de Beaurepaire, 50690 Martinvast, Basse-Normandie, France
Tel: 00 33 2 33 87 20 80 Fax: 00 33 2 33 52 03 01 (Cte et Ctesse de Pourtales-Schickler)

This landscaped listed park containing meadows, woods, ponds, waterfalls and several constructions, including an Obelisk of the 18th century, surrounds a listed neo-gothic Castle from the XI, XVI and XIX centuries. Magnificient tree-like rhododendrons and gunneras grow in the shelter of palm trees and exotic conifers. **Location:** 5km south from Cherbourg on D900. **Open:** Every day 10–12noon and 2–6pm (except Sat from Nov–March). **Admission:** Adult FF30, Teenager FF20, Child (5–12) FF10, Parents with children FF85, Groups FF25. Guided tour for groups FF30. In April and May, add FF5 per category and from November to March, deduct FF5 per category. Best season: April and May. **E-mail:** CDepourtal@aol.com

map 287
2

CHÂTEAU DE BALLEROY
14490 Balleroy
Tel: 00 33 (0) 231 216 061 Fax: 00 33 (0) 231 215 177

Balleroy, an early work of the famous architect François Mansart, was built in 1631, and remains unspoilt and unaltered to this day. The village itself was laid out at the same time and is an essay in town planning which inspired the later work at Versailles. In 1970, Malcolm S Forbes purchased Balleroy for the family's media company and created the first international Balloon Museum established in the Château's outer court. A very popular international balloon festival, the 20th, will be held on June 23–24 2001. Near Balleroy is the Normandy Coasts with nearby Mont Saint Michel, Bayeux Tapestry & D. Day beaches. **Open:** 15 Mar–15 Oct, daily 9am–12 & 2–6pm. Closed Tuesday. Open 10–6pm July–Aug & all year by appt for groups (20 pers. min). **Admission:** Château: FF35, Museum: FF28, both FF45. **E-mail:** reservation@chateau-balleroy.com **Internet:** www.chateau-balleroy.com

map287
3

CHÂTEAU DE FONTAINE–HENRY
14610 Fontaine–Henry
Tel: 00 33 2 31 80 00 42

Halfway between Caen and the D-Day beaches, the Château de Fontaine–Henry overlooks the lush green valley of the Mue. Its spectacular roofs, towering above the ancient trees of the garden, surmount a façade richly carved in the successive styles of the 15th and 16th centuries. The interior (guided tour) contains not only monumental fireplaces, carved doors and wonderful staircases, but also furniture, paintings and objets d'arts accumulated by successive generations. This family house frequently serves as a venue for cultural events. **Admission:** Adult FF35, Child (12 yrs and over) FF20. Groups: Adults FF25 per person, Children of school age FF20 per person. **Open:** Easter–15 Jun and 16 Sept–2 Nov: Sat, Sun & Bank Hols, 2.30–6.30pm. 16 June–15 Sept, afternoons (except Tues) 2.30–6.30pm. Open all year to groups by prior arrangement. **Location:** 10km from Caen.

map 287
4

CHÂTEAU FORT DE RAMBURES

80140 Rambures, France
Tel: 00 33 3 22 25 10 93 Fax: 00 33 3 22 25 07 88 (Comtesse de Blanchard)

A furnished, feudal, stronghold from the 15th century, where Henri IV once stayed, a jewel of military architecture from the end of the Middle Ages, built as a single flight of fancy to an original plan. The castle was built at a low level in order to reduce the chances of being damaged by firing. The walls are between three and seven metres thick and are pierced by 16 canon emplacements. The superb vaulted cellars were able to house the garrison. The 17th and 18th century outbuildings are still inhabited by descendants of the Rambures – La Roche Fontenilles. The construction of the interior beams bear witness to successive periods of time: very interesting Picardy furniture from the 15th, 16th and 17th centuries. An ancestral family associated with the most important fact in the history of France for a thousand years is linked to the Rambures estate. The name of Rambures first appeared in 1058 but came out into prominence from the 14th century when they occupied a high ranking position during the Hundred Years War, notably David de Rambures the Lord Rambures of Shakespeare's Henry V, Grand Master of Crossbowmen of France, who decided to build the actual castle in 1412. The Brave Rambures was the most famous from the 16th and 17th centuries. He received Henry IV as a guest whilst he was crossing Picardy to win his victory at Arques (1589) and he saved his life at the Battle of Ivry (1590). A great friendship united them. An English park and a wood planted with very old trees possessing rare oils, a true arboretum in the centre of the Vimeu Vert. **Open:** Castle & park open throughout the year (guided tours). 1 Mar–1 Nov, 10am–noon and from 2–6pm (except Wed), 2 Nov–28 Feb, 2–5pm, open Suns and Bank Hols (except 25 Dec and 1 Jan).

map 287
5

A FLEUR D'O

23, rue de la Chaussée, 80500 Davenescourt
Tel: +33 3 22 78 09 83 Fax: +33 3 22 78 39 90

A Fleur d'O is situated in the historic village of Davenescourt, where numerous ponds provide a peaceful backdrop for a 15th century church and an 18th century château. The 5-acre garden is divided into two distinct parts: an English-style garden bordered by the river Avre, and a French topiary garden. They house an important collection of roses, both old and new, irises, and scented plants, along with a huge array of bulbs, heathers and hydrangeas. **Open:** 15 Apr-31 Oct: daily 2pm-7pm (Closed 10-26 Aug). **Admission:** Adult FF35, Child (under 12) free. Groups: FF30 (by appointment). To see nearby: Folleville (20kms) houses a beautiful church, and a château built by an ancestor of Franklin Roosevelt. The cathedral at Amiens (35km). A Fleur d'O is just 100km from Paris (autoroute A16 et A1). **Special Event:** A plant festival will be held on the 2nd weekend of April. **Email:** jardi_fleurdo@hotmail.com **Internet:** www.jardinafleurdo.com

map 287
6

MUSÉE CONDÉ – CHÂTEAU DE CHANTILLY

Château de Chantilly, B.P. 70243, 60631 Chantilly Cedex, France
Tel: 00 33 3 44 62 62 62 Fax: 00 33 3 44 62 62 61 (Institut de France)

Elevated in the middle of water, Chantilly consists of a small Renaissance-style castle, which housed the apartments of the Princes of Condé (17th and 18th centuries) and the large castle, rebuilt between 1878 and 1880 by Daumet for Henri of Orléans, Duke of Aumale (1822–1897), son of Louis Philippe who gave Chantilly to the Institut de France in 1886. The exceptional collection of paintings includes works by Clouet, Poussin, Mignard, Watteau, Ingres, Delacroix, Fra Angelico, Raphaël, Van Dyck, Teniers). The sumptuous library holds miniature paintings by Jean Fouquet. Other attractions include the 17th century Parc de le Notre, the English Garden (1817) and the Anglo-Chinese garden of Hamlet (1774). **Open:** Daily (except Tues). 1 Mar–1 Nov: 10–6pm. 1 Nov–28 Feb: 10.30–12.45pm & 2–5pm. **Admission:** Adults FF42, Teenagers FF37, Children FF15.

map 287
7

THREE OUTSTANDING GARDENS AROUND DIEPPE

Le Bois des Moutiers, Le Domaine de Miromesnil and Les Jardins de Bellevue are three of the most beautiful complementary gardens in Normandy which are not to be missed. Three gardens with historical interest, botanical originality, most exceptional surrounding landscapes; Le Bois des Moutiers with its Lutyens house and its Jekyll gardens and park running down to the sea. Centenarian Rhododenrons, Azaleas... and the very first mixed borders in France.

Le Domaine de Miromesnil with a splendid beech planting shelters the 17th century château where Guy de Maupassant was born and its unique traditional floral kitchen garden surrounded by a splendid park.

Les Jardins de Bellevue, which were created 20 years ago, offer an incredible botanical trip through its national collection of Meconopsis and Helleborus in the most extraordinary landscape facing the Eawy forest.

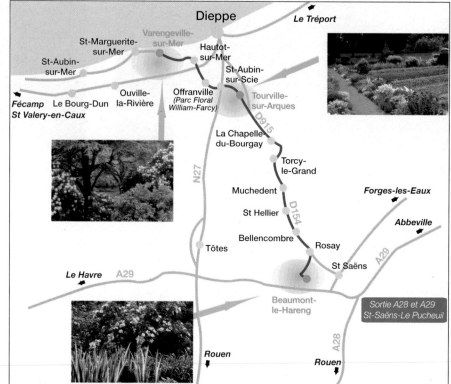

CHÂTEAU DE MIROMESNIL

76550 Tourville-sur-Arques, France
Tel: +33 2 35 85 02 80 Fax: +33 2 35 85 02 80 (Thierry de Vogue)

Typical of Henri IV and Louis XIII 'brick and stone' architecture, the Château was built (1590-1642) in the centre of a 25-acre beech grove, which hides a small chapel with lovely 18th century decoration. A 250-year-old cedar tree dominates the park and the traditional 'Potager', one of the best known in France, that still provides the family all year round with fresh vegetables and flowers. A collection of clematis grows among roses and fruits on the 17th century brick walls and the strictly ordered rows of vegetables contrast with the profusion of the flowered borders. **Location:** 6 miles south of Dieppe, by RN27 or D915. Guided visits of Château, Chapel and garden. **Open:** 28 Apr–15 Oct, daily (except Tues) 2–6pm. **Admission:** FF35 (FF25 for 10-18). Special admission and opening conditions for pre-registered groups of 20 min. on request.

map 287
8

Parc du Bois des Moutiers

76119 Varengeville-Sur-Mer, France
Tel: 00 33 2 35 85 10 02 Fax: 00 33 2 35 85 46 98 (Antoine Bouchayer-Mallet)

One of the most famous English gardens in Europe. A unique Arts and Crafts house in France built by Sir Edwin Lutyens (1869–1944) and still lived in by the family of Guillaume Mallet, creator of the walled gardens and of the park partly designed and influenced by Miss Gertrud Jekyll conceived as extensions of the house, the walled areas are carefully planned to present continuity in leading to the more natural landscape of the park. The park which covers 12 hectares, in a valley running down to the sea, is a succession of glades where a dominant species gives each a distinct character with successive flowering seasons. The acid nature of the soil allowed the introduction of an extensive collection of rare trees and shrubs coming from all over the world. (Chinese magnolias and azaleas, Himalayan rhododendrons over 15 metres high, Japanese maples, hortensias...) in total contrast to the local vegetation. **Location:** 2½ hours by boat from Newhaven to Dieppe only 8km from Dieppe by the cost (D25). **Open:** Daily from 15 Mar–15 Nov. Tickets from 10–12pm and 2–6pm. Visits from 10am–sunset. **Admission:** FF35/40 (May and June). **Facilities:** guided tour with a family member only by appointment.

map 287
9

Jardin de Bellevue

76850 Beaumont-le-Hareng, France
Tel: 00 33 2 35 33 31 37 Fax: 00 33 2 35 33 29 44 (Martine & Francis Lemonnier)

Hellebores, Prunus and Magnolias in winter, Meconopsis, Primulas and Peonies in spring, Viburnum, Roses and Hydrangeas in summer, gorgeous autumn colours together with a location is splendid: it faces the immense Eawy forest. The Stroller will seek out peace and delight. National collections: Hellebores and Meconopsis. Nursery specialised in perennials, and rare trees and shrubs (hardy for the coldest areas). **Location:** A28 or A29 exit 'Le Pucheuil', 1½ miles on N29 direction Tôtes (signposted). From Dieppe D915 Torcy turn right D154 up to Rosay (signposted). **Open:** All year: daily 10–6pm (last admission). **Admission:** FF35. **Refreshments:** Tearoom for groups (on require), B&B in the garden.

map 287
10

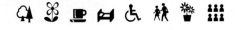

PARC DU CHÂTEAU D'ACQUIGNY

27400 Acquigny
Tel: 00 33 2 32 50 23 31 Fax: 00 33 2 32 40 46 68 (Baron d'Esneval)

Acquigny Castle, built in 1557 by Philibert Delorme for Anne de Montmorency Laval, Catherine of Médici's lady in waiting, is the epitome of Renaissance architecture. The main courtyard is graced with an ornate Italianate loggia which contrasts with the classicism of the south façade that opens out onto a large park. In its position below the wooded hills of the Eure region, and lying between the rivers Eure and Iton, the castle benefits from a favourable climate that allows Southern vegetation to prosper. Another remarkable particularity of the park is the presence of water canals, pools, waterfalls and a stone passage inspired by the works of Jean-Jacques Rousseau.

Parts of the park dating from the 18th century include a large newly restored orangery featuring a collection of citrus plants, a walled former kitchen garden, canals and trees including the historic "Sophora Japonica" that were planted in 1768. The newly restored Salon du Midi provides a wonderful 18th-century setting for a number of beautiful objects relating to the château's history. **Open:** 29 Apr–mid Oct: Sat, Sun and holidays. July & August: everyday 2–7pm. **Admission:** Adults FF35, Children FF20. Groups from 1 April–15 Nov. **Location:** 30 kms from Rouen. 15 kms from Evreux. Guided tours are available in English.

map 287
11

PARC ET JARDINS DU CHÂTEAU DE CANON

14270 Mézidon-Canon
Tel: 00 33 2 31 20 05 07 Fax: 00 33 2 31 20 65 17

Situated between the 'Pays d'Auge' and the 'Plaine de Caen' in the heart of a country rich in Roman churches, manors and castles, Canon nestles amongst ancient trees and a cluster of bubbling springs. The château is graced with balusters, Italian statues, a Chinese kiosk, a temple and neoclassic ruins and park where the formal French garden harmonises with the more natural English garden: long sweeping avenues lead to the main courtyard. Canon still has its 'Chartreuses', an exception collection of walled herbaceous borders. Jean Baptiste Jacques Elie de Beaumont, a lawyer and treasurer of 'le comte d'Artois' (later became Charles X) designed the place and in 1775 created the famous feast of 'Bonnes Gens', a name once used by the village itself. **Open:** Easter–30 Jun, Sat, Sun & BHols, 2–6pm. 1 Jul–30 Sept, daily (except Tues), 2–7pm. Interior open throughout the year.

map 287
12

CHÂTEAU DE BEAUMESNIL

Fondation Furstenberg-Beaumesnil, Beaumesnil
Tel/Fax: 00 33 2 32 444 009

Unique Louis XIII baroque style castle built from 1633–1640. Surrounded by 80 hectares landscaped by La Quintinie, who worked with Le Nôtre at Versailles. Furnished interiors and museum of ancient bookbindings. Video on bookbinding and gold decoration. **Open:** Jul, Aug, daily (except Tues), 10–12noon & 2–6pm. Apr, May, Jun, Sept, Fri–Mon, 2–6pm. **Admission:** Adults FF35, Children FF15. **Location:** 15km east of Bernay.

map 287
13

CHÂTEAU DE BIZY
27200 Vernon
Tel: 00 33 2 32 51 00 82 Fax: 00 33 2 32 21 66 54

Bizy was built in 1740, by Contant d'Ivry for the Marshal of Belle-Isle. It then belonged to the Duke of Penthièvre, Louis XIV and Madame de Montespan's grandson. Between 1822 and 1848, King Louis Philippe carried out some alterations to the castle and created a large English style park featuring lawns and large trees (beech, ash, lime, catalpa). The castle is surrounded by waterworks (under restoration) with famous sculptures depicting dolphins, sea horses and Gribouille as well as hedges and manicured yews. The large living rooms display 1st Empire relics collected by the current owners, the descendants of Marshal Suchet, Duke of Albufera. **Open:** 1 Apr–1 Nov, 10–12am and 2–6pm. Closed on Mon. Nov, Feb, March: Sat & Sun, 2–5pm. Closed Dec & Jan. **Admission:** Adults FF38, Groups FF30, Children FF20. **Location:** 70km west of Paris (A13, Junction 16). 10 mins from Giverny.

map 287 **14**

CLAUDE MONET FOUNDATION
27620, Giverny
Tel: 00 33 2 32 51 28 21 Fax: 00 33 2 32 51 54 18

Claude Monet's property opened to the public in 1980 after completion of large-scale restoration work. Claude Monet's collection of Japanese wood prints is displayed in several rooms of the House. The water lily studio opened to visitors and Monet's flowers and water-garden are as they were in his time. **Open:** 1 Apr–1 Nov, 10–6pm. Closed on Mondays except Bank Holiday Mondays. **Admission:** FF35 per person. Groups by reservation only (minimum 20 Persons) FF25 per person. **Internet:** www.foundation-monet.com.

map 287 **15**

CHÂTEAU DE THOIRY
78770, Thoiry
Tel: 00 33 1 34 87 52 25 Fax: 00 33 1 34 87 54 12 (Vicomte & Vicomtesse de la Pamouse)

The Château de Thoiry is a unique listed monument of esoteric Renaissance architecture built in 1559 by the great architect, Philibert de l'Orme. Conceived to be a transparent bridge of light, the sun rises or sets in the Castle's central arch at the summer and winter solstices. Family seat of the Counts of La Panouse for 440 years, Thoiry has fine furniture, tapestries, portraits and 950 years of family, national and international archives. The Castle's portraits, magically sonorised, reveal ancestors' secrets. The 300-acre gardens are graced by formal parterres by Le Nôtre, a bluebell wood with gigantic rhododendrons, magnolias, prunus, an Autumn Garden, flowering meadow, roses, peony border, a labyrinth and hortensias. Over 10,000 flowering trees and shrubs enhance the Botanical Gardens with many new garden creations every year. Rose Garden and Scented Garden. Thoiry's involvement in the conservation of endangered species is reinforced by "the first in France presentation" of rare Komodo dragons in a new Reptile House with hydrosaurus lizards and white crocodiles. A new river biotope of rare European otters, frogs, salamanders and fish is another big attraction. Kids "interactivate" along the new educational play circuit through the Zoological Gardens. With 'The Talking Trees' English audio guide, train tours, Giant Spiderweb Playground, and drive-through Wildlife Park, Thoiry offers hours of pleasure to all ages. **Open:** Every day of the year, 10–5/6.30pm following seasons. **Admission:** Castle only: Adult FF38, Child (9+)/Student FF30. Castle, wildlife reserve, zoo and gardens: Adult FF135, Child (3–12 yrs)/Student FF102. Group prices please contact us. **Location:** 25m W of Paris by A13, A12, N12 to Pontchartrain, then D11 to Thoiry.

map 287 **16**

France

DOMAINE DE COURSON
91680 Courson–Monteloup
Tel: 00 33 1 64 58 90 12 Fax 00 33 1 64 58 97 00

Architecture typical of the majestic country houses built in the 17th century for the wealthy officers of the Crown around Paris. Napoleonic memorabilia. Spanish, Italian and French paintings. An early 19th century beautifully landscaped park with many rare species of trees and shrubs in 80 acres of woodland. **Open:** Sun & Public Hols. Park: 1 Jan–31 Dec10-12 & 2-6pm. Château: 15 Mar–15 Nov.2-6pm **Admission:** Adult FF45, Child FF30. Reduced rates for groups and grounds only. **Events/Exhibitions:** Spectacular flower shows, third weekend of May and Oct. **Location:** Near Arpajon, 20 miles SW of Paris, 4 miles from the A10 and N20. Available for exclusive corporate entertainment. Weddings, receptions and seminars in 'Les Petites Ecuries du duc de Padoue'. Dogs allowed on lead. No access for dogs during flower shows. **E-mail:** coursondom@aol.com

map 287
17

CHÂTEAU DE VAUX LE VICOMTE
77950 Maincy
Tel: 00 33 1 64 14 41 90 Fax: 00 33 1 60 69 90 85

Vaux le Vicomte, the largest privately owned château in France is classed a historical monument. Vaux is a combination of 3 exceptional features: magnificent architecture, sumptuous decorations and a breathtaking garden. When Louis XIV was a guest at this palace and saw its refinements and exquisite gardens, he had the owner, his secretary of finance, imprisoned and the artists brought to the modest château de Versailles which became the symbol of the prestige of France. Candlelit visits, panoramic view from the dome, watery extravaganzas, rides around the gardens in electric golf cars or on the canal with the Nautils. **Open:** 31st Mar–11 Nov 2001, 10–6pm. Candlelit visits: Saturday nights from mid May to Mid Oct, 8pm–Midnight. **Admission:** Adult FF63, Teenagers/Students FF50, Children under 6 free. Self-service restaurant, tea room and gift shop. Free car parking.

map 287
18

LA PETITE ROCHELLE
22 rue du Prieuré, 61110 Rémalard
Tel: +33 02 33 73 85 38

An abundance of bulbs, perennials and shrubs from a variety of countries fill seven themed gardens. The gardens are an intriguing blend of English imagination and French equilibrium, where pools of water reflect the horticultural compositions. Form and colour are perfectly balanced throughout, revealing a deep concern for poetry and lasting beauty, whilst the owner's knowledge of rare plants is evident all around. Created in 1976, the 2½-acre garden showcases the national collection of Daphnes, along with numerous varieties of Dogwood, Pieris, Rhododendron, and rose. **Open:** Apr-Nov. **Admission:** Please note that guided tours (conducted by the Comtesse herself) are available only to groups (min 15 people) by prior appointment.

map 287
19

CHÂTEAU DE CONDÉ
DEMEURE DES PRINCES
02330 Condé-en-Brie
Tel: 00 33 3 23 82 42 25 Fax: 00 33 3 23 82 86 66 (Madame Pasté de Rochefort)

Situated on the 'Route du Champagne', this private residence will enchant you. This is a real treasure trove, crammed with thousands of surprises and delights! The Prince of Condé, Savoie, Richelieu, Watteau, Oudry, Servandoni, have successively owned, lived in, decorated and loved the castle. We invite you to come and see for yourselves. **Open:** Guided tours at 2.30, 3.30 and 4.30pm everyday throughout June, July, August and September. Sundays and Bank Holidays in May. Groups welcome throughout the year by appointment. Lunch is available for groups and only by appointment.
Internet: www.chateau–de–conde.com

map 287
20

Parks & Gardens in Brittany and the Western Loire

If you like gardens, you will love Brittany and the Western Loire region. Whether you prefer romantic, exotic or historic, these two regions have 38 parks and gardens open to the public. Some are dreamy and very English, others more formal and French. But all gardens are a living record! They tell us about the lives and attitudes of those who tamed the land; they offer us examples of the architectural style of gardens in vogue at a particular period. Together they contain a fine collection of plants and trees, but individually, each garden has its own separate purpose. Whether your aim is to discover botanical secrets or merely to take life easy, come and have a break in our regions.

The properties on pages 296 to 305 inclusive are shown in full on this map, along with the name of the nearest town. They also feature on the main French map (page 287), to which the numbered map references at the bottom right of each entry refer.

Parc Floral de la Court d'Aron

PARKS AND GARDENS IN BRITTANY

For further information on the properties that follow, please contact:

Comité Régional du Tourisme de Bretagne

1 rue Raoul Ponchon, 35069 RENNES Cedex

Tel : 00 33 2 99 36 15 15 Fax : 00 332 99 28 44 40

E-mail : tourisme-crtb@tourismebretagne.com

Alternatively, you can visit our website at **www.brittanytourism.com**

JARDIN GEORGES DELASELLE

29253 Ile de Batz

Tel : ++33 2 98 61 75 65 Fax: ++33 2 98 61 74 97

Discover the charms of a one hundred year old garden housing a rare and extraordinary collection of palm trees in remarkable surroundings. The Georges Delaselle Gardens have a special history and provide a sheltered environment where neolithic remains and contemporary sculpture come together in perfect harmony. **Location:** 15 min from Roscoff. **Open:** Apr, May, June & Sept daily (except Tues) 2–6pm; July & Aug daily 1–6pm; Oct weekends 2–6pm. **Admission:** Adults FF23, Children FF12, Group (Adults) FF16, Group (Children) F9.

map 287 **21**

JARDIN EXOTIQUE DE ROSCOFF

BP54 - 29682 Roscoff cedex

Tel: ++33 2 98 61 29 19 Fax: ++33 2 98 61 12 34

The garden's favourable climate enables it to grow 1.6 hectares of plants from the southern hemisphere: Australia, Chile and South Africa. The landscaping takes the form of a massive rock-garden, where Ficoïdes and Gazanias blaze. Waterfalls and pools add a cooling note. From the 18-metre high granite cliffs you have a panoramic view over 2 000 species, some of them very rare - a welcome change of surroundings for visitors. To take full advantage of the picturesque nature of the site, the designer has employed the natural exuberance of some plants and has created new vantage points and unexpected features within the garden. **Open:** Feb, Mar, Nov & Dec daily (exc Tues) 2–5.30pm; Apr/Oct daily 10am–12.30pm & 2–6pm; Jun–Sept daily 10am–7pm. Closed in Jan. Groups by appointment. **Admission:** Adult FF25, Child (12-18 yrs)/Retired/Student/Group FF20. Guided tour FF25. **Internet:** www.multimania.com/grapes

map 287 **22**

PARC ET CHÂTEAU DE KERGRIST

22300 Ploubezre

Tel: ++33 2 96 38 91 44 Fax: ++33 2 96 38 89 49

A typical 15th century Tregor manor house which lends itself to lasy daydreaming. In spite of being modified in the 18th century and restored in the 19th century, it remains in perfect harmony with its French-style gardens and the surrounding countryside. A charming and enchanting Breton jewel - you will be sorry to leave Kergrist. **Open:** Easter holidays 2–6pm; May, weekends & public holidays; June–Sept, daily 11am–6.30pm. **Admission:** Adults FF40 (Garden & Château), FF25 (Garden), Children/Students FF15, Group (Adults) FF20, Group (Children) FF10.

map 287 **23**

JARDIN BOTANIQUE DU DOURIC

Route de Ploudalmezeau, 29290 St Renan
Tel: ++33 6 07 08 49 15 Fax: ++33 2 98 84 27 77

A wooded valley has been transformed into an exotic botanical garden. Two hectares of bamboos, palm trees, cacti, and other plants provide a very pleasant walk for both the novice and the expert botanist. There are five water features and a beautiful stream flowing along the edge of a little oak wood. **Open:** Apr–Oct 2–7pm, weekend & holidays; Jul & Aug daily 2–7pm. **Admission:** Adults FF15, Children FF10, Group FF12.

Internet: http://perso.wanadoo.fr/michel.mauguin/douric1.htm

map 287
24

CONSERVATOIRE BOTANIQUE NATIONAL DE BREST

52, allée du Bot, 29200 Brest
Tel: ++33 2 98 41 88 95 Fax: ++33 2 98 41 57 21

The Botanical Conservatory is the first establishment in France to be entirely dedicated to the preservation of plants in danger of extinction. In its 1000 square metres of greenhouses and 22 hectares of gardens, it houses one of the largest collections in the world of threatened plant species. **Open:** Garden: 9am–6pm. Greehouse: 1 Jul–15 Sept Sun–Thurs 2–5.30pm. **Admission:** FF22. For more details please phone ++33 2 98 02 46 00.

map 287
25

JARDIN DU CENTRE CULTUREL ABBAYE DE DAOULAS

21, rue de l'Eglise, BP 34, 29460 Daoulas
Tel: ++33 2 98 25 84 39 Fax: ++33 2 98 25 89 25

The gardens, remodelled and extended in collaboration with the National Botanical Conservatory of Brest, are laid out in the style of Middle-Age and Renaissance abbey gardens. In addition to the usual medicinal, herbal and aromatic plants, they house a collection of exotic, magic and rare plants in danger of extinction. 250 pharmaceutical plants from five continents are on display. **Open:** 11 May–12 Nov daily 10am–6pm (Jul & Aug 7pm). From 12 Nov: by prior appointment. **Admission:** Abbey & Garden: Adult FF25, Child (10-18 yrs) FF15, under 10 yrs free. **E-mail:** centre.culturel.abbaye.daoulas@infini.fr

map 287
26

JARDIN DE L'ARGOAT & ARBORETUM DU POEROP

Jardin de l'Argoat: 55, rue des Cieux, 29690 Huelgoat
Tel: +33 2 98 99 71 63 Fax: +33 2 98 99 76 26
Arboretum de Poërop: Tel: +33 2 98 99 95 90

Originally a 'garden of healing' within the Huelgoat hospital grounds, this is now a fully-fledged botanical garden, thanks to the hospital director's passion for endangered plants. Several themes combine in its 3 acres - a rose garden, wetland plants around a 16th-century spring and a Himalayan woodland… A real Garden of Eden, with a 50-acre landscaped arboretum containing 2500 species of trees and shrubs. Educational farm, nursery with unusual and rare vegetables. **Open:** All year 10am–6pm. Guided tours/Groups by appointment. **Admission:** Garden or Arboretum: Adult FF15, Group/Child FF10. Garden & Arboretum: Adult FF30, Group/Child FF20. **Internet:** www.arboretum-huelgoat.com

C map 287
27

DOMAINE DE TRÉVAREZ
29520 Saint-Goazec
Tel: ++33 2 98 26 82 79 Fax: ++33 2 98 26 86 77

In the heart of a 85 ha park you can admire an exceptional collection of plants: bulbs, camellias, rhododendrons, azaleas, hydrangeas, fuchsias, and perennials are exhibited in various constantly changing garden settings. At each turn of the path, you might find an ornamental lake, fountains and waterfalls or a water garden displaying great artistry. A wonderful place in which to walk and explore, to learn and to be initiated into botany. Trévarez also organises prestigious art exhibitions and various flower shows throughout the year. A children's play area, a Breton restaurant and various shops all add to the pleasure of your visit to the Domaine de Trévarez in Brittany. **Open:** Apr, May, Jun & Sept daily 1–6pm; Jul & Aug daily 11am–6.30pm; 1 Oct–31 Mar wed, Sat, Sun & holidays 2–5.30pm. During exhibition "Noëls du Monde" daily 1.30–5.30pm. **Admission:** Adult FF28, 12–25 yrs FF22, up to 11yrs free. Groups by appointment.

map 287
28

JARDIN DU CHÂTEAU DE LANNIRON
29336 Quimper Cedex
Tel: ++33 2 98 90 62 02 Fax: ++33 2 98 52 15 56

The ancient residence of the bishops of Quimper, and a listed building, the Château overhangs the French-style 17th century gardens, which descend in terraces down to the river Odet. Presently undergoing restoration, the gardens house an interesting botanical collection. **Open:** 15 May–15 Sept, daily 2–6pm. Groups all year on appointment. **Admission:** Adult FF20, Child (10 yrs+) FF10, Residents of Quimper half price. Bar, season restaurant in the 17th century Orangerie 15 May– au 15 Sept, 12noon–1.30pm & 7–10pm. Lunch: FF59, menu from FF79, children's menu FF39. **E-mail:** jardins@lanniron.com **Internet:** www.lanniron.com

map 287
29

PARC BOTANIQUE DE CORNOUAILLE
29120 Combrit
Tel: ++33 2 98 56 44 93 Fax: ++33 2 98 51 91 96

One of the best botanical collections in Brittany. From March onwards there are flowerings of camellias, magnolias, rhododendrons, roses and water gardens. Autumn brings an Indian summer with the flamboyant colours of maples, fothergillas and pronos. Exhibition room. Expo 2000 from 2/07 to 20/08: minerals, fossils and archaeology of Brittany. **Open:** Mar–Nov daily 10am–12noon & 2–7pm; July & Aug daily 10am–7pm. Closed 20 Sept–15 Oct. Groups by prior appointment, tour with proprietor. **Admission:** Adult FF30, Child FF17. Group: Adult FF27, Child FF15.

map 287
30

JARDIN CHEVASSU
56100 Lorient
Tel (Town Hall): ++33 2 97 02 23 32

This garden consists of a 2.3-hectare valley with a river and two lakes. You can still see the old watercourse, built in the days of the India Company to supply water to the Lorient arsenal. Woodland planting consists of tall oaks, beeches and limes, with camellias, magnolias, rhododendrons, bamboos and Japanese maples. An animal park brings the scene to life. **Open:** Daily 8am–7pm. **Admission:** Free. Guided tours with gardener available.

map 287
31

PARC BOTANIQUE DE KERBIHAN
56700 Hennebont
Tel (Town Hall): +33 2 97 85 16 16

Situated right in the town centre, the 10 hectares of the Kerbihan park offer a variety of 130 species and plant materials from five continents. Its arboretum, century-old bamboo plantation and neo-romantic garden are laid out around water features interspersed with waterfalls. **Open:** All year, 24h. **Admission:** Free.

map 287
32

JARDIN DU CHÂTEAU DE KERAMBARH
56690 Landaul
Tel: ++33 2 97 24 63 86

In the grounds of the château of Kerambarh you can take a walk through the middle ages. As you wander through the park you will come across a medicinal herb garden, Charlemagne's capitulary, a liturgical garden, the garden of the "troisième fleur", a fruit orchard, and a kitchen garden of 33 "toises" (an ancient unit of measurement) laid out in nine squares. **Open:** 1 Apr–1 Nov daily 12–7pm.

map 287
33

JARDIN BOIS D'AMOUR
56120 Josselin
Tel (Town Hall): ++33 2 97 22 24 17

This garden, a pedestrian walk in the heart of the mediaeval city which respects the local vegetation, has its own very special natural look. Seven hectares of promenades with winding paths show this leisure site off to its best, with its pool and bamboo grove.

map 287
34

CHÂTEAU DU MONTMARIN
35730 Pleurtuit
Tel: ++33 2 99 88 58 79   Fax: ++33 2 99 88 55 92

A remarkable garden on the banks of the Rance, near Dinard and Saint-Malo. Le Montmarin, the only shipowner's mansion on the left bank of the Rance, looks out over a magnificent stretch of water. The six-hectare grounds consists of both formal and informal gardens with lawns, woodland, a rock garden, flower-beds, etc… **Open:** 1 May–30 Sept, daily 2–7pm. Guided visits for groups from March to October, by appointment.

map 287
35

JARDINS DU CHÂTEAU DE LA BALLUE
35560 Bazouges-la-Pérouse
Tel: ++33 2 99 97 47 86 Fax: ++33 2 99 97 47 70

This mannerist garden, recreated according to a 17th century model, holds thirteen surprises. Separated from the formal gardens by a grand arcade of wisteria, sculptures by contemporary artists lend delight and amazement to the walks. The skilful alternation of light and shadow creates extraordinary effects of perspective, and confers a special charm to the tour. **Open:** 15 Apr–15 Oct, daily 1–5.30pm. **Admission:** Adult FF35, Student FF25, Child (under12) FF15. Guided visits are available for groups. Bed & Breakfast in Château from FF650 for 2 people sharing. **E-mail:** château@laballue.com **Internet:** www.laballue.com

map 287 **36**

PARC FLORAL DE HAUTE-BRETAGNE
35133 Le Chatellier
Tel: ++33 2 99 95 48 32 Fax: +33 2 99 95 47 74

Near the mediaeval city of Fougères and famous Mont Saint-Michel, the Parc Floral of Haute-Bretagne unfolds in a romantic landscape. These superb grounds were originally laid out in the 19th century, and within them have been planted ten elegant gardens. A country stroll begins with the Persian garden, followed by the ancient city which plunges us into the Mediterranean world. Then comes Knossos with its camellias, and the Poets' Dell with its pond, little bridge and wild groves… It's up to you to discover the rest. There is a tea room in the beautiful house at the bottom of the garden, and small shrubs for sale so that you may plant your own echo of what you have seen here. **Open:** 1 Mar–12 Nov daily, 2–6pm. Sun, nat. holidays and 11 July–21 Aug: 10.30am–6.30pm. **Admission:** Adult FF43, Student/Youth (13–18 yrs) FF35, Child (4–12 yrs) FF26. **E-mail:** foltière@parcfloralbretagne.com **Internet:** www.parcfloralbretagne.com

map 287 **37**

CHÂTEAU ET PARC DE LA BOURBANSAIS
35720 Pleugueneuc
Tel: +33 2 99 69 40 07 Fax: +33 2 99 69 46 04

The park and French-style gardens of the Château de la Bourbansais recall the classicism of the great parks designed by Le Notre. The gardens extend over several hectares and have been a listed historical monument since 1959. **Open:** 1 May–15 Sept, daily 10am–7pm. April & 16–end Sept, daily 10am–12noon & 2–6pm. 1 Oct–31 Mar, daily 2–6pm. **Admission:** (Château & Gardens) Adult FF58, Child FF40. (Combined visit including zoological park) Adult FF70, Child FF45.

map 287 **38**

CARADEUC À BÉCHEREL
35190 Bécherel
Tel: +33 2 99 66 77 76

This chateau in the classical style is set in the largest park in Brittany. Numerous statues, buildings and monuments adorn the flowers beds and walks of the grounds. The château is on the supplementary list of historic monuments. It still belongs to the descendants of the celebrated procurator, Louis-René de Caradeuc de la Chalotais. **Open:** All day 25 Mar–15 Sept, afternoon only 16 Sept–31 Oct. Sat & Sun (afternoon only) 1 Nov–24 Mar.

map 287 **39**

LES JARDINS DE BROCÉLIANDE
Le Pommeret, route de Montfort, 35310 Bréal-sous-Montfort
Tel: ++33 2 99 60 51 00 Fax: ++33 2 99 60 07 94

If you were to imagine a dream garden, it would look just like the "Jardins de Brocéliande". Set in 20 hectares, with a mixture of rock gardens and flowerbeds, hills and valleys, wild flowers and plants (including the French national collection of irises). There is a 1900-style farm with poultry and animals for the children to stroke, as well as many play areas spread throughout the floral gardens. **Exhibitions:** Various exhibitions, including Franciris 2000, 13–28 May. **Open:** Spring – 1 Nov, Mon–Sun 10am–6pm. During school holidays, the gardens will be open every day. **Admission:** Adult FF35, Student FF20, free for under 16s.

map 287 / 40

JARDIN DU THABOR
Place St Mélaine, 35000 Rennes
Tel (Guided Tours): +33 2 23 20 73 76 Tel (Tourist Office): +33 2 99 67 11 11

The Thabor Garden, with ten hectares of land on a plateau overlooking the Vilaine, is one of France's finest public parks. Formerly an orchard belonging to the monastery of Saint Mélaine, it was improved and enlarged in the 19th century by Denis Bühler. Its romantic atmosphere includes scenes from hell, a grotto and a waterfall, with refreshing fountains. It contains flower-edged walks that vary with the seasons: azaleas and rhododendrons, roses, dahlias, chrysanthemums; a garden with 3120 species and 1480 genera, remarkable trees such as cedars, an aviary, a duck reserve… Nearby is the garden of the Palace of Saint-Georges, and the Parc Oberthur (2.8 hectares), also designed by Denis Bühler. **Open:** Summer, 7.15am–9.30pm. Winter, 7.30am–6pm.

map 287 / 41

JARDIN DU PARC À VITRÉ
35500 Vitré
Tel: ++33 2 99 74 43 53

Near the town centre, this informal garden reveals its many attractions as you walk through. Flowerbeds, green lawns, a splendid lake. In addition to the wealth of trees and plants, you will also enjoy the deer enclosure, the aviary, the bandstand and the play areas. **Open:** Every day, all year round.

map 287 / 42

PRÉ DES LAVANDIÈRES DE VITRÉ
35500 Vitré
Tel: ++33 2 99 74 43 53

Take the promenade du Val which leads down past the fortifications, and at the bottom of a narrow lane you will find the "Pré des Lavandières" - Washerwomen's Meadow. This naturally landscaped area of trees and flowerbeds is a blend of charm and tranquillity on the banks of the Vilaine, opposite the old washhouses. **Open:** Every day, all year round.

map 287 / 43

PARKS AND GARDENS IN THE WESTERN LOIRE

For further information on the properties that follow, please contact:

Comité Régional du Tourisme des Pays de la Loire

2, rue de la Loire, BP20411, 44204 Nantes

Tel : 00 33 2 40 48 24 20 Fax : 00 33 2 40 08 07 10

E-mail : infotourisme@crtpdl.com

Alternatively, you can visit our website at **www.cr-pays-de-la-loire.fr**

JARDINS DES RENAUDIES

Les Meserais, 53120 Colombiers-du-Plessis
Tel: 00 33 2 43 08 02 08 Fax: 00 33 2 43 08 69 83 (Mr & Mrs Renault)

The Renaudies gardens, laid out in the style of an English landscaped garden, spread over 10 acres in an enchanting valley. Trees, shrubs, bulbs, rosebushes, hardy perennials… the blooming of more than 4,000 different species lasts from May until the autumn. With the passing seasons, the rhododendrons give way to the roses, followed by the hydrangea and the heather, alongside the plants in the vegetable garden. **Open:** May 2001: Sats, Suns & public hols, 2–6.30pm. 1 June–16 Sept: every day, 10.30–6.30pm. 23–24 Sept: 2–6.30pm. 7 Oct: (pumpkins & witches festival) 11–6.30pm. **Admission:** Adult FF30, Child (12–16): FF15. Groups (20+): FF25. **E-mail:** Renault.Pepinieres@wanadoo.fr **Internet:** www.perso.wanadoo.fr/renaudies

© J. Renault

map 287
45

PARC DU CHÂTEAU DE CRAON

53400 Craon
Tel: 00 33 2 43 06 11 02 Fax: 00 33 2 43 06 05 18 (Mr & Mrs de Guébriant)

Two styles of gardens surround this XVIIIth century Château: the 'French style' garden and the 'English landscape' park bordering and enhancing the river Oudon. The 5km of pathways in this park of 100 acres take the visitors to the kitchen garden with its XIXth century greenhouses, to the icehouse, to the wash-house-laundry, to the swan lake and to the vast outbuildings with its stables. The inside of this lived in Château offers beautiful guest rooms with period furniture. **Location:** A81 (Paris–Rennes) N171/30km south of Laval (Mayenne). **Open:** Park: 1 Apr–1 Nov, 1–7pm except Tues. Château guided tour: 1 July–31 Aug, 1–7pm except Tues. Guest rooms: daily, 16 Jan–15 Dec. **Admission:** Château & park: FF45. Park only: FF30. Guest rooms FF450/person breakfast included. **E-mail:** Guébrian@club-internet.fr

map 287
46

JARDIN DU MANOIR DE LA MASSONNIÈRE

72540 Saint Christophe en Champagne
Tel: 33-2 42 88 61 26 Fax 33-1 34 73 27 89 (Anne-Marie Moulin)

A garden created in 1950 by Marguerite Weinberg and her son Pierre K. Busche in the manner of a landscaped English garden, laid out around a manor house dating from the 15th, 17th and 18th centuries. This closed area offers all the possibilities of a well-structured design: a landscaped park (with century-old trees), a formal French garden (with yews and box trees sculpted into decorative shapes), traditional kitchen garden and orchard, mixed borders (hardy perennials), and a "forest garden". The owners are currently considering plans for the creation of a maze. **Open:** Jun–Sept, on Fridays, Saturdays and Sundays, from 2–6 pm. All year for groups upon reservation. **Admission:** Adults FF25, Children under 15 free, Groups FF15/person (for groups of 10 or more).

© A. M. Moulin

map 287
47

© P. Fernandez

JARDIN DU PETIT-BORDEAUX
72220 Saint Biez-en-Belin
Tel: 33-2 43 42 15 30 (Mr & Mrs Michel Berrou)

In this garden of exquisite inspiration and exceptional botanical diversity, every season creates in the garden's 15,000 sq. m. a multitude of different places where the visitor feels impelled to pause and relish the harmony of the view, to breathe in the scented air, and admire the subtle motley of colours. All visitors who are fascinated by botany, interested in rare essences and admire the splendours of refined gardens will delight in the Garden of the Petit-Bordeaux. **Open:** 15 Apr–15 Nov 2001 from 10am–12.30 pm and from 2–7pm (closed on Tuesdays, except public holidays). **Admission:** Adults FF25, Children (12–16yrs) FF15. Groups (15 people) FF20/person.

map 287 / 48

JARDINS DU GRAND-LUCÉ
9 place de la République, 72150 Le Grand Lucé
Tel : 02 43 40 85 56 Fax : 02 43 40 94 97

The domaine, created between 1760 and 1764, offers you 30 acres to discover the castle, the formal gardens, the vegetable garden, the prairie and the forest, with its Antiquity-inspired statues. Remarkable for the reconstitution of its gardens, the domaine reflects the ideas of the French Enlightenment. From the architecture of the castle and garden, to the "uncontrolled" nature of the prairie and forest, you are invited to contemplate the path of the lonely promeneur and experience the atmosphere of life in an 18th century summer residence. A programme of special events (concerts, plays, open-air activities) will be available in April. Guided visits in English. **Open:** weekends and holidays 14–30 April, 1 May–30 September , open every day except Monday. **Admission:** Adults FF25, Seniors/Children (11–16yrs)/Groups FF20, under 11 yrs free. **E-mail:** chateaugrand-luce@wanadoo.fr **Internet:** www.sarthe.com/visiter/cult/grandluce.htm.

map 287 / 49

© Joel Tribhout

© CRT

CHATEAU DE PONCÉ
8 Rue des Côteaux, 72340 Poncé-sur-le-Loire
Tel: 00 33 2 43 44 45 39 or 00 33 2 43 44 24 02 (Mr André)

At the Château de Poncé, not far from the river Loir, strollers can discover an impressive series of leafy bowers, large and small chambers of greenery opening out onto groves of trees embellished with ornamental lakes. They can lose themselves in a labyrinth of concentric pathways leading up to the old plane tree. After passing terraces of vines and fruit trees, they enter the brick and stone-built Italian garden, to stand amazed before the large neo-gothic wall dating from 1830. **Open:** 1 Apr–30 Sept 2001: every day 10–12.30pm & 2–6.30 pm. Open on Sats & Suns in Oct and the All Saints' Day Holiday in Nov, 2–6 pm. **Admission:** Adults FF32, Children (aged 7–14) FF25, Groups (20 people) FF28.

map 287 / 50

CHÂTEAU DU LUDE
72800 Le Lude, Sarthe, France
Tel: 00 33 243 94 60 09 Fax: 00 33 243 45 27 53

An old fortress of the Anjou dukedom dominating the Loir, transformed in the Renaissance into a country retreat by King Louis XI's chamberlain. The Château du Lude is a remarkable illustration of the way French architecture has evolved, from the Renaissance to the late 18th century. Lived in by the same family for the past 200 years, the Château contains a rich interior arrangement. Formal gardens on several terraces, rose garden, kitchen garden. **Location:** 30 miles S of Le Mans and N of Tours. **Open:** 1 Apr–30 Sept: (Closed Weds in Apr, May, Jun & Sept). Open all year on request for groups upon reservation. Outside 10–12am, 2–6pm. Inside guided tour 2.30–6pm. **Admission:** FF40, reduction for children & groups. **Events:** Garden Show, 3–4 June, 'Cooking days' in the old kitchen with musical visit of the château & kitchen garden, 14 & 15 July, 15 Aug, 15 & 16 Sept.

map 287 / 51

© L.J. Nicolay

© N. de Loture

PARC ET JARDIN DU CHÂTEAU DE MONTRIOU
49460 Feneu
Tel: ++33 2 41 93 30 11 Fax: ++33 2 41 93 15 63 (Mr & Mrs de Loture)

In an unchanged rural setting of small woods, fields and hedgerows, the château stands in the midst of its grounds structured around fine old trees, box-tree borders and bushes sculpted into decorative shapes (topiaries). Not far away, the 19th-century kitchen garden, nestling within its walls, boasts a riot of vegetables and flowers. The "Princess' Garden" is entirely devoted to climbing or trailing cucurbitaceous plants, offering an eccentric display with its leafy bowers. Lastly, the so-called "Italian" garden hosts a delightful aviary. Visitors continue their stroll along avenues shaded by majestic trees or under the shadows of stately plane trees. **Open:** 1 Jun–15 Oct daily 2–6pm (closed on Mondays). Open all year for groups upon reservation. **Admission:** Adults FF20, free for children aged less than 12. Guided tours for groups: Adults FF30, Children FF10. **E-mail:** chateau-de-Montriou@wanadoo.fr **Internet:** www.chateau-de-montriou.com

map 287
52

LES CHEMINS DE LA ROSE (PATHS OF ROSES)
Route de Cholet. Parc de Courcilpleu. 49700 Doué-la-Fontaine
Tel: 00 33 2 41 59 95 95 Fax: 00 33 2 41 59 25 86 (Mr Gay)

A real innovation in a region that has long been won over to the beauty of roses (Doué-la-Fontaine is the rose-growing capital of France), the rose garden, designed along the lines of a landscaped English garden, covers a total of approximately 10 acres. Ornamental lakes, fordable streams, oaks, ash trees and willows stand alongside a fabulous collection of ancient and modern botanical species from all over the world. **Open:** from 12 May – 9 September 2001, every day from 9.30 a.m. to 7 p.m. **Admission:** Adults: FF35. Children (aged 5 to 17): FF18. Groups (20 people or more), Students and Disabled: FF28. **E-mail:** cheminsdelarose@unimedia.fr

map 287
53

© M. Denis-Hout

© Jane de la Celle

JARDINS DU PIN
Château du Pin, 49123 Champtocé-sur-Loire
Tel: 00 33 2 41 39 91 85 - 00 33 06 11 68 61 81 Fax: 00 33 2 41 39 88 41 (Mrs de la Celle)

Welcome to the land of fairy tales! At the Château du Pin in Champtocé-sur-Loire, some fifty sculpted yew trees fire the visitors' imagination: a chess board with gigantic pieces? Beyond the trees, the dream sweeps on with views over the 18 levels of terraced gardens, with the scent of rare plants, the flowering banks of the castle moat, the collection of citrus trees and the kitchen garden with its splendour of two thousand dahlias. **Open:** 15 Apr–14 Oct: 2–6 pm, Sat & Sun, and every afternoon in July & August - upon reservation. **Admission:** Entrance and tour of the garden: FF25 (free for children aged less than 12). **E-mail:** jardins@multimania.com

Internet: www.multimania.com/jardins.

map 287
54

PARC ORIENTAL DE MAULEVRIER
49360 Maulévrier
Tel: 00 33 2 41 55 50 14 Fax: 00 33 2 41 55 48 89 (Mr Chavassieux)

The Maulévrier Oriental Park is the largest Japanese garden in Europe. The stretch of the river and its different features (crane islands, Khmer temple, Bouddha, etc..) symbolise the course of the human life, from birth to death. 300 different species of spring and autumn plants transform the very nature of the park with the passing of the year, inviting guests to pause and meditate a while. **Open:** from March until November 15 2001. Every afternoon from 2 to 6 pm. Sundays and public holidays from 2–7pm. July–August, every day from 10.30–7.30 pm. Closed on Mondays (except public holidays or long holiday weekends). **Admission:** Individuals (aged 12 and above) FF 30, Groups (15 people or more) FF 25.

map 287
55

© D Drouet

© J. Renaudineau

JARDIN DES PLANTES DE NANTES
(Botanical Garden) 6 rue Stanislas Baudry, 44000 Nantes
Tel: +33 2 40 41 65 02 Fax: +33 2 40 41 65 10
(City of Nantes – Parks & Environment Services)

The horticultural tradition of Nantes is intimately bound up with the city's port which, over the centuries, favoured the introduction of plants from all over the world. The continuation of the former Apothecaries' Garden, first created in 1688, the Nantes Jardin des Plantes today is a landscaped park with undulating valleys, ornamental lakes, waterfalls and immense lawns. Of particular interest is the Botanical Garden with its flora from the western France, its collection of cactuses and epiphytes (plants depending on others for mechanical support) and its 200-year-old Hectot magnolia descending from the first magnolia graniflora brought to Nantes in 1711. **Open:** all year from 8.30am–7pm. **Admission:** Entrance and tours free of charge. **E-mail:** jardins@mairie-nantes.fr or claude.figureau@mairie-nantes.fr **Internet:** www.mairie-nantes.fr

map 287
56

PARC DE LA GARENNE LEMOT
Route Nationale 149. 44190 Gétigné Clisson
Tel: 00 33 2 40 54 75 85 Fax: 00 33 2 40 03 99 22
(Council of Department of the Loire Atlantique)

The park of Garenne Lemot is the fruit of Lemot's creative genius. On the banks of the Sèvre Nantaise, the sculptor created his romantic setting in these grounds between 1805 and 1827. Placed among the steep hillsides and the pathways winding through the park, all the "fabriques" (follies) blend harmoniously with the different natural elements: with the Villa Lemot itself, and the gardener's house, built in the Italian style. **Open:** Park: Apr–Sept 9–8pm every day. Oct–Mar 9.30–6.30pm. Gardener's house: open throughout the year. Villa: open during temporary exhibitions; please phone, fax or e-mail for opening periods and hours. **Admission:** Entrance to the park, the gardener's house, the villa and the exhibitions is free of charge. **E-mail:** contact@cg44.fr

Internet: www.cg44.fr/special/GL

map 287
57

© Conseil Général de Loire Atlantique. D. Pillet

© J. Auvinet

JARDINS DES OLFACTIES
9, rue Jean Mermoz, 85220 Coëx
Tel: 00 33 2 51 55 53 41 Fax: 00 33 2 51 55 54 10

There is more than a whiff of innovation hovering over the Floral Park of Coex, known in French as the "Jardin des Olfacties" (Garden of Scents). Indeed, the gardens were awarded the national first prize for tourist innovation in the contest for the Green Tourism Trophy. The gardens afford a perfumed journey through a variety of fragrant spaces, where expertly arranged flowers and plants evoke differing themes and a wonderful bouquet of emotions. **Open:** 15 April–15 June and 3–16 Sept 2001, from 2–7pm (closed on Saturdays). 17 June–2 Sept, open every day from 10.30am–7pm. **Admission:** Adults FF40, free for Children, Groups (on reservation). **E-mail:** parc.jardin.des.olfacties@libertysurf.fr

map 287
58

PARC FLORAL DE LA COURT D'ARON
85540 Saint-Cyr-en-Talmondais
Tel: +33 2 51 30 86 74 Fax: +33 2 51 30 87 37 (Mr & Mrs J. J. Matthijsse)

The exotic holds sway in the floral garden near the Château de la Court d'Aron! Fifty thousand rare spring flowers, along with water lilies, Iceland poppies, bamboos, banana trees, eucalyptus, Japanese lilac and other exotic plants explode in a symphony of colours between the ancient oaks and the ornemental lakes. But the most surprising sight of all is the flowering in July of the Asian Lotus as they float on their 2.5-acre lake, considered to be a unique experience in Europe. **Open:** 15 April–30 Oct 2001. Every day 10–7pm. **Admission:** Adults FF35 (1 July–30 Sept: FF47), Groups (20+) FF33, Season ticket FF100. **E-mail:** Courtdaron@aol.com **Internet:** www.domaine-des-lotus-prl.com.

map 287
59

© B. Matthijsse

France

CHÂTEAU DE GOULAINE
44115 Haute-Goulaine, Loire Atlantique
Tel: +33 2 40 54 91 42 Fax: +33 2 40 54 90 23

For over a thousand years, the Goulaine family have lived at the château, located some 11 miles south of Nantes. It was rebuilt during the 15th century, and in spite of its location, it is one of the great "Châteaux de la Loire". The lavishly decorated upstairs apartments are amongst the few that have survived intact in the Loire valley. Close to the castle, a large greenhouse shelters, in their natural environment, hundreds of tropical butterflies, flying in freedom amongst their visitors. Permanent exhibition of paintings and sculpture commissioned by the famous local biscuit firm, LU. A fascinating journey through a century of advertising, from Art Nouveau to the present day, including numerous sketches by Ronald Searle. **Open:** Easter–early Nov, 2–6pm: Sat, Sun & holidays. 15 Jun–15 Sept, 2–6pm Wed–Mon. Groups: All year round, by appointment, 10–6pm. **Admission:** Adults 45FF, Children 15FF, Children under 8 free.

map 287 60

CHÂTEAU DE SAUMUR
49400 Saumur
Tel: 00 33 2 41 40 24 40 Fax: 00 33 2 41 40 24 49

Dungeon of the Plantagenêts, fortress in the 13th century, then county residence, the castle of the Dukes of Anjou is the very image of a fairy tale. The guided tour includes: the monument's history and architecture, the Decorative Arts Collection and the Equestrian section situated in a splendid boat's hull shaped vaults room. Summer entertainments. Overlooking the Loire and the town of Saumur, the chateau offers unforgettable views onto the river and the historical places. **Open:** Every day, Oct–May: 9.30–12noon & 2–5.30pm (closed Tues 1 Oct–31 Mar, 25 Dec & 1 Jan). June–Sept: 9.30–6pm. July–August: Wed–Sat 8.30–10.30pm **Admission:** Adult FF38, Child FF27, Family FF110, Groups FF29. **Location:** Along the Loire Valley, between Angers (N147) & Tours (N152), TGV from Paris (1hr30).

map 287 61

CHÂTEAU & JARDINS DE VILLANDRY
37510 Villandry
Tel: 00 33 2 47 50 02 09 Fax: 00 33 2 47 50 12 85 (M.Carvallo)

The castle at Villandry is renowned for its architecture. Built during the reign of Francois I, the castle is constructed around an attractive courtyard and stands reflected in its surrounding moat. But it is Villandry's gardens, above all, that have won worldwide acclaim. The gardens are planted in layers, rising to a level of 30 metres: At the peak, high terraces have been cut into the hillside overlooking the castle. The next layer down comprises a huge expanse of water, which helps replenish the network of moats and fountains. At the base, you will find the ornamental gardens featuring vast box-hedges shaped into symbolic forms and edged with flowers. The castle itself, overlooks the kitchen garden. This, without doubt is the most original feature of the garden. Surrounded by vines, the garden is divided into nine squares, each of a different design. The vegetable borders are edged with dwarf box and are interspersed with fruit trees and standard roses, creating the image of a truly charming and colourful draught board. **Open:** Gardens: Every day, all year – unguided visits with leaflet. 1 Jan–28 Feb, 9–5.30pm. 1–24 Mar, 9–6pm. 25 Mar–30 Apr & 17 Sept–14 Oct, 9–7pm. 1 May–16 Sept, 9–7.30pm. 15 Oct–31 Dec, 9–5.30pm. Château: Every day, 3 Feb–11 Nov – Guided tours in French at set times or unguided visit with leaflet. 3–28 Feb, 9.30–5pm. 1–24 Mar, 9–5.30pm. 25 Mar–30 June & 1 Sept–14 Oct, 9–6pm. 1 July–31 Aug, 9–6.30pm. 15 Oct–11 Nov 9–5pm. **Admission:** Children under 8 Free. Gardens (1hr & leaflet): Adult FF33, Conc (8–18yrs, Students, large families) FF22. Château (individual/guided visit) & Gardens (2hrs): Adults FF46, Conc FF32. Groups: (min 15 paying visitors - 2 free tickets per group) Château & Gardens (2hrs) FF38, Gardens (1hr) FF26.

map 287 62

CHÂTEAU ROYAL D'AMBOISE
BP 371, 37403 Amboise Cedex
Tel: 00 33 2 47 57 00 98 Fax: 00 33 2 47 57 52 23

The cradle of the Renaissance – The Château of Amboise, one of the first truly 'royal' residences of its kind, was built during the 15th and 16th centuries on the orders of Charles VIII, Louis XII and François I. Following in the footsteps of the great kings of France, you will discover a magnificent example of Gothic and Renaissance architecture. It was at Amboise that Leonardo da Vinci lived out his last years. His body now rests in the Château's chapel of St Hubert. **Open:** Daily, throughout the year except 25 Dec & 1 Jan. **Admission:** Adults FF41, Children (7-14 yrs) FF22, Groups FF29.

map 287
63

Credit: Photoflash 41000 Blois

CHÂTEAU DE CHENONCEAU
37150 Chenonceaux, Indre-et-Loire
Tel: 00 33 2 47 23 90 07 Fax: 00 33 2 47 23 80 88 (Societe Civile Chenonceau Rentilly)

The Château at Chenonceau is a wonderful example of French Renaissance architecture. Situated in the heart of the Touraine, the castle is surrounded by a 70 Hectare park, and its two famous gardens created by Diane de Poitiers and Catherine de Medici. Diane de Poitiers was also responsible for adding the stunning galleried bridge which spans the River Cher. Built on The Cher with the waters reflecting the unique beauty of its Renaissance architecture, the Chateau de Chenonceau is the jewel of the Loire Valley. Known historically as the 'Chateau des Dames' ('Castle of Women'), it was built in 1513 by Katherine Briçonnet, beautified by Diane de Poitiers and Catherine de Médici successively and protected from the ravages of the Revolution by Madame Dupin. Thus, Chenonceau effectively owes to these ladies a part of its charm.

The enchanting setting, the French Gardens and the park which surrounds it all complete the delicate air of gracefulness which is omnipresent. **The Ladies' Gallery:** New wax museum, showing the women who built Chenonceau. Situated in the Dome building, this museum houses a sumptuous collection of costumes made according to genuine documents. Historical journey from the Renaissance to World War I (1518–1918). **Location:** Situated 214km from Paris. **Open:** 16 Mar–15 Sept, 9–7pm. 16–30 Sept, 9–6.30pm. 1–15 Oct & 1–15 Mar, 9–6pm. 16–31 Oct & 16–28 Feb, 9–5.30pm. 1–15 Nov & 1–15 Feb, 9–5pm. 16 Nov–31 Jan, 9–4.30pm. **Admission:** Adults FF50, Students FF40, Children (7–15yrs) FF40. Groups (20 or more) FF40.

map 287
64

CHATEAU DE MEUNG SUR LOIRE
45130 Meung-sur-Loire
Tel: 00 33 2 38 44 36 47 Fax: 00 33 2 38 44 29 37

The oldest chateau of the Loire Valley with over 16 centuries of history. Entirely furnished–130 rooms–plus undergrounds open to the public. The only castle in the Loire Valley with an underground chapel, prisons, torture chamber and apparatus, dungeon and prison of Villon (a 15th century poet). Headquarters of the English armies during the 100 years war. Episcopal residence of the bishops of Orleans for 6 centuries, who were administrators of the crown. Centre of justice for central France. First castle of the Loire Valley south of Paris. British owned. **Open:** 27 Nov 2000–16 Feb 2001 10.30am–12noon & 2.30–4.30pm. 17 Feb–13 Apr and 1 Oct–11 Nov daily 10am–12noon & 2–5.30pm. 14 Apr–30 Sept daily 10am–6pm. **Location:** Situated on border of river Loire off A10 Paris to Bordeaux, outlet Meung, the medieval village immediately after Orleans.

map 287
65

Photograph: F. Vallon – Kipa Press

CHÂTEAU DE CHEVERNY

41700 Cheverny
Tel: 00 33 2 54 79 96 29 Fax: 00 33 2 54 79 25 38 (Charles Antoine de Vibraye)

Travelling along the Loire Valley is like opening a book of the history of France. The principal jewels in this rich inheritance are: Chambord, Blois, Chenonceau and Cheverny. The Chateau of Cheverny, with its immaculate façade, is noted for its architecture which is both classical and majestic. For 7 centuries Cheverny has been the home of the very distinguished Hurault family, councillors to Kings Louis XII, Francois I, Henri III and Henri IV. Today their descendants preside over the fortunes of the Domaine de Cheverny. The chateau welcomes several hundred thousand visitors per year, enchanted by the richness of its decoration and the abundance of its superb furnishings. Cheverny is the most magnificently furnished chateau in the Loire Valley. Outside, be seduced by the majesty of the park and its canal....Explore the superb park of Cheverny by eletric car and boat. Observe the fauna and flora while gliding through the water in complete silence, without disturbing the enviroment (from April to November). **Location:** 13km south from Blois (D765). **Open:** daily, throughout the year. And from Apr–Nov for the park and the canal. **Admission:** Adult FF38, Child (under 14) FF17. **E-mail:** chateau.cheverny@wanadoo.fr **Internet:** www.chateau–cheverny.fr

map 287
66

PARC FLORAL DE LA SOURCE

45072 Orléans CEDEX 2
Tel: +33 2 38 49 30 00 Fax: +33 2 38 49 30 19

Once visited by Voltaire, this landscaped park was restored for the International Flower Festival in 1967, and welcomed over two million visitors in just six months. Spring sees the enchanting park burst into life, when 300 thousand bulbs flower under hundred-year-old oaks. The elegant and innovative Great Aviary stands at the shaded source of the Loiret river, and hundreds of colourful butterflies fill the air in the nearby tropical glasshouse, the only one of its kind in the region. A special video show and commentary from an entomologist help bring learning to life. A unique contemporary garden contains the breathtaking National Collection of irises, a stunning array of hues and textures. The air is heady with the scent of mysterious roses mingling with perennials in the Mirror Rose-garden. Near to the dahlia garden (180 varieties), a 49m long wicker fence encloses an experimental kitchen garden bright with flowers. Other attractions include a collection of Irises (1000 varieties), an animal park, a miniature train and various shops. Themed guided visits ("101 Trees to Discover", the Kitchen Garden, Exotic Butterflies) are available for groups of 15 or more, by prior appointment. **Location:** Situated 8km to the south-east of Orléans, exit "Orléans La Source" from A71 motorway. **Open:** April – mid November, daily 9am-7pm (last entry 6pm). Mid November – end March, daily 2–5pm. Closed 25 Dec. **Internet:** www.parcfloral-delasource.fr

map 287
67

LA CLÉ DES TEMPS

Céline Duret, Maison des Refractaires, 41250 Chambord
Tel.: +33 2 54 50 50 24

Travel back in time to the most important historical sites in the Loire valley with "La Clé des Temps" (The Key to the Past). This special season ticket, costing just 130FF, allows the bearer to visit any 10 of the 15 national monuments along the Loire, between Angers and Orléans. The following sites may be visited: Château de Oiron, Château d'Angers, **Abbaye Royale de Fontevraud**, **Château d'Azay-le-Rideau**, Cloître de la Psalette in Tours, Château de Chaumont, Château de Talcy, Château de Fougères sur Bièvre, **Château de Chambord**, Château de Châteaudun, the Cathedral in Chartres, Palais Jacques Cœur à Bourges, the Crypt and Cathedral in Bourges, the house of George Sand in Nohant-Vic and the Château de Bouges. Available at all of the above sites, it is fully transferable and valid for one year from the date of your first visit. To request a brochure, please call 00 33 2 54 50 50 24. **Internet:** www.monuments-france.fr

ABBAYE ROYALE DE FONTEVRAUD

49590 Fontevraud-l'abbaye, Anjou
Tel : 0033 2 41 51 71 41 Fax : 00 33 2 41 38 15 44

The Royal Abbey at Fontevraud was founded on a 35 acre site on the border of Anjou and the Val de Loire, and grew to become the most important monastic community in the West. Fontevraud is also the burial place of kings: the nave is crowded with the colourful tombs of the Plantagenets: Henri II, Eleanor of Aquitaine, Richard Lionheart and Isabelle of Angoulême. The enormous Romanesque kitchens are highly original, and are probably based on an English design. This is truly a living monument, widely considered one of the greatest workshops for restoration in France. Guided tours are available. The site hosts a number of regular cultural activites, including concerts, courses (Gregorian Chant, heritage workshops) and outdoor spectacles (in August). There is a hostelry in the abbey. **Open:** Daily except 1 Jan, 1 and 11 Nov, 25 Dec. **Admission:** Adult 36FF, Youth ticket (18-25) 23FF, Groups 29FF.

map 287 **68**

DOMAINE NATIONAL DE CHAMBORD

Maison des Refractaires, Val de Loire
Tel : +33 2 54 50 40 00 Fax : +33 2 54 20 34 69

Towering over the heart of a forest well stocked with game, the Château de Chambord is the largest and most sumptuous of all the Loire châteaux. Chambord's daring and innovative architecture reflects the youth of the king who built it, François I. A traditional centre for hunting, it now houses the museum of hunting and nature. More than 80 rooms are open to the public, containing collections of carpets, paintings, weapons and even carriages. The castle and surrounding forest host a variety of activities all year round. Attractions include horse-drawn carriage rides, boating, equestrian shows, wildlife hides and bicycle rides. **Open:** Daily, all year round, exc 1 Jan, 1 May & 25 Dec. **Admission:** Adult 42FF, under 18 free, Youth ticket (18-25) 26FF, Groups 33FF. **Special Event:** "Chambord in Metamorphosis", nightly from Apr–Sept. Prices: Adult FF80, Conc FF50, under 12s free.

map 287 **69**

CHÂTEAU D'AZAY-LE-RIDEAU

37190 Azay-le Rideau, Val de Loire
Tel: 00 33 2 47 45 42 04 Fax: 00 33 2 47 45 26 61
(Centre des monuments nationaux)

Built on an island in the middle of the river Indre, Azay-le-Rideau showcases all of the architectural refinements of the early Renaissance in the Loire Valley. Set in romantic parkland, this jewel of a castle has retained a remarkable unity of style. The décor of the fully furnished rooms allows the visitor to trace the lives of the château's most illustrious owners through the centuries. **Open:** All year, except 1 Jan, 1 May, 1 & 11 Nov, 25 Dec. **Admission:** Adult 36FF, under 18 free, Youth ticket (18-25) 23FF. Groups 29FF per person. **Special Event:** "Les Imaginaires" - at nightfall, wander through an enchanted park, where light and music combine to form a universal language of emotion. Nightly from mid-May to mid-Sept. **Price:** Adult 60FF, under 12 free, Youth ticket (12-25) FF35. Groups 50FF per person.

map 287 **70**

CHÂTEAU DE LA GUERCHE
37350 La Guerche
Tel: 00 33 2 47 91 02 39 Fax: 00 33 1 46 51 47 73 (Bernard de Crouy-Chanel)

La Guerche, which controlled an important bridge on the river Creuse, was fortified since the 1000s. In 1203, the marriage of the lady to a friend of the King of France urged John Lackland to take military control of the castle. The present castle was built in two stages during the 15th century (1450–1500). This ambitious construction reflects, like major castles of the Loire Valley, a concern for security (modern use of artillery), comfort and prestige. **Open:** 26 Jun–17 Sept, Mon–Sat, 10–12pm & 2–7pm. Sun 1–7pm. **Admission:** FF20, Groups FF10. Low season groups only – advance notice phone/fax: 00 33 1 46 51 47 73. English speaking guides. **Events:** 9-10 June special opening for exhibition of collectors.

map 287
71

CHÂTEAU DE TERRE NEUVE
85200 Fontenay le Comte
Tel: 00 33 2 51 69 17 75 Fax: 00 33 2 51 50 00 83 (Henri du Fontenioux)

Built in 1580 for Nicolas Rapin, comrade of King Henri IV. This castle is renowned for its fireplace featuring alchemic symbols, its coffered ceiling, sculpted in the style of the Renaissance period, its wooden structure from the Chateau de Chambord: the suns brushed in gold leaf from the bedroom of King Louis XIV and the drawing room door of King Francois I. Entirely furnished: cabinets, tableaux, clothes, armoury from the 17th and 18th centuries. The Duke of Sully, Agrippa d'Aubigne, was received there during the Renaissance and the famous writer Georges Simenon lived here from 1941 to 1943. This private castle is occupied, bedecked with flowers and open to the pubic. **Open:** 1 May–30 Sept: Daily 9–12noon & 2–6.45pm. **Admission:** Adults FF32, Children FF10. Groups FF20.

map 287
72

JARDINS DU CHÂTEAU DE VILLIERS
18800 Chassy
Tel: 00 33 2 48 77 53 20 Fax: 00 33 2 48 77 53 29

A Berry manor house dating back to the 15 C, the Château de Villiers has been a family home for 350 years. Although the house itself is closed, the gardens are open to the public. After passing the dovecote upon entering and crossing a series of courtyards, your journey takes you to the beautiful secret garden, with its flowering shrubs, clematis and hardy perennials. The large lake awaits you, dominated by an old, recently restored, windmill. In springtime, enjoy the lilacs growing in the orchard and the rose-filled clearing. New children's playground. **Location:** 38km E of Bourges by D976 to Nérondes. Then 5km N by D6. **Station:** Nérondes. **Open:** May, June, August, September, 10am–7pm. Closed on Tuesdays & 1 July – 3 August. **Admission:** FF35, Child under 7 free, half price for under 18s. FF45 for groups by written arrangement, guided visit by owner. **Refreshments:** Tea & drinks. Home-made cakes available in the afternoon.

map 287
73

PARC FLORAL ET CHATEAU D'APREMONT
18150 Apremont-sur-Allier
Tel: 00 33 2 48 77 55 00 Fax: 00 33 2 48 80 45 17 (Gilles de Brissac)

The garden at Apremont, on the banks of the Allier, is a lavish example of France's long love affair with the English Garden. Herbaceous borders, planted by Count Gilles de Brissac, are very like those he enjoyed as a child, on holiday in England. Since the climate in this area is typically continental, the choice of trees, shrubs, perennials and bulbs, had to be all thought over in a distinct manner. Other features include a cascade and ponds, a Chinese Bridge, a Turkish Pavilion, a Belvedere, a Wistaria Arch. **Location:** 15km southwest of Nevers, 60 km east of Bourges by D976 and D45 towards Apremont. **Open:** Daily, Easter–last Sunday in September 10–12noon & 2–7pm. **Admission:** Adult FF40, Children half price. **E-mail:** info@apremomt_sur_allier.com **Internet:** www.apremomt_sur_allier.com

map 287
74

CHÂTEAU D'ARLAY
39140 Arlay
Tel: 00 33 3 84 85 04 22 Fax: 00 33 3 84 48 17 96 (M et Mme R de Laguiche)

The castle was built in 1774 by the Countess of Lauraguais on the site of a Minime Convent, the only remains of which are the vaulted cellar. It was refurnished during the Restoration (1819–1835). A romantic park laid out inside the medieval ruins of the old fortress of the Princes of Orange, is an illustration of the spirit of playfulness of the late 18th century. The theme of play is also evoked by the garden created in 1996: hoops with roses on croquet lawn, with a central bell-hoop and a box-tree "ball". You can also see the four aces: hearts, spades, diamonds and clubs. Flowers, fruit and vegetables are brought together in harmony. **Open:** From 15 June–15 Sept. **Email:** chateau@arlay.com **Internet:** www.arlay.com

map 287
75

LE LABYRINTHE - JARDIN DES CINQ SENS
Rue du Lac, 74140 Yvoire
Tel: 00 33 4 50 72 88 80 Fax: 00 33 4 50 72 90 80

The castle's former kitchen garden transformed into "The Garden of the Five Senses": a labyrinth of green hedges, inspired by medieval walled gardens; a universe of colour, scent, sound and texture; a garden of full charm, which mirrors the passing hours and seasons. An excursion of discovery... where time stands still. **Location:** 15 m NE from Geneva towards Evian. Inside the medieval village of Yvoire on the South shore of Lake Geneva. **Open:** Daily mid April– mid May: 11am–6pm; mid May–mid Sept: 10am–7pm; mid Sept–mid Oct 1–5pm. **Admission:** FF45, reductions for families, children and groups. Guided tour in English for groups (20+) on reservation. **E-mail:** jardin-des-cinq-sens@wanadoo.fr

map 287
76

CHÂTEAU DE MALLE
33210 Preignac
Tel: 00 33 5 56 62 36 86 Fax: 00 33 5 56 76 82 40 (Comtesse De Bournazel)

Bordeaux area. Magnificent residence surrounded by Italian gardens, in the heart of Sauternes vineyard, Malle built by Jacques de Malle, direct ancestor of the Comte de Bournazel, dates from the early 17 C. The castle is tile-roofed, dominated by a Mansard one-storied slate covered central pavilion with two round towers at each end, topped with slate domes. The chapel is in one of the towers. Ceilings, furniture and paintings have remained as they were. The vineyard encompasses the region of Sauternes (Malle is a great classified vintage under the famous Imperial classification of 1855) and Graves (red & white wines). **Open:** 1 Apr–31 Oct, 10–12 & 2–6.30pm. Every day. Free parking. Groups by appointment. Possibility of tasting. **Location:** 35 m S Bordeaux by R.N. 113 or A62 to Langon. **E-mail:** chateaudemalle@wanadoo.fr
Internet: www.chateau–de–malle.fr

map 287
77

CHÂTEAU DU COLOMBIER
12330 Mondalazac, Salles la Source
Tel: 00 33 5 65 74 99 79 Fax: 00 33 5 65 74 99 78 (Annabelle Vicomtesse de la Panouse)

The medieval garden of Eden at the Château du Colombier is a lively depiction of the history of gardens from Charlemagne to the fifteenth century. As in times past, play croquet or chess in the flowering mead covered with violets, primroses, poppies and marguerites. Imagine maidens and their knights kissing in the folly or dancing around the May tree. Come and relive the times of yesteryear and sample moments of serenity and calm in this enchanted garden. There is a singing fountain amongst the lilies and shady walkways adorned with creeping vines. Sit on grassy banks of camomile and thyme amid a wealth of roses. The Garden of Eden will fill your senses with a thousand fragrances reminiscent of the past, and fill you with a desire to return soon. Every day an audiovisual presentation on "Man and the Animals in the Middle Ages" will entertain you. As well as a fantastic animal park, complete with lions, wolves, bears and birds of prey. **Open:** All year round: every day from 10am or 2pm–6pm or 7pm, depending on the season. **Admission:** Château, medieval gardens and live bestiary: Adults FF53 (8.07 Euros), Children FF36 (5.5 Euros).

map287
78

CHÂTEAU DE FÉNELON
Sainte Mondane, 24370 Dordogne
Tel: 00 33 5 53 29 81 45 Fax: 00 33 5 53 29 88 99 (Mr Jean-Luc Delautre)

Situated in the Valley of the Dordogne between Sarlat and Souillac. Fénelon, set in unspoiled countryside above the village, is one of the most beautiful castles in Périgord Noir. Its fortress-like appearance is a pleasing combination of mediaeval militarism and Renaissance beauty. It still looks as it did then, with its triple enclosure. Built on a series of rocky terraces, its defence system has remained intact. It is one of the rare historic buildings in Sarlat area to still have a stone roof. There is a fine collection of arms and armour, together with some beautiful furniture and objets d'art dating from the 15th to the 18th centuries. **Location:** 17km southwest of Sarlat, on the banks of the Dordogne, in Sainte-Mondane. **Open:** 1 Jan–31 May: 10–12pm & 2–6pm. 1 Jun–30 Sept: 9.30–7pm. 1 Oct–31 Dec: 10–12pm & 2–6pm. **Admission:** Adult FF40, Child FF25. Groups: Adult FF30, Child FF20.

map 287
79

CHÂTEAU-ABBAYE DE LOC-DIEU
Loc-Dieu Martiel, 12200 Villefranche de Rouergue
Tel: +33 5 65 29 51 17   Fax: +33 5 65 29 51 17

The first Cistercian abbey in Rouergue was founded by thirteen monks in 1123. What was once an inhospitable wood became a peaceful place, the place of God: Loc-Dieu. The abbey was caught up in the Hundred Years' War, and burnt to the ground in 1411. It was subsequently rebuilt and fortified. The French Revolution saw the abbey sold off along with the rest of the Church's property. After years of neglect, it was purchased by the Cibiel family who restored it and made it their family home, which it remains to this day. Da Vinci's Mona Lisa is numbered amongst the abbey's famous visitors: the painting was hidden here for some months during the Second World War. **Open:** 1 July–10 Sept, 10am-12pm and 2–6.30pm, daily except Tuesdays. Visits for groups can also be organised outside the normal opening season. Parc open all year.

map 287
80

CHÂTEAU DE LOSSE
24290 Thonac par Montignac-Lascaux, Dordogne (Périgord)
Tel/Fax: 00 33 553 50 80 08

The medieval stronghold overlooks the Vézère river, it is defended by the largest gatehouse in SW France, curtain walls linked by five towers and is surrounded by deep ditches. Within the Renaissance Hall's (1576) elegant architecture lies fine décor and exceptional period furniture (16th and 17th century). These bear witness to the way of life during the reign of the last Valois and first Bourbon kings. A walk through the green bowers in the gardens, terraced above the splendid valley and on the rose lined ramparts is a delightful conclusion to an evocative tour. **Open:** Easter–30 Sept, daily. Groups by appointment at other times. **Location:** On D706, 5km from Montignac-Lascaux to Les Eyzies. Disabled access (free access to 80% of tour), guided tours in English or with English texts. **Internet:** www.bestofPerigord.fr

map 287
81

CHATEAU DES BAUX DE PROVENCE
13520 Les Baux de Provence
Tel: 33 04 90 54 55 56 Fax: 33 04 90 54 55 00

The Baux Château was constructed on one of the most beautiful sites in France, overlooking Provence as far as the sea. The Baux Château, a historic monument, offers various centres of interest in an area of 7 hectares, ensuring a fascinating visit for all the family. The Baux history museum, which retraces the turbulent history of this 1000 yr old town, the imposing remains of the château and the ancient fortified town of Baux, (dungeon, fortified towers, columbarium, hospital, caves). At the foot of the Château, life-size medieval siege machines create a vivid impression of warfare in the middle ages. **Location:** 25km from Avignon, 15km from Arles, 40km from Nice. Off A7 at Avignon Sud or Salon de Provence exits. On A9 at Nimes exit, in direction of Arles. **Open:** Every day. Spring 9–7.30pm, Summer 9–8.45pm, Autumn 9–6.30pm. Winter 9–5pm. **Internet:** www.château-baux-provence.com

map 287
82

VILLA EPHRUSSI DE ROTHSCHILD
06230 Saint Jean Cap Ferrat
Tel: 00 33 4 93 01 33 09 Fax: 00 33 4 93 01 31 10

Built by Baroness Ephrussi de Rothschild during the Belle Epoque, the villa is surrounded by seven glorios gardens, decorated with ornamental lakes, waterfalls, patios, flower beds, shady paths and rare types of trees. Overlooking the sea and offering a unique view over the French Riveria, this palace has retained all the atmosphere of an inhabited residence. The Villa, inspired by the great residences of the Italian Renaissance, houses private function rooms and apartments with high quality works of art, collected by Beatrice Ephrussi throughout her life. A free English guide book is given to each visitor. In the summer, a series of concerts enlivens the gardens. **Location:** Between Nice & Monaco, on coast road (N 98). **Open:** Everyday throughout the year. **Internet:** www.villa-ephrussi.com

map 287
83

Germany

It was the travellers from England who started the first wave of tourism to German castles some 200 years ago. Paintings, engravings and poetry formed a lasting testament to the fascination that German rivers, vineyards and castles exercised on the early British tourist; but as soon as its invention, photography as a modern mass media was also used. Romaticism in Germany is closely associated with names like William Turner or Lord Byron. Our castles enjoyed a new revival. Prussian kings and their royal relations launched a reconstruction campaign and soon bankers and steel barons followed the trend.

In 1899, the Deutsche Burgenvereinigung (German Castles Association) was founded not only to prevent the further destruction of historic sites but also to rectify erroneous concepts and methods of restoration, which were the obvious result of a purely romantic approach to conservation. We are proud to be the oldest national and, together with the National Trust, one of the oldest European heritage organisations.

Our Marksburg situated above the Rhine and a wonderful variety of other German castles and palaces keep their doors open to visitors. A good number of them have featured in the Historic Houses, Castles and Gardens editions since 1998 and I would like to wish this partnership a successful future. Beside this selection, our association offers a wide database of about 700 castles, palaces, fortresses and historic gardens on their website www.deutsche–burgen.org. Income from tourism has become essential in maintaining our historic properties. We would be delighted to see a revival of cultural tourism from Britain and feel certain that this publication will play a successful part.

Alexander Prince zu Sayn-Wittgenstein-Sayn
President Deutsche Burgenvereinigung e.V.

BRANITZ CASTLE
Kastanienallee 11, 03042 Cottbus
Tel: 00 49 355 751 5100 Fax: 00 49 355 751 5230

Branitz Castle stands in a historic English garden. The park (approx. 100 hectares) was laid by Herman Fürst of Pückler–Muskau (1785–1871), a landscape gardener of the European circle. With their ponds, small water ways, hills, ornamental trees and bushes, the gardens have a very distinctive character. Rather unique pyramids lie deep within the garden. Inside the late Baroque-style castle and stable are the historically furnished rooms (from 19th century), which contain different exhibitions depicting the life and work of the Princes of Pückler. The Cottbus collection of the romantic painter Carl Blechen, is exhibited in the restored castle rooms. **Location:** Cottbus, c100km S of Berlin on A15. **Open:** Summer: daily 10–6pm. Winter: daily except Mon, 11–5pm. Special events include theatre, concerts and readings. **Internet:** www.pueckler–museum.de

map 313
1

CASTLES OF THE PRINCE OF HOHENLOHE – OEHRINGEN
Wald & Schlosshotel – 74639 Friedrichsruhe / Zweiflingen Tel: 00 49 7941 60870 Fax: 00 49 7941 61468
Schloss Neuenstein – 74632 Neuenstein Tel: 00 49 7942–2209/49 7941–60990 Fax: 00 49 7941–609920

Wald & Schlosshotel: This graceful hunting castle, once the summer residence of Prince Johann-Friedrich of Hohenlohe-Oehringen, is now part of an elegant hotel in a magnificent park. Visitors will appreciate the handsome reception rooms, with their splendid family portraits and gilt mirrors. The guest rooms are decorated in harmonious colours and extremely comfortable. The Michelin star restaurant, decorated with candles and chandeliers providing attractive lighting, offers a sensational international menu and first-class wines. Leisure facilities include indoor and outdoor pools, tennis, fishing, riding and an 18-hole golf course. **Location:** BAB 6, Exit Öhringen, follow signs towards Zweiflingen; find signs to the Wald & Schlosshotel at Friedrichsruhe.

Schloss Neuenstein: Schloss Neuenstein, a water castle from the 11th century, was developed 500 years later into a noble residence in the Renaissance style. The castle houses the Hohenlohe Museum which has an extensive historic collection which reflects the art and culture of the Hohenlohe region. One can, amongst other things, visit the splendid Knights Hall, the Kaiser Hall with its rich collection of weapons and the art and rarity cabinet containing finely crafted goldsmiths work and ivory carvings. A special attraction is the fully functioning castle kitchen from 1485, which remains in its original condition. **Location:** BAB 6, exit Neuenstien, B19 Burgenstrasse. **Open:** 16 Mar–15 Nov, daily except Monday (when it is not a Bank Holiday), 9–12am and 1–6pm.

map 313
2

HOHENZOLLERN CASTLE
Burg Hohenzollern–Verwaltung, 72379 Burg Hohenzollern
Tel: 00 49 7471 2428 Fax: 00 49 7471 6812

The majestic castle with its fantastic view is the ancestral seat of the Hohenzollern Dynasty, the Prussian Royal Family (Frederick the Great) and the German Emperors. Guided tours, showing a valuable collection of artwork and treasures, including the Prussian King's Crown, offer an insight into 19th century architecture and into Prussian and German history. **Location:** 5km from Hechingen town centre. **Open:** Daily all year except 24 Dec, 16 Mar–15 Oct. 9–5.30pm. 16 Oct–15 Mar, 9–4.30pm. Guided tours every 15 to 30 minutes, English tours on prior arrangement. **Admission:** Castle grounds and house: Adults DM9, Groups DM6, Children DM3. Castle grounds DM4. **Refreshments:** Snack bar, and restaurant open daily in summertime. **Internet:** www.burg–hohenzollern.com

map 313
3

ELTZ CASTLE

Burg Eltz, 56294 Münstermaifeld
Tel: 00 49 (26 72) 95 05 00 Fax: 00 49 (26 72) 950 50 50

Burg Eltz, perhaps the best known medieval castle in Germany, with its towering buildings reaching up to 10 storeys and its picturesque half-timbering, offers nearly 900 years of history to its visitors. Throughout these centuries it has been formerly, the stronghold, today, the much beloved ancestral home of the Lords and Counts of Eltz. The castle, looking down at the little Elz river from which it took its name, and cradled by the forest that surrounds it, seems very distant from the world today. Still, it is only a few miles away from some of Germany's busiest rivers and highways. It has been the favourite subject to many artists and particularly to William Turner and Edward Lear. Since it has never been destroyed or looted, it contains an interesting display of furniture and armament, reaching back to the 14th century, and some remarkable Old

Masters including Lucas Cranach and Michael Pacher. The treasury holds an impressive collection of gold and silverware, arms and pieces de vertu, all of which were in actual use of the family, some as early as the thirteenth century many bearing the Eltz coat-of-arms. **Location:** Lower Moselle river area, nearby Koblenz/Cochem. **Directions:** Car/coach by motorway A48, exit Polch, or by Federal roads B416/B49, both via Münstermaifeld. Train and boat: stop Moselkern. **Open:** 1 Apr–1 Nov, 9.30–5.30pm. **Admission:** Guided Tour: Adults DM9.50 (£2.85), Children DM6.50 (£1.95), Family DM28 (£8.40). Treasury Vault: Adults DM4 (£1.20), Children DM2 (£0.60). Groups of 20 or more: Adults DM8.50 (£2.55), Children DM5.50 (£1.65). **E-mail:** kastellanei@burg-eltz.de **Internet:** www.burg-eltz.de

map 313
4

KRONBURG CASTLE
Burgstrasse 1, 87758 Kronburg
Tel: 00 49 8394/271 Fax: 00 49 8394/1671

Built on a picturesque hill in the Allgäu, Kronburg Castle has been the property of Baron of Vequel-Westernach for 375 years. This fine four-winged Renaissance style castle is mentioned first in documents from 1227. Part of the building is open to visitors from May–Oct (if booked in advance). The Baron and Baroness guide you personally through some superb rooms. (The German Master Hall, with rich stucco work, the Red drawing room with its original Renaissance ceiling, the Hunting room, Visionary gallery, many rooms with 300 yr old linen wallpaper and the Rococo style chapel). There are chamber and castle-yard concerts during the summer. A newly built guesthouse houses exclusive holiday apartments. **Location:** Near Memmingen, 5km W on A7 (direction of Königsschlösser), taking the exit Woringen. **Admission:** Adult DM9, Child DM4.50. **E-mail:** info@schloss-kronburg.de **Internet:** www.schloss-kronburg.de

map 313
5

LANGENBURG CASTLE
Fürstliche Verwaltung, Schloss Langenburg, 74595 Langenburg
Tel: 00 49 7905 1041 Fax: 00 49 7905 1040

With parts of the castle dating back to the 12C it is remarkable that this castle is still home to the noble family Hohenlohe-Langenburg. Offering one of the nicest Renaissance courtyards in Germany, a chapel and a Baroque garden, the former stables also house a classic car museum. In an area almost 2,000m², there are approx. 80 legendary cars from 1899 up to the modern Formula 1 racing car. The castle tour displays the superb Baroque hall, different museum rooms with fine stucco ceilings and the equally splendid furnishings of the Langenburg family. **Castle Tours:** Good Fri–1 Nov, daily, 10–5pm. Tours every hour on the hour. Groups should contact the castle for advance bookings. Groups can also visit at times outside the hours above and tours can also be in English. Castle concerts, stately rooms for weddings and events. Attractive walk, museum shop and café situated in rose garden. **E-mail:** schloss.langenburg@t-online.de **Internet:** www.schlosslangenburg.de

map 313
6

LEMBECK CASTLE
46286 Dorsten-Lembeck, Nordrhein–Westfalen
Tel: 00 49 23697167 Fax: 00 49 236977391 (Ferdinand Graf von Merveldt)

A fine example of an early Baroque Westphalian moated castle built in 1692 on the foundations of a medieval fortress. The northwest wing was re-modelled in 1730 by the eminent architect Johann-Conrad Schlaun who worked extensively on other important houses in the region. The home of Graf Merveldt, whose family and ancestors have owned Lembeck since the Middle Ages, the castle is now a museum and hotel. It contains a substantial collection of Chinese porcelain, Flemish tapestries, Dutch furniture and items of local cultural and historic interest and stands in extensive grounds which include a fine rhododendron park. **Location:** From Autobahn 43 Haltern exit or Autobahn 31 Lembeck exit. Station: Lembeck, **Open:** Daily Mar–Nov from 10–6pm. **Admission:** Adult DM7, Child DM4.50.

map 313
7

MARKSBURG CASTLE
56338 Braubach
Tel: 00 49 26 27 206 Fax: 00 49 26 27 88 66

The imposing Marksburg, known as the jewel of the Rhine Valley, is the only castle on the cliffs of the Rhine that has never been destroyed. Dating back to the 12th century, the castle has maintained its medieval character. The high Keep is surrounded by the Romanesque Palace and the Gothic Hall with the Chapel-Tower. Of special interest are the horse steps carved out of the rock, the Great Battery and the medieval Herb Garden with its spectacular view, the Gothic Kitchen, Knights' Hall, Armoury Chamber and collection of torture instruments. The Marksburg is the seat of the German Castles Association. **Location:** Braubach, 12 km South of Koblenz on B42. **Open:** Daily from 10–5pm, Nov–Easter 11–4pm. **Admission:** Adult DM8, Family DM24, Child DM6. Children under 6 years free. (guided tours also in English). **E-mail:** marksburg@deutsche–burgen.org

map 313
8

PAPPENHEIM CASTLE
Neues Schloß, 91788 Pappenheim
Tel: 00 49 9143 83 890   Fax: 00 49 9143 6445 (Gräfliche Verwaltung)

An imposing 12th century castle, extension 300m long, overlooking the picturesque former residence city of the Hereditary Marshals of the Holy Roman Empire, the Marchesses Pappenheim, with important historic buildings, enlarged during the following centuries; partly destroyed since the 30-years-war, an economical building and the arsenal of the 15th century contain a small museum, torture chamber, keep, long fortification walls, herb garden (more than 400 species), arboretum with collection of trees, shrubs and plants of the area (more than 1000 species). Cafeteria. **Location:** 35 miles W of Eichstaett. **Open:** Easter–5 Nov, Tues–Sun, 10–5pm. **Admission:** Adults DM4,50, Children DM3,50.

map313 9

POSTERSTEIN CASTLE
04626 Posterstein/Thuringia
Tel: 0049 34496 22595   Fax: 0049 34496 23305

Going to Saxony's capital Dresden on the busy motorway A4, you will pass Burg Posterstein which is situated halfway between Thuringia's capital Erfurt and Dresden. Burg Posterstein is located in Eastern Thuringia, bordering on the classical Thuringia, marked by Goethe. The first information about the castle dates from 1191. The first owner, Knight Stein, got his landed property from King Friedrich I Barbarossa. In the 16th and 17th centuries the old castle was rebuilt and became a little palace. The last restoration work took place from 1984 to 1991. **Museum Open:** Tues–Sat, 10–5pm; Sun 10–6pm. Nov–Feb: Tues–Fri 10–4pm; Sat–Sun 10–5pm. **Admission:** Adults DM5, Pupils/Students DM2, Children under 14 free. **Internet:** www.burg-posterstein.de

map 313 10

QUERFURT CASTLE
06268 Querfurt
Tel: 00 49 34771/5219 0 Fax: 00 49 34771/5219 99

Gracing the southern slope of the Quernebach Valley, the castle is one of the oldest in Germany. Its first documented mention occurred in the Hersfeld tithe register (866–899). In fact, this is also one of the largest castle compounds in the land, with an area almost seven times as large as that of the Wartburg. Presumably, Querfurt Castle served as a haven for refugees in Carolingian times. Evidence of stone buildings exists from the late 10th century onwards. The most conspicuous features of the castle are its three towers: 'Dicker Heinrich', 'Marterturm' and 'Pariser Turm'. At the centre is the Romanesque church built in the latter half of the 12th century, a crosshoped edifice with three semicircular apses and an octagonal crossing tower. **Open:** Tues–Sun, 9–5pm. Closed Mon. **Admission:** DM5, Concessions DM3.

map 313 11

RITTERGUT HAUS LAER
Höfestrasse 45, 44803 Bochum
Tel: 00 49 234 383044 Fax: 00 49 234 385375

Founded in 940, it is the oldest secular building existing in the middle Ruhrgebiet. A picturesque moated castle. The reliefs of the local sovereign Henry the Lion and his spouse Mathilde, who was the daughter of King Henry II and the sister of Richard Lionheart (Robin Hood, Nottinghamshire), are situated in two Suites of Haus Laer that can be rented. In 1704 and 1709 Haus Laer fought under John Churchill, Duke of Marlborough (Blenheim Palace Woodstock), successfully against the French King Louis XIV. Reservations for the suites "Madame Pompadour" and "Prince Soubise" possible. Guest house: long and short stays in the apartments/suites. Hall of the Knights for celebrations and events. **Location:** 4.5 km from main railway station of Bochum.

map 313 12

SAYN CASTLE & BUTTERFLY GARDEN

56170 Sayn bei Bendorf/Rhein

Tel: 00 49 2622 9024 0 (The Prince & The Princess zu Sayn-Wittgenstein-Sayn)

Burg Sayn, built before 1200 by the Counts of Sayn, was destroyed in 1633 and recently restored. Spectacular view on romanesque Sayn Abbey, Rhine Valley and Eifel mountains. Falcon & Eagle Show will open in 2001. Castellated terraces descend to recently restored Schloss Sayn with its museum for cast iron art. Landscaped park with rare trees, ponds, playgrounds and Garten der Schmetterlinge, an exotic dreamland with hundreds of live tropical butterflies. **Location:** Bendorf-Sayn, 10km NE of Koblenz on A48 and B42. **Open:** Mid Mar–early Nov daily from 10am–6pm. **Admission:** Schloss-Museum & Butterfly Garden: Adult DM10, Child DM7. **Refreshments:** Restaurant in Burg and Schloss Sayn (closed Mondays). Cafeteria at Butterfly Garden. **Internet:** www.sayn.de

map 313 | 13

SIGMARINGEN CASTLE

F.H. Schlossverwaltung, 72488 Sigmaringen

Tel: 00 49 7571 729 230   Fax: 00 49 7571 729 255

Sigmaringen Castle is, to this day, the home of the descendants of the Princes of Hohenzollern. The castle majestically overlooks the town of Sigmaringen and its surrounding countryside. There are many fascinating things to see in the castle; the Hubertus hall houses a large collection of hunting trophies and over 3,000 historic weapons of all types (one of the largest private collections of its kind in Europe). Art is indestructible, but it has found a safe hiding place here in Hohenzollern's castle; valuable tapestries and paintings, priceless porcelain pieces, elegant and tasteful furniture, which capture a calm and still ambience, can be found here. **Open:** For guided tours: Nov, Feb–Apr, daily, 9.30–4.30pm; May–Oct, daily, 9–4.45pm; Dec–Jan, only organised tours with prior bookings, until 4pm. **E-mail:** schloss@hohenzollern.com

map 313 | 14

SONDERSHAUSEN CASTLE

Box 83 99702 Sondershausen (Stiftung Thüringer Schlösser und Gärten)

Tel: 00 49 36 32 6630

The former residence of the Counts (since 1697 Princes) of Schwarzburg-Sonderhausen is the many-sided and in historical and artistical terms, the most interesting building in the north of Thuringia to experience about 600 years of architecture. The castle is situated on a rise above the town, surrounded by a 19C park covering 30 hectares. **Location:** 60km N of Erfurt on B4, parking near castle; railway-line: Intercity to Erfurt, regional-line to Sondershausen. **Open:** Residence-museum Tues–Sun 10–4pm, closed Mon; guided tours 10am & 2pm and by arrangements; special tours by arrangement (contact museum Tel: 00 49 3632 663 120). **Admission:** Adult DM6, Senior/Student DM4, Child (under 6) free, Group (min 15 pers.) DM3. Restaurants in historical rooms daily 11–12pm. Concerts in historic rooms (symphonic and chamber music, organ recitals) and exhibitions.

map 313 | 15

STOLPEN CASTLE

Schlossstrasse 10, 01833 Stolpen

Tel: 00 49 35973 23410 Fax: 00 49 35973 23419

30km E of Dresden, this Medieval castle was once the secondary residence of the Bishops of Meissen and the Saxon electoral princes. The building beautifully complements the natural monument the 'Stolpener Basalt'. Stolpen castle with its striking towers dominates the landscape between the 'Lausitz' and the 'Elbsandsteingebirge'. The castle is linked with the tragic fate of Countess Cosel, the most famous of Augustus the Strong's mistresses. He was the electoral prince of Saxony and King of Poland. She was a prisoner in the castle for 49 years (1716–1765) and is buried in the chapel. The medieval character is preserved through prisons, cellars, a torture chamber and the deepest well in the world. The castle museum and events programme make Stolpen one of the liveliest historic places in Saxony. **Open:** Daily. Summer 9–5pm. Winter 10–4pm (weather permitting). **E-mail:** burg.stolpen@t-online.de **Internet:** www.burg-stolpen.de

map 313 | 16

WERNIGERODE CASTLE

Schloss Wernigerode GmbH, Am Schloss 1, 38855 Wernigerode
Tel: 00 49 39 43 55 30 30 Fax: 00 49 39 43 55 30 55

The original Romanesque castle dating from the 12th century, extensively altered over the years, was up to 1945 the residential palace of the Earls of Stolberg, who took the name 'von Stolberg-Wernigerode' from their principality, the earldom of Wernigerode. The grand turreted stone and half-timber castle with magnificent views over the medieval town of Wernigerode today ranks as a major example of the North German "Historismus" building style. The remarkable rise to political power of Earl Otto, who became Vice Chancellor of Germany under Bismarck, gave impetus to the sumptuous late 19th century remodelling seen today, including the original staterooms of Europe's highest ranking nobility of that day. Changing exhibits, a variety of events and scientific symposiums fulfil the Schlossmuseum's aim to become a centre of artistic and cultural history of the 19th

century. Weddings in the Chapel, banquets in the Dining Hall, receptions, conferences and parties in the grandly appointed staterooms by arrangement. **Location:** Above Wernigerode, 70km south of Brunswick. Transfer service every 20 minutes from the Town Centre. **Open:** May–Oct: daily 10–6pm, last admission 5.30pm, Nov–Apr: closed Mon. Tues–Fri daily 10–4pm, Sat, Sun and on holidays daily 10–6pm. **Admission:** Adults DM8, Children DM4. Gardens and panorama terrace free. **Refreshments:** Restaurant and tearoom open daily except Mondays. **Exhibitions/Events:** Open air opera, theatre, concerts and ballet on the central terrace, shop. **E-mail:** schlosswr@t-online.de **Internet:** www.schloss-wernigerode.de

map 313
17

WILHELMSBURG CASTLE

Museum Castle Wilhelmsburg, Schlossberg 9, 98574 Schmalkalden
Tel: 00 49 3683 403186 Fax: 00 49 3683 601682

Castle Wilhelmsburg was built between 1585 and 1590 by Landgraf Wilhelm IV of Hessen–Kassel. This unique monument to art and architecture is a mature example of Renaissance castle building. Renaissance ornamentation, wallpaintings and stucco are characteristic of the décor of the apartments and staterooms. The castle's church provides an example of one of the most mature Protestant church buildings of the 16th centuries. Themes of the exhibitions are Renaissance, Reformation, history of the building and its use as well as contemporary art. **Events:** Recitals on the Renaissance organ (1589); Chamber music recitals. **Location:** A4, Exit Eisenach, 40km S on B19. **Open:** (not Mons) Feb–Oct: 9–5pm, Nov–Jan: 10–4pm. **Admission:** Adults DM6, Child DM4, Groups DM5. Tours by appointment DM30. **E-mail:** museum.sm@gmx.de

map 313
18

THE PRINCELY CASTLE OF THURN UND TAXIS

Emmeramsplatz 5, 93047 Regensburg, Bavaria
Tel: 00 49 0941 5048133 Fax: 00 49 0941 5048256

Since 1812, this has been the home of the Princes of Thurn und Taxis, who reconstructed parts of the former Benedictine monastery of St. Emmeram as their residence. Besides the palace staterooms, furnished in different styles (rococo, neo-rococo, classic, historic), you can visit the medieval cloister (11–14th centuries) with the mortuary chapel (19th century) and the carriage museum (carriages, sleighs, sedan chairs, harnesses) in the former princely stables and riding hall. **Location:** A93, Exit Regensburg-Konigswiesen, then direction "Regensburg centre" **Open:** Apr–Oct daily 11am, 2, 3, 4pm, on Sats and Suns also 10am, Nov–Mar, Sats, Suns, Bank Hols 10, 11, 2, 3pm (guided tours only), tours for groups by appointment.

map 313
19

WALLERSTEIN CASTLE

D–86757 Wallerstein, Germany
Tel: +49 (0) 9081 782 300

The 'New Castle' in Wallerstein arose after the thirty year war when the Fortress on the Wallerstein Cliffs was distructed by Swedish troops. In its stately and private rooms (i.e. bedroom chamber, dining room, banquette hall) a fine Porcelain and Glass Collection as well as a unique exhibition of family uniforms of the Princes of Oettingen is on show. The adjacent English style park invites you to a relaxing stroll to the Orangerie and the impressive riding school. Location: On the Romantic Road (B25) between Dinkelsbühl and Nördlingen. Open: mid Mar–Oct, 9–5pm (closed Mons). Refreshments: Restaurant of Prince Oettingen–Wallerstein's brewery at the Wallerstein Cliff. Weddings: Chapel can be hired for weddings (80 persons). **E-mail:** schloesser@fuerst–wallerstein.de **Internet:** www.fuerst–wallerstein.de

map 313
20

The Netherlands

The Netherlands remains true to its traditions – the windmills still turn at the Zaanse Schans, the tulip gardens at Keukenhof explode in a riot of colour every Spring and the beautiful Dutch costumes are still daily wear for some people in the former fishing villages around the Ijsselmer.

The land of Rembrandt, Hals and Vermeer has more museums per square foot than any other country in the world. One of the most frequented galleries is the Van Gogh Museum, currently being refurbished. Some of the artist's 206 paintings may be seen at a special exhibition at the Rijksmuseum in Amsterdam.

The capital of The Netherlands, Amsterdam, is a fusion of both the past and present. Since the 16th century, when the diamond trade was first introduced to the city, Amsterdam has remained one of the world's most important diamond centres.

The 'Koh-I-Noor' Mountain of Light diamond was cut and polished here for the British Crown Jewels in 1852. The city is strikingly beautiful with architectural masterpieces lining the narrow streets and tall trees forming a canopy along the beautiful canals, filled with houseboats.

Situated further south along the coast is the town of Delft, famous for its blue pottery. An ideal way to explore the town is to follow the self-guided historical trail, passing the birthplace of the painter Vermeer, the old market square and the beautiful convent Het Prinsenhof.

Dutch cuisine, although largely influenced by Germanic flavours, incorporates a great deal of exquisite oysters and mussels from Zeeland.

The country's dairy farms are a source of national pride, producing the world-famous Edam cheese.

The busy port of Rotterdam is a thoroughly modern city that hosts numerous trade fairs and conferences. Nevertheless, visitors can still find quiet squares lined with fine old buildings, where pavement cafés provide a haven for the city's workers. Rotterdam is the 2001 Cultural Capital of Europe, and a number of special exhibitions and celebratory events will take place throughout the year.

The Limburg province situated in the south, near Belgium, sees a change in the landscape, as the flat plains of the north give way to a more dramatic landscape of rolling hills.

CASTLE DE HAAR

Kasteellaan 1, 3455 RR Haarzuilens
Tel: 00 31 30 677 3804 Fax: 00 31 30 677 5827 (Foundation Kasteel de Haar)

Castle de Haar dates back to the 14th century and got destroyed and rebuilt many times. By the far end of the 17th century it had become a ruin. In 1890 the ruin came into the possession of Baron Etienne van Zuylen van Nijevelt. Castle de Haar was rebuilt by a very famous Dutch architect, namely Pierre Cuypers. Castle de Haar is one of the largest castles in Holland and houses many treasures. Castle de Haar is endowed with an extensive park. Please telephone or visit our website for details of opening times and prices. **E-mail:** informatie@kasteeldehaar.nl **Internet:** www.kasteeldehaar.nl

map 321
1

KEUKENHOF

Stationsweg 166a, 2161 AM Lisse, The Netherlands
Tel: 00 31 252 465 555

Keukenhof is known as the Spring Garden of Europe. In 1949 the area was developed as a permanent showcase for the bulb and flower industry. Today, Keukenhof is the world's largest bulb flower garden, with acres of tulips, daffodils, hyacinths and other flowering bulbs, flowering shrubs, ancient trees and beautiful ponds and fountains. Keukenhof also has changing indoor flower exhibitions or parades, theme gardens and a special 'Bollebozen' route for children. Please call for details of opening times and admission prices.

map 321
2

MUIDERSLOT

Herengracht 1, 1398 AA Muiden
Tel: 00 31 (0) 294 261325 Fax: 00 31 (0) 294 261056
(Stichting Rijksmuseum Muiderslot)

The history of Muiden castle begins about 1280 when Floris V, Count of Holland, erected a stone fortress at the mouth of the river Vecht. The castle was destroyed in 1296 and rebuilt about 100 years later. The man who made the castle famous is the poet, playwright and historian Pieter Cornelisz Hooft (1581–1647). Hooft was bailiff of Muiden and reeve of Gooiland. For 39 years he summered at the castle, which he endowed with the splendour of Holland's Golden Age. Recently refurbished, the castle has regained its pristine elegance. The herb and kitchen gardens and the plum orchard also recall the sumptuous life of the castle's 17th century residents. During summer there is live falconry.

map 321
3

PALACE HET LOO NATIONAL MUSEUM

Koninklijk Park 1, NL–7315 JA Apeldoorn
Tel: 00 31 55 577 2400 Fax: 00 31 55 521 9983

Paleis Het Loo was opened to the public in 1984 after thorough restoration. The decoration and furnishing of the palace interiors (50 rooms) gives an impression of how the various members of the royal family of the House of Orange lived in the palace for three centuries. The gardens of Paleis Het Loo extend over seven hectares and contain a wealth of fountains, urns and statues. **Location:** Follow road signs; Bus 102 and 104 near Railway Station. **Open:** Palace and gardens open all year, Tue–Sun, 10–5pm; closed 1 January & Mon unless Bank Holidays. **Admission:** 6–17 years: Fl 12,50, Adults: FL 15. **Guided Tours:** In English by appointment. **Refreshments:** Tea House, Ballroom. Banquets, Meetings: 00 31 55 577 2409. **E-mail:** paleis.het.loo@wxs.nl **Internet:** www.hetloo.nl

map 321
4

SPAENSWEERD GARDENS

Bronkhorsterweg 18,6971 JA Brummen
Tel: 00 31 575 561104 Fax: 00 31 575 566160 (Diana Hummelen)

Spaensweerd dates back to the 17th century, but was altered in 1835 creating a lovely empire style. It is set in 3 acres of beautiful listed gardens with formal and informal elements. Old topiary, monumental trees and an astonishing number of rare and unusual plants in the herbaceous borders, which provides interest throughout the season. Splendid views from the garden overlooking the countryside. **Location:** 5 km south of Zutphen. **Open:** 2, 3, 4, 17 & 18 June; 8 & 9 July, 11–5pm. Groups by appointment. **Admission:** Adults FL7,50. Children under 12 free. **Refreshments** and accommodation available.

map 321
5

VALKENBURG

Grendelplein 13, Valkenburg, (Limberg), The Netherlands
Tel: 00 31 43 6090110

Visit the only castle in The Netherlands to have been built on a mountain side – these magnificent ruins are situated on the 'Falcon's Mount' – a site occupied by the castle since 1100. The castle once belonged to the ducal house of Cleves and was the setting for the marriage between Beatrice of Valkenburg and Richard of Cornwall (brother of Henry III of England) in 1269. In 1329 the castle was destroyed and rebuilt in its current shape. It was conquered by the Duke of Brabant in 1365 and was subsequently beseiged on a number of occasions until being blown up by the armies of William III in 1672. Today, it is possible to visit the network of secret passages leading to the Velvet Cave.

map 321
6

Supplementary List of Properties

The list of houses in England, Scotland and Wales printed here are those which are usually open 'by appointment only' with the owner, or open infrequently during the summer months. These are in addition to the Houses and Gardens which are open regularly and are fully classified. Where it is necessary to write for an appointment to view, see code (WA). * denotes owner/address if this is different from the property address. The majority of these properties have received a grant for conservation from the Government given on the advice of the Historic Buildings Councils. Public buildings, almshouses, tithe barn, business premises in receipt of grants are not usually included, neither are properties where the architectural features can be viewed from the street.

ENGLAND

AVON

Birdcombe Court, (Mr & Mrs P. C. Sapsed.) (WA), Wraxall, Bristol

Eastwood Manor Farm, (A. J. Gay), East Harptree

Partis College, (The Bursar.) (WA), Newbridge Hill, Bath, BA1 3QD Tel: 01225 421 532

The Refectory, (Rev. R. Salmon), The Vicarage Tel: 01934 833 126

Woodspring Priory, (WA), Kewstoke, Weston-Super-Mare.*The Landmark Trust.

BEDFORDSHIRE

The Temple, (The Estate Office) (WA), Biggleswade

Warden Abbey, (WA), Nr. Biggleswade
* The Landmark Trust.

BERKSHIRE

High Chimneys, (Mr & Mrs S. Cheetham) (WA), Hurst, Reading Tel: 01734 34517

St. Gabriel's School, (The Headmaster), Sandleford Priory, Newbury Tel: 01635 40663

BUCKINGHAMSHIRE

Bisham Abbey, (The Director), Marlow Tel: 01628 476 911

Brudenell House, (Dr H. Beric Wright) (WA), Quainton, Aylesbury, HP22 4AW

Church of the Assumption, (Friends of Friendless Churches), Harmead, Newport Pagnell Tel: 01234 39257
* For Key: Apply to H. Tranter, Manor Cottage, Hardmead, by letter or phone on 01234 39257.

Iver Grove, (Mr & Mrs T. Stoppard) (WA), Shreding Green, Iver

Repton's Subway Facade, (WA), Digby's Walk, Gayhurst Tel: 01908 551 564* JH Beverly, The Bath House, Gayhurst.

CAMBRIDGESHIRE

The Chantry, (Mrs T. A. N. Bristol) (WA), Ely, Cambridge

The Church of St. John the Baptist, (Friends of Friendless Churches), Papworth St. Agnes * For Key: Apply to Mrs P. Honeybane, Passhouse Cottage, Papworth St. Agnes, by letter or phone on 01480 830 631.

The King's School, Ely, (WA), Bursars Office, The King's School, Ely, CB7 4DB Tel: 01353 662 837, Fax: 01353 662 187

Leverington Hall, (Professor A. Barton) (WA), Wisbech, PE13 5DE

The Lynch Lodge, (WA), Alwalton, Peterborough
* The Landmark Trust

CHESHIRE

Bewsey Old Hall, (The Administrator) (WA), Warrington

Crown Hotel, (Proprietor: P. J. Martin), High Street, Nantwich, CW5 5AS Tel: 01270 625 283, Fax: 01270 628 047

Charles Roe House, (McMillan Group Plc) (WA), Chestergate, Macclesfield, SK11 6DZ

Shotwick Hall, (Tenants: Mr & Mrs G. A. T. Holland), Shotwick Tel: 01244 881 717
* P. Gardner Trustee Shotwick Manor Trust, Wychen, 17 St. Mary's Road, Leatherhead, Surrey. By appointment only with the tenants, Mr & Mrs G. A. T. Holland.

Tudor House, Lower Bridge Street, Chester Tel: 01244 20095

Watergate House, (WA), Chester Tel: 01352 713353 * Ferry Homes Ltd, 49 High Street, Holywell, Clywd, Wales, CH8 9TF.

CLEVELAND

St. Cuthbert's Church & Turner Mausoleum, (Kirkleatham Parochial Church Council), Kirkleatham Tel: Contact Mrs R. S. Ramsdale on 01642 475 198 or Mrs D. Cook, Church Warden on 01642 485 395

CORNWALL

The College, (WA), Week St. Mary
* The Landmark Trust.

Town Hall, (Camelford Town Trust), Camelford

Trecarrel Manor, (N. H. Burden), Trebullett, Launceston Tel: 01566 82286

CUMBRIA

Coop House, (WA), Netherby
* The Landmark Trust.

Preston Patrick Hall, (Mrs J. D. Armitage) (WA), Milnthorpe, LA7 7NY Tel: 01539 567 200, Fax: 01539 567 200

Whitehall, (WA), Mealsgate, Carlisle, CA5 1JS
* Mrs S. Parkin-Moore, 40 Woodsome Road, London, NW5 1RZ.

DERBYSHIRE

Elvaston Castle, (Derbyshire County Council), Nr. Derby, DE72 3EP Tel: 01332 571 342

10 North Street, (WA), Cromford
* The Landmark Trust.

Swarkestone Pavilion, (WA), Ticknall
* The Landmark Trust.

DEVON

Bindon Manor, (Sir John & Lady Loveridge) (WA), Axmouth

Bowringsleigh, (Mr & Mrs M. C. Manisty) (WA), Kingbridge

Endsleigh House, (Endsleigh Fishing Club Ltd), Milton Abbot, Nr. Tavistock Tel: 01822 870 248, Fax: 01822 870 502

Hareston House, (Mrs K. M. Basset), Brixton, PL8 2DL Tel: 01752 880 426

The Library, (WA), Stevenstone, Torrington
* The Landmark Trust.

Sanders, (WA), Lettaford, North Bovey
* The Landmark Trust.

The Shell House, (Endsleigh Fishing Club Ltd), Milton Abbot, Nr. Tavistock Tel: 01822 870 248, Fax: 01822 870 502

Shute Gatehouse, (WA), Shute Barton, Nr. Axminster
* The Landmark Trust.

Town House, (Tenant: Mr & Mrs R. A. L. Hill), Gittisham, Honiton Tel: 01404 851 041
* Mr & Mrs R. J. T. Marker

Wortham Manor, (WA), Lifton
* The Landmark Trust.

DORSET

Bloxworth House, (Mr T. A. Dulake) (WA), Bloxworth

Clenston Manor, Winterborne, Clenston, Blandford Forum

Higher Melcombe, (M. C. Woodhouse) (WA), Dorchester, DT2 7PB

Moignes Court, (A. M. Cree) (WA), Owermoigne

Smedmore House, Kimmeridge, BH20 5PG

Stafford House, (Mr & Mrs Richard Pavitt), West Stafford, Dorchester Tel: 01305 263 668

Woodsford Castle, (WA), Woodsford, Nr. Dorchester
* The Landmark Trust.

COUNTY DURHAM

The Buildings in the Square, (Lady Gilbertson) (WA), 1 The Square, Greta Bridge, DL12 9SD Tel: 01833 27276

ESSEX

Blake Hall, Battle of Britain Museum & Gardens, (Owner: R. Capel Cure), Chipping Ongar, CM5 0DG Tel: 01277 362 502

Properties by Appointment Only

Church of St. Andrews and Monks Tithe Barn, (Harlow District Council), Harlow Study & Visitors Centre, Netteswellbury Farm, Harlow, CM18 6BW Tel: 01279 446 745, Fax: 01279 421 945

Grange Farm, (J. Kirby), Little Dunmow, CM6 3HY Tel: 01371 820 205

Great Priory Farm, (Miss L. Tabor), Panfield, Braintree, CM7 5BQ Tel: 01376 550 944

The Guildhall, (Dr & Mrs Paul Sauven), Great Waltham Tel: 01245 360 527

Old All Saints, (R. Mill), Old Church Hill, Langdon Hills, SS16 6HZ Tel: 01268 414 146

Rainham Hall, (The National Trust. Tenant: D. Atack), Rainham

Rayne Hall, (Mr & Mrs R. J. Pertwee) (WA), Rayne, Braintree

The Round House, (M. E. W. Heap), Havering-atte-Bower, Romford, RM4 1QH Tel: 01708 728 136

GLOUCESTERSHIRE

Abbey Gatehouse, (WA), Tewksbury
* The Landmark Trust.

Ashleworth Court, (H. J. Chamberlayne), Gloucester Tel: 01452 700 241

Ashleworth Manor, (Dr & Mrs Jeremy Barnes) (WA), Ashleworth, Gloucester, GL19 4LA Tel: 01452 700 350

Bearland House, (The Administrator) (WA), Longsmith Street, Gloucester, GL1 2HL, Fax: 01452 419 312

Castle Godwyn, (Mr & Mrs J. Milne) (WA), Painswick

Chaceley Hall, (W. H. Lane), Tewkesbury Tel: 01452 28205

Cheltenham College, (The Bursar), The College, Bath Road, Cheltenham, GL53 7LD Tel: 01242 513 540

The Cottage, (Mrs S. M. Rolt) (WA), Stanley Pontlarge, Winchcombe, GL54 5HD

East Banqueting House, (WA), Chipping Camden
* The Landmark Trust.

Minchinhampton Market House, (B. E. Lucas), Stroud Tel: 01453 883 241

The Old Vicarage, ('Lord Weymyss' Trust), The Church, Stanway Tel: 01386 584 469
* Apply to Stanway House, Stanway, Cheltenham:

St. Margaret's Church, (The Gloucester Charities Trust), London Road, Gloucester Tel: 01452 23316
By appointment with the Warden on 01831 470 335.

Tyndale Monument, (Tyndale Monument Charity), North Nibley, GL11 4JA Tel: 01453 543 691
For Key: See notice at foot of Wood Lane.

GREATER MANCHESTER

Chetham's Hospital & Library, (The Feoffees of Chetham's Hospital & Library), Manchester, M5 1SB Tel 0161 834 9644, Fax: 0161 839 5797

Slade Hall, (Manchester & District Housing Assn.) (WA), Slade Lane, Manchester, M13 0QP

HAMPSHIRE

Chesil Theatre (formerly 12th century Church of St. Peter Chesil), (Winchester Dramatic Society), Chesil Street, Winchester, SO23 0HU Tel: 01962 867 086

The Deanery, (The Dean & Chapter), The Close, Winchester, SO23 9LS Tel: 01962 853 137, Fax: 01962 841 519

Greywell Hill, near Hook (PR FitzGerald, Wilsons)(WA) Steynings House, Fisherton Street, Salisbury SP2 7RJ

Manor House Farm, (S. B. Mason), Hambledon Tel: 01705 632 433

Moyles Court, (Headmaster, Moyles Court School) (WA), Moyles Court, Ringwood, BH24 3NF Tel: 01425 472 856

HEREFORD & WORCESTER

Britannia House, (The Alice Ottley School), The Tything, Worcester. Apply to the Headmistress.

Church House, (The Trustees), Market Square, Evesham

Grafton Manor, (J. W. Morris, Lord of Grafton), Bromsgrove Tel: 01527 31525

Newhouse Farm, (The Administrator) (WA), Goodrich, Ross-on-Wye

The Old Palace, (The Dean & Chapter of Worcester) (WA), Worcester.

Shelwick Court, (WA), Hereford * The Landmark Trust.

HERTFORDSHIRE

Heath Mount School, (The Abel Smith Trustees), Woodhall Park, Watton-at-Stone, Hertford, SG14 3NG Tel: 01920 830 286, Fax: 01920 830 162

Northaw Place, (The Administrator), Northaw Tel: 01707 44059

KENT

Barming Place, (Mr J. Peter & Dr Rosalind Bearcroft), Maidstone Tel: 01622 727 844

Bedgebury National Pinetum, (Forestry Enterprise), Nr. Goudhurst Tel: 01580 211 044, Fax: 01580 212 523

Foord Almshouses, (The Clerk to the Trustees) (WA), Rochester

Mersham-le-Hatch, (The Hon. M. J. Knatchbull), Nr. Ashford, TN25 5NH Tel: 01233 503 954, Fax: 01233 611 650. Apply to the tenant: The Directors, Caldecott Community.

Nurstead Court, (Mrs S. M. H. Edmeades-Stearns), Meopham Tel: 01474 812 121

Old College of All Saints, Kent Music Centre, Maidstone Tel: 01622 690 404
Apply to the Regional Director.

The Old Pharmacy, (Mrs Peggy Noreen Kerr), 6 Market Place, Faversham, ME13 7EH

Prospect Tower, (WA), Belmont Park, Faversham
* The Landmark Trust.

Yaldham Manor, (Mr & Mrs J. Mourier Lade) (WA), Kemsing, Sevenoaks, TN15 6NN Tel: 01732 761 029

LANCASHIRE

The Music Room, (WA), Lancaster
* The Landmark Trust.

Parrox Hall, (Mr & Mrs H. D. H. Elleston) (WA), Preesall, Nr. Poulton-le-Fylde, FY6 0NW Tel: 01253 810 245, Fax: 01253 811 223

LEICESTERSHIRE

Launde Abbey, (Rev. Graham Johnson), East Norton

The Moat House, (Mrs H. S. Hall), Appleby Magna Tel: 01530 270 301

Old Grammar School, Market Harborough
Tel: 01858 462 202

Staunton Harold Hall, (Ryder-Cheshire Foundation), Ashby-de-la-Zouch Tel: 01332 862 798

LINCOLNSHIRE

Bede House, Tattershall

The Chateau, (WA), Gate Burton, Gainsborough
* The Landmark Trust.

East Lighthouse, (Cdr. M. D. Joel R.N.) (WA), Sutton Bridge, Spalding, PE12 9YT

Fulbeck Manor, (J. F. Fane) (WA), Grantham, NG32 3JN Tel: 01400 272 231

Harlaxton Manor, (University of Evansville) (WA), Grantham. *Group Visits by appointment only*

House of Correction, (WA), Folkingham
* The Landmark Trust.

The Norman Manor House, (Lady Netherthorpe) (WA), Boothby Pagnell

Pelham Mausoleum, (The Earl of Yarborough), Limber, Grimsby

Scrivelsby Court, (Lt. Col. J. L. M. Dymoke M.B.E. DL.) (WA), Nr. Horncastle, LN9 6JA Tel: 01507 523 325

LONDON

All Hallows Vicarage, (Rev. R. Pearson), Tottenham, London, N17

69 Brick Lane, (The Administrator) (WA), London, E1

24 The Butts, 192, 194, 196, 198, 202, 204-224 Cable Street, (Mrs Sally Mills) (WA), London

11-13 Cavendish Street, (Heythrop College) (WA), London

Celia & Phillip Blairman Houses, (The Administrator) (WA), Elder Street, London, E1

Charlton House, (London Borough of Greenwich) (WA), Charlton Road, Charlton, London, SE7 8RE Tel: 020 7856 3951

Charterhouse, (The Governors of Sutton Hospital), Charterhouse Square, London, EC1

17-27 Folgate Street, (WA), London, E1

36 Hanbury Street, (WA), London, E1

Heathgate House, (Rev. Mother Prioress, Ursuline Convent), 66 Crooms Hill, Greenwich, London, SE10 8HG Tel: 020 858 0779

140, 142, 166 168 Homerton High Street, (WA), London, E5

House of St. Barnabas-in-Soho, (The Warden of the House) (WA), 1 Greek Street, Soho, London, W1V 6NQ Tel: 020 7437 1894

Kensal Green Cemetery, (General Cemetery Company), Harrow Road, London, W10 4RA Tel: 020 8969 0152, Fax: 020 860 9744

69-83 Paragon Road, (WA), London, E5

Red House, (Mr & Mrs Hollamby) (WA), Red House Lane, Bexleyheath

Sunbury Court, (The Salvation Army), Sudbury-on-Thames Tel: 01932 782 196

Vale Mascal Bath House, (Mrs F. Chu), 112 North Cray Road, Bexley, DA5 3NA Tel: 01322 554 894

Wesley's House, (The Trustees of the Methodist Church), 47 City Road, London, EC1Y 1AU Tel: 020 7253 2262, Fax: 020 7608 3825

MERSEYSIDE

The Turner Home, (R. A. Waring RGN., CGN), Dingle Head, Liverpool Tel: 0151 727 4177

NORFOLK

All Saints' Church, (Norfolk Churches Trust) , Barmer Keyholder – No 5, The Cottages.

All Saints' Church, (Norfolk Churches Trust) , Cockthorpe. Keyholder - Mrs Case at farmhouse.

All Saints' Church, (Norfolk Churches Trust) , Dunton Key of Tower at Hall Farm.

All Saints' Church, (Norfolk Churches Trust) , Frenze Keyholder - Mrs Alston at farmhouse.

All Saints' Church, (Norfolk Churches Trust) , Hargham Keyholder – Mrs Clifford, Amost, Station Road, Attleborough.

All Saints' Church, (Rector, Churchwardens and PCC) , Weston Longville, NR9 5JU Keyholder - Rev. J. P. P. Illingworth.

All Saints' Church, (Norfolk Churches Trust) , Snetterton Keyholder - at Hall Farm.

Billingford Mill, (Norfolk County Council), Scole

6 The Close, (The Dean & Chapter of Norwich Cathedral) (WA), Norwich

Fishermen's Hospital, (J. E. C. Lamb F.I.H., Clerk to the Trustees), Great Yarmouth Tel: 01493 856 609

Gowthorpe Manor, (Mrs Watkinson) (WA), Swardeston, NR14 8DS Tel: 01508 570 216

Hales Hall, (Mr & Mrs T. Read) (WA), London, NR14 6QW Tel: 0150 846 395

Hoveton House, (Sir John Blofeld), Wroxham, Norwich, NR12 8JE

Lattice House, (Mr & Mrs T. Duckett) (WA), King's Lynn Tel: 01553 777 292

Little Cressingham Mill, (Norfolk Mills & Pumps Trust), Little Cressingham, Thetford Tel: 01953 850 567

Little Hautbois Hall, (Mrs Duffield) (WA), Nr. Norwich, NR12 7JR Tel: 01603 279 333, Fax: 01603 279 615

The Music House, (The Warden), Wensum Lodge, King Street, Norwich Tel: 01603 666 021/666022, Fax: 01603 765 633

Norwich Cathedral Close, (WA), The Close, Norwich Apply to the Cathedral Steward's Office, Messrs. Percy Howes & Co, 3 The Close, Norwich.

The Old Princes Inn Restaurant, 20 Prince Street, Norwich Tel: 01603 621 043

The Old Vicarage, (Mr & Mrs H. C. Dance), Crown St. Methwold, Thetford, IP25 ANR

St. Andrew's Church, (Norfolk Churches Trust), Frenze Keyholder - Mrs Altston at farmhouse opposite.

St. Celia's Church, West Bilney Keyholder - Mr Curl, Tanglewood, Main Road, West Bilney.

St. Margaret's Church, (Norfolk Churches Trust), Morton-on-the-Hill, NR9 5JS Keyholder - Lady Prince-Smith at the Hall.

St. Mary's Church, (Norfolk Churches Trust), Dunton

St. Peter's Church, (Norfolk Churches Trust), The Lodge, Millgate, Aylsham, NR11 6HX Keyholder - Lord & Lady Romney at Wesnum Farm or Mrs Walker at Pocklethorpe Cottages.

Stracey Arms Mill, (Norfolk County Council), Nr. Acle Tel: 01603 611122 Ext 5224

The Strangers' Club, 22, 24 Elm Hill, Norwich Tel: 01603 623 813

Thoresby College, (King's Lynn Preservation Trust) (WA), Queen Street, King's Lynn, PE30 1HX

Wiveton Hall, (D. MacCarthy) (WA), Holt

NORTHAMPTONSHIRE

Courteenhall, (Sir Hereward Wake Bt. MC) (WA), Northampton

Drayton House, (L. G. Stopford Sackville) (WA), Lowick, Kettering, NN14 3BG Tel: 01832 732 405

The Monastery, (Mr & Mrs R. G. Wigley) (WA), Shutlanger, NN12 7RU Tel: 01604 862 529

Paine's Cottage, (R. O. Barber) (WA), Oundle

Weston Hall, (Mr & Mrs Francis Sitwell) (WA), Towcester

NORTHUMBERLAND

Brinkburn Mill, (WA), Rothbury * The Landmark Trust.

Capheaton Hall, (J. Browne-Swinburne) (WA), Newcastle-upon-Tyne, NE19 2AB

Causeway House, (WA), Bardon Mill

Craster Tower, (Col. J. M. Craster, Miss M. D. Craster & F. Sharratt) (WA), Alnwick

Netherwitton Hall, (J. C. R. Trevelyon) (WA), Morpeth, NE61 4NW Tel: 01670 772 219 Fax: 01670 772 332

NOTTINGHAMSHIRE

Winkburn Hall, (R. Craven-Smith-Milnes), Newark, NG22 8PQ Tel: 01636 636 465, Fax: 01636 636 717

Worksop Priory Church & Gatehouse, The Vicarage, Cheapside Tel: 01909 472 180

OXFORDSHIRE

26-27 Cornmarket Street & 26 Ship Street, (Home Bursar), Jesus College, Oxford Shop basement by written appointment to: Laura Ashley Ltd, 150 Bath Road, Maidenhead, Berks, SL6 4YS.

Hope House, (Mrs J. Hageman), Woodstock

The Manor, (Mr & Mrs Paul L. Jacques) (WA), Chalgrove, OX44 7SL Tel: 01865 890 836, Fax: 01865 891 810

Monarch's Court House, (R. S. Hine) (WA)Benson

Ripon College, (The Principal) (WA), Cuddesdon

30-43 The Causeway, (Mr & Mrs R. Hornsby), 39-43 The Causeway, Steventon

SHROPSHIRE

Bromfield Priory Gatehouse, (WA), Ludlow Tel: 01628 825 925* The Landmark Trust.

Halston, (Mrs J. L. Harvey) (WA), Oswestry

Hatton Grange, (Mrs P. Afia) (WA), Shifnal

Langley Gatehouse, (WA), Acton Burnell Tel: 01628 825 925 * The Landmark Trust, Shottesbrooke, nr. Maidenhead, Berks, SL6 3SW.

Oakley Manor, (Shrewsbury & Atcham Borough Council), Belle Vue Road, Shrewsbury, SY3 7NW Tel: 01243 231 456, Fax: 01243 271 598

St. Winifred's Well, (WA), Woolston, Oswestry * The Landmark Trust, Shottesbrooke, nr. Maidenhead, Berks, SL6 3SW.

Stanwardine Hall, (P. J. Bridge), Cockshutt, Ellesmere Tel: 01939 270 212

SOMERSET

Cothelstone Manor & Gatehouse, (Mrs J. E. B. Warmington) (WA), Cothelstone, Nr. Taunton, TA4 3DS Tel: 01823 432 200

Fairfield, (Lady Gass), Stogursey, Bridgwater, TA5 1PU Tel: 01278 732 251 Fax: 01278 732277

Gurney Manor, (WA), Cannington Tel: 01628 825 925 * The Landmark Trust, Shottesbrooke, nr. Maidenhead, Berks, SL6 3SW.

The Old Drug Store, (Mr & Mrs E. D. J. Schofield) (WA), Axbridge

The Old Hall, (WA), Croscombe * The Landmark Trust, Shottesbrooke, nr. Maidenhead, Berks, SL6 3SW.

The Priest's Hole, (WA), Holcombe Rogus, Nr. Wellington * The Landmark Trust, Shottesbrooke, nr. Maidenhead, Berks, SL6 3SW.

Stogursey Castle, (WA), Nr. Bridgwater * The Landmark Trust, Shottesbrooke, nr. Maidenhead, Berks, SL6 3SW.

West Coker Manor, (Mr & Mrs Derek Maclaren), West Coker, BA22 9BJ Tel: 01935 862 646

Whitelackington Manor, (E. J. H. Cameron), Dillington Estate Office, Illminster, TA19 9EQ Tel: 01460 54614

Properties by Appointment Only

STAFFORDSHIRE

Broughton Hall, (The Administrator) (WA), Eccleshall

Dunwood Hall, (Dr R. Vincent-Kemp FRSA), Longsdon, Nr. Leek, ST9 9AR Tel: 01538 385 071

The Great Hall in Keele Hall, (The Registrar, University of Keele) (WA), Keele

Ingestre Pavilion, (WA), Nr. Stafford
* The Landmark Trust, Shottesbrooke, nr. Maidenhead, Berks, SL6 3SW.

Old Hall Gatehouse, (R. M. Eades), Mavesyn Ridware Tel: 01543 490 312

The Orangery, (Mrs M Philips), Heath House, Tean, Stoke-on-Trent, ST10 4HA Tel: 01538 722 212

Park Hall, (E. J. Knobbs) (WA), Leigh

Tixall Gatehouse, (WA), Tixall, Nr. Stafford
* The Landmark Trust, Shottesbrooke, Nr. Maidenhead, Berks, SL6 3SW.

SUFFOLK

The Deanery, (The Dean of Bocking), Hadleigh, IP7 5DT Tel: 01473 822 218

Ditchingham Hall, (The Rt. Hon. Earl Ferrers), Ditchingam, Bungay

The Hall, (Mr & Mrs R. B. Cooper) (WA), Great Bricett, Ipswich

Hengrave Hall Centre, (The Warden), Bury St. Edmunds, IP28 6LZ Tel: 01284 701 561

Martello Tower, (WA), Aldeburgh
* The Landmark Trust.

Moat Hall, (J. W. Gray), Woodbridge, IP13 9AE
Tel: 01728 746 317

The New Inn, (WA), Peasenhall
* The Landmark Trust.

Newbourne Hall, (John Somerville) (WA), Woodbridge
* Shrubland Park Gardens (Lady de Saumarez)
(20th Dec to 3rd Jan) Tel: 01473 830221

Worlingham Hall, (Viscount Colville of Culross) (WA), Beccles

SURREY

Crossways Farm, (Tenant: C. T. Hughes) (WA), Abinger Hammer

Great Fosters Hotel, (Manager: J. E. Baumann), Egham, TW20 9UR Tel: 01784 433 822

St. Mary's Home Chapel, Church Lane, Godstone Tel: 01883 742 385

SUSSEX

Ashdown House, (The Headmaster), Ashdown House School, Forest Row, RH18 5JY Tel: 01342 822 574, Fax: 01342 824 380

Chantry Green House, (Mr & Mrs G. H. Recknell), Steyning Tel: 01903 812 239

The Chapel, Bishop's Palace, (Church Commissioners), The Palace, Chichester

Christ's Hospital, (WA), Horsham Tel: 01403 211 293

Laughton Tower, (WA), Lewes * The Landmark Trust.

WARWICKSHIRE

Bath House, (WA), Walton, Stratford-upon-Avon
* The Landmark Trust, Shottesbrooke, nr. Maidenhead, Berks, SL6 3SW.

Binswood Hall, (North Leamington School) (WA), Binswood Avenue, Leamington Spa, CV32 5SF Tel: 01926 423 686

Foxcote, (C. B. Holman) (WA), Shipton-on-Stour

Nicholas Chamberlain's Almshouses, (The Warden), Bedworth Tel: 01203 312 225

Northgate, (R. E. Phllips) (WA), Warwick, CV34 4JL

St. Leonard's Church, (WA), Wroxall
Apply to Mrs J. M. Gowen, Headmistress, Wroxall Abbey School, Warwick, CV35 7NB.

War Memorial Town Hall, (The Secretary, D. R. Young), 27 Henley Street, Alcester, B49 5QX Tel: 01789 765 198

WILTSHIRE

Bradley House, Maiden Bradley, Warminster Tel: 01803 866633 (The Estate Office)

Chinese Summerhouse, Amesbury Abbey, Amesbury Tel: 01980 622 957

Farley Hospital, (The Warden), Church Road, Farley, SP5 1AH Tel: 01722 712 231

Milton Manor, (Mrs Rupert Gentle), The Manor House, Milton Lilbourne, Pewsey, SN9 5LQ Tel: 01672 563 344, Fax: 01672 564 136

Old Bishop's Palace, (The Bursar, Salisbury Cathedral School), 1 The Close, Salisbury Tel: 01722 322 652

The Old Manor House, (J. Teed) (WA), 2 Whitehead Lane, Bradford-upon-Avon

Orpins House, (J. Vernon Burchell) (WA), Church Street, Bradford-upon-Avon

The Porch House, (Tim Vidal-Hall) (WA), 6 High Street, Potterne, Devizes, SN10 5NA

YORKSHIRE

Beamsley Hospital, (WA), Skipton
* The Landmark Trust.

Busby Hall, (G. A. Marwood) (WA), Carlton-in-Cleveland

Calverley Old Hall, (WA), Nr. Leeds
* The Landmark Trust.

Cawood Castle, (WA), Nr. Selby
* The Landmark Trust.

Chapel & Coach House, Aske, Richmond

The Church of Our Lady & St. Everilda, (WA), Everingham Tel: 01430 860 531

The Culloden Tower, (WA), Richmond
* The Landmark Trust.

The Dovecote, (Mrs P. E. Heathcote), Forcett Hall, Forcett, Richmond Tel: 01325 718 226

Home Farm House, (G. T. Reece) (WA), Old Scriven, Knaresborough

Moulton Hall, (The National Trust. Tenant: The Hon. J. D. Eccles) (WA), Richmond

The Old Rectory, (Mrs R. F. Wormald) (WA), Foston, York

The Pigsty, (WA), Robin Hood's Bay
* The Landmark Trust.

Fulneck Boys' School, (I. D. Cleland, BA, M. Phil, Headmaster) (WA), Pudsey

Grand Theatre & Opera House, (General Manager: Warren Smith), 46 New Briggate, Leeds, LS1 6NZ Tel: 0113 245 6014, Fax: 0113 246 5906

Horbury Hall, (D. J. H. Michelmore), Horbury, Wakefield Tel: 01924 277 552

Town Hall, (Leeds City Council), Leeds Tel: 0113 247 7989

Weston Hall, (Lt. Col. H. V. Dawson) (WA), Nr. Otley, LS21 2HP

WALES

CLWYD

Fferm, (Dr M. C. Jones-Mortimer), Pontblyddyn, Mold, CH7 4HN Tel: 01352 770 876

Golden Grove, (N. R. & M. M. J. Steele-Mortimer) (WA), Llanasa, Nr. Holywell, CH8 9NE Tel: 01745 854 452, Fax: 01745 854 547

Halghton Hall, (J. D. Lewis) (WA), Bangor-on-Dee, Wrexham

Lindisfarne College, (The Headmaster) (WA), Wynnstay Hall, Ruabon Tel: 01978 810 407

Pen Isa'r Glascoed, (M. E. Harrop), Bodelwyddan, LL22 9D745 583 501D Tel: 01 45 583501

DYFED

Monkton Old Hall, (WA), Pembroke
* The Landmark Trust.

Taliaris Park, (J. H. Spencer-Williams) (WA), Llandeilo

University of Wales Lampeter, (Prof. Keith Robbins), Lampeter, SA48 7ED Tel: 01570 422 351, Fax: 01570 423 423

West Blockhouse, (WA), Haverfordwest, Dale
* The Landmark Trust.

SOUTH GLAMORGAN

Fonmon Castle, (Sir Brooke Boothby, Bt.), Barry, CF6 9ZN Tel: 01446 710 206, Fax: 01446 711 687

GWENT

Blackbrook Manor, (Mr & Mrs A. C. de Morgan), Skenfrith, Nr. Abergavenny, NP7 8UB Tel: 01600 84453, Fax: 01600 84453

Castle Hill House, (T. Baxter-Wright) (WA), Monmouth

Clytha Castle, (WA), Abergavenny
* The Landmark Trust.

Great Cil-Lwch, (J. F. Ingledew) (WA), Llantilio Crossenny, Abergavenny, NP7 8SR Tel: 01600 780 206

Kemys House, (I. S. Burge) (WA), Keyms Inferior, Caerleon

Llanvihangel Court, (Mrs D. Johnson) (WA), Abergavenny, NP7 8DH

Overmonnow House, (J. R. Pangbourne) (WA), Monmouth

3-4 Priory Street, (H. R. Ludwig), Monmouth

Treowen, (John Wheelock), Wonastow, Monmouth, NP5 4DL Tel: 01600 712 031

GWYNEDD

Cymryd, (Miss D. E. Glynne) (WA), Cymryd, Conwy, LL32 8UA

Dolaugwyn, (Mrs S. Tudor) (WA), Towyn

Nannau, (P. Vernon) (WA), Dolgellau

Penmynydd, (The Rector of Llanfairpwll) (WA), Alms House, Llnafairpwll

Plas Coch, (Mrs N. Donald), Llanedwen, Llanfairpwll Tel: 01248 714272

POWYS

Abercamlais, (Mrs J. C. R. Ballance) (WA), Brecon

Abercynrig, (Mrs W. R. Lloyd) (WA), Brecon

1 Buckingham Place, (Mrs Meeres) (WA), 1 Buckingham Place, Brecon, LD3 7DL Tel: 01874 623 612

3 Buckingham Place, (Mr & Mrs A. Whiley) (WA), 3 Buckingham Place, Brecon, LD3 7DL

Maesmawr Hall Hotel, (Mrs M. Pemberton & Mrs I. Hunt), Caersws Tel: 01686 688 255

Newton Farm, (Mrs Ballance. Tenant: D. L. Evans), Brecon

Pen Y Lan, (J. G. Meade), Meifod, Powys, SY22 6DA Tel: 01938 500 202

Plasdau Duon, (E. S. Breese), Clatter

Poultry House, (WA), Leighton, Welshpool
* The Landmark Trust..

Rhydycarw, (M. Breese-Davies), Trefeglwys, Newton, SY17 5PU Tel: 01686 430 411, Fax: 01686 430 331

Ydderw, (D. P. Eckley) (WA), Llyswen

SCOTLAND

BORDERS

Old Gala House, (Ettrick & Lauderdale District Council), Galashiels Tel: 01750 20096

Sir Walter Scott's Courtroom, (Ettrick & Lauderdale District Council)), Selkirk Tel: 01750 20096

Wedderlie House, (Mrs J. R. L. Campbell) (WA), Gordon, TD3 6NW Tel: 0157 874 0223

DUMFRIES & GALLOWAY

Bonshaw Tower, (Dr J. B. Irving) (WA), Kirtlebridge, Lockerbie, DG11 3LY Tel: 01461 500 256

Carnsalloch House, (The Leonard Cheshire Foundation), Carnsalloch, Kirkton, DG1 1SN Tel: 01387 254 924, Fax: 01387 257 971

Kirkconnell House, (F. Maxwell Witham), New Abbey, Dumfries Tel: 0138 785 276

FIFE

Bath Castle, (Angus Mitchell), Bogside, Oakley, FK10 3RD Tel: 0131 556 7671

The Castle, (J. Bevan) (WA), Elie

Castle of Park, (WA), Glenluce, Galloway
* The Landmark Trust.

Charleton House, (Baron St. Clair Bonde), Colinsburgh Tel: 0133 334

GRAMPIAN

Balbithan House, (J. McMurtie), Kintore Tel: 01467 32282

Balfluig Castle, (Mark Tennant) (WA), Grampian Apply to 30 Abbey Gardens, London, NW8 9AT

Barra Castle, (Dr & Mrs Andrew Bogdan) (WA), Old Meldrum

Castle of Fiddes, (Dr M. Weir), Stonehaven Tel: 01569 740 213

Church of the Holy Rude, St. John Street, Stirling

Corsindae House, (R. Fyffe) (WA), Sauchen by Inverurie, Inverurie, AB51 7PP Tel: 01330 833 295, Fax: 01330 833 629

Drumminor Castle, (A. D. Forbes) (WA), Rhynie

Erskine Marykirk - Stirling Youth Hostel, St. John Street, Stirling

Gargunnock House, (Gargunnock Estate Trust) (WA), Stirling

Gordonstoun School, (The Headmaster) (WA), Elgin Moray

Grandhome House, (D. R. Patton), Aberdeen Tel: 01224 722 202

Guildhall, (Stirling District Council), Municipal Buildings, Stirling Tel: 01786 79000

Old Tolbooth Building, (Stirling District Council), Municipal Buildings, Stirling Tel: 01786 79000

Phesdo House, (J. M. Thomson) (WA), Laurencekirk

The Pineapple, (WA), Dunmore, Airth, Stirling
* The Landmark Trust.

Tolbooth, (Stirling District Council), Broad Street, Stirling Tel: 01786 79400

Touch House, (P. B. Buchanan) (WA), Stirling, FK8 3AQ Tel: 01786 464 278

HIGHLANDS

Embo House, (John G. Mackintosh), Dornoch Tel: Dornoch 810 260

LOTHIAN

Cakemuir, (M. M. Scott) (WA), Parthhead, Tynehead, EH3 5XR

Castle Gogar, (Lady Steel-Maitland), Edinburgh Tel: 0131 339 1234

Ford House, (F. P. Tindall ,OBE) (WA), Ford

Forth Road Bridge, (The Bridgemaster), South Queensferry Tel: 0131 319 1699

Linnhouse, (H. J. Spur(wa)y) (WA), Linnhouse, Livingstone, EH54 9AN Tel: 01506 410 742, Fax: 01506 416 591

Newbattle Abbey College, (The Principal), Dalkeith,

EH22 3LL Tel: 0131 663 1921, Fax: 0131 654 0598

Penicuik House, (Sir John Clerk, Bt.), Penicuik

Roseburn House, (M. E. Sturgeon) (WA), Murrayfield

Townhouse, (East Lothian District Council), Haddington Tel: Haddington 4161

SHETLAND ISLES

The Lodberrie, (Thomas Moncrieff), Lerwick

STRATHCLYDE

Ascog House, (WA), Rothsa* The Landmark Trust.

Barcaldine Castle, (Roderick Campbell) (WA), Benderloch

Craufurdland Castle, (J. P. Houison Craufurdland), Kilmarnock, KA3 6BS Tel: 01560 600 402

Dunstrune Castle, (Robin Malcolm of Poltallock) (WA), Lochgilphead

Kelburn Castle, (The Earl of Glasgow) (WA), Fairlie, Ayrshire, KA29 0BE Tel: Country Centre: 01475 568 685 Kelburn Castle: 01475 568 204, Fax: Country Centre: 01475 568 121 Kelburn Castle: 01475 568 328

New Lanark, (New Lanark Conservation Trust), New Lanark Mills, Lanark, ML11 9DB Tel: 01555 661 345, Fax: 01555 665 738

The Place of Paisley, (Paisley Abbey Kirk Session), Paisley Abbey, Abbey Close, Paisley, PA1 1JG Tel: 0141 889 7654

Saddell Castle, (WA), Campbeltown, Argyll
* The Landmark Trust.

Tangy Mill, (WA), Campbeltown, Kintyre, Argyll
* The Landmark Trust.

Tannahill Cottage, (Secretary, Paisley Burns Club), Queen Street, Paisley Tel: 0141 887 7500

TAYSIDE

Ardblair Castle, (Laurence P. K. Blair Oliphant), Blairgowrie, PH10 6SA Tel: 01250 873 155

Craig House, (Charles F. R. Hoste), Montrose Tel: 01674 722 239

Kinross House, (Sir David Montgomery, Bt.) (WA), Kinross

Michael Bruce Cottage, (Michael Bruce Trust), Kinnesswood

The Pavilion, Gleneagles, (J. Martin Haldane of Gleneagles) (WA), Gleneagles, Auchterarder, PH3 1PJ

Tulliebole Castle, (The Lord Moncrieff), Crook of Devon

US · Peru · London · Holland · Singapore · Beijing · Hong Kong

A warranty is only as strong as the company behind it.

TELEDEX

The First Name in Guestroom Telecommunications.

www.teledex.com

IN OUR CASE, IT'S STRONG ENOUGH TO LAST A LIFETIME.

Teledex is the only proven worldwide market leader with over 4 million guestroom phones installed, in over 110 countries. With the most comprehensive and reliable family of products, coupled with sales and product support on six continents, Teledex is pleased to introduce another truly unbeatable world standard...

A Lifetime Warranty.

For details on this "Lifetime" offer, call Teledex at 1.800.783.8353, or 408.363.3100 today!

Garden Specialists

If you have been inspired by some of the wonderful gardens contained in this guide, why not recreate some of their beauty in your own garden? Whether you seek to create the traditional elegance of the English Rose Garden, the mass of glorious colour associated with Herbaceous Borders or perhaps are looking for particular varieties, the following specialists offer a range of plants and decorative garden ornaments to enhance gardens everywhere.

ARCHITECTURAL PLANTS

Cooks Farm, Nuthurst, Nr Horsham, West Sussex RH13 6LH
Tel: 01403 891772 Fax: 01403 891056 (Angus White)

Specialising in unusual and hardy exotics from around the world, Architectural Plants is a unique nursery that grows and provides spectacular plants for adventurous gardeners. Set up by owner Angus White in the spring of 1990, the nursery has a well deserved reputation for supplying excellent quality plants, backed up by sound practical help and advice. The range of plants offered concentrate first and foremost on strong shapes, bold outlines and are mostly evergreen. Included amongst the rare and not so rare you will find bananas, bamboos, red-barked strawberry trees, giant Japanese pom-poms, green olive trees, topiary, spiky plants, Chinese cloud trees, hardy jungle plants and Lord knows what else.... **Open:** Horsham Nursery open Monday to Saturday 9am to 5pm; Chichester Nursery open from Sunday to Friday 10am to 4pm. Phone for free catalogue. **Internet**: www.architecturalplants.com

map 4
E5/6

DEACONS NURSERY (H.H)

Moor View, Godshill, PO38 3HW, Isle of Wight
Tel: 01983 840 750 or 01983 522 243 Fax: 01983 523 575 (G. D. Deacon & B. H. Deacon)

Specialist national fruit tree growers. Trees and bushes sent anywhere so send NOW for a FREE catalogue. Over 300 varieties of apples on various types of root stocks from M27 (4ft), M26 (8ft) to M25 (18ft). Plus Pears, Peaches, Nectarines, Plums, Gages, Cherries, Soft Fruits and an unusual selection of Family Trees. Many special offers. Catalogue always available (stamp appreciated). Many varieties of grapes; dessert and wine, plus Hybrid Hops and nuts of all types. **Location:** The picturesque village of Godshill. Deacons Nursery is in Moor View off School Crescent (behind the only school). **Open:** Winter – Mon–Fri, 8–4pm & Sat, 8–1pm. Summer – Mon–Fri, 8–5pm.

map 4
C7

FAMILY TREES

Sandy Lane, Shedfield, Hampshire, SO32 2HQ
Tel: 01329 834 812
(Philip House)

Wide variety of fruit for the connoisseur. Trained tree specialists; standards, espaliers, cordons etc. Other trees, old-fashioned and climbing roses, and evergreens. Free catalogue from Family Trees (as above). **Location:** See map in free catalogue. **Station(s):** Botley (2.5 miles). **Open:** Mid Oct–end Apr, Wed & Sat, 9.30am–12.30. **Admission:** No charge. No minimum order. Courier dispatch for next day delivery.

map 4
C6

HADDONSTONE SHOW GARDEN

The Forge House, Church Lane, East Haddon, Northampton, NN6 8DB
Tel: 01604 770711 Fax: 01604 770027 (Haddonstone Limited)

See Haddonstone's classic garden ornaments in the beautiful setting of the walled manor gardens – including urns, troughs, fountains, statuary, bird baths, sundials, obelisks, columns and balustrading. Featured on BBC Gardeners' World, the garden is on different levels with shrub roses, ground cover plants, conifers, clematis and climbers. In 1998 the new Jubilee Garden opened, complete with temple, pavilion and Gothic Grotto. **Location:** 7 miles NW of Northampton off A428. **Open:** Mon–Fri 9–5.30pm closed weekends, Bank Hols and Christmas period. **Admission:** Free. Groups must apply in writing for permission to visit.

map 4
D1

LANGLEY BOXWOOD NURSERY

Rake, Nr Liss, Hampshire GU33 7JL
Tel: 01730 894467 Fax: 01730 894703 (Elizabeth Braimbridge)

This small nursery, in a beautiful setting, specialises in box-growing, offering a chance to see together a unique range of old and new varieties, hedging, topiary, specimens and rarities. Some taxus also. **National Collection – Buxus.** Descriptive list available (4 x 1st class stamps). **Location:** Off B2070 (old A3) 3 miles south of Liphook. Ring for directions. **Open:** Mon–Fri 9–4.30pm, Sat 10-4. **E-mail:** langbox@msn.com **Internet:** www.boxwood.co.uk

map 4
D6

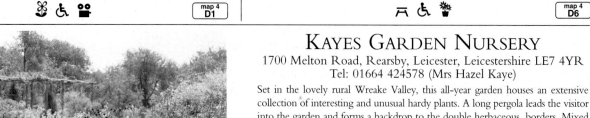

KAYES GARDEN NURSERY

1700 Melton Road, Rearsby, Leicester, Leicestershire LE7 4YR
Tel: 01664 424578 (Mrs Hazel Kaye)

Set in the lovely rural Wreake Valley, this all-year garden houses an extensive collection of interesting and unusual hardy plants. A long pergola leads the visitor into the garden and forms a backdrop to the double herbaceous borders. Mixed beds beyond are filled with a wide range of herbaceous plants, shrubs and shrub roses in subtle colour coordinated groups. A stream dissects the garden and ends in a large wild life pond alive with a myriad of dragonflies. Aromatic herbs surround a much favoured seat which looks out across one of the garden ponds towards flower beds shaded by old fruit trees, where hellebores, ferns and many other shade loving plants abound. **Open:** Mar–Oct incl. Tues–Sat 10–5pm Sun 10am–noon. Nov–Feb incl. Fri & Sat 10–4.30. Closed Dec 25–Jan 31 incl. **Admission:** Entrance to garden £2. Coach parties welcome by appointment.

map 8
D6

Hever Castle, Kent

Hatfield House, Hertfordshire

Plants for Sale

ENGLAND

BEDFORDSHIRE

Woburn Abbey, Woburn, MK43 OTP. Tel: 01525 290666
Fax: 01525 290271

BERKSHIRE

Dorney Court, Windsor SL4 6QP. Tel: 01628 604638
Fax: 01628 665772

The Savill Garden, Windsor Great Park. Tel: 01753 847518

BUCKINGHAMSHIRE

Waddesdon Manor, The Dairy, Nr Aylesbury, HP18 OJW.
Tel: 01296 651211 Fax: 01296 651142

CAMBRIDGESHIRE

The Manor Hemingford Grey PE18 9BN. Tel: 01480 463134
Fax: 01480 465026

CHESHIRE

Arley Hall, nr Great Budworth, Northwich, CW9 6NA.
Tel: 01565 777353

Cholmondeley Castle Gardens, Malpas SY14 8AH.
Tel: 01829 720383 & Fax

Dunham Massey Hall, Altrincham WA14 4SJ. Tel: 0161
9411025 Fax: 0161 929 7508

Little Moreton Hall, Congleton CW12 4SD. Tel: 01260
272018

Ness Botanic Gardens, Ness, Nesston L64 4AY. Tel: 0151
3530123 Fax: 0151 353 1004

Norton Priory Museum, Tudor Road, Manor Park, Runcorn,
WA7 1SX. Tel: 01928 569895

Rode Hall, Church Lane, Scholar Green, ST7 3QP.
Tel: 01270 873237 Fax: 01270 882962

Tatton Park, Knutsford, Cheshire WA16 6QN. Tel: 01625
534400

CORNWALL

Bosvigo House, Bosvigo Lane, Truro, TR1 3NH.
Tel: 01872 275774 Fax: 01872 275774

Burncoose Nurseries and Garden, Gwennap, Redruth, TR16
6BJ. Tel: 01209 861112

Caerhays Castle And Gardens, Gorran, St Austell PL26 6LY.
Tel 01872 501310 Fax: 01872 501870

Lanhydrock House, Bodmin, PL30 5AD. Tel: 01208 73320
Fax: 01208 74084

St. Michael's Mount, The Manor Office, Marazion, nr
Penzance, TR17 OEF. Tel: 01736 710507/710265

Pencarrow, Washway, Bodmin, PL30 5AG. Tel: 01208
841369

Trelowarren House & Chapel, Mawgan-in-Meneage,
Helston, TR12 6AD. Tel: 01326 221366

Trevarno Estate & Gardens, Trevarno Manor, Helston,
TR13 ORU. Tel: 01326 574274 Fax 01326 574282

COUNTY DURHAM

Raby Castle, Staindrop, Darlington,, DL2 3AH. Tel: 01833
660202 Fax: 01833 660169

CUMBRIA

Acorn Bank Garden, Temple Sowerby, Penrith, CA10 1SP.
Tel: 017683 61893

Dalemain, nr Penrith, CA11 OHB. Tel: 017684 86450
Fax: 017684 86223

Holker Hall and Gardens, Cark-in-Cartmel, nr Grange-over-
Sands, LA11 7PL. Tel: 015395 58328 Fax: 015395 58776

Levens Hall, Kendal, LA8 OPB. Tel: 015395 60321
Fax: 015395 60669

Muncaster Castle, Ravenglass, CA18 1RQ. Tel: 01229
717614 Fax: 01229 717010

DERBYSHIRE

Chatsworth, Bakewell, DE45 1PP. Tel: 01246 582204
Fax: 01246 583536

Lea Gardens, Lea, Matlock, DE4 5GH. Tel: 01629 534 380
Fax: 01629 534 260

Renishaw Hall, Nr Sheffield, S31 9WB. Tel: 01246 432310

DEVON

Bickleigh Castle, Bickleigh, Tiverton, EX16 8RP.
Tel: 01884 855363

Cadhay, Ottery St Mary, EX11 1QT. Tel: 01404 812432

Hartland Abbey, Hartland, Nr Bideford, EX39 6DT.
Tel: 01237 441 264/234 Fax: 01884 861134

Killerton House, Broadclyst, nr Exeter, EX5 3LE.
Tel: 01392 881345 Fax: 01392 883112

DORSET

Athelhampton House & Gardens, Athelhampton,
Dorchester,
DT2 7LG. Tel: 01305 848363 Fax: 01305 848135

Chiffchaffs, Chiffeymoor, Bourton, Gillingham, SP8 5BY.
Tel: 01747 840841

Compton Acres Gardens, Canford Cliffs, Poole BH13 7ES.
Tel: 01202 700778 Fax: 01202 707537

Cranborne Manor Gardens, Cranborne, BH21 5PP.
Tel: 01725 517248 Fax: 01725 517862

Deans Court Garden, Deans Court, Wimborne, BH21 1EE.

Forde Abbey and Gardens, nr Chard, TA20 4LU.
Tel: 01460 220231 Fax: 01460 220296

Kingston Maurawd, Dorchester DT2 8PY Tel: 01305 215003

Mapperton, Beaminster, DT8 3NR. Tel: 01308 862645

GLOUCESTERSHIRE

Barnsley House Garden, Nr Cirencester GL7 5EE.
Tel: 01285 740561 Fax: 01285 740628

Batsford Arboretum, Batsford Estate Office, Moreton-in-
Marsh, GL56 9QF. Tel: 01608 650722 Fax: 01608 650290

Berkeley Castle, Berkeley, GL13 9BQ. Tel: 01453 810332

Hodges Barn Gardens, Shipton Moyne, Tetbury, GL8 8PR.
Tel: 01666 880202 Fax: 01666 880373

Kiftsgate Court, Mickleton, nr Chipping Campden, GL55
6LW. Tel: 01386 438777 Fax: 01386 438777

Lydney Park Gardens, Estate Office, Lydney GL15 6BU.
Tel: 01594 842844 Fax: 01594 842027

Painswick Rococo Garden, The Stables, Painswick House,
Painswick, GL6 6TH. Tel: 01452 813204 Fax: 01452 813204

Sudeley Castle, Winchcombe, GL54 5JD. Tel: 01242 602308

HAMPSHIRE

Broadlands, Romsey, SO51 9ZD. Tel: 01794 505010
Fax: 01794 505040

Gilbert White's House & Garden and the Oates , The
Wakes, Selborne, GU34 3JH. Tel: 01420 511275

Highclere Castle, Newbury, RG20 9RN. Tel: 01635 253210
Fax: 01635 255315

Houghton Lodge Gardens, Stockbridge, SO20 6LQ.
Tel: 01264 810177 Fax: 01794 388072

Langley Boxwood, Rake, Nr Liss, Hampshire GU33 7JL.
Tel: 01730 894467 Fax: 01730 894703

Mottisfont Abbey Garden, Mottisfont, Nr Romsey, SO51 OLP.
Tel: 01794 340757 Fax: 01794 341492

Sir Harold Hillier Gardens and Arboretum, Ampfield, nr
Romsey SO51 0QA. Tel: 01794 368787

Stratfield Saye House, Reading, RG7 2BT. Tel: 01256 882882

HEREFORD & WORCESTER

Dinmore Manor, nr Hereford, HR4 8EE. Tel: 01432 830332

Eastnor Castle, nr Ledbury, Hereford HR8 1RL. Tel: 01531
633160 Fax: 01531 631776

Harvington Hall, Harvington, Kidderminister, DY10 4LR.
Tel: 01562 777846 Fax: 01562 777190

Hergest Croft Gardens, Kington, HR5 3EG. Tel: 01544
230160 Fax: 01544 230160

How Caple Court Gardens, How Caple, HR1 4SX.
Tel: 01989 740612 Fax: 01989 740611

Perhill Nurseries, Worcester Road, Great Witley, WR6 6JT.
Tel: 01299 896329 Fax: 01299 896 990

HERTFORDSHIRE

Aylett Nurseries Ltd, North Orbital Road, St. Albans.
Tel: 01727 822255 Fax: 01727 823024

Knebworth House, Knebworth. Tel: 01438 812661

The Gardens of the Rose, Chiswell Green, St. Albans, AL2
3NR. Tel: 01727 850461 Fax: 01727 850360

Hatfield House, Hatfield, AL9 5NQ. Tel: 01707 262823
Fax: 01707 275719

ISLE OF WIGHT

Deacons Nursery H.H. Moor View, Godshill, PO38 3HW.
Tel: 01983 840750 Fax: 01983 523575

KENT

Belmont, Throwley, nr Faversham, ME13 OHH. Tel: 01795
890202 Fax: 01795 890042

Doddington Place Gardens, Sittingbourne, ME9 OBB.
Tel/Fax: 01795 886101

Finchcocks, Goudhurst, TN17 1HH. Tel: 01580 211702
Fax: 01580 211007

Great Comp Garden, Borough Green, TN15 8QS.
Tel: 01732 886154/882 669

Great Maytham Hall, Rolvendon, Cranbrook, TN17 4NE.
Tel: 01580 241346 Fax: 01580 241038

Goodnestone Park, Canterbury CT3 IPL Tel:01304 840107

Groombridge Place Gardens, Groombridge, TN3 9QG.
Tel: 01892 863999 Fax: 01892 863996

Hall Place, Bourne Road, Bexley DA5 1PQ. Tel: 01322
526574 Fax: 01322 522 921

Hever Castle & Gardens, Hever, nr Edenbridge TN8 7NG.
Tel: 01732 865224 Fax: 01732 866796

Ladham House, Ladham Road, Goudhurst. Tel: 01580 211203
Fax: 01580 212596

Leeds Castle, Maidstone ME17 1PL. Tel: 01622 765400
Fax: 01622 735616

Lullingstone Castle, Eynsford, DA14 0JA. Tel: 01322 862114
Fax: 01322 862115

Owl House Gardens, Lamberhurst Tel:01892 890230

Penshurst Place, Penshurst, Tunbridge Wells, TN11 8DG.
Tel: 01892 870307 Fax: 01892 870866

Riverhill House Gardens, Riverhill, Sevenoaks Tel:01732
458802

LANCASHIRE

Rufford Old Hall, Rufford, Ormskirk Tel:01704 821254

Towneley Hall Art Gallery, Burnley, BB11 3RQ.
Tel: 01282 424213 Fax: 01282 436138

LEICESTERSHIRE

Kayes Garden Nursery, 1700 Melton Rd, Rearsby, Leicester,
LE7 4YR. Tel: 01664 424578

LINCOLNSHIRE

Elsham Hall, Brigg DN20 0QZ Tel:01652 688698

Marston Hall, Grantham. Tel: 01400 250225

LONDON

Chelsea Physic Garden, 66 Royal Hospital Road, Chelsea,
SW3 4HS. Tel: 020 7352 5646 Fax: 020 7376 3910

Museum of Garden History, Lambeth Palace Road, SE1 7LB.
Tel: 020 7401 8865 Fax: 020 7401 8869

Syon Park, Brentford, TW8 JF. Tel: 020 8560 0881
Fax: 020 8568 0936

Plants for Sale

NORFOLK

The Fairhaven Garden, 2 The Woodlands, Wymers Lane, South Walsam, Norwich, NR13 6EA. Tel: 01603 270449

Holkham Hall, Holkham Estate Office, Wells-next-the-Sea, NR23 1AB. Tel: 01328 710227 Fax: 01328 711707

Houghton Hall, Kings Lynn, PE31 6UE. Tel: 01485 528569

Hoveton Hall, Norwich NR12 8RJ. Tel: 01603 782798 Fax: 01603 784 564

Mannington Hall, Saxthorpe, Norwich, NR11 7BB. Tel: 01263 584175 Fax: 01263 761214

NORTHAMPTONSHIRE

Boughton House, Kettering, NN14 1BJ. Tel: 01536 515731 Fax: 01536 417255

Coton Manor Garden, Coton, Nr Guilsborough, NN6 8RQ. Tel: 01604 740219 Fax: 01604 740838

Cottesbrooke Hall and Gardens, nr Northampton, NN6 8PF. Tel: 01604 505808 Fax: 01604 505619

Haddonstone Show Garden, The Forge House, CHurch Lane, East Haddon, NN6 8BD. Tel: 01604 770711 Fax: 01604 770027

Holdenby House Gardens & Falconry Centre, Holdenby, Northampton NN6 8DJ. Tel: 01604 770074 Fax: 01604 770962

The Menagerie - Horton, Horton, Northampton, NN7 2BX. Tel: 01604 870957

NORTHUMBERLAND

Chipchase Castle, Wark on Tyne, Hexham. Tel: 01434 230203 Fax: 01434 230740

OXFORDSHIRE

Blenheim Palace Woodstock OX20 1PX. Tel: 01993 811325 24hr information Fax: 01993 813527

Waterperry Gardens, Waterperry Horticultural Centre, nr Wheatley, OX33 1JZ. Tel: 01844 339226 Fax: 01844 339 883

SHROPSHIRE

Burford House Gardens, Tenbury Wells, WR15 8HQ. Tel: 01584 810777 Fax: 01584 810673

Hodnet Hall Gardens, Hodnet, Nr Market Drayton, TF9 3NN. Tel: 01630 685202 Fax: 01630 685 853

Old Colehurst Manor, Colehurst, Market Drayton TF9 2JB Tel:01630 638833

Walcot Hall, Nr Bishops Castle, Lydbury North SY7 8AZ. Tel: 0171-581 2782 Fax: 0171 589 0195

Wollerton Old Hall, Wollerton, Market Drayton TF9 3NA. Tel: 01630 685760 Fax: 01630 685583

SOMERSET

East Lambrook Manor Garden, South Petherton TA13 5HL. Tel: 01460 240328 Fax: 01460 242 344

Gaulden Manor, Tolland, nr Taunton, TA4 3PN. Tel: 01984 667213

Hestercombe House Gardens, Cheddon Fitzpaine, Taunton, TA2 8LG. Tel: 01823 413923 Fax: 01823 413747

Milton Lodge Gardens, Milton Lodge, Wells BA5 3AQ. Tel: 01749 672168

Orchard Wyndham, Williton, nr Taunton, TA4 4HH. Tel: 01984 632309 Fax: 01984 633526

Sherborne Garden (Pear Tree House), Litton BA3 4PP. Tel: 01761 241220

STAFFORDSHIRE

Dunwood Hall, Longsdon, Nr. Leek ST9 9AR. Tel: 01538 385071

SUFFOLK

Helmingham Hall Gardens, The Estate Office, Helmingham Hall, Stowmarket, IP14 6EF. Tel: 01473 890363 Fax: 01473 890776

Hengrave Hall Centre, Hengrave Hall, Bury St Edmunds, IP28 6LZ. Tel: 01284 701561 Fax: 01284 702950

Somerleyton Hall, nr Lowestoft NR32 5QQ. Tel: 01502 730224 Fax: 01502 732143

Wingfield Old College & Gardens, Wingfield, Nr Stradbroke, IP21 5RA. Tel: 01379 384888 Fax: 01379 384034

Wyken Hall, Stanton, Bury St. Edmunds, IP31 2DW. Tel: 01359 250287 Fax: 01359 252256

SURREY

Clandon Park, West Clandon, Guildford GU4 7RQ. Tel: 01483 222482 Fax: 01483 223479

Loseley Park, Estate Office, Guildford, GU3 1HS. Tel: 01483 304440 Fax: 01483 302036

Painshill Landscape Garden, Portsmouth Road, Cobham Tel:KT11 1JE

Millais Rhododendrons, Crosswater Farm, Churt, Farnham, GU10 2JN. Tel: 01252 792698

RHS Garden Wisley, Woking, GU23 6QB. Tel: 01483 224234

SUSSEX

Borde Hill Garden, Balcombe Road, Haywards Heath, RH16 1XP. Tel: 01444 450326

Charleston Farmhouse, Firle, nr Lewes. Tel: 01323 811626 Fax: 01323 811628

Denmans Garden, Clock House, Denmans, Fontwell BN18 0SU. Tel: 01243 542808 Fax01243 544064

Fishbourne Roman Palace, Salthill Road, Fishbourne, Chichester, PO19 3QR. Tel: 01243 785859 Fax: 01243 539 266

Glynde Place, Glynde, nr Lewes, BN8 6SX. Tel: 01273 858224 Fax: 01273 858224

Great Dixter House, Northiam, Nr Rye, TN31 6PH. Tel: 01797 252878 Fax: 01797 252879

Leonardslee Gardens, Lower Beeding, Horsham, RH13 6PP. Tel: 01403 891212 Fax: 01403 891305

Michelham Priory, Upper Dicker, Hailsham BN27 3QS. Tel: 01323 844224 Fax: 01323 844030

Merriments Gardens, Hawkhurst Road, Hurst Green TN19 7RA. Tel: 01580 860666 Fax: 01580 860324

Parham House and Gardens, Parham Park Ltd, Pulborough, RH20 4HS. Tel: 01903 742021 Fax: 01903 746557

Pashley Manor Gardens, Ticehurst, Wadhurst, TN5 7HE. Tel: 01580 200692 Fax: 01580 200102

Perryhill Nurseries, Hartfield, TN7 4JP. Tel: 0892 770377

Royal Botanic Gardens, Kew at Wakehurst Place, Ardingly, Haywards Heath RH17 6TN. Tel: 01444 894066 Fax: 01444 894069

The Weald & Downland Open Air Museum, Singleton, Nr Chichester Tel:01243 811348

West Dean Gardens, West Dean Estate, nr Chichester, PO18 0QZ. Tel: 01243 818210 Fax: 01243 811342

WARWICKSHIRE

Charlecote Park, Warwick CV35 9ER Tel:01789 470277

The Hiller Garden, Dunnington Heath Farm, Alcester, B49 5PD. Tel: 01789 490991

Lord Leycester Hospital, High Street, Warwick, CV34 4BH. Tel: 01926 491422 Fax: 01926 491 422

Shakespearian Properties, Henley Street, Stratford-upon-Avon CV37 6QW. Tel: 01789 204016 Fax: 01789 269083

WEST MIDLANDS

Baddesley Clinton Hall, B93 0DQ. Tel: 01564 783294 Fax: 01564 782706

Birmingham Botanical Gardens and Glasshouses, Westbourne Road, Edgbaston, Birmingham B15 3TR. Tel: 0121 454 1860 Fax: 0121 454 7835

Castle Bromwich Hall Gardens, Chester Road, Castle Bromwich, Birmingham. Tel: 0121 749 4100

WILTSHIRE

Longleat, The Estate Office, Warminster, BA12 7NW. Tel: 01985 844400 Fax: 01985 844885

Stourhead, Stourton, nr Mere BA12 6QD. Tel: 01747 841152 Fax: 01747 841 152

YORKSHIRE

Burton Agnes Hall, Burton Agnes, Diffield, YO25 0ND. Tel: 01262 490324 Fax: 01262 490513

Castle Howard, York YO6 7DA. Tel: 01653 648444

Elsham Hall Country and Wildlife Park, The Estate Office, Brigg DN20 0QZ. Tel: 01652 688698 Fax: 01652 688240

Harewood House and Bird Garden, The Estate Office, Harewood, Leeds, LS17 9LQ. Tel: 0113 288 6331 Fax: 0113 288 6467

Harlow Carr Botanical Gardens, Crag Lane, Harrogate, HG3 1QB. Tel: 01423 565418 Fax: 01423 530663

Norton Conyers, Ripon HG4 5EQ. Tel: 01765 640333 Fax: 01765 692772.

Nunnington Hall, Nunnington, York YO62 5UY. Tel: 01439 748283 Fax: 01439 748284

Ripley Castle, Ripley HG3 3AY. Tel: 01423 770152 Fax: 01423 771745

Sewerby Hall and Gardens, Church Lane, Sewerby, Bridlington, YO15 1EA. Tel: Estate Office: 01262 673 769 Hall :01262 677874

Shandy Hall, The Laurence Sterne Trust, Coxwold, York, YO6 4AD. Tel: 01347 868465

Skipton Castle, Skipton, BD23 1AQ. Tel: 01756 792442 Fax: 01756 796100

Thorp Perrow Arboretum, Bedale DL8 2PR. Tel: 01677 425323 Fax: 01677 425 323

IRELAND

Bantry House, Bantry, Co. Cork. Tel: 00353 2 750 047 Fax: 00353 2 750 795

Benvarden Gardens, Benvarden Dervock, Co Antrim, N. Ireland. Tel: 012657 41331 Fax: 012657 41955

Birr Castle, Birr Tel:00353 50920336

Hamwood House, Hamwood, Dunboyne. Tel: 00353 1 8255210

Larchill Arcadian Gardens, Kilcock, Kildare. Tel: 00 3511 628 4580 Fax: 003511 628 7354

Powerscourt Gardens & Waterfall, Enniskerry, Co. Wicklow. Tel: 00353 1 204 6000 Fax: 00353 1 286 3561

Seaforde Gardens, Seaforde, Downpatrick BT30 3PG. Tel: +441396 811225 Fax:+441396 811370

Strokestown Park House & Gardens, Strokestown, Co. Roscommon. Tel: 00353 78 33013 Fax: 00353 78 33712

SCOTLAND

Blairquhan Castle and Gardens, Straiton,, Maybole KA19 7LZ. Tel: 016557 70239 Fax: 016557 70278

Bolfracks Garden, Aberfeldy PH15 2EX. Tel: 01887 820207

Bowhill House & Country Park, Bowhill, nr Selkirk TD7 5ET. Tel: 01750 22204 Fax: 01750 22204

Glamis Castle, Estate Office, Glamis DD8 1RT. Tel: 01307 840393 Fax: 01307 840 733

Mount Stuart House and Gardens, Mount Stuart, Isle of Bute PA20 9LR. Tel: 01700 503877 Fax: 01700 505 313

Paxton House & Gardens, Paxton, nr Berwick-upon-Tweed TD15 1SZ. Tel: 01289 386291

Traquair House, Innerleithen EH44 6PW. Tel: 01896 830323 Fax: 01896 830639

WALES

Aberglasney Gardens, East Bailiff's Lodge, Llangathen. Tel: 01558 668998 Fax: 01558 668998

Bodnant Garden, Tal Y Cafn, Colwyn Bay Tel:01492 650460

The Castle House, Usk NP5 1SD. Tel: 01291 672563

Colby Woodland Gardens, Stepaside, Narbeth SA67 8PP. Tel: 01834 811885

Dyffryn Gardens, St Nicholas, Cardiff CF5 6SU. Tel: 01222 593 328 Fax: 01222 591966

Erddig Hall, Gardens & Country Park, Nr Wrexham LL13 0YT. Tel: 01978 355314 Fax: 01978 355314

Picton Castle, Picton Castle Trust, Haverfordwest SA62 4AS. Tel: 01437 751326

Portmerion Village, Portmerion, Gwyned Tel: 01766 770000

As recommended

Universities

CAMBRIDGE

Note: Admission to the Colleges means to the Courts, not to the staircases and students' rooms. All opening times are subject to closing for College functions etc. on occasional days. Halls normally close for lunch (12–2pm) and many are not open during the afternoon. Chapels are closed during services. Libraries are not usually open, special arrangements are noted. Gardens do not usually include the Fellows' garden. Figures denote the date of foundation and existing buildings are often of later date. Daylight hours – some colleges may not open until 9.30am or later and usually close before 6pm – many as early as 4.30pm. All parties exceeding 10 persons wishing to tour the college between Easter and October are required to be escorted by a Cambridge registered Guide. All enquires should be made to the Tourist Information Centre, Wheeler Street, Cambridge CB2 3QB. Terms: Lent: Mid-January to Mid-March. Easter: April to June. Michaelmas: 2nd week October to 1st week December. Examination Period closures which differ from one college to another now begin in early April and extend to late June. Notices are usually displayed. Admission charges vary from college to college. **Visitors and especially guided parties should always call at the Porters' Lodge before entering the College.**

CHRIST'S COLLEGE (1505)
Porter's Lodge, St.Andrew's Street CB2 3BU
Tel:(01223) 334900 Fax: (01223) 334967

CLARE COLLEGE (1326)
Trinity Lane

CORPUS CHRISTI COLLEGE (1352)
Porter's Lodge, Trumpington Street CB2 1RH
Tel: (01223) 338000 Fax: (01223) 338061

DOWNING COLLEGE (1800)
Downing College, Regent Street CB2 1DQ
Tel: (01223) 334800 Fax: (01223) 467934

EMMANUEL COLLEGE (1584)
Porter's Lodge, St. Andrew's Street CB2 3AP
Tel: (01223) 334200 Fax: (01223) 334426

GONVILLE & CAIUS COLLEGE (1348)
Porter's Lodge, Trinity Street CB2 1TA
Tel: (01223) 332400

JESUS COLLEGE (1496)
Porter's Lodge, Jesus Lane CB5 8BL
Tel: (01223) 339339

KING'S COLLEGE (1441)
Porter's Lodge, King's Parade CB2 1ST
Tel: (01223) 331212 Fx:(01223) 331315

MAGDALENE COLLEGE (1542)
Porter's Lodge, Magdalene Street

NEWNHAM COLLEGE (1871)
Sidgewick Avenue

PEMBROKE COLLEGE(1347)
Trumpington Street

PETERHOUSE (1284)
Porter's Lodge, Trumpington Street CB2 1RD
Tel: (01223) 338200 Fax: (01223) 337578

QUEENS' COLLEGE (1448)
Porter's Lodge, Silver Street CB3 9ET
Tel: (01223) 335511 Fax:(01223) 335566

SIDNEY SUSSEX COLLEGE (1596)
Porter's Lodge, Sidney Street CB2 3HU
Tel: (01223) 338800 Fax: (01223) 338884

ST. CATHARINE'S COLLEGE (1473)
Porter's Lodge, Trumpington Street

ST. JOHN'S COLLEGE (1511)
Tourist Liaison Office, St. John Street CB2 1TP

TRINITY COLLEGE (1546)
Porter's Lodge, Trinity Street

TRINITY HALL (1350)
Porter's Lodge, Trinity Lane

Conducted Tours in Cambridge: Qualified badged, local guides may be obtained from: Tourist Information Centre, Wheeler Street, Cambridge CB2 3QB. Tel: (01223) 322640 or Cambridge Guide Service, 2 Montague Road, Cambridge CB4 1BX. We normally obtain the Passes and make all negotiations regarding these with the Tourist Office, so separate application is not needed. We have been providing guides for English, Foreign language and special interest groups since 1950. We supply couriers for coach tours of East Anglia, visiting stately homes etc. As an alternative to the 2 hour walking tour we can now offer half hour panoramic in clients' coach (providing there is an effective public address system) followed by a 1.5 hour tour on foot, or 1 hour panoramic only, special flat rate for up to 55 people.

OXFORD

NOTE: Admission to Colleges means to the Quadrangles, not to the staircases and students' rooms. All opening times are subject to closing for college functions etc., on occasional days. Halls normally close for lunch (12–2pm). Chapel usually closed during services. Libraries are not usually open, special arrangements are noted. Gardens do not usually include the Fellows' garden. Figures denote the date of foundation and existing buildings are often of later date. Terms: Hilary: Mid-January to Mid-March. Trinity: 3rd week April to late June. Michaelmas: Mid October to 1st week December. **Visitors and especially guided parties should always call at the Porter's Lodge before entering the College.**

ALL SOULS COLLEGE (1438)
Porter's Lodge, High Street OX1 4AL
Open: College Weekdays: 2–4.30. (2–4pm Oct–Mar).

BALLIOL COLLEGE (1263)
Porter's Lodge, Broad Street
Open: Hall Chapel & Gardens Daily 2–5. Parties limited to 25.

BRASENOSE COLLEGE (1509)
Radcliffe Square
Open: Hall Chapel & Gardens Tour parties: Daily 10–11.30 2–5 (summer) 10–dusk (winter). Individuals 2–5. College closed 11.30–2.

CHRIST CHURCH (1546)
St. Aldate's , Enter via Meadow Gate OX1 1DP
Tel: (01865) 276499
Open: Cathedral daily 9–4.30 (winter) 9–5.30 (summer). Hall daily 9.30–12,2–5.30. Picture Gallery weekdays 10.30–1, 2–4.30. Meadows daily 7–dusk. Tourist Information-(01865) 276499.

CORPUS CHRISTI COLLEGE (1517)
Porter's Lodge, Merton Street
Open: College, Chapel & Gardens Term and vacations – daily.

EXETER COLLEGE (1314)
Porter's Lodge, Turl Street OX1 3DP
Tel: (01865) 279600 Fax:(01865) 279630
Open: College & Chapel, Fellows' Garden term and vacations daily 2–5. (Except Christmas and Easter).

HERTFORD COLLEGE (1284, 1740 & 1874)
Porter's Lodge, Catte Street OX1 3BW
Tel: (01865) 279400 Fax: (01865) 279437
Open: Quadrangle & Chapel Daily 10–6

JESUS COLLEGE (1571)
Turl Street
Open: College, Hall & Chapel Daily 2.30–4.30.

KEBLE COLLEGE (1868)
Porter's Lodge, Parks Road
Open: College & Chapel Daily 10–7 (or dusk if earlier)

LADY MARGARET HALL (1878)
Porter's Lodge, Norham Gardens
Open: College & Gardens Daily 2–6 (or dusk if earlier). The chapel is also open to the public.

LINCOLN COLLEGE (1427)
Porter's Lodge, Turl Street
Open: College & Hall weekdays 2–5. Suns 11–5. Wesley Room All Saints Library Tues & Thurs 2–4.

MAGDALEN COLLEGE (1458)
High Street OX1 4AU
Tel: (01865) 276000 Fax:(01865) 276103
Open: College Chapel Deer Park & Water Walks daily 2–6 June–Sept 11–6.

MANSFIELD COLLEGE (1886)
Porter's Lodge, Mansfield Road
Open: College, May–July, Mon–Sat, 9–5.

MERTON (1264)
Merton Street OX1 4JD
Tel: (01865) 276310 Fax:(01865) 276361
Open: Chapel & Quadrangle Mon–Fri 2–4 Oct–June: Sat & Sun 10–4. Mon–Fri 2–5. Jul–Sept: Sat & Sun 10–5. Library not open on Sat Nov–Mar.

NEW COLLEGE (1379)
New College Lane
Open: Hall, Chapel, Cloister, Gardens daily. Oct–Easter in Holywell Street Gate 2–4. Easter – Early Oct, in New College Lane Gate (11–5)

NUFFIELD COLLEGE (1937)
Porter's Lodge, New Road
Open: College only, daily 9–5

ORIEL COLLEGE (1326)
Oriel Square OX1 4EW
Tel: (01865) 276555 Fax:(01865) 276532
Open: College daily 2–5.

PEMBROKE COLLEGE (1624)
Porter's Lodge, St.Aldate's
Open: College, Hall & Chapel & Gardens Term – daily on application at the Porter's Lodge.

THE QUEEN'S COLLEGE (1340)
High Street OX1 4AW
Tel: (01865) 279120 Fax:(01865) 790819
Open: Hall Chapel Quadrangles & Garden Open to public by apt.

ST. EDMUNDS HALL (1270)
Queen's Lane OX1 4AR
Tel: (01865) 279000
Open: On application to Porter

ST. JOHN'S COLLEGE (1555)
St. Giles' OX1 3JP
Tel: (01865) 277300 Fax:(01865) 277435
Open: College & Garden, Term & Vacation, daily 1–5. Hall & Chapel summer 2.30–4.30.

TRINITY COLLEGE (1554)
Main Gate, Broad Street OX1 3BH
Tel: (01865) 277300 Fax: (01865) 279898
Open: Hall, Chapel & Gardens daily during daylight hours.

UNIVERSITY COLLEGE (1249)
Porter's Lodge, High Street OX1 4BH
Open: College, Hall & Chapel Term 2–4.

WADHAM COLLEGE (1610)
Parks Road, Oxford

WORCESTER COLLEGE (1714)
Porter's Lodge, Worcester Street OX1 2HB
Tel: (01865) 278300 Fax:(01865) 278387
Open: College & Gardens Term daily, 2–6. Vacation daily 9–12 &2–6. Hall & Chapel Apply Lodge.

GUIDED WALKING TOURS OF THE COLLEGES & CITY OF OXFORD. Tours conducted by the Oxford Guild of Guides. Lectures are offered by The Oxford Information Centre, mornings for much of the year, afternoons, tours daily. For tour times please ring (01865) 726871. Tours are offered for groups in English, French, German, Spanish, Russian, Japanese, Polish and Serbo-Croat. Chinese by appointment. The most popular tour for groups, Oxford Past and Present, can be arranged at any time. The following special interest tours are available in the afternoon only: Alice in Oxford; Literary Figures in Oxford; American Roots in Oxford; Oxford Gardens; Modern Architecture in Oxford; Architecture in Oxford (Medieval, 17th century and Modern); Oxford in the Civil War and 17th century. Further details are available from the Deputy Information Officer.

Properties Used As Film Locations

ENGLAND

BERKSHIRE

Dorney Court, Dorney, Nr. Windsor, Berkshire SL4 6QP.
Tel: 01628 604638 Fax: 01628 665772 – *Children of the New Forest / Sliding Doors / The Jump / Vanishing Man / Lock, Stock & Two Smoking Barrels*

BUCKINGHAMSHIRE

Chiltern Open Air Museum, Newland Park, Gorelands Lane, Chalfont St Giles Tel:01494 871117

Claydon House, Middle Claydon, Nr. Buckingham, Bucks MK18 2EY. Tel: 01296 730349 – *Emma / Vanity Fair*

Stowe (Stowe School), Stowe MK18 5EH.
Tel: 01280 813650 – *The Avengers*

CAMBRIDGESHIRE

King's College, King's Parade, Cambridge CB2 1ST
Tel: 01223 331212

CHESHIRE

Arley Hall and Gardens, Arley, Northwich, Cheshire CW9 6NA. Tel: 01565 777353 Fax: 01565 777465 – *Good Living – Jane Asher / Brookside / Out & About*

Capesthorne Hall, Nr Macclesfield Tel:01625 861221

Little Moreton Hall, Congleton CW12 4SD Tel:01260 272018 – *Moll Flanders / Lady Jane Grey*

Peckforton Castle, Stonehouse Lane, Nr. Tarporley CW6 9TN. Tel: 01829 260930 Fax: 01829 261230. – *Robin Hood*

Tabley House, Knutsford, Cheshire. Tel: 01565 750151 Fax: 01565 653230 – *Some Coronation Street/ Sherlock Homes / Game, Set & Match*

CORNWALL

Caerhays Castle, Gorran, St Austell PL26 6LY Tel: 01872 501310 – *Rebecca, Poldark, Wycliffe, Longitude*

Godolphin House, Godophin Cross, Helston, Cornwall TR13 9RE. Tel: 01736 762409 – *Poldark / Wycliffe / Empty House*

Lanhydrock House, Bodmin, Cornwall. Tel: 01208 73320 Fax: 01208 74084 – *Twelfth Night*

Pencarrow, Washaway, Bodmin PL30 3AG Tel:01208 841369 – *The Red Robe*

CUMBRIA

Holker Hall & Gardens, Cark-in-Cartmel, Nr Grange-over-Sands LA11 7PL. Tel: 015395 58328 Fax: 015395 58776 – *The English Country Garden*

Levens, Kendal LA8 OPD Tel:015395 60321 – *Wives and Daughters (BBC)*

Mirehouse, Keswick CA12 4QE Tel:01768 772287 – *Fell Tiger, Ken Russell's 'Wordsworth'*

DERBYSHIRE

Haddon Hall, Bakewell, Derbyshire DE45 1LA.
Tel: 01629 812855 Fax: 01629 814379 – *Jane Eyre / Prince & The Pauper / Moll Flanders / Elizabeth I*

Lea Gardens, Lea, Matlock, Derbyshire ED4 5GH.
Tel: 01629 534380 Fax: 01629 534260 – *Gardeners World*

DEVON

Bickleigh Castle, Bickleigh, Nr. Tiverton, Devon EX16 8RP. Tel: 01884 855363 – *One Foot in the Past*

Cadhay, Ottery St Mary, Devon EX11 1QT.
Tel: 01404 812432 – *Miss Marple - Sleeping Murder*

Hartland Abbey, Nr Birdeford EX39 6DT
Tel:01237441234

DORSET

Athelhampton House, Athelhampton, Dorchester
Tel:01305 848363 – *Antiques Roadshow / Time Travellers*

Forde Abbey and Gardens, Forde Abbey, Chard, Somerset TA20 4LU. Tel: 01460 221290 Fax: 01460 220296 – *Restoration*

Lulworth Castle, The Lulworth Estate, East Lulworth, Wareham, Dorset BH20 5QS. Tel: 01929 400352 – *Inspector Morse / Tess of the D'Urbervilles / Red Violin*

Mapperton, Beaminster DT8 3NR Tel:01308 862645 – *Emma / Restoration / Tom Jones*

Parnham House & Gardens, Parnham, Beaminster, Dorset. Tel: 01308 862204 Fax: 01308 863494 – *French Lieutenant's Woman / Jane Austen*

CO DURHAM

Durham Castle, Durham DH1 3RW. Tel: 01913 743863 Fax: 01913 747470 – *Ivanhoe*

Raby Castle, Staindrop, Darlington, Co. Durham DL2 3AY. Tel: 01833 660202 Fax: 01833 660169 – *Elizabeth I*

ESSEX

Hedingham Castle, Halstead CO9 3DJ Tel:01787 460261 – *Ivanhoe / Lovejoy*

Ingatestone Hall, Hall Lane, Ingatestone CM4 9NR
Tel:01277 353010 – *Lovejoy*

Layer Marney Tower, Nr Colchester, Essex CO5 9US. Tel/Fax: 01206 330784 – *Canterbury Tales*

The Sir Alfred Munnings Art Museum, Castle House, Dedham CO7 6AZ. Tel/Fax: 01206 322127 – *Liza's Country / Collectors Lot / Treasure Hunt*

GLOUCESTERSHIRE

Barnsley House, Nr Cirencester GL7 5EE Tel:01285 740561 – *Greenfingers*

Chavenage, Tetbury, Gloucestershire GL8 8XP. Tel: 01666 502329 Fax: 01453 836778 – *Cider With Rosie / Berkeley Square*

Frampton Court, Frampton-on-Severn, Gloucester.
Tel: 01452 740698 – *Charge of the Light Brigade / Rocking Horse Winner / Animal Ark*

HAMPSHIRE

Avington Park, Winchester, Hampshire SO21 1DB.
Tel: 01962 779260 Fax: 01962 779864 – *Jewels / Ruth Rendell*

Breamore House, Nr. Fordingbridge, Hampshire SP6 2DF.
Tel: 01725 512468 – *Woodlanders / Florence Nightingale / Children of the New Forest / Barchester Towers*

Houghton Lodge Gardens, Stockbridge, Hampshire SO20 6LQ. Tel: 01264 810177 – *Grass Roots*

HEREFORD & WORCESTER

Eastnor Castle, Ledbury Tel:01531 633160 – *Little Lord Fauntleroy*

Moccas Court, Moccas, HR2 9LH. Tel: 01981 500381

Worcester Cathedral, College Green, Worcester, Worcestershire WR1 2LA. Tel: 01905 28854 Fax: 01905 611139 – *The Choir*

HERTFORDSHIRE

Cathedral & Abbey Church of Saint Alban, St Albans, Herfordshire AL1 1BY. Tel: 01727 860780 Fax: 01727 850944 – *First Knight*

Knebworth House, Knebworth, Hertfordshire.
Tel: 01438 812661 – *Batman / Jane Eyre / Canterville Ghost*

KENT

Cobham Hall, Cobham, Nr Gravesend DA12 3BL
Tel:01474 823371– *The Mystery of Edwin Drood / Peacock Spring*

Finchcocks, Goudhurst, Kent TN17 1HH.
Tel: 01580 211702 Fax: 01580 211007 – *Collectors Lot / French & Saunders / The Making of Pride & Prejudice*

Penshurst Place and Gardens, Penshurst, Nr Tonbridge, Kent TN11 8DG. Tel: 01892 870307 Fax: 01892 870866 – *Love on a Branch Line / Little Lord Fauntleroy / Prince & The Pauper / Young Sherlock Holmes / The Mirror Cracked / Secret Garden*

LANCASHIRE

Dalemain, Nr Penrith, Cumbria Tel: 017684 86450 Fax: 017684 86223 – *Jane Eyre / Border TV Sir Harry Secombe 'Music Is My Life'*

Towneley Hall Art Gallery & Museums, Burnley, Lancashire BB11 3RQ. Tel: 01282 424213 Fax: 01282 436138 – *Whistle Down The Wind*

LEICESTERSHIRE

Belvoir Castle, Nr Grantham NG32 IPD Tel:01476 870262 – *Little Lord Fauntleroy / Young Sherlock Holmes / The Haunting*

Stanford Hall, Lutterworth, Leicestershire LE17 6DH.
Tel: 01788 860250 Fax: 01788 860870 – *Lost without Trace / The Deep Concern / The Canal Children*

LINCOLNSHIRE

Elsham Hall, Brigg DN20 0QZ Tel:01652 688698 – *'History of Folk'*

LONDON

Southside House, 3 Woodhayes Road Wimbledon SW19 4RJ Tel:0181 946 7643 – *Dickens Christmas Special*

Mapperton, Dorset

Syon Park, Brentford TW8 8JF Tel:0181 560 0883 – *Madness of King George / Avengers / The Wings of the Dove'*

NORFOLK

Mannington Hall, Norwich Tel:01263 584175

Wolterton Park, Erpringham Tel:01263 584175

OXFORDSHIRE

Broughton Castle, Banbury, Oxfordshire OX15 5EB. Tel/Fax: 01295 276070 – *Shakespeare In Lov*

Mapledurham House, Nr Reading RG4 7TR Tel:01189 723350 – *Eagle has Landed / Children of the New Forest*

University of Oxford Botanic Garden, Rose Lane, Oxford Tel:01865 276920 – *Morse / Brideshead Revisited*

SHROPSHIRE

Ironbridge Gorge, Ironbridge, Telford, Shropshire TF8 7AW. Tel: 01952 433522 – *Feast of July / Home & Away / Dr Who / Anna of the Town / Fred Dibnah / Bill Bryson*

Old Colehurst Manor, Colehurst, Market Drayton TF9 2JB Tel:01630 638833 – *BBC Travel / Collectors Lot*

SOMERSET

Museum of Costume & Assembly Rooms, Bennett Street, Bath Tel:01225 477789 – *Persuasion*

STAFFORDSHIRE

Tamworth Castle, The Holloway, Tamworth, Staffordshire. Tel: 01827 63563 Fax: 01827 56567 – *Out & About*

SUFFOLK

Somerleyton Hall & Gardens, Somerleyton, Lowestoft, Suffolk NR32 5QQ. Tel: 01502 730224 Fax: 01502 732143 – *Garden without Borders / Lovejoy / Watercolour Challenge*

SURREY

Albury Park, Albury, Guildford, Surrey GU5 9BB. Tel: 01483 202964 Fax: 01483 205013 – *Four Weddings & A Funeral / Underworld / Unsuitable Job For A Woman*

Clandon Park, West Clandon, Guildford, Surrey, GU4 7RQ. Tel: 01483 222482 Fax: 01483 223479 – *Fashion Shoots (Hello Magazine)*

Loseley Park, Guildford, Surrey GU3 1HS. Tel: 01483 304440 Fax: 01483 302036 – *The Worst Witch / Jonathan Creek / Spice Girls Movie / The Student Prince*

Painshill Landscape Garden, Portsmouth Road, Cobham Tel:KT11 1JE– *101 Dalmations*

SUSSEX

Brickwall House & Gardens, Northiam, Rye, East Sussex TN31 6NL. Tel: 01797 253388 Fax: 01797 252567 – *Cold Comfort Farm*

Firle Place, Nr. Lewes, East Sussex BN8 6LP. Tel/Fax: 01273 858188 – *Return of Soldier / Firelight*

Parham House & Gardens, Parham Park, Nr. Pulborough, West Sussex. Tel: 01903 742021 Fax: 01903 746557 – *Prince & The Pauper / To Be The Best / Haunted*

The Royal Pavilion, Brighton, East Sussex BN1 1EE. Tel: 01273 290900 Fax: 01273 292871 – *Richard III*

WARWICKSHIRE

Arbury Hall, Nuneaton, Warwickshire CV10 7PT. Tel: 01203 382804 Fax: 01203 641147 – *Angels and Insects*

Lord Leycester Hospital, High Street, Warwick, Warwickshire CV34 4BH. Tel: 01926 491422 Fax: 01926 491422 – *Dangerfield / Songs of Praise / Surprise Gardens / Travels with Pevsner / Pride & Prejudice / Tom Jones / Moll Flanders*

WEST MIDLANDS

Baddesley Clinton Hall, Knowle, Solihull, West Midlands B93 0DZ. Tel: 01564 783294 Fax: 01564 782706 – *Sherlock Holmes*

WILTSHIRE

Corsham Court, Corsham SN13 0BZ Tel:01249 701610 – *Remains of the Day / Wives and Daughters*

Longleat, Warminster, Wiltshire BA12 7NW. Tel: 01985 844400 Fax: 01985 844885 – *Barry Lyndon / The Missionary / Adventure of a Lady*

Luckington Court, Luckington, Chippenham, Wilshire SN14 6PQ. Tel: 01666 840205 – *Pride & Prejudice / Wives and Daughters*

Wilton House, The Estate Office, Wilton, Salisbury SP2 0BJ. Tel: 01722 746720 Fax: 01722 744447 – *Madness of King George / Mrs Brown / Sense & Sensibility / Bounty*

YORKSHIRE

Aske Hall, Aske, Richmond, North Yorkshire DL10 5HJ. Tel: 01748 850391 Fax: 01748 823252 – *Collectors Lot*

Bolton Castle, Leyburn, North Yorkshire DL8 4ET. Tel: 10969 623981 Fax: 01969 623332 – *Elizabeth I / Ivanhoe / Heartbeat*

Bramham Park, Wetherby, West Yorkshire LS23 6ND. Tel: 01937 844265 Fax: 01937 845923 – *Life & Crimes of William Palmer*

Castle Howard, Nr York YO60 7DA Tel: 01653 648444 – *Brideshead Revisited / The Buccaneers*

Elsham Hall Country and Wildlife Park and Elsham Hall Barn Theatre, Brigg, East Yorkshire DN20 0Q. Tel: 01652 688698 Fax: 01652 688240 – *History of Folk*

Ripley Castle, Ripley Castle Estate, Harrogate, North Yorkshire. Tel: 01423 770152 Fax: 01423 771745 – *Jane Eyre / The Cater Street Hangman / Duchess of Duke Street / Frankenstein*

WALES

Picton Castle, Haverfordwest SA62 4AS Tel:01437 751326 – *Various Gardening Programs*

Portmerion Village, Portmerion, Gwyned Tel: 01766 770000 – *The Prisoner*

SCOTLAND

Drummond Castle Gardens, Muthill Crieff, Tayside, Scotland PH5 2AA. Tel: 01764 681257/433 Fax: 01764 681550 – *Rob Roy*

Drumlanrig Castle, Thornhill DG3 4AQ Tel:01848 330248

Scone Palace, Scone, Perth PH2 6BD. Tel: 01738 552300 Fax: 01738 552588 – *Antiques Road Show*

IRELAND

Benvarden Gardens, Benvarden, Dervock, Co. Antrim, N Ireland. Tel: 012657 41331 Fax: 012657 41955 – *Beyond The Pale*

The James Joyce Museum, The Joyce Tower, Sandycove, Co. Dublin, Ireland. Tel/Fax: 00 353 1 280 9265 – *My Friend Joe / Ulysses*

Powerscourt Gardens, Enniskerry, Co Wicklow Tel:00353 204 6000 – *BBC All for Love / Aristocrats*

Strokestown Park House & Gardens, Strokestown, Co. Roscommon, Ireland. Tel: 00 353 78 33013 Fax: 00 353 78 33712 – *Ann Devlin*

University College Dublin, Newman House, 85-86 St Stephen's Green, Dublin 2. Tel: +353 1 706 7422 / 706 7419 Fax: +353 1 706 7211 – *Aristocrats / Moll Flanders / Some Mothers Son*

Art Collections

Many properties throughout the guide contain notable works of art. The properties listed here have special collections.

ENGLAND

BEDFORDSHIRE

Woburn Abbey, Woburn, MK43 0TP
Tel: 01525 290666 – *Canaletto, Van Dyck, Reynolds*

BERKSHIRE

Dorney Court, Dorney, Nr Windsor, SL4 6QP
Tel: 01628 604638, Fax: 01628 665772

Eton College, Windsor, SL4 6DW
Tel: 01763 671177, Fax: 01753 671 265 – *Brew House Gallery, Exhibitions change*

Highclere Castle, Nr Newbury, RG20 9RN
Tel: 01635 253210. Old masters including Van Dyck

Taplow Court, Berry Hill, Taplow SL6 OER Tel:01628 591215

BUCKINGHAMSHIRE

Windsor Castle, Windsor, Berkshire SL4 1NJ
Tel: 01753 568286

CHESHIRE

Capesthorne Hall, Capesthorne, Siddington, Nr. Macclesfield, SK11 9JY. Tel: 01625 861221. Fax: 01625 861619

Dorfold Hall, Nantwich CW5 8LD Tel:01270 625245

Dunham Massey, Altrincham Tel:0161 941 1025

Norton Priory Museum & Gardens, Tudor Road, Manor Park, Runcorn, WA7 1SX. Tel: 01928 569895 – *Contemporary sculpture*

Tabley House, Knutsford, WA16 OHB
Tel: 01565 750151, Fax: 01565 653230 – *Lely, Lawrence, Opie, Ward, Owen, Devis, Turner*

Tatton Park, Knutsford, WA16 6QN
Tel: 01565 750 250, Fax: 01565 654 822

CORNWALL

Mount Edgcumbe House & Country Park, Cremyll, Torpoint PL10 1HZ Tel: 01752 822236

Pencarrow, Washway, Bodmin PL30 5AG.
Tel: 01208 841369 – *Sir Joshua Reynolds*

COUNTY DURHAM

Auckland Castle, Bishop Auckland DL14 7NR.
Tel: 01388 601627 Fax:01388 609323 – *Zurbaran*

Raby Castle, Staindrop, Darlington, Co Durham DL2 3AY Tel: 01833 660 202

CUMBRIA

Abbot Hall Art Gallery & Museum of Lakeland Life & Industry, Kirkland, Kendal LA9 5AL. Tel: 01539 722464 Fax: 01539 722494

Dalemain, nr Penrith CA11 0HB. Tel: 017684 86450 Fax 017684 86223

Hutton-in-the-Forest, Skelton, Penrith CA1 9TH. Tel: 017684 84449 Fax:017684 84571 – *Furniture / Portraits / Ceramics / Tapestry*

DERBYSHIRE

Calke Abbey, Ticknall, Derby DE73 1LE. Tel: 01332 86382 Fax: 01332 865272

Kedleston Hall, Derby, DE22 5JH. Tel: 01332 842191 Fax: 01332 841972 – *17th & 18th century Italian / Dutch collection*

Renishaw Hall, Nr Sheffield S31 9WB.
Tel: 01246 432310

DORSET

Athelhampton House & Gardens, Athelhampton, Dorchester. Tel: 01305 848363 Fax: 01305 848135 – *A.W.Pugin*

Parnham House, Parnham, Beaminster DT8 3NA.
Tel: 01308 862204 Fax 01308 863444

Sandford Orcas Manor House, Sandford Orcas, Sherbourne DT9 4SB Tel:01963 220206

Wolfeton House, Dorchester DT2 9QN.
Tel: 01305 263500

DEVON

Powderham Castle, Kenton, Exeter EX6 8JQ. Tel: 01626 890 243 Fax: 01626 890729 – *Cosway, Hudson, Reynolds*

Torre Abbey, The Kings Drive, Torquay TQ2 5JX
Tel: 01803 293593 Fax: 01803 201154 – *Pre-Raphaelites; 19th century*

ESSEX

Ingatestone Hall, Hall Lane, Ingatestone CM4 9NR
Tel:01277 353010 English Portraits

The Sir Alfred Munnings Art Museum, Castle House, Dedham CO7 6AZ Tel: 01206 322127

GLOUCESTERSHIRE

Berkeley Castle, Gloucestershire GL13 9BQ Tel: 01453 810332

Frampton Court, Frampton-on-Severn GL2 7EU. Tel: Home 01452 740 267 Office 01452 740 698

Owlpen Manor, Owlpen, nr Uley GL11 5BZ. Tel: 01453 860261 Fax 01453 860819

Sudeley Castle, Winchcombe, Gloucs. GL54 5JD
Tel: 01242 602308 – *Van Dyck, Ruben*

HAMPSHIRE

Mottisfont Abbey Garden, Mottisfont, Nr Romsey SO51 0LP. Tel: 01794 340757 Fax:01794 341492 – *Derek Hill's 20th Century picture collection*

Stratfield Saye House, Stratfield Saye, Reading, Hampshire RE7 2BT. Tel: 01256 882882

HEREFORD & WORCESTER

Eastnor Castle, Eastnor, Nr Ledbury, HR8 1RL
Tel: 01531 633160 Fax 01531 631776

HERTFORDSHIRE

Hatfield House, Hatfield, Hertfordshire AL9 5NQ.
Tel: 01707 262823, Fax: 01707 275719

KENT

Cobham Hall, Cobham, Nr Gravesend, Kent DA12 3BL.
Tel: 01474 824319 Fax: 01474 822995

Finchcocks, Goudhurst, Kent TN17 1HH.
Tel: 01580 211702 Fax: 01580 211007 – *18th century, musical theme*

Hever Castle, Nr Edenbridge TN8 7NG Tel:01732 865224

Squerryes Court, Westerham TN16 1SJ. Tel: 01959 562345/563118 Fax:01959 565949 – *Old Masters / Italian / 17th Century Dutch / 18th Century English Schools*

LANCASHIRE

Gawthorpe Hall, Padiham, Nr Burnley BB12 8UA
Tel:01282 771004

Heaton Hall, Heaton Park, Prestwich, Manchester M25 2SW. Tel: 0161 773 1231/236 5244 Fax 0161 236 7369

Towneley Hall Art Gallery & Museum and Museum of Local Crafts & Industries, Burnley BB11 3RQ. Tel: 01282 424213 Fax: 01282 436138 – *18th Century & 19th Century*

LEICESTERSHIRE

Belvoir Castle, Nr Grantham, Lincolnshire. NG32 1PD
Tel: 01476 870262

LINCOLNSHIRE

Elsham Hall, Brigg DN20 0QZ Tel:01652 688698

LONDON

Apsley House, The Wellington Museum, 149 Piccadilly, Hyde Park Corner, London SW1.
Tel: 020 7499 5676 Fax: 020 7493 6576

Boston Manor House, Boston Manor Road, Brentford TW8 9JX. Tel: 020 8560 5441 Fax: 020 8862-7602

Buckingham Palace, London SW1A 1AA.
Tel: 020 7839 1377

Greenwich Observatory, Queens House, National Maritime Museum, Romney Road, Greenwich SE10 9NF. Tel: 020 8312 6565 Fax: 020 7312 6632 – *Maritime / Seascapes / Royal Portraits*

Ham House, Ham Street, Richmond TW10 7RS Tel: 020 8940 1950

Leighton House Museum & Art Gallery, 12 Holland Park Road, London W14 8LZ. Tel: 020 7602 3316 Fax: 020 7371 2467 – *Pre-Raphaelite*

Museum of Garden History, Lambeth Palace Road, Lambeth SE1 7LB. Tel: 0171-261 1891 Fax 020 7401 8869

Orleans House Gallery, Riverside, Twickenham, TW1 3DJ. Tel: 020 8892 0221 Fax: 020 8744 0501

Osterley Park, Jersey Road, Isleworth TW7 4RB.
Tel: 020 8568 7714

St. John's Gate, St John's Lane, Clerkenwell EC1M 4DA. Tel: 020 7253 6644, Fax: 020 7336 0587

Spencer House, 27, St. James's Place SW1A 1NR Tel: 0207 514 1964

Southside House, 3 Woodhayes Road Wimbledon SW19 4RJ Tel: 020 8946 7643

Syon Park, Brentford, Middlesex TW8 8JF.
Tel: 020 860 0881

NORFOLK

Holkham Hall, Wells-next-the-Sea, Norfolk NR23 1AB
Tel: 01328 710227 Fax: 01328 711707 – *Rubens, Van Dyck, Claude, Poussin and Gainsborough*

Norwich Castle Museum, Norwich NR1 3JU.
Tel: 01603 223674

Wolterton Park, Erpingham, Norfolk. Tel: 01263 584175 Fax: 01263 761214

NORTHAMPTONSHIRE

Boughton House, Kettering NN14 1BJ. Tel: 01536 515731 Fax: 01536 417255 – *Van Dyck*

Cottesbrooke Hall & Gardens, Nr Northampton, NN6 8PF. Tel: 01604 505808 Fax: 01604 505619 – *Munnings, Gainsborough, Lionel Edwards*

Lamport Hall & Gardens, Northampton, NN6 9HD Tel: 01604 686272 Fax: 01604 686224

NORTHUMBERLAND

Alnwick Castle, Alnwick, Northumberland NE66 1NQ Tel: 01665 510777 Fax: 01665 510876 – *Titian, Van Dyck, Canelleto*

OXFORDSHIRE

Blenheim Palace, Woodstock, Oxon OX20 1PX Tel: 01993 811325 Fax: 01993 813527

Fawley Court - Marian Fathers Historic House & Museum, Marlow Road, Henley-On-Thames RG9 3AE. Tel: 01491 574917 Fax: 01491 411587

Waterperry Gardens, Nr. Wheatley, Oxon. Tel: 01844 339226/254 – *Art Gallery*

SHROPSHIRE

Burford House Gardens, Tenbury Wells WR15 8HQ. Tel: 01584 810777 Fax 01584 810673 – *Botanical, contemporary*

Ironbridge Gorge Museum, Ironbridge, Telford TF8 7AW. Tel: 01952 433522 Fax:01952 432204 – *History of Industrial Revolution*

Rowleys House Museum, Barker Street, Shrewsbury SY1 1QH. Tel: 01743 361196 Fax: 01743 358411

SOMERSET

Number One, Royal Crescent, Bath Tel:01225 428126 18th Century

STAFFORDSHIRE

Sandon Hall, Sandon, Stafford. Tel: 01889 508004 Fax: 01889 508586

The Shugborough Estate, Milford, Nr. Stafford ST17 Tel: 01889 881388

SUFFOLK

Christchurch Mansion, Christchurch Park, Ipswich Tel: 01473 253246 Fax: 01473 281274

Gainsborough's House, 46 Gainsborough Street, Sudbury, Suffolk CO10 6EU Tel: 01787 372958

Somerleyton Hall & Gardens, Somerleyton, Lowestoft, Suffolk NR32 5QQ. Tel: 01502 730224

Wingfield Old College, Wingfield, Nr Eye, Suffolk IP21 5RA. Tel: 01379 384888 Fax: 01379 384034

SURREY

Clandon Park, West Clandon, Guildford GU4 7RQ Tel: 01483 222 482 – *Gubbay Collection, Porcelain, Needlework & Furniture*

Guildford House Gallery, 155, High Street, Guildford GU1 3AJ. Tel: 01483 444740 Fax 01483 444742 – *John Russell R A / Henry J Sage / Edward Wesson*

SUSSEX

Arundel Castle, Arundel. West Sussex. Tel: 01903 883136

Bentley House & Gardens, Halland, Nr Lewes BN8 5AF. Tel: 01825 840573 – *Philip Rickman*

Charleston Farmhouse, Firle, nr Lewes. Tel: 01323 811265 Fax: 01323 811628

Firle Place, Nr Lewes, East Sussex, BN8 6LP Tel/Fax: 01273 858188. – *Van Dyck, Reynolds, Rubens, Gainsborough, Guardi, Seargeant, Tenniers, Puligo, Larkin plus many others*

Goodwood House, Goodwood, Chichester PO18 OPX. Tel: 01243 755048 Fax 01243 755005

Pallant House, 9 North Pallant, Chichester PO19 1TJ Tel: 01243 774557 – *Modern British*

Parham House and Gardens, Parham Park Ltd, Pulborough RH20 4HS. Tel: 01903 742021/ Info line 01903 744888 Fax: 01903 746557

Preston Manor, Preston Drove, Brighton BN1 6SD Tel:01273 292770

Royal Pavilion, Brighton BN1 1EE. Tel: 01273 290900 Fax 01273 292871 – *Chinoiserie, Regency Silver Gilt*

West Dean Gardens, West Dean Estate, nr Chichester PO18 0QZ. Tel: 01243 818210 Fax: 01243 811342 – *Tapestry studio*

WARWICKSHIRE

Arbury Hall, Nuneaton CV10 7PT. Tel: 01203 382804 Fax 01203 641147

Charlecote Park, Warwick CV35 9ER Tel:01789 470277

Coughton Court, Alcester, B49 5JA. Tel: 01789 400777 Fax: 01789 765544

WEST MIDLANDS

Baddesley Clinton Hall, Rising Lane, Baddesley Clinton Village, Knowle, Solihull, West Midlands. Tel: 01564 783294 Fax: 01564 782706

Birmingham Botanical Gardens & Glasshouse, Westbourne Road, Edgbaston, Birmingham B15 3TR. Tel: 0121 454 1860 Fax: 0121 454 7835

WILTSHIRE

Corsham Court, Corsham, Wilts SN13 OBZ Tel: 01249 701610/701611. – *Van Dyck, Carlo Dolei*

Longleat, The Estate Office, Warminster BA12 7NW. Tel: 01985 844400 Fax: 01985 844885 – *Alexander Thynn / Portraits*

Wilton House, Wilton, Salisbury SP2 OBJ. Tel: 01722 746720 Fax: 01722 744447 – *Van Dyck*

YORKSHIRE

Aske Hall, Aske, Richmond, North Yorkshire DL10 5HJ Tel: 01748 850391 , Fax: 01748 823252

Bramham Park, Wetherby LS23 6ND. Tel: 01937 844265 Fax:01937 845 923

Burton Agnes Hall, Buton Agnes, Driffield, nr Bridlington YO25 0ND. Tel: 01262 490324 – *Impressionists*

Cannon Hall, Cawthorne, Barnsley S75 4AT. Tel: 01226 790 270

Castle Howard, Nr York YO60 7DA Tel: 01653 648444

Elsham Hall Country and Wildlife Park, The Estate Office, Brigg DN20 0QZ. Tel: 01652 688698 Fax 01652 688240

Harewood House and Bird Garden, The Estate Office, Harewood, Leeds LS17 9LQ. Tel: 0113 288 6331 Fax: 0113 288 6467 – *Renaissance / Turner / Reynolds / Contemporary*

Lotherton Hall, Aberford, Yorkshire L25 3EB. Tel: 0113 281 3259 Fax: 0113 281 2100

Newburgh Priory, Coxwold, York YO6 4AS Tel: 01347 868435

Norton Conyers, Ripon HG4 5EQ. Tel: 01765 640333 Fax: 01765 692772 – *17th & 18th Century portraits, 19th Century hunting pictures*

Sewerby Hall & Gardens, Church Lane, Sewerby, Bridlington, East Yorks YOQT 1EA. Tel: Estate Office: 01262 673769

Temple Newsam House, Leeds LS15 OAE. Tel: 0113 264 7321, Fax: 0113 260 2285

WALES

Bodelwyddan Castle, Bodelwyddan, St Asaph, Bodelwyddan LL18 5YA. Tel: 01745 584060 Fax 01745 584563 – *National Portrait Gallery, 19th Century Collection*

Bodrhyddan Hall, Rhuddlan LL18 5SB. Tel: 01745 590414 Fax:01745 590155

Colby Woodland Gardens, Stepaside, Narbeth SA67 8PP. Tel: 01834 811885

Dinefwr Park, Llandeilo, Carmarthenshire. Tel: 01558 823902

Picton Castle, Picton Castle Trust, Haverfordwest SA62 4AS. Tel: 01437 751326

SCOTLAND

Blairquhan Castle, Straiton, Maybole KA19 7LZ Tel:016557 70239

Bowhill House & Country Park, Bowhill, Nr. Selkirk, TD7 5ET Scottish Borders. Tel/Fax: 01750 22204 – *Gainsborough, Canaletto*

Dalmeny House, South Queensferry, Edinburgh, EH30 9TQ. Tel: 0131 331 1888, Fax: 0131 331 1788

Drumlanrig Castle, Thornhill, Dumfrieshire DG3 4AQ Tel: 01848 330248

Fasque, Fettercairn, Laurencekirk AB30 1DN Tel:01561 340202

Glamis Castle, Estate Office, Glamis DD8 1RT. Tel: 01307 840393 Fax: 01307 840 733

Gosford House, Longniddry EH32 0PY. Tel: 01875 870201 Fax:01875 870620

Lennoxlove, Haddington EH41 4NZ. Tel: 01620 823720 Fax:01620 825 112

Mount Stuart House & Gardens, Mount Stuart, Isle of Bute, PA20 9LR. Tel: 01700 503877 Fax: 01700 505 313

Paxton House, Paxton, Nr Berwick upon Tweed TD15 1SZ Tel: 01289 386291

Scone Palace, Perth PH2 6BD. Tel: 01738 552300 Fax:01738 552588 – *Vernis Martin, ivories, porcelain*

Thirlestane Castle, Lauder, Berwickshire TD2 6RU. Tel: 01578 722430 Fax 01578 722761

Traquair House, Innerleithen, Peebleshire EH44 6PW Tel:01896 830323

IRELAND

Bunratty Castle and Folk Park, Bunratty, Co. Clare. Tel: 00353 61 360 788 Fax:00353 61 361 020 – *Medieval*

Glin Castle, Glin. Tel: 00353 68 34173 Fax: 00353 68 34364

Malahide Castle, Malahide, Co. Dublin. Tel: 00353 1 846 2184 Fax:00353 1 846 2537 – *Collection of Irish portrait paintings mainly from the National Gallery*

Strokestown Park House & Gardens, Strokestown, Co. Roscommon. Tel: 00353 78 33013 Fax: 00353 78 33712

Properties Licensed for Civil Marriages

ENGLAND

BEDFORDSHIRE

Woburn Abbey, Woburn, MK43 OTP.
Tel: 01525 290666 Fax: 01525 290271

BUCKINGHAMSHIRE

Stowe Landscape Gardens, Buckingham, MK18 5EH.
Tel: 01280 822850 Fax: 01280 822437

Stowe (Stowe School), Stowe, MK18 5EH.
Tel: 01280 813650

Waddesdon Manor, The Dairy, Nr Aylesbury, HP18
OJW. Tel: 01296 651211 Fax: 01296 651142

CAMBRIDGESHIRE

Kimbolton Castle, Kimbolton School, Kimbolton,
PE18 OAE. Tel: 01480 860505 Fax: 01480 861763

CHESHIRE

Arley Hall, nr Great Budworth, Northwich, CW9 6NA.
Tel: 01565 777353

Bramall Hall, Bramhall Park, Stockport, SK7 3NX.
Tel: 0161 485 3708 Fax: 0161 486 6959

Capesthorne Hall, Siddington, Macclesfield, SK11 9JY.
Tel: 01625 861221 Fax: 01625 861619

Ness Botanic Gardens, Ness, Nesston, L64 4AY.
Tel: 0151 3530123 Fax: 0151 353 1004

Peckforton Castle, Stonehouse Lane, Peckforton,
Tarporley, CW6 9TN. Tel: 01829 260930
Fax: 01829 261230

Tabley House, Knutsford, WA16 OHB. Tel: 01565
750151 Fax: 01565 653230

Tatton Park, Knutsford, WA16 6QN. Tel: 01565 654822
Fax: 01625 534403

CORNWALL

Trevarno Estate & Gardens, Trevarno Manor, Helston
TR13 ORU. Tel: 01326 574274 Fax: 01326 574282

CUMBRIA

Muncaster Castle, Ravenglass CA18 1RQ.
Tel: 01229 717614 Fax: 01229 717010

DERBYSHIRE

Eyam Hall, Hope Valley S32 5QW Tel:01433 631976

Kedleston Hall and Park, Quarndon, Derby DE22 5JH.
Tel: 01332 842191 Fax: 01332 841972

Renishaw Hall, Nr Sheffield S31 9WB. Tel: 01246
432310

DEVON

Bickleigh Castle, Bickleigh, Tiverton EX16 8RP.
Tel: 01884 855363

Buckfast Abbey, Buckfastleigh, TQ11 OEE.
Tel: 01364 642519 Fax: 01364 643891

Kingston House, Staverton, Totnes TQ9 6AR.
Tel: 01803 762235 Fax: 01803 762444

Powderham Castle, Kenton, EX6 8JQ.
Tel: 01626 890243 Fax: 01626 890729

DORSET

Kingston Maurawd, Dorchester DT2 8PY Tel: 01305
215003

ESSEX

Layer Marney Tower, Nr Colchester, CO5 9US.
Tel: 01206 330784

GREATER MANCHESTER

Heaton Hall, Heaton Park, Prestwich, M25 2SW.
Tel: 0161 773 1231/236 5244 Fax: 0161 236 7369

HAMPSHIRE

Avington Park, Winchester, SO21 1DB.
Tel: 01962 779260 Fax: 01962 779864

Highclere Castle, Newbury RG20 9RN.
Tel: 01635 253210 Fax:01635 255315

Mottisfont Abbey Garden Mottisfont, Nr Romsey,
SO51 OLP. Tel: 01794 340757 Fax: 01794 341492

The Vyne, Vyne Road, Sherborne St John, Basingstoke
Tel:01256 881337

HEREFORD & WORCESTER

Avoncroft Museum of Buildings, Stoke Heath,
Bromsgrove, B60 4JR. Tel: 01527 831886 or 831363
Fax: 02527 876934

Eastnor Castle, nr Ledbury, Hereford, HR8 1RL.
Tel: 01531 633160 Fax: 01531 631776

Hopton Court, Cleobury Mortimer, Kidderminster, DY14
OHH. Tel: 01299 270734 Fax: 01299 271132

Worcester Cathedral, College Green, Worcester,
WR1 2LH. Tel: 01905 28854 Fax: 01905 611139

HERTFORDSHIRE

Hatfield House, Hatfield ,AL9 5NQ. Tel: 01707 262823
Fax: 01707 275719

Knebworth House, Knebworth. Tel: 01438 812661

KENT

Cobham Hall, Cobham, nr. Gravesend, DA12 3BL.
Tel: 01474 824319

Down House, Downe, BR6 7JT. Tel: 01689 859119

Finchcocks, Goudhurst, TN17 1HH. Tel: 01580 211702
Fax: 01580 211007

Gad's Hill Place, Gads Hill School, Higham, Rochester
ME3 7PA. Tel: 01474 822366 Fax: 01478 822977

Groombridge Place Gardens, Groombridge, TN3 9QG.
Tel: 01892 863999 Fax: 01892 863996

Mount Ephraim Gardens, Hernhill, nr Faversham,
ME13 9TX. Tel: 01227 751496 Fax: 01227 750940

Owl House, Lamberhurst Tel:01892 890230

Penshurst Place, Penshurst, Tunbridge Wells,
TN11 8DG. Tel: 01892 870307 Fax: 01892 870866

Tonbridge Castle, Tonbridge TN9 1BG.
Tel: 01732 770929 Fax: 01732 770449

LANCASHIRE

Rufford Old Hall, Rufford, Nr Ormskirk L40 1SG
Tel:01704 821254

LINCOLNSHIRE

Elsham Hall, Brigg DN20 0QZ Tel:01652 688698

LONDON

Burgh House, New End Square, Hampstead, NW3 1LT.
Tel: 020 7431 0144 Fax: 020 7435 8817

Chiswick House, Burlington Lane, Chiswick W4.
Tel: 020 8995 0508

Greenwich Observatory, Queens House, National
Maritime Museum, Romney Road, Greenwich, London
SE10 9NF. Tel: 020 8312 6565 Fax: 020 8312 6632

Ham House, Ham Street, Richmond Tel: 020 8940 1950

Orleans House Gallery, Riverside, Twickenham,
TW1 3DJ. Tel: 020 8892 0221 Fax: 020 8744 0501

Osterley Park, Jersey Road, Isleworth, TW7 4RB.
Tel: 020 8568 7714

St. John's Gate, St John's Lane, Clerkenwell,
EC1M 4DA. Tel: 020 7253 6644 Fax: 020 7336 0587

Syon Park, Brentford ,TW8 8JF. Tel: 020 8560 0881
Fax: 020 8568 0936

NORTHAMPTONSHIRE

Lamport Hall and Gardens, Northampton, NN6 9HD.
Tel: 01604 686272 Fax: 01604 686 224

NORTHUMBERLAND

Chillingham Castle, Chillingham, Alnwick, NE66 5NJ.
Tel: 01668 215359 Fax: 01668 215643

NOTTINGHAMSHIRE

Norwood Park, Southwell, NG25 0PF.
Tel/Fax: 01636 815649

OXFORDSHIRE

Ardington House, Wantage, OX12 8QA.
Tel: 01235 821566 Fax: 01235 821151

SHROPSHIRE

Burford House Gardens, Tenbury Wells, WR15 8HQ.
Tel: 01584 810777 Fax: 01584 810673

Shrewsbury Castle & Shropshire Regimental Museum,
Castle Street, Shrewsbury, SY1 2AT.
Tel: 01743 358516 Fax: 01743 358411

Walcot Hall, Nr Bishops Castle, Lydbury North,
SY7 8AZ. Tel: 0171-581 2782 Fax: 0171 589 0195

SOMERSET

Museum of Costume & Assembly Rooms, Bennett
Street, Bath Tel:01225 477789

STAFFORDSHIRE

Ford Green Hall, Ford Green Road, Smallthorne, Stoke-
on-Trent, ST6 1NG. Tel: 01782 233195
Fax: 01782 233 194

The Shugborough Estate, Milford, Stafford, ST17 0XB.
Tel: 01889 881388 Fax: 01889 881323

SUFFOLK

Somerleyton Hall, nr Lowestoft, NR32 5QQ.
Tel: 01502 730224 Fax: 01502 732143

SURREY

Clandon Park, West Clandon, Guildford, GU4 7RQ.
Tel: 01483 222482 Fax: 01483 223479

Great Fosters Hotel, Stroude Road, Egham TW20 9UR.
Tel: 0784 433822

Loseley Park, Estate Office, Guildford GU3 1HS.
Tel: 01483 304440 Fax: 01483 302036

SUSSEX

Anne of Cleves House, 52 Southover High Street,
Lewes, BN7 1JA. Tel: 01273 474610 FX 01273 486990

Bentley House & Gardens, Halland, Nr Lewes,
BN8 5AF. Tel: 01825 840573

Brickwall House and Gardens, Northiam, Rye,
TN31 6NL. Tel: 01797 253388 Fax: 01797 252567

Glynde Place, Glynde, nr Lewes, BN8 6SX.
Tel: 01273 858224 Fax: 01273 858224

Goodwood House, Goodwood, Chichester, PO18 0PX.
Tel: 01243 755048 Fax: 01243 755005

Herstmonceux Castle, International Study Centre,
Queens University, Hailsham BN27 1RN.
Tel: 01323 833816 Fax: 01323 834499

Royal Pavilion, Brighton, BN1 1EE. Tel: 01273 290900
Fax: 01273 292871

The Weald & Downland Open Air Museum,
Singleton, Nr Chichester Tel:01243 811348

Ardington House, Oxfordshire

WARWICKSHIRE

Ragley Hall, Alcester B49 5NJ. Tel: 01789 762090
Fax: 01789 764791

WEST MIDLANDS

Birmingham Botanical Gardens and Glasshouses,
Westbourne Road, Edgbaston, Birmingham B15 3TR.
Tel: 0121 454 1860 Fax: 0121 454 7835

Hagley Hall, nr Stourbridge DY9 9LG. Tel: 0562 882408

WILTSHIRE

Longleat, The Estate Office, Warminster BA12 7NW.
Tel: 01985 844400 Fax: 01985 844885

YORKSHIRE

Bolton Castle, Leyburn, DL8 4ET. Tel: 01969 623981
Fax:01969 623332

The Bar Convent, 17 Blossom Street, York, Y02 2AH.
Tel: 01904 643238 Fax: 01904 631792

Bolton Abbey Estate, Bolton Abbey, Skipton,
BD23 6EX. Tel: 01756 7110227 Fax: 01756 710535

Duncombe Park, Helmsley, York, YO62 5EB.
Tel: 01439 770213 Fax: 01439 771114

Harewood House and Bird Garden, Harewood, Leeds
LS17 9LQ. Tel: 0113 288 6331 Fax: 0113 288 6467

Newburgh Priory, Coxwold, YO6 4AS.
Tel: 01347 868435

Oakwell Hall, Birstall, WF19 9LG. Tel: 01924 326 240

Ripley Castle, Ripley HG3 3AY. Tel: 01423 770152
Fax: 01423 771745

Sewerby Hall and Gardens, Church Lane, Sewerby,
Bridlington YO15 1EA.
Tel: Estate Office: 01262 673 769 Hall :01262 677874

WALES

Dinefwr Park, Llandeilo Tel:01558 823902

Gwydir Castle, Llanrwst. Tel: 01492 641 687
Fax: 01492 641687

Portmerion Village, Portmerion, Gwyned Tel: 01766
770000

Tredegar House, Newport NP1 9YW. Tel: 01633 815880
Fax: 01633 815895

SCOTLAND

Braemar Castle, Braemar, AB35 5XR.
Tel/Fax: 013397 41219

Dalmeny House, Charisma, South Queensferry,
EH30 9TQ. Tel: 0131-331 1888 Fax: 0131 331 1788

Duff House Country House Gallery, Banff AB45 5SX.
Tel: 01261 818181 Fax: 01261 818900

Fasque, Fettercairn, Laurencekirk AB30 1DN Tel: 01561
340 202

Lennoxlove, Haddington, EH41 4NZ. Tel: 01620 823720
Fax: 01620 825 112

Paxton House & Gardens, Paxton, nr Berwick-upon-
Tweed, TD15 1SZ. Tel: 01289 386291

Rosslyn Chapel, Roslin EH25 9PU. Tel: 0131 448 2948

Scone Palace, Perth PH2 6BD. Tel: 01738 552300
Fax: 01738 552588

Traquair House, Innerleithen, EH44 6PW.
Tel: 01896 830323 Fax: 01896 830639

IRELAND

Antrim Castle Gardens, Antrim.
Tel: 01849 428000 Fax: 01849 460360

Powerscourt Gardens, Enniskerry, Co Wicklow
Tel:00353 204 6000

Strokestown Park House & Gardens, Strokestown, Co.
Roscommon. Tel: 00353 78 33013 Fax: 00353 78
33712

Properties offering Top Teas!

ENGLAND

BEDFORDSHIRE

Woburn Abbey, Woburn MK43 OTP. Tel: 01525 290666

BERKSHIRE

Basildon Park, Lower Basildon, Reading RG8 9NR. Tel: 0118 984 3040

Dorney Court, Windsor SL4 6QP. Tel: 01628 604638

Savill Garden, Crown Estate Office, Windsor Great Park, Windsor SL7 2HT. Tel: 01753 860222

Taplow Court, Berry Hill, Taplow Tel:01628 591215

CAMBRIDGESHIRE

Ely Cathedral, The Chapter House, The College, Ely CB7 4DL. Tel: 01353 667735

CHESHIRE

Arley Hall and Gardens, Nr Great Budworth, Northwich CW9 6NA. Tel: 01565 777353

Dunham Massey, Altrincham WA14 4SJ. Tel: 0161 9411025

Little Moreton Hall, Congleton CW12 4SD. Tel: 01260 272018

Ness Botanic Gardens, Ness, Nesston L64 4AY. Tel: 0151 3530123

Tabley House Collection, Tabley House, Knutsford WA16 OHB. Tel: 01565 750151

Tatton Park, Knutsford WA16 6QN. Tel: 01565 654822

CORNWALL

Burncoose Nurseries and Garden, Gwennap, Redruth TR16 6BJ. Tel: 01209 861112

Caerhays Castle, Gorran, St Austell PL26 6LY Tel: 01872 501310

Pencarrow Washway, Bodmin PL30 5AG. Tel: 01208 841449

Trevarno Estate & Gardens, Trevarno Manor, Helston TR13 ORU. Tel: 01326 574274

Lanhydrock, Bodmin PL30 5AD. Tel: 01208 73320

CUMBRIA

Dalemain, nr Penrith CA11 OHB. Tel: 017684 86450

Hutton-in-the-Forest, Skelton, Penrith CA1 9TH. Tel: 017684 84449

Muncaster Castle, Ravenglass CA18 1RQ. Tel: 01229 717614

DERBYSHIRE

Haddon Hall, Estate Office, Bakewell DE45 1LA. Tel: 01629 812855

Lea Gardens, Lea, Matlock DE4 5GH. Tel: 01629 534 380

Renishaw Hall, Nr Sheffield, S21 3WB. Tel: 01777 860755

DEVON

Bickleigh Castle, Bickleigh, Tiverton EX16 8RP. Tel: 01884 855363

Buckfast Abbey, Buckfastleigh TQ11 OEE. Tel: 01364 643891

Killerton House, Broadclyst, nr Exeter EX5 3LE. Tel: 01392 881345

Powderham Castle Kenton, Exeter EX6 8JQ. Tel: 01626 890243

Torre Abbey, The Kings Drive, Torquay TQ2 5JX. Tel: 01803 293593

DORSET

Athelhampton House & Gardens, Athelhampton, Dorchester DT2 7LG. Tel: 01305 848363

Compton Acres Gardens, Canford Cliffs, Poole BH13 7ES. Tel: 01202 700778

Deans Court Garden, Wimborne BH21 1EE.

Forde Abbey and Gardens, nr Chard TA20 4LU. Tel: 01460 220231

Kingston Lacy House, Wimborne BH21 4EA Tel:01202 883402

Kingston Maurawd, Dorchester DT2 8PY Tel: 01305 215003

Lulworth Castle, The Lulworth Estate, East Lulworth, Wareham BH20 5QS. Tel: 01929 400352

Parnham House, Parnham, Beaminster Tel:01308 863444

Purse Caundle Manor, Purse Caundle, nr Sherborne DT9 5DY. Tel: 01963 250400

Sherborne Castle, Sherborne DT9 3PY. Tel: 01935 813182

Wolfeton House, Dorchester. Tel: 01305 263500

COUNTY DURHAM

Raby Castle, Staindrop, Darlington DL2 3AH. Tel: 01833 660202

ESSEX

Hedingham Castle, Castle Hedingham, nr Halstead CO9 3DJ. Tel: 01787 460261

Ingatestone Hall, Ingatestone CM4 9NR. Tel: 01277 353010

Layer Marney Tower, Colchester CO5 9US. Tel: 01206 330784

GLOUCESTERSHIRE

Berkeley Castle, Berkeley GL13 9BQ. Tel: 01453 810332

Chavenage, Tetbury GL8 8XP. Tel: 01666 502329

Kiftsgate Court, Mickleton, nr Chipping Campden GL55 6LW. Tel: 01386 438777

Owlpen Manor, Uley, nr Dursley GL11 5BZ. Tel: 01453 860261

Painswick Rococo Garden, The Stables, Painswick House, Painswick GL6 6TH. Tel: 01452 813204

Sudeley Castle, Winchcombe GL54 5JD. Tel: 01242 602308

HAMPSHIRE

Avington Park, Winchester SO21 1DD. Tel: 01962 779260

Gilbert White's House & Garden and the Oates Museum, The Wakes, Selborne GU34 3JH. Tel: 01420 511275

Mottisfont Abbey Garden, Mottisfont, SO51 0LP. Tel: 011794 341220

Sir Harold Hillier Gardens, Ampfield, Romsey Tel:01794 368787

The Vyne, Vyne Road, Sherborne St John, Basingstoke Tel:01256 881337

HEREFORD & WORCESTER

Burton Court, Eardisland, Leominster HR6 9DN. Tel: 01544 388231

Eastnor Castle, Nr Ledbury, Hereford HR8 1RD. Tel: 01531 633160

Harvington Hall, Harvington, Kidderminister DY10 4LR. Tel: 01562 777846

Hergest Croft Gardens, Kington. Tel: 01544 230160

How Caple Court Gardens, How Caple HR1 4SX. Tel: 01989 740612

Kentchurch Court, Nr Pontrilias, Hereford. Tel: 01981 240228

HERTFORDSHIRE

Gardens of the Rose, Chiswell Green, St. Albans AL2 3NR. Tel: 01727 850461

Hatfield House, Hatfield AL9 5NQ. Tel: 01707 262823

Knebworth House, Knebworth. Tel: 01438 812661

KENT

Belmont, Throwley, Nr Faversham ME13 0HH. Tel: 01795 890202

Cobham Hall, Cobham, Nr Gravesend DA12 3BL. Tel: 01474 824319/823371

Doddington Place Gardens, Doddington, Sittingbourne ME9 0BB. Tel: 01795 886101

Gad's Hill Place, Gad's Hill School, Rochester ME3 7AA. Tel: 01474 822366

Goodnestone Park, Canterbury CT3 IPL Tel:01304 840107

Groombridge Place Gardens, Groombridge TN3 9QG. Tel: 01892 863999

Ladham House, Goudhurst. Tel: 01580 211203

Lullingstone Castle, Eynsford DA14 0JA. Tel: 01322 862114

Owl House Gardens, Lamberhurst Tel:01892 890230

Penshurst Place, Penshurst, Tunbridge Wells TN11 8DG. Tel: 01892 870307

Squerryes Court, Westerham TN16 1SJ. Tel: 01959 562345

LANCASHIRE

Gawthorpe Hall, Padiham, Nr Burnley BB12 8UA. Tel: 011282 770353

Stonyhurst College, Stonyhurst, Clitheroe BB7 9PZ Tel:01254826345

Towneley Hall Art Gallery, Burnley BD11 3RQ.Tel: 01282 424213

LEICESTERSHIRE

Kayes Garden Nursery, 1700 Melton Rd, Rearsby, Leicester LE7 4YR. Tel: 01664 424578

The Manor House, Donington-le-Heath.

Stanford Hall, Stanford Park, Lutterworth LE17 6DH. Tel: 01788 860250

LINCOLNSHIRE

Elsham Hall, Brigg DN20 0QZ Tel:01652 688698

LONDON

Burgh House, New End Square, Hampstead NW3 1LT. Tel: 020 7431 0144

Chelsea Physic Garden, 66 Royal Hospital Road, Chelsea SW3 4HS. Tel: 020 7352 5646

Museum of Garden History, Lambeth Palace Road, Lambeth SE1 7LB. Tel: 020 7261 1891

NORFOLK

Hoveton Hall Gardens, Wroxham NR11 7BB.

NORTHAMPTONSHIRE

Boughton House, Kettering Tel:01536 515731

Coton Manor Garden, Coton, Nr Guilsborough NN6 8RQ. Tel: 01604 740219

Lamport Hall and Gardens, Northampton NN6 9HD. Tel: 01604 686272

NOTTINGHAMSHIRE

Norwood Park, Norwood Park, Southwell, NG25 0PF.

OXFORDSHIRE

Kelmscott Manor, Kelmscott, Lechlade GL7 3HJ Tel:01367 252486

Mapledurham House, Nr Reading RG4 7TR Tel:01189 723350

Waterperry Gardens, Waterperry Horticultural Centre, Nr Wheatley OX9 1SZ. Tel: 01844 339226/339254

SHROPSHIRE

Burford House Gardens, Tenbury Wells WR15 8HQ. Tel: 01584 810777

Hodnet Hall Gardens, Nr Market Drayton TF9 3NN. Tel: 01630 685202

Ironbridge Gorge Museum, Ironbridge, Telford TF8 7AW. Tel: 01952 433522

Walcot Hall, Nr Bishops Castle, Lydbury North SY7 8AZ. Tel: 0171-581 2782

Wollerton Old Hall, Wollerton, Market Drayton TF9 3NA. Tel: 01630 685760

SOMERSET

Gaulden Manor, Tolland, Nr Taunton TA4 3PN. Tel: 01984 7213

Hestercombe House Gardens, Cheddon Fitzpaine, Taunton TA2 8LQ. Tel: 01823 413923

STAFFORDSHIRE

Dunwood Hall, Longsdon, Nr. Leek ST9 9AR. Tel: 01538 385071

Sandon Hall, Sandon ST18 0BZ. Tel: 01889 508004

SUFFOLK

Helmingham Hall Gardens, The Estate Office, Helmingham Hall, Stowmarket IP14 6EF. Tel: 01473 890363

Kentwell Hall. Long Melford, Nr. Sudbury CO10 9BA. Tel: 01787 310207

Somerleyton Hall, nr Lowestoft. Tel: 01502 730224

Wingfield Old College, Wingfield, Eye IP21 5RA. Tel: 01379 384888

SURREY

Clandon Park, West Clandon, Guildford GU4 7RQ. Tel: 01483 222482

Claremont Landscape Garden, Portsmouth Road, Esher KT10 9JG. Tel: 01372 469421

Guildford House Gallery, 155 High Street, Guildford GU1 3AJ Tel:01483 444740

Hatchlands Park, West Clandon, Guildford GU4 7RT. Tel: 01483 222482

Loseley House, Estate Office, Guildford GU3 1HS. Tel: 01483 304440

RHS Garden Wisley, Woking GU23 6QB. Tel: 01483 224234

SUSSEX

Bentley House & Gardens, Halland, Nr Lewes BN8 5AF. Tel: 01825 840573

Borde Hill Garden, Haywards Heath RH16 1XP. Tel: 01444 450326

Denmans Garden, Clock House, Denmans, Fontwell BN18 0SU. Tel: 01243 542808

Firle Place, Nr Lewes BN8 6LP. Tel: 01273 858188

Fishbourne Roman Palace, Salthill Road, Fishbourne, Chichester PO19 3QR. Tel: 01243 785859

Glynde Place, Nr Lewes BN8 6SX. Tel: 01273 858224

Goodwood House, Goodwood, Chichester PO18 0PX. Tel: 01243 755048

Hammerwood Park, East Grinstead RH19 3QE. Tel: 01342 850594

Leonardslee Gardens, Lower Beeding, Horsham RH13 6PP. Tel: 01403 891212

Merriments Gardens, Hawkhurst Road, Hurst Green TN19 7RA. Tel: 01580 860666

Michelham Priory, Upper Dicker, Hailsham BN27 3QS. Tel: 01323 844224 FX- 844030

Parham House and Gardens, Parham Park Ltd, Pulborough RH20 4HS. Tel: 01903 742021

Pashley Manor Gardens, Ticehurst, Wadhurst TN5 7HE. Tel: 01580 200692

Royal Pavilion, Brighton BN1 1EE. Tel: 01273 290900

Sheffield Park Garden, TN22 3QX Tel:01825 790231

The Weald & Downland Open Air Museum, Singleton, nr Chichester PO18 OEL. Tel: 01243 811363

West Dean Gardens, West Dean Estate, Nr Chichester PO18 0QZ. Tel: 01243 818210

WARWICKSHIRE

Arbury Hall, Nuneaton CV10 7PT. Tel: 01203 382804

Charlecote Park, Warwick CV35 9ER Tel:01789 470277

The Hiller Garden, Dunnington Heath Farm, Nr Alcester Tel:01789 490439

Lord Leycester Hospital, High Street, Warwick CV34 4BH. Tel: 01926 492797

WEST MIDLANDS

Baddesley Clinton Hall, B93 0DQ. Tel: 01564 783294

Castle Bromwich Hall, Chester Road, Castle Bromwich Tel:0121 7494100

WILTSHIRE

Longleat, The Estate Office, Warminster BA12 7NW. J Tel: 01985 844400

YORKSHIRE

Aske Hall, Aske, Rickmond DL10 5HJ. Tel: 01748 823222

The Bar Convent, 17 Blossom Street, York Y02 2AH. Tel: 01904 643238

Bolton Castle, Leyburn DL8 4ET. Tel: 01969 623981

Brodsworth Hall, Brodsworth. Tel: 01302 722598

Oakwell Hall, Birstall WF19 9LG. Tel: 01924 474926

Sewerby Hall and Gardens, Church Lane, Sewerby, Bridlington YO15 1EA. Tel: Estate Office: 01262 673 769

WALES

Colby Woodland Garden, Amroth, Narbeth SA67 8PP. Tel: 01558 822800/01834 811885

Dinefwr Park, Llandeilo SA19 6RT. Tel: 011558 823902

Picton Castle, Picton Castle Trust, Haverfordwest SA62 4AS. Tel: 01437 751326

Tredegar House, Newport, Newport NP1 9YW. Tel: 01633 815880

SCOTLAND

Cawdor Castle, Nairn, Inverness IV12 5RD. Tel: 01667 404615

Dalmeny House, Charisma, South Queensferry EH30 9TQ. Tel: 0131-331 1888

Manderston, Duns, Berwickshire TD11 3PP. Tel: 01361 882636

Paxton House, Paxton, Nr Berwick upon Tweed TD15 1SZ Tel: 01289 386291

IRELAND

Bantry House, Bantry, Co. Cork. Tel: 00353 2750047

Benvarden Garden, Dervock, Ballymoney, CO. Antrim. Tel: 012657 41331

Dublin Writer's Museum, 18 Parnell Square, Dublin 1. Tel: 00353 1 872 2077

Kylemore Abbey, Kylemore, Connemara. Tel: 0195 41146

Malahide Castle, Malahide, Co. Dublin. Tel: 00353 1 846 2184

Mount Usher Gardens, Ashford. Tel: 00353 404 40205 /40116

Newbridge House, Donabate, Co. Dubin. Tel: 00353 1 8436534

Powerscourt Gardens & Waterfall, Enniskerry, Co. Wicklow. Tel: 00353 1 204 6000

Seaforde Gardens, Seaforde, Downpatrick BT30 3PG. Tel: +441396 811225

Strokestown Park House & Gardens, Strokestown, Co. Roscommon. Tel: 00353 78 33013

Tullynally Castle, Castlepollard, Co. Westmeath. Tel: 00353 44 61159

WE CHANGED FOR THE BETTER!

STILL NATURAL MINERAL WATER

HILDON SPORT
The ultimate refreshment for leisure & sport.

HILDON SPORT
The ultimate refreshment for leisure & sport.

A HELPING HAND FOR YOUNG PEOPLE: THE HILDON FOUNDATION

The Hildon Foundation has been created to help young people realise their potential – wherever their ambitions lie. **For each bottle of Hildon Sport sold, a donation of 1 p will be made to the Foundation.** The intention is to raise at least £100,000 in the first year for budding musicians, sports students, disabled causes, science and technology schemes, and other deserving projects.

"Helping young people is the best possible foundation for the future."

David Gower OBE, patron.

To find out more about the Hildon Foundation, please write to
THE HILDON FOUNDATION, PO BOX 1, BROUGHTON SO20 8WP

Properties Open All Year

ENGLAND

BERKSHIRE

Dorney Court, Windsor SL4 6QP. Tel: 01628 604638 Fax: 01628 665772
The Savill Garden, Windsor Great Park, Tel: 01753 860222 Crown Property.
Windsor Castle, Windsor, SL4 1NJ Tel: 01753 868286

BUCKINGHAMSHIRE

Cliveden, Taplow, Maidenhead SL6 OJA. Tel: 01628 605069 Fax: 01628 669461
Stowe Landscape Garden, Buckingham, Buckinghamshire MK18 5EH Tel: 01280 822850

CAMBRIDGESHIRE

Ely Cathedral, The Chapter House, The College, Ely CB7 4DL.
Tel: 01353 667735 Fax: 01353 665658
King's College, Cambridge CB2 1ST. Tel: 01223 331212
Fax: 01223 331315
The Manor, Hemingford Grey PE18 9BN. Tel: 01480 463134
Fax: 01480 465026
Oliver Cromwell's House, 29 Mary Street, Ely CB7 4DF
Tel: 01353 665555 ext.294 Fax: 01353 668518

CHESHIRE

Adlington Hall, Macclesfield SK10 4LF. Tel: 01625 820875
Fax: 01625 828756
Bramall Hall, Bramhall, Stockport SK7 3NX Tel:0161 485 3706
Ness Botanic Gardens, Ness, Nesston L64 4AY.
Tel: 0151 3530123 Fax: 0151 353 1004
Norton Priory Museum, Tudor Road, Manor Park, Runcorn WA7 1SX. Tel: 01928 569895
Tatton Park, Knutsford WA16 6QN Tel:01625 534400

CORNWALL

Burncoose Nurseries & Garden, Gwennap, Redruth
TR16 6BJ Tel: 01209 861112
Trevarno Estate & Gardens, Trevarno Manor, Helston TR13 0RU. Tel: 01326 574274 Fax: 01326 574282

CUMBRIA

Hutton-In-The-Forest, Penrith Tel: 017684 84449
Muncaster Castle, Ravenglass CA18 1RQ. Tel: 01229 717614
Fax: 01229 717010. Gardens Only

DEVON

Buckfast Abbey, Buckfastleigh TQ11 OEE. Tel: 01364 642519
Fax: 01364 643891
Killerton House, Broadclyst, nr Exeter EX5 3LE. Tel: 01392 881345 Fax: 01392 883112. Gardens Only

DORSET

Athelhampton House & Gardens, Athelhampton, Dorchester
Tel: 01305 848363 Fax: 01305 848135
Christchurch Priory, Quay Road, Christchurch, BH23 1BU.
Tel: 01202 485804 Fax: 01202 488645
Forde Abbey, Chard Tel: 01460 220231
Lulworth Castle, The Lulworth Estate, East Lulworth, Wareham BH20 5QS. Tel: 01929 400352
Wolfeton House, Dorchester, DT2 9QN Tel:01305 263500 By Apointment

GLOUCESTERSHIRE

Barnsley House Garden, The Close, Barnsley,
Nr Cirencester GL7 5EE.
Frampton Court, Frampton-on-Severn
Gloucester GL2 7EU Tel: 01452 740267

HAMPSHIRE

Beaulieu, Brockenhurst, SO42 7ZN Tel: 01590 612345
Langley Boxwood Nursery, Rake, Nr. Liss, GU33 7JL
Tel: 01730 894467 Fax: 01730 894703
Gilbert White's House & Garden & The Oates Museum, 'The Wakes' Selborne, Nr Alton, GU34 3JH
Sir Harold Hillier Gardens and Arboretum, Ampfield, nr Romsey SO51 0QA. Tel: 01794 368787

HERTFORDSHIRE

Cathedral & Abbey Church Of St. Alban, St. Albans, Hertfordshire AL1 1BY.

HEREFORD & WORCESTER

Burford House Gardens, Tenbury Wells, WR15 8HQ.
Tel 01584 810777 Fax: 01584 810673
Dinmore Manor, nr Hereford HR4 8EE. Tel: 01432 830332
How Caple Court Gardens, How Caple HR1 4SX.
Tel: 01989 740612 Fax: 01989 740611
Hopton Court, Cleobury Mortimer DY14 OEF Tel:01299 270734
Worcester Cathedral, College Green, Worcester WR1 2LH.
Tel: 01905 28854 Fax: 01905 611139

KENT

Hall Place, Bourne Road, Bexley, DA5 1PQ.
Tel: 01322 526574 Fax: 10322 522921
Ladham House, Gouldhurst, Tel: 01580 212674
Leeds Castle, Maidstone. Tel: 01622 765400
Lullingstone Castle, Eynsford, Kent DA14 OJA.
Tel: 01322 862114
The New College Of Cobham, Cobham, Nr Gravesend, DA12 3BX Tel: 01474 812503
Owl House Gardens, Lamberhurst, Tel: 01892 890962
Pattyndenne Manor, Goudhurst TN17 2QU. Tel: 01580 211361
The Theatre Royal, 102 High Street, Chatham, ME4 4BY
Tel: 01634 831028
Tonbridge Castle, Tonbridge TN9 1BG. Tel: 01732 770929
Fax: 01732 770449

LANCASHIRE

Towneley Hall Art Gallery & Museums, Burnely, BB11 3RQ
Tel: 01282 424213

LINCOLNSHIRE

Elsham Hall, Brigg DN20 0QZ Tel:01652 688698

LONDON

Apsley House, The Wellington Museum, Hyde Park Corner W1 Tel:0171 499 5676
Buckingham Palace, The Queens Gallery, SW1A 1AA
Tel: 0171 839 1377
Burgh House, New End Square, Hampstead,
Tel: 0171 431 0144
College Of Arms, Queen Victoria Stret Tel: 0171 248 2762
Greenwich – Observatory, National Maritime Museum,
Romney Road, Greenwich SE10 9NF. Tel: 0181 858 4422
Kew Gardens, Royal Botanic Gardens, Kew, Richmond
Tel: 0181 940 1171
Orleans House Gallery, Riverside, Twickenham, TW1 3DJ.
Tel: 0181-892 0221 Fax: 0181 744 0501
Osterley Park, Jersey Road, Isleworth TW7 4RB. Tel: 0181 568 7714
Pitshanger Manor Museum, Percival House, Mattock Lane, Ealing W5 5EQ. Tel: 0181-567 1227 Fax: 0181-567 0595
Syon House, Brentford TW8 8JF. Tel: 0181 560 0881
St. John's Gate, St John's Lane, Clerkenwell EC1M 4DA.
Tel: 0171-253 6644 Fax: 0171 336 0587
Tower of London, Tower Hill Tel: 0171 709 0765
Wallace Collection, Hertford House, Manchester Square
Tel: 0171 935 0687 Fax: 0171 224 2155

NORFOLK

Mannington Hall, Saxthorpe, Norwich NR11 7BB. Tel: 01263 584175 Fax: 01263 761214
Norwich Castle Museum, Norwich NR1 3JU
Tel: 01603 223624
Walsingham Abbey Grounds, Walsingham, NR22 6BP.
Tel: 01328 820 259
Wolterton Park, Erpingham Tel: 01263 584175

NORTHAMPTONSHIRE

Castle Ashby House, Castle Ashby, Northampton NN7 1LQ.
Tel: 01604 696696 Fax: 01604 696516

NOTTINGHAMSHIRE

Norwood Park, Southwell, Nottingham NG25 OP
Tel: 01636 815649 Fax: 01636 815649

OXFORDSHIRE

Broughton Castle, Banbury, OX15 5EB Tel: 01295 262624
Rousham House, Rousham, Steeple Aston, OX6 3QX.
Tel: 01869 347110
University Of Oxford Botanic Gardens, Rose Lane, Oxford OX1 4AX.
Wallingford Castle Gardens, Castle Street, Wallingford
Tel: 01491 835373
Waterperry Gardens Ltd, Nr Wheatley, Oxfordshire
Tel: 01844 339216/254

SHROPSHIRE

Burford House Gardens, Tenbury Wells WR15 8HQ.
Tel: 01584 810777 Fax: 01584 810673
Ironbridge Gorge Museum, Ironbridge, Telford TF8 7AW.
Tel: 01952 433522 Fax: 01952 432204
Ludlow Castle, Castle Square, Ludlow
Tel – Custodian: 01584 873947.
Shipton Hall, Much Wenlock TE13 6JZ. Tel: 01746 785 225
Walcot Hall, Lydbury North, Nr. Bishops Castle, SY7 8AZ
Tel: 0171 581 2782

SOMERSET

Hestercombe Gardens, Cheddon Fitzpain, Taunton,
TA2 8LG Tel: 01823 423923

STAFFORDSHIRE

Ancient High House, Greengate Street, Stafford ST16 2HS Tel:01785 619619
Dunwood Hall, Longsdon, Nr. Leek ST9 9AR
Tel: 01538 385071
Ford Green Hall, Ford Green Road Smallthorne,
Stoke-on-Trent. Tel: 01782 233195
Sandon Hall, Sandon, Stafford Tel: 01889 508004
Stafford Castle, Newport Road, Stafford ST16 1DJ. Tel: 01785 257 698
Tamworth Castle, The Holloway, Tamworth B79 7LR. Tel: 01827 709626 Fax: 01827 709630

SUFFOLK

Christchurch Mansion, Christchurch Park, Ipswich
Tel: 01473 253246 Fax: 01473 281274
Gainsborough's House, 46 Gainsborough Street, Sudbury CO10 6EU Tel: 01787 372958 Fax: 01787 376991
Hengrave Hall, Bury St Edmunds Tel:01284 701561
Ipswich Museum, Ipswich IP1 3QH Tel: 01473 213761

SURREY

Claremont Landscape Garden, Portsmouth Road, Esher
Tel: 01372 467842
Guildford House Gallery, 155, High Street, Guildford GU1 3AJ.
Tel: 01483 444740 Fax: 01483 444742

Painshill Landscape Gardens, Portsmouth Road, Cobham KT11 1JE. Tel: 01932 868113 Fax: 01932 868001
RHS Garden Wisley, Woking GU23 6QB. Tel: 01483 224234

SUSSEX

Anne Of Cleves House, 52 Southover High Street, Lewes BN7 1JA. Tel: 01273 474610 Fax: 01273 486990
Borde Hill, Balcombe Road, Haywards Heath S16 1XP.
Tel: 01444 450326
Chichester Cathedral, West Street, Chichester PO19 1PX.
Tel: 01243 782595 Fax: 01243 536190
Lewes Castle, Barbican House, 169 High Street, Lewes
BN7 1YE. Tel: 01273 486290 Fax: 01273 486990
Pallant House, 9 North Pallant, Chichester PO19 1TJ
Tel: 01243 774557
Preston Manor, Preston Drove, Brighton BN1 6SD
Tel: 01273 290900 Fax: 01273 292871
Royal Botanic Gardens, Kew At Wakehurst Place, Ardingly, Nr Haywards Heath RH17 6TN Tel: 01444 894066
The Royal Pavilion, Brighton, East Sussex BN1 1EE
Tel: 01273 290900 Fax: 01273 292871
Saint Hill Manor, Sant Hill Road, East Grinstead
RH19 4JY Tel: 01342 326711
Sheffield Park Garden, TN22 3QX Tel:01825 790231
The Weald & Downland Open Air Museum, Singleton, Nr Chichester Tel:01243 811348

WARWICKSHIRE

Lord Leycester Hospital, High Street, Warwick, CV34 4BH.
The Hiller Garden, Dunnington Heath Farm, Nr Alcester Tel:01789 490439
Shakespeare Birthplace Trust, 38/39 Henley Street, Stratford upon Avon, Tel: 01789 204016
Warwick Castle, Warwick, CV34 4QU. Tel: 01976 406600

WEST MIDLANDS

Birmingham Botanical Gardens & Glasshouses, Westbourne Road, Edgbaston, Birmingham, B15 3TR. Tel: 0121 454 1860
Fax: 0121 454 7835
Soho House, Soho Avenue, Handsworth, Birmingham
B18 5LB Tel: 0121 554 9122

WILTSHIRE

Longleat, The Estate Office, Warminster BA12 7NW.
Tel: 01985 844400 Fax: 01985 844885
Luckington Court, Luckington, Chippenham SN14 6PQ Tel:01666 840205
Stourhead, Stourton, Mere BA12 6QH Tel: 01747 841152

YORKSHIRE

Aske Hall, Aske, Richmond DL10 5HJ. Tel: 01748 850391
Bolton Abbey, Skipton, North Yorkshire BD23 6EX.
Tel: 01756 710227 Fax: 01756 710535
Harlow Carr Botanical Gardens, Crag Lane, Harrogate HG3 1QB.
Tel: 01423 565418 Fax: 01423 530663
Oakwell Hall, Nutter Lane, Birstall, Batley
Tel: 01924 326240
Red House, Oxford Road, Gomersal, Cleckheaton
Tel: 01274 335100
Sewerby Hall & Gardens, Church Lane, Sewerby, Bridlington, YO15 1EA. Tel: 01262 673769
Skipton Castle, Skipton, North Yorkshire BD23 1AQ.
Tel: 01756 792442 Fax: 01756 796100
Thorp Perrow Arboretum, Bedale DL8 2PR Tel:01677 425 32

IRELAND

Antrim Castle Gardens, Antrim Tel: 01849 428000
Birr Castle, Birr Tel:00353 50920336
Dublin Writers Museum, 18 Parnell Square, Dublin 1.
Tel: 00 353 1 872 2077 Fax: 00 353 1 872 2231
Kylemore Abbey, Conemara, Co. Galway.
Tel: 00 353 95 41146 Fax: 00 353 95 41123
Malahide Castle, Malahide, Co. Dublin.
Tel: 00 353 1 846 2184 Fax: 00 353 1 846 2537
Newbridge House, Donabate, Co Dublin.
Tel: 00 353 1 8436534 Fax: 00 353 1 8462537
Powerscourt Gardens & Waterfall, Enniskerry, Co. Wicklow. Tel: 00 353 204 6000
Fax: 00 353 28 63561

SCOTLAND

Ayton Castle, Eyemouth, Berwickshire TD14 5RD.
Tel: 018907 81212 Fax: 018907 81550
Blairquhan Castle, Straiton, Maybole KA19 7LZ Tel:016557 70239
Dalmeny House, South Queensferry, Edinburgh EH30 9TQ Tel: 0131 331 1888 Fax: 0131 331 1788
The Doune of Rothiemurchus, Rothiemurchus Estate Office, Aviemore PH22 1QH.
Tel: 01479 810858 Fax: 01479 811778
Duff House Country House Gallery, Banff AB45 5SX. Tel: 01261 818181 Fax: 01261 818900
Mirehouse, Keswick CA12 4QE Tel:01768 772287
Palace Of Holyroodhouse, Edinburgh, EH8 8DY
Tel: 0131 556 7371.

WALES

Bodelwyddan Castle, Bodelwyddan, St Asaph, Bodelwyddan LL18 5YA. Tel: 01745 584060 Fax: 01745 584563
Penhow Castle, Nr Newport NP6 3AD. Tel: 01633 400800 fax: 01633 400990
Portmerion Village, Portmerion, Gwyned Tel: 01766 770000
St. Davids Cathedral, The Deanery, The Close, St. Davids, Pembrokeshire. Tel: 01437 720202 Fax: 01437 721 885

A foundation for the future

The Hildon Foundation will provide a helping hand for young people from all walks of life to realise their full potential

Since its launch in 1999, Hildon Sport has become the mineral water of choice for young, sporty, dynamic and health-orientated individuals. At the beginning of the year 2000 Hildon Sport looked at new ways of enhancing the bond that existed between itself and those who enjoy it. The conclusion was that a charitable foundation would be the ideal vehicle and it now gives Hildon Sport great pleasure to announce the creation of The Hildon Foundation.

For each bottle of Hildon Sport sold, a donation of 1p will be made to the Foundation, with the intention of raising at least £100,000 in the first year alone. Any shortfall will be met by Hildon Limited and, unlike many charities, 100 per cent of the money raised will go directly to the Foundation as all of the administrative costs will be met by Hildon Limited itself.

The beneficiaries of the Foundation will be needy young people – both individuals and youth projects. There will be no 'preferred' cause, with applications welcome from all areas: budding musicians, sports students needing funds to continue training, disabled causes, science and technology projects; deserving cases from all walks of life will be considered by the Foundation.

It's important that the Foundation has a 'face' and a short list of suitable personalities was drawn up for the role of patron – the role requires someone who possesses the qualities that embody the Foundation and what it hopes to achieve; someone who can relate to the needs of the children involved and has demonstrated the drive to succeed in their own life. It's important, also, to note that

Courtesy of Retna

the patron will receive no financial rewards for his or her time and efforts on behalf of the Hildon Foundation.

We're thrilled that the former English cricket captain **David Gower OBE** has agreed to be our first patron. Since retiring from professional cricket, David has become an accomplished broadcaster on radio and TV, and a witty, interesting motivational and after dinner speaker. A keen sportsman in his spare time – he is a talented tennis player and skier on snow and water – David is the ideal figure to encourage youngsters, wherever their individual talents may lie.

As well as supporting and helping to communicate the concept, David and his successors will hold key roles in deciding who the first beneficiaries should be. He will have a junior counterpart, who will also reflect the aims of the Foundation, and the two will hold their positions for one year, from June 2000.

The first awards ceremony will take place in June 2001 when David will present the recipients with the first year's funds. Handing over the reins to his successor, David will remain available to provide valuable advice as the Hildon Foundation enters its second year.

Hildon Sport – creating a better future for the next generation.

Properties with Conference Facilities

ENGLAND

BEDFORDSHIRE

Woburn Abbey, Woburn MK43 OTP. Tel: 01525 290666 Fax: 01525 290271

BERKSHIRE

Dorney Court, Windsor SL4 6QP. Tel: 01628 604638 Fax: 01628 665772

Eton College, The Visits Office, WIndsor SL4 6DW. Tel: 01753 671177 Fax: 01753 671265

Highclere Castle, Nr Newbury, RG20 9RN. Tel: 01635 253210 Fax: 01635 255315

BUCKINGHAMSHIRE

Stowe Stowe School, Stowe MK18 5EH. Tel: 01280 813650

Waddesdon Manor, The Dairy, Nr Aylesbury HP18 OJW. Tel: 01296 651211 Fax: 01296 651142

CAMBRIDGESHIRE

Kimbolton Castle, Kimbolton School, Kimbolton PE18 OAE. Tel: 01480 860505 Fax: 01480 861763

King's College, Cambridge CB2 1ST. Tel: 01223 331212 Fax: 01223 331315

CHESHIRE

Adlington Hall, Macclesfield SK10 4LF. Tel: 01625 820875 Fax: 01625 828756

Arley Hall, nr Great Budworth, Northwich CW9 6NA. Tel: 01565 777353

Bramall Hall, Bramhall Park, Stockport SK7 3NX. Tel: 0161 485 3708 Fax: 0161 486 6959

Capesthorne Hall, Siddington, Macclesfield SK11 9JY. Tel: 01625 861221 Fax: 01625 861619

Ness Botanic Gardens, Ness, Nesston L64 4AY. Tel: 0151 3530123 Fax: 0151 353 1004

Peckforton Castle, Stonehouse Lane, Nr. Taporley CW6 9TN. Tel: 01829 260930 Fax: 01829 261230

Tabley House Stately Home, Tabley House, Knutsford WA16 OHB. Tel: 01565 750151 Fax: 01565 653230

Tatton Park, Knutsford, Cheshire, WA16 6QN. Tel: 01625 534400 fax: 01625 534402

CUMBRIA

Dalemain, nr Penrith CA11 OHB. Tel: 017684 86450 Fax: 017684 86223

Muncaster Castle, Ravenglass CA18 1RQ. Tel: 01229 717614 Fax: 01229 717010

DERBYSHIRE

Chatsworth, Bakewell DE45 1PP. Tel: 01246 582204 Fax: 01246 583536

Renishaw Hall, Nr Sheffield S21 3WB Tel:01246 632310

DEVON

Bickleigh Castle, Bickleigh, Tiverton EX16 8RP. Tel: 01884 855363

Buckfast Abbey, Buckfastleigh, TQ11 OEE. Tel: 01364 642519 Fax: 01364 643891

Hartland Abbey, Hartland, Nr Bideford EX39 6DT. Tel: 01237 441 264/234 Fax: 01884 861134

Kingston House, Staverton, Totnes TQ9 6AR. Tel: 01803 762235 Fax: 01803 762444

Powderham Castle, Kenton, Exeter EX6 8JQ. Tel: 01626 890243 Fax: 01626 890729

Tiverton Castle, Tiverton EX16 6RP. Tel/Fax: 01884 253200

Torre Abbey, The Kings Drive, Torquay TQ2 5JX. Tel: 01803 293593 Fax: 01803 215948

Ugbrooke House, Chudleigh TQ13 OAD. Tel: 01626 852179 Fax: 01626 853322

DORSET

Athelhampton House & Gardens, Athelhampton, Dorchester DT2 7LG. Tel: 01305 848363 Fax: 01305 848135

Forde Abbey, Chard, TA20 4LU. Tel: 01460 221290 Fax: 01460 220296

Kingston Maurawd, Dorchester DT2 8PY Tel: 01305 215003

Lulworth Castle, The Lulworth Estate, East Lulworth,

Highclere Castle, Berkshire

Wareham BH20 5QS. Tel: 01929 400352

Parnham House, Parnham, Beaminster DT8 3NA. Tel: 01308 862204 Fax: 01308 863444

Sherborne Castle, Sherborne DT9 3PY. Tel: 01935 813182 Fax: 01935 816727

Wolfeton House, Dorchester, DT2 9QN Tel:01305 263500

COUNTY DURHAM

Auckland Castle, Bishop Auckland DL14 7NR. Tel: 01388 601627 Fax: 01388 609323

ESSEX

Gosfield Hall, Halstead, CO9 1SF. Tel: 01787 472914 Fax: 01787 479551

Hylands House, Park & Gardens, Writtle, Chelmsford CM1 3HW. Tel: 01245 606812

Layer Marney Tower, Nr Colchester CO5 9US. Tel: 01206 330784

GLOUCESTERSHIRE

Chavenage, Tetbury GL8 8XP. Tel: 01666 502329 Fax: 01453 836778

Owlpen Manor, Owlpen, nr Uley GL11 5BZ. Tel: 01453 860261 Fax: 01453 860819

Sudeley Castle, Winchcombe GL54 5JD. Tel: 01242 602308

HAMPSHIRE

Avington Park, Winchester SO21 1DB. Tel: 01962 779260 Fax: 01962 779864

Beaulieu, Brockenhurst, SO42 7ZN. Tel: 01590 612345 Fax: 01590 612624

Gilbert White's House & Garden and the Oates Museum, The Wakes, Selborne GU34 3JH. Tel: 01420 511275

Mottisfont Abbey Garden, Mottisfont, Nr Romsey SO51 OLP. Tel: 01794 340757 Fax: 01794 341492

St Agatha's Church, 9 East Street, Fareham PO16 OBW. Tel: 01329 230330 Fax: 01329 230330

Sir Harold Hillier Gardens and Arboretum, Ampfield, nr Romsey SO51 0QA. Tel: 01794 368787

HEREFORD & WORCESTER

Avoncroft, Stoke Heath, Bromsgrove, B60 4JR. Tel 01527 831363 Fax: 01527 876934

Burton Court, Eardisland, Leominster HR6 9DN. Tel: 01544 388231

Dinmore Manor, nr Hereford HR4 8EE. Tel: 01432 830332

Eastnor Castle, nr Ledbury, Hereford HR8 1RL. Tel: 01531 633160 Fax: 01531 631776

Harvington Hall, Harvington, Kidderminister DY10 4LR. Tel: 01562 777846 Fax: 01562 777190

Hopton Court, Cleobury Mortimer, Kidderminster DY14 OHH. Tel: 01299 270734

Worcester Cathedral, Worcester WR1 2LA Tel: 01905 28854

HERTFORDSHIRE

The Gardens of the Rose, Chiswell Green, St. Albans AL2 3NR. Tel: 01727 850461 Fax: 01727 850360

Hatfield House, Hatfield AL9 5NQ. Tel: 01707 262823 Fax: 01707 275719

Knebworth House, Knebworth. Tel: 01438 812661

KENT

Cobham Hall, Cobham, nr. Gravesend DA12 3BL. Tel: 01474 824319

Finchcocks, Goudhurst TN17 1HH. Tel: 01580 211702 Fax: 01580 211007

Hever Castle & Gardens, Hever, nr Edenbridge TN8 7NG. Tel: 01732 865224 Fax: 01732 866796

Ladham House, Goudhurst. Tel: 01580 211203 Fax: 01580 212596

Leeds Castle, Maidstone ME17 1PL. Tel: 01622 765400 Fax: 735616

Mount Ephraim Gardens, Hernhill, nr Faversham ME13 7TX. Tel: 01227 751496 Fax: 01227 750940

Penshurst Place, Penshurst, Tunbridge Wells TN11 8DG. Tel: 01892 870307 Fax: 01892 870866

Riverhill House Gardens, Riverhill, Sevenoaks TN15 ORR. Tel: 01732 458802/452557

Squerryes Court, Westerham TN16 1SJ. Tel: 01959 562345/563118 Fax: 01959 565949

LANCASHIRE

Gawthorpe Hall, Padiham, Nr Burnley BB12 8UA Tel:01282 771004

Towneley Hall, Burnley, BB11 3RQ. Tel: 01282 424213 Fax: 01282 436138

LEICESTERSHIRE

Belvoir Castle, Nr Grantham, NG32 1PD. Tel: 01476 870262

Stanford Hall, Stanford Park, Lutterworth LE17 6DH. Tel: 01788 860250 Fax: 01788 860870

LINCOLNSHIRE

Elsham Hall, Brigg DN20 0QZ Tel:01652 688698

LONDON

Banqueting House, Whitehall Palace. Tel 020 7930 4179

Chelsea Physic Garden, 66 Royal Hospital Road, Chelsea SW3 4HS. Tel: 020 7352 5646 Fax: 020 7376 3910

Greenwich Observatory, Queens House, National Maritime Museum, Romney Road, Greenwich SE10 9NF. Tel: 020 8312 6565 Fax: 020 8312 6632

Kenwood House, Hampstead. Tel: 0181 348 1286

Museum of Garden History, Lambeth Palace Road, SE1 7LB. Tel: 020 7401 8865 Fax: 020 7401 8869

Orleans House Gallery, Riverside, Twickenham, TW1 3DJ.

Tel: 020 8892 0221 Fax: 020 8744 0501

Pitshanger Manor & Gallery, Mattock Lane, Ealing, W5 5EQ. Tel: 020 8567 1227 Fax: 020 8567 0595

St. John's Gate, Clerkenwell, EC1M 4DA. Tel: 020 7253 6644 Fax: 020 7336 0587

Strawberry Hill House, Waldegrave Road, Strawberry Hill, Twickenham. Tel: 020 8240 4114 Fax: 020 8255 6174

Syon Park, Syon House & Gardens, Brentford, TW8 8JF. Tel: 020 8560 0883 Fax: 020 8568 0936

NORFOLK

Mannington Hall, Norwich Tel:01263 584175

Wolterton Park, Erpingham NR11 7BB. Tel: 01263 584175 Fax: 01263 761214

NORTHAMPTONSHIRE

Cottesbrooke Hall, Nr Northampton NN6 8PF Tel:01604 505808

Holdenby House Gardens & Falconry Centre, Holdenby, Northampton NN6 8DJ. Tel: 01604 770074 Fax: 01604 770962

Lamport Hall and Gardens, Northampton NN6 9HD. Tel: 01604 686272 Fax: 01604 686 224

NORTHUMBERLAND

Alnwick Castle, Estate Office, Alnwick NE66 1NQ. Tel: 01665 510777 Fax: 01665 510876

Chillingham Castle, Chillingham, Alnwick NE66 5NJ. Tel: 01668 215359 Fax: 01668 215643

NOTTINGHAMSHIRE

Norwood Park, Southwell NG25 0PF. Tel: 01636 815649

Papplewick Hall, Nr Nottingham, NG15 8FE. Tel: 0115 963 3491 Fax: 0115 964 2767

OXFORDSHIRE

Ardington House, Wantage OX12 8QA. Tel: 01235 821566 Fax: 01235 821151

Blenheim Palace, Woodstock, OX20 1PX. Tel: 01993 811325 Fax: 01993 813527

Ditchley Park, Enstone, Chipping Norton OX7 4ER Tel:01608 677346

Fawley Court - Marian Fathers Historic House & Museum Marlow Road, Henley-On-Thames RG9 3AE. Tel: 01491 574917 Fax: 01491 411587

Kelmscott Manor, Kelmscott, nr Lechlade GL7 3HJ. Tel: 01367 252486 Fax: 01367 253 754

SHROPSHIRE

Burford House Gardens, Tenbury Wells, Worcestershire WR15 8HQ. Tel: 01584 810777 Fax: 01584 810673

Hawkstone Historic Park & Follies, Weston-under-Redcastle, Shrewsbury SY4 5UY. Tel: 01939 200611 Fax: 01939 200 311

Ironbridge Gorge Museum, Ironbridge, Telford TF8 7AW. Tel: 01952 433522 Fax: 01952 432204

Walcot Hall, Nr Bishops Castle, Lydbury North SY7 8AZ. Tel: 0171-581 2782 Fax: 0171 589 0195

SOMERSET

Maunsel House, North Newton, nr Bridgwater TA7 0SU. Tel: 01278 663413/661076

Museum of Costume & Assembly Rooms, Bennett Street, Bath Tel:01225 477789

The Bishop's Palace, Wells BA5 2PD. Tel: 01749 678691

STAFFORDSHIRE

Sandon Hall, Sandon ST18 0BZ. Tel: 01889 508004 Fax: 01889 508586

The Shugborough Estate, Milford, Stafford ST17 0XB. Tel: 01889 881388 Fax: 01889 881323

SUFFOLK

Hengrave Hall Centre, Hengrave Hall, Bury St Edmunds IP28 6LZ. Tel: 01284 701561 Fax: 01284 702950

Haughley Park, Nr Stowmarket IP14 3JY Tel:01359 240701

Kentwell Hall, Long Melford, nr. Sudbury CO10 9BA. Tel: 01787 310207 Fax: 01787 379318

Otley Hall, Otley, nr Ipswich IP6 9PA. Tel: 01473 890264 Fax: 01473 890803

Somerleyton Hall, nr Lowestoft NR32 5QQ. Tel: 01502 730224 Fax: 01502 732143

Wingfield Old College & Gardens, Wingfield, Nr Stradbroke IP21 5RA. Tel: 01379 384888 Fax: 01379 384034

SURREY

Clandon Park, West Clandon, Guildford GU4 7RQ.

Tel: 01483 222482 Fax: 01483 223479

Farnham Castle, Farnham GU7 0AG. Tel: 01252 721194 Fax: 01252 711283

Great Fosters Hotel, Stroude Road, Egham TW20 9UR. Tel: 0784 433822

Guildford House Gallery, 155 High Street, Guildford GU1 3AJ Tel:01483 444740

Loseley Park, Estate Office, Guildford GU3 1HS. Tel: 01483 304440 Fax: 01483 302036

Painshill Landscape Garden, Portsmouth Road, Cobham KT11 1JE. Tel: 01932 868113 Fax: 01932 868001

SUSSEX

Borde Hill Garden, Balcombe Road, Haywards Heath, RH16 1XP. Tel: 01444 450326 Fax: 01444 440427

Brickwall House and Gardens, Northiam, Rye TN31 6NL. Tel: 01797 253388 Fax: 01797 252567

Chichester Cathedral, Cathedral Cloisters, West Street, Chichester PO19 1PX. Tel: 01243 782595 Fax: 01243 536190

Firle Place, Nr Lewes BN8 6LP. Tel: 01273 858188

Goodwood House, Goodwood, Chichester PO18 0PX. Tel: 01243 755048 Fax: 01243 755005

Herstmonceux Castle, International Study Centre, Queens University, Hailsham BN27 1RN. Tel: 01323 833816 Fax: 01323 834499

Pallant House, 9 North Pallant, Chichester PO19 1TY. Tel: 01243 774557

Preston Manor, Preston Drove, Brighton BN1 6SD. Tel: 01273 292770 Fax: 01273 292871

Royal Pavilion, Brighton, East Sussex BN1 1EE. Tel: 01273 290900 Fax: 01273 292871

Saint Hill Manor, Saint hill Road, East Grinstead, RH19 4JY. Tel: 01342 325711

The Weald & Downland Open Air Museum, Singleton, Nr Chichester Tel:01243 811348

West Dean Gardens, West Dean Estate, nr Chichester PO18 0QZ. Tel: 01243 818210 Fax: 01243 811342

WARWICKSHIRE

Arbury Hall, Nuneaton CV10 7PT. Tel: 01203 382804 Fax: 01203 641147

Lord Leycester Hospital, High Street, Warwick CV34 4BH. Tel: 01926 491422 Fax: 01926 491 422

Ragley Hall, Alcester B49 5NJ. Tel: 01789 762090 Fax: 01789 764791

Warwick Castle, Warwick CV34 4QU. Tel: 01926 406600 Fax: 01926 401692

WEST MIDLANDS

Birmingham Botanical Gardens and Glasshouses, Westbourne Road, Edgbaston, Birmingham B15 3TR. Tel: 0121 454 1860 Fax: 0121 454 7835

Hagley Hall, nr Stourbridge DY9 9LG. Tel: 0562 882408

WILTSHIRE

Longleat, The Estate Office, Warminster BA12 7NW. Tel: 01985 844400 Fax: 01985 844885

Wilton House, Wilton, Salisbury SP2 0BJ. Tel: 01722 746720 Fax: 01722 744447

YORKSHIRE

Aske Hall, Aske, Richmond DL10 5HJ. Tel: 01748 850391 Fax: 01748 823252

The Bar Convent, 17 Blossom Street, York YO2 2AH. Tel: 01904 643238 Fax: 01904 631792

Bolton Abbey Estate, Bolton Abbey, Skipton BD23 6EX. Tel: 01756 7110227 Fax: 01756 710535

Bolton Castle, Leyburn, DL8 4ET. Tel: 01969 623981. Fax: 01969 623332

Duncombe Park, Helmsley, York YO62 5EB. Tel: 01439 770213 Fax: 01439 771114

Elsham Hall Country and Wildlife Park, The Estate Office, Brigg DN20 0QZ. Tel: 01652 688698 Fax: 01652 688240

Harewood House and Bird Garden, The Estate Office, Harewood, Leeds LS17 9LQ. Tel: 0113 288 6331 Fax: 0113 288 6467

Hovingham Hall, Hovingham, York YO6 4LU. Tel: 01653 628206 Fax: 01653 628668

Ripley Castle, Ripley HG3 3AY. Tel: 01423 770152 Fax: 01423 771745

Sewerby Hall and Gardens, Church Lane, Sewerby, Bridlington YO15 1EA. Tel: Estate Office: 1262 673 769 Hall :01262 677874

WALES

Cresselly, Cresselly, Kilgetty SA68 0SP. Tel: 01646 651992

Dinefwr Park, Llandeilo SA19 6RT. Tel: 01558 823902 Fax: 01558 822036

Picton Castle, Picton Castle Trust, Haverfordwest SA62 4AS. Tel: 01437 751326

Portmerion Village, Portmerion, Gwyned Tel: 01766 770000

Tredegar House, Newport NP1 9YW. Tel: 01633 815880 Fax: 01633 815895

SCOTLAND

Ayton Castle, Estate Office, Eyemouth TD14 5RD. Tel: 0189 07 81212 Fax: 018907 81550

Blairquhan Castle and Gardens, Straiton,, Maybole KA19 7LZ. Tel: 016557 70239 Fax: 016557 70278

Bowhill House & Country Park, Bowhill, nr Selkirk TD7 5ET. Tel: 01750 22204 Fax: 01750 22204

Dalmeny House, Charisma, South Queensferry EH30 9TQ. Tel: 0131-331 1888 Fax: 0131 331 1788

Doune of Rothiemurchus, By Aviemore, Inverness-shire, PH22 1QH. Tel: 01479 812345 Fax: 01479 811778

Drumlanrig Castle, Thornhill, Dumfrieshire DG3 4AQ Tel: 01848 330248

Drummond Castle Gardens, Muthill, Crieff PH5 2AA. Tel: 01764 681257/433 Fax: 01764 681 550

Duff House Country House Gallery, Banff AB45 5SX. Tel: 01261 818181 Fax: 01261 818900

Dunrobin Castle, Golspie, Sutherland KW10 6SF. Tel: 01408 633177 Fax: 01408 634081

Lennoxlove House, Haddington, East Lothian, EH41 4NZ. Tel: 01620 823720 Fax: 01620 825112

Manderston, Duns, Berwickshire TD11 3PP. Tel: 01361 883450 Fax: 01361 882010

Mount Stuart House, Isle of Bute PA20 9LR Tel:01700 503877

Paxton House & Gardens, Paxton, nr Berwick-upon-Tweed TD15 1SZ. Tel: 01289 386291

Scone Palace, Scone, Perth PH2 6BD Tel:01738 552300

Traquair House, Innerleithen EH44 6PW. Tel: 01896 830323 Fax: 01896 830639

IRELAND

Antrim Castle Gardensm, Antrim. Tel: 01849 428000 Fax: 01849 460360

Bantry Housem, Bantry, Co. Cork. Tel: 00353 2 750 047 Fax: 00353 2 750 795

Dublin Writer's Museum, 18 Parnell Square, Dublin 1. Tel: 00353 1 872 2077 Fax: 00353 1 872 2231

Glin Castlem, Glin. Tel: 00353 68 34173 Fax: 00353 68 34364

Newman House, 85/86 St. Stephens Green, Dublin 2. Tel: +353 7067422 Fax: +353 7067211

Powerscourt Gardens, Enniskerry, Co Wicklow Tel:00353 204 6000

Shannon Heritage, Bunratty Castle & Folk Park, Bunratty, Co. Clare, Ireland. Tel 00 353 61 360788 Fax: 00 353 61 361020

Strokestown Park House & Gardens, Strokestown, Co. Roscommon. Tel: 00353 78 33013 Fax: 00353 78 33712

Tullynally Castle, Castlepollard, Co. Westmeath. Tel: 00353 44 61159/ 61289 Fax: 00353 44 61856

Properties Offering Accommodation

ENGLAND

BERKSHIRE

Swallowfield Park, Swallowfield, RG7 1TG. Tel: 01734 883815
Welford Park, Newbury RG20 8HU. Tel: 01488 608203 Fax: 01488 60885

CAMBRIDGESHIRE

The Manor, Hemingford Grey PE18 9BN. Tel: 01480 463134 Fax: 01480 465026

CHESHIRE

Adlington Hall, Macclesfield SK10 4LF. Tel: 01625 820875 Fax: 01625 828756

CORNWALL

Tregrehan, Par, PL24 25J Tel: 01726 814 389/812 438.
Accommodation: Self-catering cottages available

CUMBRIA

Acorn Bank Garden & Watermill, Temple Sowerby, Nr Penrith Tel:017683 61893
Castletown House, Rockcliffe, Carlisle CA6 4BN. Tel: 01228 74792 Fax: 01228 74464
Dalemain, Nr. Penrith, CA11 0HB Tel: 017684 86450
Accommodation: B&B, Parkhouse Farm, Dalemain. Tel: 017684 86212

DEVON

Buckfast Abbey, Buckfastleigh TQ11 OEE
Tel: 01364 642519, Fax: 01364 643891
Yarde, Marlborough, Nr Salcombe TQ7 3BY
Tel: 01548 842367

DORSET

Wolfeton House, Dorchester, DT2 9QN Tel:01305 263500 By Apointment

ESSEX

Gosfield Hall, Halstead, CO9 1SF Tel: 01787 472 914

GLOUCESTERSHIRE

Frampton Court, Frampton-on-Severn GL2 7EU. Tel: Home 01452 740 267
Owlpen Manor, Uley, nr Dursley GL11 5BZ
Tel: 01453 860261 Accommodation: Nine period cottages available, including listed buildings.
Sudeley Castle and Gardens, Winchcombe, GL54 5JD
Tel: 01242 603197/602308 Accommodation: 14 romantic Cotswold Cottages on Castle Estate. Private guided tours of Castle Apartments and Gardens by prior arrangement. Schools educational pack available.

HAMPSHIRE

Gilbert White's House & Garden and the Oates Museum, The Wakes, Selborne GU34 3JH. Tel: 01420 511275
Hall Farm House, Bentworth, Alton GU34 5JU. Tel: 01420 564010
Houghton Lodge Gardens, Stockbridge SO20 6LQ. Tel: 01264 810177 Fax: 01794 388072

HEREFORD & WORCESTER

Bernithan Court, Llangarron
Accommodation: On application.
Brobury House & Garden, Borbury, Nr Hereford, HR3 6BS Tel: 01981 500 229
Burton Court, Eardisland HR6 9DN Tel: 01544 388231
Accommodation: Holiday flat, self contained – sleeps 7.
Eastnor Castle, Nr Ledbury, HR8 1RD
Tel: 01531 633160/632302, Fax: 01531 631766
Luxury accommodation for select groups.
Hergest Croft Gardens, Kington Tel: 01544 230160
Accommodation: Self-catering house – nursery sleeps 7.
Kentchurch Court, Hereford Tel: 01981 240228
Accommodation by appointment.
Moccas Court, Moccas HR2 9LH Tel: 01981 500381
Accommodation: Available at The Red Lion Hotel, Bredwardine.

KENT

Cobham Hall, Cobham, nr. Gravesend, DA12 3BL
Tel: 01474 824319/823371 Accommodation: The house, grounds, accommodation 250 beds and sports facilities are available for private hire, wedding receptions, business conferences, residential and non-residential courses and film and photographic location.
Down House, Downe BR6 7JT. Tel: 01689 859119

Great Maytham Hall, Rolvenden, Cranbrook, TN17 4NE. Tel: 01580 241 346, Fax: 01580 241 038
Goodnestone Park, Goodnestone, Canterbury CT3 1PL. Tel: 01304 840107
Ladham House, Ladham Road, Goudhurst. Tel: 01580 211203 Fax: 01580 212596
Pattyndenne Manor, Goudhurst TN17 2QU. Tel: 01580 211361

LONDON

De Morgan Foundation, Old Battersea House, 30 Vicarage Crescent, Battersea SW11 3LD.
Linley Sambourne House, 18 Stafford Terrace W8 7BH. Tel: 020 8937 0663 Fax: 020 8995 4895
Museum of Garden History, Lambeth Palace Road, Lambeth SE1 7LB. Tel: 020 7261 1891 Fax 020 7401 8869
The Traveller's Club, Pall Mall SW1Y 5EP. Tel: 020 7930 8688 Fax: 020 7930 2019

NORFOLK

Mannington Hall, Saxthorpe, Norwich NR11 7BB. Tel: 01263 584175 Fax: 01263 761214
Walsingham Abbey, Estate Office, Walsingham, NR22 6BP Tel: 01328 820259 Accommodation: Also available in the village Hotel, B&B etc..

NORTHAMPTONSHIRE

Castle Ashby House, Castle Ashby, Northampton NN7 1LQ Tel: 01604 696696
Accommodation: Holiday cottages.
The Menagerie, Horton, Horton, Northampton NN7 2BX. Tel: 01604 870957

NORTHUMBERLAND

Alnwick Castle, Alnwick, Northumberland NE66 1NQ
Tel: 01665 510777 Accommodation: Holiday cottages.
Chillingham Castle and Gardens, Alnwick
Tel: 01668 215359 Accommodation: Private family suites of rooms available.
Norwood Park, Southwell NG25 0PF. Tel: Tel/Fax: 01636 815649

NOTTINGHAMSHIRE

Carlton Hall, Carlton-On-Trent, Newark NG23 6NW
Tel: 01636 821421 Accommodation: Self-catering by appointment.
Norwood Park, Southwell, Nottingham NG25 OPF
Tel: 01636 815649
Papplewick Hall, Near Nottingham NG15 8FE
Tel: 0115 9633491 Accommodation: Country House hospitality, full breakfast and dinner, prices on request.

OXFORDSHIRE

Ardington House, Wantage OX12 8QA. Tel: 01235 821566 Fax: 01235 821151
Aynhoe Park, Suite 10, Aynho, Banbury, Oxfordshire, OX17 3BQ Tel: 01869 810 636
Ditchley Park, Ditchley Foundation, Enstone OX7 4ER. Tel: 01608 677346 Fax: 01608 677399
Mapledurham House and Watermill, Mapledurham RG4 7TR Tel: 01734 723350 Accommodation: Eleven self catering holiday cottages.

SHROPSHIRE

Fairfield, Stogursey, Bridgwater TA5 1PU. Tel: 01278 732251 Fax: 01278 732277
Hawkstone Historic Park & Follies, Weston-under-Redcastle, Shrewsbury SY4 5UY. Tel: 01939 200611 Fax: 01939 200 311
Ironbridge Gorge Museum, Ironbridge, Telford TF8 7AW. Tel: 01952 433522 Fax:01952 432204
Ludford House, Ludlow SY8 1PJ. Tel: 01584 872542 Fax: 01584 875662
Walcot Hall, Lydbury North, Nr Bishops Castle SY7 8AZ
Tel: 0171 581 2782 Accommodation: 3 flats and Ground Floor wing available all year.

SOMERSET

Barstaple House Trinity Almshouses, Old Market Street, Bristol BS2 0EU. Tel: 01179 265777 Warden
Maunsel House, North Newton, nr Bridgwater TA7 O8U. Tel: 01278 663413/661076

STAFFORDSHIRE

Dunwood Hall, Longsdon, Nr Leek, Staffordshire, ST9 9AR Tel: 01538 385071
Sandon Hall, Sandon ST18 0BZ. Tel: 01889 508004 Fax: 01889 508586
Shugborough, Stafford ST17 OXB Tel: 01889 881388
Accommodation: Details of group accommodation can be obtained from the booking office

SUFFOLK

Haughley Park, nr Stowmarket IP14 3JY. Tel: 01359 240701
Hengrave Hall Centre, Hengrave Hall, Bury St Edmunds IP28 6LZ. Tel: 01284 701561 Fax: 01284 702950

SURREY

Albury Park, Albury, Guildford GU5 9BB
Tel: 01483 202 964, Fax: 01483 205 013
Goddards, Abinger Common, Dorking RH5 6TH. Tel: 01628 825920
Great Fosters Hotel, Stroude Road, Egham TW20 9UR. Tel: 0784 433822
Greathed Manor, Dormansland, Lingfield, RH7 6PA
Tel: 01342 832 577, Fax: 01342 836 207

SUSSEX

Goddards, Abinger Common, Dorking RH5 6TH. Tel: 01628 825920
Goodwood House, Chichester PO18 OPX
Tel: 01243 774107 Accommodation: Goodwood Park Hotel, Golf and Country Club- reservations 01345 123333/01243 775537
Hammerwood Park, nr East Grinstead RH19 3QE
Tel: 01342 850594, Fax: 01342 850864
Accommodation: B&B with a difference in an idyllically peaceful location only 20 minutes from Gatwick.

WILTSHIRE

Pythouse, Tisbury, Salisbury SP3 6PB Tel: 01747 870 210, Fax: 01747 871 786

WORCESTERSHIRE

Hopton Court, Cleobury Mortimer, Kidderminster DY14 0HH. Tel: 01299 270734

YORKSHIRE

Aske Hall, Aske, Richmond DL10 5HJ. Tel: 01748 850391 Fax: 01748 823252
The Bar Convent, 17 Blossom Street, York YO2 2AH
Tel: 01904 643238
Bolton Abbey, Skipton, North Yorkshire, BD23 6EX
Tel: 01756 710 535
Broughton Hall, Skipton BD23 3AE. Tel: 01756 792267 Fax: 01756 792362
Hovingham Hall, Hovingham, York YO6 4LU. Tel: 01653 628206 Fax: 01653 628668
Elsham Hall Country and Wildlife Park, The Estate Office, Brigg DN20 0QZ. Tel: 01652 688698 Fax 01652 688240
Lindley Murray Summerhouse, The Mount School, Dalton Terrace YO24 4DD. Tel: 01904 667500 Fax: 01904 667524
The Orangery at Settrington, Settrington, Malton YO17 8NP. Tel: 01944 768345 / 768440out of hours Fax: 01944 768484
Ripley Castle, Ripley HG3 3AY Tel: 01423 770152
Accommodation: 25 deluxe bedrooms at the Estate owned Boar's Head Hotel, 100 yards from the Castle in Ripley village. The hotel is rated RAC****.
Sutton Park, Sutton-on-the-Forest, York YO61 1DP Tel:01347 81024

IRELAND

Bunratty Castle and Folk Park, Bunratty, Co. Clare. Tel: 00353 61 360 788. Knappogue Castle appartment – sleeps up to 10 people.
Bantry House, Bantry, Co. Cork. Tel: 027 50047
Accommodation: Bed & Breakfast and dinner. Nine rooms en suite.
Benvarden Gardens, Dervock, Ballymoney, CO. Antrim . Tel: 012657 41331 Fax: 012657 41955
Glin Castle, Glin Tel: 068 34173/34112
Accommodation: Overnight stays arranged. Castle can be rented.
Powerscourt Gardens & Waterfall, Enniskerry, Co. Wicklow . Tel: 00353 1 204 6000

SCOTLAND

Ayton Castle, Eyemouth, Berwickshire TD14 5RD
Tel: 018907 812812
Blairquhan Castle, Straiton, Maybole KA19 7LZ Tel:016557 70239
Dalmeny House, Charisma, South Queensferry EH30 9TQ. Tel: 0131-331 1888 Fax: 0131 331 1788
The Doune of Rothiemurchus, Rothiemurchus Estate Office, Aviemore PH22 1QH. Tel: 01479 810858 Fax: 01479 811778
Dunvegan Castle, Isle Of Skye Tel: 01470 521206
Accommodation: Self catering cottages within grounds.
Manderston, Duns, Berwickshire TD11 3PP
Tel: 01361 883450 Accommodation: By arrangement.
Sorn Castle, Sorn, Mauchline Tel: 01505 612124
Accommodation: Available - contact Cluttons.
Traquair, Innerleithan EH44 6PW Tel: 01896 830323,
Accommodation: 2 rooms B&B and Holiday flat to rent.

WALES

Cresselly, Cresselly, Kilgetty SA68 OSP. Tel: 01646 651992
Gwydir Castle, Llanrwst, Gwynedd Tel: 01492 641 687
Llanvihangel Court, Abergavenny NP7 8DH. Tel: 01873 890217
Portmerion Village, Portmerion, Gwyned Tel: 01766 770000

MINI LISTINGS
Johansens Recommended Traditional Inns, Hotels & Restaurants 2001
Here in brief are the entries that appear in full in Johansens Recommended Traditional Inns, Hotel & Restaurants – Great Britain 2001.
To order Johansens guides turn to the order forms at the back of this book.

ASHBOURNE (HOGNASTON)
Red Lion Inn

Main Street, Hognaston, Ashbourne,
Derbyshire DE6 1PR
Tel: 01335 370396
Fax: 01335 370961
lionrouge@msn.com

ASHBOURNE/UTTOXETER (WALDLEY)
Beeches Restaurant

Waldley, Doveridge, Derbyshire DE6 5LR
Tel: 01889 590288
Fax: 01889 590559
beechesfa@aol.com

BAKEWELL (ROWSLEY)
The Peacock Hotel at Rowsley

Rowsley, Derbyshire DE4 2EB
Tel: 01629 733518
Fax: 01629 732671

BELFORD
The Blue Bell Hotel

Market Place, Belford, Northumberland
NE70 7NE
Tel: 01668 213543
Fax: 01668 213787
bluebel@globalnet.co.uk

BRANCASTER STAITHE
The White Horse

Brancaster Staithe, Norfolk PE31 8BW
Tel: 01485 210262
Fax: 01485 210930
whitehorse.brancaster@virgin.net

BRIDPORT (WEST BEXINGTON)
The Manor Hotel

West Bexington, Dorchester, Dorset DT2
9DF
Tel: 01308 897616
Fax: 01308 897035
themanorhotel@bt.connect.com

BRIGHTON (BRAMBER)
**The Old Tollgate Restaurant
And Hotel**

The Street, Bramber, Steyning, West Sussex
BN44 3WE
Tel: 01903 879494 Fax: 01903 813399
otr@fastnet.co.uk

BURFORD
The Lamb Inn

Sheep Street, Burford, Oxfordshire OX18
4LR
Tel: 01993 823155
Fax: 01993 822228

BURNSALL (SKIPTON)
The Red Lion

By the bridge at Burnsall, North Yorkshire
BD23 6BU
Tel: 01756 720204
Fax: 01756 720292
redlion@daelnet.co.uk

BURTON UPON TRENT (SUDBURY)
Boar's Head Hotel

Lichfield Road, Sudbury, Derbyshire DE6
5GX
Tel: 01283 820344
Fax: 01283 820075

BURTON-ON-TRENT
Ye Olde Dog & Partridge

High Street, Tutbury, Burton upon Trent,
Staffordshire DE13 9LS
Tel: 01283 813030
Fax: 01283 813178

CALVER (NEAR BAKEWELL)
The Chequers Inn

Froggatt Edge, Derbyshire S30 1ZB
Tel: 01433 630231
Fax: 01433 631072

CAMBORNE
Tyacks Hotel

27 Commercial Street, Camborne, Cornwall
TR14 8LD
Tel: 01209 612424
Fax: 01209 612435

CAMBRIDGE (WITHERSFIELD)
The White Horse Inn

Hollow Hill, Withersfield, Haverhill, Suffolk
CB9 7SH
Tel: 01440 706081

CARLISLE (TALKIN TARN)
The Tarn End House Hotel

Talkin Tarn, Brampton, Cumbria CA8 1LS
Tel: 016977 2340
Fax: 016977 2089

CHESTERFIELD / SHEFFIELD (DRONFIELD)
**Manor House Hotel &
Restaurant**

High Street, Old Dronfield, Derbyshire
S18 1PY
Tel: 01246 413971 Fax: 01246 412104
sales@barrelsandbottles.co.uk

CHRISTCHURCH (HIGHCLIFFE ON SEA)
The Lord Bute

181 / 185 Lymington Road, Highcliffe on
Sea, Christchurch , Dorset BH23 4JS
Tel: 01425 278884
Fax: 01425 279258
mail@lordbute.co.uk

CIRENCESTER (COLN ST-ALDWYNS)
The New Inn at Coln

Coln St-Aldwyns, Gloucestershire GL7
5AN
Tel: 01285 750651
Fax: 01285 750657
stay@new-inn.co.uk

CLARE (HUNDON)

The Plough Inn

Brockley Green, Sudbury, Suffolk
CO10 8DT
Tel: 01440 786789
Fax: 01440 786710

CLAVERING (STANSTED)

The Cricketers

Clavering, Essex CB11 4QT
Tel: 01799 550442
Fax: 01799 550882
cricketers@lineone.net

COLEFORD

The New Inn

Coleford, Crediton, Devon EX17 5BZ
Tel: 01363 84242
Fax: 01363 85044
new-inn@reallyreal-group.com

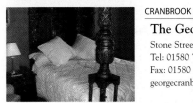

COMPTON BASSETT (NR CALNE)

White Horse Inn

Compton Bassett, Calne, Wiltshire
SN11 8RG
Tel: 01249 813118
Fax: 01249 811575

CONINGSBY

The Lea Gate Inn

Leagate Road, Coningsby, Lincolnshire
LN4 4RS
Tel: 01526 342370
Fax: 01526 345468

CRANBROOK

The George Hotel

Stone Street, Cranbrook, Kent TN17 3HE
Tel: 01580 713348
Fax: 01580 715532
georgecranbrook@aol.com

DITCHEAT (NR WELLS)

The Manor House Inn

Ditcheat, Somerset BA4 6RB
Tel: 01749 860276

themanorhouseinn@ukonline.co.uk

DORCHESTER-ON-THAMES

The George Hotel

High Street, Dorchester-On-Thames,
Oxford OX10 7HH
Tel: 01865 340404
Fax: 01865 341620

EAST WITTON (WENSLEYDALE)

The Blue Lion

East Witton, North Yorkshire DL8 4SN
Tel: 01969 624273
Fax: 01969 624189
bluelion@breathemail.net

EGTON (NR WHITBY)

The Wheatsheaf Inn

Egton, North Yorkshire YO21 1TZ
Tel: 01947 895271
Fax: 01947 895391
wheatsheaf@talk21.com

ETON (WINDSOR)

The Christopher Hotel

High Street, Eton, Windsor, Berkshire
SL4 6AN
Tel: 01753 811677 / 852359
Fax: 01753 830914
sales@christopher_hotel.co.uk

EVERSHOT

Acorn Inn

Fore Street, Evershot, Dorset DT2 0JW
Tel: 01935 83228
stay@acorn-inn.co.uk

EVESHAM (OFFENHAM)

Riverside Restaurant And Hotel

The Parks, Offenham Road, Worcestershire
WR11 5JP
Tel: 01386 446200 Fax: 01386 40021
riversidehotel@theparksoffenham.freeserve.co.uk

EXMOOR

The Royal Oak Inn

Winsford, Exmoor National Park, Somerset
EX24 7JE
Tel: 01643 851455
Fax: 01643 851009
enquiries@royaloak-somerset.co.uk

FALMOUTH (CONSTANTINE)

Trengilly Wartha Country Inn & Restaurant

Nancenoy, Constantine, Falmouth,
Cornwall TR11 5RP
Tel: 01326 340332 Fax: 01326 340332
trengilly@compuserve.com

FORDINGBRIDGE (STUCKTON)

The Three Lions Restaurant

Stuckton, Fordingbridge, Hampshire
SP6 2HF
Tel: 01425 652489
Fax: 01425 656144

GORING-ON-THAMES

The Leatherne Bottel Riverside Inn & Restaurant

The Bridleway, Goring-On-Thames,
Berkshire RG8 0HS
Tel: 01491 872667
Fax: 01491 875308

GRIMSTHORPE (BOURNE)

The Black Horse Inn

Grimsthorpe, Bourne, Lincolnshire
PE10 0LY
Tel: 01778 591247
Fax: 01778 591373
dine@blackhorseinn.co.uk

GRINDLEFORD

The Maynard Arms

Main Road, Grindleford, Derbyshire
S32 2HE
Tel: 01433 630321
Fax: 01433 630445
info@maynardarms.co.uk

HALIFAX/HUDDERSFIELD

The Rock Inn Hotel

Holywell Green, Halifax, West Yorkshire
HX4 9BS
Tel: 01422 379721
Fax: 01422 379110
THE.ROCK@DIAL.PIPEX.COM

HANDCROSS (SLAUGHAM)

The Chequers At Slaugham

Slaugham, West Sussex RH17 6AQ
Tel: 01444 400239/400996
Fax: 01444 400400

HARROGATE

The George

Wormald Green, North Yorkshire HG3 3PR
Tel: 01765 677214
Fax: 01765 676201

HARROGATE (RIPLEY CASTLE)

The Boar's Head Hotel

Ripley, Harrogate, North Yorkshire
HG3 3AY
Tel: 01423 771888
Fax: 01423 771509
boarshead@ripleycastle.co.uk

HATHERSAGE

The Plough Inn

Leadmill Bridge, Hathersage, Derbyshire
S30 1BA
Tel: 01433 650319
Fax: 01433 651049

HAYFIELD (HIGH PEAK)

The Waltzing Weasel

New Mills Road, Birch Vale, High Peak,
Derbyshire SK22 1BT
Tel: 01663 743402
Fax: 01663 743402

HELMSLEY

The Feathers Hotel

Market Place, Helmsley, North Yorkshire
YO6 5BH
Tel: 01439 770275
Fax: 01439 771101

HELMSLEY (NEAR YORK)

The Feversham Arms Hotel

Helmsley , North Yorkshire YO6 5AG
Tel: 01439 770766
Fax: 01439 770346

HINDON (NR SALISBURY)

The Grosvenor Arms

Hindon, Salisbury, Wiltshire SP3 6DJ
Tel: 01747 820696
Fax: 01747 820869

HOLT (AYLMERTON)

The Roman Camp Inn

Holt Road, Aylmerton, Norwich, Norfolk
NR11 8QD
Tel: 01263 838291
Fax: 01263 837071

HONITON (WILMINGTON)

Home Farm Hotel

Wilmington, Devon EX14 9JR
Tel: 01404 831278
Fax: 01404 831411
homefarmhotel@breathemail.net

HUDDERSFIELD (GOLCAR)

The Weavers Shed Restaurant with Rooms

Knowl Road, Golcar, Huddersfield, West
Yorkshire HD7 4AN
Tel: 01484 654284 Fax: 01484 650980
stephen@weavers-shed.demon.co.uk

KENILWORTH

Clarendon House Bar Brasserie Hotel

Old High Street, Kenilworth, Warwickshire
CV8 1LZ
Tel: 01926 857668 Fax: 01926 850669
ch@nuthurst-grange.co.uk

KNUTSFORD

Longview Hotel And Restaurant

51/55 Manchester Road, Knutsford,
Cheshire WA16 0LX
Tel: 01565 632119 Fax: 01565 652402
Longview_hotel@compuserve.com

LEEK (BLACKSHAW MOOR)

The Three Horseshoes Inn & Kirk's Restaurant

Buxton Road, Blackshaw Moor, Staffordshire
ST13 8TW
Tel: 01538 300296
Fax: 01538 300320

LONGLEAT (HORNINGSHAM)

The Bath Arms

Horningsham, Warminster, Wiltshire
BA12 7LY
Tel: 01985 844308
Fax: 01985 844150

LYMINGTON (HORDLE)

Gordleton Mill Inn

Silver Street, Hordle, Hampshire SO41 6DJ
Tel: 01590 682219
Fax: 01590 683073
bookings@gordleton-mill.co.uk

LYNMOUTH

The Rising Sun

Harbourside, Lynmouth, Devon EX35 6EQ
Tel: 01598 753223
Fax: 01598 753480
risingsunlynmouth@easynet.co.uk

MAIDSTONE (RINGLESTONE)

Ringlestone Inn and Farmhouse Hotel

'Twixt Harrietsham and Wormshill, Kent
ME17 1NX
Tel: 01622 859900 Fax: 01622 859966
bookings@ringlestone.com

MALMESBURY

The Horse And Groom Inn

Charlton, Wiltshire SN16 9DL
Tel: 01666 823904
Fax: 01666 823390

MELLS (NR BATH)

The Talbot Inn at Mells

Mells, Somerset BA11 3PN
Tel: 01373 812254
Fax: 01373 813599
talbot.inn@lineone.net

MILDENHALL

The Bell Hotel

High Street, Mildenhall, Suffolk IP28 7EA
Tel: 01638 717272
Fax: 01638 717057
info@the-bell-hotel.co.uk

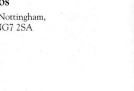

NEWBY BRIDGE

The Swan Hotel

Newby Bridge, Cumbria LA12 8NB
Tel: 015395 31681
Fax: 015395 31917
swanhotel@aol.com

NOTTINGHAM

Hotel Des Clos

Old Lenton Lane, Nottingham,
Nottinghamshire NG7 2SA
Tel: 01159 866566
Fax: 01159 860343

OXFORD (BANBURY)

Holcombe Hotel

High Street, Deddington, Oxfordshire
OX15 0SL
Tel: 01869 338274
Fax: 01869 337167

OXFORD (MIDDLETON STONEY)

The Jersey Arms

Middleton Stoney, Oxfordshire OX6 8SE
Tel: 01869 343234
Fax: 01869 343565
jerseyarms@bestwestern.co.uk

PADSTOW

The Old Custom House Hotel

South Quay, Padstow, Cornwall PL28 8BL
Tel: 01841 532359
Fax: 01841 533372

PANGBOURNE (NR READING)

The George Hotel

The Square, Pangbourne, Berkshire
RG8 7AJ
Tel: 01189 842237
Fax: 01189 844354
info@georgehotelpangbourne.co.uk

PELYNT (NR LOOE)

Jubilee Inn

Pelynt, Cornwall PL13 2JZ
Tel: 01503 220312
Fax: 01503 220920
rickard@jubileeinn.freeserve.co.uk

PENZANCE

The Summer House

Cornwall Terrace, Penzance, Cornwall
TR18 4HL
Tel: 01736 363744
Fax: 01736 360959
summerhouse@dial.pipex.com

PICKERING

The White Swan

The Market Place, Pickering, North
Yorkshire YO18 7AA
Tel: 01751 472288
Fax: 01751 475554
welcome@white-swan.co.uk

PORT GAVERNE

The Port Gaverne Inn

North Cornwall PL29 3SQ
Tel: 01208 880244
Fax: 01208 880151
pghotel@telinco.co.uk

PRESTON (GOOSNARGH)

Ye Horn's Inn

Horn's Lane, Goosnargh, Lancashire
PR3 2FJ
Tel: 01772 865230
Fax: 01772 864299
enquiries@YEHORNSINN.co.uk

RUGBY (EASENHALL)

The Golden Lion Inn of Easenhall

Easenhall, Warwickshire CV23 0JA
Tel: 01788 832265 Fax: 01788 832878
Goldenlioninn@aol.co.uk

SADDLEWORTH (DELPH)

The Old Bell Inn Hotel

Huddersfield Road, Delph, Saddleworth,
Greater Manchester OL3 5EG
Tel: 01457 870130
Fax: 01457 876597

SHIPTON UNDER WYCHWOOD

The Shaven Crown Hotel

High Street, Shipton Under Wychwood,
Oxfordshire OX7 6BA
Tel: 01993 830330
Fax: 01993 832136

SNETTISHAM (NR KING'S LYNN)

The Rose & Crown

Old Church Road, Snettisham, Norfolk
PE31 7LX
Tel: 01485 541382
Fax: 01485 543172

STAMFORD

The Crown Hotel

All Saints Place, Stamford, Lincolnshire
PE9 2AG
Tel: 01780 763136
Fax: 01780 756111
thecrownhotel@excite.com

STAMFORD (NR GRANTHAM)

Black Bull Inn

Lobthorpe, Lincolnshire NG33 5LL
Tel: 01476 860086
Fax: 01476 860796

STANTON WICK (NR BATH)

The Carpenters Arms

Stanton Wick, Somerset BS39 4BX
Tel: 01761 490202
Fax: 01761 490763
carpenters@dial.pipex.com

STOW-ON-THE-WOLD (BLEDINGTON)

The Kings Head Inn & Restaurant

The Green, Bledington, Oxfordshire OX7
6XQ
Tel: 01608 658365 Fax: 01608 658902
kingshead@orr-ewing.com

TELFORD (NORTON)

The Hundred House Hotel

Bridgnorth Road, Norton, Nr Shifnal,
Telford, Shropshire TF11 9EE
Tel: 01952 730353
Fax: 01952 730355
hundredhouse@compuserve.com

THAXTED

Recorders House Restaurant (With Rooms)

17 Town Street, Thaxted, Essex CM6 2LD
Tel: 01371 830438 Fax: 01371 831645

THIRSK

Crab & Lobster

Asenby, North Yorkshire YO7 3QL
Tel: 01845 577286
Fax: 01845 577109
reservations@crabandlobster.co.uk

THORNHAM

The Lifeboat Inn

Ship Lane, Thornham, Norfolk PE36 6LT
Tel: 01485 512236
Fax: 01485 512323
reception@lifeboatinn.co.uk

THORPE MARKET

Green Farm Restaurant And Hotel

North Walsham Road, Thorpe Market,
Norfolk NR11 8TH
Tel: 01263 833602 Fax: 01263 833163
GRFARMH@AOL.COM

TINTAGEL (TREBARWITH STRAND)

The Port William

Trebarwith Strand, Cornwall PL34 0HB
Tel: 01840 770230
Fax: 01840 770936
william@eurobell.co.uk

TOTNES (STAVERTON)

The Sea Trout Inn

Staverton, Devon TQ9 6PA
Tel: 01803 762274
Fax: 01803 762506

UPTON-UPON-SEVERN, NR MALVERN

The White Lion Hotel

High Street, Upton-Upon-Severn,
Worcestershire WR8 0HJ
Tel: 01684 592551
Fax: 01684 593333
reservations@whitelionhotel.demon.co.uk

WEST AUCKLAND

The Manor House Hotel & Country Club

The Green, West Auckland, County
Durham DL14 9HW
Tel: 01388 834834 Fax: 01388 833566
manorhousehotel.net

WHITEWELL

The Inn At Whitewell

Forest Of Bowland, Clitheroe, Lancashire
BB7 3AT
Tel: 01200 448222
Fax: 01200 448298

WISBECH (OUTWELL)

Crown Lodge Hotel

Downham Road, Outwell, Wisbech,
Cambridgeshire PE14 8SE
Tel: 01945 773391
Fax: 01945 772668
crownlodgehotel@hotmail.com

WOOLER

The Tankerville Arms Hotel

Wooler, Northumberland NE71 6AD
Tel: 01668 281581
Fax: 01668 281387
enquiries@tankervillehotel.co.uk

BRIDGEND (LALESTON)

The Great House

High Street, Bridgend, Laleston,
Mid-Glamorgan CF32 0HP
Tel: 01656 657644
Fax: 01656 668892
greathse1@aol.com

LLANARMON DYFFRYN CEIRIOG

The West Arms Hotel

Llanarmon D C, Denbighshire LL20 7LD
Tel: 01691 600665
Fax: 01691 600622
gowestarms@aol.com

PRESTEIGNE

The Radnorshire Arms

High Street, Presteigne, Powys LD8 2BE
Tel: 01544 267406
Fax: 01544 260418

ANNAN (POWFOOT)

The Powfoot Hotel

Powfoot, Dumfriesshire DG12 5PN
Tel: 01461 700254
Fax: 01461 700288

EDINBURGH

Bank Hotel

1 South Bridge, Edinburgh EH1 1LL
Tel: 0131 556 9940
Fax: 0131 558 1362

ISLE OF SKYE (EILEAN IARMAIN)

Hotel Eilean Iarmain

Sleat, Isle Of Skye IV43 8QR
Tel: 01471 833332
Fax: 01471 833275
hotel@eilean-iarmain.co.uk

KYLESKU (SUTHERLAND)

Kylesku Hotel

Kylesku, Via Lairg, Sutherland IV27 4HW
Tel: 01971 502231/502200
Fax: 01971 502313
kylesku.hotel@excite.co.uk

LOCH EARN (PERTHSHIRE)

Achray House on Loch Earn

Loch Earn, St Fillan, Perthshire PH6 2NF
Tel: 01764 685231
Fax: 01764 685320
achrayhotelsltd@btinternet.com

MOFFAT

Annandale Arms Hotel

High Street, Moffat, Dumfriesshire
DG10 9HF
Tel: 01683 220013
Fax: 01683 221395

OLDMELDRUM

The Redgarth

Kirkbrace, Oldmeldrum, Aberdeenshire
AB51 0DJ
Tel: 01651 872 353
redgath1@aol.com

PLOCKTON (BY KYLE OF LOCHALSH)

The Plockton Hotel & Garden Restaurant

Harbour Street, Plockton, Wester Ross
IV52 8TN
Tel: 01599 544274
Fax: 01599 544475

POOLEWE (WESTER ROSS)

Pool House Hotel

Poolewe, Achnasheen, Wester Ross
IV22 2LD
Tel: 01445 781272
Fax: 01445 781403
Poolhouse@inverewe.co.uk

STIRLING (NR DUNBLANE)

Sheriffmuir Inn

Sheriffmuir, Perthshire FK15 0LN
Tel: 01786 823285
Fax: 01786 824418

TIGHNABRUAICH (ARGYLL)

Royal Hotel

Tighnabruaich, Argyll , Argyllshire
PA21 2BE
Tel: 01700 811239
Fax: 01700 811300
royalhotel@btinternet.com

GUERNSEY (ST PETER PORT)

Les Rocquettes Hotel

Les Gravees, St Peter Port GY1 1RN
Tel: 01481 722176
Fax: 01481 714543
rocquettes@sarinahotels.co.uk

MINI LISTINGS
Johansens Recommended Hotels – Belgium, France, Germany, The Netherlands 2001
Here in brief are the entries that appear in full in Johansens Recommended Hotels – Europe & The Mediterranean 2001.
To order Johansens guides turn to the order forms at the back of this book.

FRANCE/BRITTANY (MOELAN-SUR-MER)

Manoir de Kertalg

Route de Riec sur Belon, 29350 Möelan-sur-Mer, France
Tel: 33 2 98 39 77 77
Fax: 33 2 98 39 72 07

FRANCE/BRITTANY (PLEVEN)

Manoir du Vaumadeuc

22130 Pleven, France
Tel: 33 2 96 84 46 17
Fax: 33 2 96 84 40 16

FRANCE/BRITTANY (PLOERDUT)

Château du Launay

56160 Ploerdut, France
Tel: 33 2 97 39 46 32
Fax: 33 2 97 39 46 31

FRANCE/BURGUNDY (AVALLON)

Château de Vault de Lugny

11 Rue du Château, 89200 Avallon, France
Tel: 33 3 86 34 07 86
Fax: 33 3 86 34 16 36

FRANCE/BURGUNDY (AVALLON)

Hostellerie de la Poste

13 place Vauban, 89200 Avallon, France
Tel: 33 3 86 34 16 16
Fax: 33 3 86 34 19 19

FRANCE/BURGUNDY (BEAUNE)

Ermitage de Corton

R.N. 74, 21200 Chorey-les-Beaune, France
Tel: 33 3 80 22 05 28
Fax: 33 3 80 24 64 51

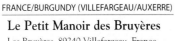

FRANCE/BURGUNDY (VILLEFARGEAU/AUXERRE)

Le Petit Manoir des Bruyères

Les Bruyères, 89240 Villefargeau, France
Tel: 33 3 86 41 32 82
Fax: 33 3 86 41 28 57

FRANCE/CHAMPAGNE (ÉPERNAY)

Hostellerie La Briqueterie

4 Route de Sézanne, 51530 Vinay-Epernay, France
Tel: 33 3 26 59 99 99
Fax: 33 3 26 59 92 10

FRANCE/CHAMPAGNE (FÉRE-EN TARDENOIS)

Château de Fére

Route de Fismes, 02130 Fére-en-Tardenois, France
Tel: 33 3 23 82 21 13
Fax: 33 3 23 82 37 81

FRANCE/CHAMPAGNE (TINQUEUX-REIMS)

L'Assiette Champenoise

40, Avenue Paul Vaillant Couturier, 51430 Tinqueux, France
Tel: 33 3 26 84 64 64
Fax: 33 3 26 04 15 69

FRANCE/LOIRE VALLEY (AMBOISE)

Château de Pray

Route de Chargé, 37400 Amboise, France
Tel: 33 2 47 57 23 67
Fax: 33 2 47 57 32 50

FRANCE/LOIRE VALLEY (AMBOISE)

Le Manoir des Minimes

34 Quai Charles Guinot, 37400 Amboise, France
Tel: 33 2 47 30 40 40
Fax: 33 2 47 30 40 77

FRANCE/LOIRE VALLEY (LANGEAIS)

Château de Rochecotte

Saint Patrice, 37130 Langeais, France
Tel: 33 2 47 96 16 16
Fax: 33 2 47 96 90 59

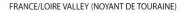

FRANCE/LOIRE VALLEY (NOYANT DE TOURAINE)

Château de Brou

37800 Noyant de Touraine, France
Tel: 33 2 47 65 80 80
Fax: 33 2 47 65 82 92

FRANCE/LOIRE WEST (CHAMPIGNE)

Château des Briottières

49330 Champigné, France
Tel: 33 2 41 42 00 02
Fax: 33 2 41 42 01 55

FRANCE/LOIRE WEST (MISSILLAC)

Domaine de la Bretesche

44780 Missillac, France
Tel: 33 2 51 76 86 96
Fax: 33 2 40 66 99 47

FRANCE/NORMANDY (BREUIL-EN-BESSIN)

Château de Goville

14330 Le Breuil-en-Bessin, France
Tel: 33 2 31 22 19 28
Fax: 33 2 31 22 68 74

FRANCE/NORMANDY (ETRETAT)

Le Donjon

Chemin de Saint Claire, 76790 Etretat, France
Tel: 33 2 35 27 08 23
Fax: 33 2 35 29 92 34

FRANCE/NORMANDY (FORGES-LES-EAUX)

Folie du Bois des Fontaines

Route de Dieppe, 76440 Forges-les-Eaux, France
Tel: 33 2 32 89 50 68
Fax: 33 2 32 89 50 67

FRANCE/NORMANDY (HONFLEUR)

La Chaumière

Route du Littoral, 14600 Honfleur, France
Tel: 33 2 31 81 63 20
Fax: 33 2 31 89 59 23

FRANCE/NORMANDY (HONFLEUR)

La Ferme Saint-Siméon

Rue Adolphe-Marais, 14600 Honfleur,
France
Tel: 33 2 31 81 78 00
Fax: 33 2 2 31 89 48 48

FRANCE/NORMANDY (HONFLEUR)

Le Manoir du Butin

Phare du Butin, 14600 Honfleur, France
Tel: 33 2 31 81 63 00
Fax: 33 2 31 89 59 23

FRANCE/PARIS (CHAMPS-ELYSÉES)

Hôtel de la Trémoille

14 rue de la Trémoille, 75008 Paris, France
Tel: +33 1 47 23 34 20
Fax: +33 1 40 70 01 08

FRANCE/PARIS (CHAMPS-ELYSÉES)

Hôtel Franklin D. Roosevelt

18 rue Clement Marot, 75008 Paris, France
Tel: 33 1 53 57 49 50
Fax: 33 1 47 20 44 30

FRANCE/PARIS (CHAMPS-ELYSÉES)

Hôtel Plaza Athénée

25 Avenue Montaigne, 75008 Paris, France
Tel: 33 1 53 67 66 65
Fax: 33 1 53 67 66 66

FRANCE/PARIS(CHAMPS-ELYSEES)

Hôtel San Regis

12, rue Jean Goujon, 75008 Paris, France
Tel: 33 1 44 95 16 16
Fax: 33 1 45 61 05 48

FRANCE/PARIS (CONCORDE)

Hôtel de Crillon

10 Place de la Concorde, 75008 Paris,
France
Tel: 33 1 44 71 15 00
Fax: 33 1 44 71 15 02

FRANCE/PARIS (INVALIDES)

Hôtel Le Tourville

16 Avenue de Tourville, 75007 Paris, France
Tel: 33 1 47 05 62 62
Fax: 33 1 47 05 43 90

FRANCE/PARIS (MADELEINE)

Hôtel de L'Arcade

9 Rue de l'Arcade, 75008 Paris, France
Tel: 33 1 53 30 60 00
Fax: 33 1 40 07 03 07

FRANCE/PARIS (MADELEINE)

Hôtel le Lavoisier

21 rue Lavoisier, 75008 Paris, France
Tel: 33 1 53 30 06 06
Fax: 33 1 53 30 23 00

FRANCE/PARIS (PORTE MAILLOT)

L'Hôtel Pergolèse

3 Rue Pergolèse, 75116 Paris, France
Tel: 33 1 53 64 04 04
Fax: 33 1 53 64 04 40

FRANCE/PARIS (PORTE MAILLOT)

La Villa Maillot

143 Avenue de Malakoff, 75116 Paris,
France
Tel: 33 1 53 64 52 52
Fax: 33 1 45 00 60 61

FRANCE/PARIS (SAINT -GERMAN)

Hôtel le Saint-Grégoire

43 rue de l'Abbé Grégoire, 75006 Paris,
France
Tel: 33 1 45 48 23 23
Fax: 33 1 45 48 33 95

FRANCE/PARIS (SAINT-GERMAIN)

Hôtel Buci Latin

34 rue de Buci, 75006 Paris, France
Tel: 33 1 43 29 07 20
Fax: 33 1 43 29 67 44

FRANCE/PARIS-OUTSKIRTS (BOUTIGNY NR
BARBIZON)

Domaine de Belesbat

Courdimanche-sur-Essonne, 91820
Boutigny-sur-Essonne, France
Tel: 33 1 69 23 19 00
Fax: 33 1 69 23 19 01

FRANCE/PARIS-OUTSKIRTS (GRESSY-EN-
FRANCE/CHANTILLY)

Le Manoir de Gressy

77410 Gressy-en-France, France
Tel: 33 1 60 26 68 00
Fax: 33 1 60 26 45 46

FRANCE/POITOU-CHARENTES (CRAZANNES-
SAINTES)

Château de Crazannes

17350 Crazannes, France
Tel: 33 6 80 65 40 96
Fax: 33 5 46 91 34 46

FRANCE/POITOU-CHARENTES (SAINT MAIXENT
L'ECOLE)

Le Logis St Martin

Chemin de Pissot, 79400 St Maixent
L'Ecole, France
Tel: 33 5 49 05 58 68
Fax: 33 5 49 76 19 93

FRANCE/PROVENCE-CÔTE D'AZUR (BEAULIEU-
SUR-MER)

La Réserve de Beaulieu

5 boulevard Général Leclerc, 06310
Beaulieu-sur-Mer, France
Tel: 33 4 93 01 00 01
Fax: 33 4 93 01 28 99

FRANCE/PROVENCE-CÔTE D'AZUR (EZE
VILLAGE)

Château Eza

Rue de la Pise, 06360 Eze Village, France
Tel: 33 4 93 41 12 24
Fax: 33 4 93 41 16 64

FRANCE/PROVENCE-CÔTE D'AZUR (LES BAUX DE PROVENCE)

Mas de l'Oulivié

13 520 Les Baux de Provence, France
Tel: 33 4 90 54 35 78
Fax: 33 4 90 54 44 31

FRANCE/PROVENCE-COTE D'AZUR (LORGUES)

Château de Berne

Chemin de Berne, Flayosc, 83510 Lorgues, France
Tel: 33 4 94 60 48 88
Fax: 33 4 94 60 48 89

FRANCE/PROVENCE-CÔTE D'AZUR (MANDELIEU-CANNES)

Ermitage du Riou

Avenue Henri Clews, 06210 Mandelieu-la-Napoule, France
Tel: 33 4 93 49 95 56
Fax: 33 4 92 97 69 05

FRANCE/PROVENCE-CÔTE D'AZUR (MOUGINS-CANNES)

Le Mas Candille

Boulevard Rebuffel, 06250 Mougins, France
Tel: 33 4 92 28 43 43
Fax: 33 4 92 28 43 40

FRANCE/PROVENCE-CÔTE D'AZUR (RAMATUELLE)

La Ferme d'Augustin

Route de Tahiti, 83 350 Ramatuelle, France
Tel: 33 4 94 55 97 00
Fax: 33 4 94 97 40 30

FRANCE/PROVENCE-CÔTE D'AZUR (SAINT-PAUL-DE-VENCE)

Le Grande Bastide

Route de la Colle, 06570 Saint-Paul-de-Vence, France
Tel: 33 4 93 32 50 30
Fax: 33 4 93 32 50 59

FRANCE/PROVENCE-CÔTE D'AZUR (SAINT-RÉMY-DE-PROVENCE)

Château des Alpilles

Route Départementale 31, Ancienne route du Grés, 13210 St-Rémy-de-Provence
Tel: 33 4 90 92 03 33
Fax: 33 4 90 92 45 17

FRANCE/PROVENCE-CÔTE D'AZUR (SAINT-TROPEZ)

Hôtel Sube

15 Quai Suffren, 83990 Saint-Tropez, France
Tel: 33 4 94 97 30 04
Fax: 33 4 94 54 89 08

FRANCE/PROVENCE-CÔTE D'AZUR (SAINT TROPEZ)

La Résidence de la Pinède

Plage de la Bouillabaisse, 83990 Saint-Tropez, France
Tel: 33 4 94 55 91 00
Fax: 33 4 94 97 73 64

FRANCE/PROVENCE-CÔTE D'AZUR (SAINTE-MAXIME/BAY OF SAINT TROPEZ)

Hôtel Le Beauvallon

Baie de Saint-Tropez, Beauvallon-Grimaud, 83120 Sainte-Maxime, France
Tel: 33 4 94 55 78 88
Fax: 33 4 94 55 78 78

FRANCE/PROVENCE-CÔTE D'AZUR (SERRE-CHEVALIER)

L'Auberge du Choucas

Serre-Chevalier 1500, 05220 Monetier-les-Bains, France
Tel: 33 4 92 24 42 73
Fax: 33 4 92 24 51 60

FRANCE/PROVENCE-CÔTE D'AZUR (UZÉS)

Château d'Arpaillagues

Hôtel Marie d'Agoult, 30 700 Uzés, France
Tel: 33 4 66 22 14 48
Fax: 33 4 66 22 56 10

FRANCE/CORSICA (PORTICCIO)

Hôtel Le Maquis

BP 94, 20166 Porticcio-Corsica, France
Tel: 33 4 95 25 05 55
Fax: 33 4 95 25 11 70

FRANCE/RHÔNE VALLEY (GRIGNAN)

Manoir de la Roseraie

Route de Valréas, 26230 Grignan, France
Tel: 33 4 75 46 58 15
Fax: 33 4 75 46 91 55

FRANCE/RHÔNE VALLEY (LYON)

La Tour Rose

22 rue du Boeuf, 69005 Lyon, France
Tel: 33 4 78 37 25 90
Fax: 33 4 78 42 26 02

FRANCE/SOUTH WEST (BIARRITZ)

Hôtel du Palais

Avenue de l'Impératrice, 64200 Biarrritz, France
Tel: 33 5 59 41 64 00
Fax: 33 5 59 41 67 99

FRANCE/SOUTH WEST (CASTRES)

Château d'Aiguefonde

Rue du Château, 81200 Aiguefonde, France
Tel: 33 5 63 98 13 70
Fax: 33 5 63 98 69 90

GERMANY (BADENWEILER)

Hotel Römerbad

Schlossplatz 1, 79410 Badenweiler, Germany
Tel: 49 7632 700
Fax: 49 7632 70200

GERMANY (MUNICH)

Hotel Königshof

Karlsplatz 25, 80335 Munich, Germany
Tel: 49 8955 1360
Fax: 49 8955 136113

GERMANY (OBERWESEL/RHEIN)

Burghotel Auf Schönburg

55430 Oberwesel/Rhein, Germany
Tel: 49 6744 93930
Fax: 49 6744 1613

GERMANY (ROTHENBURG OB DER TAUBER)

Hotel Eisenhut

Herrngasse 3-7, 91541 Rothenburg ob der Tauber, Germany
Tel: 49 9861 7050
Fax: 49 9861 70545

GERMANY (SYLT)

Christian VIII

Heleeker 1, 25980 Archsum/Sylt, Germany
Tel: 49 4651 97070
Fax: 49 4651 970777

GERMANY (SYLT)

Landhaus Nösse

Nösistieg 13, Morsum 25980 Sylt, Germany
Tel: 49 4651 9722 0
Fax: 49 4651 891658

GERMANY (SYLT)

Hotel Restaurant Jörg Müller

Süderstrasse 8, 25980 Westerland/Sylt, Germany
Tel: 49 4651 27788
fax: 49 4651 201 471

GERMANY (TRIBERG)

Romantik Parkhotel Wehrle

Gartenstr.24, 78094 Triberg, Germany
Tel: 49 7722 86020
Fax: 49 7722 860290

GERMANY (WASSENBERG)

Hotel Burg Wassenberg

Kirchstrasse 17, 41849 Wassenberg, Germany
Tel: 49 2432 9490
Fax: 49 2432 949100

NETHERLANDS (AMSTERDAM)

Ambassade Hotel

Herengracht 341, 1016 AZ Amsterdam, Netherlands
Tel: 31 205 55 02 22
Fax: 31 205 55 02 77

NETHERLANDS (AMSTERDAM)

The Canal House Hotel

Keizersgracht 148, 1015 CX, Amsterdam, The Netherlands
Tel: 31 206 22 51 82
Fax: 31 206 24 13 17

NETHERLANDS (AMSTERDAM)

Seven One Seven

Prinsengracht 717, 1017 JW, Amsterdam, The Netherlands
Tel: 31 204 27 07 17
Fax: 31 204 23 07 17

NETHERLANDS (DE LUTTE)

Landhuishotel & Restaurant Bloemenbeek

Beuninger Straat 6, 7587 ZG De Lutte, The Netherlands
Tel: 31 541 55 12 24
Fax: 31 541 55 22 85

NETHERLANDS (DRUNEN)

Hotel De Duinrand

Steergerf 2, 5151 RB Drunen, The Netherlands
Tel: 31 416 37 24 98
Fax: 31 416 37 49 19

NETHERLANDS (MOLENHOEK)

Jachtslot de Mookerheide

Heumensebaan 2, 6584 CL Molenhoek, The Netherlands
Tel: 31 243 58 30 35
Fax: 31 243 58 43 55

NETHERLANDS (OOTMARSUM)

Hotel de Wiemsel

Winhofflaan 2, 7631 HX Ootmarsum, The Netherlands
Tel: 31 541 29 21 55
Fax: 31 541 29 32 95

NETHERLANDS (VOORBURG)

Restaurant Hotel Savelberg

Oosteinde 14, 2271 EH Voorburg, The Netherlands
Tel: 31 703 872 081
Fax: 31 703 87 77 15

PREFERRED PARTNERS

Preferred partners are those organisations specifically chosen and exclusively recommended by Johansens for the quality and excellence of their products and services for the mutual benefit of Johansens recommendations, readers and independent travellers. For further details, please contact Fiona Patrick at Johansens on +44 (0)1344 306650.

Johansens Recommendations
Alphabetical list of Johansens Recommendations

HOTELS
ENGLAND

BRISTOL

Hotel Du Vin & Bistro	Bristol	0117 925 5577

BEDFORDSHIRE

The Bedford Arms	Woburn	01525 290441
Flitwick Manor	Woburn	01525 712242
Moore Place Hotel	Milton Keynes	01908 282000
Woodlands Manor	Bedford	01234 363281

BERKSHIRE

The Berystede	Ascot	0870 400 8111
The Castle Hotel	Windsor	0870 400 8300
Chauntry House Hotel & Restaurant	Bray-on-Thames	01628 673991
Cliveden	Maidenhead	01628 668561
Donnington Valley Hotel & Golf Club	Newbury	01635 551199
Fredrick's Hotel & Restaurant	Maidenhead	01628 581000
The French Horn	Sonning-On-Thames	01189 692204
Monkey Island Hotel	Bray-on-Thames	01628 623400
Newbury Manor Hotel	Newbury	01635 523838
Royal Berkshire	Ascot	01344 623322
Sir Christopher Wren's Hotel	Windsor	01753 861354
The Swan Diplomat Hotel	Streatley-On-Thames	01491 873737
Taplow House Hotel	Maidenhead	01628 670056
The Vineyard At Stockcross	Newbury	01635 528770

BUCKINGHAMSHIRE

Danesfield House	Marlow-On-Thames	01628 891010
Hartwell House	Aylesbury	01296 747444
The Priory Hotel	Aylesbury	01296 641239
Stoke Park Club	Heathrow	01753 717171
Compleat Angler	Marlow	0870 400 8100

CAMBRIDGESHIRE

The Haycock	Peterborough	01780 782223

CHESHIRE

The Alderley Edge Hotel	Alderley Edge	01625 583033
The Bridge Hotel	Prestbury	01625 829326
Broxton Hall Country House Hotel	Chester	01829 782321
The Chester Grosvenor	Chester	01244 324024
Crabwall Manor	Chester	01244 851666
Crewe Hall	Crewe	01270 253333
Mere Court Hotel	Knutsford	01565 831000
Nunsmere Hall	Chester	01606 889100
Rookery Hall	Nantwich	01270 610016
Rowton Hall Hotel	Chester	01244 335262
The Stanneylands Hotel	Manchester	01625 525225
Woodland Park Hotel	Altrincham	0161 928 8631

CORNWALL

Budock Vean - The Hotel on the River	Falmouth	01326 250288
Fowey Hall Hotel & Restaurant	Fowey	01726 833866
The Garrack Hotel & Restaurant	St. Ives	01736 796199
The Greenbank Hotel	Falmouth	01326 312440
Meudon Hotel	Falmouth	01326 250541
The Nare Hotel	Carne Beach	01872 501111
Penmere Manor	Falmouth	01326 211411
Rose-in-Vale Country House Hotel	St Agnes	01872 552202
The Rosevine Hotel	St.Mawes	01872 580206
Talland Bay Hotel	Polperro	01503 272667

Treglos Hotel	Padstow	01841 520727
The Well House	St Keyne	01579 342001

COUNTY DURHAM

Headlam Hall	Darlington	01325 730238
Lumley Castle Hotel	Durham	0191 389 1111

CUMBRIA

Appleby Manor Country House Hotel	Appleby-in-Westmorland	017683 51571
The Borrowdale Gates Hotel	Keswick	017687 77204
The Derwentwater Hotel	Keswick	017687 72538
Farlam Hall Hotel	Brampton	016977 46234
Gilpin Lodge	Windermere	015394 88818
Graythwaite Manor	Grange-Over-Sands	015395 32001
Holbeck Ghyll Country House Hotel	Ambleside	015394 32375
Lakeside Hotel On Lake Windermere	Windermere	0541 541586
Langdale Chase	Windermere	015394 32201
Langdale Hotel & Country Club	Ambleside	015394 37302
Linthwaite House Hotel	Windermere	015394 88600
Lovelady Shield Country House Hotel	Alston	01434 381203
Michaels Nook	Grasmere	015394 35496
Miller Howe	Windermere	015394 42536
Nanny Brow Country House Hote	Ambleside	015394 32036
Rampsbeck Country House Hotel	Lake Ullswater	017684 86442
Rothay Manor	Ambleside	015394 33605
Sharrow Bay Country House Hotel	Lake Ullswater	017684 86301/86483
Storrs Hall	Windermere	015394 47111
Tufton Arms Hotel	Appleby-in-Westmorland	017683 51593
The Wordsworth Hotel	Grasmere	015394 35592

DERBYSHIRE

Callow Hall	Ashbourne	01335 300900
The Cavendish Hotel	Baslow	01246 582311
East Lodge Country House Hotel	Bakewell	01629 734474
Fischer's	Baslow	01246 583259
The George at Hathersage	Hathersage	01433 650436
Hassop Hall	Bakewell	01629 640488
The Izaak Walton Hotel	Ashbourne	01335 350555
The Lee Wood Hotel & Restaurant	Buxton	01298 23002
Riber Hall	Matlock	01629 582795
Ringwood Hall Hotel	Chesterfield	01246 280077
Risley Hall Country House Hotel	Risley	0115 939 9000
Riverside House	Ashford-In-The-Water	01629 814275

DEVON

The Arundell Arms	Lifton	01566 784666
Bolt Head Hotel	Salcombe	01548 843751
Buckland-Tout-Saints	Kingsbridge Estuary	01548 853055
Combe House at Gittisham	Exeter	01404 540400
The Edgemoor	Bovey Tracey	01626 832466
Fairwater Head Country House Hotel	Hawkchurch	01297 678349
Gidleigh Park	Chagford	01647 432367
Hotel Barcelona	Exeter	01392 281000
Hotel Riviera	Sidmouth	01395 515201
Ilsington Country Hotel	Ilsington	01364 661452
Kitley House Hotel & Restaurant	Plymouth	01752 881555
Mill End Hotel	Chagford	01647 432282
Northcote Manor Country House Hotel	Burrington	01769 560501
Orestone Manor Hotel & Restaurant	Maidencombe	01803 328098
The Osborne Hotel & Langtry's Restaurant	Torquay	01803 213311
The Palace Hotel	Torquay	01803 200200
The Queens Court Hotel & The Olive Tree Restaurant	Exeter	01392 272709
Soar Mill Cove Hotel	Salcombe	01548 561566
The Tides Reach Hotel	Salcombe	01548 843466

Watersmeet Hotel	Woolacombe	01271 870333
Woodbury Park Hotel	Exeter	01395 233382
Woolacombe Bay Hotel	Woolacombe	01271 870388

DORSET

Bridge House Hotel	Beaminster	01308 862200
The Dormy	Bournemouth	01202 872121
Langtry Manor - Lovenest of a King	Bournemouth	01202 553887
Moonfleet Manor	Weymouth	01305 786948
The Norfolk Royale Hotel	Bournemouth	01202 551521
Plumber Manor	Sturminster Newton	01258 472507
The Priory	Wareham	01929 551666
Summer Lodge	Evershot	01935 83424

EAST SUSSEX

Ashdown Park Hotel & Country Club	Forest Row	01342 824988
Buxted Park Country House Hotel	Buxted	01825 732711
Dale Hill	Ticehurst	01580 200112
The Grand Hotel	Eastbourne	01323 412345
Netherfield Place Hotel	Battle	01424 774455
Newick Park	Lewes	01825 723633
PowderMills Hotel	Battle	01424 775511
White Lodge Country House Hotel	Alfriston	01323 870265

EAST YORKSHIRE

Willerby Manor Hotel	Hull	01482 652616

ESSEX

Five Lakes Hotel Golf Country Club	Colchester	01621 868888
Maison Talbooth	Dedham	01206 322367
The Pier At Harwich	Harwich	01255 241212
Pontlands Park Country Hotel	Chelmsford	01245 476444
Whitehall	Stansted	01279 850603

GLOUCESTERSHIRE

The Bear of Rodborough Hotel	Cirencester	01453 878522
Calcot Manor	Tetbury	01666 890391
Charingworth Manor	Chipping Campden	01386 593555
The Cheltenham Park Hotel	Cheltenham	01242 222021
Corse Lawn House Hotel	Tewkesbury	01452 780479 / 771
Cotswold House	Chipping Campden	01386 840330
The Grapevine Hotel	Stow-On-The-Wold	01451 830344
The Greenway	Cheltenham	01242 862352
Hotel Kandinsky	Cheltenham	01242 527788
Hotel On The Park	Cheltenham	01242 518898
Lords Of The Manor Hotel	Stow-on-the-Wold	01451 820243
Lower Slaughter Manor	Lower Slaughter	01451 820456
The Manor House Hotel	Moreton-In-Marsh	01608 650501
The Noel Arms Hotel	Chipping Campden	01386 840317
The Painswick Hotel	Painswick	01452 812160
The Queen's	Cheltenham	0870 400 8107
The Swan Hotel At Bibury	Bibury	01285 740695
Three Ways Hotel	Chipping Campden	01386 438429
The Unicorn Hotel	Stow-on-the-Wold	01451 830257
Washbourne Court Hotel	Lower Slaughter	01451 822143
Wyck Hill House	Stow-on-the-Wold	01451 831936

GREATER MANCHESTER

Etrop Grange	Manchester Airport	0161 499 0500

HAMPSHIRE

Careys Manor Hotel	Brockenhurst	01590 623551
Esseborne Manor	Andover	01264 736444
Fifehead Manor	Andover	01264 781565
Hotel Du Vin & Bistro	Winchester	01962 841414
Lainston House Hotel	Winchester	01962 863588

Le Poussin at Parkhill ....Lyndhurst 023 8028 2944
The Master Builder's House ....Beaulieu 01590 616253
The Montagu Arms Hotel ....Beaulieu 01590 612324
New Park Manor ....Brockenhurst ..01590 623467
Passford House Hotel ....Lymington 01590 682398
Rhinefield House Hotel ....Brockenhurst ..01590 622922
Stanwell House ....Lymington 01590 677123
Tylney Hall ....Basingstoke ...01256 764881

HEREFORDSHIRE
The Chase Hotel ....Ross-On-Wye ..01989 763161
Pengethley Manor ....Ross-On-Wye ..01989 730211

HERTFORDSHIRE
Down Hall Country House Hotel ....Stansted 01279 731441
Hanbury Manor...................Ware 01920 487722
Pendley Manor Hotel ....Tring 01442 891891
Sopwell House Hotel Country Club ....St Albans 01727 864477
The St Michael's Manor ....St Albans 01727 864444
West Lodge Park ....Hadley Wood ...020 8216 3900

ISLE OF WIGHT
The George Hotel..................Yarmouth 01983 760331
The Priory Bay Hotel ....Seaview 01983 613146

KENT
Chilston Park ....Maidstone 01622 859803
Eastwell Manor ....Ashford 01233 213000
Hotel Du Vin & Bistro ....Tunbridge Wells .01892 526455
Howfield Manor ....Canterbury 01227 738294
Rowhill Grange Hotel & Spa.........Dartford 01322 615136
The Spa Hotel....................Tunbridge Wells ..01892 520331

LANCASHIRE
Astley Bank Hotel ....Blackburn 01254 777700
The Gibbon Bridge Hotel............Preston 01995 61456
The Imperial Hotel ....Blackpool.......01253 623971

LEICESTERSHIRE
Barnsdale Lodge ....Rutland Water....01572 724678
Quorn Country Hotel ....Loughborough ...01509 415050
Sketchley Grange Hotel ....Leicester 01455 251133
Stapleford Park Country House Hotel ..Melton Mowbray..01572 787522

LINCOLNSHIRE
The George Of Stamford ....Stamford 01780 750750
Kenwick Park Hotel & Leisure Club ....Louth 01507 608806

LONDON
The Academy, The Bloomsbury Town House ..Bloomsbury.........020 7631 4115
41 Buckingham Palace Road ....Buckingham Palace 020 7300 0041
The Rubens at the Palace...............Buckingham Palace ..020 7834 6600
The Club Suites ....Chelsea 020 7730 9131
Draycott House Apartments..............Chelsea 020 7584 4659
The Sloane Hotel ....Chelsea 020 7581 5757
Great Eastern Hotel ....City 020 7618 5000
London Bridge Hotel & Apartments ....City 020 7855 2200
The Rookery ....City 020 7336 0931
Kingsway Hall ....Covent Garden ..020 7309 0909
One Aldwych ....Covent Garden ..020 7300 1000
Hendon Hall ....Hendon 020 8203 3341
The Halcyon ....Holland Park 020 7727 7288
Harrington Hall ....Kensington 020 7396 9696
The Lexham Apartments ....Kensington 020 7559 4444
The Milestone Hotel ....Kensington 020 7917 1000
Twenty Nevern Square ....Kensington 020 7565 9555
Basil Street Hotel ....Knightsbridge ...020 7581 3311
The Beaufort ....Knightsbridge ...020 7584 5252
Beaufort House Apartments ....Knightsbridge ...020 7584 2600
The Cadogan ....Knightsbridge ...020 7235 7141
The Cliveden Town House ....Knightsbridge ...020 7730 6466
Number Eleven Cadogan Gardens.......Knightsbridge ...020 7730 7000

The Hempel ....Lancaster Gate ...020 7298 9000
The Colonnade
  - The Little Venice Town House.......Little Venice......020 7286 1052
The Leonard ....Marble Arch......020 7935 2010
The Ascott Mayfair.................Mayfair 020 7499 6868
Brown's Hotel ....Mayfair 020 7493 6020
The Dorchester ....Mayfair 020 7629 8888
Westbury Hotel ....Mayfair 020 7629 7755
Pembridge Court Hotel..............Notting Hill Gate 020 7229 9977
The Petersham Hotel ....Richmond Upon Thames..020 8940 7471
Number Sixteen ....South Kensington 020 7589 5232
Shaw Park Plaza ....St Pancras..........020 7666 9000
The Royal Horseguards ....Whitehall 020 7839 3400
Cannizaro House..................Wimbledon Common..020 8879 1464

NORFOLK
Barnham Broom ....Barnham Broom ..01603 759393
Congham Hall....................King's Lynn 01485 600250
The Hoste Arms Hotel ....Burnham Market..01328 738777
Lynford Hall Hotel & Business Centre .Thetford 01842 878351
Park Farm Hotel & Leisure..........Norwich 01603 810264
Petersfield House Hotel ....Norwich 01692 630741

NORTH YORKSHIRE
Ambassador Hotel.................York 01904 641316
The Balmoral Hotel ....Harrogate.......01423 508208
The Boar's Head Hotel ....Harrogate.......01423 771888
Crab Manor ....Thirsk 01845 577286
Crathorne Hall ....Crathorne 01642 700398
The Devonshire Arms Hotel ....Bolton Abbey 01756 710441
The Grange Hotel.................York 01904 644744
Grants Hotel ....Harrogate.......01423 560666
Hackness Grange ....Scarborough 01723 882345
Hazlewood Castle Hotel ....Leeds 01937 535353
Hob Green Hotel & Restaurant.........Harrogate.......01423 770031
Middlethorpe Hall ....York 01904 641241
Monk Fryston Hall Hotel ....York 01977 682369
Mount Royale Hotel ....York 01904 628856
Rudding Park House & Hotel ....Harrogate.......01423 871350
The Worsley Arms Hotel ....Hovingham 01653 628234
Wrea Head Country Hotel ....Scarborough 01723 378211
Simonstone Hall ....Hawes 01969 667255

NORTHAMPTONSHIRE
Fawsley Hall Hotel ....Daventry 01327 892000
Kettering Park Hotel...............Kettering 01536 416666
Whittlebury Hall...................Northampton 01327 857 857

NORTHUMBERLAND
Linden Hall Hotel.................Newcastle-Upon-Tyne 01670 50 00 00
Marshall Meadow Hotel ....Berwick-Upon-Tweed..01289 331133
Matfen Hall ....Newcastle-Upon-Tyne 01661 886 500
Tillmouth Park ....Berwick-Upon-Tweed 01890 882255

NOTTINGHAMSHIRE
Langar Hall ....Nottingham 01949 860559

OXFORDSHIRE
The Bay Tree Hotel & Restaurant ....Burford.............01993 822791
The Cotswold Lodge Hotel ....Oxford 01865 512121
Fallowfields........................Oxford 01865 820416
The Feathers Hotel ....Woodstock 01993 812291
Le Manoir aux Quat' Saisons ....Oxford 01844 278881
Mill House Hotel ....Kingham 01608 658188
Phyllis Court Club ....Henley-On-Thames 01491 570500
The Plough at Clanfield ....Clanfield 01367 810222
The Randolph ....Oxford 0870 400 8200
The Spread Eagle Hotel ....Thame 01844 213661
Studley Priory ....Oxford 01865 351203
Weston Manor ....Oxford 01869 350621
Wroxton House Hotel ....Banbury 01295 730777

RUTLAND
Hambleton Hall ....Oakham........01572 756991
The Lake Isle ....Uppingham 01572 822951

SHROPSHIRE
Dinham Hall ....Ludlow 01584 876464
Madeley Court ....Telford 01952 680068
The Old Vicarage Hotel ....Wolverhampton ..01746 716497
Prince Rupert Hotel ....Shrewsbury 01743 499955

SOMERSET
The Bath Priory Hotel and Restaurant .Bath 01225 331922
The Bath Spa Hotel ....Bath 0870 400 8222
Bindon Country House Hotel ....Taunton 01823 400070
Charlton House....................Shepton Mallet 01749 342008
Combe Grove Manor & Country Club Bath .01225 834644
Daneswood House Hotel ....Bristol South 01934 843145
Holbrook House Hotel ....Wincanton 01963 32377
Homewood Park ....Bath 01225 723731
Hunstrete House ....Bath 01761 490490
The Market Place Hotel ....Wells 01749 672616
The Mount Somerset Hotel ....Taunton 01823 442500
Periton Park Hotel ....Middlecombe 01643 706885
The Queensberry.................Bath 01225 447928
The Royal Crescent Hotel ....Bath 01225 823333
Ston Easton Park ....Bath 01761 241631

SOUTH GLOUCESTERSHIRE
Thornbury Castle ....Bristol 01454 281182
Charnwood Hotel ....Sheffield 0114 258 9411
Whitley Hall Hotel ....Sheffield 0114 245 4444

STAFFORDSHIRE
Hoar Cross Hall Health Spa Resort ......Lichfield 01283 575671
The Moat House ....Stafford 01785 712217

SUFFOLK
The Angel Hotel...................Bury St Edmunds..01284 714000
Bedford Lodge Hotel ....Newmarket 01638 663175
Belstead Brook Hotel ....Ipswich 01473 684241
The Black Lion Hotel ....Long Melford.....01787 312356
The Cornwallis Country Hotel ......Eye 01379 870326
Hintlesham Hall ....Ipswich 01473 652268
The Marlborough Hotel ....Ipswich 01473 257677
Ravenwood Hall ....Bury St Edmunds..01359 270345
Seckford Hall ....Woodbridge 01394 385678
The Swan Hotel ....Southwold 01502 722186
Swynford Paddocks Hotel..........Newmarket 01638 570234
Wentworth Hotel ....Aldeburgh 01728 452312

SURREY
The Angel Posting House And Livery ..Guildford 01483 564555
The Burford Bridge ....Box Hill 0870 400 8283
The Carlton Mitre Hotel ....Hampton Court ..020 8979 9988
Foxhills ....Heathrow 01932 704500
Great Fosters ....Egham 01784 433822
Langshott Manor..................Gatwick 01293 786680
Lythe Hill Hotel ....Haslemere 01428 651251
The Manor House ....Guildford 01483 413021
Nutfield Priory ....Redhill 01737 824400
Oatlands Park Hotel ....Weybridge 01932 847242
Pennyhill Park Hotel ....Ascot 01276 471774
The Richmond Gate Hotel ....Richmond-Upon-Thames 020 8940 0061
Woodlands Park Hotel ....Cobham 01372 843933

WARWICKSHIRE
Alveston Manor ....Stratford-Upon-Avon..0870 400 1818
Coombe Abbey ....Coventry 024 76450450
Ettington Park ....Stratford-Upon-Avon ..01789 450123
The Glebe At Barford..............Warwick 01926 624218
Mallory Court ....Leamington Spa ..01926 330214
Nailcote Hall ....Coventry 024 7646 6174

Nuthurst Grange ....Hockley Heath 01564 783972
Welcombe Hotel & Golf Course ....Stratford-Upon-Avon ..01789 295252

WEST MIDLANDS

The Burlington Hotel ....Birmingham 0121 643 9191
New Hall ....Birmingham 0121 378 2442

WEST SUSSEX

Alexander House ....Gatwick 01342 714914
Amberley Castle ....Amberley 01798 831992
The Angel Hotel ....Midhurst 01730 812421
Bailiffscourt ....Arundel 01903 723511
Ghyll Manor Country Hotel ....Rusper 01293 871571
The Millstream Hotel ....Chichester 01243 573234
Ockenden Manor ....Cuckfield 01444 416111
South Lodge Hotel ....Horsham 01403 891711
The Spread Eagle Hotel & Health Spa Midhurst 01730 816911

WEST YORKSHIRE

42 The Calls ....Leeds 0113 244 0099
Chevin Lodge Country Park Hotel ......Otley 01943 467818
Haley's Hotel & Restaurant ....Leeds 0113 278 4446
Holdsworth House ....Halifax 01422 240024
Oulton Hall ....Leeds 0113 282 1000
Wood Hall ....Wetherby 01937 587271

WILTSHIRE

Bishopstrow House ....Warminster 01985 212312
Howard's House ....Salisbury 01722 716392
Ivy House Hotel ....Marlborough 01672 515333
Lucknam Park ....Bath 01225 742777
The Manor House Hotel & Golf Club Castle Combe 01249 782206
The Old Bell ....Malmesbury 01666 822344
The Pear Tree at Purton ....Swindon 01793 772100
Woolley Grange ....Bradford-On-Avon 01225 864705

WORCESTERSHIRE

The Broadway Hotel ....Broadway 01386 852401
Brockencote Hall ....Chaddesley Corbett ..01562 777876
Buckland Manor Hotel ....Broadway 01386 852626
Colwall Park Hotel ....Malvern 01684 540000
Cottage In The Wood..........................Malvern Wells 01684 575859
Dormy House ....Broadway 01386 852711
The Elms ....Worcester 01299 896666
The Evesham Hotel ....Evesham 01386 765566
The Lygon Arms ....Broadway 01386 852255
Salford Hall Hotel..............................Stratford-Upon-Avon ..01386 871300
Stone Manor Hotel............................Kidderminster 01562 777555
Wood Norton Hall ....Evesham 01386 420007

WALES

CEREDIGION

Conrah Country House Hotel ....Aberystwyth 01970 617941
Ynyshir Hall ....Machynlleth 01654 781209

CLWYD

Llyndir Hall Hotel ....Wrexham 01244 571648

DENBIGHSHIRE

Tyddyn Llan Country House Hotel ......Corwen 01490 440264

GWYNEDD

Bodysgallen Hall................................Llandudno 01492 584466
Bontddu Hall......................................Barmouth 01341 430661
Hotel Maes-Y-Neuadd........................Harlech 01766 780200
Palé Hall ....Bala 01678 530285
Penmaenuchaf Hall............................Dolgellau 01341 422129
Porth Tocyn Country House Hotel ......Abersoch 01758 713303

The Portmeirion and Castell Deudraeth ....Portmeirion Village..01766 770000
St Tudno Hotel ....Llandudno 01492 874411
Trearddur Bay Hotel ....Anglesey 01407 860301
Ye Olde Bull's Head ....Beaumaris 01248 810329

HEREFORDSHIRE

Allt-Yr-Ynys Hotel ....Abergavenny 01873 890307

MID GLAMORGAN

Miskin Manor Country House Hotel ....Cardiff 01443 224204
Ty Newydd Country Hotel ....Aberdare 01685 813433

MONMOUTHSHIRE

The Cwrt Bleddyn Hotel ....Usk 01633 450521
Llansantffraed Court Hotel..................Abergavenny 01873 840678

MONTGOMERYSHIRE

Lake Vyrnwy Hotel ....Lake Vyrnwy 01691 870 692

PEMBROKESHIRE

The Court Hotel & Restaurant ....Pembroke....01646 672273
Penally Abbey ....Tenby 01834 843033
Warpool Court Hotel ....St David's 01437 720300

POWYS

Gliffaes Country House Hotel ....Crickhowell....01874 730371
The Lake Country House ....Llangammarch Wells ..01591 620202
Llangoed Hall ....Brecon 01874 754525
Nant Ddu Lodge Hotel ....Brecon Beacons 01685 379111
Peterstone Court ....Brecon 01874 665387

SCOTLAND

ABERDEENSHIRE

Ardoe House Hotel & Restaurant ....Aberdeen 01224 860600
Darroch Learg Hotel ....Ballater 013397 55443
Kildrummy Castle Hotel......................Kildrummy....019755 71288
Raemoir House Hotel ....Banchory 01330 824884
Thainstone House Hotel ....Aberdeen 01467 621643

ARGYLL

Ardanaiseig ....Kilchrenan by Oban ..01866 833333
Enmore Hotel ....Dunoon 01369 702230
Knipoch Hotel ....Oban 01852 316251

AYRSHIRE

Glenapp Castle ....Ballantrae 01465 831212
Lochgreen House ....Troon 01292 313343
Piersland House Hotel ....Troon 01292 314747

BANFFSHIRE

Craigellachie Hotel............................Craigellachie 01340 881204

DUMFRIES & GALLOWAY

Balcary Bay Hotel ....Auchencairn 01556 640311
Cally Palace Hotel ....Gatehouse Of Fleet ..01557 814341
The Dryfesdale Country House Hotel ..Lockerbie....01576 202427
Corsewall Lighthouse Hotel ....Stranraer 01776 853220

EDINBURGH

Dalhousie Castle & Spa ....Edinburgh 01875 820153
The Howard ....Edinburgh....0131 557 3500
Prestonfield House ....Edinburgh 0131 668 3346
The Roxburgh ....Edinburgh....0131 240 5500
The Scotsman ....Edinburgh 0131 556 5565

FIFE

The Inn at Lathones............................St Andrews....01334 840 494

GLASGOW

Carlton George Hotel ....Glasgow 0141 353 6373

INVERNESS-SHIRE

Arisaig House ....Beasdale By Arisaig 01687 450622
Bunchrew House Hotel........................Inverness 01463 234917
Culloden House Hotel ....Inverness 01463 790461
Loch Torridon Hotel ....Torridon 01445 791242
Mansion House Hotel ....Elgin 01343 548811

LANARKSHIRE

Shieldhill Castle ....Biggar....01899 220035

MID LOTHIAN

The Bonham ....Edinburgh 0131 226 6050
Borthwick Castle ....Edinburgh 01875 820514
Channings ....Edinburgh 0131 315 2226
The Norton House Hotel ....Edinburgh 0131 333 1275

MORAYSHIRE

Muckrach Lodge Hotel & Restaurant ..Grantown-on-Spey 01479 851257

PEEBLESHIRE

Cringletie House Hotel........................Peebles 01721 730233

PERTHSHIRE

Auchterarder House ....Auchterarder 01764 663646
Ballathie House Hotel ....Perth 01250 883268
Cromlix House ....Kinbuck 01786 822125
Dalmunzie House ....Glenshee 01250 885224
Huntingtower Hotel ....Perth 01738 583771
Kinfauns Castle ....Perth 01738 620777
Kinloch House Hotel ....Blairgowrie 01250 884237
Kinnaird ....Dunkeld 01796 482 440
Pine Trees Hotel ....Pitlochry 01796 472121

RENFREWSHIRE

Gleddoch House ....Glasgow 01475 540711

ROXBURGHSHIRE

Ednam House Hotel ....Kelso 01573 224168
The Roxburghe Hotel & Golf Course ..Kelso 01573 450331

SCOTTISH BORDERS

Dryburgh Abbey Hotel ....St Boswells 01835 822261

STRATHCLYDE

Macdonald Crutherland House Hotel ..East Kilbride 01355 577000

STIRLING

Stirling Highland Hotel ....Stirling 01786 272727
Forest Hills ....Aberfoyle 01877 387277

SUTHERLAND

Inver Lodge Hotel..............................Lochinver 01571 844496

WEST LOTHIAN

Houstoun House ....Uphall 01506 853831

WIGTOWNSHIRE

Fernhill Hotel ....Portpatrick 01776 810220
Kirroughtree House............................Newton Stewart ..01671 402141

IRELAND

BELFAST

The McCausland Hotel ....Belfast 028 9022 0200

CO. CLARE

Dromoland Castle ....Newmarket-On-Fergus 00 353 61 368144
Woodstock Hotel ....Ennis 00 353 65 684 6600

CO CORK
Longueville House
& Presidents' Restaurant .... Mallow 00 353 22 47156

CO DONEGAL
The Sand House Hotel .... Rossnowlagh 00 353 72 51777

CO DOWN
Culloden Hotel .... Belfast 028 9042 5223

CO DUBLIN
The Merrion Hotel .... Dublin 00 353 1 603 0600

CO GALWAY
Renvyle House Hotel .... Connemara 00 353 95 43511

CO KERRY
Aghadoe Heights Hotel .... Killarney 00 353 64 31766
The Killarney Park Hotel .... Killarney 00 353 64 35555
The Park Hotel Kenmare .... Kenmare 00 353 64 41200
Parknasilla Hotel .... Parknasilla 00 353 64 45122
Sheen Falls Lodge .... Kenmare 00 353 64 41600

CO KILDARE
Kildare Hotel & Country Club .... Dublin 00 353 1 601 7200

CO.KILKENNY
Kilkenny Ormonde Hotel .... Kilkenny 00 353 56 23900

CO. MAYO
Ashford Castle .... Cong 00 353 92 46003
Knockranny House Hotel .... Westport 00 353 98 28600

CO MONAGHAN
Nuremore Hotel & Country Club .... Carrickmacross 00 353 429
661438

CO WEXFORD
Kelly's Resort Hotel .... Rosslare 00 353 53 32114
Marlfield House .... Gorey 00 353 55 21124

CO WICKLOW
Hunter's Hotel .... Rathnew 00 353 404 40106
Tinakilly Country House Hotel .... Wicklow 00 353 40469274

CORK
Hayfield Manor Hotel .... Cork 00 353 21 4315600

DUBLIN
Brooks Hotel .... Dublin 00 353 1 670 4000
The Davenport Hotel .... Dublin 00 353 1 607 3500
The Hibernian .... Dublin 00 353 1 668 7666
Stephen's Green Hotel .... Dublin 00 353 1 607 3600
The Fitzwilliam Hotel .... Dublin 00 353 1 478 7000

GALWAY
Connemara Coast Hotel .... Galway 00 353 91 592108

WEST CORK
The Lodge & Spa at Inchydoney Island .... Clonakilty 00 353 23 33143

CHANNEL ISLANDS

GUERNSEY
Old Government House Hotel .... Guernsey 01481 724921
St Pierre Park Hotel .... Guernsey 01481 728282

JERSEY
The Atlantic Hotel .... Jersey 01534 744101
Château La Chaire .... Jersey 01534 863354
Hotel L'Horizon .... Jersey 01534 743101
Longueville Manor .... Jersey 01534 725501

COUNTRY HOUSES
ENGLAND

CAMBRIDGESHIRE
Melbourn Bury .... Cambridge 01763 261151

CHESHIRE
Green Bough Hotel .... Chester 01244 326241
Willington Hall Hotel .... Tarporley 01829 752321

CO.DURHAM
Grove House .... Hamsterley Forest 01388 488203
Horsley Hall .... Stanhope 01388 517239

CORNWALL
The Cormorant Hotel .... Golant by Fowey .. 01726 833426
The Countryman At Trink Hotel .... St Ives 01736 797571
Cross House Hotel .... Padstow 01841 532391
The Hundred House Hotel .... St Mawes 01872 501336
Nansloe Manor .... Helston 01326 574691
The Old Rectory Country House Hotel .. St Keyne 01579 342617
Penhallow Manor Country House Hotel .. Launceston 01566 86206
Trebrea Lodge .... Tintagel 01840 770410
Tredethy House .... Wadebridge 01208 841262
Trehellas House &
Memories of Malaya Restaurant .... Wadebridge 01208 72700
Trelawne Hotel-The Hutches Restaurant .. Falmouth 01326 250226
Tye Rock Country House & Apartments .. Porthleven 01326 572695

CUMBRIA
Aynsome Manor Hotel .... Cartmel 015395 36653
Broadoaks Country House .... Windermere 01539 445566
Crosby Lodge Country House Hotel .... Carlisle 01228 573618
Dale Head Hall Lakeside Hotel .... Keswick 017687 72478
Fayrer Garden House Hotel .... Windermere 015394 88195
Hipping Hall .... Kirkby Lonsdale .. 015242 71187
Lakeshore House .... Windermere 015394 33202
Nanny Brow Country House Hotel ...... Ambleside 015394 32036
The Old Vicarage Country House Hotel .. Witherslack 015395 52381
Sawrey House Country Hotel .... Hawkshead 015394 36387
Swinside Lodge Hotel .... Keswick 017687 72948
Temple Sowerby House Hotel .... Penrith 017683 61578
White Moss House .... Grasmere 015394 35295
Winder Hall .... Lorton 01900 85107

DERBYSHIRE
Biggin Hall .... Biggin-By-Hartington .. 01298 84451
The Homestead .... Derby 01332 544300
Santo's Higham Farm .... Higham 01773 833812
The Wind In The Willows .... Glossop 01457 868001

DEVON
Ashelford .... Combe Martin ... 01271 850469
Bel Alp House .... Dartmoor 01364 661217
Blackaller .... North Bovey 01647 440322
Browns Hotel Wine Bar & Brasserie .... Tavistock 01822 618686
Coombe House Country Hotel .... Crediton 01363 84487
Downrew House Hotel .... Barnstaple 01271 342497
Ilsington Country Hotel .... Ilsington 01364 661452
Kingston House .... Staverton 01803 762 235
Moor View House .... Lydford 01822 820220
Oxenways .... Membury 01404 881785
Preston House Hotel .... Saunton 01271 890472
The White House .... Kingsbridge 01548 580580
Wigham .... Morchard Bishop.. 01363 877350
Beechleas .... Wimborne Minster 01202 841684
The Grange Hotel & Restaurant .... Sherborne 01935 813463
Yalbury Cottage Hotel .... Dorchester 01305 262382

EAST SUSSEX
The Granville .... Brighton 01273 326302
Hooke Hall .... Uckfield 01825 761578
White Vine House .... Rye 01797 224748

ESSEX
The Pump House Apartment .... Billericay 01277 656579

GLOUCESTERSHIRE
Bibury Court .... Bibury 01285 740337
Burleigh Court .... Minchinhampton 01453 883804
Charlton Kings Hotel .... Cheltenham 01242 231061
Dial House Hotel .... Bourton-On-The-Water .. 01451 822244
Lower Brook House .... Blockley 01386 700286
The Malt House .... Chipping Campden 01386 840295
Owlpen Manor .... Owlpen 01453 860261
Three Choirs .... Newent 01531 890223
Tudor Farmhouse Hotel & Restaurant .. Clearwell 01594 833046

GREATER MANCHESTER
Eleven Didsbury Park .... Manchester 0161 448 7711

HAMPSHIRE
The Beaufort Hotel .... Portsmouth 023 92823707
Langrish House .... Petersfield 01730 266941
Moortown Lodge .... Ringwood 01425 471404
The Nurse's Cottage .... Lymington 01590 683402
Thatched Cottage Hotel & Restaurant .. Brockenhurst 01590 623090
Whitley Ridge & Country House Hotel .. Brockenhurst 01590 622354

HEREFORDSHIRE
Glewstone Court .... Ross-On-Wye 01989 770367
Lower Bache House .... Leominster 01568 750304
The Steppes .... Hereford 01432 820424
Wilton Court Hotel .... Ross-on-Wye 01989 562569

HERTFORDSHIRE
Little Offley .... Luton 01462 768243
Redcoats Farmhouse Hotel & Restaurant .. Stevenage 01438 729500

ISLE OF WIGHT
Rylstone Manor .... Isle of Wight 01983 862806

KENT
Romney Bay House .... New Romney 01797 364747
Sandgate Hotel at Restaurant La Terrasse .. Folkestone 01303 220444
Wallett's Court .... Dover 01304 852424

LANCASHIRE
Tree Tops Country House Hotel .... Southport 01704 572430

LEICESTERSHIRE
Abbots Oak .... Coalville 01530 832 328
The Old Manor Hotel .... Loughborough 01509 211228
Sutton Bonnington Hall .... Nottingham 01509 672355

LINCOLNSHIRE
Washingborough Hall .... Lincoln 01522 790340

MIDDLESEX
Oak Lodge Hotel .... Enfield 020 8360 7082

NORFOLK
The Beeches Hotel & Victorian Gardens .. Norwich 01603 621167
Beechwood Hotel .... North Walsham 01692 403231
Broom Hall Country Hotel .... Thetford 01953 882125
Catton Old Hall .... Norwich 01603 419379
Elderton Lodge .... North Walsham 01263 833547
Felbrigg Lodge .... Holt 01263 837588

Johansens Recommendations

The Great Escape Holiday Company ....North Norfolk Coast 01485 518717
Norfolk Mead Hotel ....Norwich 01603 737531
The Old Rectory ....Great Snoring 01328 820597
The Old Rectory ....Norwich 01603 700772
Sea Marge Hotel ....Overstrand 01263 579579
The Stower Grange ....Norwich 01603 860210

NORTH YORKSHIRE
Appleton Hall ....Appleton-Le-Moors 01751 417227
The Parsonage Country House Hotel ..York 01904 728111
The Pheasant ....Helmsley 01439 771241
Rookhurst Country House Hotel ....Hawes 01969 667454
Shallowdale House ....Ampleforth 01439 788325
Waterford House ....Middleham 01969 622090
The White House ....Harrogate............01423 501388

NORTHUMBERLAND
The Otterburn Tower ....Otterburn 01830 520620
Waren House Hotel ....Bamburgh 01668 214581

NOTTINGHAMSHIRE
Cockliffe Country House Hotel ....Nottingham..........01159 680179
The Cottage Country House Hotel ......Nottingham 01159 846882
Langar Hall ....Nottingham 01949 860559

OXFORDSHIRE
The George Hotel..............................Dorchester-On-Thames 01865 340404
Fallowfields ....Oxford 01865 820416
The Shaven Crown Hotel ....Shipton 01993 830330
The Tollgate Inn ....Stow-On-The-Wold 01608 658389
Westwood Country House ....Oxford 01865 735408

SHROPSHIRE
The Brompton...................................Shrewsbury 01743 761629
Overton Grange Hotel ....Ludlow 01584 873500
Pen-y-Dyffryn Country Hotel..............Oswestry 01691 653700
Rowton Castle Hotel ....Shrewsbury 01743 884044
Soulton Hall ....Wem 01939 232786

SOMERSET
Andrew's On The Weir ....Porlock Weir 01643 863300
Apsley House ....Bath 01225 336966
Ashwick Country House Hotel ....Dulverton 01398 323868
Bath Lodge Hotel ....Bath 01225 723040
Beryl ....Wells 01749 678738
The County Hotel ....Bath 01225 425003
Daneswood House Hotel ....Cheddar 01934 843145
Glencot House ....Wells 01749 677160
The Old Priory Hotel ....Bath 01761 416784
The Old Rectory ....Ilminster 01460 54364
Paradise House ....Bath 01225 317723
Periton Park Hotel ....Middlecombe 01643 706885
Porlock Vale House ....Porlock Weir 01643 862338
Villa Magdala ....Bath 01225 466329
Woolverton House ....Bath 01373 830415

STAFFORDSHIRE
The Grange Hotel..............................Albrighton 01902 701711

SUFFOLK
Chippenhall Hall ....Diss 01379 588180
'Edge Hall' Hotel...............................Hadleigh 01473 822458
The Elms ....Beccles 01502 677380

SURREY
Chalk Lane Hotel ....Epsom 01372 721179
Chase Lodge ....Hampton Court ...020 8943 1862
The Hautboy ....Ockham 01483 225355
Stanhill Court Hotel..........................Gatwick 01293 862166

WARWICKSHIRE
The Ardencote Manor Hotel ....Warwick 01926 843111
Arrow Mill Hotel And Restaurant ....Alcester 01789 762419
Chapel House ....Atherstone 01827 718949
Glebe Farm House ....Stratford-upon-Avon ..01789 842501

WEST SUSSEX
Burpham Country House Hotel ....Arundel 01903 882160
Chequers Hotel ....Pulborough 01798 872486
Crouchers Bottom Country Hotel ....Chichester 01243 784995
The Mill House Hotel ....Ashington 01903 892426

WILTSHIRE
Stanton Manor ....Chippenham 01666 837552
Widbrook Grange ....Bath 01225 864750

WORCESTERSHIRE
Grafton Manor Country House Hotel ..Bromsgrove 01527 579007
The Old Windmill ....Alcester 01386 792801

WALES

CARMARTHENSHIRE
The Cawdor Arms Hotel ....Llandeilo 01558 823500

CONWY
The Old Rectory Country House ....Conwy 01492 580611
Tan-y-Foel ....Betws-y-Coed 01690 710507

GLAMORGAN
Llechwen Hall..................................Cardiff 01443 742050

GWYNEDD
Abergwynant Hall..............................Dolgellau 01341 422160
Plas Dolmelynllyn ....Dolgellau 01341 440273
Plas Penhelig Country House Hotel......Aberdovey 01654 767676
Ty'n Rhos Country Hotel ....Caernarfon 01248 670489
Tyddyn Iolyn ....Criccieth01766 522509 /522537

MONMOUTHSHIRE
The Crown At Whitebrook ....Monmouth 01600 860254
Parva Farmhouse and Restaurant ....Tintern................01291 689411

PEMBROKESHIRE
Waterwynch House Hotel ....Tenby 01834 842464

WEST GLAMORGAN
Norton House Hotel & Restaurant ......Swansea 01792 404891

SCOTLAND

ABERDEENSHIRE
Balgonie Country House......................Ballater 013397 55482
Banchory Lodge Hotel ....Banchory 01330 822625
Castle of Park ....Cornhill 01466 751111

ARGYLLSHIRE
Ardsheal House.................................Kentallen Of Appin ..01631 740227
Dungallan House Hotel ....Oban 01631 563799

AYRSHIRE
Culzean Castle -
   The Eisenhower Apartment ....Maybole 01655 884455

DUNFRIESSHIRE
Trigony House Hotel...........................Dunfries 01848 331211

FIFE
Balgeddie House Hotel ....Leslie 01592 742511
Garvock House Hotel ....Edinburgh 01383 621067
The Inn on North Steet ....St. Andrews.........01334 473387

INVERNESS-SHIRE
Boath House ....Nairn 01667 454896
Corrour House...................................Rothiemurchus 01479 810220
Culduthel Lodge ....Inverness 01463 240089
Mullardoch House Hotel ....Glen Cannich 01456 415460

PERTHSHIRE
The Four Seasons Hotel ....St Fillans 01764 685333
The Killiecrankie Hotel ....Killiecrankie........01796 473220
Knockendarroch House ....Pitlochry 01796 473473
The Lake Hotel..................................Port Of Menteith ..01877 385258
The Pend..Dunkeld..............01350 727586

ROSS-SHIRE
Glenmorangie House at Cadbol ....Tain 01862 871671

STIRLING & TROSSACHS
Culcreuch Castle Hotel & Country Park ....Fintry 01360 860555

WESTERN ISLES
Ardvourlie Castle ....Isle Of Harris........01859 502307

IRELAND

CO DONEGAL
Castle Grove Country House Hotel......Letterkenny 00 353 745 1118

CO GALWAY
Ross Lake House Hotel.......................Connemara 00 353 91 550109
St. Clerans......................................Craughwell ..00 353 91 846 555

CO KERRY
Caragh Lodge ....Caragh Lake 00 353 66 9769115
Earls Court House ....Killarney 00 353 64 34009
Killarney Royal Hotel ....Killarney 00 353 64 31853

CO SLIGO
Coopershill House ....Riverstown 00 353 71 65108
Markree Castle ....Sligo 00 353 71 67800

CO TIPPERARY
Cashel Palace Hotel ....Cashel 00 353 62 62707

CO WATERFORD
The Old Rectory - Kilmeaden House....Kilmeaden 00 353 51 384254

CHANNEL ISLANDS

GUERNSEY
Bella Luce Hotel & Restaurant ....Guernsey 01481 238764
La Favorita Hotel ....Guernsey 01481 35666
La Favorita Hotel ....Guernsey 01481 35666

HERM ISLAND
The White House ....Herm Island 01481 722159

SARK ISLAND
La Sablonnerie ....Sark Island 01481 832061

EUROPE & THE MEDITERRANEAN

AUSTRIA

Almdorf "Seinerzeit"	Patergassen	+43 4275 7201
Ana Grand Hotel Wien	Vienna	+43 1515 80726
Arlberg Hospiz	Sankt Christoph	+43 5446 2611
Das Moser	Bad Hofgastein	+43 6432 6209
Hotel Auersperg	Salzburg	+43 662 88 944
Hotel Gasthof Gams	Bezau	+43 5514 2220
Hotel Goldener Berg	Lech	+43 5583 22050
Hotel im Palais Schwarzenberg	Vienna	+43 1 798 4515
Hotel Klosterbräu	Seefeld	+43 521 226210
Hotel Palais Porcia	Klagenfurt	+43 463 51 15 90
Hotel Schloss Dürnstein	Dürnstein	+43 2711 212
Hotel Schloss Mönchstein	Salzburg	+43 662 84 85 55 0
Hotel & Spa Haus Hirt	Bad Gastein	+43 64 34 27 97
Romantik Hotel Almtalhof	Grünau	+43 7616 82040
Romantik Hotel Böglerhof	Alpbach	+43 5336 5227
Romantik Hotel im Weissen Rössl	St Wolfgang am See	+43 6138 23060
Romantik Hotel Schwarzer Adler	Innsbruck	+43 512 587109
Romantik Hotel Tennerhof	Kitzbühel	+43 53566 3181
RomantikHotel Gasthof Hirschen	Schwarzenberg im Bregenzerwald	+43 5512 29 44 0
Schlossberg Hotel	Graz	+43 316 80700
Schlosshotel Igls	Igls	+43 512 37 72 17
Seeschlössl Velden	Velden	+43 4274 2824
Sporthotel Igls	Igls	+43 512 37 72 41
Sporthotel Kristiania	Lech	+43 55 83 25 610
Thurnhers Alpenhof	Zürs	+43 5583 2191

CYPRUS

Le Meridien Limassol Spa and Resort	Limassol	+357 5 634 000
The Four Seasons Hotel	Limassol	+357 5 310 222

CZECH REPUBLIC

Hotel Hoffmeister	Prague	+420 2 510 17 111
Sieber Hotel & Apartments	Prague	+420 2 242 50 025
Hotel U Krale Karla	Prague	+420 2 575 31 211

DENMARK

Hotel Hesselet	Nyborg	+45 65 31 30 29
Steensgaard Herregårdspension	Faaborg	+45 62 61 94 90

ESTONIA

Park Consul Schlössle	Tallinn	+372 699 7700

GIBRALTER

The Rock Hotel	Gibralta	+350 73 000

GREECE

Doryssa Bay Hotel-Village	Samos Island	+30 273 88 300
Hotel Club Montana	Karpenisi	+30 237 80400
Hotel Pentelikon	Athens	+30 1 62 306506
St Nicolas Bay Hotel	Crete	+30 841 25041

HUNGARY

Danubius Hotel Gellért	Budapest	+36 1 385 2200

IRELAND

Adare Manor Hotel & Golf Resort	Adare	+353 61 396 566

ITALY

Albergo Annunziata	Ferrara	+39 0532 20 11 11
Albergo Quattro Fontane	Venice Lido	+39 041 52 60 227
Albergo San Lorenzo	Mantova	+39 037 62 20 500
Albergo Terminus	Como	+39 031 32 91 11
Capitol Millennium	Milan	+39 024 38 591
Castello Di Spaltenna	Gaiole In Chianti	+39 057 77 49 483
Grand Hotel Cocumella	Sorrento	+39 081 87 82 933
Grand Hotel Excelsior Vittoria	Sorrento	+39 081 80 71 044
Grand Hotel Villa Balbi	Sestri Levante	+39 018 54 29 41
Hellenia Yachting Hotel	Giardini Naxos	+39 094 25 1737
Hotel Auriga	Milan	+39 026 69 85 851
Hotel Baia Taormina	Marina d'Agro	+39 094 27 56 292
Hotel Farnese	Rome	+39 063 21 25 53
Hotel Giulio Cesare	Rome	+39 063 21 07 51
Hotel J and J	Florence	+39 055 26 31 21
Hotel Lorenzetti	Madonna di Campiglio	+39 046 54 41 404
Hotel Montebello Splendid	Florence	+39 055 23 98 051
Hotel Punta Est	Finale Ligure	+39 019 60 06 11
Hotel Relais La Suvera	Pievescola	+39 057 79 60 300
Hotel Roma	Siracusa	+39 093 14 65 626
Hotel Tosco Romagnolo	Bagno Di Romagna	+39 054 39 11 260
Hotel Victoria	Torino	+39 011 56 11 909
Hotel Villa Flori	Como	+39 031 57 3105
Hotel Villa Paradiso Dell' Etna	Etna	+39 095 75 12 409
Hotel Villa Sant' Andrea	Taormina Mare	+39 094 22 31 25
Hotel Villa Undulna	Cinquale	+39 058 58 07 788
Il Pellicano	Porto Ercole	+39 056 48 58 111
La Posta Vecchia	Palo Laziale-Rome	+39 069 94 95 01
Palazzo Vivani-Castello Di Montegridolfo	Castello Di Montegridolfo	+39 0541 85 53 50
Park Hotel Mignon	Merano	+39 047 32 30 353
Parkhotel Sole Paradiso	San Candino	+39 047 49 13 120
Posthotel Weisses Rössl	Nova Levante	+39 047 16 13 113
Relais Villa Pomela	Novi Ligure	+39 014 33 29 910
Ripagrande Hotel	Ferrara	+39 053 27 65 250
Romantic Hotel Oberwirt	Marling-Méran	+39 047 34 47 111
Romantik Hotel Barocco	Rome	+39 064 87 20 01
Romantik Hotel Le Silve di Armenzano	Assisi	+39 075 80 19 000
Romantik Hotel Poseidon	Positano	+39 089 81 11 11
Romantik Hotel Stafler	Mauls	+39 047 27 71 136
Romantik Hotel Tenuta Di Ricavo	Castellina In Chianti	+39 057 77 40 221
Romantik Hotel Turm	Völs am Schlern	+39 047 17 25 014

LATVIA

Hotel de Rome	Riga	+371 708 7600
Hotel Grand Palace	Riga	+371 704 4000
Hotel Konventa Seta	Riga	+371 708 7501

LUXEMBOURG

Hotel Saint Nicolas	Remich	+352 26 663

MONACO

Hôtel Hermitage	Monte-Carlo	+377 92 16 40 00

NORWAY

Dalen Hotel	Dalen	+47 35 07 70 00
First Hotel Bastion	Oslo	+47 22 47 77 00
Fleischers Hotel	Voss)	+47 56 52 05 00
Gloppen Hotel	Sandane	+47 57 86 53 33
Hotel Refsnes Gods	Moss	+47 69 27 83 00
Walaker Hotell	Solvorn	+47 57 68 42 07

PORTUGAL

A Forte de S. Francisco	Chaves	+351 276 33 37 00
Casa D'Azurara	Mangualde	+351 232 612010
Casa Domilu	Carvoeiro	+351 282 358 404
Convento de Sao Paulo	Redondo	+351 266 98 91 60
Monte do Casal	Estoi	+351 289 99 0 1 40
Pousada De Alijó- Barão de Forrester	Alijó	+351 259 95 92 15
Pousada de Condeixa-a Nov Santa Cristina	Condeixa-a-Nova	+351 239 94 40 25
Pousada de São Brás d e Alportel	São Brás de Alportel-Algarve	+351 28 98 42 305
Pousada De Vila Viçosa-D.João IV	Vila Viçosa- D.João I	+351 268 98 07 42
Quinta Da Bela Vista	Madeira	+351 291 764 144
Reid's Palace	Madeira	+351 291 7171 71
Romantik Hotel Vivenda Miranda	Lagos	+351 282 763 222

SPAIN

Almenara Hotel - Golf	Sotogrande	+34 956 58 20 00
Ca's Xorc	Mallorca	++34 971 63 8091
Cortijo Aguila Real	Seville	+34 955 78 50 06
Gran Hotel Bahia Del Duque	Tenerife	+34 922 74 69 00
Hacienda Benazuza	Seville	+34 955 70 33 44
Hacienda El Santiscal	Arcos De La Frontera	+34 956 70 83 13
Hotel Botánico	Tenerife	+34 922 38 14 00
Hotel Byblos Andaluz	Mijas-Costa	+34 952 47 30 50
Hotel Claris	Barcelona	+34 934 87 62 62
Hotel Colon	Barcelona	+34 933 01 14 04
Hotel Estela Barcelona	Sitges	+34 938 11 45 45
Hotel Grevol	Camprodon	+34 972 74 10 13
Hotel Jardin Tropical	Tenerife	+34 922 74 60 00
Hotel La Costa	Pals	+34 972 66 77 40
Hotel Monnaber Nou	Mallorca	+34 971 87 71 76
Hotel Rector	Salamanca	+34 923 21 84 82
Hotel Rigat Park	Lloret de Mar	+34 972 36 52 00
Hotel Sa Pedrissa	Mallorca	+34 971 63 91 11
Hotel San Roque	Tenerife	+34 922 13 34 35
Hotel Suites Albayzin Del Mar	Almuñecar	+34 958 63 21 61
Hotel Termes Montbrío Resort	Tarragona	+34 977 81 40 00
Hotel Vistamar De Valldemosa	Mallorca	+34 971 61 23 00
La Parada Del Compte	Teruel	+34 978 76 90 72
La Posada Del Torcal	Malaga	+34 952 03 11 77
Las Dunas Suites	Marbella	+34 952 79 43 45
Marbella Club Hotel, Golf and Spa Resort	Marbella	+34 952 82 22 11
Monasterio de San Miguel	Puerto de Santa Maria-Cádiz	+34 956 54 04 40
The Gallery	Barcelona	+34 93 415 99 11
Villa Real	Madrid	+34 914 20 37 67
Xalet La Coromina	Viladrau	+34 938 84 92 64

SWEDEN

Halltorps Gästgiveri	Borgholm	+46 485 85 000
Hotel Eggers	Gothenburg	+46 318 06 070
Romantik Hotel Åkerblads	Tällberg	+46 247 50 800
Romantik Hotel Söderköpings Brunn	Söderköping	+46 121 10 900
Toftaholm Herrgård	Lagan	+46 370 44 055

SWITZERLAND

Grand Hotel Zermatterhof	Zermatt	+41 27 966 6600
Hostellerie Bon Accueil	Chateau d'Oex	+41 26 924 6320
Hotel Stadthaus	Burgdorf-Bern	+41 34 428 8000
Le Grand Chalet	Gstaad	+41 33 748 7676
Posthotel Engiadina	Zouz	+41 81 854 1021
Royal Park ***** Hotel	Kandersteg	+41 33 675 8888

TURKEY

Hillside Beach Club	Fethiye-Mugla	+90 252 614 8360
Hotel Villa Mahal	Kalkan	+90 242 844 3268
Marina Residence and Restaurant	Antalya	+90 242 247 5490
Savile Residence	Kas	++44 207 625 3001

Calendar of Events

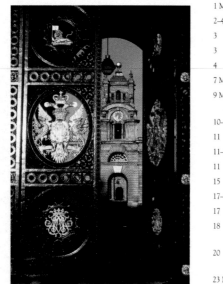

Ardington House, Oxfordshire

FEBRUARY

1 Feb–31 May	Hampstead Museum Exhibition – Historic Pubs & Taverns of Hampstead	Burgh House, London. (020) 7431 0144
1 Feb–28 Feb	Snowdrop Sunday – 1pm – 3 pm – £2 per person Including NT members, See Press for Details	Rievaulx Terrace & Temples, North Yorkshire. (01439) 748 283
10 Feb–8 July	Riverworks	River & Rowing Museum, Oxfordshire tel:(01491) 415610
11	Snow Drop, 11am – 3pm	Chelsea Physic Garden, London. (020) 7352 5646
11	Snowdrop Sunday, 11 am – 5 pm, Admiss. A £4 C £3. (01707) 262 823.	Hatfield House, Herts. (01707) 262 823
17–25	Half – Term Children's Activity Week	Royal Pavilion, Sussex. (01273) 290 900
17–25	Springtime Safari	Painshill Park, Surrey. 01932 868113
18	French Art Family Fun Day	The Bowes Museum, Co Durham. (01833) 690 606
18	Snowdrop Sunday, 11 am – 5 pm, Admiss. A £4 C £3. (01707) 262 823.	Hatfield House, Herts. (01707) 262 823
19–23	Half –Term Theatre	Leeds Castle, Kent. (01622) 765 400
20 Feb–1 Apr	Exhibition – Way Out! Art & Design in the Space Age	Cecil Higgins Art Gallery & Museum, Bedfordshire. (0234) 211 222
23–25	Antique Fair	Stoneyhurst College Delco Ltd, Lancashire. (01254) 826 345
23–24	Bonsai at Wisley. Lectures & Demonstrations Beginners as well as Enthusiats, Specialist Nurseries	RHS Garden Wisley, Surrey. (01483) 224 234
25	Snowdrop Sunday, 11 am – 5 pm, Admiss. A £4 C £3. (01707) 262 823.	Hatfield House, Herts. (01707) 262 823
28	Stately Home Experience' – Lecture, Personal guided tour, Lunch & Wine 10am–4pm £44.50	Ardington House, Oxfordshire. (01235) 821566

MARCH

1 Mar–3 Jun	Peter Lanyon: Coastal Journey	Tate Gallery St Ives, Cornwall. (01736) 796 226
2–4	Antiques Fair	Scone Palace, Scotland. 01738 552300
3	Craft Market	The Bowes Museum, Co Durham. (01833) 690 606
3	Winston Churchill Memorial Concert, Palace	Blenheim Palace, Oxfordshire, Admissions– Rosie Lewis – 01869 350049
4	Winter Events – Games & Gambling, Living History at the Royal Pavilion	Royal Pavilion, Sussex. (01273) 290 900
7 Mar–13 Aug	Florence Nightingale's Biographers	The Florence Nightingale Museum Trust, London. Tel 020 7620 0374
9 Mar–11	Bailey Antique Fair, Held in the Riding School with Free Admission to the Park (House & Gardens Closed), 11 am – 5 pm, Admiss. A £3 C £1.50	Hatfield House, Herts. (01707) 262 823
10–11	Pruning & Spring Bulb Weekend	The Gardens of the Rose, Hertfordshire. (01727) 850 461
11	Donn Fair	Woburn Abbey, Bedfordshire. (01525) 290 666
11–15	Celebration of Fine Art in Teesdale, Short Break	The Bowes Museum, Co Durham. (01833) 690 606
11	Northern Chamber Orchestra Concert	Tatton Park, Cheshire. 01635 534400
15	Deceiving the Eye– Lecture by Dr Helen Clifford	Somerset House, London. 020 7420 9406
17–18	Craft Fair	Doddington Hall, Lincolnshire. (01522) 694 308
17	Concert, 7.30 pm	St Davids Cathedral, Pembrokeshire. (01437) 720202
18	Book Fair, Held in the Riding School with Free Admission to the Park (House & Gardens Closed), 10 am – 4.30 pm, Admiss. A £1 C Free.	Hatfield House, Herts. (01462) 685 985
20	Stately Home Experience – Lecture, Personal guided tour, Lunch & Wine 10am–4pm £44.50	Ardington House, Oxfordshire. (01235) 821566
23 Mar–5 May	Art Exhibition: 'David Royle'	Pitshanger Manor Museum, London 0208 567 1227
24	Choir of St. John's College, Cambridge in Concert at Ely Cathedral – 7.30pm. For tickets call – 01353 66 77 35	Ely Cathedral, Cambs. (01353) 667 735
24–25	Rare Plants Sale (East Gardens Open), 11 am – 6 pm. Admiss. A £4 C £3.	Hatfield House, Herts. (01707) 260 228
25	Gardens Open Day (National Gardens Scheme/SSAFA)	Little Malvern Court & Gardens, Hereford & Worcester. (01684) 892 988
25	National Science in Education Week – Let There be Light	The Bowes Museum, Co Durham. (01833) 690 606
25	Mother's Day Afternoon	Charlecote Park, Warwickshire. (01789) 470277
27–29	Phillips Sale	Powderham Castle, Devon
27 Mar–3 Apr	Li Yuan–chia Exhibition	Abbot Hall, Cumbria
29	The Birthplace of Science and the Royal Soociety. A lecture by Joanna Cordon	Somerset House, London. 020 7420 9406
31 Mar–1 Apr	Gardeners Weekend	Leeds Castle, Kent. (01622) 765 400
31 Mar–1 Apr	Craft Weekend	Shibden Hall, West Yorkshire. (01422) 352 246
31 Mar–1 Apr	April Fool Weekend including Tom Fool Spectral Supper	Muncaster Castle, Cumbria. (01229) 717614

Blenheim Palace, Oxfordshire

APRIL

4	Easter EGGSTRAVAGANZA	Shibden Hall, West Yorkshire. (01422) 352 246
4 Apr–4 Jan 02	Greenwich Exhibition	Queen's House, London
4 Apr–4 Jan 02	Naval Portraits Exhibition	Queen's House, London

Craft Fair

Calendar of Events

Kentwell Manor, Suffolk

Pashley Manor, Sussex

Eastnor Castle, Herefordshire

3–30 Anne Frank – 'A History for Today'. An acclaimed exhibition on the life of Anne Frank ....Ely Cathedral, Cambs. (01353) 667 735

4 Open for the National Gardens Scheme, 9am– 5pm ....Cranborne Manor Gardens, Dorset. (01725) 517 248

4–6 Ely Experience Weekend with Esther de Waal looking at the Benedictine Tradition.
To Book Call – 01353 66 77 35...Ely Cathedral, Cambs. (01353) 667 735

6–8 Galloway Antique Fair...Ripley Castle, North Yorkshire. (01423) 770 152

7–8 Rainbow Craft Fair ....Capesthorne Hall,Cheshire. (01625) 861221

7 Craft Market...The Bowes Museum, Co Durham. (01833) 690 606

7–22 Painshill Easter Quest...Painshill Park, Surrey. 01932 868113

8 MGB Car Rally ....Sudeley Castle, Gloucestershire. (01242) 602 308

8 Beaulieu Boat Jumble ....Beaulieu, Hants. (01590) 612 345

8 Bluebell Walk at Arley ....Arley Hall, Cheshire. 01565 777353

9 House & Park Open for the Season...Ragley Hall, Warwickshire. (01789) 762 090

10 Apr–8 Jul Exhibition – Pressed For Time: The History of Printmaking ....Cecil Higgins Art Gallery & Museum, Bedfordshire. (0234) 211 222

11 Devotional Evening for Holy Week. Stainer 'Crucifixion' with Ely Cathedral Choir Admission Free ....Ely Cathedral, Cambs. (01353) 667 735

13–16 Great Easter Egg Quiz, 11a.m – 6 p.m. ....Kentwell Hall, Suffolk. (01787) 310 207

13–16 Re–creation of Tudor Life, 11a.m – 6 p.m. ....Kentwell Hall, Suffolk. (01787) 310 207

13–16 The Medway Craft Fair ....Cobham Hall, Kent

14–16 An Easter Celebration ....Leeds Castle, Kent. (01622) 765 400

14 Primrose Fair – Rare & Unusual Plant Fair, From 10 am,
Ring House Manager On : 01522 694 308 For Details.................................Doddington Hall, Lincolnshire. (01522) 694 308

14–16 Gardeners Weekend ....Ragley Hall, Warwickshire. (01789) 762 090

14 Balloon Race ....Charlecote Park, Warwickshire. (01789) 470277

14–16 Easter Events ....Tatton Park, Cheshire. 01635 534400

15 Easter Egg Hunt Challenge ....Herstmonceux Castle, East Sussex. (01323) 833 816

15 Apr–15 May The Stunning 5 – Acre Blue Bell Wood will be in Flower Until Mid – May
(Depending on the Season) ....Coton Manor Garden, Northamptonshire. (01604) 74 0219

15–16 Easter Egg Hunts ....Sudeley Castle, Gloucestershire. (01242) 602 308

15–16 Easter Egg Trail – £1. 00 per person, Normal Opening Times & Prices Apply ..Rievaulx Terrace & Temples, North Yorkshire. (01439) 748 283

15–16 Foolhardy Folk Circus & Workshop, Easter Egg Hunt & Quiz, 11 am – 6 pm ....Layer Marney Tower, Essex. (01206) 330 784

15–16 Festival of Transport ....Weston Park, Shropshire

15 Easter Egg Extravaganza ....Traquair House, Scotland. (01896) 830323

16 Concert ....St Davids Cathedral, Pembrokeshire. (01437) 720202

19 'Stately Home Experience' – Lecture, Personal guided tour, Lunch & Wine 10am–4pm £44.50 Ardington House, Oxfordshire. (01235) 821566

21–22 Home Design Interiors Event (Goodwood House) ....Goodwood House, West Sussex. (01243) 755 040

21 Vacation Chamber Orchestras Concert ....The Bowes Museum, Co Durham. (01833) 690 606

22 Special Plant Fair, 11 am – 5 pm ....Spetchley Park, Hereford & Worcester. (01905) 345 224

22 Apr–9 Jul Three American Painters ....Wingfield Old College, Suffolk. (01379) 384505

23–24 Medieval Combat ....Kenilworth Castle, Warwickshire

23–24 Captain Hook – 12.30pm & 3pm...Stokesay Castle, Shropshire

23–24 Civil War Music and Dance ....Boscobel House, Shropshire

26–28 Spring Grand Sale ....Sudeley Castle, Gloucestershire. (01242) 602 308

27–29 Country Homes & Gardens Show ....Highclere Castle, Berkshire. 01635 253210

29 Specialist Charity Plant Fair ....Mapperton, Dorset. (01308) 862 645

29 National Garden Scheme Day ....Sudeley Castle, Gloucestershire. (01242) 602 308

29 Apr–1 May Civil War Living History, from noon...Goodrich Castle, Herefordshire

MAY

1 May–20 Jun Botanical Art Exhibition ....Pashley Manor, Sussex. 01580 200692

3–7 Tulip Festival..Pashley Manor, Sussex. 01580 200692

5 Craft Market...The Bowes Museum, Co Durham. (01833) 690 606

5–7 Living Heritage Oxfordshire Craft Fair.............................Blenheim Palace, Oxfordshire, Admissions– Marge Needham– 01283 820548

5–7 Water Play..Painshill Park, Surrey. 01932 868113

5 Bluebell Walk, meet at 10.30am ....Stourhead, Wiltshire. 01747 841152

5–6 Central Scotland Horse Trials ....Scone Palace, Scotland. 01738 552300

5–7 Bonsai Weekend...Leonardslee Gardens, Sussex. 01403 891212

5–6 May Festival...Avoncroft Museum of Historic Building, Worcs. 01527 831363

6–7 Tulip Festival ....Constable Burton Hall Gardens,North Yorkshire. (01677) 450428

6–7 Spring Bank Holiday – Feed the Lambs, Tractor Rides,
Plant Sales & Animal Shows, 11 am – 6 pm..Layer Marney Tower, Essex. (01206) 330 784

6–7 Spring Craft Festival..Eastnor Castle, Hereford & Worcester. (01531) 633 160

6–7 Tatton May Fair..Tatton Park, Cheshire. 01635 534400

6–7 Knebworth Country Show ....Knebworth House, Hertfordshire. 01438 812661

7 Gardens Open Day (National Gardens Scheme/SSAFA) ....Little Malvern Court & Gardens, Hereford & Worcester. (01684) 892 988

7 Medieval Fun Day ....Sudeley Castle, Gloucestershire. (01242) 602 308

Leeds Castle, Kent

Leonardslee Gardens, Sussex

Blair Castle, Scotland

7	May Day Celebrations ....Shibden Hall, West Yorkshire. (01422) 352 246
7	May Day Celebrations with Maypole Dancing 2pm & 3.15pm ....Charlecote Park, Warwickshire. (01789) 470277
9	History & Horticulture of Rievaulx Terrace, Explore this important 18th Century Landscape Garden 2 pm Booking Essential – 01439 798 340 ....Rievaulx Terrace & Temples, North Yorkshire. (01439) 748 283
10–13	Living Crafts, 10 am – 6 pm, Admiss. A £7 G £6 C £3.30. (023) 9242 6523.....................Hatfield House, Herts. (01707) 262 823
12–13	Festival of English Food & Wine ....Leeds Castle, Kent. (01622) 765 400
12	Ely Cathedral Choir/ Trinity College of Music. Dupre De Profundis. For Tickets Call – 01353 66 77 35Ely Cathedral, Cambs. (01353) 667 735
12	Rare Plant Fair ....Savill Garden, Berkshire. (01753) 847 518
12–13	Antique Fair (Goodwood House) ....Goodwood House, West Sussex. (01243) 755 040
12	Ghost of the Night (Evening) ....Sudeley Castle, Gloucestershire. (01242) 602 308
12–13	Spring AutoJumble ....Beaulieu, Hants. (01590) 612 345
12–13	International Horse Trials ....Chatsworth, Derbyshire
12–27	Rhododendron & Azalea Fortnight ....Leonardslee Gardens, Sussex. (01403) 891212
13	Plant Fair in Paddock ....Charlecote Park, Warwickshire. (01789) 470277
13–31	'Fantasia of Rhododendrons' and 'Meet the Gardener' – Mons & Fris.............Muncaster Castle, Cumbria. (01229) 717614
14	Attics and Cellars– Looking behind the scenes at Stourhead House ....Stourhead, Wiltshire. 01747 841152
16	History & Horticulture of Rievaulx Terrace, Explore this important 18th Century Landscape Garden £5 per person Normal Admission Applies 2 pm Booking Essential – 01439 798 341................Rievaulx Terrace & Temples, North Yorkshire. (01439) 748 283
16 May–3 Jun	Pirate Treasure Hunt ....Painshill Park, Surrey. 01932 868113
16	Family Fun Day ....Belvoir Castle, Leics. 01476 870262
18 May–7 Jul	Art Exhibition: 'Utakumari Prints by John Tran' ....Pitshanger Manor Museum, London 0208 567 1227
19–20	New Homes Exhibition ....Ingatestone Hall, Essex. (01277) 353 010
19	Sail Fiesta by the Lake ....Ragley Hall, Warwickshire. (01789) 762 090
19–20	Angling Fair ....Chatsworth, Derbyshire
20	Model Soldiers Day, 11 am – 4.30 pm, Admiss. A £2 C £1. (020) 8979 7137. ....Hatfield House, Herts. (01707) 262 823
20 May–24 Sep	Sculpture by Derek Morris & Robin Welch ....Wingfield Old College, Suffolk. (01379) 384505
20	Spring Plant Fair..Pashley Manor, Sussex. 01580 200692
21–25	Special Chelsea Show Week Opening, 12 noon – 5 pm ....Chelsea Physic Garden, London. (020) 7352 5646
23	'Bluebell Heaven' Walks and Trails ....Muncaster Castle, Cumbria. (01229) 717614
24	'Stately Home Experience' – Lecture, Personal guided tour, Lunch & Wine 10am–4pm £44.50 Ardington House, Oxfordshire. (01235) 821566
24–28	The Charleston Festival ....Charleston, Sussex. 01273 709709
25	Perth Festival of the Arts Concert..................................Scone Palace, Scotland. 01738 552300
25–28	Rainbow Craft Fair ....Burghley House, Lincs. 01529 414793
26–28	The Red Wyvern Society will re-enact life in Skipton Castle in the 15th Century ....Skipton Castle, Nyorkshire. (01756) 792 442
26 May–3 Jun	Half –Term Amazing Mazes Week ....Leeds Castle, Kent. (01622) 765 400
26 May–3 Jun	St. Davids Cathedral Festival ....St Davids Cathedral, Pembrokeshire. (01437) 720202
26–28	Whitsuntide Tudor Re-creation, 11a.m – 6 p.m.....................Kentwell Hall, Suffolk. (01787) 310 207
26–27	Scottish Beer Festival..Traquair House, Scotland. (01896) 830323
26–28	Crafts at Arley ....Arley Hall, Cheshire. 01625 430519
26–28	Spring Craft Fair ....Shugborough Estate, Staff. 01889 881388
26	Atholl Highlands Parade..Blair Castle, Scotland. 01796 481207
27–28	Cheshire Classic Car & Motorcycle Show ....Capesthorne Hall,Cheshire. (01625) 861221
27–28	Steam & Country Festival. Steam Engines, Field Events, Activities; Crafts & Trade Stands ....Lamport Hall and Gardens, Northamptonshire. (01604) 686 272
27–28	A Long Running Traditional Country Fair, 10a.m – 5 p.m...........Lamport Hall and Gardens, Northamptonshire. (01604) 686 272
27 May–29 Jul	Traditional Skills Day ....Shibden Hall, West Yorkshire. (01422) 352 246
27–28	Farm Festival, Sheep Shearing and Demonstrations by the Romany Shepherdess, Church Fete (Monday Only), 11 am – 6 pm ....Layer Marney Tower, Essex. (01206) 330 784
27	The Great Farm Shop Open Day...................................Powderham Castle, Devon
27–28	The Stowe Garden Show ....Stowe House, Bucks. 01280 818282
27–28	Southern Counties Game & Country Fair........................Highclere Castle, Berkshire. 01635 253210
27	Atholl Gathering and Highland Games ....Blair Castle, Scotland. 01796 481207
28 May–10 Jun	June Craft Exhibition..St Davids Cathedral, Pembrokeshire. (01437) 720202
28	Steam Fair & Country Show With Fred Dibnah.............Eastnor Castle, Hereford & Worcester. (01531) 633 160
28–29	The Fury of the Norsemen – The Vikings ....Kenilworth Castle, Warwickshire
28	NCCPG Rare Plant Sale ....Sausmarez Manor, Guernsey. 01481 235571
30	Paint the garden! Come try your hand at painting– help provided. Meet at 10.30am ....Stourhead, Wiltshire. 01747 841152

JUNE

1–3	Home Design & Interiors Exhibition ....Ingatestone Hall, Essex. (01277) 353 010
1–30	Classical Concerts to be held in the Long Gallery. Please Ring House Manager On : 01522 694 308 For Details. Date to be Confirmed ....Doddington Hall, Lincolnshire. (01522) 694 308
2–3	Garden & Craft Fair ....Stoneyhurst College Delco Ltd, Lancashire. (01254) 826 345

Calendar of Events

Stourhead, Wiltshire

Warwick Castle, Warwick

Leeds Castle, Kent

2–3	Special Gardens Weekend Guided Tours of Gardens with Head Gardener & Bluebell Walks Through Cawdor Big Wood with Estate Ranger.	Cawdor Castle, Inverness–shire. (01667) 404 615
2	Craft Market	The Bowes Museum, Co Durham. (01833) 690 606
3	Stationary Engine Rally	Woburn Abbey, Bedfordshire. (01525) 290 666
3	The MSA Classic	Boughton House, Northamptonshire. 01536 515731
3	Motor Show	Normanby Hall County Park, Lincs. 01724 720588
4–10	Shakespeare at Traquair – Twelfth Night	Traquair House, Scotland. (01896) 830323
7–10	Grand Summer Sale	Ripley Castle, North Yorkshire. (01423) 770 152
8–10	Garden Show	Woburn Abbey, Bedfordshire. (01525) 290 666
9–10	Belvoir Ballooning Festival	Belvoir Castle, Leics. 01476 870262
9–10	Children's Festival – Music, Dancing, Entertainers	Museum of Welsh Life. 02920 573471
10	Forfar Highland Games	Glamis Castle, Angus. (01307) 840 393/ 842 242
10	Lydbrook Band	Sudeley Castle, Gloucestershire. (01242) 602 308
10	Mini Cooper Rally	Beaulieu, Hants. (01590) 612 345
10	History Day – Guided Tours of Layer Marney Tower, Including Private Areas of the House that are not Open to the Public. These Tours are usually only Available to Groups, but on History Day will be open to Individuals, 12 noon – 5 pm	Layer Marney Tower, Essex. (01206) 330 784
10–11	Medieval Siege and Joust	Kenilworth Castle, Warwickshire
12 Jun–7 Oct	Paula Rego – One of Britain's foremost resident figurative artists	Abbot Hall Art Gallery, Cumbria. 01539 722464
14	The Grand Tour – meet at 2.30pm at Stourhead House	Stourhead, Wiltshire. 01747 841152
14–17	Summer Flower Festival	Pashley Manor, Sussex. 01580 200692
15–17	Scottish Caravan Club, Golden Jubilee Rally	Glamis Castle, Angus. (01307) 840 393/ 842 242
16	Open for the National Gardens Scheme, 9am– 5pm	Cranborne Manor Gardens, Dorset. (01725) 517 248
16 Jun–2 Sep	Anthony Gormley: Critical Mass, Field for the British Isles & New Work	Tate Gallery St Ives, Cornwall. (01736) 796 226
16–17	Medieval Jousting	Sudeley Castle, Gloucestershire. (01242) 602 308
16–17	Medieval Fair	Tatton Park, Cheshire. 01635 534400
17 Jun–8 Jul	The Greater Annual Re–creation of Tudor Life, 11a.m – 5 p.m.	Kentwell Hall, Suffolk. (01787) 310 207
17	Beamish Vintage Car Rally	The Bowes Museum, Co Durham. (01833) 690 606
17	Shakespeare in the Park: 'The Tempest' by Theatre Setup, 4 pm – 7 pm, Admiss. A £8.50 C £5 (01707) 262 823 or Tel:(01707) 332 880.	Hatfield House, Herts. (01707) 262 823
18–24	Waterloo Week	Apsley House, London. (020) 7499 5676
18–22	Special Chelsea Festival Opening, 12 noon – 5 pm	Chelsea Physic Garden, London. (020) 7352 5646
18–24	Rose Week	Sudeley Castle, Gloucestershire. (01242) 602 308
20	Midsummer Indoor Concert with Beverley Davidson Dazzling Digits	Charlecote Park, Warwickshire. (01789) 470277
21–24	Blenheim Palace Flower Show	Blenheim Palace, Oxfordshire, Admissions – 0208547 30060
22 Jun–27 Jul	Sculpture Trail	Eastnor Castle, Hereford & Worcester. (01531) 633 160
22	Concert: Classics in the Park – An American Dream with Fireworks, Deer Park	Eastnor Castle, Hereford & Worcester. (01531) 633 160
23–24	Hopton Court Horse Trials	Hopton Court, Worcs. (01299) 270 734
23–24	Festival Of Gardening, 10 am – 6 pm, Admiss. A £7.50 G £6.50 C £4. (01707) 262 823.	Hatfield House, Herts. (01707) 262 823
23–24	Arley Garden Festival	Arley Hall, Cheshire. 01565 777353
23–24	Annual Craft Fair	Leonardslee Gardens, Sussex. 01403 891212
23	Outdoor performance of Mid-Summer Night's Dream –booking essential	Renishaw Hall, Derbyshire. 01264 432310
24	Veteran Car Rally	Leeds Castle, Kent. (01622) 765 400
24	Bicycle Day – as part of National Bike Week, Everyone Arriving by Bicycle May Enter for just £1. Special Cycling Events & Workshops going on throughout the day, 12 noon – 5 pm	Layer Marney Tower, Essex. (01206) 330 784
29 Jun–1 Jul	British Touring Shakespeare Company	Powderham Castle, Devon
30	Open Air Concert	Leeds Castle, Kent. (01622) 765 400
30 Jun–9 Aug	Sculpture Exhibition	Savill Garden, Berkshire. (01753) 847 518
30	Gloucestershire Youth Music Event	Sudeley Castle, Gloucestershire. (01242) 602 308
30	Outdoor Opera – Mozart's The Magic Flute	Weston Park, Shropshire
30	Craft Fair	Glynde Place, Sussex

JULY

1–30	Gardens Open	Stoneyhurst College Delco Ltd, Lancashire. (01254) 826 345
1	Caspian Horse Society	Ragley Hall, Warwickshire. (01789) 762 090
1	Austin 750 Rally	Beaulieu, Hants. (01590) 612 345
1	Festival of Wood	Eastnor Castle, Hereford & Worcester. (01531) 633 160
1–31	Classical Concerts to be held in the Long Gallery. Please Ring House Manager On : 01522 694 308 For Details. Date to be Confirmed	Doddington Hall, Lincolnshire. (01522) 694 308
1–2	From Hawkeye to GI	Witley Court, Worcestershire
4	Children's Prom Concert	Leeds Castle, Kent. (01622) 765 400
6–8	Festival of Speed	Goodwood House, West Sussex. (01243) 755 040
6–7	Open Air Rock Concert in the Park	Powderham Castle, Devon
6–8	Live Craft Fair	Highclere Castle, Berkshire. 01635 253210
7	Open–Air Charity Jazz Concert	Ingatestone Hall, Essex. (01277) 353 010

Powderham Castle, Devon

Claremont Landscape Garden, Surrey

Ragley Hall, Warwickshire

Date	Event	Venue
7	Anglican Pilgrimage	Glastonbury Abbey, Somerset. (01458) 832 267
7	Concert, 7.30 pm	St Davids Cathedral, Pembrokeshire. (01437) 720202
7	Craft Market	The Bowes Museum, Co Durham. (01833) 690 606
7	English Folk Dance Festival, 11 am – 5 pm, Admiss. A £4 C £3. (01727) 851 987	Hatfield House, Herts. (01707) 262 823
7	Craft Fair	Glynde Place, Sussex
7–8	Scottish Game Conservancy Fair	Scone Palace, Scotland. 01738 552300
7–8	Tudor Living History	Avoncroft Museum of Historic Building, Worcs. 01527 831363
8	Roman Catholic Pilgrimage	Glastonbury Abbey, Somerset. (01458) 832 267
8	Warwick Courtiers	Sudeley Castle, Gloucestershire. (01242) 602 308
8	Open Air Concert by Local Choral Group Voicebox, 2 – 4 Normal opening times & prices apply	Rievaulx Terrace & Temples, North Yorkshire. (01439) 748 283
8	International Co-op Day – Family Fun Day	New Lanark Visitor Centre. (01555)661345
9	Walk & Dine	Renishaw Hall, Derbyshire. 01264 432310
10	Castle Theatre – Shakespeare in the Park	Highclere Castle, Berkshire. 01635 253210
11–14	A Midsummer Night's Dream, Open Air Theatre	The Bowes Museum, Co Durham. (01833) 690 606
11 Jul–16 Sep	Ana Maria Pacheco:Dark Night of the Soul	Ashmolean Museum, Oxford. 01865 288298
12–15	Claremont Fete Champetre	Claremont Landscape Garden, Surrey. (01372) 469 421
12	Open – Air Shakespeare Performance – Mad Dogs & Englishmen, Hamlet. 7.30 pm, Tickets £8/£6	Layer Marney Tower, Essex. (01206) 330 784
13–15	Galloway Antique Fair	Ripley Castle, North Yorkshire. (01423) 770 152
13	Open – Air Shakespeare Performance – Mad Dogs & Englishmen, Hamlet. 7.30 pm, Tickets £8/£7	Layer Marney Tower, Essex. (01206) 330 784
13	A Midsummer Night's Dream	Boughton House, Northamptonshire. 01536 515731
13–15	Food Lovers Fair	Highclere Castle, Berkshire. 01635 253210
14–15	Vintage Vehicle Extravaganza	Glamis Castle, Angus. (01307) 840 393/ 842 242
14–15	Hot Air Balloon Meet & Jousting Tournament, Deer Park	Eastnor Castle, Hereford & Worcester. (01531) 633 160
14–15	Historic Vehicle Gathering	Powderham Castle, Devon
14–15	Summer Concerts in the Gardens	Arley Hall, Cheshire. 01925 601112
14–15	Model Boat Regatta	Leonardslee Gardens, Sussex. 01403 891212
14	Tribute Bands Concert	Highclere Castle, Berkshire. 01635 253210
15 Jul–9 Sep	Summer Exhibition of Wood Engravings Myth & Magic British Native Plants, Free During Normal Opening Hours	Chelsea Physic Garden, London. (020) 7352 5646
15	Rain or Shine Theatre company, Evening	Sudeley Castle, Gloucestershire. (01242) 602 308
15 Jul–17 Sep	Fleeting Arcadias	Wingfield Old College, Suffolk. (01379) 384505
17 Jul–28 Oct	Exhibition – Wonderland Children's Book Illustrations	Cecil Higgins Art Gallery & Museum, Bedfordshire. (0234) 211 222
17 Jul–28 Oct	Exhibition – The Great Wave	Cecil Higgins Art Gallery & Museum, Bedfordshire. (0234) 211 222
18 Jul–9 Sep	The Knights of Powderham – Family Entertainment, joust	Powderham Castle, Devon
19–22	Festival of Summer Floral Art	Leeds Castle, Kent. (01622) 765 400
19	Love's Labour's Lost	Charlecote Park, Warwickshire. (01789) 470277
21–22	Hole in the Wall Open Air Rock Concert	Hopton Court, Worcs. (01299) 270 734
21	Outdoor Concert	Ragley Hall, Warwickshire. (01789) 762 090
21	Concert: Kenny Ball & Syd Lawrence & His Orchestra, Deer Park	Eastnor Castle, Hereford & Worcester. (01531) 633 160
21–22	Holkham County Fair (Hall & Museum closed)	Holkham Hall, Norfolk
21	Outdoor Concert with Fireworks	Shugborough Estate, Staff. 01889 881388
22	Classic Car Rally	Ingatestone Hall, Essex. (01277) 353 010
22	National Archaeology Family Fun Day	The Bowes Museum, Co Durham. (01833) 690 606
22	Concert: Bootleg Beatles & Abba Magic, Deer Park	Eastnor Castle, Hereford & Worcester. (01531) 633 160
22	Shakespeare in the Park: 'As You Like It' by Play On, 4 pm – 7 pm, Admiss. A £8.50 C £5 (INCL. Free Admission from 10.30 am). (01707) 262 823 or Tel:(01707) 332 880.	Hatfield House, Herts. (01707) 262 823
22–23	A Civil War Surgeon – The Ringwoods of History	Boscobel House, Shropshire
22	Medieval Jousting	Belvoir Castle, Leics. 01476 870262
23	As You Like It – 6.30pm, bring a picnic	Belvoir Castle, Leics. 01476 870262
26	Teddy Bears Picnic & Charlecote Creepies and Crawlies	Charlecote Park, Warwickshire. (01789) 470277
26–27	Outdoor Production of 'Macbeth'	Scone Palace, Scotland. 01738 552300
27–29	Game Fair	Woburn Abbey, Bedfordshire. (01525) 290 666
27–28	Miracle Play Entitled Legends, Open Air Theatre in the Evening	Glastonbury Abbey, Somerset. (01458) 832 267
27	Bat Walk – 8.30 pm – £2. 00 per adult £1 per child including NT Members, Booking Essential	Rievaulx Terrace & Temples, North Yorkshire. (01439) 748 283
27	Antique Valuation Day, 10 am – 4 pm, Admiss. A £4 C £3. (01707) 260 228	Hatfield House, Herts. (01707) 262 823
28	Grand Scottish Prom	Glamis Castle, Angus. (01307) 840 393/ 842 242
28–29	Craft Fair	Ingatestone Hall, Essex. (01277) 353 010
28–29	The National Show For Miniature Roses, St Albans.	The Gardens of the Rose, Hertfordshire. (01727) 850 461
28	Newfoundland Dog Trials	Ragley Hall, Warwickshire. (01789) 762 090
28 Jul–12 Aug	Family Fortnight. Story Telling, Botanical Art & Pot Painting Workshops, Creepy Crawly Lectures & Competitions	RHS Garden Wisley, Surrey. (01483) 224 234
28	Gala Concert in the Park	Burghley House, Lincs. 01625 560000
28	Halle Fireworks & Light Spectacular Concert	Tatton Park, Cheshire. 01635 534400

Calendar of Events

Traquair House, Scotland

Hatfield House, Hertfordshire

Stourhead, Wiltshire

29   Family Fun Day ....Herstmonceux Castle, East Sussex. (01323) 833 816

29   RSGB Radio & Computer Show, 10 am – 6 pm, Admiss. A £3 C £1. (01707) 659 015.........................Hatfield House, Herts. (01707) 262 823

29–30   Medieval Music, Richard York – from noon ....Kenilworth Castle, Warwickshire

31 Jul–4 Aug   Race Week: Goodwood Racecourse ....Goodwood House, West Sussex. (01243) 755 040

AUGUST

1–27   Gardens Open ....Stoneyhurst College Delco Ltd, Lancashire. (01254) 826 345

1–31   Exhibition of Craft & Art ....St Davids Cathedral, Pembrokeshire. (01437) 720202

1–8   History & Horticulture of Rievaulx Terrace, Explore this important 18th
     Century Landscape Garden £5 per person
     Normal Admission Aplies 2 pm Booking Essential – 01439 798 340 ......Rievaulx Terrace & Temples, North Yorkshire. (01439) 748 283

1 Aug–30 Sep   Exhibition of Kilms ....Doddington Hall, Somerset

2–4   Music Festival ....Weston Park, Shropshire

3–5   ART IN CLAY, 10 am – 5 pm, Admiss. A £5.50 C £3. (0115) 987 3966. ....Hatfield House, Herts. (01707) 262 823

3–5   The British Clematis Society Annual Meeting & 3–day Event.....................Burford House Gardens, Worcestershire. 01584 810777

4–5   World War Two Recreation, 11a.m – 6 p.m. ....Kentwell Hall, Suffolk. (01787) 310 207

4   Firework & Light Extravaganza – Outdoor Concert ....Ragley Hall, Warwickshire. (01789) 762 090

4   Gloucestershire Youth Jazz Orchestra, Evening ....Sudeley Castle, Gloucestershire. (01242) 602 308

4   Craft Market..The Bowes Museum, Co Durham. (01833) 690 606

4   Open Air Concert – 70's Revival Night ....Powderham Castle, Devon

4–5   Traquair Fair ....Traquair House, Scotland. (01896) 830323

4–26   Teddies in trouble! ....Painshill Park, Surrey. 01932 868113

4   Battle Proms – picnic concert ....Highclere Castle, Berkshire. 01635 253210

5   Open for National Gardens Scheme Charity, Cream Teas only today. ....Heale Garden and Plant Centre, Wiltshire. (01722) 782 260

5   Jaguar National Rally ....Woburn Abbey, Bedfordshire. (01525) 290 666

5   Classic Car Show ....Sudeley Castle, Gloucestershire. (01242) 602 308

5–26   Muncaster 'Family Fun Month' includes Fairly Famous Family Aug 26th ....Muncaster Castle, Cumbria. (01229) 717614

5   Victorian Day ....Normanby Hall County Park, Lincs. 01724 720588

6   Walk & Dine ....Renishaw Hall, Derbyshire. 01264 432310

7–9   Country Homes & Gardens Show, 10 am – 5 pm, Admiss. A £5.50 C £3. (01628) 631 131. ....Hatfield House, Herts. (01707) 262 823

10   Merchant of Venice, Open – Air Theatre ....The Bowes Museum, Co Durham. (01833) 690 606

11   Craft Fair..Stoneyhurst College Delco Ltd, Lancashire. (01254) 826 345

11   The Tempest. Gates open at 6pm ....Stourhead, Wiltshire. 01747 841152

11   Proms Concert with Fireworks...Shugborough Estate, Staff. 01889 881388

12   Victoria Day ....Sudeley Castle, Gloucestershire. (01242) 602 308

12–13   Sheepdog Demonstrations – Will Gray, from noon ....Boscobel House, Shropshire

13–17   Children's Fun Week ....Eastnor Castle, Hereford & Worcester. (01531) 633 160

18–19   The Feudal Archers will provide a medieval display and encampment in the 12th Century ....Skipton Castle, Nyorkshire. (01756) 792 442

18   Mapperton Court Fair ....Mapperton, Dorset. (01308) 862 645

18–19   Scottish Horse Trial Championship ....Thirlestane Castle, Borders. (01578) 722 430

18–19   Warwickshire & West Midlands Game Fair ....Ragley Hall, Warwickshire. (01789) 762 090

18   Classical Extravaganza with Royal Philharmonic Orchestra, Fireworks & Dancing Water ....Glastonbury Abbey, Somerset. (01458) 832 267

18–19   Festival Players, Evening..Sudeley Castle, Gloucestershire. (01242) 602 308

18–19   Craft Weekend (Demonstrating Selling) ....Shibden Hall, West Yorkshire. (01422) 352 246

19–20   Soldiers of George III, from noon...Stokesay Castle, Shropshire

19   Summer Plant Fair ....Pashley Manor, Sussex. 01580 200692

21–23   Wisley Flower Show ....RHS Garden Wisley, Surrey. (01483) 224 234

23–26   Bowmore Blair Castle International Horse Trials & County Fair ....Blair Castle, Scotland. 01796 481207

24–27   High Summer Tudor Recreation, 11a.m – 6 p.m. ....Kentwell Hall, Suffolk. (01787) 310 207

24   Classical Concert with Fireworks ....Blenheim Palace, Oxfordshire, Admissions – 01625 560000

25–27   Shakespeare on the Lawn ....Leeds Castle, Kent. (01622) 765 400

25   Peacock & Dragon Workshop, Starts at 12. 00 pm Art & Craft – £2. 00 per person –
     Normal Opening Times & Prices Apply ....Rievaulx Terrace & Temples, North Yorkshire. (01439) 748 283

25–27   Living Heritage Oxfordshire Craft Fair ....Blenheim Palace, Oxfordshire, Admissions –Marge Needham, 01283 820548

25–27   The Festival of the Horse & International Horse Trials ....Highclere Castle, Berkshire. 01635 253210

25–27   Countrywide Events Fair ....Tatton Park, Cheshire. 01635 534400

26   Massed Pipes & Drums Day, Featuring Over 200 Pipers & Drummers Performing in
     Front of the Castle. Wide Variety of Events for the Whole Family ....Floors Castle, Borders. (01573) 223 333

26–27   Medieval Fun Day..Sudeley Castle, Gloucestershire. (01242) 602 308

26–27   Craft Fair Organised by KC Craft Fairs, 11 am – 6 pm ....Layer Marney Tower, Essex. (01206) 330 784

26–27   Berkeley Household & Arms & Armour Exhibition/Demonstration ....Eastnor Castle, Hereford & Worcester. (01531) 633 160

26   Rare and Unusual Plant Fair ....Renishaw Hall, Derbyshire. 01264 432310

26–28   Manor Car Club Rally ....Sausmarez Manor, Guernsey. 01481 235571

26–27   Knebworth '01 – The Classic Car Show ....Knebworth House, Herts

27   Vacation Chamber Orchestras Concert ....The Bowes Museum, Co Durham. (01833) 690 606

RHS Garden Wisley, Surrey

27–28	Medieval Entertainment, from 11.30am	Kenilworth Castle, Warwickshire
27	Children's Day	Normanby Hall County Park, Lincs. 01724 720588
30	Tribal Rhythms Workshop, Starts at 12. 00 pm Music & Dance – £2. 00 per person – Normal opening Times & Prices Apply	Rievaulx Terrace & Temples, North Yorkshire. (01439) 748 283
30 Aug–2 Sep	The Burghley Horse Trials	Burghley House, Lincs. 01780 752451
31	Last Night of the Ragley Proms – Outdoor Concert	Ragley Hall, Warwickshire. (01789) 762 090

SEPTEMBER

1	Last Night of the Proms	Ripley Castle, North Yorkshire. (01423) 770 152
1 Sept–3 Nov	Craft Market	The Bowes Museum, Co Durham. (01833) 690 606
1–26	Sculpture Trial – Trial Features Over 50 Pieces Within Garden. Sculpture is Available to Purchase	RHS Garden Wisley, Surrey. (01483) 224 234
1–2	Country Fair	Chatsworth, Derbyshire
2	Victorian Fair	New Lanark Visitor Centre. (01555)661345
2	Prom Concert	Belvoir Castle, Leics. 01476 870262
3–24	Muncaster Castle Celebration King Lear, Tom Fool, John Ruskin	Muncaster Castle, Cumbria. (01229) 717614
6–9	The Blenheim International Horse Trials	Blenheim Palace, Oxfordshire, Admissions –01993 813335
8–9	Balloon & Vintage Car Weekend	Leeds Castle, Kent. (01622) 765 400
8–9	Garden Fair	Ragley Hall, Warwickshire. (01789) 762 090
8–9	Beaulieu International AutoJumble	Beaulieu, Hants. (01590) 612 345
8–9	Open for National Gardens Scheme Charity	Squerryes Court, Kent
9	National Garden Schemes Day	Sudeley Castle, Gloucestershire. (01242) 602 308
9	County Fair	Boughton House, Northamptonshire. 01536 515731
10 Sept–27 Oct	Craft Exhibition	St Davids Cathedral, Pembrokeshire. (01437) 720202
14–16	Historic Motor circuit Event	Goodwood House, West Sussex. (01243) 755 040
15–16	Rainbow Craft Fair	Capesthorne Hall,Cheshire. (01625) 861221
15–16	Game Fair	Weston Park, Shropshire
16	History Day – Guided Tours of Layer Marney Tower, Including Private Areas of the House that are not Open to the Public. These Tours are usually only Available to Groups, but on History Day will be open to Individuals, 12 noon – 5 pm	Layer Marney Tower, Essex. (01206) 330 784
29–30	Elizabethan Weekend	Shibden Hall, West Yorkshire. (01422) 352 246
30	House & Park Closes for the Season	Ragley Hall, Warwickshire. (01789) 762 090

Burghley House, Lincolnshire

OCTOBER

5–7	Antique Porcelain & Pottery Fair, Held in the Riding School with Free Admission to the Park (House & Gardens Closed), 11 am – 5 pm , Admiss. A £3 C £1.50. (01303) 258 635.	Hatfield House, Herts. (01707) 262 823
6–7	Festival of Fine Food & Drink	Eastnor Castle, Hereford & Worcester. (01531) 633 160
7	Charity Day – All the Gate Money Goes to East Anglian Children's Hospice & St. John Ambulance, 12 noon – 5 pm	Layer Marney Tower, Essex. (01206) 330 784
13–14	Craft Fair	Ragley Hall, Warwickshire. (01789) 762 090
13–14	Living Heritage Country Show, Deer Park	Eastnor Castle, Hereford & Worcester. (01531) 633 160
13–14	Christmas Craft Show	Shugborough Estate, Staff. 01889 881388
14	Donn Fair	Woburn Abbey, Bedfordshire. (01525) 290 666
14	Dolls House Fair, 10.30 am – 4.30 pm , Admiss. A £2.50 C £1. (01753) 890 794	Hatfield House, Herts. (01707) 262 823
16 Oct–30 Dec	Brazilian Baroque	Ashmolean Museum, Oxford. 01865 288298
18	Autumn Colour – A morning walk	Stourhead, Wiltshire. 01747 841152
20–21	Gifts & Craft Fair. Over 100 Stalls, something for everyone	Lamport Hall and Gardens, Northamptonshire. (01604) 686 272
20–28	Sammy Squirrels Survival Trail – £1. 00 per Tail Normal Admission Applies. Forage in the Wood for Acorns to Help you make it through the Winter	Rievaulx Terrace & Temples, North Yorkshire. (01439) 748 283
20–21	Apple Days	Waterperry Gardens. 01844 3392276
20–21	The Medway Flower Festival & Craft Show	Cobham Hall, Kent
21–23	Programme of Demonstrations, Walks & Fruit Tasting in Celebration of Britain's Favourite Fruit	RHS Garden Wisley, Surrey. (01483) 224 234
21–22	Craft Fair	Belvoir Castle, Leics. 01476 870262
22–26	Half– Term Halloween Week	Leeds Castle, Kent. (01622) 765 400
26–28	Antique Fair	Stoneyhurst College Delco Ltd, Lancashire. (01254) 826 345
26–27	Gothic Ghost Tours of Knebworth House	Knebworth House, Herts. (01438) 812661
27	Halloween Fireworks	Beaulieu, Hants. (01590) 612 345
27	Witches, Fireworks & Pumpkins, 5.45 am – 8 pm (Fireworks 6.45), Admiss. A £5 C £2.50. (01707) 260 228 or Tel:(01707) 332 880	Hatfield House, Herts. (01707) 262 823

Beaulieu, Hampshire

Calendar of Events

Waterperry Gardens, Oxfordshire

Knebworth House, Hertfordshire

Victorian Christmas,
Church Farmhouse Museum, London

27–28	Crafts at Arley	Arley Hall, Cheshire. 01625 430519
27–28	The Stowe Christmas Fayre	Stowe House, Bucks. 01280 818282
27–28	Countrywide Events Fair	Tatton Park, Cheshire. 01635 534400
28	Book Fair, Held in the Riding School with Free Admission to the Park (House & Gardens Closed), 10 am – 4.30 pm, Admiss. A £1 C Free. (01462) 685 985	Hatfield House, Herts. (01707) 262 823
30	Christmas Shopping Fair – In aid of Service charities	Powderham Castle, Devon
31	Hallowe'en	Charlecote Park, Warwickshire. (01789) 470277

NOVEMBER

3	Grand Firework Spectacular	Leeds Castle, Kent. (01622) 765 400
4	Autumn Colours (All Gardens Open), 11 am – 5 pm, Admiss. A £4 C £3. (01707) 262 823.	Hatfield House, Herts. (01707) 262 823
4	Bonfire & Firework Spectacular	Weston Park, Shropshire
6 Nov–1 Mar	Exhibition – Watercolours from the Higgins Collection	Cecil Higgins Art Gallery & Museum, Bedfordshire. (0234) 211 222
9–16	Botanical Art Exhibition	RHS Garden Wisley, Surrey. (01483) 224 234
10	Christmas Market, Held in the Riding School with Free Admission to the Park (House & Gardens Closed), 10.30 am – 4.30 pm, Admiss. A £2 C Free. (01707) 659 407.	Hatfield House, Herts. (01707) 262 823
11	Autumn Colours (All Gardens Open), 11 am – 5 pm, Admiss. A £4 C £3. (01707) 262 823.	Hatfield House, Herts. (01707) 262 823
16–18	Bailey Antique Fair, Held in the Riding School with Free Admission to the Park (House & Gardens Closed), 11 am – 5 pm, Admiss. A £3 C £1.50. (01277) 214 677.	Hatfield House, Herts. (01707) 262 823
16–18	Antiques Fair	Scone Palace, Scotland. 01738 552300
17 Nov–16 Dec	Christmas Shopping, 11 am – 4.30 pm, Free Entry to Park. (01707) 262 823.	Hatfield House, Herts. (01707) 262 823
17 Nov–24 Dec	The New Christmas Experience	New Lanark Visitor Centre. (01555)661345
17–18	Oak Crafts Fair	Tatton Park, Cheshire. 01635 534400
17–18	Craft Show	Avoncroft Museum of Historic Building, Worcs. 01527 831363
24–25	Yuletide Craft Fair	Ragley Hall, Warwickshire. (01789) 762 090
24	Craft Weekend (Demonstrating Selling)	Shibden Hall, West Yorkshire. (01422) 352 246
25	Book Fair, Held in the Riding School with Free Admission to the Park (House & Gardens Closed), 10 am – 4.30 pm, Admiss. A £1 C Free. (01462) 685 985	Hatfield House, Herts. (01707) 262 823
26	A Medieval Christmas, from 11am	Kenilworth Castle, Warwickshire
30 Nov– 2 Dec	Christmas Fair	Leeds Castle, Kent. (01622) 765 400

DECEMBER

1	Craft Market	The Bowes Museum, Co Durham. (01833) 690 606
1–15	Xmas at Wisley. Xmas Plant & Trees. Plants Gifts Available in Plant Centre & Shop	RHS Garden Wisley, Surrey. (01483) 224 234
1	St. Etheldreda's Church Fair, Held in the Riding School with Free Admission to the Park (House & Gardens Closed), 11 am – 4.30 pm, Admiss. A £2 C Free. (01707) 262 072	Hatfield House, Herts. (01707) 262 823
1–16	Father Christmas in the Summer House	Charlecote Park, Warwickshire. (01789) 470277
1–20	Christmas Crafts	Ayscoughfee Hall Museum, Lincs
1–20	Christmas Party Nights	Weston Park, Shropshire
3–23	Christmas Tree Sales, 10 am – 4 pm, Free Entry To Park. (01707) 273 315.	Hatfield House, Herts. (01707) 262 823
5–7	Christmas Tree Festival	Museum of Welsh Life. 02920 573471
7	Christmas Concert	Shibden Hall, West Yorkshire. (01422) 352 246
8	Victorian Christmas Evening	Charlecote Park, Warwickshire. (01789) 470277
8	Christmas Concert	Stourhead, Wiltshire. 01747 841152
8–9	Christmas Opening Weekend	Scone Palace, Scotland. 01738 552300
10–24	Christmas in Max Meadowvole's Santa's Grotto	Muncaster Castle, Cumbria. (01229) 717614
15	Christmas Carol Concert	Charlecote Park, Warwickshire. (01789) 470277
15–16	Winter Wonderland	Painshill Park, Surrey. 01932 868113
16	Christmas at Shibden	Shibden Hall, West Yorkshire. (01422) 352 246
16–17	The Tudor Toymaker, from 10.30am	Kenilworth Castle, Warwickshire
17	Christmas Carol Concert	Glamis Castle, Angus. (01307) 840 393/ 842 242

ORDER FORM

order 3 titles get £5 off · order 4 titles get £10 off · order 5 titles get £20 off

or you can order the Chairman's collection and save £35

Simply indicate the quantity of each title you wish to order, total up the cost and then make your appropriate discount. Complete your order below and choose your preferred method of payment. Then send it to Johansens, FREEPOST (CB 264), 43 Millharbour, London E14 9BR (no stamp required). FREE gifts will automatically be dispatched with your order. Fax orders welcome on 0207 537 3594.

ALTERNATIVELY YOU CAN ORDER IMMEDIATELY ON FREEPHONE 0800 269 397 and quote ref   B18

Recommended Hotels - Great Britain & Ireland 2001
I wish to order
QUANTITY
copy/ies priced at £19.95 each.
Total cost
£

Recommended Country Houses - Great Britain & Ireland 2001
I wish to order
QUANTITY
copy/ies priced at £11.95 each.
Total cost
£

Recommended Traditional Inns, Hotels & Restaurants - Great Britain 2001
I wish to order
QUANTITY
copy/ies priced at £11.95 each.
Total cost
£

Historic Houses, Castles & Gardens 2001 incorporating Museums & Galleries
I wish to order
QUANTITY
copy/ies priced at £7.95 each.
Total cost
£

Recommended Hotels - Europe & The Mediterranean 2001
I wish to order
QUANTITY
copy/ies priced at £16.95 each.
Total cost
£

Recommended Hotels - North America, Bermuda & The Caribbean 2001
I wish to order
QUANTITY
copy/ies priced at £12.95 each.
Total cost
£

Recommended Hotels, Country Houses & Game Lodges – Southern Africa, Mauritius, The Seychelles 2001
I wish to order
QUANTITY
copy/ies priced at £9.95 each.
Total cost
£

Recommended Hotels & Lodges Australia, New Zealand, The Pacific 2001
NEW
I wish to order
QUANTITY
copy/ies priced at £9.95 each.
Total cost
£

Recommended Business Meeting & Conference Venues 2001
I wish to order
QUANTITY
copy/ies priced at £25.00 each.
Total cost
£

Johansens Worldwide Recommendations 2001 (Pocket Guide)
NEW
I wish to order
QUANTITY
copy/ies priced at £7.95 each.
Total cost
£

The Chairman's Collection

order the complete collection of Johansens Recommended Guides
for only **£99.55** a saving of **£35**
PLUS FREE **P&P** worth £4.50
PLUS FREE **Luxury Luggage Tag** worth £15
PLUS FREE **Privilege Card** worth £20

The Chairman's Collection contains the following titles:
•Business Meetings & Conference Venues •Traditional Inns, Hotels & Restaurants - GB •Hotels - GB & Ireland •Country Houses - GB & Ireland •Historic Houses, Castles & Gardens •Hotels, Country Houses & Game Lodges - Southern Africa •Hotels - North America, Bermuda, The Caribbean •Hotels - Europe & The Mediterranean •Hotels & Lodges - Australia, New Zealand, The Pacific • Johansens Worldwide Recommendations 2001

Now please complete your order and payment details

I have ordered 3 titles - £5 off   −£5.00

I have ordered 4 titles - £10 off   −£10.00

I have ordered 5 titles - £20 off   −£20.00

Total cost of books ordered minus discount
(not including the Chairman's Collection)   £

Privilege Card - FREE WITH ANY ORDER
Additional cards can be ordered for £20   £

Luxury Luggage Tag - Johansens branded polished
steel tag at £15. Quantity and total cost: £

POSTAGE & PACKING
(UK) for a single item add £2.50
More than one item add £4.50
(Outside) UK for a single item add £4.00
More than one item add £6.00   £

I wish to order the Chairman's collection at £99.55
(no P&P required) Enter quantity and total cost: £

Johansens Gold Blocked SLIP CASE at £5 for the
Chairman's Collection. Quantity and total cost: £

GRAND TOTAL £

I have chosen my Johansens Guides and (please tick)

I enclose a cheque payable to Johansens ☐
I enclose my order on company letterheading, please invoice (UK only) ☐
Please note that books will be sent upon payment being received
Please debit my credit/charge card account (please tick) ☐

☐ **MasterCard**   ☐ **Amex**   ☐ **Visa**   ☐ **Switch** (Issue Number)

Card Holders Name   (Mr/Mrs/Miss)

Address

Postcode

Telephone

Card No.

Exp Date

Signature

NOW simply detach the order form and send it to Johansens,
FREEPOST (CB264), 43 Millharbour, London E14 9BR (no stamp required)
FREE gifts will be dispatched with your order. Fax orders welcome on 0207 537 3594
The information given may be used for direct marketing purposes. If you do not wish to receive other information please
tick this box ☐. (Your phone number will only be used to ensure the fast and safe delivery of your order)

Index of Properties

D

E

F

G

H

I

J

Key to Map Pages

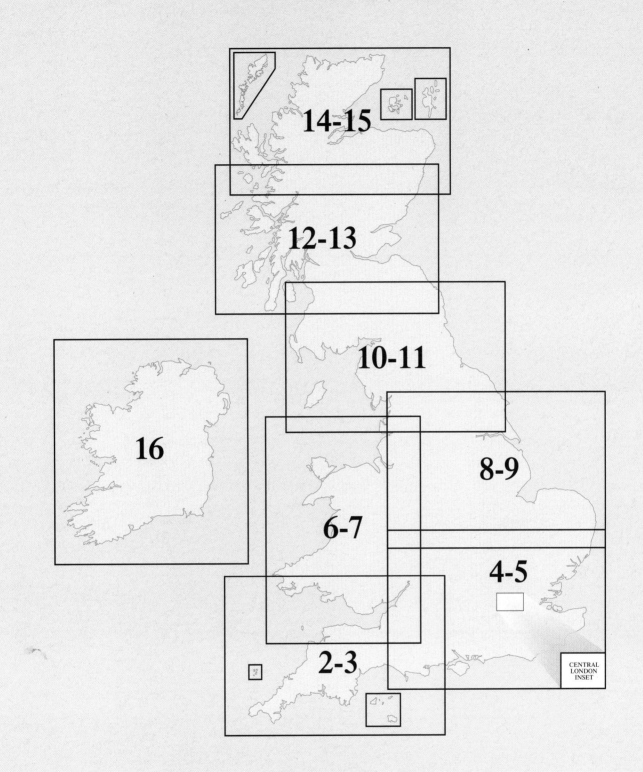

14-15

12-13

10-11

16

8-9

6-7

4-5

2-3

CENTRAL
LONDON
INSET

CARTOGRAPHY BY EUROPEAN MAP GRAPHICS LTD. COPYRIGHT © EUROPEAN MAP GRAPHICS LTD 2001

Key to Map Symbols

M62 12 Motorway	⌗ Property in the care of English Heritage	🏠 House with or without garden
A50 Primary Route		🏰 Castle with or without garden
A Roads	❦ Property in the care of The National Trust	🅼 Museum
B Roads	❧ Property in the care of The National Trust for Scotland	✺ Garden

Channel Islands

Alderney

St. Anne's

Guernsey

Herm

Vazon Bay

St. Peter Port

Sausmarez Manor

Sark

To Alderney & Torquay (Summer only)

To Poole

To Portsmouth (Summer only)

To Jersey

To Cherbourg (Summer only)

To St. Malo (Summer only)

Jersey

St. Helier

To Poole & Guernsey

To Alderney & Torquay (Summer only)

0   4   8 miles

0   5   10   15 km

Scale 1 : 730 000

0   10   20 miles

0   10   20   30 kilometres

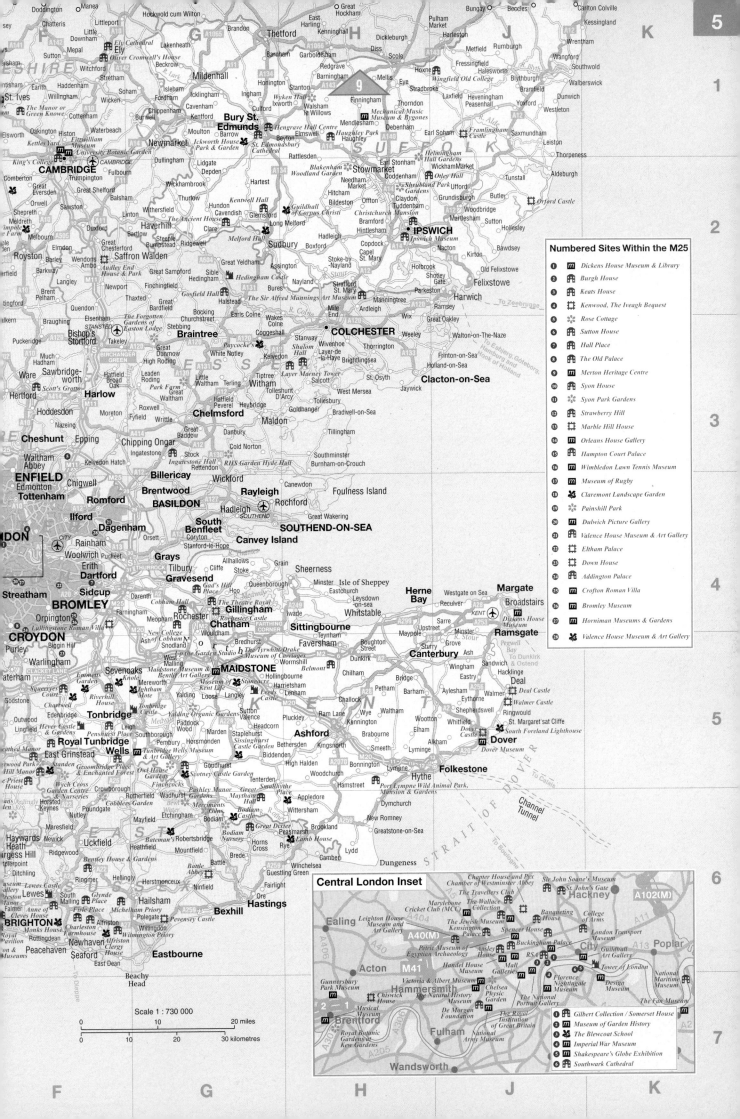

Numbered Sites Within the M25

1. Dickens House Museum & Library
2. Burgh House
3. Keats House
4. Kenwood, The Iveagh Bequest
5. Rose Cottage
6. Sutton House
7. Hall Place
8. The Old Palace
9. Merton Heritage Centre
10. Syon House
11. Syon Park Gardens
12. Strawberry Hill
13. Marble Hill House
14. Orleans House Gallery
15. Hampton Court Palace
16. Wimbledon Lawn Tennis Museum
17. Museum of Rugby
18. Claremont Landscape Garden
19. Painshill Park
20. Dulwich Picture Gallery
21. Valence House Museum & Art Gallery
22. Eltham Palace
23. Down House
24. Addington Palace
25. Crofton Roman Villa
26. Bromley Museum
27. Horniman Museums & Gardens
28. Valence House Museum & Art Gallery

Central London Inset

1. Gilbert Collection / Somerset House
2. Museum of Garden History
3. The Blewcoat School
4. Imperial War Museum
5. Shakespeare's Globe Exhibition
6. Southwark Cathedral

Scale 1 : 730 000

0   10   20 miles
0   10   20   30 kilometres

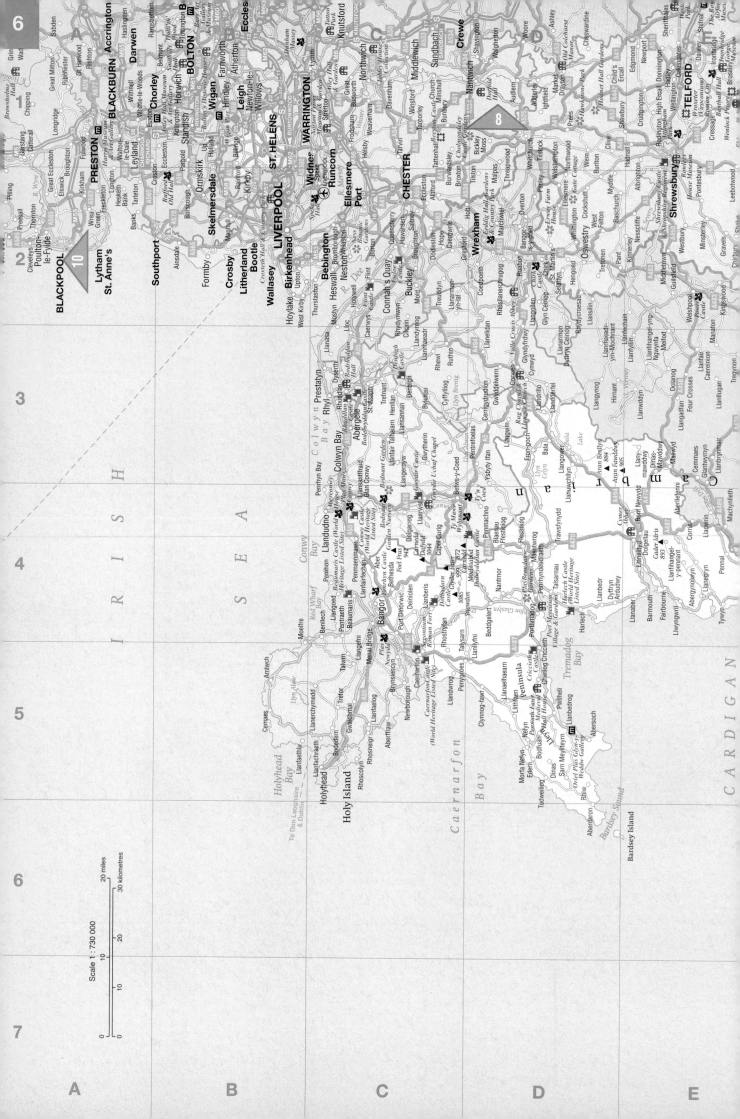

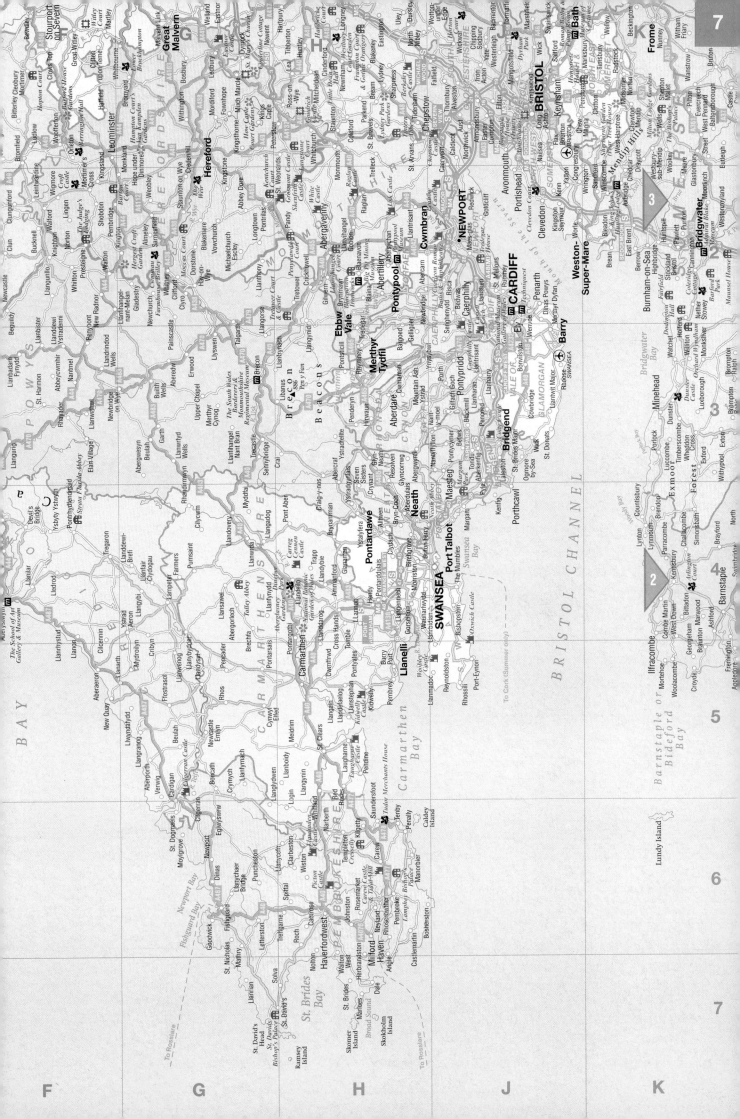

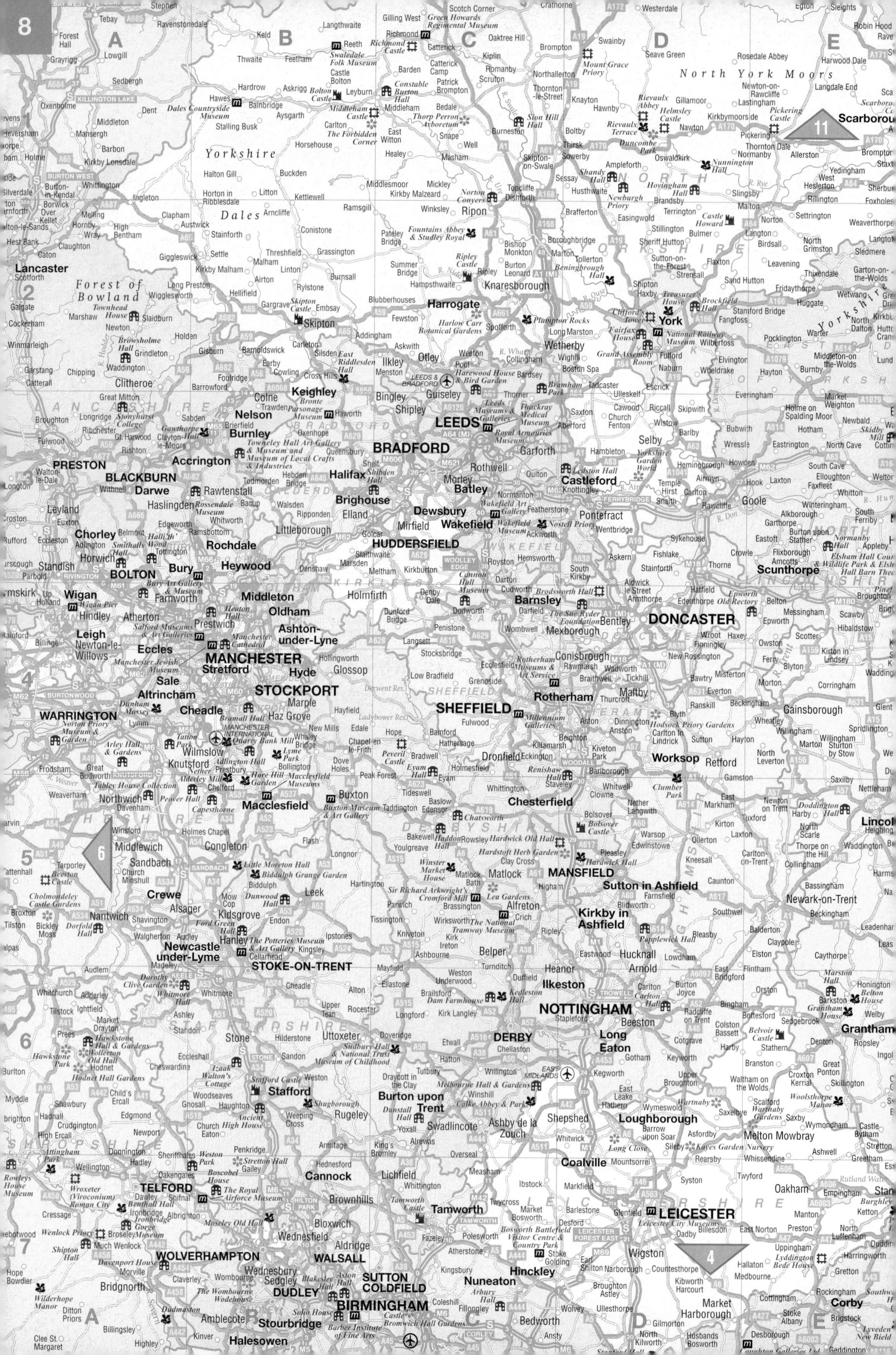

North York Moors
Yorkshire Dales
Forest of Bowland
11
Scarborough
6
4
Lancaster
PRESTON
BLACKBURN
Darwen
Burnley
Nelson
Accrington
Keighley
Skipton
Harrogate
Knaresborough
Ripon
York
LEEDS
BRADFORD
Halifax
HUDDERSFIELD
Dewsbury
Wakefield
Pontefract
Castleford
Selby
Goole
Scunthorpe
DONCASTER
Barnsley
Rotherham
SHEFFIELD
Chesterfield
MANSFIELD
Worksop
Gainsborough
Lincoln
Newark-on-Trent
NOTTINGHAM
DERBY
Ilkeston
Loughborough
Melton Mowbray
LEICESTER
Hinckley
Nuneaton
Tamworth
Lichfield
BIRMINGHAM
SUTTON COLDFIELD
WALSALL
WOLVERHAMPTON
DUDLEY
Stourbridge
Halesowen
TELFORD
Cannock
Stafford
STOKE-ON-TRENT
Newcastle under-Lyme
Macclesfield
Buxton
Crewe
Nantwich
Northwich
Knutsford
Wilmslow
Altrincham
Cheadle
STOCKPORT
MANCHESTER
Stretford
Sale
Eccles
Oldham
Ashton-under-Lyne
Rochdale
Bury
BOLTON
Wigan
Leigh
WARRINGTON
Chorley
Leyland
Grantham
Corby
Market Harborough
Oakham
Burton upon Trent
Uttoxeter
Matlock
Alfreton
Belper
Hucknall
Coalville
Ashby de la Zouch

F   G   H   J   K

1

Scale 1 : 730 000

0   10   20 miles

0   10   20   30 kilometres

Bridlington

Bempton
Flamborough
Flamborough Head
Sewerby Hall & Gardens
Hilderthorpe

Bridlington Bay

Barmston
Skipsea
North Frodingham
Atwick
Hornsea
Brandesburton
Sigglesthorne

Withernwick
Aldbrough
South Skirlaugh
Sproatley
Garton
KINGSTON UPON HULL
Burton Pidsea
Tunstall
Roos
Withernsea
Halsham
Hollym
Ottringham
Patrington
Sunk Island
Easington
East Halton
Sutton Curtis
Kilnsea

Immingham
Habrough
Great Coates
Spurn Head
Keelby
Grimsby
Cleethorpes
Humberston
To Zeebrugge & Rotterdam

SOUTH EAST LINCOLNSHIRE
Laceby
Waltham
Swallow
Humberstone
Cabourne
North Thoresby
Tetney
Marshchapel
Caistor
Wold Newton
Fulstow
Grainthorpe
North Somercotes
Ludborough
Saltfleet
Binbrook
Fotherby

NORTH SEA

Market Rasen
Grimoldby
Saltfleetby St. Peter
Louth
Great Carlton
Legbourne
Mablethorpe
Scamblesby
Withern
Maltby le Marsh
Sutton on Sea

West Barkwith
Belchford
Huttoft
Brinkhill
Alford
Chapel St. Leonards
Baumber
Ulceby
Willoughby
Ingoldmells
Thimbleby
Horncastle
Partney
Seathorne
Bucknall
Spilsby
Gunby Hall
Burgh le Marsh

LINCOLNSHIRE
Haltham
East Keal
Skegness
Coningsby
Revesby
Stickford
Tattershall Castle
Dogdyke
Stickney
Eastville
Wainfleet All Saints
North Kyme
Sibsey
Friskney
Wrangle

South Kyme
Langrick
Hubbert's Bridge
Boston Guildhall Museum
Benington
Butterwick

The Wash

Boston
Swineshead
Kirton
Holme next the Sea
Brancaster
Wells-next-the-Sea
Blakeney
Sheringham
Cromer
Overstrand
Trimingham
Bicker
Sutterton
Fosdyke
Hunstanton
Burnham
Holkham Hall
Binham
Weybourne
Felbrigg Hall
Donington
Billingborough
Gosberton
Heacham
Ringstead
Market Docking
North Creake
South Creake
Little Walsingham
Holt
Roughton
Mundesley
Bacton
Matlaske
Trunch
North Walsham
Happisburgh
Pinchbeck West
Gedney Drove End
Dersingham
Sedgeford
Syderstone
Sculthorpe
Melton Constable
Mannington Gardens Countryside
Wolterton Park
Hindolveston
Saxthorpe
Honing
Stalham
Sea Palling
Ayscoughfee Hall Museums
Whaplode
Holbeach St. Matthew
Lutton
Long Sutton
Great Bircham
Houghton Hall
East Rudham
Fakenham
Great Ryburgh
Blickling Hall
Aylsham
Cawston
Smallburgh
Hickling
Horsey
Spalding
Cowbit
Moulton
Sutton St. James
Sutton Bridge
Terrington St. Clement
South Wootton
Harpley
East Raynham
Guist
Foulsham
Reepham
Buxton
Coltishall
Hoveton
Ludham
Winterton-on-Sea
Deeping St. Nicholas
Holbeach St. Johns
Walpole St. Peter
King's Lynn
Grimston
Rougham
North Elmham
Bawdeswell
Hevingham
Martham
Hemsby
Baston
Gayton
Castle Rising Castle
Middleton
Litcham
Swanton Morley
Lyng
Horsford
Wroxham
Hoveton Hall Gardens
Ormesby St. Margaret
Billockby
Market Deeping
Crowland
Gedney Hill
Walpole St. Andrew
Wiggenhall St. Germans
Setchey
Castle Acre
Attlebridge
Horsham St. Faith
Costessey
Filby
Caister-on-Sea
Peakirk
Helpston
Thorney
Peckover House and Garden
Emneth
Narborough
Marham
East Dereham
Wendling
Honingham
Bawburgh
NORWICH
Sprowston
PETERBOROUGH
Peterborough Cathedral
Old Fletton
Murrow
Guyhirn
Friday Bridge
Upwell
Outwell
Shouldham
Swaffham
Cockley Cley
Necton
Shipdham
Barnham Broom
Hethersett
Acle
Great Yarmouth
Halvergate
Burgh Castle
Belton
Gorleston-on-Sea
Hopton
Farcet
Yaxley
Wimblington
March
Christchurch
Welney
Downham Market
Stoke Ferry
Fincham
Stradsett
Oxburgh Hall
Hilborough
Watton
Caston
Ashwellthorpe
Wymondham
Swardeston
Newton Flotman
Brooke
Reedham
Loddon
Corton
Whittlesey
Doddington
Manea
Southery
Methwold
Northwold
Mundford
Wretham
Great Hockham
Attleborough
Hempnall
New Buckenham
Long Stratton
Haddiscoe
Lowestoft
Stilton
Holme
Chatteris
Littleport
Brandon
Grime's Graves
Hockwold cum Wilton
Feltwell
East Harling
Kenninghall
Bungay
Beccles
Somerleyton Hall
Carlton Colville
Sawtry
Ramsey
Little Downham
R. Little Ouse
Thetford
Harleston
Kessingland

NORFOLK

F   G   H   J   K

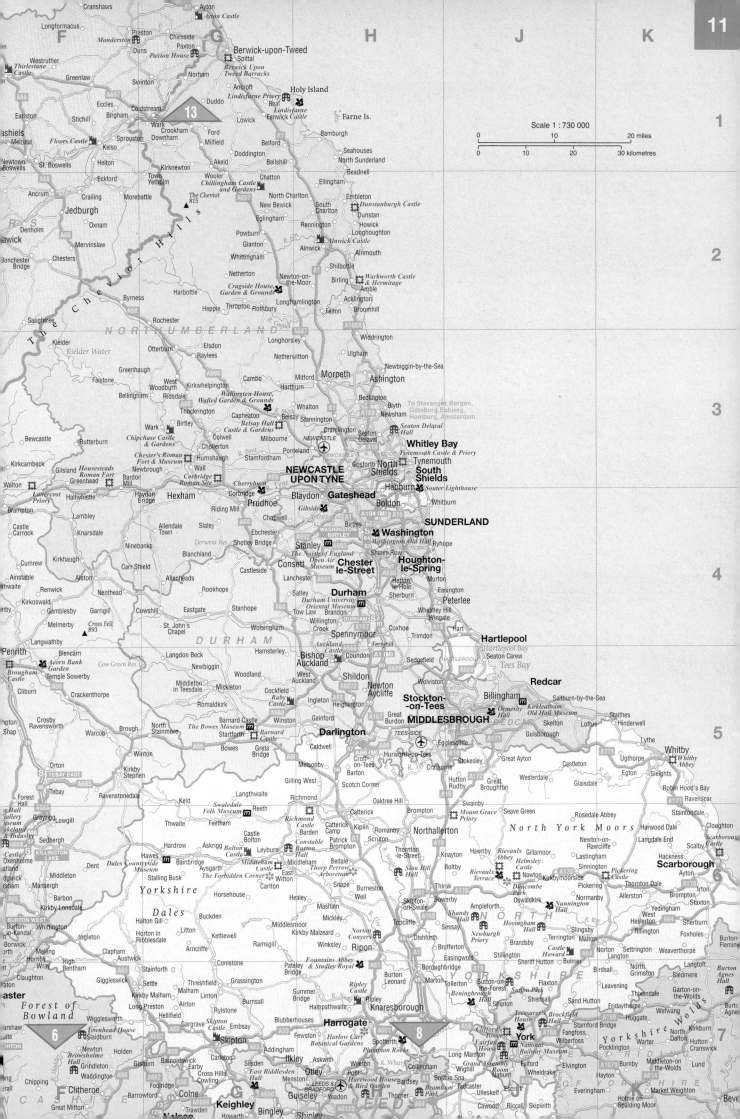

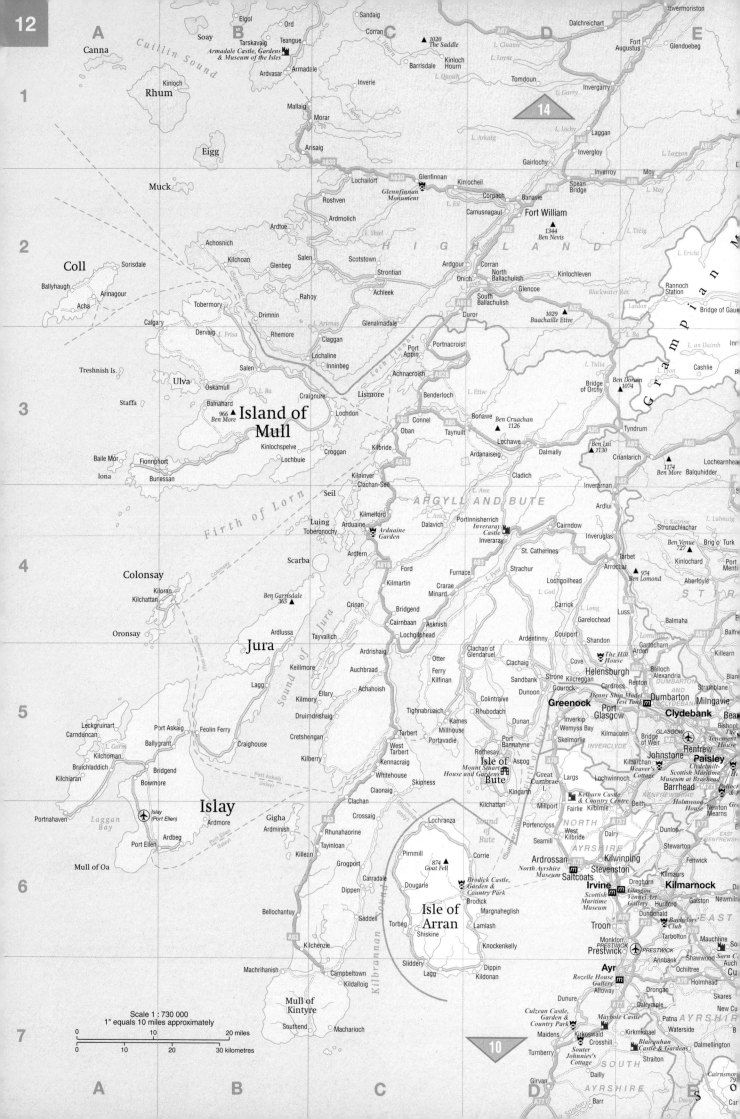

A B C D E

Canna

Cuillin Sound

Elgol
Soay
Ord
Sandaig
Invermoriston

Tarskavaig
Teangue
Corran
L. Cluanie
Dalchreichart

Armadale Castle, Gardens
& Museum of the Isles
L. Hourn
1020 ▲
The Saddle
L. Loyne
Fort
Augustus
Glendoebeg

Rhum
Kinloch
Ardvasar
Armadale
Inverie
Barrisdale
Kinloch
Hourn
L. Quoich
Tomdoun
Invergarry

1

L. Garry

Mallaig
Morar
L. Arkaig
L. Lochy
Inverroy
Moy

Eigg
Arisaig
Invergloy
L. Laggan
L. Laggan

Muck
A830
Lochailort
A830
Glenfinnan
Kinlocheil
Gairlochy
L. Lochy
Inverroy
Spean
Bridge
L. Moy

Glennfinnan
Monument
Corpach
Banavie

Roshven
L. Eil
Camusnagaul
Fort William

Ardmolich
Ardtoe
L. Shiel
H I G H L A N D
1344 ▲
Ben Nevis
L. Treig

2
Achosnich
Kilchoan
Glenbeg
Salen
Scotstown
Ardgour
Corran
North
Ballachulish
Kinlochleven
Rannoch
Station
L. Ericht

Coll
Sorisdale
Tobermory
Drimnin
Rahoy
Achleek
Onich
Glencoe
Blackwater Res.
Laidon
Bridge of Gau

Ballyhaugh
Arinagour
Calgary
Dervaig
Rhemore
L. Arienas
Glenalmadale
Duror
1029 ▲
Buachaille Etive
L. an Daimh
Inn

Acha
L. Frisa
Claggan
Lochaline
Port
Appin
Portnacroish
L. Lyon
Ben Dorain
1074 ▲
Cashlie

Treshnish Is.
Ulva
Oskamull
Salen
Lochaline
Inninbeg
Achnacroish
Benderloch
L. Etive
Bridge
of Orchy

3
Staffa
Balnahard
966 ▲
Ben More
Craignure
Lochdon
Lismore
Bonawe
Ben Cruachan
1126 ▲
Ben Lui
1130 ▲
Tyndrum

**Island of
Mull**
Kinlochspelve
Croggan
Kilbride
Oban
Connel
Taynuilt
Lochawe
Dalmally
Crianlarich
Lochearnhea

Baile Mór
Fionnphort
Lochbuie
Kilninver
Clachan-Seil
Ardanaiseig
Cladich
Inverarnan
1174 ▲
Ben More
Balquhidder

Iona
Bunessan
Seil
A R G Y L L   A N D   B U T E
L. Awe
Ardlui
L. Katrine
Stronachlachar

Kilmelford
Arduaine
L. Avich
Portinnisherrich
Cairndow
Ben Venue
727 ▲
Brig o' Turk

Firth of Lorn
Luing
Toberonochy
Arduaine
Garden
Dalavich
*Inveraray
Castle*
Inveraray
L. Lubnaig

4
Colonsay
Scarba
Ardfern
Ford
Furnace
St. Catherines
Inveruglas
Tarbet
Arrochar
974 ▲
Ben Lomond
Aberfoyle
S T R

Kiloran
Kilchattan
Ben Garrisdale
365 ▲
Kilmartin
Crarae
Minard
L. Pyne
Strachur
Lochgoilhead
L. Long
Luss
Lochlochard
Port
Menti

Oronsay
Crinan
Bridgend
Cairnbaan
Asknish
Carrick
Garelochead
Balmaha
Balfr

Jura
Ardlussa
Taynuilt
Tayvallich
Lochgilphead
Otter
Ferry
Clachan of
Glendaruel
Ardentinny
Coulport
Shandon
L. Lomond
Gartocharn
Killearn

Keillmore
Ardrishaig
Kilfinan
Clachaig
Cove
The Hill
House
Arden
Balfr

Ellary
Auchbraad
Achahoish
Ferry
Sandbank
Strone
Kilcreggan
Helensburgh
Balloch
Alexandria
DUMBARTON

5
Lagg
Kilmory
Druimdrishaig
Tighnabruaich
Rhubodach
Dunoon
Inverkip
Gourock
Cardross
Renton
Strathblane

Leckgruinart
Carnduncan
Port Askaig
Feolin Ferry
Cretshengan
Kames
Millhouse
Dunan
Wemyss Bay
Port
Glasgow
Bridge
of Weir
INVERCLYDE

Kilchoman
Ballygrant
Craighouse
Kilberry
West
Tarbert
Portavadie
Port
Bannatyne
Skelmorlie
Kilmacolm
GLASGOW
Johnstone
Paisley

Bruichladdich
Bridgend
Whitehouse
Kennacraig
Rothesay
**Isle of
Bute**
Ascog
Largs
Lochwinnoch
Beith
Barrhead

Kilchiaran
Bowmore
Kilberry
Skipness
Mount Stuart
House and Gardens
Great
Cumbrae I.
Kingarth
Millport
Fairlie
Kilbirnie

Portnahaven
*Laggan
Bay*
Islay
Gigha
Claonaig
Clachan
Kilchattan
N O R T H
Dalry
Dunlop

Islay
(Port Ellen)
Ardmore
Ardminish
Crossaig
Lochranza
*Sound
of
Bute*
West
Kilbride
Stewarton
Fenwick

Ardbeg
Tayinloan
Rhunahaorine
Corrie
Portencross
Seamill
Dalry
Dundonald

6
Port Ellen
Killean
874 ▲
Goat Fell
Ardrossan
North Ayrshire
Museum
Kilwinning
Kilmaurs

Mull of Oa
Grogport
Dougarie
Brodick
Stevenston
Saltcoats
Irvine
Kilmarnock

Carradale
Pirnmill
*Brodick Castle,
Garden & Country Park*
Scottish
Maritime
Museum
Glasgow
Vennel Art
Gallery
Hurlford

Dippen
Margnaheglish
Troon
Dundonald
Galston

Bellochantuy
Saddell
**Isle of
Arran**
Lamlash
Bachelors'
Club
Tarbolton
Mauchline

Torbeg
Shiskine
Knockenkelly
PRESTWICK
Ayr
Prestwick
Annbank
Sorn

Sliddery
Lagg
Dippin
Kildonan
Monkton
Ochiltree
Auch

Machrihanish
Campbeltown
Kildalloig
*Rozelle House
Gallery*
Alloway
Drongan
Holmhead
Skares

Machrioch
Dunure
Dalrymple
Patna
New Cu

7
**Mull of
Kintyre**
Southend
*Culzean Castle,
Garden & Country Park*
Maybole Castle
Maidens
Kirkoswald
Crosshill
Kirkmichael
Dalmellington

0   10   20 miles

0   10   20   30 kilometres
*Souter
Johnnie's
Cottage*
Turnberry
*Blairquhan
Castle & Gardens*
S O U T H
Straiton
Cairnsm

Girvan
A77
A713
AYRSHIRE

A B C D E

▲14

▼10

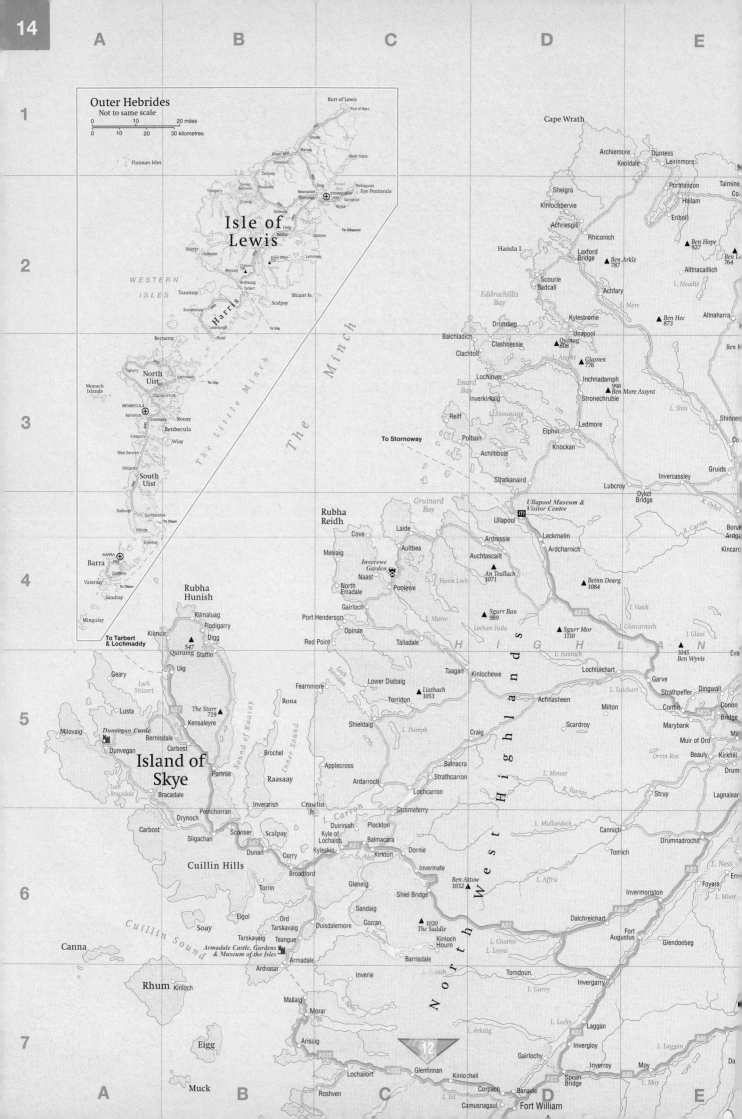

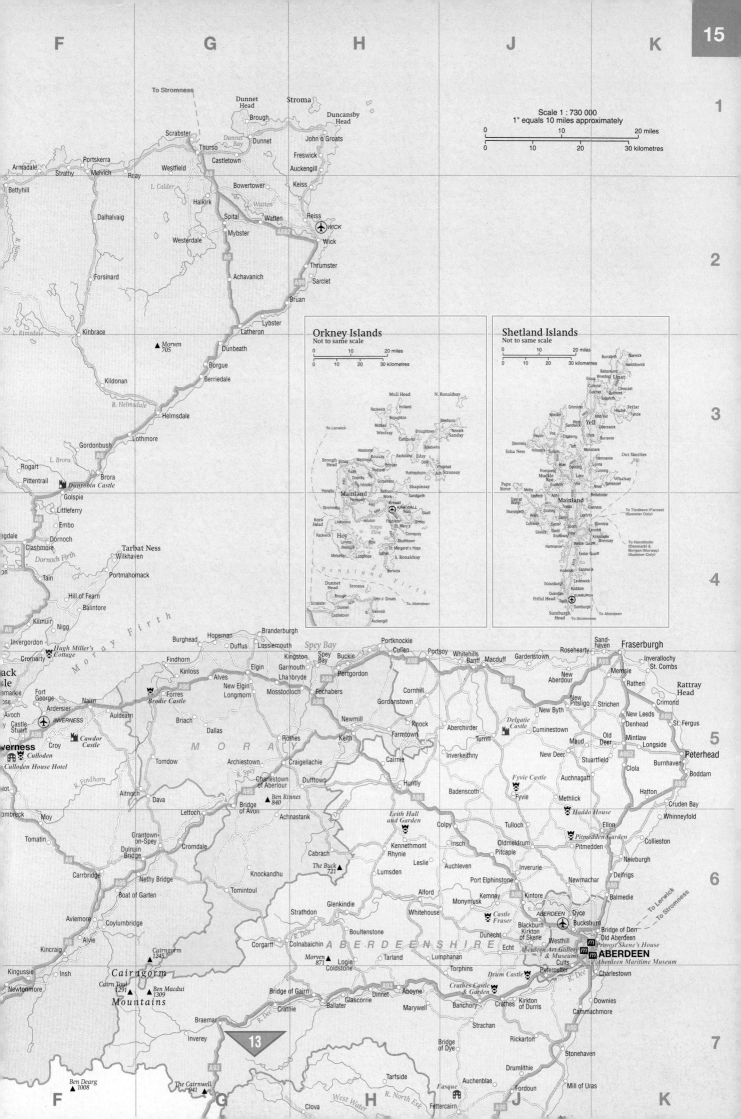

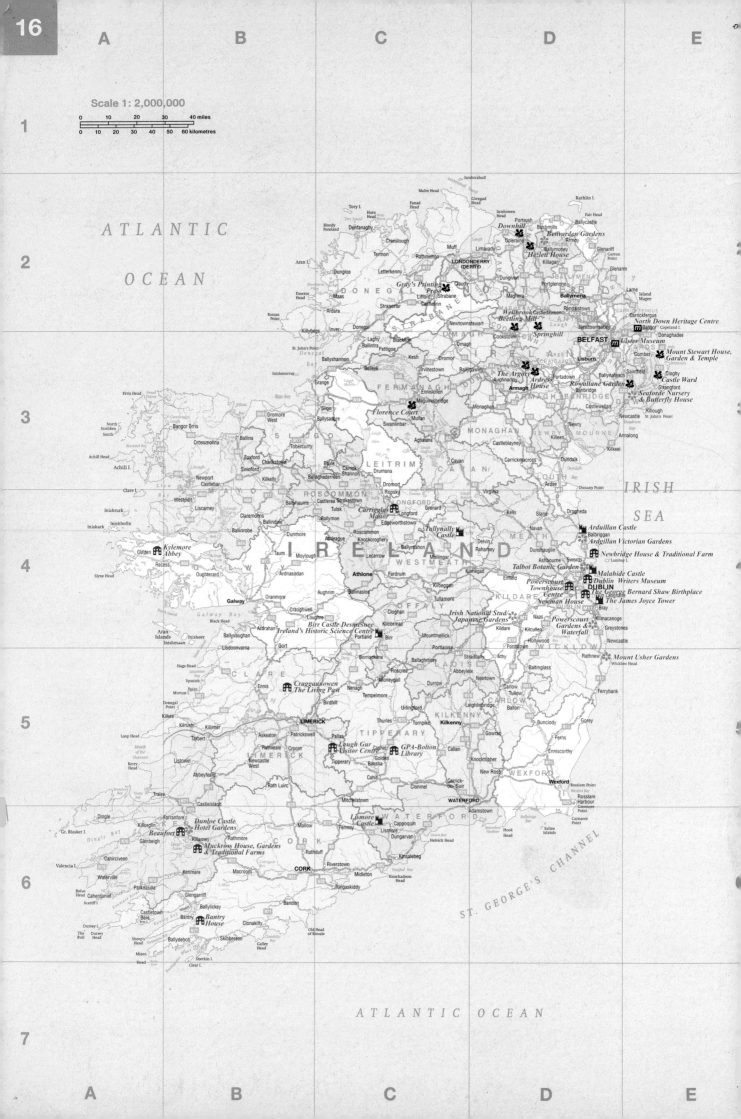